Peace and Conflict Studies

Peace and Conflict Studies: A Reader is a comprehensive and intensive introduction to the key works in this growing field.

Presenting a range of theories, methodologies and approaches to understanding peace and to transforming conflict, this edited volume contains both classic and cutting-edge contemporary analyses. The text is divided into six general sections:

PART 1: Peace studies, peace education, peace research, and peace
PART 2: Peace theories and peace movements
PART 3: The meanings and nature of conflict
PART 4: Conflict analysis, transformation and prevention
PART 5: Nonviolent action and political change
PART 6: Building institutions and cultures of peace

With an extensive introduction, as well as recommendations for further reading and questions for the classroom, *Peace and Conflict Studies: A Reader* will be essential reading for students, teachers, and practitioners of peace and conflict studies, and conflict resolution. It is also highly recommended for students of peace operations, peacebuilding, sociology, international security and IR in general.

Charles P. Webel has recently taught at the Honors College of the University of South Florida, the University of New York in Prague, and the University of California at Berkeley, where he received his Ph.D. in Philosophy, Political and Social Thought. He has also studied and taught at Harvard University and is a research graduate of the Psychoanalytic Institute of Northern California. He is the author/editor of six books, including, as author, of *Terror, Terrorism and the Human Condition* (2005); the *Handbook of Peace and Conflict Studies* (2007, co-edited with Johan Galtung); *Peace and Conflict Studies* (2002, 2009, co-authored with David P. Barash); and, of *The Ethics and Efficacy of the Global War on Terrorism* (2011, co-edited with John Arnaldi).

Jørgen Johansen has 30 years' experience as a consultant and trainer in conflict prevention and resolution. Johansen has published six books and contributed to numerous volumes. He is a researcher at the Resistance Studies Network, Gothenburg University, and lecturer at several universities, such as Syracuse University, Strasbourg, France, Transcend Peace University, Gothenburg University, Sweden, and World Peace Academy, Basel, Switzerland.

D1141526

Peace and Conflict Studies

A Reader

Edited by
Charles P. Webel and Jørgen Johansen

Routledge
Taylor & Francis Group

LONDON AND NEW YORK

First published 2012
by Routledge
2 Park Square, Milton Park, Abingdon, Oxon OX14 4RN

Simultaneously published in the USA and Canada
by Routledge
711 Third Avenue, New York, NY 10017

Routledge is an imprint of the Taylor & Francis Group, an informa business

British Library Cataloguing in Publication Data
A catalogue record for this book is available from the British Library

Library of Congress Cataloging-in-Publication Data
Peace and conflict studies: a reader/edited by Charles Webel and
Jørgen Johansen.
p. cm.
Includes bibliographical references and index.
1. Peace–Research. 2. Peace-building–Research. 3. Peace.
4. Peace-building. I. Webel, Charles. II. Johansen, Jørgen.
JZ5534.P4 2011
303.6'6–dc23
2011026806

ISBN13: 978–0–415–59128–7 (hbk)
ISBN13: 978–0–415–59129–4 (pbk)

Typeset in Baskerville by
Swales & Willis Ltd, Exeter, Devon

MIX
Paper from
responsible sources
FSC® C004839
www.fsc.org

Printed and bound in Great Britain by
TJ International Ltd, Padstow, Cornwall

Contents

The reasons for violent conflicts and terrorism

PART 4
CONFLICT ANALYSIS, TRANSFORMATION AND PREVENTION

Conflict dynamics, resistance and democracy

Reconciliation

Disarmament

Acknowledgements

The publisher would like to thank the following for permission to reprint their material:

Conrad Brunk. 'Shaping a Vision – The Nature of Peace Studies', in *Patterns of Conflict, Paths to Peace*, eds. Larry J. Fisk and John L. Schellenberg, © Broadview Press, 2000, excerpts from pp. 11–33. Reprinted with permission of the publisher (University of Toronto Press).

Gavriel Salomon. 'Four Major Challenges Facing Peace Education in Regions of Intractable Conflict', in *Peace and Conflict: Journal of Peace Psychology*, Vol. 17, Issue no. 1. Online publication date: 28 January 2011. Reprinted with permission of the publisher (Taylor & Francis).

Oliver Richmond. *Peace in International Relations*. From the Introduction, 'Peace in IR', excerpts from pp. 2–17. © 2008 Routledge. Reproduced by permission of Taylor & Francis.

Vision of Humanity (Sydney). 2011 Global Peace Index: http://www.visionofhumanity.org/contact/ And from the GPI 2011 Discussion Paper, 'New Dimensions of Peace – Society, Economy, and the Media', pp. 4–11.

Charles Webel. 'Thinking Peace', revision of 'Introduction: Toward a Philosophy and Meta-psychology of Peace', in *Handbook of Peace and Conflict Studies*, eds. Webel and Galtung. © Routledge 2009, pp. 5–13. Reproduced by permission of Taylor & Francis.

Johan Galtung. 'Positive and Negative Peace', from *A Theory of Peace*, © Transcend Press, 2010.

Immanuel Kant. 'Eternal Peace', reprinted by permission of the publisher from *Inevitable Peace* by Carl Joachim Friedrich, pp. 245–247, 248–250, 254–260, 262–266, Cambridge, Mass.: Harvard University Press, © 1948 by the President and Fellows of Harvard College. © renewed 1975 by Carl Joachim Friedrich.

Leo Tolstoy. 'Address to The Swedish Peace Congress in 1909', in Aylmer Maude's translation of *The Kingdom of God and Peace Essays*, Oxford University Press, 1935, pp. 583–591.

William James. 'The Moral Equivalent of War', 1906.

The Russell–Einstein Manifesto, 1955. http://www.pugwash.org/about/manifesto.htm

His Holiness the Dalai Lama. 'A Human Approach to World Peace', 1984.

David Cortright. *Peace. A History of Movements and Ideas*. From Ch. 1, 'What is Peace?', excerpts from pp. 1–21. © David Cortright 2008, published by Cambridge University Press, reproduced with permission.

April Carter. 'Introduction', in *Peace Movements in International Protest and World Politics Since 1945*, Longman, 1992, pp. 1–12.

Nigel Young. 'From Protest to Cultural Creativity: Peace Movements Identified and Revisited', in *Patterns of Conflict, Paths to Peace*, eds. Larry J. Fisk and John L. Schellenberg, © Broadview Press, 2000, excerpts from pp. 143–158. Reprinted with permission of the publisher (University of Toronto Press).

Hannah Arendt. Excerpt from *On Violence*, © 1969, 1970 by Hannah Arendt, reprinted by permission of Houghton Mifflin Harcourt Publishing Company, pp. 3–11 and 59–69.

'Geneva Declaration on Armed Violence and Development', Geneva: Geneva Declaration, 2006. http://www.genevadeclaration.org/fileadmin/docs/Geneva-Declaration-Armed-Violence-Development-091020-EN.pdf

'An Internationally Accepted Definition of Violence' (Box 1.1), from *Preventing Violence and Reducing its Impact: How Developmental Agencies Can Help*, by Alexander Butchart, David Brown, Andrew Wilson and Christopher Mikton, Geneva: World Health Organization, 2008, p. 5.

'Violence Prevention: The Evidence, Overview'. Geneva: World Health Organization, 2009, pp. 1–5.

Albert Einstein. 'Letter to Sigmund Freud, 30 July 1932', in *Einstein on Politics*, eds. David Rowe and Robert Schulmann, Princeton University Press, 2007, pp. 216–220. Reprinted by permission of Princeton University Press.

Sigmund Freud. 'Why War?' (1932), excerpts pp. 273–287, from *The Standard Edition of the Complete Psychological Works of Sigmund Freud*, translated and edited by James Strachey, published by The Hogarth Press. Reprinted by permission of the Random House Group Ltd and Basic Books, a member of Perseus Books Group.

UNESCO. 'Seville Statement on Violence', 1986: http://portal.unesco.org/education/en/ev.php-URL_ID=3247&URL_DO=DO_TOPIC&URL_SECTION=201.html

Charles Webel and Viera Sotakova. 'Psychological Contributions to Understanding Peace and Conflict', 2010.

Noam Chomsky. 'The Evil Scourge of Terrorism: Reality, Construction, Remedy', (the Erich Fromm Lecture), 2010.

Bruce Dayton and Louis Kriesberg, eds. *Conflict Transformation and Peacebuilding: Moving from Violence to Sustainable Peace*, excerpts. © 2009 Routledge. Reproduced by permission of Taylor & Francis.

Richard Falk. 'Nonviolent Geopolitics; Rationality and Resistance', taken from *Experiments with Peace*, eds. Jørgen Johansen and John Y. Jones, 2010, pp. 33–40. Reprinted by kind permission of Pambazuka Press.

Steven Zunes. 'The United States and the Prospects for Democracy in Islamic Countries'.

Andrew Rigby. 'How do Post-Conflict Societies Deal with a Traumatic Past and Promote National Unity and Reconciliation?'

Marc Pilisuk. 'Disarmament and Survival', in *Handbook of Peace and Conflict Studies*, eds. Charles Webel and Johan Galtung, Routledge, 2009, pp. 94–105.

Christine Schweitzer. 'Overcoming War', taken from *Experiments with Peace*, eds. Jørgen Johansen and John Y. Jones, 2010, pp. 315–326. Reprinted by kind permission of Pambazuka Press.

Mohandas Karamchand Gandhi. *Hind Swaraj or Indian Home Rule and other Writings*, ed. Anthony Parel. Cambridge University Press, 1997, excerpts from pp. 34–38, 66–71, 79–87 and 88–94.

Martin Luther King, Jr. 'Pilgrimage to Nonviolence', in *A Testament of Hope: The Essential Writings of Martin Luther King, Jr.*, ed. James Melvin Washington. San Francisco: Harper & Row Publishers, 1986, pp. 35–40. © 1963 Dr. Martin Luther King, Jr; copyright renewed 1991 Coretta Scott King. Reprinted by arrangement with The Heirs to the Estate of Martin Luther King, Jr., c/o Writers House as agent for the proprietor New York, NY.

Brian Martin. 'How Non-violence Works'. This article was first published in Borderlands Vol. 4, No. 3, 2005, and is reproduced with permission. http://www.borderlands.net.au/

Gene Sharp. Excerpts from *From Dictatorship to Democracy*, 4th US Edition, Boston: The Albert Einstein Institution, 2010.

Jørgen Johansen. 'Waves of Nonviolence and The New Revolutionary Movements', in *Seeds of New Hope, Pan-African Peace Studies for the Twenty-First Century*, Matt Meyer, Elavie Ndura-Ouedraogo and editors. Africa World Press, 2009, excerpts from pp. 69–124.

Thierry Tardy. 'A Critique of Robust Peacekeeping in Contemporary Peace Operations', in *International Peacekeeping*, Vol. 18, Issue no. 2. Online publication date: 22 March 2011. Reprinted with permission of the publisher (Taylor & Francis).

Ryszard Praszkier, Andrej Nowak and Peter T. Coleman. 'Social Entrepreneurs and Constructive Change: The Wisdom of Circumventing Conflict', in *Peace and Conflict: Journal of Peace Psychology*, Vol. 16, Issue no. 2. Online publication date: 30 April 2010. Reprinted with permission of the publisher (Taylor & Francis).

Peter Haldén. 'Systems-Building before State-Building: On the Systemic Preconditions of State-Building', in *Conflict, Security & Development*, Vol. 10, Issue no. 4. Online publication date: 19 August 2010. Reprinted with permission of the publisher (Taylor & Francis).

Tony Jenkins and Betty Reardon. Revision of 'Gender and Peace: Towards a Gender-Inclusive, Holistic Perspective', in *Handbook of Peace and Conflict Studies*, eds. Charles Webel and Johan Galtung, Routledge, 2009, pp. 209–231.

Majken Jul Sørensen. 'Competing Discourses on Aggression and Peacefulness', in *Peace Review: A Journal of Social Justice*, Vol. 19, Issue no. 4, pp. 603–609. Online publication date: 10 January 2007. Reprinted with permission of the publisher (Taylor & Francis).

Maja Korac. 'Gender, Conflict, and Social Capital; Bonding and Bridging in War in the former Yugoslavia', in *Social Capital and Peace-Building: Creating and Resolving Conflict with Trust and Social Networks*, ed. Michaelene Cox, © Routledge, 2009, pp. 107–121.

Elise Boulding. 'Peaceful Societies and Everyday Behavior', in *Cultures of Peace: The Hidden Side of History*, Syracuse University Press, 2000, pp. 89–106.

Introduction

Charles P. Webel and Jørgen Johansen

Peace studies in higher education has come of age. As a trans-disciplinary enquiry into the nature of peace and the reasons for wars and other forms of human conflict, peace studies, or peace and conflict studies, has grown exponentially since its birth about a half-century ago. Since 2000, there has been a sharp increase in peace and conflict studies curricula, particularly in the number of postgraduate peace studies programmes. Peace studies journals, conferences and professional associations continue to proliferate and periodically to intersect movements for peace and social justice. And peace education and peace research, as complements to PCS, strive not just to study, but also to achieve peace.

Peace and conflict studies, incorporating anthropology, sociology, political science, ethics, theology and history, aims to uncover the roots of conflict, transform the underlying causes, develop preventive strategies, and teach conflict transformation skills. The field is growing and is ripe for a new book to meet the increasing demand for information on these topics. Our *Peace and Conflict Studies: A Reader* is designed to do just this.

Peace and Conflict Studies: A Reader is a comprehensive and intensive introduction to the field. It presents a range of theories, methodologies and approaches to understanding peace and to transforming conflict. Both classic and contemporary analyses are featured. And the selections include pieces by Kant, Tolstoy, Einstein, Freud, William James, Martin Luther King, Jr., Gandhi, the Dalai Lama, Hannah Arendt, Johan Galtung, Elise Boulding, Nigel Young, April Carter, Andrew Rigby, Richard Falk, Betty Reardon and Noam Chomsky.

The book has six general sections, commencing with 'Peace Studies, Peace Education, Peace Research and Peace', which provides seminal philosophical, religious, social-scientific and historical perspectives on the genealogy, history and somewhat contested nature of peace and its study. The second section surveys peace theories and movements, from Kant, Tolstoy and the Dalai Lama to contemporary, cutting-edge analyses of the history, strengths and weaknesses of past and present peace and other nonviolent social movements. In the third part of the book, we present important theoretical and empirical pieces that focus on the reasons for violent conflicts, wars and terrorism, including significant portions of the legendary Einstein – Freud correspondence and a new piece by Noam Chomsky.

The fourth section focuses on contending approaches to conflict management, resolution and transformation. New theories and ideas for understanding and acting in conflicts are presented. This section includes assessments of diplomacy, realpolitik, nonviolent revolutionary movements, disarmament and reconciliation.

The fifth section includes classic essays on nonviolence in theory and as a way of life, as well as contemporary assessments of nonviolence as a means of political transformation. The nonviolent social protest traditions stemming from Gandhi and Martin Luther King, Jr. and their relevance today are explored.

And in the final part of the book, we look forward. The focus is on building institutions and cultures of peace via peacekeeping and peacemaking. Societies that have sustained peace are central elements in this analysis.

The *PCS Reader* is unique in a number of ways. First, it is specifically designed either to stand alone as the core text in PCS and related courses or to accompany other books in the field. Second, in addition to the sections on the nature, meanings and history of peace and conflict, the book prominently features classic and contemporary, cutting-edge readings on conflict management, resolution and transformation, as well as recent analyses of peaceful societies and cultures of sustainable peace. In other words, this book is not just about 'negative peace', or the avoidance of war, but also about the viability of 'positive' peace. In addition, there are in-depth, scholarly treatments, including empirical and quantitative measures, of the many topics covered, not just brief and sometimes superficial opinion-pieces. And finally, there are numerous contributions by outstanding women scholars, as well as a selection that focuses on ongoing Islamic struggles for peace and nonviolent political change.

Central to peace studies, peace education and peace research is a concern not just with understanding the world but with changing it. This is a bone of contention for academics who espouse 'value neutrality and scientific impartiality'. Inter- (or multi-) disciplinary approaches are also frequently employed, as are innovative pedagogical and scholarly techniques, which may also be contested by conventional disciplines, notably political science/international relations.

The inclusion of the analysis of (violent) conflict within peace studies has sparked a debate not only with mainstream international relations and its dominant realpolitik orientation, but also in the field of peace studies itself. Some peace researchers decry the apparent focus on 'war studies' by PCS at the possible cost of understanding and building sustainable nonviolent cultures of peace. But the history of peace discourse and movements is intertwined with opposition to war and the advocacy of conflict reduction, dating back to the ancient Romans and Chinese. Accordingly, for PCS, analysis of the reasons for war and other forms of violent conflict is linked to its aspiration for violence prevention, reduction and possible elimination. A necessary but insufficient condition for peace is the absence of war. The main task for peace researchers should be to help in building peace with peaceful means. It seems natural for avowed peace researchers to study the most peaceful cases of conflict transformation in order to learn how to handle similar conflicts in the future.

Within PCS there are, of course, disagreements. Many PCS observers and critics smile when they hear about conflicts between those studying conflicts. Just as doctors sometimes get diseases, researchers of PCS will of course now and then have conflicts and disagreements. If we use the ABC-triangle developed by Johan Galtung, conflicts have three main components: Attitudes, Behaviour and Contradiction/Content. Different schools of thought within PCS focus on different elements. Many will say that if we just can persuade people to have more tolerant and open-minded attitudes, conflicts will no longer be harmful or may even disappear. Others peace researchers focus on how people behave; it is their use of violent and aggressive means of trying to 'resolve' conflicts that is the problem. And some conflict transformers will argue that what matters is that the contradictions be resolved or transcended. All three schools have some 'fundamentalists', but a growing majority of PCS researchers and conflict specialists see the need to include all three perspectives.

One old debate regarding PCS is the relation between inner and outer peace; peace within yourself and/or God, or peace in society? Which comes first, 'healing oneself' to gain 'inner peace', or changing a violent to a peaceful world? Despite different views, many peace researchers and activists view this as a 'false dilemma' and see the need for both inner and outer peace.

As in other social sciences, there is a serious debate about methodology within PCS. Do we focus on quantitative or qualitative studies in order to get the best understanding of a conflict? At present, the majority of those who are close to the 'political science/IR side' are using more quantitative methodologies, while the 'social movement/nonviolent side' publish more qualitative studies. There is no doubt that both contribute importantly to the field.

When initiatives are taken to have new PCS programmes at universities, there have often been spirited discussions about whether the 'best' way to create a PCS degree is to include PCS in already existing fields (like IR) and institutions (like departments of social science), or to set up separate PCS centres? What we see around the world is an expansion of both types.

Many academic fields have a theoretical focus – PCS included. Good theories are essential for anyone who wants to understand the world. The complexity of conflicts makes it a challenge to have a full understanding of a complex political reality. As with most social sciences, PCS finds it difficult to do experiments and tests that can be repeated. That is not to say that empirical observation and facts are useless. The more and better case studies we have, the more accurate should be the theories based on these observations.

Comparing PCS with meteorology may help us to understand some of the problems we are facing. The complexity of weather forecasting is probably similar to understanding the complexity of many conflicts. Meteorologists today are pretty good at predicting a five-day weather forecast. By identifying, measuring and analysing the thousands of variables that influence the weather, they are able to forecast today the probability of how weather will develop in the near future. Early warning systems for predicting the development of conflicts face similar or even more difficult challenges. Humans significantly influence the Earth's climate, especially global warming, but have little influence on day-to-day weather. Natural forces create weather and human behaviour creates conflicts. To understand human behaviour is essential, but not sufficient, for students of PCS. For PCS is an ethical and applied social science as well as an analytical one. Peace scholars, researchers and students are encouraged to contribute to transforming the world, not just to understanding it.

Even very good theories are not enough to guarantee that action will be either good or wise. Even if you have read books and know all the theories on how to build houses, there is no guarantee that your first house will be of high quality. Experience and skills are often just as important as theoretical knowledge – for builders of houses and of peace. In addition to a good education in PCS it is good for those who want to act, in any capacity, to have good intentions. But good intentions are not enough! This is one reason why PCS instructors tell their students that they need to study diligently and develop good skills prior to acting in real conflicts. This is not to discourage students from being active; on the contrary, practice is essential for the learning process. But we are aware of the possible damage one can do if one acts before one has sufficient skills. For a medical student doing surgery this is obvious; we hope one day it will be for PCS students as well. Many soldiers are given at least a year of training prior to being sent to a conflict zone. We see no reason that a conflict worker with a toolbox of conflict resolution skills and nonviolent techniques should need less.

All tools, theories and kinds of knowledge can be misused. Medical science is a gift to humanity, but was misused by some doctors in Nazi Germany. Many of those who employ torture are using legally, psychologically and medically trained personnel to 'help them' be more efficient. There is a need to include a humanitarian ethic in the teaching of PCS. Johan

Galtung has suggested a version of the Hippocratic Oath, which may as useful for students of PCS as it can be for medical students.[1]

The future for PCS looks bright. More universities around the world are offering PCS programmes of some sort. The variety is impressive, and a wide range of perspectives courses, programmes and institutions are being implemented – from new introductory courses to doctoral programmes. Traditional academic disciplines, especially political science and international relations, include some PCS, and new independent institutions are being created. The combination of new programmes and methodologies has created a field bursting with creativity, energy, theories and skills – attracting a growing number of students.

And the job market for PCS grads is also expanding. State ministries, civil society actors, businesses and religious communities are just a few of those who today employ students from PCS. Almost all social constituencies are involved in conflicts of some sort. Skills and theories of how to act wisely in conflicts are, and will increasingly be, in demand. Conflicts are in most cases today seen as problematic, costly and disturbing. If we can learn how to act wisely, conflicts might be transformed into a resource for the future development of PCS.

The enormous expansion of PCS since the first early attempts to study wars and conflicts make a Reader like this one incomplete. It is not possible to give adequate space to all the relevant disciplines (like law, medicine and the biological sciences) and important and influential theoretical frameworks (like those of Albert Camus and John Burton) that have contributed to PCS cannot be included in a single volume without adding many more pages.

Still, you are reading a book we are proud of, and we hope will be useful for the students, scholars and activists who want to help the field progress.

So what can we expect from PCS in the years to come? Our conviction is that the field will continue to expand and PCS theories and skills will be refined and useful for more stakeholders in conflicts. Theories of conflicts are based on knowledge of what most conflicts have in common – from individual conflicts, via group and national conflicts, to international and global disputes. With new generations of students graduating from PCS and many moving on to Ph.D. programmes in peace and conflict, recognition of the field as a legitimate, evidence-based discipline should grow. For judicious and effective action to take place, theories need to be combined with in-depth knowledge of the actual case. Critical evaluations of past conflicts will help us to act more appropriately to address future ones.

We look forward to a shift of the main focus of PCS from traditional war studies to a critical examination of nonviolent options in inter- and intrastate conflicts, as well as in global structural conflicts. When Gandhi said that he saw the theory and practice of nonviolence to be at same level as electricity in Edison's day, he was probably right. 'Peace by peaceful means' has taken the first step on the long road from being a slogan to becoming a reality. With serious research, creative action and compassion, PCS educators, activists and students can better address future global challenges. We hope this Reader will be a useful tool for those taking that path.

Notes

1 http://www.pbs.org/wgbh/nova/body/hippocratic-oath-today.html

Part 1

Peace studies, peace education, peace research and peace

SUMMARY

Precursors of peace studies, peace education and peace research go back to ancient times. But the systematic practice of peace education began in the early twentieth century, partly in reaction to World War I, and took off after World War II, as did the earliest higher education-based peace studies programmes. Similarly, while the origins of peace research date back to religious and ethical debates on peace and war scattered across various world cultures and traditions, and the forerunners of scientific approaches to investigating war and peace also emerged in conjunction with World War I, peace and conflict research as a distinct scholarly discipline took off soon after World War II.

The first initiatives to develop peace education focused on the horrors of war and facts about weapon systems. Today we see a wide variety of courses and programmes aimed at giving students tools to reduce violence and oppression. Strategies for avoiding bullying and increasing empowerment are popular forms of peace education in schools in many parts of the world.

In this part of the book, we invite you to examine the issues and assumptions central to peace and conflict studies, peace research and peace education. We begin with a more detailed introduction to the field, present some classic philosophical and religious contributions to peace, and conclude Part I with several contemporary analyses of the history, strengths and weaknesses of peace and related social movements.

What are peace and conflict studies and peace education?

This section provides an overview and analysis of some key issues central to contemporary developments, and controversies, in peace and conflict studies and peace education. Conrad Brunk argues in 'Shaping a Vision – The Nature of Peace Studies' that the explicit value commitment of peace studies to peace, 'the belief that peaceful relations among peoples and nations are better than unpeaceful ones', requires another 'value central to the very definition of Peace Studies – that violence is undesirable, and that where the same human goods can be achieved by them, nonviolent means are preferable to violent ones' (Brunk, Chapter 1). Brunk shows how the 'normative' components of the field are no different from many other scholarly endeavours, so what distinguish PCS from most academic fields are principally its subject matter – peace, violence, conflict and power – its inter- (or multi-) disciplinary methodology, and its aim of identifying, testing and implementing many different strategies for dealing with conflict situations.

Gavriel Salomon adumbrates some major challenges facing peace educators around the world, especially those working in zones of ongoing and seemingly intractable conflict (such as Israel/Palestine). In addition to political opposition to their programmes, peace education practitioners also face such challenges as conflicting collective narratives, historical memories, contradictory beliefs and severe socioeconomic inequalities. Salomon focuses on four additional challenges 'that appear to concern the heart of peace education…the need to create a societal "ripple effect" whereby the impact of peace education programs spreads to wider social circles…; increasing the endurance of desired program effects…; the need for diverse programs…; [and] the need to find ways to bridge the gap that divides the cultivation of desired general dispositions, principles, and values and their application in specific situations' (Salomon, Chapter 2). To maximize the enduring social impact of peace education, Salomon calls for such programmes to take ethnic and social differences into account and to combine general dispositions to peace with specific context-sensitive applications.

Like peace itself, peace studies and peace education are very much works-in-progress. We invite you to discuss and debate the values and methods used by these fields to propagate their vision and mission of creating more peace on earth via education, research and lifestyle change.

What is peace?

'Peace' is a five-letter word in English, a proper noun. But like many abstract terms, peace is difficult to define, a challenge to comprehend, and seemingly impossible to achieve, at least for any significant amount of time. To understand what peace means, it is important to see how the word is used, and abused.

The English word *peace* came into use during the late thirteenth and early fourteenth centuries. It apparently derives from the Anglo-Norman *pas*, meaning 'freedom from civil disorder', a translation of the Latin *pax* and Greek *eirene*. These were approximations of the Hebrew *shalom*, a cognate of the Arabic *salaam*, meaning safety, prosperity and security.[1]

Like other abstract terms, peace is intangible. But like 'happiness', 'justice' and 'freedom', *we recognize peace by its absence*. Hence peace has a 'negative' dimension – the absence of war, injustice and widespread violence. Peace denotes the opposite of things we don't like, that 'disturb' our 'peace'.

But peace also has 'positive' dimensions. It is a linchpin of social harmony, economic equity and political justice. Unfortunately, peace is constantly ruptured by wars and other forms of violent conflict.

Peace has 'outer' and 'inner' referents as well as 'negative' and 'positive' meanings. 'Outer' peace tends to denote the absence of war and presence of harmony in the social and political realms, while 'inner' peace refers to a tranquil state of mind.

To increase peace and decrease violence, it is important to understand its various dimensions – political, socio-cultural, psycho-philosophical and task-oriented. Here we present four frames or discourses of peace.

Oliver Richmond tackles the contested relationship between peace and international relations (IR) theories and practices head on. He claims that peace is both a process and a goal: mutual preservation. Richmond aims to 'establish a broader, interdisciplinary reading of peace and to embed this within IR.' He advocates connecting discussions of peace and war with research and policy on development, justice and environmental sustainability. And he argues that the dominant concept of peace today, what Richmond calls 'liberal peace', is in crisis. Richmond assesses the ways in which peace is characterized within the liberal IR tradition, and considers such paradigmatic alternatives as conservative realpolitik, idealism, Marxism, critical theory and post-structuralism. He highlights 'the contested' nature of peace and from this concludes that peace 'is a subjective concept', constructed as a 'result of the interplay of different actors' attempts to define peace and according to their relative interests, identities, power and resources' (Richmond, Chapter 3).

The Global Peace Index (GPI), produced by the Institute for Economics and Peace in Sydney, Australia, is an empirical gauge of domestic and international conflict, social safety and security, and militarization in 153 countries, which are rank ordered. The GPI takes into account 23 separate indicators of the existence or absence of peace, operationally defined 'negatively' in terms of 'harmony achieved by the absence of war or… violence' (Vision of Humanity, GPI, Chapter 4). The GPI is weighted according to indicators of internal (domestic) peace (60%) and external (international) peace (40%). The rankings indicate the relative peacefulness of advanced industrial societies, primarily in Europe, compared with war-torn and impoverished nations, predominantly African and Asian.

The United States was chosen for the GPI's first national peace index, and the results indicate that states in the northern part of that country were in general more peaceful than those in the south, and also that the U.S. performs well on the majority of 'internal indicators' compared with the rest of the world. However, on measures of global peace, the United States ranks 82nd. The 2011 edition of the GPI also demonstrates how greater or lesser peace depends importantly on society, economy and the media.

Charles Webel addresses some of the philosophical and depth-psychological (psychoanalytic) challenges in 'Thinking Peace' and obstacles to mainstreaming such enquiries in the academy and professions. He elucidates the complexities of peace theory and adds to peace discourse the dimensions of 'interpersonal' (intersubjective) and 'divine' peace. Webel's 'dialectical' determination of peace contextually and historically situates this ethical ideal. He claims the antithesis of peace is not conflict, or even most forms of violence, but rather the terrorising use of violence for criminal and/or political purposes. He shows how the three zones of inner, outer and intersubjective peace are interactive, not static. And he delineates a *continuum*, or spectrum, of states of mind and cultures ranging from 'strong' to 'weak' peace. Webel concludes by advocating 'imperfect' rather than 'unending' peace.

The Norwegian peace scholar and conflict transformer, a founder of peace studies, Johan Galtung, reformulates his classic distinction between 'positive' and 'negative' peace. Galtung posits 'six peace tasks: eliminating the direct violence that causes suffering; eliminating the structures that cause suffering through economic inequity; eliminating the cultural themes that justify one or the other; [and] building direct, structural, and cultural peace' (Galtung, Chapter 6). Galtung's paradigmatic actor for building peace is Gandhi, whose 'theory and practice went far beyond Western security theory and practices'.

These diverse and sophisticated 'language games' of peace frame peace as unequivocally desirable. This seems self-evident, but it is an assumption that may need to be called into question, given the appropriation of 'peace talk' by political and military decision-makers from time immemorial, who say they are all 'for peace' but orchestrate campaigns of mass violence ostensibly to attain it. What ultimately matters is not how we *talk* about peace but what *do* to achieve peace in all its important dimensions.[2]

Talking peace meaningfully is a necessary but insufficient condition for making peace. We encourage you to do both.

Notes

1 For the words for peace in other languages see: http://www.columbia.edu/~fdc/pace/
2 See Anat Biletski, 'The Language-Games of Peace', in Charles Webel and Johan Galtung, eds., *Handbook of Peace and Conflict Studies* (London and New York: Routledge, 2009), 345–354.

1   Shaping a vision

The nature of peace studies

Conrad G. Brunk

Why study peace?

The twentieth century has been described by many historians as the bloodiest century in recorded human history. Judging simply by the numbers of people who have suffered violent death or the many other terrors of warfare and social strife, they are surely justified in their claim. The majority of those killed in the two major world wars, like most of the victims of the many regional wars that followed, were terrified, innocent civilians. The latter half of the century was dominated by a "cold war" in which the superpower nations of the world, having developed weapons of mass destruction, threatened massive genocide upon each other's populations. Their weapons, many scientists believed, held the potential to terminate human life on the planet. Although this "cold war" came to an end in the last decade, the nuclear, chemical, and biological weapons it produced remain in existence and continue to place the peoples of the world at risk.

This is only a part of the bloody story of the twentieth century, however. The rest includes chapter upon chapter of border wars between smaller nations, and ethnic, religious, and revolutionary conflict, in which acts of terrorism, guerilla war, and even genocide have become commonplace. The human race has achieved many apparent economic, scientific, and political advances in the modern era, but when it comes to managing our conflicts our most recent record demonstrates that we have made little, if any, progress. Indeed, it appears that the human race has a decided penchant for turning its most impressive technological achievements to the task of finding ever more painful and destructive ways of dealing with its conflicts.

Surely one of the most important tasks for humanity in the new millennium is to learn how to handle individual, social, and national or international strife in more constructive and peaceful ways. The toll in human misery and the threat to our survival on this planet have become far too great. Rather than continuing to rely on entrenched procedures, we need to find less destructive, less violent ways of dealing with conflict at every level, from the family and the neighbourhood all the way up to the community of nations and states.

For this reason increasing numbers of educators and scholars have developed the conviction in recent years that the problem of conflict and violence in our world requires focused attention to the conditions that can turn human conflicts so quickly and easily to violence and war, as well as new ways of thinking about the alleviation of these conditions. After seeing the horrible power of the atomic bombs dropped upon the Japanese people at the end of World War II, Albert Einstein observed that nuclear weapons technology had "changed everything, except our way of thinking." What he meant by this was that the awesome power this technology introduced had radically changed the world, especially humanity's ability to threaten the life of the planet. This, of course, should have altered just as dramatically the way we think about the place of violence and war in dealing with human conflicts, but it did not. Many people concluded that the only serious way to respond to the problem noted by Einstein was to set issues of peace and conflict apart as a special area of research and education in the university.

Of course, problems of conflict and its resolution have always been the subject of study and research by the traditional disciplines represented in the university. Historians study the history of conflict. In fact, many people think that historians tend to focus too much of their attention on wars and violence, as if these were the only important events in history, psychologists study human behaviour at the individual level, to try to understand what influences us to choose violent or nonviolent means of handling our disputes. Social psychologists, anthropologists, and sociologists focus their attention on the behaviour of social groups; political scientists try to understand the behaviour of nations and political organisations. Philosophers and theologians are interested in the moral and religious significance of conflicts and the most appropriate means of dealing with them. Even some of the so-called "hard sciences" like biology, zoology, and ethology claim insights into the problems of human violence.

But each of these disciplines tends to study only a narrow aspect of human behaviour; that is, the one that most naturally fits its own methodological approaches and assumptions. And it is clear that the problems of human conflict and their peaceful resolution are much larger than any single discipline can capture. Each discipline has important insights to offer, but none can understand these problems fully in their real-life contexts. Further, there are aspects of these problems that can fall in the cracks between disciplines. This is why the proper study of human conflict and its resolution is *interdisciplinary* – understanding the problem requires the insights both contained in and overlooked by many disciplines. Only by setting the study of conflict and peace apart as a separate *problem area* is it possible to stimulate the "new ways of thinking" necessary for our radically changed world.

Objections to peace studies

Is it really a discipline?

The points just mentioned indicate the usual rationale for the development of "Peace Studies" as an independent course of study in many colleges and universities. But some traditional academics have argued that Peace Studies really isn't a "discipline" in the commonly understood sense of that term, and therefore should not really be a separate field of study. This argument is not very persuasive, because it is not at all clear what defines academic "disciplines" in the first place. They are not identified by a common methodology, since in many disciplines there are lively debates about the proper methods to use (especially in the humanities and social sciences). Nor are they characterized by common assumptions shared by their members, since these too are constantly debated. It appears that many disciplines are defined by the range of problems, or the *subject matter,* they study. History is defined by its concern with events in the past, psychology with human behaviour, anthropology with practices of different cultures, and so on.

In this respect, Peace Studies, which takes as its subject matter the problem of human conflict and its peaceful resolution, is no less a *discipline* than many of the well-recognized academic disciplines which have emerged over time, especially in the twentieth century. But it is not necessary to establish Peace Studies as a distinct academic discipline in order to establish its value as a separate course of study, because it is clear that some of the most significant and

highly respected courses of study to emerge in colleges and universities in the past several decades are, like Peace Studies, attempts to explore highly important social issues which require
the perspectives of many disciplines.

Take, for instance, the emergence of Environmental Studies in universities around
the world in the past forty years. Environmental issues have come to be recognized as
demanding immediate, well-founded responses in personal behaviour and in economic
and political policy. Understanding these issues requires input from many sciences, as well
as disciplines in the humanities; physics, biology, geology, zoology, ecology, psychology,
sociology, geography, political science, economics, ethics, and religious studies, just to
name the most relevant. But these disciplines cannot tackle environmental problems in
an integrated and coherent way in their own isolated corners. They need to be brought
together around real environmental problems, where the solutions require insights from
each and require each to recognize the limitations and possibilities identified by the others. Environmental Studies is one of the best examples of the importance *of interdisciplinary*
research and education in dealing with critical social problems. Other similar examples in
the university include Development Studies, Area Studies (e.g., Canadian Studies, African
Studies), and Ethnic Studies (e.g., Aboriginal Studies). Few people today would argue that
these do not have a legitimate place in the university, even though many of the traditional
"disciplinarians" were highly suspicious of them when they were first proposed because
they infringed on their "disciplinary turf."

Is peace studies too political?

Even though Environmental Studies is now an accepted and highly respected course of study,
when it was first introduced into college and university curricula many people opposed it on
the grounds that it was not an "objective" science. It was, they said, merely an excuse for
introducing environmentalist political activism into the academic curriculum, and this was
a violation of the scholarly commitment to maintaining a neutral or "objective" attitude. It
is not appropriate for colleges and universities to be supporting items on the "green" agenda
(like "limited growth," sustainability, or "saving the spotted owl"), which are controversial
and challenge many entrenched ways of thinking and acting within our society.

Peace Studies programs meet with the same arguments. They, too, are charged with
being "too political" because they are often critical of mainstream ways of thinking about
government behaviour and policy. Thus they are often seen as promoting pacifism, socialism, or other "left-wing" political agendas and providing a platform for engaging students in
anti-war protests and other forms of activism, rather than maintaining the appropriate level
of scholarly "objectivity."[1] Now it is certainly true that Peace Studies, like Environmental
Studies, looks for new ways of thinking about conflict and violence that often are critical of
entrenched ways of thinking about these things. But there is nothing inherently more "political" about this than other accepted forms of critical scholarly inquiry. Indeed, most people
would argue that this is just what the university is all about: the promotion of new, and often
very unpopular, ways of thinking. "Politicization" *is* something to worry about in universities,
but the "politicization" to be feared is not that of ideas critical of mainstream politics. It is
rather that which suppresses the free expression of unpopular viewpoints for political reasons.
We might also ask which is the greater threat to the objectivity of the university: a research
grant of millions from a government defence department to a physics professor to study the
feasibility of a laser weapon, or a Peace Studies course which investigates nonviolent alternatives for national defence or international peacekeeping?

Is peace studies value-free?

An important related question is whether Peace Studies is defined by a commitment to a certain set of values. Some of its academic critics have claimed that it is defined *primarily* by such a value commitment, and that this is the sense in which it is really the inappropriate introduction of a moral or political agenda into scholarly research and education. Thus it is often said that Peace Studies is defined by a common commitment to pacifism or nonviolence as a moral or political ideology, or that it shares a common opposition to patriotic nationalism in favour of trans-nationalist or internationalist sentiments. Some of its harshest critics have even claimed that it is motivated by strong socialist or Marxist ideology.

There is an important sense in which it is true that Peace Studies is defined by certain values. One of these is certainly the value of peace itself; that is, the belief that peaceful relations among people and nations are better than unpeaceful ones. This implies another closely related value central to the very definition of Peace Studies – that violence is undesirable, and that where the same human goods can be achieved by them, nonviolent means are preferable to violent ones. But these two values are, as just stated, hardly controversial ones. They would be shared by most people and should not be identified with any particular "political" agenda.

With respect to these value commitments, Peace Studies is no different from many, probably most, other academic and scholarly endeavours, which are also motivated by underlying values or goals. For example, the whole point of Environmental Studies is to find ways to ameliorate destructive impacts upon the environment. This distinguishes it from Geology, which is more often taught with an eye towards facilitating the extraction of resources from the environment (this, after all, is what most geology graduates do). Administrative and Management Studies have as underlying values such things as efficiency and profitability. Aboriginal Studies is premised upon the explicit value of preservation of cultural and ethnic traditions and practices. Even Strategic Studies, often hailed by its proponents as a "value-free" or "realistic" enterprise, is based upon national interest. These are, in each case, values appropriate to the community served by the area of study and appropriate to the area of study itself. Peace Studies is committed, equally appropriately, to the values of peace.

The subject matter of peace studies

As already suggested, Peace Studies is defined, not so much in terms of its methods and assumptions, but in terms of its *subject matter*, the problems with which it is concerned, This problem area has been loosely identified as that of "human conflict and its peaceful resolution." The domain of human conflict is, of course, extremely broad, because we are very conflict-prone creatures who construct many levels of social interaction and generate conflict at every level of that interaction. Individuals find themselves in conflict with others in a variety of social contexts: in families, in schools, in the workplace, and in the community. We organize ourselves within racial, religious, ethnic, economic, and political groupings which regularly come into conflict with each other. And we also form nation states and alliances in the international arena which vie with each other for power, influence, resources, and territory. If we ever encounter beings from other galaxies, we will surely add intergalactic conflict to the list!

That humans come into conflict with each other at various levels of individual and group interaction is normal and expected. Conflict is itself inevitable among beings who live together in situations where common interests meet finite resources, and where different interests lead to incompatible activities. There is nothing particularly bad, or even undesirable, about the inevitability of conflict. It is, in itself, neither had nor good, though it can have both good and bad consequences. It can lead to misunderstanding, hostility, alienation, and violence. But conflict can also be a stimulus to creative thinking and the development of new ideas, new technologies, or new forms of social interaction, all of which can make things better for everyone. Nothing would be more boring and unsatisfying than life without conflict. The only human community without conflict, it has been said, is to be found in a cemetery!

Conflict can be defined (and usually is defined in conflict theory) simply as what results from the existence, real or imagined, of incompatible interests, goals, beliefs, or activities. It is a situation in which one party's interests cannot be fully realized without their impinging upon the realization of some other party's interests – or a situation in which one of them *thinks* that the interests are incompatible. Defined this way, it should be clear that conflict among finite beings on this earth is inevitable. It would be inevitable even if humans were perfectly good beings. It is not our failure to be good that brings us into conflict with others. It is simply the fact that, being the same kinds of beings, with similar interests, we will naturally want the same things when there is not enough for everyone at the same time. But we also have different beliefs and values, and these too come into conflict with the beliefs and values of others. This is normal and natural – there is nothing bad about it at all.

The important thing about human conflicts, then, is not so much the conflicts themselves as the *means we choose to deal with them*. These means largely determine whether the conflict leads to good or ill. Not only do we generate strife at various levels of social interaction, from the individual to the international, we also have developed habits, practices, and institutions for dealing with it at all these levels. Some of these work better than others, are better at *preventing* hostility and violence, while others seem *to promote* hostility and violence or even depend upon them.

The primary concern of Peace Studies is to understand how conflicts among human beings arise, what causes them to become harmful for some or all the parties, and what means are most likely to deal with them in less harmful ways. Adam Curle, founder of one of the first Peace Studies programs in Britain, defined the function of Peace Studies as identifying and analyzing "unpeaceful relationships" in order to "devise means of changing unpeaceful into peaceful relationships."[2] A useful aspect of Curle's definition is the way it points out that human conflicts can be handled in "unpeaceful" as well as "peaceful" ways, and that the point is to find ways of turning conflicts of the former type into conflicts of the latter type. What this amounts to depends, of course, upon what is meant by "peaceful relationships," and, as we shall see in a moment, this is a matter of much interesting debate within the Peace Studies community.

Another useful aspect of Curle's definition is that it defines Peace Studies very broadly, since it includes the study of peaceful and unpeaceful relations at every one of the levels of human conflict from the individual to the international. Peace Studies is interested in the analysis of conflict between individuals and groups in communities and in finding methods of transforming violent and harmful relations arising in these conflicts into more constructive or "peaceful" relations. This is the focus of what is often called "Community Conflict Resolution Studies."

But Peace Studies is interested in conflicts at the more "political" levels as well. These include the unpeaceful relations that often arise in conflicts between the diverse racial, religious, ethnic, and political groups within our communities and nations. While most states have legal and political institutions for dealing with these conflicts – police, courts, prisons, social agencies, elected councils, and legislatures, which are designed to "keep the peace" – they often do not perform in ways that resolve the underlying conflicts or transform them into more peaceful relationships between the parties. Creative nonviolent means of confrontation and conflict transformation, such as those used by Mohandas Gandhi and Martin Luther King, Jr., have therefore been a major subject for study.

Conflict between nations and between ethnic or nationalist groups within nations, which typically leads to the organized violence of civil or international war, has been a major focus of Peace Studies in the past. Indeed, during the past several decades the major impetus for the establishment of such programs in European and North American universities and colleges has often been concern about the growing destructiveness of regional wars around the world, the high risks of nuclear war during the cold war period, and the emergence of ever more horrifying military technologies, such as chemical and biological weapons. The search for more peaceful ways of managing regional and national conflicts rightfully remains a high priority. There is a desperate need for investigating new methods of intervention in highly volatile situations: peacebuilding or peacekeeping roles which do not simply multiply the violence and suffering of the people in conflict, as traditional military methods of intervention so often do.

Peace Studies researchers and educators have also been interested in undertaking critical examination of the prevailing doctrines and ideologies that shape the mainstream ways of thinking about human conflict. This is especially true at the level of international conflict, where international relations theory has been strongly dominated by debates between "realism" and "idealism," Marxism and capitalism, liberalism and fascism, and similar dichotomies. Many people think that these debates are based upon assumptions about individual, group, and national behaviour that are outmoded and prevent the emergence of new, creative solutions to conflict at this level. Perhaps these assumptions – the identification of political power with force and violence, the idea that human individual or group behaviour is essentially egoistically motivated, that social order is dependent upon the monopoly of violence, and so on – need to be challenged. Here Peace Studies provides a useful service by examining the evidence from the many sciences which may call these assumptions into question. For example, the "political realist" assumption that social order and cooperation can only be maintained by the existence of a scheme of centralized enforcement has been called into serious question by recent research on the emergence of cooperation and altruism among insects and animals in their natural evolutionary adaptation to their environment.[3] There is reason to believe that the same might be true of the human animal in social contexts.

So we see that Peace Studies is defined by concerns with human conflicts and their peaceful resolution across a broad spectrum of human interaction. The chapters in this book speak to this wide variety of conflict issues and introduce critical challenges to entrenched ways of thinking. It is thus clear in what ways Peace Studies can be distinguished from many other disciplines and research programs. For instance, Strategic Studies, a growing area of research in universities and non-academic research institutes, generally limits its focus to international conflict situations, and it views them from the point of view of the national interest of a particular national actor or government. It tends to make certain assumptions about the interests of states and their use of power and examines conflict situations with the aim of finding the most effective "strategy" for maximizing the interests of the particular state. It provides useful input for policy-makers who are interested in serving the particular interests of their own country, however these interests may be defined (and they are usually defined in terms of economic advantage and political influence). Peace Studies, on the other hand, attempts to take a broader view, which may include the critical assessment of assumptions made by Strategic Studies and their implications for peaceful relations among nations.

Central concepts in peace studies

Peace

The best evidence against the claim that Peace Studies is defined by any particular ideology lies in the existence of an ongoing vigorous debate within the field about how to define "peace," the concept central to Peace Studies as a field of research and education. If we accept anything like Adam Curle's definition of the field, as the analysis of unpeaceful relationships and the means of transforming them into peaceful ones, then the first question we must address when undertaking our study is: What do we mean by "unpeaceful" and "peaceful" relationships between people?

Curle himself defines these terms in the following way. "Peaceful relationships," he says, are "those in which individuals or groups are enabled to achieve together goals which they could not have reached separately." In contrast, "unpeaceful relationships are those in which the units concerned damage each other so that, in fact, they achieve less then they could have done independently, and in one way or another harm each other's capacity for growth, maturation or fulfilment."[4] Curle clearly includes more within the concept of "peace" than is usual in newspapers and popular language. He does not mean merely the absence of war or other forms of overt violence which kill or maim persons and does not believe that a situation is "peaceful" simply when there is a ceasefire or temporary truce in hostilities between parties, There are many subtle and inconspicuous ways in which people can harm each other psychologically, socially, and economically even though they are not actually engaged in acts of violence in the usual sense of this term.

Curle's definition of peace is an example of what has come to be known as "positive peace," because it is said to define peace in terms of the *presence* of a state of affairs that is beneficial for all the parties in a relationship. "Positive peace" is contrasted with "negative peace," which defines peace negatively – as the *absence* of certain kinds of specific violent actions, like those which physically maim or kill other persons. From the point of view of "negative peace," a situation is peaceful among individuals and groups if they are not engaging in specific acts of physical or psychological violence, such as occur in assaults in which people are seriously injured or even killed. Among nations there is "negative peace" if they are not at war or are not using the threat of war to advance their diplomatic objectives. The concept of "negative peace" is the one that we typically use in our ordinary speech when we talk about peace among nations or among conflicting political groups within a society.

Curle prefers to use a "positive" as opposed to a "negative" conception of peace because he thinks that there are many ways in which relations among individuals and groups can be harmful to some or all the parties to the relationship even when they do not involve overt acts of violence. A situation should not be called "peaceful" if persons are suffering harm from the nature of the relationship. A marriage is not "peaceful" if one of the partners is being exploited, oppressed, or prevented from realizing his or her potential as a person because of power imbalances or simply habitual ways of structuring the roles, even when these are unrecognized or unintended. A society is not "peaceful" if, as in a slaveholding society, its laws or social practices demean or impoverish certain groups or exclude them from the opportunities and benefits available to others. Those who, like Curle, prefer the notion of "positive peace" would say that any relationship of extreme injustice should hardly be considered "peaceful." Furthermore, a situation that places people in such positions is a fertile breeding ground for overt forms of violence, and thus is not likely to be peaceful even in the "negative" sense for very long,

The well-known Scandinavian peace researcher, Johan Galtung, has defended an even stronger conception of positive peace than Curle's. He calls any situation unpeaceful in which "human beings are being influenced so that their actual (physical) and mental realizations are below their potential realization."[5] Galtung has been much criticized for this view because it suggests that we have peace only when we have reached a perfect Utopia! Others have pointed out that on this definition there is no difference between the concept of peace and the concept of perfect justice. We will return to this criticism a bit later.

Violence

Johan Galtung also has an interesting way of explaining the distinction between positive and negative peace by pointing out that really each of them has a "negative" definition – peace is the *absence* of something," which can be called "violence." But negative and positive peace, it may be said, refer to the absence of two *different kinds* of violence. The violence with which negative peace is concerned Galtung calls "direct, personal violence." This is what we normally think of when we hear the word. Violence in this sense has four essential elements: a) an identifiable *actor* or groups of actors, b) an identifiable physical *action* or behaviour, c) a clear physical or psychological *harm* which results from the action, and d) an identifiable *victim* who suffers the harm. The usual things that come to mind when we hear the word "violence" – such as physical assaults, stabbings, shootings, bombings – have all four of these elements.

But Galtung points out that some of the most pernicious ways people are harmed do not have all these elements, and hence they tend to be ignored or not recognized as "violent," even though they should be. People can be harmed, not only by the actions of others, but also as a result of the way the relevant relationships or social practices are structured. In these cases it is not anybody's particular *actions* but the structures themselves that cause the harm. The examples cited earlier of the lack of "positive peace" – slavery, apartheid, or an oppressive marriage – are for Galtung perfect examples of what he calls "structural violence." In these cases there is a clear "victim" who is being harmed in some way in the situation, or *by* the situation, but the victim may be unable to identify any particular *action* of any particular *person* or group as the cause of the harm. It is the way things go as a result of the relevant social arrangements that puts the person in the disadvantaged situation. The poverty and dehumanization of the slave is the result of the *system of slavery*, not the result of any identifiable act of violence on the part of the slavemaster. The fact that a specific slavemaster may be very "nonviolent" (in the sense of direct, personal violence), or even unusually benevolent, in the treatment of his or her slaves does not mean that the situation of the slaves is not extremely detrimental to them. There is a sense in which slavery "does violence" to the slaves, even though no one nay be "acting violently" toward them. This is what Galtung means by structural violence."

This distinction between direct, personal violence and structural violence makes it easier to clarify the distinction between negative peace and positive peace. Negative peace can simply be understood as the absence of direct, personal violence. Positive peace is the absence of structural violence. When viewed this way, it becomes evident that the common element in both conceptions of peace and violence is the element of *harm*. How broadly we understand the notion of peace depends in large part upon what we include as the types of harm that are "violent" or "unpeaceful."

This is not just an academic question about terminology, as it might appear to be on the surface. Very important debates about the nature of peace studies, peace research, and peacemaking turn on this issue. Consider, for example, the debate that raged among peace researchers in the 1960s and 1970s, when Galtung and Curle were writing about the issue. Many of the most visible wars occurring in the world then were "wars of liberation," in which dissident groups fought revolutionary guerilla wars against very oppressive, undemocratic regimes. Even if we agree that the goal of peace research is to find ways to help these societies restore a peaceful situation (to "turn unpeaceful relationships into peaceful ones," as Curle puts its), we must still ask whether this means finding ways to end the wars (restoring negative peace) or finding ways to end the oppression of the governments, against which the wars were being fought (restoring or creating positive peace).

Not surprisingly, peace researchers did not agree about this, nor did many of the people involved directly in the violent situation. Some people (like Galtung and Curle) argued that merely to focus on the direct, personal violence of the fighting and to advocate ways of stopping it was to take sides with the oppressive status quo which the people were fighting to end, to side with the political and economic structures that were structurally violent, and to prefer a negative peace to a positive peace. If one wanted to contribute to peacemaking in this situation, it was argued, then one should focus upon ways of ending the oppression, not just on ways of ending the war. Further, the revolutionaries fighting these wars claimed that they were not the ones who should be criticized for being "unpeaceful". They were, in fact, fighting against the structural violence of the oppressive regime and for positive peace (as well as for negative peace in the long run). They needed to break the negative peace (with direct, personal violence) in order to achieve positive peace. Those who were truly on the side of "real" (positive) peace should, they said, side with the revolutionaries. Those who merely wanted to stop the fighting weren't really on the side of peace.

Other peace researchers, like the well-known American economist Kenneth Boulding, were strongly critical of this position. They argued that this emphasis on positive peace confuses the issues. By defining "peace" and "violence" so broadly, they said, the ideas become indistinguishable from the concepts of "justice" and "injustice," thus obscuring an important and enduring moral question that arises when we face the need to choose between peace and justice. We value negative peace too, the critics argued, and sometimes it comes into conflict with justice. When it does, we simply have to make a moral decision about which value is more important: whether the injustice is so great that ending it justifies breaking the peace by using direct, personal violence. Recognizing that this is a real choice between two *values* also forces us to look seriously for the least violent (or as we should say, most "peaceful") ways of struggling against injustice. This, Boulding argued, was exactly that Peace Studies and peace research should be seeking to do – to find effective nonviolent ("negatively peaceful") ways of fighting against injustice. So, negative peace should be the central conception of peacemaking.

Those who in this way prefer the concept of negative peace as the controlling idea in Peace Studies point out an important fact about human beings and their propensity to violence in dealing with conflict. The fact that people nearly always believe in the rightness of their own cause. So, when they fight, they are fighting "for justice." If the injustice against which they fight is perceived to be grave, then the temptation is to use whatever means are considered necessary to succeed. This is why intense conflicts have the well-known tendency to spiral into ever-increasing levels of violence and horror. And as they do, the parties on both sides become ever more firmly convinced that their horrible deeds are justified by the end of the justice they seek. The more people use the term "structural violence" to describe the injustice of their opponents, the easier it becomes for them to think of themselves as "peacemakers" and the more difficult it becomes for them to see the violence of their own actions. The language of "structural violence" and "positive peace" helps warriors to avoid making an explicit moral choice about the justification of their own violent actions, or about whether there might be morally preferable, nonviolent ways of dealing with the conflict.

The debate about justice and peace cannot be resolved here. Perhaps the best thing to say at this point is simply that the two concepts of violence and peace call our attention to importantly different aspects of conflict and its peaceful resolution. We know that situations of structural violence are often fertile breeding grounds for the outbreak of many kinds of direct, personal violence and that, in most cases, structural violence is maintained by the regular use or threat of direct personal violence, which often incites those who suffer to employ violent resistance. So there is a clear sense in which it is true that the only real peace is a positive peace. It is also clear that to be concerned about negative peace, without taking into account the underlying conditions that produce the direct, personal violence, is to take too narrow a view, Those who seek negative peace as a goal must also be concerned about how to achieve positive peace (or justice) peacefully.

Different "peacemaking" approaches can give high priority to both these values.

This allows us to suggest an alternative definition of Peace Studies to that provided by Adam Curle. Perhaps we can say that its aim is to analyze human conflicts in order to find the most peaceful (negatively peaceful) ways to turn unjust relationships into more just (positively peaceful). This definition has the advantage of capturing the full importance of the concept of positive peace without losing sight of the distinction between peace and justice.

Conflict

We often think of conflict among human beings as a bad thing – something to be avoided at all costs. Partly as a result of this perception many people avoid conflict as much as possible. We might even think that peace is the absence of conflict, and that the aim of Peace Studies is to find ways of avoiding or reducing conflict among human individuals, groups, and nations. This would be a mistake, however. The reader will notice that the definitions of "peace" we have reviewed so far have referred to the absence of violence – both direct and personal and structural – but not the absence of conflict.

This is because conflict is not necessarily a bad thing, although it is the *occasion* for the well-known unpleasant things people may do when they are not very good at handling it. In fact, conflict can cause many good things, Loraleigh Keashly and William Warters point out the many positive functions that conflict can play in human relations, such as fostering creative solutions to problems, facilitating personal and social change, and maintaining personal and social identities. In addition, it can be exciting and fun. This is the whole point of competitive games, of course – to engage in a contrived, but controlled, conflict for the enjoyment of the participants and the spectators.

Many people think that if they find themselves in a conflict with another person or group, it must be because someone – me, another person, or both of us – is doing something wrong. Psychologists have found that people have tendencies toward one or other of these alternatives. Some people tend to assume that they, themselves, are doing something wrong when they find themselves in a conflict. They feel guilty and tend to resolve the conflict by giving in immediately to the other party. Others assume the opposite. They feel threatened by the conflict, blame the other party, and are more likely to be combative and aggressive. Still others blame themselves *and* others. These people are either very pessimistic and fatalistic about conflict and avoid or withdraw from it, or they look for ways to reach quick compromises. None of these are very constructive ways to deal with the problem. None of them motivate the person to engage in constructive problem-solving. A person who does not immediately assume that conflict is a sign of someone doing something wrong is less likely to engage in blaming (oneself or the other) and is therefore less likely to be aggressive and competitive and more likely to look for constructive ways of dealing with the situation.

So the point of Peace Studies and peacemaking is not necessarily to find ways to end conflicts, but to handle them more constructively. Because conflict is so often the occasion for people to become nasty toward one another – to become hateful, distrustful, alienated, aggressive, and violent – we need to find ways to carry on conflicts without becoming nasty ourselves.

Power

Another central concept in Peace Studies, power, is like conflict, commonly understood in many different ways. Throughout human history there has been a tendency to think of power (especially political power) as synonymous with force and violence or the threat of force or violence. Western political theorists from the Greek historian Thucydides to the seventeenth-century philosopher Thomas Hobbes and modern social theorists like Max Weber and Mao Zedong have all claimed that the use or threat of force or violence was the source and measure of political power. They believed that the greater the ability of a person or state to wreak violence upon others, the greater its power. Hobbes, for example, believed that all forms of social cooperation and trust, including moral relations between people (and presumably all animals), were possible only because a strong leader could punish with violence those who refused to cooperate.[6] Apparently he had never observed "social" animals and insects, who seem to cooperate regularly, without threat from such a centralized leader.

However, throughout this same history there have also been thinkers such as Socrates, Jesus, and the Buddha, and such influential modern political theorists as Gandhi, Hannah Arendt, and Gene Sharp, who have seriously questioned this equation of power and violence. They define power in broader, more general terms, as the ability to organize persons and groups into cooperative enterprises for the accomplishment of social goals. When power is defined as *cooperation*, it leaves open the question of its relationship with violence. Threat of violence or force may be one way to exercise power, but it may not be the only or even the most effective way. As Arendt puts it, violence may be an efficient means of exercising *destructive power*, but it is an extremely inefficient and often ineffective way of exercising *constructive power*.[7]

At the centre of the argument for nonviolent action is the view, shared by Gandhi, King, and Sharp, that there are forms of social power, made possible by the willingness of people to stand up to threats of violence against them, which can undermine the power of those who depend upon the threat of force and violence. The argument is based upon a simple but often ignored fact: a person who threatens others with violence in order to get them to cooperate and do his or her will is powerless if those others refuse to give in to the threat. All that is left for the threatener to do is to wreak his violence upon the refusers. In doing so, he or she destroys those who are needed to carry out the purpose. This is what Leo Tolstoy taught Gandhi about the British subjugation of India: the British colonizers needed cooperative Indian colonists to do their labour and buy their goods. When Gandhi gave the Indian people the courage to resist the British threats of violence, there was nothing the latter could do to get the cooperation they sought. It is the subjugated, Gandhi realized, who ultimately have the power over the subjugators.

Part of the task of Peace Studies is to understand the dynamics and uses of power. It is one of the most important elements in conflict, since balances of power among conflicting parties have a significant impact upon the "outcome" of the conflict or the way it is handled. If peacemaking is concerned with both peace and justice (or "negative" and "positive" peace), then it is concerned to find ways of managing conflict which do not simply allow powerful parties to impose unfair settlements upon weaker parties.

Approaches to peacemaking

One of the primary objectives of Peace Studies is to identify, test, and implement many different strategies for dealing with conflict situations. Human beings have had such strategies for as long as they have experienced conflicts. However, some are more violent than others, and some are more effective at achieving positive peace, or justice. Some aim at "winning" the conflict or imposing a loss on the opponent; others try to find some way of ending the conflict altogether by finding a "win-win" solution. Some attempt to "manage" the conflict through agreed-upon procedures (like tossing a coin or voting) or systems of rules, while others aim at actually intensifying the conflict in order to motivate one or more of the parties to resolve it in a constructive way.

Some conflicts are between parties that are relatively equal in power and resources; some are not. A strategy likely to reach a fair resolution between parties (such as a mediated negotiation) is not nearly as likely to do so if they are highly unequal. The outcome of a negotiation between two unequal parties is predictable; it will favour the interests of the party who has the greater power. So an unrestrained negotiation between unequals will not necessarily produce a more just, or positively peaceful, outcome than will an unrestrained fight between two parties of unequal strength. Negotiation is a more negatively peaceful means than fighting or war between parties, but it does not necessarily guarantee that the resulting relationship will be good (or even better). This is why methods of conflict resolution that may be good in one type of conflict may not be as good in others.

Figure 1 provides a helpful way to understand important ways in which strategies of peacemaking define their objectives differently and employ different procedures with different implications for "peacefulness," in both of the senses we have discussed. It distinguishes three very different approaches, each defined by a different underlying conception of the "peace" to be attained. Within each of these three general approaches both coercive (and violent) and noncoercive (and nonviolent) methods can be used. The bottom row provides some examples of actual conflict resolution techniques that can be used to achieve the goals of each approach. You will notice that some techniques, such as bargaining and debating, can be used to accomplish quite different goals.

The most important things to notice in Figure 1 are the three very different aims that a peacemaking approach might have. In the first, which I have called "Conflict Resolution," the goal of the approach is to end the conflict between the parties altogether. There are many ways to do this, of course, some more constructive than others. Conflict resolution is most appropriate and constructive in those situations where the parties may *perceive* their interests to be incompatible, but where there is a "win-win" solution available which would allow them both fully to achieve their goals. Careful problem-solving through negotiation, often with the help of a mediator, can be the most constructive or "peaceful" approach. A typical way to "end the conflict" is for one of the parties simply to inflict defeat on the other and

	Conflict Resolution		Conflict Management		Conflict Transformation	
	Non-coercive	Coercive	Non-coercive	Coercive	Non-coercive	Coercive
Definition of Peace	Ending Conflict		Controlling Destructive Conflict "Negative Peace"		Justice, Equal Power, Etc. "Positive Peace"	
Intermediate Goals	Avoidance of Conflict Solve Problem Exchange Capitulation (Giving in)	Eliminate or Defeat Opponent "Winning"	Establish System of Rules With Sanctions	Without Sanctions	Strengthen the Weak Party	Weaken the Strong Party
			Avoid Stereotypes, Prejudice, Alienation, and Violence		Change the System Controntation of Power Organizing	
			Share Power Compromise	Maintain Power Compromise		
Means Used	Debate Bargaining (with Offers) Mediation Withdrawal (Mutual or Unilateral) Negotiation (Problem Solving)	Fighting Threatening Bargaining (with Threats) Force	Debate Negotiation Bargaining (with Offers) Mediation Voting Ritual (dice, coin-tossing) Voluntary Arbitration Compromise	Bargaining (with Threats) Policing (Law Enforcement) Enforcement of Vote Coercive Arbitration/ Adjudication	Education Moral Persuasion Demonstration Parallel Rule Non-cooperation Fasting Negotiation Bargaining (with Offers)	Strike Boycott Fighting Sabotage Threat Fasting Force Negotiation Bargaining (with Threats)

Figure 1 Types of conflict resolution

"win" by imposing terms in its own favour. Complete elimination of the opponent will end a conflict, of course, but hardly in a constructive way.

In the second peacemaking approach, "Conflict Management," the aim is not to end the conflict, but rather to get the parties to live with it or to carry it on in ways that keep it within limits that are beneficial to both parties. What else is a recreational competitive game like hockey or chess but a contrived conflict that is carried on by the opponents because they both derive certain benefits (fun, exercise, thrill of competition, etc.)? The success of the game rests upon keeping the conflict within the rules that regulate it. Many real-life conflicts are like competitive games in this respect. For example, most of the political conflicts within societies can never be terminated completely. People's political beliefs and preferences don't change that easily. What a good political system does is to find effective rules and mechanisms for deciding what laws and policies to follow, without actually ending the diversity of opinion and disagreement about these things.

Democracy, for example, is a system of conflict management. It resolves questions by a set of rule-governed mechanisms like voting (majority rule), establishing rules to protect the minority (or minorities), and so on. Courts are rule-governed institutions that decide disputes by imposing an arbitrated settlement on the parties (which does not necessarily end the conflict between them). One of the best-known mechanisms for settling conflicts between good friends is through some "ritual", such as coin-tossing, straw-drawing, or dice-throwing, which the parties consider a fair procedure.[8] Another common, and very effective, conflict management device is that of compromise. In a compromise, both parties agree not to end the conflict, but to "live with it" in a way that allows each to get some of what they want. Negotiation and problem-solving cannot always end a conflict by finding a complete win-win solution; sometimes parties have to settle for compromise.

What about the third approach to peacemaking, "Conflict Transformation"? Some people find it hard to understand how *intensifying* a conflict can be called "peacemaking" or conflict resolution. Sometimes, however, it is necessary to intensify conflict before it can be resolved in a fair and constructive way. Earlier we discussed the problem of the apparent conflict between negative peace and positive peace, or between peace and justice. There we saw that a negative peace between parties that is destructive or oppressive for one of them is hardly an acceptable peace: it is not peace in the fullest sense of the word. Conflict Transformation models attempt to deal with this issue. They recognize that often, before a conflict can be resolved (regulated or terminated) in an acceptable way, it may have to be intensified first. Maybe the power balance between the conflicting parties is extremely unequal, so that one has the power to impose terms on the other in negotiation, bargaining, debating, voting – or fighting. In such cases, one must try to restore a more equal balance of power between them. Or, maybe, one party gains much more from the conflict than the other. In such cases the party getting the benefits may find it hard to see that there is a conflict to be resolved, and even if they see it they may not be motivated to enter into any resolution. These are cases in which the first step of conflict resolution has to include ways of "getting the attention" of the other party.

That is why Conflict Transformation approaches to peacemaking are usually confrontational in nature. They are concerned with finding ways to motivate unwilling parties to make peace. Often they are aimed at either strengthening the power of the weaker party or weakening the power of the stronger party. Various forms of persuasive or even coercive pressure, such as demonstrations, strikes, boycotts, non-cooperation or civil disobedience, and other tactics associated with nonviolent resistance have power equalization and motivation as their intermediate goal. The primary goal is to achieve a "positive peace." This is what distinguishes Conflict Transformation from Conflict Resolution that aims merely at beating or eliminating one's opponents.

Notes

1 A summary of these criticisms can be found in the *International Peace Studies Newsletter*, 15.2 (Winter 1986). One of the strongest criticisms of Peace Studies as a politicization of education is made by Caroline Cox and Roger Scruton, *Peace Studies: A Critical Survey* (London: Institute for European Defense and Strategic Studies, 1985).
2 Adam Curle, "The Scope and Dilemmas of Peace Studies," inaugural lecture at the University of Bradford, 4 February 1975 (Bradford: School of Peace Studies, University of Bradford).
3 See, for example, Robert M, Axelrod, *The Evolution of Cooperation* (New York; Basic Books, 1984). See also, M. Nowak, R. May, and K. Sigmund, "The Arithmetics of Mutual Help," *Scientific American* (June 1995): 76–81.
4 Curle.
5 Johan Galtung, "Violence, Peace, and Peace Research," *Journal of Peace Research* 6.3 (1969): 167–91.
6 Thomas Hobbes, *Leviathan: Or the Matter, Form and Power of a Commonwealth Ecclesiastical and Civil* (Paris, 1651; New York: Collier Books, 1962).
7 Hannah Arendt, *On Violence* (New York: Harcourt Bruce Jovanovich, 1970).
8 Rituals like these are common ways of settling important disputes within certain so-called primitive tribes and cultures, often with great success. More "advanced," scientific cultures are suspicious of ritualistic ways of deciding disputes, since we believe that conflict resolution should be "rational." But maybe our modern societies would be better off if we tossed coins to decide very tense political disputes between warring parties!

2 Four major challenges facing peace education in regions of intractable conflict

Gavriel Salomon

Although peace education all over the world faces numerous challenges, such as conflicting collective narratives, historical memories, contradictory beliefs, and severe inequalities, there are additional challenges that transcend content and method. Four such major challenges that pertain to the very core of peace education are discussed: (a) the creation of a "ripple effect" whereby the impact of peace education programs spreads to wider social circles of society; (b) increasing the endurance of desired program effects in light of their easy erosion; (c) the need for differential programs given the differences in culture and in the role that each adversary plays in a conflict; and (d) the need to find ways to bridge between general dispositions, principles, and values and their application in specific situations where competing motivations are dominant. I argue that the four major challenges are also common to other kinds of programs, such as human rights, antiracism, and tolerance.

Peace education in regions of intractable conflict is often carried out in sociopolitical contexts that essentially negate the messages of such programs (e.g., Barash, 1997) and which are sometimes described as subversive activities during ongoing intractable conflict (Minow, 2002). However, beyond political opposition, there are other challenges facing peace education: contradictory collective narratives, charged negative emotions, severe inequalities, and more (Salomon, 2004, 2006). Some of these are dealt with head-on, as in the case of historical memories that fuel the conflict (e.g., McCully, 2005; Roe & Cairns, 2003), or opposing identity constructions that, likewise, underlie the conflict (Halabi & Sonnenschein, 2004).

However, there are other challenges that need to be dealt with. In this article, I discuss four such challenges that appear to concern the very heart of peace education. The discussion of these challenges is based on research and experience of peace education in Israel–Palestine, but seems to be equally relevant to other settings and locations where peace education is carried out within the context of an intractable conflict. The challenges are as follows: (a) the need to create a societal "ripple effect" whereby the impact of peace education programs spreads to wider social circles of non-program participants; (b) increasing the endurance of desired program effects in the face of their easy erosion; (c) the need for diverse programs, given the differences among groups' needs and the role those needs play in the conflict; and (d) the need to find ways to bridge the gap that divides the cultivation of desired general dispositions, principles, and values and their application in specific situations where competing motivations are dominant. I believe these four challenges transcend questions of specific goals, methods, contents, ages of participants, or the surrounding sociopolitical contexts.

The creation of a ripple effect

The United Nations called for the promotion of a culture of peace by educating people to see themselves as peaceful with norms that emphasize cooperation and the resolution of conflicts through dialogue, negotiation, and nonviolence. Two issues are involved here. One pertains to peace education of youngsters with the purpose of developing them into peace-supporting adults (e.g., Oppenheimer, 2009). This is a developmental issue. The other, of greater concern here, is the creation of a more peaceful society. This can be achieved

> . . . when citizens of the world understand global problems, have the skills to resolve conflicts and struggle for justice non-violently, live by international standards of human rights and equity, appreciate cultural diversity, and respect the Earth and each other. Such learning can only be achieved with systematic education for peace. (Hague Appeal, 1999, para. 6)

Clearly, the idea was to educate not only individuals, but to affect whole societies. Thus, a major challenge facing peace education programs must be the concern for a ripple effect whereby program effects spread to wider circles of society.

The perceptions, attitudes, and dispositions to be changed are rooted in a social ethos and, more specifically, in a collective narrative and "ethos of the conflict" (Bar-Tal & Salomon, 2006; Rouhana & Bar-Tal, 1998). It follows that if peace education is to have any lasting effect, it must affect the social ethos. If society does not express its desire to live in peace with an adversary, or does not condemn intolerance of a minority, or fails to promote human rights, affecting the hearts and minds of a few individuals to become more peace oriented or more tolerant may not matter much in the larger social context.

The issue here pertains to levels of influence – the level of individual psychology and the level of society. However, lest we exercise reductionism, the two levels need to be examined together; neither alone is a sufficient explanation of the spread of ideas. Changing the attitudes, beliefs, and perceptions of an individual, and the inter-individual spread of these changes – the ripple effect – are two different processes that require two different, although interrelated, sets of explanatory concepts.

Recent research concerns the way the fruits of intergroup contact can spread. This line of research focuses on the extended contact hypothesis (e.g., Pettigrew, Christ, Wagner, & Stellmacher, 2007), whereby participation in contact groups affects non-participating friends of participants. However, this line of research has only rarely examined the spreading effects of indirect contact in the context of social tension or actual conflict (one exception is the Northern Ireland study of Paolini, Hewstone, Cairns, & Voci, 2004). The context of real tension or conflict between groups is qualitatively different from less-threatening contexts as it entails strong feelings of anxiety, hatred, distrust, and anger (Coleman, 2003; Salomon, 2002). It is an open question whether findings of studies carried out in the United States concerning relationships between ethnic groups (Wright, Aaron, McLaughlin-Vlope, 1997), or in Finland about relationships with foreigners (Liebkind & McAlister, 1999), apply also to Kashmir or Lebanon or other regions where tension is high between majority and a profoundly discriminated ethnic minority.

According to the extended contact theory, when an ingroup person (A) learns that another ingroup friend (B) has close contacts with an outgroup person (C), then this leads, under certain conditions, to A's more positive attitudes, reduced anxiety, and weaker prejudices toward C's outgroup (Pettigrew et al., 2007). This argument has been supported in a variety of countries and contexts with a variety of means, ranging from reading friendship stories in the United Kingdom (Cameron, Rutland, Brown, & Douch, 2006) to knowledge of real face-to-face contact (Turner, Hewstone, Voci, Paolini, & Christ, 2007). A number of underlying mechanisms have been suggested and supported: reduced intergroup anxiety (Paolini et al., 2004), changed ingroup norms with respect to the outgroup (Wright et al., 1997), vicarious experience (Turner, Rihannon, Hewstone, Voci, & Vonafakou, 2008), and self-disclosure (Turner et al., 2007).

However, one factor that has been studied so far only partly concerns different degrees of proximity to the actual contact. Not all candidates to be part of the extended contact are equally close to the contact itself or equally emotionally involved with the person who is in contact with an outgroup member. It can be hypothesized that the effects of the extended contact and the need to establish balance (Heider, 1958) are stronger for those who are emotionally or physically closer to the individuals involved in real contact with adversaries than those who are farther away or less emotionally involved.

The challenge of the ripple effect of peace education programs in contexts of intractable conflict is twofold. First, there are the psychological questions of whether ripple effects resulting from peace or similar educational programs do actually take place, how potent they are, what mechanisms underlie them, and what conditions facilitate or hinder their creation. Are the mechanisms and conditions more or less similar to the ones observed in less conflicted contexts? Second, there are the more applied questions of how ripple effects can be created, facilitated, and sustained. We would also need to distinguish short-from long-term ripple effects. Short-term effects may be attained through the mechanism of extended contacts; but, if not reinforced by continued peace education efforts, it would remain short-lived (see the next section). Still, although extended contact and continued reinforcements may be two of the necessary conditions to attain a longer-range ripple effect, it is quite likely that peace education alone in the absence of top-down political changes would be insufficient.

Paolini et al. (2004) and others studied the effects of extended contact as they unfold without intervention. The question in the realm of peace education is how to engineer such effects and what audience is most likely to serve as an effective lever for advancing a ripple effect. Seen in this context, one may ask whether children and youths, the most common participants in peace education programs, are the most suitable target audiences. This issue has not often been discussed (as an exception, see Cox & Scruton, 1984). However, when considered in the context of social psychological literature on the spread of persuasion, children would not be considered the most influential social agents in society at large. Alternatively, what would distinguish peace education for the young from peace education for adults when the attainment of social ripple effects is the goal? How could school children be helped to serve as influential gatekeepers, opinion leaders, and agenda setters as suggested by the two-step flow of communication theory (Brosius & Weimann, 1996), given their unique social contexts? It might well be the case that if one aims at initiating a social ripple effect, then the approach for adults – the kind of influential ones studied by Kelman (2002) – ought to be radically changed when applied to younger audiences.

Increasing the endurance of desired program effects

There is ample research to show that peace education and similar programs have a positive, albeit differential, impact on program participants' attitudes, prejudices, desires for contact, and legitimizations of the "other side" (e.g., Salomon, 2004; A. Smith, 1999). However, these positive results are more often than not obtained when measured right after the completion of programs. When measured a while later, the effects appear to have eroded and returned to their original state (Kupermintz & Salomon, 2005).[1] Whether there is a long-term implicit sleeper effect is, so far, an open question.

Apparently, sociopolitical events can suppress previously attained effects, suggesting that that which can be changed by a "shot in the arm" kind of intervention can as easily be changed back by external forces, as shown, for example, in Northern Ireland (Kilpatrick & Leitch, 2004) and in Israel (Salomon, 2006). A similar fate has faced other short "technological" interventions, such as attempts to change teachers' understandings of "good learning" (Strauss & Shilony, 1994) and mothers' ways of handling substance-dependent infants (Dakof, Quille, & Tejeda, 2003). Such interventions, as contrasted with "natural" ones that are more akin to socialization processes, often have only short-lived effects (L. D. Smith, 1993).

The research and theoretical literature pertaining to attitude change is rich, yet there is far less research on the issue of maintaining changes (for an exception, see Schimmel, 2009). Two fields are much concerned with this issue: the medical (e.g., Mccrady, Epstein, & Hirsch, 2002) and the therapeutic fields (e.g., McGuire, 2003). Different models of diffusion and social adoption of medical and technological innovations have been suggested (e.g., Kempe, Kleinberg, & Tardos, 2003), including word-of-mouth and the two-step flow of communication. However, it may well be the case that the models developed for the fields of medicine and technological innovation may not fit issues concerning the impact of peace education, with its potential negation of prevailing views and the dominance of the received collective narrative.

Three attempts to restore the eroded attainments of peace education programs were successfully carried out 2 or 3 months after the completion of peace education programs. Field experimental interventions have shown that when even brief interventions, such as forced compliance (a form of role playing; Leippe & Eisenstadt, 1994), peer teaching of lessons learned during a peace education program to younger peers, or writing reflections on the programs, are carried out, the initial changes are restored and endure for at least another 3 months. Such experimental interventions suggest that the changes may not have totally eroded, allowing for a certain degree of recovery. However, settings that enable such interventions are limited, such as school programs, and, thus, not an answer to the question of how to maintain changes on a larger social scale. Moreover, we do not know whether the revived changes would overcome truly dramatic or painful sociopolitical events, so common in situations of intractable conflict.

An important element may be the depth of the attitudinal and perceptual change. It can be assumed that the deeper the change, the more durable it would be. This may depend on a number of factors. One is the extent to which peace education programs satisfy the collective needs of participants. This can be implied from a study by Shnabel and Nadler (2008), who found that, although a minority (Arabs in Israel) are driven by a need for empowerment, the majority (Jews in Israel) are driven by a need for moral justification. Kelman (1958) suggested another set of factors: compliance, identification, and internalization. Ajzen and Sexton (1999) spoke of depth of processing, belief congruence, and attitude–behavior correspondence as relevant factors for the maintenance of change. Indeed, Ajzen and Sexton's research on depth of processing would predict that deeper processing – more elaboration and more controlled, rather than automatic, connections to existing cognitive schemata – would increase the chances of accessing the acquired attitudes and perceptions. However, deeper processing is less likely to take place when the desired attitudinal and perceptual changes and one's belief system are incongruent, suggesting that deeper processing is more likely among those already partly converted.

Another factor that seems to contribute to the sustainability of peace educational effects is the affective component – the arousal of positive affect and empathy vis-à-vis the adversary (Schimmel, 2009; Stephan, 2008). Positive affect also implies the reduction of negative feelings, such as threat and anxiety (Paolini et al., 2004), which facilitate the effects of contact. To the extent that positive emotions sustain the effect of the persuasion (Petty, Gleicher, & Baker, 1991) and facilitate changes in organizations (Forgas & George, 2001), they can be expected to help sustain the effects of peace education.

An important implication that follows from the previous list of desired intra-individual changes is that they cannot be easily attained and sustained with short-term programs. Depth of processing, empathy, internalization, taking the other side's role, and the like require time (e.g., Nisbett & Ross, 1980). However, intra-individual changes of cognition and emotions may not suffice to sustain the kinds of changes that peace education desires. As is commonly known, one's attitudes, feelings, and perceptions vis-à-vis the other side in the conflict are deeply rooted in the collective narrative and its dictates. Social support is one of the conditions for the success of intergroup contact (e.g., Pettigrew, 1998). It appears to also be a necessary condition for sustaining the effects of peace education programs. However, this entails a paradox: Although social support may be a necessary condition for sustaining a program's effects, it is itself a result of the spreading effects of peace education. As pointed out earlier, peace education programs often take place in social contexts colored by that kind of conflict-related ethos that negates the very messages of peace education (e.g., Magal, 2009); and hence, one cannot assume the a priori existence of social support that might help sustain program effects.

The solution may well lie in the combination of incremental bottom-up, intra-individual processes generated by peace education and top-down, policy-based governmental promotion of peace processes. In this respect, Gallagher (2007) concluded that what made Northern Ireland progress more than Cyprus is that

> bolstered by formal diplomatic efforts toward peace agreement in the society at large, the educational system of Northern Ireland has been able to pursue many incremental peace education efforts that have helped to move its society along thus far. (p. 31)

Whereas the top-down processes provide the needed social support, the grassroot peace education efforts provide the impetus for change through the intra-individual factors mentioned earlier: satisfaction of needs, identification, internalization, depth of processing, and positive affect.

The need for a differential approach

So far, many of the contents and methods of peace education programs are the same for all sides of a conflict. This is particularly pronounced where the contact hypothesis is applied (Mania et al., 2009). The underlying assumption appears to be that the processes of reconciliation, mutual understanding, humanization, and empathy are similar for all involved, regardless of whether they are majority or minority, conqueror or conquered, natives or immigrants.

In a few cases, programs have been administered in uni-national or uni-ethnic groups. However, even then, the contents and the methods are quite uniform; but, as research shows, they are not (Yablon, 2007). In one study (Biton & Salomon, 2005) involving about 800 Israeli Jewish and Palestinian youngsters, we found that, whereas the former entered the program with a conception of peace as the absence of violence ('negative peace'), the latter assumed that peace means independence and freedom ('structural peace'). The effects of that year-long, school-based program were far stronger on the Jews than on the Palestinians because it mainly dealt with the psychological aspects of reconciliation, not with any political solution; and, as other research has shown, the Jews, being the majority, shun the political and prefer the interpersonal (Suleiman, 2004).

Rosen (2008), applying a forced compliance intervention with peace education graduates, found positive effects that restored earlier attitudinal changes for the Israeli Jewish participants, but found no effect on the Israeli–Palestinians. This suggests that, whereas the Jews engaged in trying to convey the ideas acquired during the peace education workshop, the Palestinians engaged in asserting their position and becoming empowered. This was supported by yet another study (Hussesi, 2009) where it was found that in the same year-long, school-based peace education program, the Jews learned to give somewhat more legitimacy to the Palestinian collective narrative, whereas the Palestinians came to reinforce their own narrative. No legitimization of the Jewish collective narrative took place. Maoz (2000) found that, whereas the Jewish participants rely on formal power that emanates from institutionally provided powers, the Palestinians rely on informal factors: their knowledge of the local history of the conflict and their sense of deprivation and injustice. Gallagher (2007) reached the same kind of conclusion: Cultural contexts, different needs, conflicting narratives and expectations, and opposing political agendas affect what each side brings to and takes from a program. One size definitely does not fit all.

Such distinctions require a differential approach to peace education. However, the challenge is to find some formulae in light of which different programs, based on different psychological principles, can be designed. Halabi, Sonnenschein, and Friedman (2004) indeed developed differential programs, the emphasis of which was to strengthen the identity of the so-called oppressed minority and to liberate the so-called oppressor from its illusion of superiority. This then suggests that, rather than striving to attain a common goal – such as mutual acknowledgment, empathy, or reduced prejudices – peace education would need to accept the possibility that programs serve very different needs and goals for the parties involved, allowing one side to "have a voice," strengthen its adherence to its own collective narrative, or become empowered; and the other side to acknowledge its role in the conflict and give legitimacy to the other's collective narrative (Salomon, 2002). This might well be a variation on what Ross (2000) called 'good enough conflict resolution."

Facilitating the application of general dispositions and values to specific situations

Bar-Tal, Rosen, and Nets-Zehngut (2009) questioned the value of direct peace education as commonly practiced while a conflict is in full force, as is the current situation in Israel–Palestine and elsewhere. Instead, the authors suggested engaging in indirect peace education: cultivating general abilities, dispositions, and values such as tolerance, critical thinking, and ethnoempathy. Although this appears as a sound idea, there is room for some questions. How effectively can *general* abilities, dispositions, and values be applied in highly *specific* situations where strong counter-motivations are at play? Do believers offer their cheeks even to those whom they hate and despise? Are victims, even those with high morals, willing to show tolerance to their aggressors?

It is commonly accepted in social psychology that general values, dispositions, and abilities are not easily applied in specific situations, especially when alternative motivations – for example, to comply with the scientist (Milgram, 1974), to avoid responsibility (Latané, 1968), to avoid effort (Salomon, 1984), and so forth – are at play. Would the acquired disposition to be tolerant apply when it concerns a threatening adversary? Would the ability to think critically be utilized when anger is aroused by news about a terror activity?

All this does not mean that general abilities, dispositions, principles, and values are not to be cultivated. The challenge is to make them more accessible when motivations that negate them come into play. This is particularly important in the case of peace education, first, because indirect peace education – the cultivation of general abilities and dispositions – is proposed to replace direct peace education under certain conditions (Bar-Tal et al., 2009). Second, it is also important for peace education because even direct peace education needs to be accompanied by a wider context of more general abilities, beliefs, and dispositions that provide justification and support for the more specific attitudes and perceptions that dialogue and conflict management skills are designed to cultivate.

Cognitions, as Kruglanski (1989) pointed out, differ from each other in terms of content and certitude. Knowledge that is held with greater certitude, values that are more central, and attitudes that are held with greater strength are likely to be more tightly related to actual behaviors and are far more difficult to change (e.g., Abelson, 1988; Petty & Krosnick, 1995). Does this mean that the strength and certitude with which a cognition is held contributes to one's application of cognitions to situations that include competing motivations? The answer is a mixed one. Forsythe (1992), studying the morality (or rather, immorality) of business practices, found that those who espoused lofty moral values tended to behave most immorally, whereas those who perceived these values conditionally were more likely to apply them. Also, Langer (1997) did not support the idea of strongly held convictions, concepts, and beliefs. These, she claimed, are mindlessly applied even when the application is inappropriate. For Langer, practice and, thus, increased certitude make *im*perfect. In an interesting experiment, Langer showed that acquiring categorical knowledge ("this *is* X") debilitates its application to a new situation. On the other hand, conditional knowledge ("this *could be* X") makes applications to new situations possible.

Is then the implication that coming to hold certain beliefs and attitudes to a high degree of centrality and, hence, certitude may facilitate its application in situations in which one faces tempting alternatives and competing motivations, as is the case, say, with applying knowledge of mathematics to physics (Bassok & Holyoak, 1989)? Research on transfer of learning would support this view. Firm mastery of the principles to be transferred is needed, says some old research. Alternatively, is the implication that doubt, uncertainty, and conditional, rather than categorical, knowledge are better suited for application to novel situations, as the research by Langer (1997) suggests?

The answer seems to be "it depends." There is room to hypothesize that solidly held knowledge, firmly embraced beliefs, strongly held attitudes, and centrally placed values are, of course, easily applicable to concrete situations, but this application is generally to routine cases, it is automatically carried out, and it is therefore quite inflexible; or, in Langer's (1997) words, it is automatically and mindlessly applied. Having acquired socially shared and reinforced stereotypes about 'colored' people, the very observation of one of them automatically brings up the stereotype that is then easily applied in the form of an avoiding behavior. On the other hand, when knowledge is conditional, held with less certitude, it is more likely to be mindfully applied in a wide range of novel situations. One way or another, the very acquisition of certain socially oriented beliefs, values, and attitudes, in and of itself, does not guarantee its application to real-life situations involving an adversary.

Discussion

The four challenges I chose to discuss are not the only ones that face peace education. Other challenges, like severe inequalities built into the social fabric of societies in conflict, are as challenging as the ones previously mentioned. However, most other challenges do not pertain to the very core of peace education as do the challenges of the ripple effect, the endurance of effects, the need to provide differential approaches, and the relations between general dispositions and their specific application. In the absence of any one of the four, peace education may likely be a local, well-intended activity, but with little enduring social impact.

Revisiting the challenges discussed here raises the question of whether they apply only to peace education in the context of intractable conflict or whether they also apply, partly or wholly, to education for human rights, antiracism, tolerance, and the like. The differences between peace education and the other programs are clear enough, but there is also an important commonality. All pertain to changing hearts and minds in social environments that are not very supportive of their messages: human rights and civic education in certain developing countries (e.g., Fok, 2001), tolerance for minorities in particular minority-rich countries (e.g., Weldon, 2006), and antiracism in multinational countries (e.g., Penketh, 2000). Such programs – explicitly or implicitly – aim at having a societal impact, with enduring effects, taking ethnic and social group differences into account, and combining general dispositions and specific applications. In these respects, the challenges discussed here appear to apply to them as well.

Biographical note

Gavriel Salomon received his PhD at Stanford. He is past Dean of the Faculty of Education at the University of Haifa, is the founder and co-director of the Center for Research on Peace Education and a fellow of the AERA and APA. He has published six books on mind and technology, computers in education, and research on peace education, and numerous research and theory articles in international journals. He served as editor of the journal *Educational Psychologist* and is the recipient of an honorary doctorate from the Catholic University of Leuven, Belgium, the Israel National Award for scientific achievements in educational research, the AERA Scribner Award, and the Clervinga Chair at the University of Leiden, The Netherlands.

Notes

1 A rare exception is the study carried out in Sri Lanka by Malhotra and Liyanage (2005), where positive effects of a 4-day program were detected 1 year later.

References

Abelson, R. P. (1988). Conviction. *American Psychologist, 43*, 267–275.
Ajzen, I., & Sexton, J. (1999). Depth of processing, belief congruence, and attitude–behavior correspondence. In S. Chaiken & Y. Trope (Eds.), *Dual-process theories in social psychology* (pp. 117–140). New York, NY: Guilford.
Barash, P. D. (1997). *Beloved enemies: Our need for opponents.* Amherst, NY: Prometheus.
Bar-Tal, D., Rosen, Y., & Nets-Zehngut, R. (2009). Peace education in societies involved in intractable conflicts: Goals, conditions and directions. In G. Salomon & E. Cairns (Eds.), *Handbook of peace education* (pp. 21–44). New York, NY: Taylor & Francis.

Bar-Tal, D., & Salomon, G. (2006). Israeli-Jewish narratives of the Israeli–Palestinian conflict: Evolvement, contents, functions and consequences. In R. I. Rotberg (Ed.), *Israeli and Palestinian narratives of conflict: History's double helix* (pp. 19–46). Bloomington, IN: Indiana University Press.

Bassok, M., & Holyoak, K. J. (1989). Interdomain transfer between isomorphic topics in algebra and physics. *Journal of Experimental Psychology: Learning, Memory, and Cognition, 15*,153–166.

Biton, I., & Salomon, G. (2005). Peace in the eyes of Israeli and Palestinian youths: Effects of collective narratives and peace education programs. *Journal of Peace Research, 43*, 167–180.

Brosius, H. B., & Weimann, G. (1996). Who sets the agenda? Agenda-setting as a two-step flow. *Communication Research, 23*, 561–580.

Cameron, L., Rutland, A., Brown, R., & Douch, R. (2006). Changing children's intergroup attitudes towards refugees: Testing different models of extended contact. *Child Development, 77*, 1208–1219.

Coleman, P. T. (2003). Characteristics of protracted, intractable conflict: Toward the development of a metaframework–I. *Peace and Conflict: Journal of Peace Psychology, 9*, 1–38.

Cox, C., & Scruton, R. (1984). *Peace studies: A critical survey* (Paper No. 7). New York, NY: Institute for European Defence and Strategic Studies.

Dakof, G., Quille, T., & Tejeda, M. (2003). Enrolling and retaining mothers of substance-exposed infants in drug abuse treatment. *Journal of Consulting & Clinical Psychology, 71*, 764–772.

Fok, S. C. (2001). Meeting the challenge of human rights education: The case of Hong Kong. *Asia Pacific Educational Review, 2*, 56–65.

Forgas, J. P., & George, J. M. (2001). Affective influences on judgments and behavior in organizations: An information processing perspective. *Organizational Behavior and Human Decision Processes, 86*, 3–34.

Forsyth, D. (1992). Judging the morality of business practices: The influence of personal moral philosophies. *Journal of Business Ethics, 11*, 461–470.

Gallagher, T. (2007, March). *Social inclusion and education in Northern Ireland.* Invited keynote presentation to a Save the Children Conference on Social Inclusion, Belfast, Ireland.

Hague Appeal for Peace Global Campaign for Peace Education. (1999). *Global campaign for peace education.* Retrieved from http://www.haguepeace.org/index.php?action=pe

Halabi, R., & Sonnenschein, N. (2004). The Jewish-Palestinian encounter in a time of crisis. *Journal of Social Issues, 60*, 373–387.

Halabi, R., Sonnenschein, N., & Friedman, A. (2004). Liberate the oppressed and their oppressors. In R. Halabi (Ed.), *Israeli and Palestinian identities in dialogue* (pp. 59–78). New Brunswick, NJ: Rutgers University Press.

Heider, F. (1958). *The psychology of interpersonal relations.* New York, NY: Wiley.

Hussesi, R. (2009). *The relationship between legitimizing the adversary's collective narrative and adherence to one's own collective narrative, as a function of participation in a peace education program* (Unpublished doctoral dissertation). University of Haifa, Israel.

Kelman, H. C. (1958). Compliance, identification, and internalization: Three processes of attitude change. *Journal of Conflict Resolution, 2*, 51–60.

Kelman, H. C. (2002). Interactive problem solving: Informal mediation by the scholar-practitioner. In J. Bercovitch (Ed.), *Studies in international mediation* (pp. 167–193). New York, NY: Palgrave Macmillan.

Kempe, D., Kleinberg, J., & Tardos, E. (2003, April). *Maximizing the spread of influence through a social network.* Paper presented at the International Conference on Knowledge Discovery and Data Mining, Washington, DC.

Kilpatrick, R., & Leitch, R. (2004). Teachers' and pupils' educational experiences and school-based responses to the conflict in Northern Ireland. *Journal of Social Issues, 60*, 563–586.

Kruglanski, A. W. (1989). *Lay epistemics and human knowledge: Cognitive and motivational bases.* New York, NY: Plenum.

Kupermintz, H., & Salomon, G. (2005). Lessons to be learned from research on peace education in the context of intractable conflict. *Theory to Practice, 44*, 293–302.

Langer, E. J. (1997). *The power of mindful learning.* Reading, MA: Addison-Wesley.

Latané, B. (1968). Group inhibition of bystander intervention in emergencies. *Journal of Personality and Social Psychology, 10*, 215–221.

Leippe, M., & Eisenstadt, D. (1994). Generalization of dissonance reduction: Decreasing prejudice through induced compliance. *Journal of Personality and Social Psychology, 67*, 395–413.

Liebkind, K., & McAlister, A. L. (1999). Extended contact through peer modeling to promote tolerance in Finland. *European Journal of Social Psychology, 29*, 765–780.

Magal, T. (2009, March). *The media's role as a barrier to ethos challenging beliefs.* Paper presented at the annual meeting of the International Society of Political Psychology, Dublin, Ireland. Retrieved from http://www.allacademic.com/meta/p305570_index.html

Malhotra, D., & Liyanage, S. (2005). Long-term effects of peace workshops in protracted conflicts. *Journal of Conflict Resolution, 49*, 908–924.

Mania, E. W., Gaertner, S. L., Riek, B. M., Dovidio, J. F., Lomereaux, M. L., & Direso, S. A. (2009). Intergroup contact: Implications for peace education. In G. Salomon & E. Cairns (Eds.), *Handbook of peace education* (pp. 87–102). New York, NY: Taylor & Francis.

Maoz, I. (2000). Power relations in intergroup encounters: A case study of Jewish–Arab encounters in Israel. *International Journal of Intercultural Relations, 24*, 259–277.

Mccrady, B., Epstein, E., & Hirsch, L. (2002). Maintaining change after conjoint behavioral alcohol treatment for men: Outcomes at 6 months. *Addiction, 94*, 1381–1396.

McCully, B. K. (2005). History, identity, and the school curriculum in Northern Ireland: An empirical study of secondary students' ideas and perspectives. *Journal of Curriculum Studies, 37*, 85–116.

McGuire, J. (2003). Maintaining change: Converging legal and psychological initiatives in a therapeutic jurisprudence framework. *Western Criminology Review, 4*, 108–123.

Milgram, S. (1974) *Obedience to authority: An experimental view.* New Brunswick, NJ: Rutgers University Press.

Minow, M. (2002). Education for co-existence. *Arizona Law Review, 44*, 1–29.

Nisbett, R., & Ross, L. (1980). *Human inference: Strategies and shortcomings of social judgment.* Englewood Cliffs, NJ: Prentice Hall.

Oppenheimer, L. (2009). Contribution of developmental psychology to peace education. In G. Salomon & E. Cairns (Eds.), *Handbook of peace education* (pp. 103–121). New York, NY: Taylor & Francis.

Paolini, S., Hewstone, M., Cairns, E., & Voci, A. (2004). Effects of direct and indirect cross-group friendships on judgments of Catholics and Protestants in Northern Ireland: The mediating role of an anxiety-reduction mechanism. *Personality and Social Psychology Bulletin, 30*, 770–786.

Penketh, L. (2000). *Tackling institutional racism: Anti-racist policies and social work education and training.* Bristol, England: Policy Press.

Pettigrew, T. (1998). Intergroup contact theory. *Annual Review of Psychology, 49*, 65–85.

Pettigrew, T., Christ, O., Wagner, U., & Stellmacher, J. (2007). Direct and indirect intergroup contact effects on prejudice: A normative interpretation. *International Journal of Intercultural Relations, 31*, 411–425.

Petty, R. E., Gleicher, F., & Baker, S. M. (1991). Multiple roles for affect in persuasion. In J. Forgas (Ed.), *Emotion and social judgments* (pp. 181–200). Oxford, England: Pergamon.

Petty, R. E., & Krosnick, J. A. (Eds.). (1995). *Attitude strength: Antecedents and consequences.* Mahwah, NJ: Lawrence Erlbaum Associates, Inc.

Roe, M. D., & Cairns, E. (2003). Memories in conflict: Review and a look to the future. In E. Cairns & M. D. Roe (Eds.), *The role of memory in ethnic conflict* (pp. 171–180). New York, NY: Palgrave Macmillan.

Rosen, I. (2008). Perception of collective narrative of the conflict: Challenges of peace education. In S. Zamir & A. Aharoni (Eds.), *The voice of peace in the process of education* (pp. 49–68). Shikmim, Israel: Achva Academic College of Education.

Ross, M. (2000). "Good-enough" isn't so bad: Thinking about success and failure in ethnic conflict management. *Journal of Peace Psychology, 6*, 27–47.

Rouhana, N., & Bar-Tal, D. (1998). Psychological dynamics of intractable ethnonational conflicts: The Israeli–Palestinian case. *American Psychologist, 53*, 761–770.

Salomon, G. (1984). Television is "easy" and print is "tough": The differential investment of mental effort in learning as a function of perceptions and attributions. *Journal of Educational Psychology, 76*, 647–658.

Salomon, G. (2002). The nature of peace education: Not all programs are created equal. In G. Salomon & B. Nevo (Eds.), *Peace education: The concept, principles, and practices around the world* (pp. 3–15). Mahwah, NJ: Lawrence Erlbaum Associates, Inc.

Salomon, G. (2004). Does peace education make a difference? *Peace and Conflict: Journal of Peace Psychology, 10,* 257–274.

Salomon, G. (2006). Does peace education *really* make a difference? *Peace and Conflict: Journal of Peace Psychology, 12,* 37–48.

Schimmel, N. (2009). Towards a sustainable and holistic model of peace education: A critique of conventional modes of peace education through dialogue in Israel. *Journal of Peace Education, 6,* 51–68.

Shnabel, N., & Nadler, A. (2008). A needs-based model of reconciliation: Satisfying the differential emotional needs of victim and perpetrator as a key to promoting reconciliation. *Journal of Personality and Social Psychology, 94,* 116–132.

Smith, A. (1999, April). *Education and the peace process in Northern Ireland.* Paper presented to the annual conference of the American Education Research Association, Montreal, Canada.

Smith, L. D. (1993). Natural science and unnatural technology. *American Psychologist, 48,* 588–589.

Stephan, W. G. (2008). Psychological and communication processes associated with intergroup conflict resolution. *Small Group Research, 39,* 28–41.

Strauss, S., & Shilony, T. (1994). Teachers' models of children's minds and learning. In L. A. Hirschfeld & S. A. Gelman (Eds.), *Mapping the mind* (pp. 455–473). New York, NY: Cambridge University Press.

Suleiman, R. (2004). Jewish-Palestinian relations in Israel: The planned encounter as a microcosm. In R. Halabi (Ed.), *Israeli and Palestinian identities in dialogue* (pp. 31–46). New Brunswick, NJ: Rutgers University Press.

Turner, R. N., Hewstone, M., Voci, A., Paolini, S., & Christ, O. (2007). Reducing prejudice via direct and extended cross-group friendship. *European Review of Social Psychology, 18,* 212–255.

Turner, R. N., Rihannon, N., Hewstone, M., Voci, A., & Vonafakou, C. (2008). A test of the extended intergroup contact hypothesis: The mediating role of intergroup anxiety, perceived intergroup and outgroup norms, and inclusion of the outgroup on the self. *Journal of Personality and Social Psychology, 95,* 834–860.

Weldon, S. (2006). The institutional context of tolerance for ethnic minorities: A comparative, multi-level analysis of Western Europe. *American Journal of Political Science, 50,* 331–349.

Wright, S. C., Aaron, A., McLaughlin-Vlope, T., & Ropp, S. A. (1997). The extended contact effect: Knowledge of cross-group friendship and prejudice. *Journal of Personality and Social Psychology, 73,* 73–90.

Yablon, Y. B. (2007). Cognitive rather than emotional modification in peace education programs: Advantages and limitations. *Journal of Moral Education, 36,* 51–65.

3   Peace in international relations

Oliver P. Richmond

Peace can be seen in more critical terms as both a process and a goal. This opens up a particular focus on the process by which peace as a self-conscious and reflexive goal may be achieved. If peace is taken as a strategic goal it would tend towards a focus on mutual preservation and never move beyond preliminary stages relating to security, but there are further, more inspiring, possibilities.

This is certainly not to dismiss the importance of mainstream IR, but to caution against its representation as a 'complete' discipline, which it clearly is not. Indeed, there is a serious question as to whether aspects of orthodox approaches (by which I mean positivist debates derived from realism, liberalism and Marxism) to IR are anti-peace, sometimes purposively, and sometimes carelessly. The three main orthodox theories are often taken to offer determinist grand narratives: realism offers an elite and negative peace based on inherency; liberalism offers a one-size-fits all progressive framework of mainly elite governance with little recognition of difference; and Marxism offers grassroots emancipation from determinist structures of the international political economy via violent revolution. Yet, as this study shows, in the context of peace other possible narratives emerge.

This study is informed by an attempt to establish a broader, interdisciplinary reading of peace and to embed this within IR. It is worth noting that peace has preoccupied a broad range of thinkers, activists, politicians and other figures in various ways, often to do with an interest in, or critique of, violence, influence, power and politics. These include, to name but a few, Thucydides, Hobbes, Machiavelli, Kant, Locke, Paine, Jefferson, John Stuart Mill, Gandhi, Freud, Einstein, Lorenz, Mead, Martin Luther King, Thoreau, Foucault, Galtung, Boulding, Freire, Tolstoy and Camus. Many other public figures, religious figures, cultural figures, politicians and officials, as well as many obscured from Western post-Enlightenment thought by their linguistic or cultural difference, also turned their hands to describing peace. Yet, there remains a surprising lack of an explicit debate on peace in IR theory.

More than ever, research and policy informed by a contextual understanding of peace is needed, rather than merely a focus on fear reproduced by worst case security scenarios stemming from a balance of power or terror derived from military, political or economic analytical frameworks that assume violence and greed to be endemic. Indeed, in the contemporary context it is also clear that any discussion of peace as opposed to war and conflict must also connect with research and policy on development, justice and environmental sustainability. These are the reasons why, for example, the liberal peace – the main concept of peace in circulation today – is in crisis.

Much of the debate about war that dominates IR is also indicative of assumptions about what peace is or should be. This ranges from the pragmatic removal of overt violence, an ethical peace, ideology, to a debate about a self-sustaining peace. Anatol Rapoport conceptualised 'peace through strength'; 'balance of power'; 'collective security'; 'peace through law'; 'personal or religious pacifism'; and 'revolutionary pacifism'. Hedley Bull saw peace as the absence of war in an international society, though of course war was the key guarantee for individual state survival. These views represent the mainstream approaches and indicate why the creation of an explicit debate about peace is both long overdue and vital in an international environment in which major foreign policy decisions seem to be taken in mono-ideational environment where ideas matter, but only certain, hegemonic ideas.

With the exception of orthodox versions of realism and Marxism, approaches to IR theory offer a form of peace that many would recognise as personally acceptable. Realism fails to offer much for those interested in peace, unless peace is seen as Darwinian and an unreflex-ive, privileged concept only available to the powerful and a commonwealth they may want to create. Most realist analysis expends its energy in reactive discussions based upon the inherency of violence in human nature, now discredited in other disciplines, which are ultimately their own undoing. This is not to say that other approaches do not also suffer flaws, but the focus on individuals, society, justice, development, welfare, norms, transnationalism, institutionalism or functionalism offers an opportunity for a negotiation of a form of peace that might be more sustainable because it is more broadly inclusive of actors and issues. In other words, parsimony, reductionism and rationalism run counter to a peace that engages fully with the diversity of life and its experiences.

Methodological considerations

Any discussion of peace is susceptible to universalism, idealism and rejection-ism, and to collapse under the weight of its own ontological subjectivity. This study is indebted to a genealogical approach that can be used to challenge the common assumption of IR theorists that peace as a concept is ontologically stable, in terms of representing an objective truth (plausible or not), legitimating the exercise of power, and representing a universal ethic. To rehearse this, a genealogical approach allows for an investigation of the subject without deference to a meta-narrative of power and knowledge in order to unsettle the depiction of a linear projection from 'origin' to 'truth'. The camouflaging of the subjective nature of peace disguises ideology, hegemony, dividing practices and marginalisation. Concepts of peace should be a cornerstone of IR interdisciplinary investigation of international politics and everyday life.

For the purposes of this study, peace is viewed from a number of perspectives. It can be a specific concept (one among many): it infers an ontological and epistemological position of being at peace, and knowing peace; it infers a methodological approach to accessing knowledge about peace and about constructing it; and it implies a theoretical approach, in which peace is a process and outcome defined by a specific theory.

The concepts of peace

What is peace? This would seem to be an obvious question deserving an obvious answer. Yet, the reluctance to open this debate could be merely an oversight, it could be because the answer is too obvious to waste time upon it, or it could be because once opened up, the debate upon peace offers all kind of possibilities, liberal, illiberal or radical, and possibly subversive. This is not to say that there is a conspiracy of silence when it comes to peace, because two World Wars and the Cold War would seem to have settled this basic question of modernity in favour of the 'liberal peace', made up of a victor's peace at its most basic level, an institutional peace to provide international governance and guarantees, a constitutional peace to ensure democracy and free-trade, and a civil peace to ensure freedom and rights within society. This, in Anglo-American terms, places the individual before the state, though in Continental varieties it sees the individual as subordinate to the state (a little noted, but significant point). Both variations rest upon a social contract between representatives and citizens. Yet, events since 1989 indicate that peace is not as it seems. There may be a liberal consensus on peace, but there are many technical, political, social, economic and intellectual issues remaining, and the very universality of the post-Cold War liberal peace is still contested in terms of components, and the methods used to build it (from military intervention to the role of NGOs, international organisations, agencies and international financial institutions).

One approach to thinking about peace that is commonly used is to look back at its historical, international, uses. These generally include the following: an Alexandrian peace, which depended upon a string of military conquests loosely linked together; a Pax Romana, which depended upon tight control of a territorial empire, and also included a 'Carthaginian peace' in which the city of Carthage was razed to the ground and strewn with salt to make sure it would not re-emerge; an Augustine peace dependent upon the adoption and protection of a territorial version of Catholicism, and the notion of just war; the Westphalian peace, dependent upon the security of states and the norms of territorial sovereignty; the Pax Britannia, dependent upon British domination of the seas, on trade and loose alliances with colonised peoples; the Paris Peace Treaty of 1919, dependent upon an embryonic international organisation, collective security, the self-determination of some, and democracy; the United Nations system, dependent upon collective security and international cooperation, a social peace entailing social justice, and the liberal peace, including upon democratisation, free markets, human rights and the rule of law, development, and, perhaps most of all, the support both normative and material, of the United States and its allies.

Though peace was supposed to be one of IR's key agendas when the discipline was founded in 1919, and certainly was explicitly part of the main institutional frameworks of the modern era, IR as a discipline tends to deal with peace implicitly, through its theoretical readings of international order, of war, and history. The empirical events that mark IR tend to be associated with violence, rather than peace. Most thinkers in a Western, developed context assume that they know peace and would never take on an ontological position that violence is a goal, though it may be an acknowledged side-effect. This adds the sheen of legitimacy, not to say legality, in both a juridical and normative sense to the discipline, despite its very limited engagement with peace.

The following dynamics are characteristic of the way in which peace is often thought of and deployed in IR:

1 peace is always aspired to and provides an optimum, though idealistic, point of reference;
2 it is viewed as an achievable global objective, based on universal norms;
3 it is viewed as a geographically bounded framework defined by territory, culture, identity and national interests;
4 it is presented as an objective truth, associated with complete legitimacy;
5 it is related to a certain ideology or political or economic framework (liberalism, neo-liberalism, democracy, communism or socialism, etc.);
6 it is viewed as a temporal phase;
7 it is based upon state or collective security;
8 it is based upon local, regional or global forms of governance, perhaps defined by a hegemonic actor or a specific multilateral institution;

9 it is viewed as a top-down institutional framework or a bottom-up civil society-oriented framework;

10 there needs to be little discussion of the conceptual underpinnings of peace because it is one ideal liberal form;

11 most thinking about peace in IR is predicated on preventing conflict, and at best creating an externally supported peace, not on creating a self-sustaining peace.

These dynamics have meant that the most important agenda in IR has not been subject to a sustained examination. Even in the realms of peace and conflict studies, the focus has been on preventing violence rather than on a sustained attempt to develop a self-sustaining order. Where attempts have been made to reflect on a viable world order in a number of different quarters, the liberal peace has often emerged as the main blueprint approach. What is most important about this treatment is that as an objective point of reference, it is possible for the diplomat, politician, official of international organisations, regional organisations or international agencies, to judge what is right and wrong in terms of aspirations, processes, institutions and methods, in their particular areas of concern. The liberal peace is the foil by which the world is now judged, in its multiple dimensions, and there has been little in terms of the theorisation of alternative concepts of peace.

How does international theory develop concepts of peace? This happens only indirectly in most cases. Implicit in thought and practice relating to the international are multiple perspectives on the nature, scope and plausibility of certain kinds of peace. What is more, in this age of globalisation the deferral of a debate on peace in favour of reductive and expedient debates on war, power, conflict and violence, is dangerously anachronistic if IR theory is to be seen as part of a broader project leading to viable and sustainable forms of peace.

Perspectives on peace in IR theory

Realism implies a peace found in the state-centric balance of power, perhaps dominated by a hegemon. Peace is limited if at all possible. Idealism and utopianism claim a future possibility of a universal peace in which states and individuals are free, prosperous and unthreatened. Pluralism, liberalism, internationalism, liberal institutionalism and neo-liberalism see peace as existing in the institutionalisation of liberal norms of economic, political and social institutionalisation of cooperation, regulation and governance. These approaches offer functional networks and organisation, and transnationalism, between and beyond states, and the ensuing liberal peace is believed not to be hegemonic, but universal. Structuralism and Marxist approaches see peace as lying in the absence of certain types of structural violence, often in structures which promote economic and class domination. Cosmopolitanism extends the liberal argument to include the development of a universal discourse between states, organisations and actors for mutual accord. Constructivism combines these understandings, allowing identities and ideas to modify state behaviour but retaining the core of realism which sees states as underpinning order and peace as limited to institutional cooperation and a limited recognition of individual agency. Critical approaches see peace as a consequence of a cosmopolitan, communicative transcendence of parochial understandings of global responsibility and action. Post-structuralism represents peace as resulting from the identification of the deep-rooted structures of dominance and their revolutionary replacement as a consequence of that identification by multiple and coexisting concepts of peace which respect the difference of others.

One common thread within many of the implicit debates about peace is its use as something close to the Platonic 'ideal form'. In *The Republic,* Socrates argued that truth is found in an ideal form, associated with 'goodness' rather than in subjective perceptions and interests. This type of thinking indicates that there could be an objective reality of peace, but because it is an ideal form it is probably not fully attainable. Yet, it is often assumed that history is driven by a linear, rational, progression towards that ideal form. The notion of peace as an ideal form has different implications for different approaches to IR theory, spanning the implicit acceptance that peace is a guiding objective even though it cannot be achieved to a belief that rational progress will lead to peace.

Debates about peace span both classical and contemporary literatures, and a range of intellectual debates. These include what modern realists often described as the realism of Thucydides, Augustine, Hobbes and Schmitt, in which peace was to be found in bounded and often tragic strategic thinking in which unitary actors delineate their own versions of peace within the framework provided by sovereign states. The tragedy of these approaches lies in their unitary internal assumptions of a shared peace within political units based upon common interests and values, and the difficulties in maintaining peaceful relations with other external polities that have their own notions of peace. Peace in these terms is derived from territorial units determined to protect their identities and interests, and is therefore extremely limited. For this reason, an international system comprising states pursing their interests is said to exist, which denotes few shared values beyond domestic politics, and rests upon the hierarchical ordering of international relations. This is based upon relative power and alliances derived from shared interests rather than shared values. Peace is conceptualised as very basic, or as a Utopian ideal form, which is unobtainable.

A less harsh version of peace is to be found in the idealist, liberal and liberal interventionist strands of international thought. These also focus on territorially bounded identity and interest units – mainly states – but see their interests defined in terms of cooperation and shared norms rather than power. Consequently, these approaches engender a concern with the nature of the domestic polity and the best way of creating domestic political harmony to ensure peaceful relations between polities at the same time. This type of thinking has given rise to major projects to construct international regimes, laws, and norms to limit war and engineer peace between polities, including states and multilateral organisations. Here questions of justice begin to emerge at a normative level in relation to peace between and within political units. Subsequent debates about justice revolve around the discovery and construction of legal frameworks based upon universal norms and so acceptable to the majority of states within an international society or community. This latter concept denotes the liberal belief that shared values at the international level indicates a community of states rather than merely a system of states as realists would have it. For those interested in what happens inside states rather than between them, peace may rest upon the preservation of a socioeconomic order, or the use of a particular type of constitution, or the construction of an equal and just society. Democratic peace theorists are able to extend this domestic peace to an international community. The liberal peace is the widely used term to describe this broad framework.

Lying behind such thinking is one of the core implicit debates in IR theory. Peace is seen to be something to aspire to though it is perhaps not achievable. This failure rests on human nature for realists, or the failure of institutions for liberals, and is reflected in the nature of states and organisations, which at best can attain a negative peace. This is the hallmark of conservative and realist thought, though for liberals, a positive peace is plausible through the adoption of certain domestic and international practices that are aimed at guaranteeing the rights and needs of individuals. For some, idealism could also be pragmatic, and merely rest upon the discovery of the obstacles to peace, and then upon the deployment of the correct methods required to overcome these obstacles. The Westphalian international system represents a compromise upon both positions. This is indicative of Galtung's negative and positive peace framework, which is the most widely used conceptualisation of peace. This can be extended, as Rasmussen has indicated, into a negative and positive epistemology of peace, meaning that ontological assumptions are made about whether a negative or positive peace can exist. The dominant mode of thought, however, which informs most IR theorists and policymaking today is that 'the logic of strategy pervades the upkeep of peace as much as the making of war'. In other words, a negative epistemology of peace arises from strategic thinking, and even the application of force or threat. War can even therefore be seen as the 'origin of peace' by exhausting opponents and their resources.

The Marxist-derived orthodoxy offers a concept of peace relating to the international political economy, the problem of economic exploitation of its weakest actors, and the subsequent need for radical reform. It posits that the international economic system defines the behaviour of its key actors. From this perspective, peace can be seen in terms of development and the just division of resources. Social and economic justice provides the dominant focus of significance for peace within Marxist-influenced approaches in IR. This raises the issues of the emancipation of the individual, the provision of welfare and the sharing of resources equitably across society without regard to political, economic or social hierarchies. Beyond the state, Marxist-inspired approaches focus on the division of resources through an equitable international economy and the reform of neo-liberal strategies of trade and development, as well as transnational approaches to global political and social communication designed to produce fairer communication, dialogue and interaction.

For contemporary realists such as Waltz or Mearshimer, peace is very limited, delineated by a natural confluence of interests rather than a mechanistic reform or management of interests or resources. For contemporary and broadly liberal thinkers like Falk or Keohane, or pluralist thinkers like Burton, the latter provides the basis for a more humane peace guided by liberal norms and human needs. For English School thinkers, and for constructivists, peace is equated with the liberal nature of the state, which provides security and manages equitable and transparent transnational mechanisms of exchange and communication. In terms of social constructivism, peace could be both pragmatic and ideational, and constructed by actors with the resources and broad consensus to provide both social legitimacy and material value. To some degree, critical theorists and certainly post-structuralists see more ambiguity in peace and war and recognised that peace would only be achieved in pluralist forms by uncovering the relationship between power and discourse, and the ways in which behaviour is constrained and conditioned by the hidden exercise of hegemonic power. Peace is impeded by hegemony, 'Orientalism', or by methodological, ontological barriers erected by the tradition of liberal-inspired post-Enlightenment rationalism and institutionalism. Critical theorists and post-structuralists are interested in identifying the structures of hegemony and domination and, in the case of the former, neo-liberal creating universal programmes providing a cosmopolitan response.

A major criticism of the 'agenda for peace' in IR is that it has been strongly influenced by idealism or utopianism, rather than reflecting a pragmatic engagement with the problems of IR. However, the democratic peace project, and the broader forms of the liberal peace, illustrate that this is not the case. The now dominant concept of liberal peace has practical implications, and can be conceptualised without necessarily entering into the realms of fantasy. Yet this has occurred without much debate about the possible variants of the concept of peace. Because thinking about peace is dominated by a set of key assumptions, most theorists, policymakers and practitioners assume that the concept of peace they deploy is ontologically stable. By extension this means that peace can be engineered in environments where it may not yet be present. As a result peace is constructed according to the preferences of those actors who are most involved in its construction. This confirms the pragmatism inherent in an agenda for peace, but also the interests that may lurk behind it.

For a complex set of reasons, it has become the orthodoxy that attaining peace is a long-term process, which is probably not achievable but is worth working towards. As a result, intellectual energy tends to be focused upon problem-solving from the perspective of achieving a minimalist version of peace in the short-term. This then provides the basis for a longer term refinement of the concept. In the short-term, stopping violence and providing basic security is often the focus, with more sophisticated attempts to provide rights, resources and democratic institutions seen as a longer term process. The hope is that the short-term peace will be superseded in the longer term by a self-sustaining peace according to a universally agreed formula. International theorists, political scientists, diplomats, officials, politicians and citizens rarely question whether they understand these short-term and long-term concepts of peace, but instead take them a predetermined givens, which should simply be implemented when the opportunity arises. Certainly, amongst groups united by common interests, this appears to be a plausible position. What becomes clear when one examines the views of actors that are divided by interests, culture, conflict, ideology, religion, or other forms of identity, is that these assumptions of peace break down very easily. An assumption of peace tied up in the framework of a group's position on a particular piece of territory, or the superiority of one culture, identity or religion over another, can easily become a source of conflict. One could make a strong argument that IR is actually about conflicting images of peace, as opposed to conflicting interests.

War and peace are seen as separate concepts, which are the antitheses of each other, particularly for pluralists, liberals, constructivists and critical theorists (peace may masquerade as war for some post-structuralists). Yet, this separation has always been weak. For example, in the debate on peace-enforcement or humanitarian intervention, and on state-building, there has been much tension. This is partly why the debates over state-building in Afghanistan and Iraq in the early 2000s have been so controversial. The contemporary concept of the liberal peace, which is expressed in different ways throughout much of IR theory, also makes this separation. The liberal peace provides the 'good life' if its formulas are followed, for all, and without exception, and even if it rests on a coercive introduction through invasion or peace enforcement. This has occurred within a Western context, which immediately points to a major flaw in thinking about peace (and indeed in the capacity of this study), which is firmly rooted in a critique within this Western, secular context. Peace rests upon a set of cultural, social and political norms, often dressed up as being secular, though closely reflecting the non-secular religious writings on the issue. The Christian notion of crusades for peace, or the use of force to construct peace, is taken for granted in this context. Lawful self-defence and just war remain integral to the preservation of this tranquil order, once all peace efforts have failed. From this have sprung the great peace conferences that marked the nineteenth and twentieth centuries, and which contributed to the emergence of the United Nations. Also visible have been the various social movements, charities and NGOs campaigning for human rights, voting rights, the banning of certain weapons, and more recently advocating and practical multiple forms of humanitarian assistance in conflict and disaster zones. Yet, where and when IR theorists do attempt to engage with peace as a concept, they often focus upon ending war, or preventing war, and in the context of units such as states, IOs or even empires. The role and agency of individuals and societies in the creation of peace tends to be less valued, the focus instead being on grand scale political, economic, military, social and constitutional peace projects undertaken beyond the ken and capacity of the individual.

The liberal peace is closely associated with the orthodoxy of IR theory, and can be seen as an outcome of a hybridisation of liberalism and realism. This can be described as axis denoting *liberal-realism* in which force, controlled by states, underpins the democratic and liberal political, social and economic institutions of a liberal polity. This axis explains both violence and order, and how they are related in the maintenances of domestic and international order. Structural thinking adds to this a concern with social justice and legitimacy, but this is mainly dealt with in a liberal-realist context by democratisation rather than the promotion of social justice. So while the structuralist or Marxist agenda has been partially incorporated, it lacks the affinity of liberal-realism, where hierarchies, states and groups accept certain levels of dominance and intrusive governance in order to also receive related, progressive freedoms. Equality is not a key issue, rather security and stability discursively construct international life.

A number of strategies for the conceptualisation of peace can be identified in the literature on IR, and its sub-disciplines. These can be summarised as follows:

1   Idealism depicts a future, complete peace incorporating social, political and economic harmony (of which there are no examples) represented by internationalism, world government and federation. This type of peace is represented as desirable but effectively unobtainable. It is an 'ideal form', though for idealists this does not mean that attempts to achieve it should be abandoned. Some idealists saw the League of Nations, and later the UN, attempts at disarmament, and the outlawing of war, as an attempt to attain this peace.

2   Liberalism, liberal-internationalism/institutionalism, neo-liberalism and liberal imperialism, and ultimately *liberal-realism* depict an achievable general peace derived from international institutions and organizations representing universal agreements and norms. This provides a basis for individualism, and social, political and/or economic rights and responsibilities, based upon significant levels of justice and consent. It is generally acknowledged that this form of peace will probably be marred by injustice, terrorism, secessionism or guerilla warfare perpetrated by marginalised actors which do not accept the norms and frameworks engendered in such universal agreements. Still, this represents a form of peace that is believed to be plausible and achievable, though often geographically limited by boundaries that exclude actors who do not conform to such a view of what is essentially an inter national society. Peace in this framework can be constructed by actors with the necessary knowledge and resources, probably resembling a Kantian 'Perpetual Peace'. This is commonly referred to as the liberal peace, embodied in the UN system and a post-Cold War 'international society'.

3   Realism (and other power/interest focused theories) represents IR as relative anarchy managed by a powerful hegemon or an international system, which produces a basic international, though not necessarily domestic, order. This imposes a limited temporal and geographically bounded order, which attempts to manage or assuage border conflicts, territorial conflicts, ethnic, linguistic, religious (and other identity) conflicts. The resulting type of peace rests upon the balance of power, or domination, perceptions of threat and the glorification of national interest in relation to military might. There have been many examples of this type of peace, from Alexander's conquest of the ancient world, the Pax Romana (and the destruction of Carthage), the Pax Britannia and the Paris Peace Treaty of 1919.

4   Marxist inspired structuralist insights into peace represent it as resting on social justice, equality and an equitable system of international trade, where states and actors

are not hierarchically organised according to socioeconomic class indicators. Peace in these terms is achievable, but probably only after massive, and probably revolutionary, upheaval in the international economy and in traditional class and economic hierarchies and systems which reorder states and the international in a way which better represents in the interests of workers and society, rather than wealthy elites.

5   Critical theory and post-structuralism, resting to some degree upon the intellectual legacy of points 1, 2 and 4, depicts an emancipatory peace, in multiple forms, in which consideration of forms of justice, identity and representation allows for marginalised actors (such as women, children, and minorities) and environmental factors to be considered. Critical theory seeks a universal basis to achieve such an outcome through ethical forms of communication, whereas post-structural approaches are wary of accepting its plausibility in the light of the dangers of universalism, the problem of relativism and the genealogical scale of the obstacles to emancipation. Hypothetically, both approaches concur that marginalised actors and discourses should be recognised, and discourses and practices of domination should be removed through radical reform. Whether there can be a universal peace or multiple states of peace, reflecting pluralism/relativism is heavily contested. However, there is still a strong sense that peace as an ideal form could be achieved within critical theory. Post-structuralism certainly does not deny the possibility of peace, but sees it reflecting difference, everyday life, hybridity and personal agency.

One peace or many peaces?

One of the ways in which IR theory and international practices related to the ending of war can be evaluated is by opening up the conceptualisation of peace by asking the question, one peace or many? Clearly, the liberal peace is the dominant conceptualisation deployed in these processes, and represents an amalgam of mainstream approaches to IR theory, though IR theory and associated debates also offers a powerful critique of this conceptualisation, and offers a glimpse of alternatives. These alternatives are as yet not comparable to the liberal peace in their intellectual conceptualisation, and have had little impact on the policy world. However, the liberal peace is far from being uncontested and indeed is theoretically rather incoherent. A debate between it and other forms of peace, and a negotiation between the different actors, levels of analysis and many issues involved is necessary. Indeed, for IR to contribute to its original agenda for peace it must become more fully involved in this process of theorisation of peace and a negotiation between its possible concepts. By developing a clear idea of the type of peace that each theoretical perspective envisages, and also developing theoretical approaches in the light of this debate, this process of evaluation and development could begin, setting peace and its variants at the centre of IR theory rather than at its periphery, as is currently the case. For this process to be meaningful, however, there also needs to be a debate about what basis such evaluation would rest on. Would it aspire to a cosmopolitan and universal set of basic norms? Would it aspire to a communitarian version of peace? Would it give rise to one peace or many peaces? If the latter, how would the *via media*, or process of negotiation and mediation, between them operate? Would peace be limited simply to the prevention of open violence, or would it aim to respond to structural violence, inequality, domination and marginalisation? What are the factors that create a sustainable peace in this case, how might such a peace be theorised, and then constructed? Or, perhaps, even more ambitiously, how can a self-sustaining peace be created?

IR theory, conflict theory and, indeed, policy debates often make the mistake of assuming that the project of peace is so apparent as to not require detailed explanation. This is part of the problem of peace. What is peace, why, who creates and promotes it, for what interests, and who is peace for? IR theory makes a number of key assumptions across its spectrum of approaches. The essentialisation of human nature regardless of culture, history, politics, economy or society, is common. The extrapolation of state behaviour from a flawed view of human nature as violent assumes that one reflects the other. This also rests on the assumption that one dominant actor, in this case often the state, is the loci around which power, interest, resources and societies revolve, in this sense, IR is often perceived to be immutable, reflecting the forces which drive it and their permanence, ranging from structures, the state, IOs and other key influences. Alternatively, these immutable forces may simply disguise an intellectual conservativism in which individuals as agents simply repeat the errors of old as they believe that nothing can change. This 'self-fulfilling prophecy' argument is often reflective of both an acceptance of the key difficulties of IR, as well as a reaction against them. Furthermore, all of this assumes that there can be value-free investigation in the discipline. Or is all knowledge effectively discursive and ideational? By attempting to understand and interpret peace, are we empowered to bring about change, or destined to be confronted only by our inability to do so?

This study underlines the view that a universal, single form of peace will inevitably be seen by some as hegemonic and oppressive, and though there may indeed be a dominant version or agenda for peace in IR theory and in practice (currently the liberal peace) this reflects the intellectual limitations of the orthodoxy of the discipline, its culture, ontology and methods, rather than its achievements. It is clear that peace is essentially contested as a concept. Inevitably, and following on from this, it is a subjective concept, depending on individual actors for definition, different methods and ontologies, and indeed different epistemological approaches. Its construction is a result of the interplay of different actors' attempts to define peace and according to their relative interests, identities, power and resources. For this reason, different approaches to IR theory produce different discourses about peace, some within the liberal peace framework, and some outside of it both as rhetorical devices and as practices. In the context of such inter-subjective concepts, theory is inevitably intertwined with practice, and cannot merely be read as representing an orthodoxy, hegemonic or otherwise, hi practice, in different political, social and economic environments around the world, there are rich variants of peace known to other disciplines or perhaps awaiting discovery. Yet, the liberal peace has become a hegemonic concept.

To counter this universal and hegemonic discourse, peace might instead be contextualised more subtly, geographically, culturally, in terms of identity, and the evolution of the previous socioeconomic polity. This means that one should be wary of a theoretical approach, or an empirical analysis, or a policy, which suggests that the institutions, norms, regimes and constitutions associated with peace can be applied equally across the world. There needs to be a differentiation between international order and peace in a global context, as well as local order and peace in a local or indigenous context. This means that peace as a concept can subjected to very specific interpretations, determined by politics, society, economy, demography, culture, religion and language. It should not merely be a legitimating trope applied to bolster a specific theory, policy or form or organisation, but conceptually and theoretically, should represent a detailed engagement with the multiple dynamics of conflict, war and disorder as well as the social, political and economic expectations, practices and identities of its participants. Engaging with the multiple concepts of peace forms the heartland of IR's quest to contribute to an understanding of stability and order and the 'good life'.

4 Global peace index

2011 Methodology, results and findings

Institute for Economics and Peace

The results of the Global Peace Index (GPI) for 2011 suggest that the world has become slightly less peaceful in the past year. The deterioration is smaller than that which occurred between the 2009 and 2010 editions of the GPI, when some nations experienced an intensification of conflicts and growing instability linked to rapid rises in food, fuel and commodity prices and the global economic downturn. The 2011 GPI, which gauges ongoing domestic and international conflict, safety and security in society and militarisation in 153 countries, registered overall score increases for several indicators, the largest of which were in the potential for terrorist acts and the likelihood of violent demonstrations. The indicator showing the most substantial year-on-year score decline (improvement) was military expenditure as a percentage of GDP, reflecting the impact of the global financial and economic crisis on defence budgets. While several countries experienced improved levels of peacefulness that appear to be linked with their economic recoveries, others, notably those in North Africa and the Middle East that have been swept up in the political turmoil of the "Arab Spring", have experienced sharp falls in their peacefulness.

This is the fifth edition of the Global Peace Index (GPI). It has been expanded to rank 153 independent states and updated with the latest-available figures and information. The index is composed of 23 qualitative and quantitative indicators from respected sources, which combine internal and external factors ranging from a nation's level of military expenditure to its relations with neighbouring countries and the level of respect for human rights. These indicators were selected by an international panel of academics, business people, philanthropists and members of peace institutions. As before, we have explored the possibility of correlations between the GPI and other economic and societal indicators - including measures of democracy and transparency, education and material wellbeing. The GPI brings a snapshot of relative peacefulness among nations while continuing to contribute to an understanding of what factors help create or sustain more peaceful societies. The GPI was founded by Steve Killelea, an Australian international technology entrepreneur and philanthropist. It forms part of the Institute for Economics and Peace, a global think tank dedicated to the research and education of the relationship between economic development, business and peace. The GPI is collated and calculated by the Economist Intelligence Unit, with whom this report is written in co-operation.

Highlights

In the Global Peace Index 2011 Iceland is ranked as the country most at peace, replacing New Zealand. Iceland topped the GPI in 2008, but dropped to fourth place in 2009 amid the country's unprecedented economic collapse and political crisis. Small, stable and democratic countries are consistently ranked highest; 14 of the top 20 countries are western or central European nations. This is, however, a reduction from 15 last year, and reflects both an improvement in Malaysia's score and a deterioration in Slovakia's, which lifts the South- East Asian nation into the top 20 for the first time. Qatar rises two places to 12th position and remains the highest-ranked Middle-eastern country by some margin (Kuwait is the next highest in 29th place). The recent waves of uprisings and revolutions in the Middle East have been reflected in sharply deteriorating GPI scores across the region, notably in Bahrain, Egypt, Libya and Tunisia, which were previously ranked in the top half of the GPI. Island nations generally fare well – most are in the top half of the GPI, with Sri Lanka a notable exception, although its score has improved since the defeat of the Tamil Tigers in May 2009 and it rose by 11 places in the 2011 index. Madagascar and Jamaica are accorded relatively low ranks (105th and 106th respectively), with the former experiencing a sharp deterioration in its score for the second successive year amid an ongoing political and economic crisis. War-torn Somalia drops one place to replace Iraq as the country ranked least at peace, although its score improved slightly. This is chiefly because of a more substantial improvement in Iraq's GPI score compared with last year, lifting the country from the foot of the index for the first time since 2007. Sudan and Afghanistan follow. The average score for the 153 states surveyed in the 2011 GPI is 2.05 (based on a 1–5 scale), a slight rise (reduction in peacefulness) compared with last year, when the average reached 2.02, up from 1.96 in 2009. The more substantial deterioration between 2009 and 2010 appears to have reflected rising conflict in several countries, triggered by rapidly increasing food and fuel prices in 2008 and the subsequent dramatic global economic downturn.

There is little variance (0.347) between the overall scores of the top 20 countries (from 1.148 for Iceland to 1.495 for Hungary), although slightly more than last year. The 20 lowest-ranked countries exhibit a far greater spread of 0.821 (from 2.558 for Georgia to 3.379 for Somalia), a drop from 0.832 last year.

Changes to the methodology for 2011

The international panel of experts that oversees the compilation of the Global Peace Index chose to include five additional countries in the 2011 edition: Eritrea, Guinea, Kyrgyz Republic, Niger and Tajikistan. Subsequent editions of the GPI will include other nations, but not micro-states: the panel decided that countries in the GPI must either have a population of more than 1 million or a land area greater than 20,000 sq km, which means that Luxembourg is no longer ranked. This brings the total number of countries covered in the 2011 GPI to 153, encompassing around 99% of the world's population and over 87% of the planet's land mass.

The dramatic events unfolding in the Middle East in 2010–11 prompted discussion about whether the eight qualitative indicators scored by Economist Intelligence Unit analysts could be undertaken at a slightly later stage – in previous editions the scoring had been carried out in January, referring to the previous calendar year. The panel decided it was both beneficial and practicable to update the period of analysis, and it will henceforth start and end on March 15th. Thus the eight qualitative indicators for the 2011 GPI relate to the period of 15th March 2010 to 15th March 2011.

Defining peace

The concept of peace is notoriously difficult to define. The simplest way of approaching it is in terms of harmony achieved by the absence of war or conflict. Applied to nations, this would suggest that those not involved in violent conflicts with neighbouring states or suffering internal wars would have achieved a state of peace. This is what Johan Galtung1 defined as a "negative peace" – an absence of violence. The concept of negative peace is immediately intuitive and empirically measurable, and can be used as a starting point to elaborate its counterpart concept, "positive peace". Having established what constitutes an absence of violence, is it possible to identify which structures and institutions create and maintain peace? The Global Peace Index (GPI) is a first step in this direction; a measurement of peace as the "absence of violence" that seeks to determine what cultural attributes and institutions are associated with states of peace. In 1999 the UN General Assembly launched a programme of action to build a "culture of peace" for the world's children, which envisaged working towards a positive peace of justice, tolerance and plenty. The UN defined a culture of peace as involving values, attitudes and behaviours that:

- Reject violence
- Endeavour to prevent conflicts by addressing root causes
- Aim at solving problems through dialogue and negotiation

It proposed that such a culture of peace would be furthered by actions promoting education for peace and sustainable development, which it suggested was based on human rights, gender equality, democratic participation, tolerant solidarity, open communication and international security. However, these links between the concept of peace and the causes of them were presumed rather than systematically measured. For example, while Doyle2 and advocates of his liberal peace theory have held that democratic states rarely attack each other, the ongoing war in Iraq demonstrates how some democratic countries can be militant or belligerent – the justification for war often being that peace is ultimately secured through violence or the threat of violence.

Measuring states of peace

The difficulties in defining the concept of peace may partly explain why there have been so few attempts to measure states of peace across nations. This project has approached the task on two fronts – the first aim is to produce a scoring model and Global Peace Index that ranks 153 nations by their relative states of peace using 23 indicators. The indicators have been selected as being the best available datasets that reflect the incidence or absence of peace, and contain both quantitative data and qualitative scores from a range of trusted sources. The second aim is to use the underlying data and results from the Global Peace Index to undertake investigations into the relative importance of a range of potential determinants or "drivers" that may influence the creation and nurturance of peaceful societies, both internally and externally.

Methodology and data sources

The indicators

Twenty-three indicators of the existence or absence of peace were chosen by the panel, which are divided into three broad categories:

- Ongoing domestic and international conflict;
- Safety and security in society;
- Militarisation.

All scores for each indicator are "banded", either on a scale of 1–5 (for qualitative indicators) or 1–10 (for quantitative data, such as military expenditure or the jailed population, which have then been converted to a 1–5 scale for comparability when compiling the final index). Qualitative indicators in the index have been scored by the Economist Intelligence Unit's extensive team of country analysts, and gaps in the quantitative data have been filled by estimates by the same team. Indicators consisting of quantitative data such as military expenditure or jailed population have been measured on the basis of the distribution of values across all countries between the maximum and minimum values (we assume that the 153 countries measured for the Global Peace Index (GPI) are a representative sample of all countries). Since the 2008 GPI the data for each indicator has been divided into ten bands based on the full range of the data set and a country's corresponding score results in its ranking position.

Measures of ongoing domestic and international conflict

The Global Peace Index is intended as a review of the state of peace in nations over the previous calendar year, although several indicators are based on data covering the previous two years (2009–10 in the case of the 2011 GPI). The advisory panel decided against including data reflecting a country's longer-term historical experience of domestic and international conflict on the grounds that the GPI uses authoritative statistics on ongoing civil and transnational wars collated by the Uppsala Conflict Data Program and the International Peace Research Institute, Oslo. These, combined with two indicators scored by the Economist Intelligence Unit's analysts, comprise five of the 23 indicators:

- Number of external and internal conflicts fought: 2004–09
- Estimated number of deaths from organised conflict (external)
- Number of deaths from organised conflict (internal)
- Level of organised conflict (internal)
- Relations with neighbouring countries

Measures of societal safety and security

Ten of the indicators assess the levels of safety and security in a society (country), ranging from the perception of criminality in society, to the level of respect for human rights and the rate of homicides and violent crimes. Crime data is from the UN Office of Drugs and Crime. The difficulties of comparing international crime statistics are discussed in detail in Annex A. Five of these indicators have been scored by the Economist Intelligence Unit's team of country analysts:

- Perceptions of criminality in society
- Number of refugees and displaced people as a percentage of the population
- Political instability
- Political Terror Scale
- Potential for terrorist acts
- Number of homicides per 100,000 people
- Level of violent crime
- Likelihood of violent demonstrations
- Number of jailed population per 100,000 people

- Number of internal security officers and police
- per 100,000 people

Measures of militarisation

Eight of the indicators are related to a country's military build-up – reflecting the assertion that the level of militarisation and access to weapons is directly linked to how at peace a country feels internationally. Comparable data are readily available from sources such as the International Institute of Strategic Studies (IISS):

- Military expenditure as a percentage of GDP
- Number of armed services personnel per 100,000 people
- Volume of transfers (imports) of major conventional weapons per 100,000 people
- Volume of transfers (exports) of major conventional weapons per 100,000 people
- Budgetary support for UN peacekeeping missions: percentage of outstanding payments versus annual assessment to the budget of the current peacekeeping missions
- Aggregate number of heavy weapons per 100,000 people
- Ease of access to small arms and light weapons
- Military capability/sophistication

Weighting the index

The advisory panel apportioned scores based on the relative importance of each of the indicators on a 1–5 scale. The consensus scores for each indicator are given in Table 1. Two sub-component weighted indices were then calculated from the GPI group of indicators:

1) a measure of how at peace internally a country is;
2) a measure of how at peace externally a country is (its state of peace beyond its borders).

The overall composite score and index was then formulated by applying a weight of 60% to the measure of internal peace and 40% for external peace. The heavier weight applied to internal peace was agreed within the advisory panel, following robust debate. The decision was based on the innovative notion that a greater level of internal peace is likely to lead to, or at least correlate with, lower external conflict.

GPI 2011 discussion paper: new dimensions of peace – society, economy, and the media

Executive Summary

Since the first release of the Global Peace Index in 2007 the Institute for Economics and Peace (IEP) has been consistently improving our shared knowledge of peace and of the economic benefits that flow from improvements in peace. During the last twelve months the Institute has produced a number of reports and white papers. This year's Discussion Paper focuses on three of them: the United States Peace Index, the Peace & the Media report and a white paper on the relationship between social sustainability and peace. IEP recently released the United States Peace Index (USPI), the first in a series of national peace indices, which

Table 1

Indicator (1 to 5) Internal Peace 60%	Weight External Peace 40%
Perceptions of criminality in society	4
Number of internal security officers and police per 100,000 people	3
Number of homicides per 100,000 people	4
Number of jailed population per 100,000 people	3
Ease of access to weapons of minor destruction	3
Level of organised conflict (internal)	5
Likelihood of violent demonstrations	3
Level of violent crime	4
Political instability	4
Level of disrespect for human rights (Political Terror Scale)	4
Volume of transfers of major conventional weapons, as recipient (Imports) per 100,000 people	2
Potential for terrorist acts	1
Number of deaths from organised conflict (internal)	5
Military expenditure as a percentage of GDP	2
Number of armed services personnel per 100,000 people	2
Funding for UN peacekeeping missions	2
Aggregate number of heavy weapons per 100,000 people	3
Volume of transfers of major conventional weapons as supplier (exports) per 100,000 people	3
Military capability/sophistication	2
Number of displaced people as a percentage of the population	4
Relations with neighbouring countries	5
Number of external and internal conflicts fought: 2003–08	5
Estimated number of deaths from organised conflict (external)	5

Table 2

Rank	Country	Score
1	Iceland	1.148
2	New Zealand	1.279
3	Japan	1.287
4	Denmark	1.289
5	Czech Republic	1.320
6	Austria	1.337
7	Finland	1.352
8	Canada	1.355
9	Norway	1.356
10	Slovenia	1.358
11	Ireland	1.370
12	Qatar	1.398
13	Sweden	1.401
14	Belgium	1.413
15	Germany	1.416
16	Switzerland	1.421
17	Portugal	1.453
18	Australia	1.455
19	Malaysia	1.467
20	Hungary	1.495
21	Uruguay	1.521
22	Poland	1.545

Table 2 Continued

23	Slovakia	1.576
24	Singapore	1.585
25	Netherlands	1.628
26	United Kingdom	1.631
27	Taiwan	1.638
28	Spain	1.641
29	Kuwait	1.667
30	Vietnam	1.670
31	Costa Rica	1.681
32	Laos	1.687
33	United Arab Emirates	1.690
34	Bhutan	1.693
35	Botswana	1.695
36	France	1.697
37	Croatia	1.699
38	Chile	1.710
39	Malawi	1.740
40	Romania	1.742
41	Oman	1.743
42	Ghana	1.752
43	Lithuania	1.760
44	Tunisia	1.765
45	Italy	1.775
46	Latvia	1.793
47	Estonia	1.798
48	Mozambique	1.809
49	Panama	1.812
50	South Korea	1.829
51	Burkina Faso	1.832
52	Zambia	1.833
53	Bulgaria	1.845
54	Namibia	1.850
55	Argentina	1.852
56	Tanzania	1.858
57	Mongolia	1.880
58	Morocco	1.887
59	Moldova	1.892
60	Bosnia and Hercegovina	1.893
61	Sierra Leone	1.904
62	The Gambia	1.910
63	Albania	1.912
64	Jordan	1.918
65	Greece	1.947
66	Paraguay	1.954
67	Cuba	1.964
68	Indonesia	1.979
69	Ukraine	1.995
69	Swaziland	1.995
71	Cyprus	2.013
72	Nicaragua	2.021
73	Egypt	2.023
74	Brazil	2.040
75	Equatorial Guinea	2.041
76	Bolivia	2.045
77	Senegal	2.047

Table 2 Continued

78	Macedonia	2.048
79	Trinidad and Tobago	2.051
80	China	2.054
81	Gabon	2.059
82	United States of America	2.063
83	Bangladesh	2.070
84	Serbia	2.071
85	Peru	2.077
86	Cameroon	2.104
87	Angola	2.109
88	Guyana	2.112
89	Montenegro	2.113
90	Ecuador	2.116
91	Dominican Republic	2.125
92	Guinea	2.126
93	Kazakhstan	2.137
94	Papua New Guinea	2.139
95	Nepal	2.152
96	Liberia	2.159
96	Uganda	2.159
98	Congo (Brazzaville)	2.165
99	Rwanda	2.185
100	Mali	2.188
101	Saudi Arabia	2.192
102	El Salvador	2.215
103	Tajikistan	2.225
104	Eritrea	2.227
105	Madagascar	2.239
106	Jamaica	2.244
107	Thailand	2.247
108	Turkmenistan	2.248
109	Armenia	2.260
109	Uzbekistan	2.260
111	Kenya	2.276
112	Belarus	2.283
113	Haiti	2.288
114	Kyrgyz Republic	2.296
115	Cambodia	2.301
116	Syria	2.322
117	Honduras	2.327
119	Iran	2.356
119	Niger	2.356
121	Mexico	2.362
122	Azerbaijan	2.379
123	Bahrain	2.398
124	Venezuela	2.403
125	Guatemala	2.405
126	Sri Lanka	2.407
127	Turkey	2.411
128	Cote d' Ivoire	2.417
129	Algeria	2.423
130	Mauritania	2.425
131	Ethiopia	2.468
132	Burundi	2.532
133	Myanmar	2.538

Table 2 Continued

134	Georgia	2.558
135	India	2.570
136	Philippines	2.574
137	Lebanon	2.597
138	Yemen	2.670
139	Colombia	2.700
140	Zimbabwe	2.722
141	Chad	2.740
142	Nigeria	2.743
143	Libya	2.816
144	Central African Republic	2.869
145	Israel	2.901
146	Pakistan	2.905
147	Russia	2.966
148	Democratic Republic of Congo	3.016
149	North Korea	3.092
150	Afghanistan	3.212
151	Sudan	3.223
152	Iraq	3.296
153	Somalia	3.379

ranks the states of the U.S. by their peacefulness. The study made two unique contributions to the public debate on crime. The first was estimating of the additional economic activity and the number of jobs that would be created through improvements in peace. These estimates include the direct costs associated with policing, justice, incarceration and crime. The study also conservatively estimated the flow-on effects to the overall economy if the U.S. could achieve the same level of peacefulness as Canada.

The other unique contribution of the U.S. Peace Index was the statistical analysis between a number of socioeconomic indicators and the index to derive the types of environments that are associated with peace within the U.S. Fifteen data sets were correlated and the significant factors could be grouped by three categories: economic opportunity, education, and health.

Peace & the Media is a study jointly conducted by the IEP and Media Tenor which is a leading organisation on analysing global media coverage. The report, which was used to form the central part of the book "2010 Peace Report", analyses the media coverage from news and current affairs programs for 37 television networks from four continents on their coverage of peace. It also analyses the global media coverage of the "Structures of Peace". These structures have been derived through statistical analysis and describe the environment that creates a peaceful society. There is a important section that analyses what is missing in the media coverage of Afghanistan when compared to the Structures of Peace. It provides a useful insight into some of the reasons why peace in Afghanistan has been elusive as it appears that little attention has been paid to some of the key structures of peaceful societies.

The social sustainability and peace white paper focuses on the new and emerging area of social sustainability. The concept of social sustainability has increasingly become the focus of intergovernmental organizations, academics, global think tanks, and policymakers within government. While sustainability has for some time been a prominent concept in environmental currents, the social dimension of sustainability has previously been overshadowed by economic and environmental aspects. The recent shift of focus to social sustainability is recognition of the interdependent nature of social, economic and environmental factors in determining progress and the importance of social institutions in helping to shape economic, political and environmental outcomes. This is also true for peace.

This section of the 2011 GPI Discussion Paper sets out to explain how the environments that shape peace are also the same environments that create the appropriate conditions for social sustainability. This study draws on recently published research from the Indices for Social Development (ISD) to correlate their measures of social sustainability with the GPI.

Peace is one of the most used and esteemed words in the human vocabulary. Yet if we wish to create peace then we must first pose the question; "what do we know about peace?" Although great strides have been made in improving our common understanding of peace and its causes, with many universities now having peace and conflict centres, peace is still not common to the major academic disciplines. There are no courses on the literature of peace in the literature departments of the major universities in the world yet most people know profound works on peace. Nor is there a chair in Peace Economics in any major university. However, surveys conducted by the United Nations Global Compact found that 80% of business leaders believe that the size of their markets expands with peace and 79% believe that their costs decrease with improvements in peace. Knowledge is the key to creating the correct sets of initiatives to solve any problem; if we live in a world that desires peace then *how can the optimum level of peace be created if we do not fully understand it?* We live in an age that is different to any other epoch in human history. We are more interconnected than ever before yet finding finite constraints on many of the basic resources needed to sustain life. These challenges are occurring globally and are multi-faceted; encompassing economic management, environmental sustainability and a wide variety of social ills. Global challenges do call for global actions but compounding these challenges is the inability of our institutions to adequately address their causes and to then create the remedies. This has been demonstrated by the inability to find global solutions to many pressing problems as is exemplified by the breakdown of the Copenhagen Climate Change talks, burgeoning government and private sector debt, lack of regulation of the speculative aspects of the financial system or indeed our inability to even articulate good capitalist models that aren't totally based on consumption.

Yet such imminent and urgent challenges do provide a unique opportunity for us to reconsider and redefine our institutions, relationships and values so that we can create a viable future in which humanity can meet its shared challenges and continue to prosper. Peace is one of these essential elements. One of the more remarkable findings from the Global Peace Index in 2010 was that societies that are highly peaceful also perform exceptionally well in many other ways. The most peaceful societies also have higher per capita income, higher levels of well-being, more freedom, perform better at sustainability, and appear to have a more equitable distribution of social spending. What is important is not whether peace creates these abundances, rather the realization that what creates a peaceful society also allows for a fuller expression of human potential, and in many diverse forms. The Structures of Peace describe this environment and therefore create much more than peace.

The United States Peace Index is the first in a series of national peace indices that will build on the work of the Institute for Economics and Peace in measuring and understanding the fabric of peace. It is envisaged that by producing a series of national peace indices using the same methodology across many nations the patterns that are associated with peace will emerge. This will enable politicians and policy makers to consult and legislate in areas that will lead to more stable, affluent and peaceful societies.

The U.S. Peace Index consists of a composite set of five indicators. These indicators were chosen because they can be measured across many countries with a methodology that would allow for the data to be consistently collected by state, district or region. The definition of

peace that was chosen for these studies is the "absence of violence". This is a simple definition, intuitive to most people and is the same definition used for the GPI. The indicators
that have been selected relate to violent crime, homicides, incarceration rates, policing and
availability of small arms.

In the U.S. there are many benefits that would flow from improvements in peace, either
physically, emotionally or socially, but one of the key benefits that is often overlooked is the
substantial positive economic impact that even small improvements in peace can have. Violence creates costs for both business and government. It also reduces productivity, which if
unleashed will create substantial additional economic growth.

This study estimates that if the U.S. had similar levels of peacefulness to Canada, the
conservative economic benefit on the U.S. economy would be $361 billion per annum. This
would consist of $89 billion in direct savings and $272 billion from additional economic activity. This additional economic activity, if recouped, would have a stimulatory effect capable
of generating approximately 2.7 million additional jobs. States that rank higher on the social
and economic factors that significantly correlated with the USPI tend to have higher scores
in peace, indicating that having access to basic services, having an education, being in good
health and ultimately being given the opportunity to succeed, are linked to peace. Improving these factors would also create additional economic activity. Contrary to popular belief
peace in the U.S. has been on the increase, recording an 8% improvement since 1991. The
improvement in peacefulness has been driven by a substantial decrease in homicides and
violent crime. This however, has been somewhat offset by large and progressive increases in
the incarceration rate from 1991 onwards.

Media is one of the most influential aspects in any society yet using deep multi-national
datasets to analyse global media patterns on societal issues is relatively new. Therefore the
combination of the Media Tenor datasets and the Global Peace Index made for an original
study in analysing the different patterns of coverage between continents, countries and networks with the emphasis on highlighting the accuracy of coverage, the tenor of the coverage
as well as breadth of coverage. Media accuracy is a much debated subject but how accurate
is the media on reporting peace and conflict and is it more accurate than people would commonly believe?

The starting point for the analysis was to determine how closely the global media coverage
of violence matched the measured levels of violence within each country. To accomplish this,
the percentage of "violence" stories was tallied for all television programs by country, other
than for the country in which the television network was domiciled. This dataset was then
statistically analysed against the GPI to determine its alignment. It was striking how aligned
the data sets were. However ,there were some notable exceptions with over reporting of
violence for Austria, Ireland, Portugal and Finland. Despite their high levels of peacefulness,
over half of all TV reports on these countries focused on violence issues. Russia, Israel and
Sudan are identified as another set of outliers. These countries are ranked at 143, 144 and
146 (out of 149) respectively on the 2010 Global Peace Index. Yet, they had lower levels of
violence reporting than would be expected.

Executive summary

By categorising topics according to the Structures that build peace it was possible to further
analyse media coverage of these crucial areas. In order to help facilitate an increase in peacefulness, coverage of these topics is essential as it would encourage a more informed global
debate on matters of key strategic significance. It is encouraging to find that there are 20%

more stories covering topics related to the Structures of Peace than stories that focused on conflict. The analysis was not concerned with whether the reports were positive or negative; rather the emphasis is on the subject matter as that is what will create awareness.

When analysing the least peaceful countries, a different picture emerges. As would be expected there is a higher percentage of reporting on Violence related topics, at 75%. Defence and Crime had by far the largest levels of coverage. The distribution of stories across the Violence topics was well spread while the distribution of stories across the Peace topics had a wide variance. For the 10 least peaceful countries, reports on topics relating to the Structures of Peace are roughly a third of the reports on conflict. However, there is a relative paucity of reports on 'education', 'equitable distribution of resources', the 'free flow of information' and 'corruption'. Other than Israel, all the countries in the group of the 10 least peaceful countries have high levels of corruption. Without an adequate focus on these topics building a sustainable society will be difficult because the citizens of many of the least peaceful countries do not have the knowledge to know what is needed.

This paper also shows for the first time that measures of social sustainability are linked to indicators of peacefulness as measured by the GPI. The research demonstrates measures of civic activism, inter-group social cohesion and interpersonal safety and trust as measured by ISD are highly correlated with the GPI. The paper also fits these informal institutions into the Structures of Peace and discusses their interaction within such a model.

The approach adopted by the IEP is not to aim at isolating single causal factors that drive peace, but rather, via statistical means, to holistically describe the environments that are associated with peace. Through focusing on all of these factors as being interdependent a holistic approach can be used to define the optimum conditions that create peace. Additionally, the environment that is optimal for creating peace is also optimal for many other desirable aspects of human activity to flourish, such as the arts or business. In summary our knowledge of peace is improving and one of the most important contributions that the IEP has made to it is to statistically determine what structures build a peaceful society. The U.S. Peace Index has confirmed that the same aspects identified globally, also play a key role in the U.S. The Peace and the Media report further builds on this theme by analysing the global coverage of these structures and then compares them to the media coverage of Afghanistan where there is little to no coverage of some of these essential structures. Social sustainability is also analysed to determine how it statistically relates to peace and where it is included within the Structures of Peace.

The United States peace index

The U.S. Peace Index is the first in a series of national peace indices that will be produced by the Institute for Economics and Peace (IEP). These studies will analyse the level and composition of peace within selected nations by state, district or region.

The aim of the research will be to further our understanding of what types of environments are associated with peace sub-nationally and to further define the positive economic impact of peace. Since producing the first Global Peace Index in 2007, the Institute for Economics and Peace has been asked to develop a number of national peace indices. As the empirical basis for the GPI has progressively developed, research by the IEP has found that many large nations have substantial internal variances in their levels of peacefulness. This is especially true for nations with marked social and cultural diversity combined with variable economic conditions. It is predominantly for this reason that the IEP has decided to produce national peace indices, with the U.S. Peace Index being the first in the series.

Through analysing national peace indices a better understanding of the fabric of peace is possible. If trends and statistical relations can be found between the level of internal peacefulness of different nations, then new approaches to creating peace may emerge. In order to undertake comparable national peace studies, it was decided to adopt a minimal number of indicators and to develop a methodology that could be applied to all future studies. This will provide a comparable framework for cross country analysis. It was also important to adopt a measurement framework underpinned by a proven and familiar philosophical foundation.

Why select the U.S. for the first national peace index?

The United States makes an ideal case study for the first national peace index principally due to the high quality of state-level data dating back to the early 1980s and the existence of a large literature of related studies which estimate the various costs of violence as well as the costs associated with the containment of violence. Compared to other nations on the Global Peace Index, the U.S. is a middle ranking nation with a peace measure of 2.06 very close to the global average of 2.05.1 The combination of economic size, the substantial capabilities and resources of government, and the middle level ranking, means trapped economic potential and productivity within the country is greater and has more opportunity of being realised than in any other region or nation in the world.

The U.S. was also attractive because it is commonly characterized as having a higher rate of violence than many other developed economies and also because trends in crime over the past twenty years have been the subject of much debate and curiosity. It is interesting to note that at the beginning of the 1980s the U.S.'s crime rate was comparable to that of other developed nations and violence steadily increased to a peak in the mid-1990s and has since been falling. However, this fall has been accompanied by a steadily increasing incarceration rate which has significant economic consequences associated with it.

The excellent availability of time series data allows these correlation trends to be compared with the U.S. Peace Index so changes in correlations can be seen over time. Additionally, the large pool of available literature on the cost of the items associated with this study meant that reasonably good estimates could be made on the savings or costs from either improvements in peace or losses in peacefulness. Estimated savings have been broken down by state. It is acknowledged that with better data and more time the estimates could be refined even further. Furthermore, the U.S., being the largest economy in the world and having a relatively lower level of peacefulness than other developed economies means the potential economic gains are of a much higher magnitude than in other nations. In the context of the lingering effects of the Global Financial Crisis this is especially pertinent, because the additional economic activity that would be created through improvements in peace can provide a powerful economic stimulus to aid economic recovery.

The opportunity to move expenditure from violence-containment industries to more economically productive industries is significant. This can be exemplified by the opportunity to build a highway instead of a jail, or the expansion of employment in teachers rather than prison guards. While such efforts would not necessarily generate additional economic activity in themselves, they would create the foundation for a more productive economy. The realisation of additional economic activity is defined as the 'dynamic peace dividend' and can result in a substantial lift in GDP and employment. The concept is further explained in the economic analysis section.

Definition of peace

For the purpose of this study, peace has been defined as "the absence of violence". This definition is easily understood while also being relatively open to empirical quantification. The methodological framework was based on envisaging a society that is perfectly at peace; a society where there is no violence, no police and no one in jail. Evidently, this does not exist in any modern developed nation. Without police crime would be rampant, while violence can be reduced by increasing the number of police and/or jailing large numbers of individuals. This study does not seek to make any moral or value judgments about the appropriate levels of policing or incarcerations. It is acknowledged that without police higher levels of crime would exist and that it is necessary to incarcerate individuals who pose a danger to society.

The indicators are interdependent, well-recorded, and measurable across states and provide a solid foundation from which to develop measures of peace.

Identifying the potential determinants of peace

To further the understanding of the economic and social factors associated with peace, the IEP compiled a secondary dataset composed of 37 secondary factors grouped into four categories of education, health, economic conditions, politics and demographics. The composite USPI score was correlated with each factor to determine statistical significance. The correlation coefficients are calculated across the 50 states plus Washington D.C. and values where $r > 0.5$ and $r < -0.5$ were considered to be statistically significant. A high positive correlation suggests a factor is associated with violence, while a high negative correlation suggests that the factor is associated with increasing peacefulness.

Economic measurements and benefits of peace

To understand the economic impact of peace the economic costs associated with homicides, violent crime, policing, judicial services and incarceration have been estimated. The figures chosen were based on a review of the existing literature and the sources used are mentioned in the study in the relevant commentary. The estimated costs are considered to be conservative as there are many additional costs associated with violence that have not been included due to the difficulty in finding accurate statistics. These include: higher insurance premiums, lost management time dealing with defensive measures against crime, additional security costs, and the productivity loss from investing in less productive assets.

Two of the main economic losses caused by violence are the value lost of life-time employment of homicide victims and the lost value of employment when an employed person is imprisoned. It is estimated that 70% of people imprisoned had full-time employment for a year prior to their incarceration.

In order to realise the peace dividend investments will need to be made, but some actions can have quick returns. As an illustrative example let's consider incarceration as it has significant economic effects. Lowering the rates of incarceration of low risk nonviolent offenders who are employed in full-time work would have an immediate economic benefit to both state government budgets and the economy. For each person imprisoned tax receipts are lost while the state also has to fund their imprisonment. Additionally, the value of their wage is lost to the economy. This also has flow on effects as their spending employs others. Management programs would be self-funding through reductions in state expenditure on incarceration and increased tax receipts. Estimating the costs or recommending the programs is beyond the scope of this study but lessening new incarcerations of non-violent offenders who are currently employed would have immediate benefits to state government budgets as well the economy.

Methodology and data sources

Five indicators reflecting the absence of peace have been selected to construct the index because of the ability to scale these indicators in a consistent way across many nations.

In addition, data for these five indicators was readily available in the U.S. without the need to make qualitative assessments. Owing to the purely quantitative nature of these measurements, it has been possible to collect data from 1991 onwards, and construct U.S. peace indices for almost 20 consecutive years. This has allowed for the development of a detailed trend analysis which is included in this report and will hopefully serve as a useful resource for academics interested in further research.

The indicators

Each of the five indicators is a quantitative measure. The five indicators are:

• Number of homicides per 100,000 people

Source: FBI Uniform Crime Reports, 1991–2009

The USPI uses the same definition of homicide as the U.S. Bureau of Justice Statistics, wherein homicide is defined as "murder or non-negligent manslaughter"..

• Number of violent crimes per 100,000 people

Source: FBI Uniform Crime Reports, 1991–2009

The U.S. Peace Index measure uses the Bureau of Justice Statistics definition of violent crime and the associated quantitative measures. In the U.S., the measure of violent crime includes homicide, forcible rape, robbery, and aggravated assault. The USPI measure of violent crime excludes homicide from this group, as it is already included in the first indicator.

• Number of jailed population per 100,000 people

Source: U.S. Bureau of Justice Statistics, 1991–2009

In order to allow for meaningful comparisons across states, the USPI only includes prisoners under state jurisdiction who have been sentenced to more than one year in prison. This means that both federal prisoners and prisoners in jail are excluded from this indicator.

• Number of police officers per 100,000 people

Source: FBI Uniform Crime Reports, 1991–2009

This number includes both sworn officers and civilian employees. The USPI uses the census population estimates for all states and indicators for the sake of consistency.

• Availability of small arms

Source: Centre for Disease Control and Prevention, National Centre for Injury Prevention and Control, Fatal Injury Reports, 1991–2007

Although the U.S. has excellent data for many statistics, there is no reliable data on small arms availability, small arms ownership, or small arms sales within the U.S. or within the states of the U.S.. An accurate measure of gun prevalence cannot be calculated from administrative records alone. For this reason many studies on gun prevalence use a quantitative proxy. The proxy used in the USPI is: firearm suicides as a percentage of total suicides (FS/S). As this indicator varied significantly from year to year for some states, a five year moving average was used in order to smooth out the variance. For example, the figure used for Alabama for 2008 was an average of FS/S for 2003–2007.

All indicators are scored between 1 and 5, with 1 being the most peaceful possible score, and 5 being the least peaceful. Scores are calculated to two decimal places.

Weighting the index

In order to maintain consistency, the weights assigned to each indicator mirror those used in the GPI for the equivalent measures. GPI indicators weights were agreed upon by an international panel of experts based on a consensus view of their relative importance. The weights assigned to the 5 indicators are presented in Table 3.

Key findings

1. From 1995 to 2009, the United States has become more peaceful

Peace improved by 8% from 1995 to 2009, driven by a substantial decrease in the rates of homicide and violent crime. However, these improvements have been largely offset by large and progressive increases in the incarceration rate, which has seen a slight decline only in the last two years.

There have been three trends; the first was from 1997 to 2000 when there was dramatic decrease in homicides and violent crime. This was followed by a plateau effect with no change in homicides and violent crime from 2000 to 2007, and finally the improving trend resumed from 2008 onwards.

From 1991 to 2009, 28 states improved their peacefulness while 10 of these states experienced an increase in peacefulness beyond 15%. Overall, the average USPI score moved from an average of 2.74 in 1991, to 2.62 in 2009, with most of the improvement coming from the bottom 30 ranked states.

Table 3 The indicators and their scores

Indicator	Weight
Number of homicides per 100,000 people	4
Number of violent crimes per 100,000 people	4
Number of jailed population per 100,000 people	3
Number of police officers per 100,000 people	3
Availability of small arms	1

Note: As incarceration data is not available post 2002 for Washington D.C., it has been excluded from the USPI.

2. The five most peaceful states are Maine, New Hampshire, Vermont, Minnesota and North Dakota
The Northeast is the most peaceful region in the U.S., with all of its states ranking in the top half of the U.S. Peace Index, including the heavily populated states of New York, Pennsylvania, and New Jersey. The least peaceful states are Louisiana, Tennessee, Nevada, Florida and Alabama.

3. Peace is linked to opportunity, health, education and the economy
Statistically significant correlations were found with fifteen different social and economic factors. These related to health, education, demographics and economic opportunity, but not to political affiliation. The key correlants were:

- % With at least high school diploma (2009)
- High school graduation rate (2007)
- PEW State of the States – Educational Opportunities
- % Without health insurance (2008–2009)
- % With diabetes (2008)
- Life expectancy at birth (2007)
- Teenage pregnancy rate (2008)
- Infant mortality rate (2007)
- Teenage death rate (2007)
- Household income Gini coefficient (2009)
- % Households in poverty (2009)
- Gallup State of the States (2009) Basic Access
- Labor force participation rate (2009)
- % Children in single parent families (2009)
- % Females in Labor force (2009)

Many of these factors can be seen as measures of opportunity. States that ranked higher on these social and economic factors tended to have higher scores in peace – indicating access to basic services, having an education, good health, and ultimately the opportunity to succeed, are key pre-requisites to a more peaceful society.

4. Peace is not linked to political affiliation
Neither the groupings of Republican nor Democratic states had a discernible advantage in peace. Although the top five states are predominantly Democratic and the bottom five states are predominantly Republican, once the other states were included in the analysis they neutralised out any effect.

5. The potential economic gains from improvements in peace are significant
Improvements in peace would result in the realisation of substantial savings for both governments and society. If the U.S. reduced its violence to the same levels as Canada then the general community and state governments would collectively save in the region of $89 billion while the same reductions in the level of violence would provide an economic stimulus of approximately $272 billion. The release of trapped productivity through the abatement of violence would create a stimulus that could generate an additional 2.7 million new jobs, effectively lowering the U.S. unemployment rate by 20% from 8.9% to 7.1%.

6. On a per capita basis, the top five states with the most to gain from reductions in violence are Louisiana, Florida, Nevada, Alaska and New Mexico

The total economic effect of violence tends to be greatest in the most violent states; however several states have a structurally higher cost of violence because of the composition of their violence. For instance, lost productivity from assault and lost productivity from incarceration are the largest shares of the total cost of violence, so states with high levels of incarceration and assault tend to have a higher per capita cost. In outright dollar terms, the large populous states with high levels of incarceration have the most to gain, such as California, Florida and Texas.

7. Growing incarceration is a drag on the economy and in recent years has not had a significant effect on violent crime

While homicide and violent crime rates have fallen, the economic benefits to flow from these decreases have been largely offset by the costs associated with the increase in the incarceration rate. In recent years there has been no statistically meaningful relationship between increases in incarceration rates and decreases in violent crime. While from 1991 to 1999 increases in incarceration were met with falls in violent crime, from 2000 to 2007 increases in the incarceration rate had no impact on the level of violent crime. Furthermore for 2008 and 2009 both the violent crime and incarceration rates dropped.

8. The Gallup Basic Access sub-index is the strongest correlating qualitative measure, linking the perception of how satisfied people are with their access to basic services to peace

The Gallup Basic Access sub-index has a correlation of $r = -.75$. This sub-index is based on 13 questions gauging access to basic needs for a healthy life – specifically, access to clean water, medicine, a safe place to exercise, and affordable fruits and vegetables; enough money for food, shelter, and healthcare; having health insurance, having a doctor, having visited a dentist recently, satisfaction with the community, the community getting better as a place to live, and feeling safe walking alone at night. This strong correlation shows further research into qualitative attitudinal factors such as feeling comfortable in a community and feeling optimistic about the community one lives in are also important factors not necessarily captured in quantitative studies.

9. Six of the top ten most populous states were also in the top ten percentage improvers of peace

These states included New York, California, Texas, Georgia, Illinois and Michigan. This is an interesting finding which requires further qualitative research and potentially provides a novel insight into why Pennsylvania as the sixth most populous state, also ranked in the bottom ten for declines in peace. Further research could perhaps better reveal common demographic, economic and governance related trends in these populous states.

10. The three Midwestern states, North Dakota, South Dakota and Montana, all experienced the three most significant declines in peacefulness

This result stands out as the three Midwestern states all declined in peacefulness by over 40%. However, these states are still relatively peaceful states and in the top half of the USPI. Understanding commonalities between them may improve understanding as to why these states have declined in peacefulness and what they can do to improve.

Table 4 U.S. vs. global average, internal indicators

Internal Indicators Average	USA	Difference	
OVERALL SCORE 2.05	2.06	−0.01	
Internal Indicators	Average	USA	Difference
Perceptions of criminality in society	3.1	2	1.1
Number of internal security officers and police per 100,000 people	2.3	2	0.3
Number of homicides per 100,000 people	2.6	2	0.6
Number of jailed population per 100,000 people	1.5	5	−3.5
Ease of access to small arms and light weapons	3.1	3	0.1
Level of organised conflict (internal)	2.4	1	1.4
Likelihood of violent demonstrations	2.9	2	0.9
Level of violent crime	2.7	1	1.7
Political instability	2.5	1	1.5
Respect for human rights	2.7	3	−0.3
Potential for terrorist acts	2.3	3	−0.7
Number of deaths from organised conflict (internal)	1.4	1	0.4

The U.S. and the global average

The peacefulness of the U.S. can be further analysed by comparing the internal U.S. 'peace score' from the Global Peace Index with the average GPI score for each of the categories measured. Indicators that are not shaded are those where the U.S. performed better than the global average while indicators shaded red are those where the U.S. scored below the global average.

It is interesting to note how relatively well the U.S. performs on the majority of the internal indicators when compared to the rest of the world. The U.S. performs particularly well on measures of internal cohesion with low levels of organised internal conflict and a high level of political stability. The country also performs well on the perception of crime within the country and the likelihood of violent demonstrations.

5 Thinking peace

Charles P. Webel

The importance of securing international peace was recognized by the really great men of former generations. But the technical advances of our times have turned this ethical postulate into a matter of life and death for civilized mankind today, and made the taking of an active part in the solution to the problem of peace a moral duty which no conscientious man can shirk.

Albert Einstein (1984: 43)

Nonviolence is a weapon of the strong. . . . The law of love will work, just as the law of gravitation will work, whether we accept it or not. . . . The more I work at this law the more I feel the delight in life, the delight in the scheme of the universe. It gives me a peace and a meaning of the mysteries of nature that I have no power to describe.

M.K. Gandhi (1930/2002: 46)

And how long shall we have to wait before the rest of mankind becomes pacifists too? There is no telling. . . . But one thing we can say: whatever fosters the growth of culture works at the same time against war.

Sigmund Freud (1932/1959: 287)

Preface

For millennia, philosophers, religious thinkers and political activists have written about and demonstrated for 'peace' and decried war. Yet a 'philosophy' of peace is still in its infancy. And while theorists, strategists, tacticians and planners of war and 'security studies' dominate both the academy and the halls of power, philosophers who profess and march for peace do so outside the mainstream philosophical curriculum, far removed from those with the power to make and enforce important political decisions, and often to the dismay and castigation of their more 'echt philosophical' colleagues.

For over a century, psychologists and psychoanalysts have attempted to illuminate the often elusive and murky depths of the human psyche. But a 'depth psychology' of peace is also merely inchoate. Psychologists who research and teach peace, like their philosophical comrades, do so on the margins of their discipline, and usually as a supplement to more 'rigorous, scientific' investigations.

Philosophers and psychologists are all 'for' peace. But those who attempt to bring peace studies and peace research into their 'professional' work, at least in much of the Anglophonic world, risk marginalization and even exclusion from their disciplinary practices, powers and perks. As a result, scholars who wish to study, research, teach and practice peace have begun in the past half century to create their own counter-institutions, where they may do so without the risk of continued academic and professional isolation.

And psychoanalysts, perhaps modernity's most acute probers of conflicts unconscious and interpersonal, are shunned almost entirely by the halls of academic learning and medical research and shun, almost entirely, a depth analysis of the emotional and cognitive hallmarks of inner peace (or harmony) and outer discord (or conflict). Unlike Freud, who engaged in an epistolary discussion with Albert Einstein about the depth-psychological origins of war and mass violence, most analysts in the mainstream 'object relations' and 'drive-theoretical' traditions are reluctant to stray from the inner sanctum of the clinical case conference and take a public stand on the unconscious sources of bellicose and peaceful behaviour. In contrast, an earlier generation of analysts, including Wilhelm Reich and Erich Fromm, actively sought to understand and transform the characterological and cultural sources of authoritarianism and militarism. But in our time, analytic 'silence' tends to extend far beyond the analytic hour with the analysand.

There are some hopeful contraindications, however. In the US and the UK, progressive and peace-oriented philosophers have banded together in such organizations as Concerned Philosophers for Peace, Radical Philosophy and International Philosophers for the Prevention of Nuclear War (created by John Somerville as a sister group of International Physicians for the Prevention of Nuclear War). Several journals and many conferences have been held by these organizations. And psychologists have their own division of 'Peace Psychology' in the American Psychological Association and have recently published two books about peace psychology (Christie et al. 2001; Macnair 2003).

Psychoanalysts, while speaking as individuals in favour of peaceful means of conflict resolution and in opposition to war in general and to recent wars in particular, still tend, at least in the English-speaking world, to shy away from 'politicization' of their 'science'. Many Latin American and European analysts are less reluctant to publicize their privately held pacifist sentiments. On the whole, however, most contemporary philosophers, psychologists and psychoanalysts remain publicly mute about war and peace.

Consequently, in large part because of the modernist and postmodernist shifting of peace analysis and research to the fringes of 'elite' professional discourse and outside the institutional reward structure of mainstream academia and politics, a philosophical theory of 'outer' peace and a depth-psychological comprehension of 'inner' peacefulness seem as desirable today as they did thousands of years ago. And just as evasive and elusive.

Hence we are confronted with a seeming paradox – peace is something we all desire, and yet, except for relatively brief intervals between wars, seem unable to attain (except on paper). And peace studies, peace research, peacekeeping and peacemaking are almost universally acclaimed to be laudable activities, but not for 'serious' scholars and clinicians doing their 'day' jobs.

Is an ontology, a metaphysics, of peace possible, or even desirable? If so, what might it look like? Can a deep psychological account of emotional well-being, and its opposite(s), be offered, possibly on scientific principles rooted in contemporary psychoanalysis and neuroscience? If so, what might this contribute to contemporary theories and practices of nonviolence and peacemaking?

What is, and might be, peace?

Perhaps 'peace' is like 'happiness', 'justice', 'health' and other human ideals – something every person and culture claims to desire and venerate but which few, if any, achieve, at least on an enduring basis. Why are peace, justice and happiness so desirable, but also so intangible and elusive? But perhaps peace is different from happiness, since it seems to require social harmony and political enfranchisement, whereas happiness appears, at least in Western culture, to be largely an individual matter.

Alternatively, perhaps peace does indeed resemble individual happiness – always there, implicit in our psychological make-up and intermittently explicit in our social behaviour and cultural norms. Peace is a pre-condition for our emotional well-being, but a peaceful state of mind is subject to cognitive disruptions and aggressive eruptions. Peace is a linchpin of social harmony, economic equity and political justice, but peace is also constantly ruptured by wars and other forms of violent conflict. Like happiness, peace remains so near . . . and yet, like enduring love, so far. . . .

Spiritual and religious leaders from the Buddha and Jesus to Gandhi and the Dalai Lama have been inclined to equate peace and love, both in their inner dimensions and in the manner in which people who are spiritually developed interact with others, most acutely with those who may hate and envy them. In the twentieth century, Freud and other depth psychologists explored the vicissitudes of our loving and hating feelings, both toward our 'selves', and to others both near and dear (especially our mothers), and to those distant and often dangerous (the 'enemy' within and without).

Eros and aggression, love and hate, are intermingled from birth to burial. Understanding and pacifying our conflicted inner worlds – our need for and flight from love of our selves and others – is an intellectual and political project of the highest and most urgent order. This undertaking must run in tandem with the necessity of comprehending and transforming the conflicts rampant in our interpersonal and political realms of interaction and division.

If peace, like happiness, is both a normative ideal in the Kantian sense (a regulative principle and ethical virtue indicating how we should think and act, even if we often fail to do so) as well as a psychological need (something of which we are normally unaware but sporadically conscious), then why are violence and war (the apparent contraries of social, or outer, peace), as well as unhappiness and misery (the expressions of a lack of inner peace), so prevalent, not just in our time but for virtually all of recorded human history? Given the facts of history and the ever-progressing understanding of our genetic and hormonal nature, is peace even conceivable, much less possible?

These are issues that have been addressed from time immemorial, in oral form since the dawn of civilization and in written form since at least the periods of the great Greek and Indian epochs. But they seem no closer, and perhaps even farther, from resolution than they were at the times of the *Iliad* and the *Mahabharata*.

What does peace mean?

'Peace', like many theoretical terms, is difficult to define. But, as with 'happiness', 'harmony', 'love', 'justice' and 'freedom', we often recognize it by its absence. Consequently, Johan Galtung and others have proposed the important distinction between 'positive' and 'negative' peace. 'Positive' peace denotes the simultaneous presence of many desirable states of mind and society, such as harmony, justice, equity, etc. 'Negative' peace has historically denoted the 'absence of war' and other forms of wide-scale violent human conflict.

Many philosophical, religious and cultural traditions have referred to peace in its 'positive' sense. In Chinese, for example, the word *heping* denotes 'world peace', 'peace among nations', while the words *an* and *mingsi* denote an 'inner peace', a tranquil and harmonious state of mind and being, akin to a meditative mental state. Other languages also frame peace in its 'inner' and 'outer' dimensions.

The English lexicon is quite rich in its supply of terms that refer to and denote peace. In *Webster's Third New International Dictionary*, for example, the meanings of peace are clearly defined.

Initially, in Webster's, peace is defined negatively, as 'freedom from civil clamor and confusion', and positively as 'a state of public quiet' (Webster's 1993: 1660). This denotes –peace and +peace in their political or 'outer' sense. Webster's proceeds further to define (political or outer) peace positively as 'a state of security or order within a community provided for by law, custom, or public opinion' (Ibid.).

Webster's second distinct definition of peace is a 'mental or spiritual condition marked by freedom from disquieting or oppressive thoughts or emotions' (–peace in its personal or 'inner' sense) as well as 'calmness of mind and heart: serenity of spirit' (+inner peace) (Ibid.). Third, peace is defined as 'a tranquil state of freedom from outside disturbances and harassment (+inner peace resulting from –peace) (Ibid.). Fourth, peace denotes 'harmony in human or personal relations: mutual concord and esteem' (this is what I will call interpersonal or intersubjective peace) (Ibid.).

Next, peace is defined by Webster's as (1) 'a state of mutual concord between governments: absence of hostilities or war' (+outer peace caused by –outer peace) and (2) 'the period of such freedom from war' (–outer peace) (Ibid.). The sixth definition of peace is the 'absence of activity and noise: deep stillness: quietness' (+inner peace caused by –inner peace) (Ibid.). And the final lexicographical meaning of peace in the English language (American version) personifies peace as 'one that makes, gives or maintains tranquility' (as God being the ultimate cause of peace on earth and as identified with peace, or Peace, itself) – 'divine peace' (or Peace?) (Ibid.).

Dictionary definitions of abstract terms can only go so far. But in the case of the English lexicon, the semantics of peace gets us remarkably far. For in this important dictionary, the meanings of peace are clearly classified into both + and –, as well as 'inner and outer' components. Two additional denotations are what I am calling 'interpersonal or intersubjective' peace, and 'divine peace' or the divine peacemaker (God, or in polytheistic and mythological cosmologies, the gods). I will not go into various spiritual, theological and/or religious views of peace and Peace, but I will explore some aspects of intersubjective peace, especially in what I shall call its 'dialectical' determination. For it is in this intersubjective zone that some important contemporary and cutting-edge philosophical, psychological and psychoanalytic theories and research strategies converge.

A dialectical determination of peace

Peace is often defined or determined negatively. Peace is 'the absence of war'. Peace is 'non-violence'. Etc. *We know peace by its absence.*

We would agree that World War II was certainly not a time of peace, at least for much of the northern hemisphere. But what about much of the southern hemisphere from 1919 to 1945 – were sub-Saharan Africa, most of Latin America, and the homelands of the Anzus countries 'at peace' because they were not battlegrounds? And what about the period of the 'Cold War' – was that a 'Cold Peace' as well?

These historical considerations lead us back to first, perhaps to 'ultimate', principles, regarding not just the meaning(s) of peace, but its 'essence', its ontology. Is peace like other theoretical terms – justice, freedom, virtue and equality, to name a few? Something intangible but which virtually all rational people prize? Or is it even less tangible, less perceptible – an ideal without an essence, an 'ideal type' (in Max Weber's formulation) but still bearing a 'family resemblance' to other, more tangible human desiderata? *Perhaps peace is both an historical ideal and a term whose meaning is in flux, sometimes seemingly constant (as in 'inner peace of mind') but also noteworthy for its relative absence on the field of history (as in 'world peace').*

Peace is dialectical. In this world, peace is neither a timeless essence – an unchanging ideal substance – nor a mere name without a reference, a form without content. Peace should neither be reified by essentialist metaphysics nor rendered otiose by postmodernist and sceptical deconstruction.

Peace is also not the mere absence of war in a Hobbesian world of unending violent conflict. *Peace is both a means of personal and collective ethical transformation and an aspiration to cleanse the planet of human-inflicted destruction.* The means and the goal are in continual, dialectical evolution, sometimes regressing during periods of acute violent conflict and sometimes progressing nonviolently and less violently to actualize political justice and social equity. Like history and life, peace is a terrestrial creation struggling for survival in a constantly changing, and sometimes threatening environment.

Thinking peace

In thinking about and thinking peace, it is helpful to make clear distinctions between what peace is and might be, and what peace is not and should not be. Thinking 'negatively' (critically or dialectically), it is important to note that peace is not mere pacification: it is not active or subtle domination and manipulation of less by more powerful actors (or –pacification). Peace is also not quiescence and acquiescence by a 'pacified' population fed 'bread and circuses' by a 'benevolent' empire or autocrat.

On the contrary, peace in its progressive or dialectical mode denotes active individual and collective self-determination and emancipatory empowerment. Peace entails continuous peacekeeping and peacemaking. And peacemaking requires active and continual personal and collective transformation, pacifistic rather than pacifying in its means of psychological and political development.

Similarly, the belief system of those who both think and practise peace and who actively seek to attain it by peaceful (nonviolent) means – true pacifism – is not passivism. Genuine pacifism is transformative and activist, employing nonviolent means of social and personal change to resist oppression, war and injustice and to promote personal and social moral integrity and radical, peaceful means of transforming conflicts and actors.

Given the history of the recent past and the current parlous state of our world, one might understandably be tempted to be sceptical about the prospects for enduring peace on earth in an era (error?) of potential instantaneous global war with weapons of mass and vast destruction. But it is worth recalling that other political ideals once thought unachievable also came to pass.

It took centuries, even millennia, to outlaw slavery and legitimize human rights. It might take at least as long to delegitimize political violence, both from above (by the state) and from below (by non-state actors).

And 'peace on earth' might in fact be unachievable, at least for a sustained period of time. That does not invalidate the struggle to achieve a world with greater justice and equity and without violence, or at least with significantly less violence, injustice and inequity. On the contrary, the nonviolent struggle to liberate humanity from its means of self-destruction and self-enslavement is its own end. The absence of a guarantee of 'success' in the effort to bring peace to humanity, and the real possibility of the failure of the human experiment, do not undermine the effort to pacify existence but instead bestow on it a kind of existential nobility and political virtue.

Peace and its antitheses: terror and terrorism

The antithesis of peace is not conflict. Conflicts appear historically inevitable and may be socially desirable if they result in personal and/or political progress. Conflicts may, perhaps paradoxically, promote and increase peace and diminish violence if the conflicting parties negotiate in good faith to reach solutions to problems that are achievable and tolerable, if not ideal.

And sometimes the antithesis of peace is not violence, even political violence, since violent means (such as World War II and wars of independence/national liberation) have sometimes historically helped to bring about periods of less violence and fragile peace. During the long Cold War from 1945–1991, for example, the major powers – the US and its NATO allies on the one hand, and the former Soviet Union and its Warsaw Pact allies on the other hand – did not attack each other directly. Simultaneously, the defeated World War II axis powers – Germany, Italy and Japan – experienced unprecedented political and economic development with vastly less militarism than before 1939.

War-prone nations can become peace-prone (Switzerland, the Scandinavian countries and Costa Rica come to mind) if their real and perceived security and resource needs are met and their standing armies are dramatically reduced or are retired. Even the most striking personal example of the unification of peace thinking and peacemaking – M.K. Gandhi – believed that under certain circumstances it is preferable to act violently on behalf of a just cause than not to act at all. Gandhi said,

> It is better for a man to be violent, if there is violence in our breasts, than to put on the cloak of nonviolence to cover impotence. Violence is any day preferable to impotence. There is hope for a violent man to become nonviolent. There is no such hope for the impotent.
>
> (Gandhi, in Webel 2004/2007: 141)

Rather the polar opposite of peace is violence, or the threat of violence, employed either for its own sake – that is, on behalf of political and/or criminal terrorism – or for the primary purpose of achieving, maintaining and/or expanding personal and/or political power for the sake of conquest and domination. Peace and reflexive acts of interpersonal violence, perpetrated on the spur of the moment against real and/or perceived threats to one's or one's loved ones' existence, are not always mutually exclusive. Similarly, certain acts of political violence may at times advance peaceful ends, as during revolutionary struggles employing controlled and generally non-lethal violence against clear state representatives of tyranny and oppression. The less violence the better. But in a world of murder and murderers, it is often not possible, no matter how ethically desirable, simultaneously to have justice and 'clean hands'.

On the other hand, there is a kind of political and psychological violence that seems always to be reprehensible and avoidable. For this kind of violence – terrifying, terroristic violence – almost always increases human pain and suffering and usually diminishes personal safety and peace of mind, without accomplishing 'higher order' political goals, such as national liberation and political or socioeconomic emancipation.

Some kinds of violence may, especially if non-lethal and not directed intentionally or foreseeably at civilians and other non-combatants, at least in the short run, seem to augment national security or to promote 'just causes'. But in the long run, the chronic use of violence for political and/or criminal means turns back on those who deploy it (as the film *Munich* concretely illustrates at the international level and *A History of Violence* shows at the interpersonal level) and ultimately decreases both the psychological and political security of those who use violence ostensibly to protect themselves from real and/or perceived antagonists or as a means of retaliation to avenge attacks on them, their families and/or their property.

Peace and conflict are not antagonists, especially if the conflicting parties use nonviolent, less violent and non-lethal means of conflict resolution and transformation. Even peace and war are not always antitheses if parties who find themselves reluctantly pulled into war make every effort to reduce the incidence and lethality of violent conflicts and operations during a war and in good faith resolve to end the violence as expeditiously as possible and not to inflict violence on civilian and military non-combatants (*jus in bello*).

Terror and terrorism, however, are incompatible with peace, peacemaking and the struggle to pacify existence. Terrorism is a dual phenomenon, a tactic used by states (terrorism from above) and by non-state actors (terrorism from below) to induce fear in terrorized people for the purpose of influencing another, less vulnerable, population, such as government officials (Webel 2004; Barash and Webel 2009: 43–66; Webel and Arnaldi 2011). *To be at peace in our inner worlds means, inter alia, to be free from the anxiety and terror that are induced or threatened both from above and from below.*

Being at peace: toward a metapsychology of peace

'Metapsychology' is a term used by Freud to denote a number of essays he wrote just after the start of World War I, commencing with two papers written in 1915, 'Instincts and their Vicissitudes' and 'The Unconscious', and continuing two years later with 'Mourning and Melancholia'. In his 'Autobiographical Study', Freud said that what is meant by 'metapsychology' is

> a method of approach according to which every mental process is considered in relation to three coordinates, which I described as dynamic, topographical, and economic, respectively; and this seemed to me to represent the furthest goal that psychology could achieve.
>
> (Freud 1925/1995: 37).

Freud's 'metapsychology' was his theoretical effort to provide a three-dimensional portrait of the dynamics of emotional life, as 'determined' by mostly unconscious mental processes. Here, I am appropriating and revising the Freudian notion of 'metapsychology' and am using it to denote a three-dimensional portrayal of the political psychology of peace and conflict formation.

There are three dialectical, dynamic 'spheres' or 'spectra' of greater or lesser peace. The first is the realm of 'inner', or psychobiological peace (IP). I will use IP to correspond to the 'topographical' (or 'inner spatial') representation of Freud's metapsychological theory. Unconscious, pre-conscious and conscious thoughts, impulses, needs, desires and perceptions constitute the mental and emotional lives of sentient beings.

The second part of this spectrum is the 'outer' sphere of sociopolitical, domestic and international peace (OP). This is the 'economic' arena, both in the psychodynamic sense of 'economy' (drives, instincts and their vicissitudes operating, roughly, according to and beyond the pleasure principle), and in the literal sense of the term. Macro-economic and political forces constitute the commonly understood field of global and local market and power-driven agents and agencies.

And the third, and least discussed, sphere in peace studies and conflict research, is inter-subjective or interpersonal peace (ITP). This corresponds to the 'dynamic' element of Freud-ian metapsychological theory. It is the behavioural field of human interaction in daily life and work.

Like Freud's tripartite 'structural theory', in which the ego, the superego and the uncon-scious are in continuous interaction, IP, OP and ITP are similarly dynamic processes. States of inner peace, or psychological harmony and well-being, are characterized by low degrees of 'inner conflict' and malignant aggression (directed either against oneself, as in masochism, or against others, as in sadism), and by high ego functioning, successful sublimation and non-pathological object relations with significant (and even insignificant) others.

But even the most psychologically healthy persons have difficulty maintaining their equilib-rium in pathogenic environments. Their tranquility may be undermined and even uprooted by pathology-inducing familial, organizational, social and political systems, ranging from conflict-laden interactions with kith and kin, bosses and subordinates, to such stress- and potentially violence-inducing structural factors as under- and unemployment, racism, sex-ism, injustice, need-deprivation, famine, natural catastrophes, poverty, exploitation, inequity and militarism. The intersubjective zone mediates and straddles the zones of inner and outer peace. It is accordingly the catalyst for environmental and interpersonal agents, energies and institutions that reinforce or subvert psychological equilibrium, or inner peace.

But being-at-peace is possible but improbable in an environment that is impoverished. Being peaceful is an enormous challenge when others with whom one interacts are hostile, aggressive, very competitive, and violent. And living in peace is almost inconceivable in desperately poor and war-ridden cultures.

Accordingly, the three zones of inner, outer and intersubjective peace are never static and are always in interaction. A metapsychology of peace would lay out the structural dynamics of these interactions (the descriptive component), assess the strengths and weaknesses of their current historical alignment (the analytic component), and propose a practicable strategy for remediating the inequities and infelicities in the respective spheres of IP, OP, ITP and their interactions (the prescriptive or therapeutic component).

A spectral theory of peace as a continuum

Peace is like light – intangible but discernible either by its absence or by its sporadic and often startling appearances (like a flash of lightning against a black sky). *Peace is a background condition for the perception of everything else, a physical phenomenon affecting all sentient beings, something whose pres-ence or absence is best measured on a continuum or spectrum.*

Peace ranges from what I shall call 'Strong, or Durable, Peace' (roughly equivalent to Johan Galtung's term 'positive peace' – a condition in which there is relatively robust justice, equity and liberty, and relatively little violence and misery at the social level) – to weak or fragile peace. *Strong, peaceful cultures and societies reflexively promote personal harmony and satisfaction.*

At the other end of the spectrum is what I will call 'Weak, or Fragile, Peace' ('negative peace' in Galtung's formulation), where there may be an overt absence of war and other widespread violence in a particular culture, society or nation-state, but in which there is also pervasive injustice, inequity and personal discord and dissatisfaction. Very few human cultures and societies historically have qualified for the designation of Strong Peace, while very many tend toward Weak Peace. The spectrum that measures the relative presence or absence of the necessary and sufficient conditions for sociocultural and national Strong or Weak Peace illuminates what I call 'Outer Peace.'

At times of Weak Peace, peace is a background condition for social existence in general and of personal happiness in particular, something taken for granted – until it is no longer present. During times of war, people yearn for peace in ways they could not have imagined during less violent times. They imagine and desire an often idealized and all-too-evanescent 'peaceable kingdom', a blissful condition, a status quo *ante bellum*, to which they long to return and for which they would pay literally any price.

Personal survival is the absolutely necessary condition, the *sine qua non*, for peace at the personal level. And 'national security', or the collective survival of a culture, people or nation-state, has in modern times become the macroscopic extension of individual 'defensive' struggles, sometimes ruthless, unscrupulous and murderous during times of perceived and real threats to individual and familial existence.

This spectrum is also descriptive of the mental/emotional lives of individuals, which range from extremely conflicted, or Weak Harmony (similar but not identical to psychotic) to conflict free, or Strong Harmony (what ego psychologists once referred to as 'the conflict-free zone' of ego-syntonicity). This is a measure of an individual person's 'Inner Peace'.

Similarly, cultures and societies also range on a spectrum from 'very violent and warlike' to 'very nonviolent and warfree' in terms of their intercultural and international behaviour. The United States, especially since 1941, has vacillated between periods of Weak Peace and 'very violent and war-like' behaviour, both internally (domestically) and internationally. The spectrum that places nation-states and cultures on a continuum ranging from continual and high-casualty warfare to no warfare and no casualties is a measure of Outer Peace.

Finally, individual persons, when interacting with others, exhibit a range of behaviours ranging from 'very conflicted' to 'very unconflicted'. There are a variety of reasons and motivations, from the intrapsychic and hormonal to the sociocultural, why certain individuals behave in antagonistic and hyper-competitive ways on the one hand, to peaceable and cooperative on the other hand. And the continuum of personal feelings, needs, inclinations and desires manifested in behaviours ranging from very conflicted to very unconflicted is a measure of Inner Peace.

The zone of Intersubjective Peace comprises the public and familial spheres, in which people's most aggressive and compassionate qualities are elicited, reinforced or rejected by their peers and bosses. Inner peace can often be made or unmade by interpersonal and socio-economic (or class) conflict.

But peace is also spectral in another way. Peace seems very illusory, almost ghost-like. It is sometimes fleeting and barely visible, like an apparition, especially during times of continual warfare and collective violence.

Peace is a future end-point and 'goal' of war in virtually all cultures and societies. War has been allegedly conducted 'for the sake of peace' from Homeric to present times. As such, *peace is a vision, often otherworldly, of a human and individual condition that is violence and terror free.*

Absolute peace, like absolute pacifism, may also be ghost-like in that it may not exist at all. It may be an illusion or delusion, something for which we are inclined by our natures and cultures to yearn for and idealize, but also something deeply resisted by those same natures and cultures.

Instead of desiring and idealizing what may be unachievable – 'Perfect Peace', or, in Kant's formulation, 'Unending Peace' – might it be more prudent and realistic to think of peace as what Kant sometimes called a 'regulative ideal', a norm (like the Platonic form of perfect virtue or complete happiness) that ought to guide and regulate our behaviour but which is also unlikely to be universally observed? So instead of vainly trying to achieve the impossible – a world completely without war and violence – should we be willing instead to strive for 'Imperfect Peace'?

Conclusion: imperfect but durable peace?

Peace is not and probably cannot be either perfect or unending – at least not on this island Earth as we now know it. But that does not imply that peace is also chimerical and 'not in our genes'. *Rather peace, like justice and happiness, is an historically shifting condition of our individual and collective natures, of our psyches and polities, that at some times is less intangible and at other historical moments shines in the most distant horizons of our imaginations and desires.*

Peace is, like all desired and desirable human ideals and needs, always potentially within us, even if difficult to discern and seemingly impossible to accomplish. The quest for peace may seem quixotic, but that is part of it allure.

Peacemaking is and ought to be heroic. Peace is and must be the heroic quest of this new millennium – if we are to survive.

Bibliography

Ackerman, P. and J. DuVall (2000). *A Force More Powerful: A Century of Nonviolent Conduct.* New York: Palgrave.

Barash, D. and C. Webel (2009). *Peace and Conflict Studies.* Thousand Oaks, CA: Sage.

Christie, D., R. Wagner and D. Winter (2001). *Peace, Conflict, and Violence: Peace Psychology in the 21st Century.* Upper Saddle River, NJ: Prentice Hall.

Einstein, A. (1984). *The World as I See It.* Secausus, NJ: Citadel Press.

Fornari, F. (1974). *The Psychoanalysis of War.* Garden City: Doubleday Anchor Books.

Frank, J.D. (1968). *Sanity and Survival: Psychological Aspects of War and Peace.* New York: Random House Vintage Books.

Freud, S. (1959). *Collected Papers*, Volumes 4 and 5. New York: Basic Books.

Galtung, J. and D. Ikeda (1995). *Choose Peace: A Dialogue between Johan Galtung and Daisaku Ikeda* (translated and edited by R.L. Gage.). London: Pluto Press.

Galtung, J., C.G. Jacobsen and K.F. Brand-Jacobsen (2002). *Searching for Peace: The Road to TRANSCEND.* London: Pluto Press.

Gay, P., ed. (1989). *The Freud Reader.* New York: W.W. Norton.

Kant, I. (1983). *Perpetual Peace and Other Essays on Politics, History, Morals.* Indianapolis, IN: Hackett Publishing Company.

Kernberg, O.F. (1992). *Aggression in Personality Disorders and Perversions.* New Haven: Yale University Press.

Macnair, R.M. (2003). *The Psychology of Peace: An Introduction.* Westport: Praeger.

Merton, T., ed. (1965). *Gandhi on Non-Violence.* New York: New Directions Press.

Reich, W. (1971). *The Mass Psychology of Fascism.* New York: Farrar, Straus & Giroux.

Rose, J. (1993). *Why War? Psychoanalysis, Politics, and the Return to Melanie Klein.* Oxford: Blackwell.

Somerville, J. (1954). *The Philosophy of Peace.* New York: Liberty Press.

Thich Nhat Hanh in Kotler, A. (1991). *Peace is Every Step, the Path of Mindfulness in Everyday Life.* New York: Bantam Books.

Webel, C. (2004/2007). *Terror, Terrorism, and the Human Condition.* New York: Palgrave Macmillan.

Webel, C. and J. Arnaldi, J. (2011). *Fighting Fire with Fire: The Ethics and Efficacy of The Global War on Terrorism.* New York: Palgrave Macmillan.

Webster's Third New International Dictionary of the English Language Unabridged (1993). Springfield, ILL: Merriam-Webster, Inc.

6 Positive and negative peace

Johan Galtung

Any concept of peace includes the absence of direct violence between states, engaged in by military and others in general; and the absence of massive killing of categories of humans in particular. All these absences of types of violence add up to negative peace; as by mutual isolation, unrelated by any structure and culture. This situation is better than violence, but it is not fully peaceful, because positive peace is missing in this conceptualization. Indeed, peace would be a strange concept if it did not include relations between genders, races, classes and families; and did not also include absence of structural violence, the non-intended slow, massive suffering caused by economic and political structures of exploitation and repression (Galtung, 1985); and if it excluded the absence of the cultural violence that legitimizes direct and/or structural violence (Galtung, 1990). Table 1 shows an overview of key terms about positive and negative peace.

This gives us six peace tasks: eliminating the direct violence that causes suffering; eliminating the structures that cause suffering through economic inequity, or, say, walls once placing Jews, now Palestinians, in ghettos; and eliminating cultural themes that justify one or the other. The task known as ceasefire is only one-sixth of a complete peace process.

But then come the three tasks of building direct, structural and cultural peace. The parties exchange goods, not 'bads', not violence. The structural version of that builds cooperation and sustainability into the structure, with equity for the economy, and equality for the polity.

The goal is to build a structure based on reciprocity, equal rights, benefits and dignity, 'what you want for yourself you should also be willing to give the Other'; and a culture of peace, confirming and stimulating an equitable economy and an equal polity. Economic equity stands as a very weak, undeveloped field, in economic theory and practice, with the

Table 1 Matrix of key terms about positive and negative peace

VIOLENCE	DIRECT VIOLENCE= intended harming, hurting	STRUCTURAL VIOLENCE = unintended harming, hurting	CULTURAL VIOLENCE = intended or unintended justifying violence
NEGATIVE PEACE	[1] absence of = ceasefire	[2]absence of = no exploitation; or no structure=atomie	[3] absence of = no justification; or no culture=anomie
POSITIVE PEACE	[4] presence of= cooperation	[5] presence of= equity, equality	[6] presence of= culture of peace, and dialogue
PEACE	negative + positive	negative + positive	negative + positive

social, economic and cultural rights of the 16 December 1966 Human Rights Convention being an effort, but not yet ratified by a leading state in the state system, the United States. Political equality covers issues of democracy (one person one vote) and human rights, not only within countries, but also among them. Political scientists have been far ahead of economists in giving meaning to equity.

Applying the concepts of positive and negative peace to a couple: violence can be physical, like wife-battering, or verbal, bad-mouthing; negative peace is the absence of all that, passive co-existence; positive peace is active love, the union of body, mind and spirit. Thus, negative peace is like a point, neither violence, nor positive peace. Violence is a region of actors exchanging 'bads', and positive peace another region of actors exchanging 'goodies'.

This idea can be developed further, with two actors, X and Y, avoiding suffering, *dukkha* (Sanksrit) and pursuing fulfilment, *sukha* (Sanskrit). X and Y can now relate to each other in three ways: they go up or down the *dukkha-sukha* gradient together; when one goes up the other goes down, and vice versa; or there is no relation between X and Y. In other words, high positive correlation, high negative correlation, or little or no correlation. The correlations are diachronic, not synchronic, identifying trajectories; or symbiosis, antibiosis, abiosis.

Figure 1 presents a diagram with an X-axis and Y-axis, each axis running from −9, extreme suffering (I want to leave this life) to +9, extreme fulfilment (I want to stay here forever), cutting each other in the origin of neither-nor.

The diagram has a main diagonal from −9,−9 through the origin to +9, +9 where the two parties enjoy maximum fulfilment, singly, or jointly in positive harmony (in Quadrant I), and maximum suffering, singly or jointly in negative harmony (in Quadrant III). 'Harmony', then, does not mean joy, happiness, but 'swinging in tact', 'attuned', for good as also for bad.

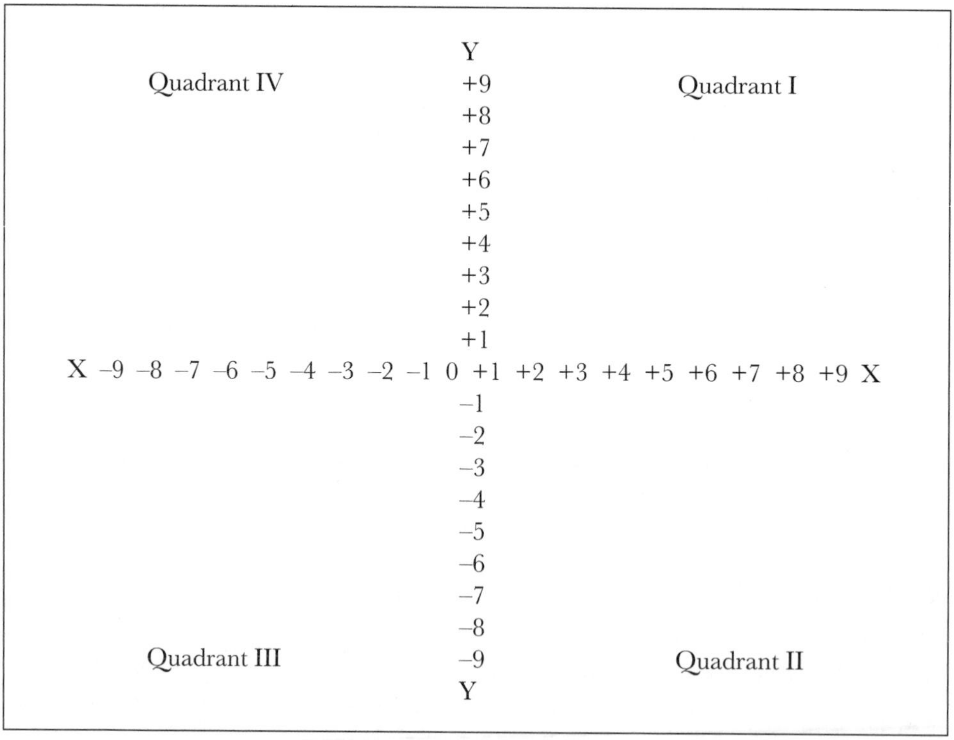

Figure 1 Reference diagram on which to map the concepts of coupling, decoupling, recoupling

But, on the diagram's bi-diagonal, from –9,+9 in Quadrant IV to +9,–9 in Quadrant II, the dyad, singly or jointly, experiences the disharmony of fulfilment for one and suffering for the other, with origin as neither-nor.

Let us now tilt the diagonals toward the X axis, starting with the main diagonal. They still grow or suffer together. But a great gain for X is now a small gain for Y; and a great loss for X a small loss for Y. There is asymmetry, inequity, parasitism. For the bi-diagonal, a great gain for X is only a small loss for Y, and vice versa. So also for Quadrant III: tilting links a great suffering increase for one to a small one for the other, and in the asymmetric Quadrants II and IV even more so.

If we focus on the main diagonal in Quadrant I we get the 'peace diagonal' in the transcend method, with 0,0 as negative transcendence (neither-nor), passing through compromises to +9,+9, positive transcendence (both/and in terms of goal-fulfilment). The bi-diagonal in Quadrant I is the 'war diagonal' of the either/or: at +9,0 X prevails, at 0,+9 Y prevails, with stalemate in the middle, on the peace diagonal known as compromise. To this can then be added curvilinear trajectories telling more complex stories. In short, this intellectual space can accommodate 'grand' peace theory, and *dukkha/sukha* enables us to identify and locate its components.

But we need a concept bridging the singly versus jointly divided above; coupling, showing up as diachronic correlation, X and Y tracing a trajectory in this diagram jointly, like a couple, in harmony or not. High covariation means strong coupling, low means weak and zero/no coupling. Decoupling is the process from high to no coupling, the reverse process is recoupling; like a married couple separating, divorcing and then remarrying.

A couple breaking up decouples, explicitly or implicitly, telling each other that 'my *sukha/dukkha* is now mine, yours is yours, should they coincide it is by chance only'. They may delude themselves and each other, and in the despair over their inability to produce joint fulfilment produce joint suffering, negative instead of positive harmony. Alternatively, they may recouple, or hope for a better coupling to come with the help of 'time'. But 'time' is no substitute for hard work on the relationship. An adolescent leaving the parental home 'to go his/her own way' is obviously decoupling. This may last forever, but with sufficient maturity on both sides, recoupling at higher levels may happen.

Here is one image of coupling, not only in marriage, from Daoism: 'Share in the suffering of others. Delight in the joy of others. . . . View the good fortune of others as your good fortune. View the losses of others as your own loss.' Another is in the Zulu *ubuntu*, 'I am in you, you are in me, we are in each other'. Both tap definitions of a strong spiritual coupling in a we-culture. The unit of suffering and joy is a we, not two I's.

Compare this to the Golden Rule, positive (or negative): 'Do (not do) unto others what you (do not) want them to do unto you.' The subject for *sukha*, and for *dukkha* avoidance, is an individual, 'you'. The rule is ego-centric, an ethical device for self-satisfaction, highly compatible with Abrahamitic individualism. The ethical budget is individual, I-culture, not collective, we-culture oriented. It may not even be very smart; as G. B. Shaw pointed out: 'their tastes may be different'.

Something of the same applies to the Kantian dictum, *Handle so dass die Maxime deines Willens jederzeit zugleich als Prinzip eines allgemeines Gesetzgebung gelten könne* ('Always act so that the thesis underlying your will could serve as a general law'). What Kant introduces here is not a we-culture but a traffic rule for individualist co-existence: the validity of an act is linked to its generalizability. Kant wants a multilateral normative umbrella; the Golden Rule is more bilateral. That rule may be useful, if attention is paid to individual and cultural differences, for positive co-existence in an I-culture, but does not produce the *sui generis* union of a we-culture in the Daoist sense above, as exemplified in the definition of love.

So far we have degree of coupling, strong versus weak, as illustrated by the perfect versus worn-out clutch, and positive versus negative coupling. But how does coupling come about? Using the pillars of peace studies – nature, culture and structure – there are three types of answers. Nature produces coupling, the extreme case being Siamese twins, or one-egged twins in general, and siblings; in short, genetic sharing. Being of the same species is already a (weak) coupling. Culture produces coupling as internalized harmony, like in friendship and love. Primary relations (family, school) produce stronger internalization, but also stronger disharmony 'when things go wrong'. Structure produces coupling as institutionalized coop-eration, in secondary relations (school, at work), and in tertiary relations (belonging to the same category, gender, generation, race, class, nation, territory).

Thus, there are inner versus outer couplings, steering us from within by good and bad conscience, and from without by reward and punishment. We-cultures would produce very strong inner couplings. But I-cultures, guided by the Golden Rule and/or Kantianism, also produce inner couplings, only of a different nature. Love is based on inner we- and I-cultures, and a marriage on an outer social pact, triggering sanctions from all kinds of structures. If one fails, the other coupling devices may still be there.

We can now reap the harvest of all this by linking the concepts of positive and negative peace to the idea of coupling, using the quadrants in Figure 1. Quadrant I is positive peace when there is coupling, positive harmony and symbiosis; and more symmetric, equitable, the closer to the diagonal. Quadrant III is violence when there is coupling, negative harmony and symbiosis; and more symmetric, equitable, the closer to the main diagonal. Quadrants II and IV are fulfilment for one and suffering for the other, negative coupling, disharmony, antibiosis; and more asymmetric, inequitable, the closer to the bi-diagonal, a good illustra-tion of structural violence. The origin is negative peace with both X and Y at the 'no peace, no war' point of no coupling-indifference-abiosis.

Quadrant I accommodates not only direct, intended, but also structural, institutionalized peace. Quadrant IV accommodates direct and structural violence. In Quadrants II and IV there must be something strong on the side of the party extracting benefit: structural violence. But the structural elements in Quadrants I and III should not be underestimated: a ritualized marriage may be good for both; wars may be institutionalized like vendettas.

From this we can already draw some conclusions. Positive peace and violence-war are similar in having positive inner or outer (or both) couplings in common, in other words a joint project like a European community, or a world (meaning European) war. Conflict and struc-tural violence are similar in having negative inner or outer (or both) couplings in common, in other words a joint anti-project. Negative peace, like a ceasefire, is a limited and limiting category suitable for dualist minds: violence versus its absence. Thus, the road from war to positive peace may not be that difficult to travel. Joint projects buoyed by passion are in both; only the content has to be changed. But in negative peace there is little passion, abstention from any joint project, and withdrawal into mutual indifference.

Peace theory and practice are about getting out of Quadrant III direct violence, of Quad-rants II and IV structural violence, and into Quadrant I, direct and structural, positive peace, beyond bland, negative peace. But how? Gandhi's answer: by decoupling in Quadrants III and II–IV, using nonviolence instead of violence in Quadrant II; using non-cooperation, even civil disobedience, in Quadrants II and IV; using constructive action, recoupling, build-ing peace, for Quadrant I.

Gandhi's theory and practice went far beyond Western security theory and practice with clearly paranoid features. To Gandhi, the level of coupling was the key variable as opposed to praising peace, and blaming violence. The work for positive, or as a minimum negative, peace implies changing interaction relations more than actor attributes, and that is exactly what decoupling and recoupling are about. Great. A genius.

References

Galtung, J. (1990). 'Cultural Violence' in *Journal of Peace Research*, *27*(3), 291–305.
Galtung, J. (1985). 'Twenty-five Years of Peace Research: Ten Challenges and Some Responses' in *Journal of Peace Research*, 22(2), 141–158.

Additional resources

Galtung, J. (1998). *Peace by Peaceful Means*. London: Sage.
Galtung, J. (1992). *The Way is the Goal: Gandhi Today*. Ahmedabad: Navajivan, Gujarat Vidyapith.
Galtung, J. (2004). *Transcend and Transform*. London: Pluto and Boulder, CO: Paradigm Press.

PART 1 PEACE STUDIES, PEACE EDUCATION, PEACE RESEARCH AND PEACE

Suggestions for further reading

Adolf, Antony (2009). *Peace A World History*. Cambridge, U.K.: Polity Press.
Barash, David, ed. (2010). *Approaches to Peace A Reader in Peace Studies*. Second edition. New York and Oxford: Oxford University Press.
Barash, David and Charles Webel (2009). *Peace and Conflict Studies*. Second edition. Los Angeles and London: SAGE Publications.
Cortright, David (2009). *Peace A History of Movements and Ideas*. Cambridge and New York: Cambridge University Press.
Galtung, Johan, Carl G. Jacobsen and Kai Fritjof Brand-Jacobsen (2002). *Searching for Peace: The Road to TRANSCEND*. London: Pluto Press.
Harris, Ian M., and Amy L. Shuster, eds. (2006). *Global Directory of Peace Studies and Conflict Resolution Programs*. San Francisco: Peace and Justice Studies Association (PJSA) and the International Peace Research Association Foundation (IPRAF).
Jeong, Ho-Won (2000). *Peace and Conflict Studies: An Introduction*. Burlington, VT: Ashgate.
McElwee, Timothy A., B. Welling Hall, Joseph Liechty and Julie Garber, eds. (2009). *Peace, Justice, and Security Studies: A Curriculum Guide*. Boulder and London: Lynne Rienner.
Richmond, Oliver (2007). *The Transformation of Peace*. New York: Palgrave Macmillan.
Webel, Charles and Johan Galtung, eds. *Handbook of Peace and Conflict Studies*. London and New York: Routledge, 2009.
Young, Nigel, J., editor in chief (2010). *The Oxford International Encyclopedia of Peace*, four volumes. Oxford and New York: Oxford University Press.

Journals

Journal of Peace Research (JPR): http://jpr.sagepub.com/
Peace and Change: http://www.wiley.com/bw/journal.asp?ref=0149-0508
Peace Review: http://www.tandf.co.uk/journals/titles/10402659.asp

Websites

PUGWASH: http://www.pugwash.org/
Stockholm International Peace Research Institute: http://www.sipri.org/
Transcend International: http://www.transcend.org/

Questions for reflection and discussion

1   Consider the various meanings and definitions of peace. Which one(s) do you prefer and why?

2   From what you've now read about peace and conflict studies, what would you consider to be the strengths and weaknesses of this field?

3   If you were to design a peace education programme for your community/nation, what would you include?

4   Assess the strengths and weaknesses of such empirical tools as the Global Peace Index (GPI) for measuring peace.

5   Do you think global peace is achievable in your lifetime? Why/why not?

Part 2

Peace theories and peace movements

SUMMARY

It is not unusual to read and hear about war defined as a form of conflict, often expressed as 'war is a conflict with at least one state involved ...' This formulation is problematic and can have serious consequences. War is a *means* that can be used in a conflict. If we are not able to separate the means used from the content of the dispute, we risk seeing war as the only *tool* to be used during such a conflict, and it is seldom the wisest one. There are of course many other ways to act in times of conflict than to order military troops into action. To make other options visible, we should make a clear distinction between the 'seemingly incompatible goals' and the means to be used.

Most conflicts between states are probably solved without the use of war as a means. Negotiations, mediations, courts and sanctions are just a few examples of other means used to address international disputes. But most of them are badly documented and poorly analysed. Just compare the division of the former Yugoslavia with the division of the former Czechoslovakia. The two cases of division were carried out with very different means. The former has many serious scholarly analyses on the shelves of major research libraries; the latter has few.

There are almost as many theories of peace and war as there are definitions. And throughout recorded history, there has been a plethora of peace and anti-war movements, both explicit and implicit. In modern English, 'theory' is a term originally stemming from classical Greek philosophy, especially from Plato. The term is derived from the ancient Greek *theoria*, which originally meant 'a looking at, viewing, beholding', and refers to contemplation or speculation, as opposed to action. Theory is often contrasted with 'practice' (Greek *praxis*), an Aristotelian concept used to refer to anything done for the sake of any action, in contrast with theory, which is not.

A theory is a system of ideas intended to explain something, and it is generally based on general principles independent of the thing to be explained, such Darwin's theory *of* evolution, Marx's theory *of* capitalism, or Einstein's theory *of* relativity. Theories are sets of principles on which the practice of an activity is based, such as legal or political theories, including such influential theories of war and peace as 'realpolitik' (political realism), 'just war theory' and 'pacifism'.

In English, the noun 'movement' refers to a move, a change of place or position or posture; a tactical or strategic shifting of a military unit, a manoeuvre; to an action or activity – usually used in the plural, 'movements'. A movement also refers to a tendency or trend. And it importantly denotes *a series of organized activities working to promote or attain an end*, especially such political and social movements as the civil rights movement, the anti-war movement and the peace movement.

With reference to peace, the distinction between 'theory' and 'movement' is somewhat arbitrary, since peace denotes *both the idea of peace and the action* needed to bring it about. This 'unity' of theory and practice is exemplified by the life and work of Mohandas K. Gandhi, for whom peace, or individual and collective nonviolence, was religious, philosophical, psychological, legal and political at the same time. Gandhi, in turn, was deeply influenced by spiritual and secular theories and traditions, both those indigenous to India (Hinduism) and Western.

Recorded religious, legal and/or philosophical theories of peace and war date back to the Code of Hammurabi, during the eighteenth century BCE in ancient Babylon. There are similar roots to be found in the Vedic tradition in India dating from 5500–2600 BCE[1] and in other civilizations.

These early irenic and belligerent discourses were developed further by the Greeks and Romans in numerous treatises and legislative codes. For example, in his *History of the Peloponnesian War*, the great Greek historian Thucydides fashions a heart-rending dialogue between morally appealing magistrates of the small city-state of Melos (a Spartan colony without the means to defend itself) and the politically tough-minded generals of Athens, who attacked this island in 416 BCE, ostensibly because of Melos' association with Athens' mortal rival, Sparta.

Thucydides constructs his dialogue to highlight the glaring gap between the Melian appeals to such quintessential ethical ideals as 'justice and fairness', and what the ancient Greek critic Dionysius calls the 'depraved shrewdness' of the Athenian imperialists. From the standpoint of virtually all ethical, religious and legal traditions, the Melians had 'right' on their side, but the Athenians had something vastly more important in the political realm – might. Consequently, hoping to preserve their peace and independence, the Melians did not try to resist, relying, imprudently, on the Athenians' presumed compassion and sense of 'fair play'. The Athenians slaughtered all Melian males of military age, enslaved their women and children, and colonized Melos. High-minded theoretical appeals to justice and peaceful coexistence fell on deaf ears. The view that 'might' (or the use or threatened use of deadly force on behalf of political aims) trumps right (ethical, legal and/or religious appeals to such moral ideals as justice and peace) underpins the most influential Western theory and practice of peace and war – realpolitik (political realism). Modest efforts to limit the 'collateral damage' (civilian casualties) of wars spawned by realpolitik are exemplified by the theory of 'just war'.

About 700 years after the Peloponnesian War, during the waning days of the Roman Empire, the Christian philosopher/theologian Augustine, to justify Christian participation in the defence of Rome against its 'barbaric' enemies, proposed the distinction between *jus ad bellum* (Latin for the 'the justice of going to war') and *jus in bello* ('justice during a war'). This doctrine of 'just and unjust wars' was refined by philosophers and theologians from Aquinas and the Second Lateran Council in the thirteenth century, to the Second Vatican Council in 1966. The idea of 'just war' has been cited for almost two millennia by decision makers and world leaders as a rationale for 'going to war to preserve the peace', including by President Barack Obama in his Nobel Peace Prize acceptance speech in 2009.[2]

It is not too long time ago in human history that slavery was considered to be acceptable and 'Just Slavery' was an integrated part of the global economy. Just as such notions as 'Just Patriarchy' and 'Just Wife Beating' are challenged today, perhaps in the future the institution of war and the rationale of 'Just War' will also be seen as unacceptable ways of handling and justifying conflicts.

When the term 'Peace Movement' is used, many people think of those organizations that oppose wars. But most peace researchers and activists alike will argue that peace must be understood as much more than absence of war. They regard domestic violence and structural violence (unjust world order, etc.) as just as important as the absence of war.

The Western intellectual and cultural tradition is rich in 'war talk' and 'just' wars, and, compared with certain non-Western traditions, especially East Asian ones, comparatively poor in peace theories.[3] In this part of the book, we present some powerful theoretical alternatives to the language games of just war and realpolitik. Here you will be exposed to some of the most significant philosophical and religious/spiritual approaches to understanding peace as more than the absence of war, and you will also read three important contemporary analyses of the history, strengths and weaknesses of peace and other protest movements.

Philosophical and religious contributions to peace

Throughout recorded history, philosophers have speculated on the nature of peace and the meanings of war. And religion has served both as a force for peace and as a source of conflict. This is as true today as it has been in the past. For even now, invocations of divine sanction serve as justifications for violence against one's enemies ('we're on God's side; they're evil'), while such spiritual leaders as the Dalai Lama preach and practise nonviolence.

For much of the Western philosophical and theological tradition, especially for idealists and rationalists (such as Plato and Kant), peace denotes *both* a well-coordinated body politic – a republic of virtue – *and* a harmonious psyche, a mind that is rational and a will governed by rational laws. Philosophically speaking, peace is an ethical virtue indicating how we *should* think and act, individually and collectively, even if we often fail to do so. And for many social scientists and psychoanalysts, peace is also a psychological need for a tranquil mental and emotional life – something of which we are normally unaware but sporadically conscious, as well as a cessation of hostilities within and between nations.

Peace and war are issues that have been addressed from time immemorial, in oral form since the dawn of civilization and in written form since at least the periods of the great Greek and Indian epochs. But they seem no closer, and perhaps even farther, from resolution than they were at the times of the *Iliad* (ca. eighth century BCE) and the *Mahabharata* (ca. fifth century BCE).

Immanuel Kant, one of the greatest philosophers of modern times, is best known for his complex analyses of the nature and limits of human knowledge and for his postulates of what he called the 'Categorical Imperative(s)', or moral law, a modern philosophical version of 'The Golden Rule'. In 'Eternal Peace', Kant posits the 'evil nature of man' and the 'state of nature' as a 'state of war', not 'the state of peace'. But he argues that 'natural' but nonetheless unethical human weaknesses might be contained, especially when they impel states to wage war. The vehicle of containment is a federalist world order, 'the law of nations . . . based upon a *federalism* of free states'. This is an idea that found applications in such twentieth-century institutions as the League of Nations and the United Nations. The establishment of such a 'union of nations', under the rule of law, and the disappearance of all standing armies, 'the cause of wars of aggression', should, in Kant's estimation, lead to a state of (negative) peace, 'the end of all hostilities'.

In his 'Address to the Swedish Peace Congress in 1909', the great Russian writer Leo Tolstoy poses to Christians and others troubled by war the simple truth, known as 'the law of God: Thou shalt not kill'. Based on what Tolstoy regarded as the 'binding' nature of this truth, 'man may not and should not in any circumstances or under any pretext kill his fellow man'. Tolstoy's absolute (Christian) pacifism deemed war 'evil' and implied the abolition of armies and the governments that wage war. In choosing love over murder, Christians, according to Tolstoy, must demand 'a different social order', and change 'the cruel and irrational' (militarized) 'life of our time'.

Writing at the same time as Tolstoy, the American psychologist and pragmatist philosopher William James, in his essay 'The Moral Equivalent of War', noted the 'militant enthusiasm' of humans to rally around the military flag, and he challenged the simplistic view that war was an inevitable result of human nature, even though 'history is a bath of blood'. James, a pacifist, called for pacifists 'to enter more deeply into the aesthetical and ethical point of view of their opponents', the 'militarists'. And he argued for 'the moral equivalent of war', 'a substitute for war's disciplinary function' – a non-military conscription for young people – because he claimed that war gives people an opportunity to express their spiritual inclinations towards self-sacrifice and personal honour, and to create peace it is necessary to express these sentiments in another, less bellicose way.

Following World War II and the development of nuclear weapons, a group of Nobel Prize-winning scientists, led by Albert Einstein (*Time Magazine's* 'Man of the 20th century') and the distinguished English writer-philosopher Bertrand Russell, wrote a Manifesto to the 1955 Pugwash Conference on Science and World Affairs. They presented the 'stark and dreadful and inescapable problem . . . Shall we put an end to the human race or shall mankind renounce war?' And they called for an agreement to renounce and abolish nuclear weapons 'as a first step' toward a general reduction or armaments. In addition, to further the continued existence of mankind, what has come to be known as 'The Russell – Einstein Manifesto' calls for a 'new way of thinking' and urges the world's governments 'to find peaceful means for the settlement of all matters of dispute between them'.

His Holiness the 14th Dalai Lama of Tibet concurs that the greatest single danger facing humankind is the threat of nuclear destruction and also calls for a new (nonviolent) approach to global problems. Coming from the Mahayana Buddhist tradition, the Dalai Lama believes that 'love and compassion are the moral fabric of world peace'. These spiritual qualities can not only provide us with peace of mind, but can also be useful for those 'in whose hands lie the power and the opportunity to create the structure of world peace'. According to the Dalai Lama, compassion and wisdom are in accord with the ethical teachings of all world religions, which should promote better interfaith understanding and bring about a global consensus on basic spiritual values to effectively reduce hatred, fighting and violence. The globalization of such humanitarian ideals as compassion, decency and wisdom 'can enable us to create the spiritual conditions for world peace'.

We encourage you to contemplate and discuss the ideas and ideals promoted in the articles that follow.

Peace and social justice movements

A political movement is a social movement in the political arena. Social movements are a type of group action. They are large, often informal groupings of individuals and/or organizations focused on specific political or social issues, on carrying out, or resisting, a social change or a political state of affairs. A political movement may be organized around a single issue or set of issues, or around a set of shared concerns of a social group. In contrast with a political party, a political movement is usually not organized to elect members of the movement to government office; instead, a political movement aims to convince citizens and/or government officials to take action on the issues and concerns that are the focus of the movement. They are often represented by non- or even anti-state groups. A political movement may be local, regional, national or international in scope. Some aim to change government policy, such as the anti-war movement, the ecology movement, the anti-globalization movement and the peace movement.

Social and political movements for peace owe a great deal to religion and philosophy. For example, the Anabaptists and Catholic humanists influenced mass political upheavals during the sixteenth and seventeenth centuries. The Quakers merged spiritual inspiration with secular democratic ideals and nonviolence. And the writings of Immanuel Kant, Jean-Jacques Rousseau and other Enlightenment theorists were influenced by the theological and political events of the late eighteenth century (such as the French, American and Industrial Revolutions) and in turn influenced the first modern peace societies and 'peace movements' of the nineteenth century.

David Cortright responds to challenges faced by pacifism by exploring the history of movements and ideas for peace – what he calls 'peace history' and 'peacemaking ideas' – and by arguing for 'pragmatic pacifism'. This is what Cortright claims to be 'the dominant position of those who consider themselves peace supporters', in contrast with 'absolute pacifists', whom Cortright says are a minority within peace movements. Specifically, 'pragmatic pacifism can be understood as a continuum of perspectives, beginning on the one hand with the rejection of military violence and extending across a range of options that allow for some limited use of force under specific conditions'. Cortright hopes to combine the pacifist and just war traditions, thereby 'taking into account the full range of peacemaking options and traditions', which he argues 'conforms with the original definition and meaning of pacifism'.

April Carter outlines the religious and philosophical origins of peace activity, especially from the humanists and the Quakers. She indicates that the first organized peace groups were founded in the U.S. and Britain in the early nineteenth century as 'part of the new spirit of democracy which prompted popular agitation . . . for a range of social and humanitarian reforms and created aspirations for the transformation of society'. A representative case of the tension in nineteenth-century peace societies between maintaining peace and securing justice occurred among American pacifists over the issue of slavery. Subsequently, World War I, 'while a disaster for groups committed to work for peace', proved to be a 'powerful impetus to peace sentiment and peace campaigning for the subsequent twenty years'. World War II led to the creation of the United Nations, a new supra-national organization designed to promote international order and peace.

Nigel Young, editor in chief of *The Oxford International Encyclopedia of Peace*, distinguishes between peace studies, 'an intellectual endeavour', and peace movements, modern social movements emerging from the Enlightenment. Since these movements rise and fall at different times and in different societies, Young finds it 'difficult to discern one continuous movement for peace over the past century'. He assesses April Carter's criteria for peace movements, which Young finds problematic because 'a movement could . . . be autonomous, nonaligned, and nonviolent and yet not seek *peace* . . . .' Young concludes that the 'great nonviolent campaigns are peace movements', quintessentially the Gandhian movement from 1917 through the 1940s, the U.S. Civil Rights movement (1956–65), and the 'people's power' movements of resistance to Communist governments in Eastern Europe in the 1980s. He supports the construction of a global 'peace culture'.

The relations between peace and peace movements are complex and in flux. We invite you to consider such contemporary manifestations of this phenomenon as the 'Arab Spring' movements for change in 2011.

Notes

1 Nikhilananda, Swami (1990), *The Upanishads: Katha, Iśa, Kena, and Mundaka*, I (5th ed.). New York: Ramakrishna-Vivekananda Center.
2 For the full text of Obama's speech, see: http://www.msnbc.msn.com/id/34360743/ns/politics-white_house/t/full-text-obamas-nobel-peace-prize-speech/
3 For a summary of some Western classical and Eastern concepts of peace, see David Barash and Charles Webel, *Peace and Conflict Studies*, op. cit., 4–7.

7 Eternal Peace

Immanuel Kant

"To eternal peace"

Whether the above satirical inscription, once put by a certain Dutch innkeeper on his sign-board on which a graveyard was painted, holds of men in general, or particularly of the heads of states who are never sated with war, or perhaps only of those philosophers who are dreaming that sweet dream of peace, may remain undecided. However, in presenting his ideas, the author of the present essay makes, one condition. The practical statesman should not, in case of a controversy with the political theorist, suspect that any danger to the state lurks behind the opinions which such a theorist ventures honestly and openly to express. Consistency demands this of the practical statesman, for he assumes a haughty air and looks down upon the theorist with great self-satisfaction as a mere theorizer whose impractical ideas can bring no danger to the state, since the state must be founded on principles derived from experience. The worldly-wise statesman may therefore, without giving himself great concern, allow the theorizer to throw his eleven bowling balls all at once. By this "saving clause" the author of this essay knows himself protected in the best manner possible against all malicious interpretation.

First section

Which contains the preliminary articles of an eternal peace between states

1. "No treaty of peace shall be held to be such, which is made with the secret reservation of the material for a future war."

For, in that event, it would be a mere truce, a postponement of hostilities, not *peace*. Peace means the end of all hostilities, and to attach to it the adjective "eternal" is a pleonasm which at once arouses suspicion. The preexisting reasons for a future war, including those not at the time known even to the contracting parties, are all of them obliterated by a genuine treaty of peace; no search of documents, no matter how acute, shall resurrect them from the archives. It is Jesuitical casuistry to make a mental reservation that there might be old claims to be brought forward in the future, of which neither party at the time cares to make mention, because both are too much exhausted to continue the war, but which they intend to assert at the first favorable opportunity. Such a procedure, when looked at in its true character, must be considered beneath the dignity of rulers; and so must the willingness to attempt such legal claims be held unworthy of a minister of state.

But, if enlightened notions of political wisdom assume the true honor of the state to consist in the continual increase of power by any and every means, such a judgment will, of course, evidently seem academic and pedantic.

2. "No state having an independent existence, whether it be small or great, may be acquired by another state, through inheritance, exchange, purchase, or gift."

A state is not a possession (*patrimonium*) like the soil on which it has a seat. It is a society of men, which, no one but they themselves is called upon to command or to dispose of. Since, like a tree, such a state has its own roots, to incorporate it as a graft into another state is to take away its existence as a moral person and to make of it a thing. This contradicts the idea of the original contract, without which no right over a people can even be conceived.[1] Everybody knows into what danger, even in the most recent times, the supposed right of thus acquiring states has brought Europe. Other parts of the world have never known such a practice. But in Europe states can even marry each other. On the one hand, this is a new kind of industry, a way of making oneself predominant through family connections without any special effort; on the other, it is a way of extending territorial possessions. The letting out of troops of one state to another against an enemy not common to the two is in the same class. The subjects are thus used and consumed like things to be handled at will.

3. "Standing armies shall gradually disappear."

Standing armies incessantly threaten other states with war by their readiness to be prepared for war. States are thus stimulated to outdo one another in number of armed men without limit. Through the expense thus occasioned peace finally becomes more burdensome than a brief war. These armies are thus the cause of wars of aggression, undertaken in order that this burden may be thrown off. In addition to this, the hiring of men to kill and be killed, an employment of them as mere machines and tools in the hands of another (the state), cannot be reconciled with the rights of humanity as represented in our own person. The case is entirely different where the citizens of a state voluntarily[2] drill themselves and their fatherland against attacks from without. It would be exactly the same with the accumulation of a war fund if the difficulty of ascertaining the amount of the fund accumulated did not work a counter effect. Looked upon by other states as a threat of war, a big fund would lead to their anticipating such a war by making an attack themselves, because of the three powers – the power of the army, the power of alliance, and the power of money – the last might well be considered the most reliable instrument of war.

[. . .]

5. "No state shall interfere by force in the constitution and government of another state."

For what could justify it in taking such action? Could perhaps some offense do it which that state gives to the subjects of another? Such a state ought rather to serve as a warning, because of the example of the evils which a people brings upon itself by its lawlessness. In general, the bad example given by one free person to another (is a *scandalum acceptum)* is no violation of the latter's rights. The case would be different if a state because of internal dissension should he split into two parts, each of which, while constituting a separate state, should lay claim to the whole. An outside state, if it should render assistance to one of these, could not be charged with interfering in the constitution of another state, as that state would then be in a condition of anarchy. But as long as this inner strife was not decided, the interference of outside powers would be a trespass on the rights of an independent people struggling only with its own inner weakness. This interference would be an actual offense which would so far tend to render the autonomy of all states insecure.

6. "No state at war with another shall permit such acts of warfare as must make mutual confidence impossible in time of future peace: such as the employment of assassins, of poisoners, the violation of articles of surrender, the instigation of treason in the state against which it is making war, etc."

These are dishonorable stratagems. Some sort of confidence in an enemy's frame of mind must remain even in time of war for otherwise no peace could be concluded, and the conflict would become a war of extermination. For after all, war is only the regrettable instrument of asserting one's right by force in the primitive state of nature where there exists no court to decide in accordance with law. In this state neither party can be declared an unjust enemy, for this presupposes a court decision. The outcome of the fight, as in the case of a so-called "judgment of God," decides on whose side the right is. Between states no, war of punishment can be conceived, because between them there is no relation, of superior and subordinate.

From this it follows that a war of extermination, in which destruction may come to both parties at the same time, and thus to all rights too, would allow eternal peace only upon the graveyard of the whole human race. Such a war, therefore, as well as the use of the means which might be employed in it, is wholly forbidden.

But that the methods of war mentioned above inevitably lead to such a result is clear from, the fact that such hellish arts, which are in themselves degrading, when once brought into use do not continue long within the limits of war but are continued in time of peace, and thus the purpose of the peace is completely frustrated. A good example is furnished by the employment of spies, in which only the dishonorableness of others (which unfortunately cannot be exterminated) is taken advantage of.

Although all the laws above laid down would objectively – that is, in the intention of the powers, be negative laws (*leges prohibitirae*), yet some of them are strict laws, which are valid without consideration of the circumstances. They insist that the abuse complained of be abolished at once. Such are our rules number 1, 5, and 6. The others, namely rules number 2, 3, and 4, though not meant to be permitting exception from the "rule of law," yet allow for a good deal of subjective discretion in respect to the application of the rules. They permit delay in execution without their purpose being lost sight of. The purpose, however, does not admit of delay till doomsday – "to the Greek Calends," as Augustus was wont to say. The restitution, for example, to certain states of the freedom of which they have been deprived, contrary to our second article, must not be indefinitely put off. The delay is not meant to prevent restitution, but to avoid undue haste which might be contrary to the intrinsic purpose. For the prohibition laid down by the article relates only to the mode of acquisition, which is not to be allowed to continue, but it does not relate to the present state of possessions. This present state, though not providing the needed just title, yet was held to be legitimate at the time of the supposed acquisition, according to the then current public opinion.

Second section

which contains the definitive articles for eternal peace among states

The state of peace among men who live alongside each other is no state of nature *(status naturalis)*. Rather it is a state of war which constantly threatens even if it is not actually in progress. Therefore the state of peace must be *founded;* for the mere omission of the threat of war is no security of peace, and consequently a neighbor may treat his neighbor as an enemy unless he has guaranteed such security to him, which can only happen within a state of law.

Second definitive article of the eternal peace

The law of nations (Völkerrecht) should be based upon a *federalism* of free states.

Nations may be considered like individual men which hurt each other in the state of nature, when they are not subject to laws, by their very propinquity. Therefore each, for the sake of security, may demand and should demand of the other to enter with him into a constitution similar to the civil one where the right of each may be secured. This would be a *union of nations [Völkerbund]* which would not necessarily have to be a *state of nations [Völkerstaat]*, A state of nations contains a contradiction, for every state involves the relation (of a superior (legislature) to a subordinate (the subject people), and many nations would, in a single state, constitute only one nation, which is contradictory since we are here considering the right of nations toward each other as long as they constitute different states and are not joined together into one.

We look with deep aversion upon the way primitive peoples are attached to their lawless liberty – a liberty which enables them to fight incessantly rather than subject themselves to the restraint of the law to be established by themselves; in short, to prefer wild freedom to a reasonable one. We look upon such an attitude as raw, uncivilized, and an animalic degradation of humanity. Therefore, one should think, civilized peoples (each united in a state) would hasten to get away from such a depraved state as soon as possible. Instead, each *state* insists upon seeing the essence of its majesty (for popular majesty is a paradox) in this, that it is not subject to any external coercion. The luster of its ruler consists in this, that many thousands are at his disposal to be sacrificed for a cause which is of no concern to them, while he himself is not exposed to any danger. Thus a Bulgarian Prince answered the Emperor who good naturedly wanted to settle their quarrel by a duel: "A smith who has prongs won't get the hot iron out of the fire with his bare hands." The difference between the European savages and those in America is primarily this, that while some of the latter eat their enemies, the former know how better to employ their defeated for than to feast on them – the Europeans rather increase the number of subjects, that is the number of tools for more extended wars.

In view of the evil nature of man, which can be observed clearly in the free relation between nations (while in a civil and legal state it is covered by governmental coercion), it is surprising that the word *law* [R*echt*] his not been entirely banned from the politics of war as pedantic, and that no state has been bold enough to declare itself publicly as of this opinion. For people in *justifying* an aggressive war still cite HUGO GROTIUS, PUFENDORF, VATTEL and others (all of them miserable consolers). This is done, although their code of norms, whether stated philosophically or juristically does not have the least *legal* force; nor can it have such force, since states as such are not subject to a common external coercion. There is not a single case known in which a state has been persuaded by arguments reinforced by the testimony of such weighty men to desist from its aggressive design.

This homage which every state renders the concept of law (at least in words) seems to prove that there exists in man a greater moral quality (although at present a dormant one), to try and master the evil element in him (which he cannot deny), and to hope for this in others. Otherwise the words *law* and *right* would never occur to states which intend to fight with each other, unless it were for the purpose of mocking them, like the Gallic prince who declared: "It is the advantage which nature has given the stronger over the weaker that the latter ought to obey the former."

In short, the manner in which states seek their rights can never be a suit before a court, but only war. However, war and its successful conclusion, *victory*, does not decide what is law and what right. A *peace treaty* puts an end to a particular war, but not to the state of war which consists in finding ever new pretexts for starting a new one. Nor can this be declared strictly unjust because in this condition each is the judge in his own cause. Yet it cannot be maintained that states under the law of nations are subject to the same rule that is valid for individual men in the lawless state of nature: "that they ought to leave this state." For states have internally a legal constitution and hence [their citizens] have outgrown the coercion of others who might desire to put them under a broadened legal constitution conceived in terms of their own legal norms. Nevertheless, reason speaking from the throne of the highest legislative power condemns war as a method of finding what is right. Reason makes [the achievement of] the state of peace a direct duty, and such a state of peace cannot be established or maintained without a treaty of the nations among themselves. Therefore there must exist a union of a particular kind which we may call the *pacific union (foedus pacificum)* which would be distinguished from a *peace treaty (pactum pacis)* by the fact that the latter tries to end merely *one* war, while the former tries to end *all* wars forever. This union is not directed toward the securing of some additional power of the state, but merely toward maintaining and making secure the *freedom* of each state by and for itself and at the same time of the other states thus allied with each other. And yet, these states will not subject themselves (as do men in the state of nature) to laws and to the enforcement of such laws.

It can be demonstrated that this idea of *federalization* possesses objective reality, that it can be realized by a gradual extension to all states, leading to eternal peace. For if good fortune brings it to pass that a powerful and enlightened people develops a republican form of government which by nature is inclined toward peace, then such a republic will provide the central core for the federal union of other states. For they can join this republic and can thus make secure among themselves the state of peace according to the idea of a law of nations, and can gradually extend themselves by additional connections of this sort.

It is possible to imagine that a people says: "There shall be no war amongst us; for we want to form a state, i.e., to establish for ourselves a highest legislative, executive, and juridical power which peacefully settles our conflicts." But if this state says: "There shall be no war between myself and other states, although I do not recognize a highest legislative authority which secures my right for me and for which I secure its right," it is not easy to comprehend upon what ground I should place my confidence in my right, unless it be a substitute [*Surrogat*] for the civil social contracts, namely, a free federation. Reason must necessarily connect such a federation with the concept of a law of nations, if authority is to be conceived in such terms.

On the other hand, a concept of the law of nations as a right *to make* war is meaningless; for it is supposed to be a right to determine what is right not according to external laws limiting the freedom of each individual, but by force and according to one-sided maxims. Unless we are ready to accept this meaning: that it serves people who have such views quite right if they exhaust each other and thus find eternal peace in the wide grave which covers all the atrocities of violence together with its perpetrators. For states in their relation to each other there cannot, according to reason, be any other way to get away from the lawless state which contains nothing but war than to give up (just like individual men) their wild and lawless freedom, to accept public and enforceable laws, and thus to form a constantly growing world *state of all nations (civitas centium)* which finally would comprise all nations. But states do not want this, as not in keeping with their idea of a law of nations, and thus they reject in fact what is true in theory.[2] Therefore, unless all is to be lost, the positive idea of a *world republic* must be replaced by the negative substitute of a *union* of nations which maintains itself, prevents wars, and steadily expands. Only such a union may under existing conditions stem the tide of the law-evading, bellicose propensities in man, but unfortunately subject to the constant danger of their eruption (*furor, impius intus – fremit horridus ore cruento*. VIRGIL).

Third definitive article of the eternal peace

"The Cosmopolitan or World Law shall be limited to conditions of a universal hospitality."

We are speaking in this as well as in the other articles not of philanthropy, but of *law*. Therefore *hospitality* (good neighborliness) means the right of a foreigner not to be treated with hostility when he arrives upon the soil of another. The native may reject the foreigner if it can be done without his perishing, but as long as he stays peaceful, he must not treat him hostilely. It is not the right of becoming a permanent guest [*Gastrecht*] which the foreigner may request, for a special beneficial treaty would be required to make him a fellow inhabitant [*Hausgenosse*] for a certain period. But it is the right to visit [*Besuchsrecht*] which belongs to all men – the right belonging to all men to offer their society on account of the common possession of the surface of the earth. Since it is a globe, they cannot disperse infinitely, but must tolerate each other. No man has a greater fundamental right to occupy a particular spot than any other.

Uninhabitable parts of the earth's surface, the oceans and deserts, divide this community. But *ship* or *camel* (the ship of the desert) enable men to approach each other across these no-man's regions, and thus to use the right of the common *surface* which belongs to all men together, as a basis of possible intercourse. The inhospitable ways of coastal regions, such as the Barbary Coast, where they rob ships in adjoining seas or make stranded seamen into slaves, is contrary to natural law, as are the similarly inhospitable ways of the deserts and their Bedouins who look upon the approach (of a foreigner) as giving them a right to plunder him. But the right of hospitality, the right, that is, of foreign guests, does not extend further than to the conditions which enable them to attempt the developing of intercourse with the old inhabitants.

In this way, remote parts of the world can enter into relationships which eventually become public and legal and thereby may bring mankind ever nearer to an eventual world constitution.

If one compares with this requirement the *inhospitable* conduct of the civilized, especially of the trading, nations of our continent, the injustice which they display in their *visits* to foreign countries and peoples goes terribly far. They simply identify visiting with *conquest*. America, the lands of the Negroes, the Spice Islands, the Cape of South Africa, etc., were countries that belonged to nobody, for the inhabitants counted for nothing. In East India (Hindustan) they brought in foreign mercenaries, under the pretense of merely establishing trading ports. These mercenary troops brought suppression of the natives, inciting the several states of India to extended wars against each other. They brought famine, sedition, treason and the rest of the evils which weigh down mankind.

China[3] and Japan, who had made an attempt to get along with such guests, have wisely allowed only contact, but not settlement – and Japan has further wisely restricted this privilege to the Dutch only, whom they exclude, like prisoners, from community with the natives. The worst (or viewed from the standpoint of a moral judge the best) is that the European nations are not even able to enjoy this violence. All these trading companies are on the point of an approaching collapse; the sugar islands, which, are the seat of the most cruel and systematic slavery, do not produce a yield – except in the form of raising recruits for navies; thus they in turn serve the conduct of war – wars of powers which make much ado about their piety and who want themselves to be considered among the morally elect, while in fact they consume [the fruits of] injustice like water.

The narrower or wider community of all nations on earth has in fact progressed so far that a violation of law and right in one place is felt in *all* others. Hence the idea of a cosmopolitan or world law is not a fantastic and utopian way of looking at law, but a necessary completion of the unwritten code of constitutional and international law to make it a public law of mankind. Only under this condition can we flatter ourselves that we are continually approaching eternal peace.

First addition

On the guarantee of eternal peace

No one less than the great artist *nature* (*natura daedala rerum*) offers such a *guarantee*. Nature's mechanical course evidently reveals a teleology: to produce harmony from the very disharmony of men even against their will. If this teleology and the laws that effect it is believed to be like an unknown cause compelling us, it is called *fate*. But if it is considered in the light of its usefulness for the evolution of the world, it will be called *providence* – a cause which, responding to a deep wisdom, is directed toward a higher goal, the objective final end [*Endzweck*] of mankind which predetermines this evolution.[4] We do not really *observe* this providence in the artifices of nature, nor can we *deduce* it from them. But we can and must *add this thought* (as in all relations of the form of things to ends in general), in order to form any kind of conception of its possibility. We do this in analogy to human artifices. The relation and integration of these factors into the end (the moral one) which reason directly prescribes is very sublime in *theory*, but is axiomatic and well-founded in practice, e.g., in regard to the concept of a duty toward eternal peace which that mechanism promotes.

[. . .]

War itself does not require a special motivation, since it appears to be grafted upon human nature. It is even considered something noble for which man is inspired by the love of honor, without selfish motives. This martial courage is judged by American savages, and European ones in feudal times, to be of great intrinsic value not only *when* there is a *war* (which is equitable), but also so *that* there may be war. Consequently war is started merely to show martial courage, and war itself invested with an inner *dignity*. Even philosophers will praise war as ennobling mankind, forgetting the Greek who said: "War is bad in that it begets more evil people than it kills." This much about what nature does in pursuit of its own purpose in regard to mankind as a species of animal.

Now we face the question which concerns the essential point in accomplishing eternal peace: what does nature do in relation do the end which man's reason imposes as a duty, in order to favor thus his *moral intent?* In other words: how does nature guarantee that what man ought to do according to the laws of freedom, but does not do, will be made secure regardless of this freedom by a compulsion of nature which forces him to do it? The question presents itself in all three relations: *constitutional* law, *international* law, and cosmopolitan or world law, – And if I say of nature: she wants this or that to take place, it does not mean that she imposes a *duty* to do it – for that only the non-compulsory practical reason can do – but it means that nature itself does it, whether we want it or not (*fata volentem ducunt, nolentem trahunt*).

1. If internal conflicts did not compel a people to submit itself to the compulsion of public laws, external wars would do it. According to the previously mentioned arrangement of nature, a people discovers a neighboring people who are pushing it, against which it must form itself into a *state* in order to be prepared as a *power* against its enemy. Now the *republican* constitution is the only one which is fully adequate to the right of man, but it is also the hardest to establish, and even harder to maintain. Therefore many insist that it would have to be a state of angels, because men with their selfish propensities are incapable of so sublime

a constitution. But now nature comes to the aid of this revered, but practically ineffectual general will which is founded in reason. It does this by the selfish propensities themselves, so that it is only necessary to organize the state well (which is indeed within the ability of man), and to direct these forces against each other in such wise that one balances the other in its devastating effect, or even suspends it. Consequently the result for reason is as if both selfish forces were nonexistent. Thus mm, although not a morally good man, is compelled to be a good citizen. The problem of establishing a state is solvable even for a people of devils, if only they have intelligence, though this may sound harsh. The problem may be stated thus: "To organize a group of rational beings who demand general laws for their survival, but of whom each inclines toward exempting himself, and to establish their constitution in such a way that, in spite of the fact that their private attitudes are opposed, these private attitudes mutually impede each other in such a manner that the public behavior [of the rational beings] is the same as if they did not have such evil attitudes." Such a problem *must* be solvable. For it is not the moral perfection of mankind, but merely the mechanism of nature, which this task seeks to know how to use in order to arrange the conflict of unpacific attitudes in a given people in such a way that they impel each other to submit themselves to compulsory laws and thus bring about the state of peace in which such laws are enforced. It is possible to observe this in the actually existing, although imperfectly organized states. They approach in external conduct closely to what the idea of law prescribes, although an inner morality is certainly not the cause of it (just as we should not expect a good constitution from such morality, but rather from such a constitution the good moral development of a people). These existing states show that the mechanism of [human] nature, with its selfish propensities which naturally counter-act each other, can be employed by reason as a means. Thus reason's real purpose may be realized, namely, to provide a field for the operation of legal rules whereby to make secure internal and external peace as far as the state is concerned. In short, we can say that nature *wants* irresistibly that law achieve superior force. If one neglects to do this, it will be accom-plished anyhow, albeit with, much inconvenience. "If you bend the stick too much, it breaks; and he who wants too much, wants nothing" (Bouterwek).

2. The idea of a law of nations presupposes the separate existence of many states which are independent of each other. Such a situation constitutes in and by itself a state of war, unless a federative union of these states prevents the outbreak of hostilities. Yet such a situ-ation is from the standpoint of reason better than the complete merging of all these states in one of them which overpowers them and is thereby in turn transformed into a universal monarchy. This is so, because the laws lose more and more of their effectiveness as the government increases in size, and the resulting soulless despotism is plunged into anarchy after having exterminated all the germs of good [in man]. Still, it is the desire of every state (or of its ruler) to enter into a permanent state of peace by ruling if possible the entire world. But *nature* has decreed differently. Nature employs two means to keep peoples from being mixed and to differentiate them, the difference of *language* and of *religion*.[5] These differences occasion the inclination toward mutual hatred and the excuse for war; yet at the same time they lead, as culture increases and men gradually come closer together, toward a greater agreement on principles for peace and understanding. Such peace and understanding is not brought about and made secure by the weakening of all other forces (as it would be under the aforementioned despotism and its graveyard of freedom), but by balancing these forces in a lively competition.

3. Just as nature wisely separates the nations which the will of each state would like to unite under its sway either by cunning or by force, and even in keeping with the reasoning of the law of nations, so also nature unites nations which the concept of a cosmopolitan or

world law would not have protected from violence and war, and it does this by mutual self-interest. It is the *spirit of commerce* which cannot coexist with war, and which sooner or later takes hold of every nation. For, since the money power is perhaps; the most reliable among all the powers subordinate to the state's power, states find themselves impelled (though hardly by moral compulsion) to promote the noble peace and to try to avert war by mediation whenever it threatens to break out anywhere in the world. It is as if states were constantly leagued for this purpose; for great leagues *for* the purpose of making war can only come about very rarely and can succeed even more rarely. – In this way nature guarantees lasting peace by the mechanism, of human inclinations; however the certainty [that this will come to pass] is not sufficient to *predict* such a future (theoretically). But for practical purposes the certainty suffices and makes it one's duty to work toward this (not simply chimerical) state.

Second addition

A secret article concerning Eternal Peace

A secret article in negotiations pertaining to *public* law is a contradiction objectively, i.e., as regards its substance or content; subjectively, however, i.e., as regards the quality of the person which formulates the article, secrecy may occur when such a person, hesitates to declare himself publicly as the author thereof.

   The sole article of this kind [in the treaty on eternal peace] is contained in the following sentence: *The maxims of the philosophers concerning the conditions of the possibility of public peace shall be consulted by the states which are ready to go to war.* Perhaps it would seem like belittling the legislative authority of a state to which one should attribute the greatest wisdom to suggest that it should seek instruction regarding the principles of its conduct from its *subjects* (the philosophers); nevertheless this is highly advisable. Hence the state will *solicit* the latter *silently* (by making it a secret) which means that it will *let them talk* freely and publicly about the general maxims of the conduct of war and the establishment of peace (for they will do it of their own accord, if only they are not forbidden to do so). The agreement of the states among themselves regarding this point does not require any special stipulation but is founded upon an obligation posited by general morality legislating for human reason. This does not mean that the state must concede that the principles of the philosopher have priority over the rulings of the jurist (the representative of governmental power); it only means that the philosopher be *given a hearing*. The jurist who has made the *scales* of law and right his symbol, as well as the *sword* of justice, commonly employs the sword not only toward off all outside influence from the scales, but also to put it into one of the scales if it will not go down (*vae victis*). A jurist who is not at the same time a philosopher (morally speaking) has the greatest temptation to do this, because it is only his job to apply existing laws, and not to inquire whether these laws need improvement. In fact he counts this lower order of his faculty to be the higher, simply because it is the concomitant of power (as is also the case of the other two faculties). – The philosophical faculty occupies a low place when confronted by all this power. Thus, for example, it is said of philosophy that she is the *handmaiden* of theology (and something like that is said regarding the other two). It is not very clear however "whether she carries the torch in front of her gracious lady or the train of her dress behind."

   It is not to be expected that kings philosophize or that philosophers become kings, nor is it to be desired, because the possession of power corrupts the free judgment of reason inevitably. But kings or self-governing nations will not allow the class of philosophers to disappear or to become silent, but will let them speak publicly, because this is indispensable for both in order to clarify their business. And since this class of people are by their very nature incapable of forming gangs or clubs they need not be suspected of carrying on *propaganda*.

Notes

1 An hereditary monarchy is not a state which can be inherited by another state. Only the right to govern it may be transferred by heredity to another person. Thus the state acquired a ruler, not the ruler a state.
2 After the end of a war, at the conclusion of a peace, it would not be improper for a people to set a day of atonement after the day of thanks so as to pray to heaven asking forgiveness for the heavy guilt which mankind is under, because it will not adapt itself to a legal constitution in its relation to other nations. Proud of its independence, each nation will rather employ the barbaric means of war by which that which is being sought, namely the right of each state, cannot be discovered. The celebrations of victory, the hymns which in good Old Testament style are sung to the Lord of Hosts, contrast equally sharply with the moral idea of the father of mankind; because besides the indifference concerning the manner in which people seek their mutual right which is lamentable enough, they rejoice over having destroyed many people and their happiness.
3 [I am omitting a lengthy and obsolete footnote on the origin of the word *China*, in spite of its interest in showing Kant's keen personal delight in concrete historical detail. – C.J.F.]
4 [In a lengthy footnote at this point, Kant discusses the concept of *providence* as something necessary to explain the basic "form" of events in their totality. He rejects the idea as illogical, when applied to specific events, but allows it as a general founding, governing, and directing providence. The discussion follows the treatment in the *Critique of Practical Reason*. – C.J.F.]
5 *Difference of religion*: a strange expression! as if one were to speak of different *morals*. There may be different *kinds of faith* which are historical and which hence belong to history and not to religion and are part of the means in the field of learning. Likewise there may be different *religious books* (Zendavesta, Vedam, Koran, etc.). But there ran only be one *religion* valid for all men and for all times. Those other matters are nothing but a vehicle of religion, accidental and different according to the difference of time and place.

8 Address to the Swedish Peace Congress in 1909

Leo Tolstóy

Dear brothers

We have met here to fight against war. War, the thing for the sake of which all the nations of the earth – millions and millions of people – place at the uncontrolled disposal of a few men or sometimes only one man, not merely milliards of rubles, talers, francs, or yen (representing a very large share of their labour), but also their very lives. And now we, a score of private people gathered from the various ends of the earth, possessed of no special privileges and above all having no power over anyone, intend to fight – and as we wish to fight we wish also to conquer – this immense power not of one government but of all the governments, which have at their disposal these milliards of money and millions of soldiers and who are well aware that the exceptional position of those who form the governments rests on the army alone: the army which has a meaning and purpose only if there is a war, the very war against which we wish to fight and which we wish to abolish.

For us to struggle, the forces being so unequal, must appear insane. But if we consider our opponents' means of strife and our own, it is not our intention to fight that will seem absurd but that the thing we mean to fight against can still exist. They have millions of money and millions of obedient soldiers; we have only one thing, but that is the most powerful thing in the world – Truth.

Therefore, insignificant as our forces may appear in comparison with those of our opponents, our victory is as sure as the victory of the light of the rising sun over the darkness of night.

Our victory is certain, but on one condition only – that when uttering the truth we utter it all; without compromise, concession, or modification. The truth is so simple, so clear, so evident, and so incumbent not only on Christians but on all reasonable men, that it is only necessary to speak it out completely in its full significance for it to be irresistible.

The truth in its full meaning lies in what was said thousands of years ago (in the law accepted among us as the Law of God) in four words: *Thou Shalt Not Kill*. The truth is that man may not and should not in any circumstances or under any pretext kill his fellow man.

That truth is so evident, so binding, and so generally acknowledged, that it is only necessary to put it clearly before men for the evil called war to become quite impossible.

And so I think that if we who are assembled here at this Peace Congress should, instead of clearly and definitely voicing this truth, address ourselves to the governments with various proposals for lessening the evils of war or gradually diminishing its frequency, we should be like men who having in their hand the key to a door, should try to break through walls they know to be too strong for them. Before us are millions of armed men, ever more and more efficiently armed and trained for more and more rapid slaughter. We know that these millions of people have no wish to kill their fellows and for the most part do not even know why they are forced to do that repulsive work, and that they are weary of their position of subjection and compulsion; we know that the murders committed from time to time by these men are committed by order of the governments; and we know that the existence of the governments depends on the armies. Can we, then, who desire the abolition of war, find nothing more conducive to our aim than to propose to the governments which exist only by the aid of armies and consequently by war – measures which would destroy war? Are we to propose to the governments that they should destroy themselves?

The governments will listen willingly to any speeches of that kind, knowing that such discussions will neither destroy war nor undermine their own power, but will only conceal yet more effectually what must be concealed if wars and armies and themselves in control of armies are to continue to exist.

'But,' I shall be told, 'this is anarchism; people never have lived without governments and States, and therefore governments and States and military forces defending them are necessary for the existence of the nations.'

But leaving aside the question of whether the life of Christian and other nations is possible without armies and wars to defend their governments and States, or even supposing it to be necessary for their welfare that they should slavishly submit to institutions called governments (consisting of people they do not personally know), and that it is necessary to yield up the produce of their labour to these institutions and fulfil all their demands – including the murder of their neighbours – granting all that, there yet remains in our world an unsolved difficulty.

This difficulty lies in the impossibility of making the Christian faith (which those who form the governments profess with particular emphasis) accord with armies composed of Christians trained to slay. However much you may pervert the Christian teaching, however much you may hide its main principles, its fundamental teaching is the love of God and one's neighbour; of God – that is of the highest perfection of virtue, and of one's neighbour – that is of all men without distinction. And therefore it would seem inevitable that we must repudiate one of the two, either Christianity with its love of God and one's neighbour, or the State with its armies and wars.

Perhaps Christianity may be obsolete, and when choosing between the two – Christianity and love or the State and murder – the people of our time will conclude that the existence of the State and murder is so much more important than Christianity, that we must forgo Christianity and retain only what is more important: the State and murder.

That may be so – at least people may think and feel so. But in that case they should say so! They should openly admit that people in our time have ceased to believe in what the collective wisdom of mankind has said, and what is said by the Law of God they profess: have ceased to believe in what is written indelibly on the heart of each man, and must now believe only in what is ordered by various people who by the accident of birth have happened to become emperors and kings, or by various intrigues and elections have become presidents or members of senates and parliaments – even if those orders include murder. That is what they ought to say!

But it is impossible to say it; and yet one of these two things has to be said. If it is admitted that Christianity forbids murder, both armies and governments become impossible. If it is admitted that the government acknowledges the lawfulness of murder and denies Christianity, no one will wish to obey a government that exists merely by its power to kill. And besides, if murder is allowed in war it must be still more allowable when a people seeks its rights in a revolution. And therefore the governments, being unable to say either the one thing or the other, are anxious only to hide from their subjects the necessity of solving the dilemma.

And for us who are assembled here to counteract the evil of war, if we really desire to attain our end, only one thing is necessary: namely to put that dilemma quite clearly and definitely both to those who form the governments and to the masses of the people who compose the army. To do that we must not only clearly and openly repeat the truth we all know and cannot help knowing – that man should not slay his fellow man – but we must also make it clear that no considerations can destroy the demand made by that truth on people of the Christian world.

Therefore I propose to our Meeting to draw up and publish an appeal to all men, and especially to the Christian nations, in which we clearly and definitely express what everybody knows but hardly anyone says: namely that war is not – as most people now assume – a good and laudable affair, but that like all murder, it is a vile and criminal business not only for those who voluntarily choose a military career but for those who submit to it from avarice or fear of punishment.

With regard to those who voluntarily choose a military career, I would propose to state clearly and definitely in that appeal that notwithstanding all the pomp, glitter, and general approval with which it is surrounded, it is a criminal and shameful activity; and that the higher the position a man holds in the military profession the more criminal and shameful is his occupation. In the same way with regard to men of the people who are drawn into military service by bribes or by threats of punishments, I propose to speak clearly and definitely of the gross mistake they make – contrary to their faith, morality, and common sense – when they consent to enter the army; contrary to their faith, because by entering the ranks of murderers they infringe the Law of God which they acknowledge; contrary to morality, because for pay or from fear of punishment they agree to do what in their souls they know to be wrong; and contrary to common sense, because if they enter the army and war breaks out they risk having to suffer consequences as bad or worse than those they are threatened with if they refuse. Above all they act contrary to common sense in that they join that caste of people which deprives them of freedom and compels them to become soldiers.

With reference to both classes I propose in this appeal to express clearly the thought that for men of true enlightenment, who are therefore free from the superstition of military glory (and their number is growing every day) the military profession and calling, notwithstanding all the efforts to hide its real meaning, is as shameful a business as an executioner's and even more so. For the executioner only holds himself in readiness to kill those who have been adjudged harmful and criminal, while a soldier promises to kill all whom he is told to kill, even though they be those dearest to him or the best of men.

Humanity in general, and our Christian humanity in particular, has reached a stage of such acute contradiction between its moral demands and the existing social order, that a change has become inevitable, and a change not in society's moral demands which are immutable, but in the social order which can be altered. The demand for a different social order, evoked by that inner contradiction which is so clearly illustrated by our preparations for murder, becomes more and more insistent every year and every day. The tension which demands that alteration has reached such a degree that, just as sometimes only a slight shock is required to change a liquid into a solid body, so perhaps only a slight effort or even a single word may be needed to change the cruel and irrational life of our time – with its divisions, armaments, and armies – into a reasonable life in keeping with the consciousness of contemporary humanity. Every such effort, every such word, may be the shock which will instantly solidify the super-cooled liquid. Why should not our gathering be that shock? In Andersen's fairy tale, when the King went in triumphal procession through the streets of the town and all the people were delighted with his beautiful new clothes, a word from a child who said what everybody knew but had not said, changed everything. He said: 'He has nothing on!' and the spell was broken and the King became ashamed and all those who had been assuring themselves that they saw him wearing beautiful new clothes perceived that he was naked! We must say the same. We must say what everybody knows but does not venture to say. We must say that by whatever name men may call murder – murder always remains murder and a criminal and shameful thing. And it is only necessary to say that clearly, definitely, and loudly, as we can say it here, and men will cease to see what they thought they saw and will see what is really before their eyes. They will cease to see the service of their country, the heroism of war, military glory, and patriotism, and will see what exists: the naked, criminal business of murder! And if people see that, the same thing will happen as in the fairy tale: those who do the criminal thing will feel ashamed, and those who assure themselves that they do not see the criminality of murder will perceive it and cease to be murderers.

But how will nations defend themselves against their enemies, how will they maintain internal order, and how can nations live without an army?

What form the life of men will take if they repudiate murder, we do not and cannot know; but one thing is certain: that it is more natural for men to be guided by the reason and conscience with which they are endowed, than to submit slavishly to people who arrange wholesale murders; and that therefore the form of social order assumed by the lives of those who are guided in their actions not by violence based on threats of murder but by reason and conscience, will in any case be no worse than that under which they now live.

That is all I want to say. I shall be very sorry if it offends or grieves anyone or evokes any ill feeling. But for me, a man eighty years old, expecting to die at any moment, it would be shameful and criminal not to speak out the whole truth as 1 understand it – the truth which, as I firmly believe, is alone capable of relieving mankind from the incalculable ills produced by war.

9 The moral equivalent of war

William James

The war against war is going to be no holiday excursion or camping-party. The military feelings are too deeply grounded to abdicate their place among our ideals until better substitutes are offered than the glory and shame that come to nations as well as to individuals from the ups and downs of politics and the vicissitudes of trade. There is something highly paradoxical in the modern man's relation to war. [. . .] In modern eyes, precious though wars may be, they must not be waged solely for the sake of the ideal harvest. Only when forced upon one, only when an enemy's injustice leaves us no alternative, is a war now thought permissible.

It was not thus in ancient times. The earlier men were hunting-men, and to hunt a neighbouring tribe, kill the males, loot the village and possess the females, was the most profitable, as well as the most exciting, way of living. Thus were the more martial tribes selected, and in chiefs and peoples a pure pugnacity and love of glory came to mingle with the more fundamental appetite for plunder.

Modern war is so expensive that we feel trade to be a better avenue to plunder; but modern man inherits all the innate pugnacity and all the love of glory of his ancestors. Showing war's irrationality and horror is of no effect upon him. The horrors make the fascination. War is the *strong* life; it is life *in extremis*; war taxes are the only ones men never hesitate to pay, as the budgets of all nations show us.

History is a bath of blood. The *Iliad* is one long recital of how, Diomedes and Ajax, Sarpedon and Hector *killed*. No detail of the wounds they made is spared us, and the Greek mind fed upon the story. Greek history is a panorama of jingoism and imperialism – war for war's sake, all the citizens being warriors. It is horrible reading, because of the irrationality of it all – save for the purpose of making 'history' – and the history is that of the utter ruin of a civilization in intellectual respects perhaps the highest the earth has ever seen.

[. . .]

Such was the gory nurse that trained societies to cohesiveness. We inherit the warlike type; and for most of the capacities of heroism that the human race is full of we have to thank this cruel history. Dead men tell no tales, and if there were any tribes of other type than this they have left no survivors. Our ancestors have bred pugnacity into our bone and marrow, and thousands of years of peace won't breed it out of us. The popular imagination fairly fattens on the thought of wars. Let public opinion once reach a certain fighting pitch, and no ruler can withstand it. [. . .]

At the present day, civilized opinion is a curious mental mixture. The military instincts and ideals are as strong as ever, but are confronted by reflective criticisms which sorely curb their ancient freedom. Innumerable writers are showing up the bestial side of military service. Pure loot and mastery seem no longer morally avowable motives, and pretexts must be found for attributing them solely to the enemy. [. . .] 'Peace' in military mouths today is a synonym for 'war expected'. The word has become a pure provocative, and no government wishing peace sincerely should allow it ever to be printed in a newspaper. Every up-to-date dictionary should say that 'peace' and 'war' mean the same thing, now *in posse*, now *in actu*. It may even reasonably be said that the intensely sharp competitive *preparation* for war by the nations *is the real war*, permanent, unceasing; and that the battles are only a sort of public verification of the mastery gained during the 'peace' interval.

[. . .]

In my remarks, pacificist though I am, I will refuse to speak of the bestial side of the war regime (already done justice to by many writers) and consider only the higher aspects of militaristic sentiment. Patriotism no one thinks discreditable; nor does any one deny that war is the romance of history. But inordinate ambitions are the soul of every patriotism, and the possibility of violent death the soul of all romance. The militarily patriotic and romantic-minded everywhere, and especially the professional military class, refuse to admit for a moment that war may be a transitory phenomenon in social evolution. The notion of a sheep's paradise like that revolts, they say, our higher imagination. Where then would be the steeps of life? If war had ever stopped, we should have to reinvent it, on this view, to redeem life from flat degeneration.

Reflective apologists for war at the present day all take it religiously. It is a sort of sacrament, its profits are to the vanquished as well as to the victor; and quite apart from any question of profit, it is an absolute good, we are told, for it is human nature at its highest dynamic. Its 'horrors' are a cheap price to pay for rescue from the only alternative supposed, of a world of clerks and teachers, of co-education and zoophily, of 'consumer's leagues' and 'associated charities', of industrialism unlimited, and femininism unabashed. No scorn, no hardness, no valour any more! Fie upon such a cattleyard of a planet!

So far as the central essence of this feeling goes, no healthy-minded person, it seems to me, can help to some degree partaking of it. Militarism is the great preserver of our ideals of hardihood, and human life with no use for hardihood would be contemptible. Without risks or prizes for the darer, history would be insipid indeed; and there is a type of military character which everyone feels that the race should never cease to breed, for everyone is sensitive to its superiority. The duty is incumbent on mankind, of keeping military characters in stock – of keeping them, if not for use, then as ends in themselves and as pure pieces of perfection.

[. . .]

This natural sort of feeling forms, I think, the innermost soul of army writings. Without any exception known to me, militarist authors take a highly mystical view of their subject, and regard war as a biological or sociological necessity, uncontrolled by ordinary psychological checks and motives. When the time of development is ripe the war must come, reason or no reason, for the justifications pleaded are invariably fictitious. War is, in short, a permanent human *obligation*. [. . .]

The virtues that prevail, [. . .] are virtues anyhow, superiorities that count in peaceful as well as in military competition; but the strain on them, being infinitely intenser in the latter case, makes war infinitely more searching as a trial. No ordeal is comparable to its winnowings. Its dread hammer is the welder of men into cohesive states, and nowhere but in such states can human nature adequately develop its capacity. The only alternative is 'degeneration'.

[. . .]

Turn the fear over as I will in my mind, it all seems to lead back to two unwillingnesses of the imagination, one aesthetic, and the other moral; unwillingness, first to envisage a future in which army life, with its many elements of charm, shall be for ever impossible, and in which the destinies of peoples shall nevermore be decided quickly, thrillingly, and tragically, by force, but only gradually and insipidly by 'evolution'; and, secondly, unwillingness to see the supreme theatre of human strenuousness closed, and the splendid military aptitudes of men doomed to keep always in a state of latency and never show themselves in action. These insistent unwillingnesses, no less than other aesthetic and ethical insistencies, have, it seems to me, to be listened to and respected. One cannot meet them effectively by mere counter-insistency on war's expensiveness and horror. The horror makes the thrill; and when the question is of getting the extremest and supremest out of human nature, talk of expense sounds ignominious. The weakness of so much merely negative criticism is evident – pacificism makes no converts from the military party. The military party denies neither the bestiality nor the horror, nor the expense; it only says that these things tell but half the story. It only says that war is *worth* them; that, taking human nature as a whole, its wars are its best protection against its weaker and more cowardly self, and that mankind cannot *afford* to adopt a peace economy.

Pacificists ought to enter more deeply into the aesthetical and ethical point of view of their opponents. [. . .] So long as anti-militarists propose no substitute for war's disciplinary function, no *moral equivalent* of war, analogous, as one might say, to the mechanical equivalent of heat, so long they fail to realize the full inwardness of the situation. And as a rule they do fail. The duties, penalties, and sanctions pictured in the utopias they paint are all too weak and tame to touch the military-minded. Tolstoy's pacificism is the only exception to this rule, for it is profoundly pessimistic as regards all this world's values, and makes the fear of the Lord furnish the moral spur provided elsewhere by the fear of the enemy. [. . .]

Having said thus much in preparation, I will now confess my own utopia. I devoutly believe in the reign of peace and in the gradual advent of some sort of a socialistic equilibrium. The fatalistic view of the war function is to me nonsense, for I know that war-making is due to definite motives and subject to prudential checks and reasonable criticisms, just like any other form of enterprise. And when whole nations are the armies, and the science of destruction vies in intellectual refinement with the sciences of production, I see that war becomes absurd and impossible from its own monstrosity. Extravagant ambitions will have to be replaced by reasonable claims, and nations must make common cause against them, I see no reason why all this should not apply to yellow as well as to white countries, and I look forward to a future when acts of war shall be formally outlawed as between civilized peoples.

All these beliefs of mine put me squarely into the anti-militarist party. But I do not believe that peace either ought to be or will be permanent on this globe, unless the states pacifically organized preserve some of the old elements of army discipline. A permanently successful peace economy cannot be a simple pleasure-economy. In the more or less socialistic future towards which mankind seems drifting we must still subject ourselves collectively to those severities which answer to our real position upon this only partly hospitable globe. We must make new energies and hardihoods continue the manliness to which the military mind so faithfully clings. Martial virtues must be the enduring cement; intrepidity, contempt of softness, surrender of private interest, obedience to command, must still remain the rock upon which states are built – unless, indeed, we wish for dangerous reactions against commonwealths fit only for contempt, and liable to invite attack whenever a centre of crystallization for military-minded enterprise gets formed anywhere in their neighbourhood.

The war party is assuredly right in affirming and reaffirming that the martial virtues, although originally gained by the race through war, are absolute and permanent human goods. Patriotic pride and ambition in their military form are, after all, only specifications of a more general competitive passion. They are its first form, but that is no reason for supposing them to be its last form. Men now are proud of belonging to a conquering nation, and without a murmur they lay down their persons and their wealth, if by so doing they may fend off subjection. But who can be sure that *other aspects of one's country* may not, with time and education and suggestion enough, come to be regarded with similarly effective feelings of pride and shame? Why should men not some day feel that it is worth a blood tax to belong to a collectivity superior in *any* ideal respect? Why should they not blush with indignant shame if the community that owns them is vile in any way whatsoever? Individuals, daily more numerous, now feel this civic passion. It is only a question of blowing on the spark till the whole population gets incandescent, and on the ruins of the old morals of military honour, a stable system of morals of civic honour builds itself up. What the whole community comes to believe in grasps the individual as in a vice. The war function has grasped us so far; but constructive interests may some day seem no less imperative, and impose on the individual a hardly lighter burden.

Let me illustrate my idea more concretely. There is nothing to make one indignant in the mere fact that life is hard, that men should toil and suffer pain. The planetary conditions once for all are such, and we can stand it. But that so many men, by mere accidents of birth and opportunity, should have a life of *nothing else* but toil and pain and hardness and inferiority imposed upon them, should have *no* vacation, while others natively no more deserving never get any taste of this campaigning life at all – *this* is capable of arousing indignation in reflective minds. It may end by seeming shameful to all of us that some of us have nothing but campaigning, and others nothing but unmanly ease. If now – and this is my idea – there were, instead of military conscription a conscription of the whole youthful population to form for a certain number of years a part of the army enlisted against *Nature*, the injustice would tend to be evened out, and numerous other goods to the commonwealth would follow. The military ideals of hardihood and discipline would be wrought into the growing fibre of the people; no one would remain blind as the luxurious classes now are blind, to man's relations to the globe he lives on, and to the permanently sour and hard foundations of his higher life. To coal and iron mines, to freight trains, to fishing-fleets in December, to dishwashing, clothes-washing, and window-washing, to road-building and tunnel-making, to foundries and stoke-holes, and to the frames of skyscrapers, would our gilded youths be drafted off, according to their choice, to get the childishness knocked out of them, and to come back into society with healthier sympathies and soberer ideas. They would have paid their blood tax, done their own part in the immemorial human warfare against nature; they would tread the earth more proudly, the women would value them more highly, they would be better fathers and teachers of the following generation.

Such a conscription, with the state of public opinion that would have required it, and the many moral fruits it would bear, would preserve in the midst of a pacific civilization the manly virtues which the military party is so afraid of seeing disappear in peace. We should get toughness without callousness, authority with as little criminal cruelty as possible, and painful work done cheerily because the duty is temporary, and threatens not, as now, to degrade the whole remainder of one's life. I spoke of the 'moral equivalent' of war. So far, war has been the only force that can discipline a whole community, and until an equivalent discipline is organized, I believe that war must have its way. But I have no serious doubt that the ordinary prides and shames of social man, once developed to a certain intensity, are capable of organizing such a moral equivalent as I have sketched, or some other just as effective for preserving manliness of type. It is but a question of time, of skilful propagandism, and of opinion-making men seizing historic opportunities.

The martial type of character can be bred without war. Strenuous honour and disinterestedness abound elsewhere. Priests and medical men are in a fashion educated to it, and we should all feel some degree of it imperative if we were conscious of our work as an obligatory service to the state. We should be *owned*, as soldiers are by the army and our pride would rise accordingly. We could be poor, then, without humiliation, as army officers now are. The only thing needed henceforward is to inflame the civic temper as past history has inflamed the military temper.

[. . .]

It would be simply preposterous if the only force that could work ideals of honour and standards of efficiency into English or American natures should be the fear of being killed by the Germans or the Japanese. Great indeed is Fear; but it is not, as our military enthusiasts believe and try to make us believe, the only stimulus known for awakening the higher ranges of men's spiritual energy. The amount of alteration in public opinion which my utopia postulates is vastly less than the difference between the mentality of those black warriors who pursued Stanley's party on the Congo with their cannibal war cry of 'Meat! Meat!' and that of the 'general staff' of any civilized nation. History has seen the latter interval bridged over: the former one can be bridged over much more easily.

10 The Russell–Einstein manifesto issued in London, 9 July 1955

Bertrand Russell and Albert Einstein

In the tragic situation which confronts humanity, we feel that scientists should assemble in conference to appraise the perils that have arisen as a result of the development of weapons of mass destruction, and to discuss a resolution in the spirit of the appended draft.

We are speaking on this occasion, not as members of this or that nation, continent, or creed, but as human beings, members of the species Man, whose continued existence is in doubt. The world is full of conflicts; and, overshadowing all minor conflicts, the titanic struggle between Communism and anti-Communism.

Almost everybody who is politically conscious has strong feelings about one or more of these issues; but we want you, if you can, to set aside such feelings and consider yourselves only as members of a biological species which has had a remarkable history, and whose disappearance none of us can desire.

We shall try to say no single word which should appeal to one group rather than to another. All, equally, are in peril, and, if the peril is understood, there is hope that they may collectively avert it.

We have to learn to think in a new way. We have to learn to ask ourselves, not what steps can be taken to give military victory to whatever group we prefer, for there no longer are such steps; the question we have to ask ourselves is: what steps can be taken to prevent a military contest of which the issue must be disastrous to all parties?

The general public, and even many men in positions of authority, have not realized what would be involved in a war with nuclear bombs. The general public still thinks in terms of the obliteration of cities. It is understood that the new bombs are more powerful than the old, and that, while one A-bomb could obliterate Hiroshima, one H-bomb could obliterate the largest cities, such as London, New York, and Moscow.

No doubt in an H-bomb war great cities would be obliterated. But this is one of the minor disasters that would have to be faced. If everybody in London, New York, and Moscow were exterminated, the world might, in the course of a few centuries, recover from the blow. But we now know, especially since the Bikini test, that nuclear bombs can gradually spread destruction over a very much wider area than had been supposed.

It is stated on very good authority that a bomb can now be manufactured which will be 2,500 times as powerful as that which destroyed Hiroshima. Such a bomb, if exploded near the ground or under water, sends radio-active particles into the upper air. They sink gradually and reach the surface of the earth in the form of a deadly dust or rain. It was this dust which infected the Japanese fishermen and their catch of fish. No one knows how widely such lethal radio-active particles might be diffused, but the best authorities are unanimous in saying that a war with H-bombs might possibly put an end to the human race. It is feared that if many H-bombs are used there will be universal death, sudden only for a minority, but for the majority a slow torture of disease and disintegration.

Many warnings have been uttered by eminent men of science and by authorities in military strategy. None of them will say that the worst results are certain. What they do say is that these results are possible, and no one can be sure that they will not be realized. We have not yet found that the views of experts on this question depend in any degree upon their politics or prejudices. They depend only, so far as our researches have revealed, upon the extent of the particular expert's knowledge. We have found that the men who know most are the most gloomy.

Here, then, is the problem which we present to you, stark and dreadful and inescapable: Shall we put an end to the human race; or shall mankind renounce war? People will not face this alternative because it is so difficult to abolish war.

The abolition of war will demand distasteful limitations of national sovereignty. But what perhaps impedes understanding of the situation more than anything else is that the term "mankind" feels vague and abstract. People scarcely realize in imagination that the danger is to themselves and their children and their grandchildren, and not only to a dimly apprehended humanity. They can scarcely bring themselves to grasp that they, individually, and those whom they love are in imminent danger of perishing agonizingly. And so they hope that perhaps war may be allowed to continue provided modern weapons are prohibited.

This hope is illusory. Whatever agreements not to use H-bombs had been reached in time of peace, they would no longer be considered binding in time of war, and both sides would set to work to manufacture H-bombs as soon as war broke out, for, if one side manufactured the bombs and the other did not, the side that manufactured them would inevitably be victorious.

Although an agreement to renounce nuclear weapons as part of a general reduction of armaments would not afford an ultimate solution, it would serve certain important purposes. First, any agreement between East and West is to the good in so far as it tends to diminish tension. Second, the abolition of thermo-nuclear weapons, if each side believed that the other had carried it out sincerely, would lessen the fear of a sudden attack in the style of Pearl Harbour, which at present keeps both sides in a state of nervous apprehension. We should, therefore, welcome such an agreement though only as a first step.

Most of us are not neutral in feeling, but, as human beings, we have to remember that, if the issues between East and West are to be decided in any manner that can give any possible satisfaction to anybody, whether Communist or anti-Communist, whether Asian or European or American, whether White or Black, then these issues must not be decided by war. We should wish this to be understood, both in the East and in the West.

There lies before us, if we choose, continual progress in happiness, knowledge, and wisdom. Shall we, instead, choose death, because we cannot forget our quarrels? We appeal as human beings to human beings: Remember your humanity, and forget the rest. If you can do so, the way lies open to a new Paradise; if you cannot, there lies before you the risk of universal death.

Resolution

We invite this Congress, and through it the scientists of the world and the general public, to subscribe to the following resolution:

"In view of the fact that in any future world war nuclear weapons will certainly be employed, and that such weapons threaten the continued existence of mankind, we urge the governments of the world to realize, and to acknowledge publicly, that their purpose cannot be furthered by a world war, and we urge them, consequently, to find peaceful means for the settlement of all matters of dispute between them."

Max Born
Percy W. Bridgman
Albert Einstein
Leopold Infeld
Frederic Joliot-Curie
Herman J. Muller
Linus Pauling
Cecil F. Powell
Joseph Rotblat
Bertrand Russell
Hideki Yukawa

11 A human approach to world peace

The Dalai Lama

When we rise in the morning and listen to the radio or read the newspaper, we are confronted with the same sad news: violence, crime, wars, and disasters. I cannot recall a single day without a report of something terrible happening somewhere. Even in these modern times it is clear that one's precious life is not safe. No former generation has had to experience so much bad news as we face today; this constant awareness of fear and tension should make any sensitive and compassionate person question seriously the progress of our modern world.

It is ironic that the more serious problems emanate from the more industrially advanced societies. Science and technology have worked wonders in many fields, but the basic human problems remain. There is unprecedented literacy, yet this universal education does not seem to have fostered goodness, but only mental restlessness and discontent instead. There is no doubt about the increase in our material progress and technology, but somehow this is not sufficient as we have not yet succeeded in bringing about peace and happiness or in overcoming suffering.

We can only conclude that there must be something seriously wrong with our progress and development, and if we do not check it in time there could be disastrous consequences for the future of humanity. I am not at all against science and technology – they have contributed immensely to the overall experience of humankind; to our material comfort and well-being and to our greater understanding of the world we live in. But if we give too much emphasis to science and technology we are in danger of losing touch with those aspects of human knowledge and understanding that aspire towards honesty and altruism.

Science and technology, though capable of creating immeasurable material comfort, cannot replace the age-old spiritual and humanitarian values that have largely shaped world civilization, in all its national forms, as we know it today. No one can deny the unprecedented material benefit of science and technology, but our basic human problems remain; we are still faced with the same, if not more, suffering, fear, and tension. Thus it is only logical to try to strike a balance between material developments on the one hand and the development of spiritual, human values on the other. In order to bring about this great adjustment, we need to revive our humanitarian values.

I am sure that many people share my concern about the present worldwide moral crisis and will join in my appeal to all humanitarians and religious practitioners who also share this concern to help make our societies more compassionate, just, and equitable. I do not speak as a Buddhist or even as a Tibetan. Nor do I speak as an expert on international politics (though I unavoidably comment on these matters). Rather, I speak simply as a human being, as an upholder of the humanitarian values that are the bedrock not only of Mahayana Buddhism but of all the great world religions. From this perspective I share with you my personal outlook – that:

1.   Universal humanitarianism is essential to solve global problems;
2.   Compassion is the pillar of world peace;
3.   All world religions are already for world peace in this way, as are all humanitarians of whatever ideology;
4.   Each individual has a universal responsibility to shape institutions to serve human needs.

Solving human problems through transforming human attitudes

Of the many problems we face today, some are natural calamities and must be accepted and faced with equanimity. Others, however, are of our own making, created by misunderstanding, and can be corrected. One such type arises from the conflict of ideologies, political or religious, when people fight each other for petty ends, losing sight of the basic humanity that binds us all together as a single human family. We must remember that the different religions, ideologies, and political systems of the world are meant for human beings to achieve happiness. We must not lose sight of this fundamental goal and at no time should we place means above ends; the supremacy of humanity over matter and ideology must always be maintained.

By far the greatest single danger facing humankind – in fact, all living beings on our planet – is the threat of nuclear destruction. I need not elaborate on this danger, but I would like to appeal to all the leaders of the nuclear powers who literally hold the future of the world in their hands, to the scientists and technicians who continue to create these awesome weapons of destruction, and to all the people at large who are in a position to influence their leaders: I appeal to them to exercise their sanity and begin to work at dismantling and destroying all nuclear weapons. We know that in the event of a nuclear war there will be no victors because there will be no survivors! Is it not frightening just to contemplate such inhuman and heartless destruction? And, is it not logical that we should remove the cause for our own destruction when we know the cause and have both the time and the means to do so? Often we cannot overcome our problems because we either do not know the cause or, if we understand it, do not have the means to remove it. This is not the case with the nuclear threat.

Whether they belong to more evolved species like humans or to simpler ones such as animals, all beings primarily seek peace, comfort, and security. Life is as dear to the mute animal as it is to any human being; even the simplest insect strives for protection from dangers that threaten its life. Just as each one of us wants to live and does not wish to die, so it is with all other creatures in the universe, though their power to effect this is a different matter.

Broadly speaking there are two types of happiness and suffering, mental and physical, and of the two, I believe that mental suffering and happiness are the more acute. Hence, I stress the training of the mind to endure suffering and attain a more lasting state of happiness. However, I also have a more general and concrete idea of happiness: a combination of inner peace, economic development, and, above all, world peace. To achieve such goals I feel it is necessary to develop a sense of universal responsibility, a deep concern for all irrespective of creed, colour, sex, or nationality.

The premise behind this idea of universal responsibility is the simple fact that, in general terms, all others' desires are the same as mine. Every being wants happiness and does not want suffering. If we, as intelligent human beings, do not accept this fact, there will be more and more suffering on this planet. If we adopt a self-centred approach to life and constantly try to use others for our own self-interest, we may gain temporary benefits, but in the long run we will not succeed in achieving even personal happiness, and world peace will be completely out of the question.

In their quest for happiness, humans have used different methods, which all too often have been cruel and repellent. Behaving in ways utterly unbecoming to their status as humans, they inflict suffering upon fellow humans and other living beings for their own selfish gains. In the end, such shortsighted actions bring suffering to oneself as well as to others. To be born a human being is a rare event in itself, and it is wise to use this opportunity as effectively and skillfully as possible. We must have the proper perspective that of the universal life process, so that the happiness or glory of one person or group is not sought at the expense of others.

All this calls for a new approach to global problems. The world is becoming smaller and smaller – and more and more interdependent – as a result of rapid technological advances and international trade as well as increasing trans-national relations. We now depend very much on each other. In ancient times problems were mostly family-size, and they were naturally tackled at the family level, but the situation has changed. Today we are so interdependent, so closely interconnected with each other, that without a sense of universal responsibility, a feeling of universal brotherhood and sisterhood, and an understanding and belief that we really are part of one big human family, we cannot hope to overcome the dangers to our very existence – let alone bring about peace and happiness.

One nation's problems can no longer be satisfactorily solved by itself alone; too much depends on the interest, attitude, and cooperation of other nations. A universal humanitarian approach to world problems seems the only sound basis for world peace. What does this mean? We begin from the recognition mentioned previously that all beings cherish happiness and do not want suffering. It then becomes both morally wrong and pragmatically unwise to pursue only one's own happiness oblivious to the feelings and aspirations of all others who surround us as members of the same human family. The wiser course is to think of others also when pursuing our own happiness. This will lead to what I call 'wise self-interest', which hopefully will transform itself into 'compromised self-interest', or better still, 'mutual interest'.

Although the increasing interdependence among nations might be expected to generate more sympathetic cooperation, it is difficult to achieve a spirit of genuine cooperation as long as people remain indifferent to the feelings and happiness of others. When people are motivated mostly by greed and jealousy, it is not possible for them to live in harmony. A spiritual approach may not solve all the political problems that have been caused by the existing self-centered approach, but in the long run it will overcome the very basis of the problems that we face today.

On the other hand, if humankind continues to approach its problems considering only temporary expediency, future generations will have to face tremendous difficulties. The global population is increasing, and our resources are being rapidly depleted. Look at the trees, for example. No one knows exactly what adverse effects massive deforestation will have on the climate, the soil, and global ecology as a whole. We are facing problems because people are concentrating only on their short-term, selfish interests, not thinking of the entire human family. They are not thinking of the earth and the long-term effects on universal life as a whole. If we of the present generation do not think about these now, future generations may not be able to cope with them.

Compassion as the pillar of world peace

According to Buddhist psychology, most of our troubles are due to our passionate desire for and attachment to things that we misapprehend as enduring entities. The pursuit of the objects of our desire and attachment involves the use of aggression and competitiveness as supposedly efficacious instruments. These mental processes easily translate into actions, breeding belligerence as an obvious effect. Such processes have been going on in the human mind since time immemorial, but their execution has become more effective under modern conditions. What can we do to control and regulate these 'poisons' – delusion, greed, and aggression? For it is these poisons that are behind almost every trouble in the world.

As one brought up in the Mahayana Buddhist tradition, I feel that love and compassion are the moral fabric of world peace. Let me first define what I mean by compassion. When you have pity or compassion for a very poor person, you are showing sympathy because he or she is poor; your compassion is based on altruistic considerations. On the other hand, love towards your wife, your husband, your children, or a close friend is usually based on attachment. When your attachment changes, your kindness also changes; it may disappear. This is not true love. Real love is not based on attachment, but on altruism. In this case your compassion will remain as a humane response to suffering as long as beings continue to suffer.

This type of compassion is what we must strive to cultivate in ourselves, and we must develop it from a limited amount to the limitless. Undiscriminating, spontaneous, and unlimited compassion for all sentient beings is obviously not the usual love that one has for friends or family, which is alloyed with ignorance, desire, and attachment. The kind of love we should advocate is this wider love that you can have even for someone who has done harm to you: your enemy.

The rationale for compassion is that every one of us wants to avoid suffering and gain happiness. This, in turn, is based on the valid feeling of 'I', which determines the universal desire for happiness. Indeed, all being are born with similar desires and should have an equal right to fulfill them. If I compare myself with others, who are countless, I feel that others are more important because I am [. . .] one person whereas others are many. [. . .]

Whether one believes in religion or not, there is no one who does not appreciate love and compassion. [. . .]

When we take into account a longer perspective, the fact that all wish to gain happiness and avoid suffering, and keep in mind our relative unimportance in relation to countless others, we can conclude that it is worthwhile to share our possessions with others. When you train in this sort of outlook, a true sense of compassion – a true sense of love and respect for others – becomes possible. Individual happiness ceases to be a conscious self-seeking effort; it becomes an automatic and far superior by-product of the whole process of loving and serving others.

Another result of spiritual development, most useful in day-to-day life, is that it gives a calmness and presence of mind. Our lives are in constant flux, bringing many difficulties. When faced with a calm and clear mind, problems can be successfully resolved. When, instead, we lose control over our minds through hatred, selfishness, jealousy, and anger, we lose our sense of judgement. Our minds are blinded and at those wild moments anything can happen, including war. Thus, the practice of compassion and wisdom is useful to all, especially to those responsible for running national affairs, in whose hands lie the power and opportunity to create the structure of world peace.

World religions for world peace

The principles discussed so far are in accordance with the ethical teachings of all world religions. I maintain that every major religion of the world – Buddhism, Christianity, Confucianism, Hinduism, Islam, Jainism, Judaism, Sikhism, Taoism, Zoroastrianism – has similar ideals of love, the same goal of benefiting humanity through spiritual practice, and the same effect of making their followers into better human beings. All religions teach moral precepts for perfecting the functions of mind, body, and speech. All teach us not to lie or steal or take others' lives, and so on. The common goal of all moral precepts laid down by the great teachers of humanity is unselfishness. The great teachers wanted to lead their followers away from the paths of negative deeds caused by ignorance and to introduce them to paths of goodness.

All religions agree upon the necessity to control the undisciplined mind that harbours selfishness and other roots of trouble, and each teaches a path leading to a spiritual state that is peaceful, disciplined, ethical, and wise. It is in this sense that I believe all religions have essentially the same message. Differences of dogma may be ascribed to differences of time and circumstance as well as cultural influences; indeed, there is no end to scholastic argument when we consider the purely metaphysical side of religion. However, it is much more beneficial to try to implement in daily life the shared precepts for goodness taught by all religions rather than to argue about minor differences in approach.

There are many different religions to bring comfort and happiness to humanity in much the same way as there are particular treatments for different diseases. For, all religions endeavour in their own way to help living beings avoid misery and gain happiness. [. . .]

While pointing out the fundamental similarities between world religions, I do not advocate one particular religion at the expense of all others, nor do I seek a new 'world religion.' All the different religions of the world are needed to enrich human experience and world civilization. Our human minds, being of different calibre and disposition, need different approaches to peace and happiness. [. . .] Thus, the point is clear: humanity needs all the world's religions to suit the ways of life, diverse spiritual needs, and inherited national traditions of individual human beings.

[. . .]

There are two primary tasks facing religious practitioners who are concerned with world peace. First, we must promote better interfaith understanding so as to create a workable degree of unity among all religions. This may be achieved in part by respecting each other's beliefs and by emphasizing our common concern for human well-being. Second, we must bring about a viable consensus on basic spiritual values that touch every human heart and enhance general human happiness. This means we must emphasize the common denominator of all world religions – humanitarian ideals. These two steps will enable us to act both individually and together to create the necessary spiritual conditions for world peace.

We practitioners of different faiths can work together for world peace when we view different religions as essentially instruments to develop a good heart – love and respect for others, a true sense of community. The most important thing is to look at the purpose of religion and not at the details of theology or metaphysics, which can lead to mere intellectualism. I believe that all the major religions of the world can contribute to world peace and work together for the benefit of humanity if we put aside subtle metaphysical differences, which are really the internal business of each religion.

[. . .]

Whether we will be able to achieve world peace or not, we have no choice but to work towards that goal. If our minds are dominated by anger, we will lose the best part of human intelligence – wisdom, the ability to decide between right and wrong. Anger is one of the most serious problems facing the world today.

Individual power to shape institutions

Anger plays no small role in current conflicts such as those in the Middle East, Southeast Asia, the North-South problem, and so forth. These conflicts arise from a failure to understand one another's humanness. The answer is not the development and use of greater military force, nor an arms race. Nor is it purely political or purely technological. Basically it is spiritual, in the sense that what is required is a sensitive understanding of our common human situation. Hatred and fighting cannot bring happiness to anyone, even to the winners of battles. Violence always produces misery and thus is essentially counter-productive. It is, therefore, time for world leaders to learn to transcend the differences of race, culture, and ideology and to regard one another through eyes that see the common human situation. To do so would benefit individuals, communities, nations, and the world at large.

[. . .]

To improve person-to-person contact in the world at large, I would like to see greater encouragement of international tourism. Also, mass media, particularly in democratic societies, can make a considerable contribution to world peace by giving greater coverage to human interest items that reflect the ultimate oneness of humanity. With the rise of a few big powers in the international arena, the humanitarian role of international organizations is being bypassed and neglected. I hope that this will be corrected and that all international organizations, especially the United Nations, will be more active and effective in ensuring maximum benefit to humanity and promoting international understanding. It will indeed be tragic if the few powerful members continue to misuse world bodies like the UN for their one-sided interests. The UN must become the instrument of world peace. This world body must be respected by all, for the UN is the only source of hope for small oppressed nations and hence for the planet as a whole.

As all nations are economically dependent upon one another more than ever before, human understanding must go beyond national boundaries and embrace the international community at large. Indeed, unless we can create an atmosphere of genuine cooperation, gained not by threatened or actual use of force but by heartfelt understanding, world problems will only increase. If people in poorer countries are denied the happiness they desire and deserve, they will naturally be dissatisfied and pose problems for the rich. If unwanted social, political, and cultural forms continue to be imposed upon unwilling people, the attainment of world peace is doubtful. However, if we satisfy people at a heart-to-heart level, peace will surely come.

[. . .]

The achievement of justice, harmony, and peace depends on many factors. We should think about them in terms of human benefit in the long run rather than the short term. I realize the enormity of the task before us, but I see no other alternative than the one I am proposing – which is based on our common humanity. Nations have no choice but to be concerned about the welfare of others, not so much because of their belief in humanity, but because it is in the mutual and long-term interest of all concerned. [. . .]

I question the popular assumption that religion and ethics have no place in politics and that religious persons should seclude themselves as hermits. Such a view of religion is too one-sided; it lacks a proper perspective on the individual's relation to society and the role of religion in our lives. Ethics is as crucial to a politician as it is to a religious practitioner. Dangerous consequences will follow when politicians and rulers forget moral principles. Whether we believe in God or karma, ethics is the foundation of every religion.

Such human qualities as morality, compassion, decency, wisdom, and so forth have been the foundations of all civilizations. These qualities must be cultivated and sustained through systematic moral education in a conducive social environment so that a more humane world may emerge. The qualities required to create such a world must be inculcated right from the beginning, from childhood. We cannot wait for the next generation to make this change; the present generation must attempt a renewal of basic human values. If there is any hope, it is in the future generations, but not unless we institute major change on a worldwide scale in our present educational system. We need a revolution in our commitment to and practice of universal humanitarian values.

It is not enough to make noisy calls to halt moral degeneration; we must do something about it. Since present-day governments do not shoulder such 'religious' responsibilities, humanitarian and religious leaders must strengthen the existing civic, social, cultural, educational, and religious organizations to revive human and spiritual values. Where necessary, we must create new organizations to achieve these goals. Only in so doing can we hope to create a more stable basis for world peace.

Living in society, we should share the sufferings of our fellow citizens and practise compassion and tolerance not only towards our loved ones but also towards our enemies. This is the test of our moral strength. We must set an example by our own practice, for we cannot hope to convince others of the value of religion by mere words. We must live up to the same high standards of integrity and sacrifice that we ask of others. The ultimate purpose of all religions is to serve and benefit humanity. This is why it is so important that religion always be used to effect the happiness and peace of all beings and not merely to convert others.

[. . .]

Finally, a few words about material progress. I have heard a great deal of complaint against material progress from Westerners, and yet, paradoxically, it has been the very pride of the Western world. I see nothing wrong with material progress per se, provided people are always given precedence. It is my firm belief that in order to solve human problems in all their dimensions, we must combine and harmonize economic development with spiritual growth.

However, we must know its limitations. Although materialistic knowledge in the form of science and technology has contributed enormously to human welfare, it is not capable of creating lasting happiness. In America, for example, where technological development is perhaps more advanced than in any other country, there is still a great deal of mental suffering. This is because materialistic knowledge can only provide a type of happiness that is dependent upon physical conditions. It cannot provide happiness that springs from inner development independent of external factors.

For renewal of human values and attainment of lasting happiness, we need to look to the common humanitarian heritage of all nations the world over. May this essay serve as an urgent reminder lest we forget the human values that unite us all as a single family on this planet.

> I have written the above lines
> To tell my constant feeling.
> Whenever I meet even a 'foreigner',
> I have always the same feeling:
> 'I am meeting another member of the human family.'
> This attitude has deepened
> My affection and respect for all beings.
> May this natural wish be
> My small contribution to world peace.
> I pray for a more friendly,
> More caring, and more understanding
> Human family on this planet.
> To all who dislike suffering,
> Who cherish lasting happiness –
> This is my heartfelt appeal.

12 What is peace?

David Cortright

Jesus said that peacemakers are to be blessed as children of God, but in the real world they are often dismissed as utopian dreamers or worse, quaking defeatists who live in denial of reality. Jane Addams was one of the most admired persons in the United States in the years before World War I, but when she opposed US entry into the war she was ridiculed and reviled.[1] Those who advocated peace during the 1930s were accused of helping Hitler and aiding appeasement. Disarmament activists during the cold war were sometimes considered dupes of the Soviet Union. Throughout history the cause of peace has been on trial, standing like a forlorn defendant before the court of established opinion, misunderstood and maligned on all sides. Peace is "naked, poor, and mangled," wrote Shakespeare.[2] To be called a pacifist is almost an insult, to be labeled cowardly or selfish, unwilling to fight for what is right. It is easy to arouse people to war, said Hermann Goering at the Nuremberg trials. "All you have to do is tell them they are being attacked and denounce the pacifists for lack of patriotism . . ."[3]

This piece is a response to the charges against pacifism. It is an attempt to set the record straight by exploring the history of movements and ideas for peace – an opportunity for the cause of peace to have its day in court. This is not an apologia for or paean to pacifism, however – far from it. I am often critical of peace advocacy, especially absolute pacifism, and I try to present both the strengths and weaknesses of the various movements and theories for peace that have emerged over the centuries. I write as one who has been engaged with these issues for decades. I strive for rigorous scholarly standards and objective analysis but I am hardly neutral in this debate. Questions of war and peace intruded into my life when I was drafted for the Vietnam War, and they have remained with me ever since. I spoke out against that war as an active duty soldier, was the director of the National Committee for a Sane Nuclear Policy (SANE) during the disarmament campaigns of the 1980s, and helped to found the Win Without War coalition to oppose the US invasion and occupation of Iraq. I have written about nuclear disarmament, economic sanctions, and nonviolent social change and have taught peace studies courses. I know only too well the many limitations of movements for peace and the inadequacy of theories on the causes and prevention of war. It is precisely because of my engagement with these issues that I feel qualified to offer this witness for the defense, to present the case of peace, and to examine its practices and principles.

Idealism and realism

The book of Isaiah called believers to study war no more but offered little instruction about learning peace. The study of peace has been neglected over the ages and has emerged as a proper discipline only in recent decades.[4] The first academic programs and scholarly institutes dedicated to peace did not appear until after World War II, and refereed journals such as the *Journal of Conflict Resolution* and the *Journal of Peace Research* did not begin publication until 1957 and 1964 respectively. Pioneers in the field included Kenneth and Elise Boulding, who helped create the Center for Research on Conflict Resolution at the University of Michigan in the 1950s; Johan Galtung, who founded the International Peace Research Institute in Norway in 1959; and Adam Curle, the first chair of a peace studies program in Britain, at the University of Bradford in 1973. Major studies and books about peace appeared in earlier decades, of course, but the systematic application of rigorous scholarship and empirical analysis to the problems of peacemaking did not begin until quite recently.

This partly explains the inadequacies of many of the theories of peace. For much of history the cause of peace has predominantly been a religious concern. Moral reformers embraced the teachings of love and compassion in religious doctrine, but they often overlooked the challenges of political realism. Classical liberals extolled the virtues of democracy and free trade, but they underestimated the virulence of nationalism and the power of imperialism. Immanuel Kant probably came closest to crafting a comprehensive philosophy of peace, but his theory did not address questions of social equality. Socialists and feminists brought these issues to the fore and broadened the peace agenda to include problems of economic injustice and patriarchy. In recent decades social scientists and political theorists have made progress in verifying and explaining the components of the so-called Kantian triad – mutual democracy, economic interdependence, and international cooperation – as predicates of peace. Links have been discovered between gender equality and a lessening of violence. Unresolved political grievances and a lack of economic development have been identified as factors that contribute to armed conflict. Many questions remain unanswered, but progress has been made in understanding the causes of and cures for war.

Peace societies emerged in the nineteenth century, but it was only in the twentieth century that peace movements as we presently understand them came into existence. Large-scale mobilizations against war took place in the years before and after World War I, during the 1930s, and especially in response to the Vietnam and Iraq wars. These movements challenged government policy, particularly that of the United States, and were generally antiimperialist in outlook. Mobilizations for disarmament occurred during the interwar years and re-emerged in the cold war as a response to the threat of nuclear war. Disarmament activism reached a peak with the massive nuclear freeze and disarmament campaigns of the 1980s. Some of those organizing antiwar and disarmament campaigns were absolute pacifists, rejecting the use of force for any purpose, but most were more pragmatic and conditional in their rejection of war. They opposed dangerous weapons policies and unjust wars, but not all uses of force. Still the purist position often predominated, conveying an impression of implicit pacifism that limited the peace movement's public appeal.

Many opponents of war have emphasized the need for constructive alternatives. During the 1934–5 Peace Ballot in Britain the League of Nations Union (LNU) organized an informal vote on British security policy in which 11.6 million citizens participated. Among the options presented and endorsed was the use of multilateral sanctions, economic and even military, to counter aggression by one nation against another. The ballot results pressured the British government to propose League of Nations sanctions against Italy. During the nuclear freeze campaign of the 1980s US activists urged a bilateral halt to the testing, production, and deployment of nuclear weapons. European disarmament campaigners urged an end to both Soviet and US intermediate-range nuclear forces (INF) in Europe, which NATO officials effectively adopted as the "double zero" proposal, with zero INF weapons in Europe on both sides. During the Iraq antiwar debate many activists called for continued weapons inspections and targeted sanctions as alternatives to war and effective means of containing

Saddam Hussein. In the debate over the so-called "war on terror" peace scholars and activists have insisted that terrorism as a tactic cannot be defeated by war. They have advocated alternative strategies for countering terrorism based on multilateral action, cooperative law enforcement, and the amelioration of political grievances.

The strategies and proposals of peace scholars and activists are often fully compatible with the requirements of sound security policy. Throughout the cold war disarmament advocates insisted that a nuclear war could never be won and must never be fought; this became Ronald Reagan's mantra during the 1980s. Those who opposed the Vietnam and Iraq wars did so not only on humanitarian grounds but on the basis of solid political reasoning. Hans Morgenthau spoke out against the Vietnam War because it was based on an erroneous theory of monolithic communism, was justified with false information, and ignored the history of southeast Asia.[5] John Mearsheimer and Stephen Walt opposed the war in Iraq for similar reasons: it misjudged the terrorist threat, was based on deceptive claims about Iraqi capabilities, and risked eroding US power and prestige in the world.[6] Peace advocates warned that the invasion and occupation of Iraq would play into the hands of Osama bin Laden and lead to an increase in terrorist violence. Warmakers are often wrong – disastrously so in the cases of Vietnam and Iraq. Peace advocates are sometimes right, especially when their ideas are not only morally sound but politically realistic.

New wars

The nature of war has changed dramatically in recent decades. The old paradigm of industrial interstate war "no longer exists," declared General Rupert Smith in 2006.[7] Raimo Väyrynen, John Mueller, and other political scientists have written of the "waning of major war."[8] No instances of full-scale war have occurred between major industrialized states since the end of World War II. This is in part because of the extreme lethality of all forms of modern weaponry, nuclear and non-nuclear. It is also the result of the development of an integrated community of prosperous, secure, and interdependent nations in the heart of Europe where previous world wars originated. While interstate war has largely disappeared, intrastate conflicts have increased markedly. The new paradigm, wrote Smith, is "war amongst the people."[9] Of the thirty-one wars in the world in 2005 (as measured by the Uppsala Conflict Data Program), all were armed conflicts fought within nations between communities divided by ethnicity, language, religion, and/or geography.[10] Nearly all military deployments, UN peacekeeping operations, and peace-building missions in recent decades have taken place in settings of intrastate conflict.

This change in the nature of war has not meant an end to the scourge of deadly violence. On the contrary the number of people dying in war in recent years has been extremely high. Since the 1990s millions have died in the Congo, Sudan, and other African countries, and hundreds of thousands in former Yugoslavia and Iraq, In today's "new wars," to use peace scholar Mary Kaldor's phrase, methods of terror, ethnic cleansing, and genocide are deliberate strategies to target civilians. The result is that more than 80 percent of the casualties are civilian, and the number of refugees and displaced persons has increased sharply. "Violations of humanitarian and human rights law are not a side effect" of armed violence, wrote Kaldor, "but the central methodology of new wars."[11] The strategy of violence in the new paradigm utilizes terror and destabilization to displace populations and gain control of territory and sources of income.[12]

In response to the rise of intrastate war international humanitarian action and peace-building efforts have increased. Those who seek to prevent war have recognized the need to act in the midst of violent conflict to ameliorate its consequences and prevent its recurrence. The responsibility to protect civilians has emerged as a new principle of global action, part of what Kaldor has termed "cosmopolitan politics." The urgency of stemming genocide, oppression, and terrorism has sparked a new wave of action and inquiry, and has led to an intensified search for ways to resolve and prevent deadly conflict.

At the international level peacemaking programs have expanded and become institutionalized at the United Nations and in other multilateral and regional organizations. In the 1992 report *An Agenda for Peace* UN Secretary-General Boutros Boutros-Ghali identified four phases of inter-national action to prevent and control armed violence: preventive diplomacy, which includes early warning, mediation, and confidence-building measures; peacemaking efforts such as arbitration and the negotiation of peace accords; peacekeeping, the deployment of impartial forces to monitor and implement peace settlements; and peace-building, which the UN defines as post-conflict efforts to rebuild war-torn societies and prevent the recurrence of violence.[13] These contemporary strategies correspond directly to peace principles and traditions in earlier periods of history.

Defining terms

At the outset we face definitional challenges and the need to differentiate among different terms and concepts. What exactly do we mean by peace? The term is highly emotive, historian Michael Howard wrote, and is often abused as a tool of political propaganda.[14] When peace is defined narrowly it can imply passivity and the acceptance of injustice.[15] During the cold war the word had subversive implications and was often associated with communism. Moscow sponsored ersatz "peace councils," which gave the word a negative connotation. Hesitancy about the meaning of peace existed long before the cold war. In the years before World War I Andrew Carnegie lavishly funded programs to prevent war and advance international cooperation, but he was uncomfortable with the word peace and wanted to leave it out of the title of the international endowment he left as his legacy.[16]

Peace is more than the absence of war. It is also "the maintenance of an orderly and just society," wrote Howard – orderly in being protected against the violence or extortion of aggressors, and just in being defended against exploitation and abuse by the more powerful.[17] Many writers distinguish between negative peace, which is simply the absence of war, and positive peace, which is the presence of justice. "Peace can be slavery or it can be freedom; subjugation or liberation," wrote Norman Cousins. Genuine peace means progress toward a freer and more just world.[18] Johan Galtung developed the concept of "structural violence" to describe situations of negative peace that have violent and unjust consequences.[19] Violence in Galtung's expansive definition is any condition that prevents a human being from achieving her or his full potential. Leonardo Boff, the Brazilian priest and theologian, employed the term "originating violence," which he defined as an oppressive social condition that preserves the interests of the elite over the needs of dispossessed and marginalized populations.[20] Originating or structural violence can include impoverishment, deprivation, humiliation, political repression, a lack of human rights, and the denial of self-determination. Positive peace means transcending the conditions that limit human potential and assuring opportunities for self-realization.

Gandhi spoke of nonviolence rather than peace and emphasized the necessity of overcoming injustice. Gandhi's meaning was deftly summarized by Jonathan Schell: "Violence is a method by which the ruthless few can subdue the passive many. Nonviolence is a means by which the active many can overcome the ruthless few." Yet the word nonviolence is "highly imperfect," wrote Schell. It is a word of "negative construction," as if the most important thing that can be said about nonviolence is that it is *not* something else. It is a negation of the negative force of violence, a double negative which in mathematics would yield a positive result. Yet English has no positive word for it. Schell attempted to resolve this dilemma by defining nonviolence as "cooperative power" – collective action based on mutual consent, in contrast to coercive power, which compels action through the threat or use of force.[21]

Peace does not mean the absence of conflict, argued peace researcher and former Australian ambassador John W. Burton. Conflict is intrinsic in human relationships, although it does not have to be and usually is not violent. The challenge for peace practitioners is to find ways in which communities can resolve differences without physical violence. In this context peace is understood as a dynamic process not an absolute end point. The goal of peacemakers is to develop more effective ways of resolving disputes without violent conflict, to identify and transform the conditions that cause war.

What's in a word?

The term "pacifism" especially needs deconstruction. It entered the lexicon at the beginning of the twentieth century as a general term to describe the stance of those opposed to war. After World War I the term became synonymous with an earlier, more specific tradition of religiously based refusal to condone or participate in war in any form, also known as nonresistance. This purist position was distinct from the more widely accepted traditions of pragmatic or conditional pacifism, which opposed war in principle but accepted the possibility of using force for self-defense or the protection of the vulnerable. It also contrasted with internationalism, which along with political realism traced the causes of war to the condition of anarchy among nations, and which advocated transnational cooperation and the strengthening of international law and institutions as the means of preventing armed conflict. Absolute pacifism also differed from "just war" principles, developed by Augustine in the fifth century and accepted by official Christianity, which set limits on war but gave it justification.

Pacifism existed as a movement and set of ideas long before the actual word was coined in 1901. The term emerged during the tenth Universal Peace Congress in Glasgow, at a time when organizations seeking to prevent war were spreading throughout Europe and the United States. Proposals for arbitration and the development of international law were gaining support among political leaders on both sides of the Atlantic. Bertha von Suttner's book *Lay Down Your Weapons* was an international bestseller, published in thirty-seven editions and translated into more than a dozen languages. The ideology of the peace movement was maturing. The narrow religious base of the early Anglo-American peace societies was giving way to more secular, humanitarian perspectives, especially in continental Europe.

Prior to the Glasgow congress members of the various peace societies and international organizations generally referred to themselves as "peace workers," "peace advocates," or, most commonly, "friends of peace." These were awkward terms that satisfied no one. Activists sought to develop a better term that would more effectively convey the growing maturity and sophistication of the movement. It was Emile Arnaud of France, president of the *Ligue internationale de la paix et de la liberté*, who first introduced the word "pacifism." He and others used it in a generic sense to describe the broad international peace movement. It was meant to suggest a coherent body of thought and developed set of political beliefs and policies for preventing war and assuring peace. The term elevated the philosophy of peace into an official "ism." It had international appeal and could be integrated easily into different languages. The term was officially adopted at the Glasgow congress. Thereafter those who participated in the various peace organizations and societies around the world began to refer to themselves as "pacifists." It was a term of distinction and had a broad social connotation. It was meant to encompass all of those who worked to preserve peace and prevent war.

Pacifism also meant social action. It was not merely a philosophy but a political program and a commitment to social change. It was distinct from the quietist tradition of some religious sects, whose members tended to withdraw from public life and cede to the state the realm of practical politics. This was not what the early twentieth-century pacifists had in mind. Arnaud sought to distinguish pacifists from those who merely hope or pray for peace. "We are not passive types . . . we are pacifists."[22] Pacifism included a personal commitment to take action, to work for peace. It implied, historian Roger Chickering wrote, a "high degree of engagement in activity" to help reduce the level of violence in international relations.[23] The study of peace is thus a history of social action as well as of ideas, an examination of social movements and of intellectual development.

Soon after the term pacifism emerged debates developed over its exact meaning and application. Should it encompass the traditional peace societies, which were often quite conservative and in some cases supported military "preparedness?" Did it apply to internationalism, which tended to focus narrowly on promoting arbitration and international law and institutions? Internationalists could be either conservative or progressive, favoring the status quo (including the system of imperialism) or advocating greater equality of status among nations. Was the term pacifism appropriate for the socialist parties, which opposed imperialist war but were prepared to support the class war? What about the democratic nationalists who supported the use of force for the just cause of national liberation? Could all of these diverse approaches, each in its distinctive way claiming to embody the path to peace, fit within one broad pacifist movement? These differences came to a head with the outbreak of war in 1914, when the peace movement collapsed and fractured. Most peace advocates, including internationalists and socialists, abandoned their commitment to transnational solidarity and marched off to war. Only a small remnant of the previously broad international movement stood apart from the nationalist frenzy and remained steadfast in opposing war.

In the years after World War I there was much recrimination and debate about the meaning of pacifism. The purists who had opposed the march to war claimed the term for themselves. They narrowed its definition to the unconditional rejection of war in all its forms. As revulsion at the horrific bloodletting of the war deepened, a growing number of people pledged never again to participate in or support war. These "pacifists" played a major role in the peace movement of the interwar era, which grew to unprecedented scale. Internationalists remained an important force, especially in Britain, where the LNU attracted widespread public support, but the influence of those who rejected war under all circumstances was substantial. The restrictive meaning of pacifism became the accepted standard and was adopted by A. C. F. Beales in his influential 1931 volume, *The History of Peace*[24] Thereafter it became the standard in both scholarly and popular discourse.

This narrow definition of pacifism left most of the peace community out in the cold. Many of those who considered themselves pacifist were uncomfortable with the absolutist stand. As the menace of fascism mounted pacifism became increasingly marginalized and associated with isolationism. The term sank into disrepute and was largely abandoned, even by those who considered themselves advocates of peace. Many peace supporters, especially the internationalists, urged vigorous action to confront aggression. Some, such as Albert Einstein, tried to redefine pacifism to include rearmament and collective military resistance against Hitler. Others adopted a "peace with justice" perspective, arguing that the prevention of war depended on resolving political and economic grievances. The majority of peace advocates found themselves in a state of confusion and uncertainty. They were part of a broad social movement amorphously defined as for peace, but they lacked a coherent program for preventing the impending war and had no commonly accepted "ism" to describe the prevailing philosophy.

Scholars have attempted to remedy this frustrating imprecision by providing definitions for the various philosophies and political tendencies that exist within the peace community. The most elaborate and sophisticated attempt to parse the meaning of pacifism was provided by historian Martin Ceadel in his masterful volume, *Thinking about Peace and War*. Ceadel identified five distinct theories of war and peace, ranging from militarism to pacifism. He differentiated absolute pacifism from "pacificism." The latter term was coined by the historian A.J.P. Taylor to describe those who believe that war is always irrational and inhumane and should be prevented, but who accept that it may be necessary at times.[25] Ceadel defined pacificists as those who believe that war can be prevented and with sufficient commitment to justice can be abolished, or nearly so.[26] This is an apt description of the position of most peace advocates. The distinction that Ceadel and others make between absolute and pragmatic pacifism is vital, although often obfuscated. Few have adopted the "pacificist" label, however, which is awkward, confusing, and difficult to write or pronounce. It will not appear again in this volume. The general concept of pragmatic or conditional pacifism is nonetheless valuable, and will serve as the foundation for the definition employed here.

"Pacifist" Japan ?

In Japan absolute pacifism is official national policy, as enshrined in Article 9 of the postwar Constitution:

> Aspiring sincerely to an international peace based on justice and order, the Japanese people forever renounce war as a sovereign right of the nation and the threat or use of force as means of settling international disputes.
>
> In order to accomplish the aim of the preceding paragraph, land, sea, and air forces, as well as other war potential, will never be maintained. The right of belligerence of the state will not be recognized.

This extraordinary and unequivocal rejection of war has no precedent in history. Other countries have renounced war in their constitutions but never with such totality. Japan's Constitution was imposed by US occupation authorities, but many Japanese nonetheless supported its rejection of war, and a vigorous peace and disarmament movement developed over the decades – although the traditions of nationalism also retained their appeal among some conservatives.

Support for peace in Japan is understood as both a personal moral commitment and a social-political position that is linked to human rights, democracy, and economic well-being. The common term for peace advocacy is *heiwa shugi*, which is a combination of the Japanese words for "peace" and "ism." The ambiguity of the term makes it difficult to differentiate between absolute and conditional pacifism, and for many the meanings overlap and often coexist. The term *heiwa shugi* has no equivalent in English, although the original Glasgow definition of pacifism was intended precisely to convey the principled yet pragmatic commitment to peace conveyed by the Japanese term.[27]

Article 9 is absolute in its language, but the political and legal interpretation of the clause has been more pragmatic. In practice pacifism in Japan has meant a "presumption against the employment of force, rather than its absolute rejection," according to scholar Robert Kisala.[28] The common understanding is that force may be used in self-defense or in humanitarian or peacekeeping missions authorized by the United Nations, but that other uses of military force are unacceptable. The government has pursued its foreign policy objectives mostly through economic means, principally through overseas development assistance.[29]

Latin American and African traditions

In Latin America absolute pacifism is rare, but the use of nonviolent action as a method of social change is widespread. The commitment to nonviolence is often more pragmatic than principled, based on the calculation that violence leads to further oppression, and that *firmeza permanente* ("relentless persistence") can be a powerful means of achieving justice. The use of active nonviolence is rooted in the historical example of Latin America's indigenous communities, which struggled over the centuries to resist assimilation, by Spanish conquerors and national governments, often through nonviolent methods of mass noncooperation. In recent decades numerous Latin American social movements have utilized nonviolent action to overcome repression, end military dictatorship, and defend human rights. The commitment to nonviolent action gained momentum after the Second Vatican Council of 1962–5 and the Latin American bishops conference in Medellín, Colombia, in 1968, as liberation theology emerged to proclaim a "preferential option for the poor." Some appropriated the new theology to justify armed revolution, but most agreed with Leonardo Boff that liberation theology and active nonviolence were "two facets of a single reality." Both are rooted in the Gospel and seek to transform a society of violence and oppression into one of compassion and justice.[30]

In African traditions peace means order, harmony, and equilibrium, not merely preventing war.[31] Western concepts of absolute pacifism or non-resistance have little meaning in societies that place primary value on maintaining social harmony. Peace is a function of social justice. It depends on preserving the integrity of communities. This concept of shared humanity is embodied in the African phrase *ubuntu*, which literally means "I am because we are." The truth of *ubuntu*, wrote philosopher Augustine Shutte, is that we become ourselves by belonging to community.[32] Peace can only be realized in community with others, through the embrace of the other. Community elders are often called upon to preserve peace by adjudicating and resolving conflicts.

Africa remains deeply scarred by the brutal legacies of colonialism. In recent decades no continent has suffered more from war and pervasive economic deprivation. The presence of conflict and the absence of development are bound together in a downward spiral of violence and misery. In response African leaders have argued that peace is impossible without economic development and political freedom. Tanzanian president Julius Nyerere wrote: "for the sake of peace and justice, these economic inequalities in the world must be reduced and the mass of the people must be able to relieve themselves from the burden of poverty."[33] Bishop Desmond Tutu said in his Nobel Peace Prize speech in 1984: "There can be no real peace and security [in South Africa] until there be first justice enjoyed by all the inhabitants of that beautiful land."[34] In Africa, as in Latin America and Asia, peace is inextricably linked to economic and social justice.

Pacifism and "just war"

Pacifism and the just war tradition are analytically distinct and are often considered opposites. The concept of pragmatic pacifism helps to bridge the gap and provides a more holistic framework for understanding peace advocacy. It reflects the dominant position of those who consider themselves peace supporters. Absolute pacifists have always been a minority, even within peace movements. The majority of those who work for peace seek to avoid war but are willing to accept some limited use of force for self-defense or to uphold justice and protect the innocent. Some uses of military force are more objectionable than others. This is evident from the fact that certain wars, such as those in Vietnam and Iraq, arouse vociferous movements of protest, while other uses of force, such as the multinational operation in Bosnia, are broadly accepted, even by many peace supporters. As the United States prepared to take military action in Afghanistan following the September 2001 terrorist attacks, Scott Simon of National Public Radio wrote "Even Pacifists Must Support This War."[35] Some peace advocates accepted the attack against Al Qaida as justified self-defense, but many cautioned against militarizing the struggle against terrorism. Because just war language is often abused by political leaders to justify military aggression there is concern that misuse of the framework can be a slippery slope toward the legitimation of indiscriminate violence. As Michael Walzer emphasized, just war reasoning is a challenge to political realism.[36] The just war doctrine establishes a rigorous set of moral conditions that must be met before armed conflict can be considered. If thoroughly and honestly applied these criteria would rule out most of the armed conflicts that political leaders claim to be just and would make war a rare occurrence.

Pragmatic pacifism can be understood as a continuum of perspectives, beginning on one end with the rejection of military violence and extending across a range of options that allow for some limited use of force under specific conditions. The presumption is always against the use of force and in favor of settling differences without violence, but reality dictates that some uses of force may be necessary at times to assure justice and prevent the greater violence that often results when exploitation and aggression are unconstrained. Even strict pacifists acknowledge that at times soldiers can play a role in preventing the spread of violence. I once asked a class of Mennonite students who described themselves as pacifist if they would support the continued deployment of NATO troops in Bosnia to keep the peace among the previously warring factions. All but one of the twenty students said yes. Pacifists may accept the use of force if it is constrained, narrowly targeted, and conducted by proper authority within the rule of law.[37] Mennonite theologian John Howard Yoder differentiated between war and the use of police power; the latter is subject to legal and moral constraints and is ethically superior to war.[38] Distinctions matter, and a vast difference exists between unilateral, unprovoked military aggression and multilateral peace operations to protect civilian populations. No one who considered herself pacifist would accept the former but a great many would accept the latter.

The just war position also contains a continuum of perspectives, extending from limited police action to all-out war, based on a set of moral criteria that can vary significantly in different settings. Views on whether a particular use of force is justified range from a restrictive interpretation that permits military action only under narrowly constrained circumstances, to more expansive claims that seek to justify large-scale military operations and even the unprovoked invasion of other countries. Analysts often differ on whether a particular use of force, such as the 1991 Gulf War, meets the classic moral criteria of a just war.[39] Most ethicists within the tradition agree, however, that the just war framework is based on a presumption against the use of military force. All share Walzer's insistence on addressing the moral reality of war.[40] The use of military force is not merely an extension of politics. It is a moral act of supreme importance that must be judged according to the strictest ethical standards.

The continuum of pacifism can be combined with that of just war to form a continuous range of options extending from absolute nonviolence at the one end to the justification of war at the other. All the differing perspectives on war and peace thus can be considered in relation to one another. This is the approach employed by Ceadel in his classification of five major perspectives on peace and war.[41] John Howard Yoder also combined the two traditions in a standard lecture I had the privilege of hearing on several occasions. Yoder argued that a systematic and rigorous application of just war principles – just cause, right authority, last resort, probability of success, proportionality, discrimination – would make war extremely rare. Philosopher John Rawls wrote that justice demands a form of "contingent pacifism." The possibility of just war is conceded in principle, but the far greater likelihood is that war will be unjust, especially when waged by large and powerful states against weaker nations. Given the often predatory aims of state power the demands of justice may require resistance to war.[42]

An honest appraisal of war through the lens of just war criteria would forbid any consideration of nuclear strikes and would rule out virtually all forms of large-scale, unilateral military intervention. It would leave only self-defense and limited, legally constrained uses of multilateral force to protect civilians and restore conditions of justice. The "responsibility to protect" principles that have recently gained international endorsement embody this perspective. Walzer argued that the only morally justified reason for fighting is the defense of rights, most essentially the right of self-defense.[43] Rawls likewise acknowledged the principle of self-defense and the right of people to determine their own affairs without the intervention of foreign powers.[44] Combining the pacifist and just war traditions allows for a broader and richer examination of the peace tradition, one that more accurately reflects the thinking of those who consider themselves part of the peace movement. It takes into account the full range of peacemaking options and traditions that are part of the history of peace. It also conforms with the original definition and meaning of pacifism.

An outline of peace history

Peace societies first emerged in the United States and Britain in the early part of the nineteenth century and later spread across Europe and beyond. Peace advocates focused on proposals for the arbitration of interstate disputes and the strengthening of international law. The internationalist agenda was partly realized in Woodrow Wilson's vision of the League of Nations. Although the League was flawed in design and fatally weakened by the lack of US participation, it established a precedent for the gradual strengthening of international institutions and laid the foundations for the United Nations.

Pacifism and internationalism attracted very broad public support during the interwar era. Peace advocates and internationalists were early opponents of fascist aggression in Manchuria and Abyssinia, and many urged the defense of the Spanish republic. They demanded League of Nations action to impose sanctions against Japan and Italy. The LNU organized the Peace Ballot as a way of demonstrating support for mutual disarmament and collective action against aggression. The decisions to betray Ethiopia and the Spanish republic and appease Hitler were taken by Western government leaders not peace advocates. Interwar pacifists can be faulted for many things – clinging too long to the failed promise of the League of Nations, supporting the illusion of neutrality, believing that diplomacy could stop the Nazi menace – but they were not culpable for war.

In the early years of the cold war peace advocacy fell to its lowest ebb of the century. Anticommunism and a suffocating atmosphere of political conformity combined with a backlash against pacifism to undermine the legitimacy of progressive internationalism. A significant movement for world federalism emerged in the late 1940s but rapidly declined with the onset of the Korean War. Peace scholars and activists addressed the problem of militarization and the growing tendency toward military interventionism. The development of atomic weapons and their terrifying spread created new dangers and sparked significant waves of disarmament activism. The first wave of anti-nuclear action was initiated by the atomic scientists who created the bomb. The second wave came in the late 1950s in response to atmospheric nuclear testing. Led by groups such as the Campaign for Nuclear Disarmament (CND) in Britain and SANE in the United States, the ban the bomb movement exerted significant pressure that led to the 1963 atmospheric test ban treaty. The arms race continued and intensified in the 1980s, prompting a third and even larger wave of disarmament activism. The nuclear freeze campaign in the United States and disarmament movements in Europe paved the way for significant nuclear reductions and the end of the cold war.

The movement against the Vietnam War was one of the largest and most intensive peace campaigns in history. Antiwar efforts influenced the Johnson and Nixon administrations and exerted sustained pressure for US military withdrawal. Antiwar activism developed even among active-duty soldiers and veterans, as I personally experienced. Conscientious objection reached an unprecedented scale and spread not only in the United States during the Vietnam era but in Europe and beyond in subsequent decades. Antiwar activism rose again in response to the US invasion and occupation of Iraq. In February 2003 an estimated 10 million people demonstrated against the Iraq war in hundreds of cities across the globe. This vast movement was unable to stop the US-led invasion, but it prevented the Bush administration from gaining UN endorsement and contributed to the political defeat of the administration's war policy.

An overview of peacemaking ideas

The religious traditions of Hinduism, Buddhism, Judaism, Islam, and Christianity all contain principles and practices to sustain peacemaking – although justifications for war can also be found in many sacred texts. The Gospel of Jesus is unequivocal in its commitment to love and nonretaliation for injury, as reflected in the absolute pacifism of the early Christian communities. Although the just war tradition replaced pacifism within official Christianity, the tradition of nonresistance continued and reemerged during and after the Reformation in the Anabaptist and Quaker movements. The Social Gospel of the late nineteenth and twentieth centuries brought peace and social justice issues into the mainstream of Christianity, but it also sparked renewed debate about the limitations of pacifism. The leading voice in this reappraisal was Reinhold Niebuhr, whose philosophy of Christian realism became a dominant influence in the twentieth century. John Howard Yoder's response to Niebuhr sought to preserve the integrity of pacifism through a more realistic, minimalist understanding of the possibilities for Christian perfectionism.

Niebuhr and Yoder were influenced by the achievements of Gandhi and the power of nonviolent action to achieve social justice. The Gandhian method inspired Martin Luther King, Jr. and the US civil rights movement. Nonviolent citizen movements have since become a "force more powerful," bringing democracy to the Philippines, a "velvet revolution" to eastern Europe, the end of apartheid in South Africa, and the overthrow of corrupt regimes in Serbia, Ukraine, and other former Soviet republics. Nonviolent action is the key to mote realistic pacifism, a bridge between idealism and realism. Assertive nonviolence as developed by Gandhi provides an answer to the challenge of Niebuhr, transcending the passivity of nonresistance while offering a strategy for fighting effectively to resist social evil.

The rise of peace advocacy in recent centuries is directly tied to the spread and deepening of democracy. It is no accident that peace societies first emerged in democratic Britain and the United States, and that the largest peace mobilizations have occurred in democratic countries. Pacifism is by its very nature an activist commitment that depends for its expression on the right of people to assemble and speak freely. The rise of socialism influenced pacifism by focusing attention on issues of equality and social justice. Relations between pacifism and socialism were decidedly cool at first, the result of different theories about the causes of war and the requirements for peace. Gradually the movements began to converge, as peace advocates broadened their agenda and socialists became less doctrinaire. In recent decades peace advocates and Internationalists have supported more equitable economic development as an essential strategy for preventing war.

The advent of feminism and the growing involvement of women significantly influenced the agenda for peace. Women tended to give greater emphasis to the social dimensions of peace, and linked the concerns of family and community life with the larger realm of state and international affairs. In the late nineteenth and early twentieth centuries feminists noted the heavy burden of war on women, including impoverishment from the toss of male breadwinners. In the twentieth century they emphasized the rising death toll among women and children caused by the increased lethality of war and the spread of civil conflict. Feminists pointed to the connection between the institutionalized violence of war and violence against women. They sought to achieve greater equality for women as an essential requirement for creating a more just and peaceful world. They enlarged the definition of peace beyond narrow legalistic and institutional concerns to encompass a more holistic social, economic, cultural, and political strategy for preventing violence.[45]

Support for human rights has become an essential element of the strategy for peace and was a key factor in ending the cold war. The cause of political freedom is sometimes misused by governments, however, as when US and British leaders claimed a human rights argument for the invasion of Iraq. More legitimate human rights challenges were posed by genocide and the abuse of civilians in Bosnia, Kosovo, and Darfur – although in these instances the response from the major powers was initially timid. The moral and political imperative of responding to the slaughter of innocents has sparked an intense international debate about the responsibility to protect. Peace and human rights advocates are finding common ground in advocating mote vigorous international action, including the use of force under specified conditions, as necessary means of ending oppression and securing peace with justice.

Patriotism is often pitted against pacifism. Throughout history the call to arms has trumped the appeal for peace. The phenomenon of mass belligerence was the subject of a famous 1932 correspondence between Einstein and Freud and motivated philosopher William James's search for "a moral equivalent of war" a generation earlier. Gandhi sought to harness the desire for patriotic service into a commitment to social justice through the idea of a nonviolent army. His concept echoes today in various citizen nonviolent peacemaking initiatives and conciliation programs in conflict zones around the world. Recent trends toward greater peacemaking duties for armed forces and proposals for a "human security response force" within the European Union suggest that the gap between traditional military service and peacemaking may be narrowing. Peace advocacy is itself a form of patriotic service, not only to nation but to the wider human community.

My goal is to forge a synthesis among peacemaking traditions, giving the principles of nonviolence cardinal importance. This synthesis incorporates advances in the theory and practice of international peace-building, while also drawing from the contributions of democracy theory, feminism, socialism, and human rights. It addresses the rise of antiwar movements, the imperative of disarmament, and the contemporary challenges of countering terrorism and nuclear proliferation. Over the decades new possibilities have emerged for resolving conflict and achieving justice through nonviolent means. History's most violent era has also seen the dawning of an age of nonviolence. While the dominant narrative has been and continues to be written in blood, a different, more hopeful story has emerged in the development of movements and ideas for peace. Gandhian principles of nonviolence have inspired new strategies and possibilities for achieving justice and overcoming social evil while remaining true to religious principles of peace. Growing numbers of people now recognize and act upon the realization that the peaceful resolution of conflict is both necessary and possible.

Notes

1 Victoria Bissell Brown, "Addams, Jane," February 2000. Available online at American National Biography Online, www.anb.org/articles/15/15–00004.html (accessed 22 November 2006).
2 *The Life of King Henry V*, act V, scene ii, line 34.
3 G. M, Gilbert, *Nuremberg Diary* (New York: Farrar, Straus, and Co., 1947), 279.
4 Sec George A, Lopez, special editor, "Peace Studies: Past and Future," *The Annals of the American Academy of Political and Social Science* 504 (July 1989).
5 Hans J. Morgenthau, "We are Deluding Ourselves in Vietnam," *The New York Times Magazine.* 18 April 1965, SM25.
6 John J. Mearsheimer and Stephen M. Walt, "An Unnecessary War," *Foreign Policy* no. 134 (January–February 2003): 50.
7 Rupert Smith, *The Utility of Force: The Art of War in the Modern World* (London: Penguin Books,2006), 1–2.
8 Raimo Väyrynen, ed., *The Waning of Major War: Theories and Debates* (London: Routledge, 2006).
9 Smith, *The Utility of Force*, 3.
10 Lotta Harbom, Stina Högbladh, and Peter Wallensteen. "Armed Conflict and Peace Agreements," *Journal of Peace Research* 43, no. 5 (2006): 617–31.
11 Mary Kaldor, "Beyond Militarism, Arms Races and Arms Control" (essay prepared for the Nobel Peace Prize Centennial Symposium, 6–8 December 2001). Available online at the *Social Science Research Council*, www.ssrc.org/septn/essays/kaldor.htm (accessed 22 November 2006).
12 Mary Kaldor, *New and Old Wars: Organized Violence in a Global Era* (Stanford, CA: Stanford University Press, 2001), 115.
13 Boutros Boutros-Ghali, *An Agenda for Peace: Preventive Diplomacy, Peacemaking, and Peace-keeping*, Report of the Secretary-General Pursuant to the Statement Adopted by the Summit Meeting of the Security Council on 31 January 1992, A/47/277 – S/24III (New York: United Nations, 1992).
14 Michael Howard, "Problems of a Disarmed World," in *Studies in War and Peace* (New York: Viking Press, 1971), 225.
15 David P. Barash, *Introduction to Peace Studies* (Belmont, CA: Wadsworth Publishing, 1991), 6.
16 Charles Chatfield, *The American Peace Movement: Ideals and Activism* (New York: Twayne Publishers, 1992), 23.
17 Howard. "Problems of a Disarmed World," 226.
18 Norman Cousins, *Modern Man is Obsolete* (New York: Viking Press, 1946), 45–6.
19 Johan Galtung, "Violence. Peace, and Peace Research," *Journal of Peace Research* 6, no.3 (1969): 167–97.
20 Leonardo Boff, "Active Nonviolence: The Political and Moral Power of the Poor," in *Relentless Persistence: Nonviolent Action in Latin America*, ed. Philip McManus and Gerald Schlabach (Philadelphia, PA: New Society Publishers, 1991), vii.
21 Jonathan Schell, *The Unconquerable World: Power, Nonviolence, and the Will of the People* (New York; Metropolitan Books, 2003), 144, 227, 351.

22 Sandi E. Cooper, *Patriotic Pacifism: Waging War in Europe, 1815–1914* (New York: Oxford University Press, 1991), 60.

23 Roger Chickering, *Imperial Germany and a World without War: The Peace Movement and German Society, 1892–1914* (Princeton, NJ: Princeton University Press, 1975), 16–17.

24 A. C. F. Beales, *The History of Petite: A Short Account if the Organised Movement; for International Peace* (London: G. Bell, 1931).

25 Martin Ceadel, *Pacifism in Britain 1914–1945: The Defining of a Faith* (Oxford: Clarendon Press, 1980), 3.

26 Martin Ceadel, *Thinking about Peace and War* (Oxford; Oxford University Press, 1987), 4–5.

27 Mari Yamamoto, *Grassroots Pacifism in Post-war Japan: The Rebirth of a Nation* (London: RoutledgeCurzon, 2004), 10.

28 Robert Kisala, *Prophets of Peace: Pacifism and Cultural Identity in Japan's New Religions* (Honolulu: University of Hawai'i Press, 1999), 8.

29 Peter J. Katzenstein and Nobuo Okawara, *Japan's National Security; Structures, Norms, and Policy Responses in a Changing World* (Ithaca, NY: East Asia Program, Cornell University, 1993), 105–7.

30 Boff, "Active Nonviolence," ix–x.

31 Godfrey Igwebuike Onah, "The Meaning of Peace in African Traditional Religion and Culture" (lecture, Pontifical Urban University, Rome, n.d.). Available online at Afrika World, www.afrikaworld.net/afrel/goddionah.htm (accessed 5 March 2007).

32 Augustine Shutte, *Ubuntu: An Ethic for a New South Africa* (Pietermaritzburg, South Africa: Cluster Publications, 2001), 9.

33 Julius K. Nyerere, *Freedom and Unity: Uhuru na umoja: A Selection from Writings and Speeches, 1952–65* (London: Oxford University Press, 1967), 235.

34 *The Nobel Peace Prize Lecture: Desmond M. Tutu* (New York; Anson Phelps Stokes Institute for African, Afro-American, and American Indian Affairs, 1986).

35 Scott Simon, "Even Pacifists Must Support This War," *Wall Street Journal,* 11 October 2001.

36 Michael Walzer, *Arguing about War* (New Haven, CT: Yale University Press, 2004), ix.

37 Gerald Schlabach, "Just Policing, Not *War,*" *America* 189, no. 1 (7–14 July 2003): 19–21.

38 John Howard Yoder, *The Politics of Jesus,* 2nd edn (Grand Rapids, MI: Eerdmans, 1994), 204.

39 See Jean Bethke Elshtain and David E. DeCosse, eds., *But Was It Just? Reflections on the Morality of the Persian Gulf War* (New York: Doubleday, 1992).

40 Michael Walzer, *Just and Unjust Wars: A Moral Argument with Historical Illustrations* (New York: Basic Books, 1992), 15.

41 Ceadel, *Thinking about Peace and War.*

42 John Rawls, *A Theory of Justice,* rev. edn (Cambridge, MA: The Belknap Press of Harvard University Press, 1999), 335.

43 Walzer, *Just and Unjust Wars,* 72.

44 Rawls, *A Theory of Justice,* 332.

45 Harriet Hyman Alonzo, *Peace as a Women's Issue: A History of the US Movement for World Peace and Women's Rights* (Syracuse, NY: Syracuse University Press, 1993), 8–14.

13 Introduction from *Peace Movements in International Protest and World Politics Since 1945 (the Postwar World)*

April Carter

The peace protests which captured public attention in the years since 1945 took place in response to immediate dangers, but they were nevertheless, linked to a much longer history of peace campaigning. Some of the organizations now active in opposing war and war preparations date from earlier in this century. Some go back very much further: the Quakers, for example, arose in the seventeenth century. Moreover, recent campaigners not only respond to contemporary concerns and arguments but draw also on a much longer tradition of thinking about the problems of war and peace. There are many continuities between past and present peace action, and to gain a full understanding of the present we need to begin by looking very briefly at the history of thought and action relating to peace before the Second World War.

Origins of peace activity

The belief that war is immoral is rooted in early Christianity, which at first prompted a pacifist refusal to take part in war. In due course Christian belief was adapted to political realities and the requirements of rulers, as St Augustine and later Catholic philosophers elaborated the doctrine of Just War. In addition to a specifically Christian rejection of war there is a humanist strand of thought, which stresses the brutalizing and corrupting nature of warfare, that can be traced back to classical Greece Humanism surfaced in the Renaissance and led thinkers like Erasmus to denounce the barbarities of war. Later, secular rationalism prompted theorists in early eighteenth-century Europe to propose forms of international organization to secure permanent peace. One of the best-known treatises was by St Pierre, who published his essay on *Perpetual Peace* in 1712. Towards the end of the century both Rousseau and Kant produced their own critical reflections on this topic, raising questions about the relevance of the internal organization of states if the aim of international peace was to be realized.

The first organized peace groups, however, were founded immediately after the Napoleonic Wars, in the USA and in Britain. The growth of peace activity might be seen as part of the new spirit of democracy which prompted popular agitation not only for extension of the franchise but for a range of social and humanitarian reforms, and created aspirations for the transformation of society. It is, nonetheless, significant that the new peace societies were founded after a Europe-wide conflict that had effectively lasted twenty-five years. The Napoleonic Wars are often seen as marking a critical change in the nature of modern war, popularizing the idea of 'the nation in arms' and promoting a new form of total war. Certainly the wars prompted a romantic nationalism and a glorification of war and the figure of the soldier. But there was also awareness of the destructiveness and waste of war, of the thousands of fighting men killed, the ravages of famine and the burned and sacked towns and villages.[1] Goya's etchings of 'The Disasters of War' depicted the mutual atrocities resulting from the Spanish people's guerrilla resistance to the Napoleonic army of occupation.

The first peace societies also drew upon a much earlier commitment to oppose war, since Quakers played a key role in founding them, aided by Unitarians and other free-thinking Protestants. The Quaker commitment to peace stemmed from their belief in recapturing the spirit of early Christianity and conviction that waging war was incompatible with respecting 'that of God in every man'. While a number of religious sects which arose at the time of the Reformation believed bearing arms was forbidden by the Christian gospels, most of these were primarily concerned about personal morality and salvation, and so avoided compromise with the world of polities. The Quakers, however, were formed during the religious and political ferment of the English Civil War in the 1640s, and under one of their leaders, William Penn, were able to found a Quaker government in America. So they always had a concern with the politics of this world. Indeed, Penn anticipated St Pierre in drawing up his own plan for a league of states to preserve international peace. Quakers therefore quite naturally sponsored peace groups, which also drew on the ideas of early nineteenth-century liberalism.

The first peace societies stressed that differences between states could be settled without recourse to war, and relied heavily on the role of enlightened public opinion and on rational discussion of conflicting interests. The American Peace Society, created in 1828 through the merger of thirty-six societies from different areas, called in its constitution for 'amicable discussion and arbitration' between states, and for 'settling all controversies by an appeal to reason'. The institutional basis for devising such settlements was to be a 'Congress of Nations whose decrees shall be enforced by public opinion that rules the world'.[2] In order to promote and mobilize public opinion, the new peace societies engaged in extensive pamphleteering, sent speakers on long lecture tours and founded their own periodicals. The British Society, which laid particular emphasis on the power of the press, began to publish the *Herald of Peace* in 1819, and the first American peace paper was the *Friend of Peace,* founded in 1821. The franchise was still restricted, but the peace societies did not limit themselves to mobilizing those who had the vote. Women were involved early on in peace activity, while campaigners like the American Elihu Burritt set out to recruit workers in both the USA and Britain.

From the 1840s to the Crimean War

Thinking about peace acquired a more radical tinge when William Lloyd Garrison, best known for his efforts to abolish slavery, spelled out the implications of Christian 'non-resistance' and called for non-cooperation with all government preparations for war. Garrison drew up a Declaration of Principles for the New England Non-Resistance Society, which he helped to found in 1838. One of his colleagues, Adin Ballou, explained in more detail what was meant in a book entitled *Christian Non-Resistance,* published in 1846. Both Garrison and Ballou stressed that they were advocating not passivity, but an active moral resistance to evil, a resistance which did not involve inflicting physical violence.[3] Garrison came to condone the use of violence to end slavery, but the idea of non-resistance was later to influence Tolstoy, who had read Ballou. Tolstoy himself had an impact on the young Gandhi, who translated non-violent resistance into an effective form of political action, first in South Africa and then in India. Through Gandhi peace activists were in turn inspired by the potential of non-violent resistance to oppose injustice, occupation and war.

The original Quaker-influenced peace groups acquired a new ally in the 1840s in the Free Trade Movement, led in Britain by Richard Cobden and in the USA by Charles Sumner and William Ellery Channing. Theorists of free trade believed that trade would create such a strong economic interest in peace that even governments adhering to obsolete attitudes would be prevented from launching wasteful and destructive wars. The Free Traders gained support from businessmen for their economic defence of free trade, and were able to ally with the peace societies on a limited programme and help finance a number of international peace congresses, starting in London in 1843.

Peace societies flourished in countries where Protestantism in religion, liberalism in politics and a free enterprise economy provided a favourable setting. Hence the predominance of peace activity in Britain and the USA. The relative isolation of both these countries from the rivalries and conflicts of Europe encouraged opposition to war, although Britain could not entirely escape its great power 'obligation' to maintain a European balance of power, and the USA was to face similar dilemmas in the twentieth century. Peace organizations did spread to various parts of continental Europe, but were in the early nineteenth century often initiated by British or American activists; and the international congresses were organized and dominated by the Anglo-American groups. Continental Europeans had a different view of the ideal international order. After the Napoleonic Wars much of Europe was subjected to the enforced stability laid down at the Congress of Vienna. The Concert of Europe was designed to settle territorial boundaries, but under Austrian and Russian influence it also meant that peace was purchased at the price of suppressing liberal, democratic and nationalist aspirations. So, in the short run, armed rebellion seemed the obvious means of securing freedom from autocratic and imperial rulers. In the long run, European thinkers looked to the goal of a United States of Europe.

The Anglo-American concept of internationalism did not embrace any form of supranational organization: its vision was rather of independent sovereign states meeting in periodic conference and resolving their disputes by reasoned negotiation or voluntary acceptance of arbitration. By 1848 the theme of disarmament had been added to the platform of the second Universal Peace Congress, and an appeal was made to the two major liberal powers, Britain and the USA, to give a lead in reducing their arms. It was the ideas of the British and American peace societies which prevailed in international congresses up to 1853, though they themselves were split between the more committed pacifists and the conventional liberalism of the free trade movement. The former wished oppose all wars and promote Christian non-resistance, the latter to give primacy to free trade. Both emphases were omitted from compromise policies designed to gain support in Europe.

Despite the very moderate programmes adopted at these congresses and the generally respectable middle-class character of the peace societies, they attracted the hostility and contempt of the political establishment and its press. *The Times* denounced the 1843 Universal Peace Congress as a particularly extreme and pernicious example of the 'disease' of the 'fanaticism of association'. It commented scathingly on 'the vagaries and delusions of those unhappy individuals who . . . profess no less than the total abolition throughout the terrestrial globe of war. . .'[4]

The settlement of Europe imposed by the Congress of Vienna was challenged by the wave of revolutions which swept across Europe in 1848–49, and asserted democratic and nationalist justifications for violent rebellion and wars of liberation. Belief that some types of war were just and necessary, and that democratic or nationalist freedoms must be secured as the basis for just and lasting peace, had (as noted above) separated many European radicals from the Anglo-American ideology of the early peace societies. But the conflict between maintaining peace and securing justice caused a crisis among American pacifists, also, over the issue of slavery. Some committed abolitionists, such as William Garrison, abandoned their pacifism and the Civil War divided the peace societies.

From the Crimean War to the First World War

The collapse of the first international peace movement was directly caused, however, not by the problems posed by just wars but by the outbreak of another European war based on the balance of power principle of curbing Russian territorial ambitions: the Crimean War of 1854–56. There followed a period of wars in Europe for Italian and German unification, and no international peace congress was held between 1853 and 1871. Nevertheless, new peace groups were springing up in Europe, representing the democratic republicanism which had been suppressed. The developing socialist movement also had a commitment to resist war. The convergence of various strands of radical thought with the more traditional pacifist internationalism of the early peace societies was demonstrated by the appearance of the flamboyant anarchist Bakunin at the Peace Congress of 1871. The development of the independent Socialist Internationals marked a divergence between the liberal and pacifist peace societies and the more militant war resistance espoused by the Second international. But the peace societies and the socialists held certain views in common, assuming peace would ensue once arbitrary and corrupt forms of government and sinister interests had been overthrown by popular democratic pressure. The liberals, however, relied primarily on an enlightened middle class, whereas socialists looked to the working class and the overthrow of capitalism. By the turn of the century both the peace groups and socialist parties were specifically pointing to the role of imperialist rivalries, the vested interests of armament manufacturers and the momentum of the arms race as threats to peace.

Peace societies multiplied after 1870. By 1900 there were 425 in existence, concentrated mainly, but not exclusively, in north-west Europe and the USA. Parallel to this growth of peace groups, many lawyers and parliamentarians became increasingly interested in promoting international law and international arbitration of disputes, creating their own international organizations. The predominant emphasis of the peace movement represented by the Universal Peace Congresses, held annually after 1892, was on negotiations between governments and arbitration to settle conflicts. The International Peace Bureau was set up as a permanent coordinating body to promote these aims, and it still has a secretariat in Geneva a century later. Even governments themselves were receptive to this approach in the late nineteenth century, and were often willing to accept arbitration. They met for the first time specifically to discuss peace at the Hague Conferences of 1899 and 1907, which issued Declarations prohibiting use of some particularly inhumane weapons, dum-dum bullets and poison gas. The 1907 convention also sought to prohibit deliberate killing of civilians during the course of war.

Belief in the possibility of securing peace, or at least of limiting the horrors of wars if it occurred, was destroyed by the First World War. It exposed the inadequacy of the liberal peace groups' reliance on rational compromise and awareness of common economic interests in peace, and demonstrated the strength of nationalist and *realpoilitik* arguments for going to war. The outbreak of war demonstrated too that public opinion was not necessarily a force for peace, and showed how powerfully nationalism and martial attitudes could grip the popular imagination, as had the Crimean War sixty years earlier.[5] The utopian nature of socialist hopes for united working-class action to prevent war was also revealed in 1914. Many socialists were convinced, once war seemed inevitable, that a victory for Germany (or in the case of German socialists, a victory for Tsarist Russia) would disastrously strengthen the forces of reaction. Most socialist parliamentarians in all the belligerent countries voted for war credits. The Second International collapsed.

The peace movements from 1914 to 1945

War is often the greatest test of the convictions of chose committed to oppose resort to armed violence. Despite the change in popular mood in 1914 many individuals did speak and write against the war, and some men refused to fight. One of the strongest grounds for resisting conscription was Christian pacifism, but men also disobeyed orders to enlist on socialist or anarchist grounds. There were liberals, too, who opposed the principle of conscription. The best known was Bertrand Russell, who helped to found the No Conscription Fellowship in Britain, and was jailed for an article opposing the war. Conscientious objection was adopted on the largest scale in Britain and the USA. After conscription was introduced, in 1916 in Britain, 16,500 men became COs, about 6,000 were court-martialled and over 800 of the most uncompromising resistors suffered more than two years of very harsh imprisonment – while a few were threatened with execution. The USA only entered the war in 1917, but nearly three million men were conscripted and about 4,000 refused on conscientious grounds, despite often brutal army measures to force them to obey orders. Christian pacifism was espoused by the Fellowship of Reconciliation, set up in 1914 in Britain and in 1915 in the USA. A minority of socialists continued to oppose the war, and forty-two delegates from Western and Eastern Europe met at Zimmerwald, Switzerland, in September 1915, in an attempt to reconstruct socialist internationalism.

If the outbreak of war in 1914 was disastrous for groups committed to work for peace, the total experience of the First World War proved a powerful impetus to peace sentiment and peace campaigning for the subsequent twenty years. The static trench warfare on the Western Front rapidly disillusioned the soldiers who suffered the constant shelling and horrors of the trenches, and who knew that each offensive for a small strip of ground brought mass slaughter and mutilation. The change in mood is illustrated by contrasting the poems of Rupert Brooke and their romantic patriotism with the bitter verses of Wilfred Owen and Siegfried Sassoon. The increasing anger among the common soldiers was expressed in 1917 by mutiny in the French army and by revolt on the Eastern Front among the ill-clothed and ill-fed Russian troops who supported revolution inside Russia. Although civilians were insulated from knowledge of the conditions under which the soldiers fought, the mounting death toll and casualties affected millions of families who lost sons, brothers, husbands, fathers and friends. After the war, novels, plays, films and autobiographies dramatized battles such as those fought on the Somme and at Passchendacle, recreating the terror of poison gas and helping to promote popular revulsion against war.

A succession of progressive movements and modes of thought had embraced the quest for creating permanent peace: liberalism, democratic republicanism, socialism and anarchism. The rise of feminism, which became politically significant by the 1900s, also embodied the hope that womanly influence in politics would result in an end to the peculiarly masculine pursuit of war. Women had been active in the peace campaigns of the previous century and had their own peace organizations, but by 1900 the cause of votes for women had been linked to anti-war sentiment. Feminists, like other progressives, split when war broke out in 1914, with some suffrage campaigners becoming ardent patriots and others moving into the ranks of war resisters. The First World War in fact evoked the first explicit feminist initiatives to end the fighting. One such initiative took place within the socialist movement. Clara Zetkin, a prominent anti-war socialist in Germany, managed to organize an International Women's Socialist Conference in Switzerland in 1915, bringing together women from both the warring alliances and from the neutral states. An international women's conference was also held at The Hague in 1915, initiated by a leading Dutch suffrage campaigner, to reaffirm the struggle for women's right to vote and to explore peaceful means of settling international conflicts. The women returned home to lobby their own governments. The Hague Conference gave rise to the Women's International League for Peace and Freedom (WILPF), which remained active after 1918 and mounted a major campaign round the 1932 World Disarmament Conference.[6]

After the First World War widespread anti-war sentiment was expressed in No More War demonstrations in Germany, but in the political and economic turmoil of the early 1920s only a few gave priority to peace campaigning.[7] A new anti-war international body, based on resistance to conscription, was founded in 1921 when groups from Germany, Austria, The Netherlands and Britain met in Holland to form PACO (Esperanto for 'peace'). The Dutch group was primarily inspired by anarchism, the others by a mixture of pacifism and socialism. This grouping soon changed its name to the War Resisters' International (WRI) and at its first proper international conference in 1925 there were representatives from twenty countries. The WRI could claim sections in an impressive range of countries: during the 1920s groups were allowed to exist in the Soviet Union and by the Fourth International Conference of 1934 the Secretary reported that new sections had been formed in Japan, Hong Kong, Mexico and Canada. Lithuania had been added to a long list of European countries where the WRI had groups. The WRI also had some influential supporters – Einstein cooperated with it for a time. Nevertheless, the absolutes of WRI's position in not only opposing military service but all forms of alternative service meant that its support in most countries was limited to a small minority, and it was not in agreement with other peace organizations. The WRI concentrated on support for conscientious objectors (COs) often treated harshly by military courts. (In France, for example, objectors were sent to the notorious prison camp on Devil's Island, made famous by the earlier incarceration there of Alfred Dreyfus.) The spread of fascism and the German occupation of much of Europe meant that war registers had to confront extreme political repression. One of the founder members of PACO, a German Catholic priest, was hanged by the Gestapo in April 1944; others, for example in Holland and Norway, were active in non-violent resistance to Nazi rule.[8]

The International Fellowship of Reconciliation (IFOR) was founded in 1919. It was an explicitly Christian body, and primarily based on Protestant support, although a few Catholics cooperated with it. The IFOR was a response to the failure of the churches to transcend national interests in the First World War and an attempt to promote Christian pacifism. Despite the rather purist and exclusivist approach implied by this goal, the American section of the IFOR had some importance in the wider politics of the Left. It embraced the goal of the social transformation of society and increasingly saw capitalism as the primary cause of injustice and war. Leaders of the American FOR included a number of figures known as socialists or social reformers, including Norman Thomas and Jane Addams. But the extent of FOR's social commitment led some of its members to question whether non-violent methods were adequate to secure social justice. Reinhold Niebuhr, who became one of the most eminent theological critics of Christian pacifism, left the organization in the mid-1930s calling for violent resistance to overthrow capitalism.[9] A. J. Muste, another leading figure in the FOR, also left to become a Trotskyist, but after visiting Europe in 1936 reverted to his belief in non-violence. A. J. had come with his parents from Holland in the 1890s to the Mid-West, become a Minister in the Reformed Church in 1909, but embarked upon a life-long career of radical protest when he opposed the War in 1917 and found himself leading a major textile strike in Massachusetts in 1919. After he returned to his Christian pacifism in 1936 he became one of the most respected figures in both American and international peace circles until he died in 1967. At eighty-two he was one of the 'few social activists and theorists over thirty' to whom an impatient generation of radical youth was prepared to listen.[10]

A much greater political impact was achieved by groups which during and after the First World War revived the liberal internationalist and legalistic proposals for resolving conflict. For example, a League of Nations Society was formed in Britain as early as 1915, and towards the end of the war there was increasing sympathy with the idea of an international body to prevent aggression and to arbitrate or adjudicate disputes. These ideas did influence governments and led to the creation of the League of Nations and the International Court of Justice. The League was based on the concept of collective security and so embodied willingness to use force to prevent aggression. Support for the League was therefore natural to those who sought to avoid further wars, but did not imply a strict pacifism.

The pacifist commitment not to fight in or support any war did win surprisingly widespread support for a period in the 1930s in Britain, where memories of the First World War influenced the attitudes of many to the prospect of any new war. The movement was launched when Canon Dick Sheppard issued a public appeal in 1934 for signatories to a pledge to renounce war. It became an organized campaign in 1936, with eminent support, up to 800 local groups, mass meetings and its own newspaper. The Peace Pledge Union (as it became known) was, however, founded at a time when pacifist policies became increasingly difficult to uphold, as the Left committed itself to oppose the victory of fascism in the Spanish Civil War and Hitter's aggressive ambitions became more obvious. Some eminent supporters of the pacifist cause, such as Albert Einstein and Bertrand Russell, became convinced of the need to fight fascism by military means. After war began in 1939 many former peace campaigners decided that they had to fight, although a significant minority remained committed to opposing the war and became COs. The Peace Pledge Union itself and its journal, *Peace News*, continued to uphold pacifist principles and when necessary defied wartime restrictions to do so. Provisions for conscientious objection were much more liberal than in the previous war, and about 60,000 men and 1,000 women applied to tribunals to be registered as COs.[11] Some took an absolutist stand and refused to do anything which might directly or indirectly assist the war effort; others, such as members of the Friends' Ambulance Unit, gave medical and humanitarian aid to both soldiers and civilians wherever their services were required.

During the late 1930s the failure to impose economic sanctions against Italy, after it invaded Abyssinia in 1935, and the inability of the League of Nations to halt the Japanese invasion of China destroyed the hopes of those who had looked to international organization to prevent war. Peace campaigners who believed in collective security could, however, without any crisis of conscience support a war against the Axis Powers. Moreover, despite the weaknesses displayed by the League, Allied governments had decided before the Second World War was over to create a new body designed to promote international order and peace – the United Nations. During and after the war groups pursued the idea of supranational organization as a means of ensuring peace: this belief motivated the founders of the European Community and in the early post-war years inspired the campaign for world government. The World Federalists tended, however, to oppose the campaigns of the later 1950s against nuclear weapons. The more broadly based United Nations Associations supported negotiations for nuclear and conventional disarmament, but also diverged from more radical anti-nuclear and pacifist organizations.

Notes and references

1 See, for example, letter written by a young officer in 1813, quoted in Geoffrey Best, *War and Society in Revolutionary Europe, 1770–1870* (London, Fontana, 1982), p. 194.
2 Quoted in F.H. Hinsley, *Power and the Pursuit of Peace: Theory and Practice in the History of Relations between*

States (Cambridge, Cambridge University Press, 1967), p. 94. See also, Merle Eugene Curti, *The American Peace Crusade 1815–1860* (Durham, N. Carolina, Duke University Press, 1929).

3 Extracts from Garrison and Ballou and brief comments on their position can be found in Peter Mayer (ed), *The Pacifist Conscience* (Harmondsworth, Penguin, 1966).

4 Quoted in Hinsley, p. 98.

5 Michael Howard, *War and the Liberal Conscience* (London, Temple Smith, 1978), pp. 45–6.

6 Jill Liddington, 'The Women's Peace Crusade: the History of a Forgotten Campaign', in Dorothy Thompson (ed.). *Over Our Dead Bodies: Woman Against the Bomb* (London, Virago, 1983), pp. 180–98.

7 Martin Ceadel, *Pacifism in Britain 1914–1945* (Oxford, The Clarendon Press, 1980), p. 72.

8 Peter Brock, *Twentieth Century Pacifism* (New York, Van Nostrand Reinhold Co., 1970), pp. 110–12 and *The War Resister*, 50, 1945 and 51, 1946.

9 Brock, pp. 142–50.

10 Nat Hentoff (ed.), *The Essays of A.J. Muste* (Indianapolis, Bobbs Merrill, 1967), p. xiv. The essays include Muste's 'Sketches for an Autobiography'. See also Nat Hentoff, *Peace Agitator; the Story of A.J. Muste* (New York, Macmillan, 1963).

11 Brock, pp. 158–60.

14 From protest to cultural creativity

Peace movements identified and revisited

Nigel Young

A. Distinguishing study and action

A central part of peace and conflict research is the study of those social movements called *peace* movements. One way to begin a discussion of this area of study (arguably a good way, because of the confusion that often arises here) is to note that Peace Studies is not itself a peace movement. It might seem to be otherwise. It might be claimed, for example, that peace education (to all appearances a part of Peace Studies) did for a while constitute something of a social movement when its advocates became a substantial lobby among teachers in schools – for example, in the early 1980s. But while peace educators may at times combine peace study and peace action, Peace Studies is by definition an intellectual endeavour, not a social movement. Though, like some other disciplines (e.g., sociology), it springs from deeply rooted social concerns and pragmatism, it is part of a project that goes beyond movements and parties, pressure groups and campaigns. While peace movements are phenomena concerned with political action or protest, Peace Studies, by definition, involves theory, analysis, and explanation and is not as such an agent or instigator of political change.

Peace Studies as a field has developed separately, in different conditions, and at different times from the peace movements, but, like them, in a context of growing peace concerns – especially during the "nuclear age." Clearly, specific peace movements and traditions have had an organizational impact in developing, motivating, and funding the field. At times the agenda of Peace Studies has been altered by the history of peace ideas, and the agendas of the movements. Equally, some findings of peace research and study have filtered into peace movements – especially factual information for policy campaigns – and through them into political decisions.

But while such factors sometimes lead students, activists, and antagonists of Peace Studies to confuse and conflate them, peace study or research and peace action remain conceptually distinct. Peace Studies is an academic phenomenon, a truth-seeking – even if not a narrowly scientific – enterprise. And it seeks truths in a way that is different from, say, Gandhian non-violence and its experiments with truth, or any seeking of "truth" through action and change. (Sometimes, indeed, peace movements have shunned truth in search of change.)

B. Why study peace movements?

Studying the failures and successes, however defined, of the peace action movements enables us to sharpen our knowledge of the interaction of states and society, ideals and realities, of ideology and utopia.[1] It illuminates the links between theory and practice, research and action, analysis and "publicism" – the latter perhaps serving as a euphemism for propaganda.

In my view, new forms of social movement have become an emergent expression or an external dimension of *all social life*. Political systems or states left to themselves may be incapable of creative human change – indeed, they are often the main obstacle to it. If this is the case then human change has to come from outside and from below, from the non-state sector or so-called *civil society*, especially non-governmental organizations. Comparatively researching these processes, and the role of peace movements within them, thus becomes a crucial part of our intellectual responsibility in the new millennium.

Insofar as inherited systems fail to represent adequately new forces and aspirations, social movements – some benign, and others problematic or pathological – emerge and become a central focus of attention. Such movements exist throughout the world and are a key fact of modern transnational life. They are a dominant factor in a multiplicity of global communities. Both overt and covert movements working within institutions, states, churches, and at the grassroots level see globalism or transnationalism as a fundamental part of their identity. Issues they raise – issues of culture, identity, and not least, language – clearly ought to be addressed by any attempt to understand the ways and means of peace.

C. The origins of peace movements

What is clear is that many of the present movements and movement organizations have their roots in the universalist ideas of the enlightenment and in the first peace societies after 1815. Advocacy for what we today call negative peace can be recognized in opposition to the kind of butchery seen in the Napoleonic Wars between 1793 and 1815. But an emphasis on *positive* peace also emerged in the form of enlightenment principles, as support for peace linked to social and human rights and justice, as well as visions of social harmony and schemes of universal cooperation, principles, and utopias.

Modern public protest arose in the eighteenth century and as the labour movement truly established the idea of a modern social movement. Along with other forms of political agitation from the late eighteenth century onwards, the problem of war became an issue attracting public gatherings and protest. There were popular peace organizations often rooted in Western, usually Anglo-Saxon, and usually Protestant, radicalism. These organizations were particularly linked to nonconformist Christianity and to the emergent idea of the role of the democratic political *lobby* or public pressure group or campaign, such as Chartism in England.

The particular issue of compulsory military service, an institution which was spreading rapidly and globally throughout the nineteenth century, also became a focal point for protest. It precipitated substantial migrations to non-conscripting countries, especially in the Americas. By the second half of the nineteenth century, the first social opposition to specific wars and atrocities took to the streets and the public halls. Notable orators from a range of traditions began to denounce war, the arms race, and national chauvinisms, already predicting by the 1890s the catastrophe of 1914 – and initiating what is really the first peace movement, properly so-called.

An interesting element of this movement was the way in which notable figures spoke out to large gatherings in a number of countries. Women like Rosa Luxemburg on the left, or Berta von Suttner, a conservative liberal, and men like Keir Hardie, leader of the Labour Party, and Jean Jaures, the great French Internationalist and anti-militarist, all spoke against the arms race, national chauvinisms, and the possibility of war. Each represented a different tradition, as did the young Bertrand Russell or as had Leo Tolstoy. Yet they all shared a sense of the scourge of war, years before Emperor Franz Josef signed the warrant at his desk in Bad Ischl and the German army entered Luxembourg. Indeed, Hardie embarked on world speaking tours in the preceding years. By 1914 four of these six were dead, and Luxemburg, a prisoner during the war, was to be murdered early in 1919. Russell, despite incarceration, survived to participate in five subsequent, significant phases of the increasingly international twentieth-century peace movement.

D. The nature of peace movements

Some points relevant to the nature of peace movements have already been made. Here I want to enter a little more fully into that discussion. Perhaps the first thing to note is that, if we wish to be most accurate, we *do* need to speak in the plural: while writers (including the present writer) sometimes refer loosely to "the" peace movement, in most periods and in many countries, "the" movement has been made up of a disparate set of organizations and movements. Some of these agencies had a general following, and others specific memberships. Many, like the anti-nuclear and anti-Vietnam War movements, have had both specific memberships and public manifestations. Their numbers expand and contract by the hundreds of thousands, even millions, within a few years. Moreover, there are a number of distinct approaches: religious and secular movements, political and ethical movements, single issue and multi-issue movements. They adopt diverse programs and address various constituencies in different areas and countries. Individuals join and rejoin; their priorities and ideologies change. Since these movements rise and fall at different times, and at a different *pace*, in various societies and even on the same issue, it is difficult to discern *one continuous social movement for peace* over the past century.

Recognizing that there are really many peace movements, and noticing certain general features they share (e.g., some form of mass activity on peace issues over some period of time), we still face the question whether a more precise definition can be fashioned: What exactly *makes* a peace movement a peace movement? It is an important, though difficult, question. And it is not just theoretically, but practically, important. We can see this when we consider how the issue of "official" and "unofficial" Vietnamese Buddhists arose to divide peace movements in the context of the Vietnam War. The independent, non-sponsored, essentially oppositional peace organizations emerging in Eastern and Central Europe by the 1980s raised similar issues. They were unofficial, often illegal, banned or underground. One had the situation of international peace movement conferences where debate arose as to whether to seat the delegates of official or of unofficial (dissident) peace movements or organizations or both. In these situations, sometimes both were represented, sometimes a painful or tactical choice was made, or empty chairs were symbolically left. The question of what is a *real* peace movement is not just academic. Certainly by the 1980s it was also highly charged, strategic, and political!

Academics have attempted to clarify the issue. April Carter proposes the following criteria as a litmus test by which to judge whether a movement is a peace movement; 1) its oppositional autonomy from a state or party, 2) its critical nonalignment with any state or military alliance, and 3) its adherence to nonviolence as a methodology of action or protest.[2] As a student of Eastern European resistance and change it is perhaps no accident that Carter should settle on these points. For her, the symmetric relationship between independent, nonaligned, and nonviolent peace groups critical of governments, both East and West, is obvious. This is true even though their agendas greatly differed.

But while helpful, provocative, and likely to be influential, Carter's scheme faces certain problems. A movement could after all be autonomous, nonaligned, and nonviolent and yet not seek *peace* in any recognized sense. (This is perhaps why Gandhi's movement and that of his successors like Vinoba Bhave are sometimes not seen as peace movements.) Without defining peace goals or aims, the Carter criteria seem insufficient as a defining statement.

Let us consider this in a little greater detail. The anti-Vietnam War coalitions of 1964–73, for example, included absolute and relative pacifists, as well as non-pacifists. It included those opposed to war as an institution, those opposed to this war in particular, those opposed to specific acts (bombing the north, invading Cambodia), those opposing military service (the draft), those supporting the Buddhists, those supporting wars of national liberation, those campaigning against specific weapons (e.g., napalm), those supporting the counter-culture and nonviolent revolution, and, finally, those supporting anti-imperialist class struggle and revolution. Clearly some of these, goals fall outside the peace movement as Carter would define it.[3] Some of the groups mentioned would use violence, were state- or party-sponsored, or were aligned; and some would not legitimately have been part of the peace movement of the time even if they had joined meetings and demonstrations. (I have argued at length that this confusion of identity in the New Left brought about a loss of its identity and its collapse and disintegration.[4])

The Hague peace conferences of 1899 and 1909, and many international organizations since then, were in part state-sponsored, A visit to the Peace Palace at the Hague, later to be home of the International Court of Justice, quickly reveals the degree to which this was not only an organization of state representatives. In addition to the private benefactors such as Carnegie, state gifts were also an important part of the enterprise. The irony of World War I's outbreak shortly after the completion of the palace, suggests the limitations of that episode. Like the *Palais des Nations* in Geneva it stands as a monument to one of the frustrated phases of liberal internationalism.

Communist internationalism, or *cominternationalism*, as I have termed it, was also born in the light of internationalist principles, however distorted they may have become in practice. Like liberal internationalism, cominternationalism was prepared to use force if necessary, and revolutionary force in particular, to abolish the perceived causes of war – which were notably capitalism and imperialism. The ideas of uniting the working people who lacked any fatherland, the abolition of the arms industries, and the eventual withering away of the state were not so far from the ideals of peace movements. In practice, Communist internationalism after Lenin became a pragmatic extension of the foreign policy exigencies of the USSR. It used "entrism" into existing peace movements, or created its own peace fronts, which were ostensibly coalitions under party control. But one cannot deny the genuine idealism of many of those who joined such groups.

Even liberal democracies have found it convenient at times to use "peace" as a public relations term. The Strategic Air Command, for example, announced that "peace is our profession," and several right wing "peace through strength" groups emerged. Why should we not include these under our definition of twentieth-century peace movements? They certainly were not overtly "pro-war" groups in the sense of some fascist or militarist movements. Nor did they share the irrationalist glorification of war prevalent amongst some intellectual and artistic groups at the outset of the 1914 war (e.g., Futurism). They simply believed the classical dictum: "If you want peace, prepare for war."

Thus it seems that Carter's definition is incomplete. What we can learn from it is that if we wish to be accurate and properly inclusive we need to also make some mention, in our definition, of *peace* as the goal of any social movement properly called by that name, while at the same time recognizing that views as to the nature of peace and how best to pursue it vary enormously. (More on this later.) Given the great diversity we face here, it seems that a precise and *convincing* analysis or definition of "peace movement," though perhaps desirable for some purposes, is difficult to attain.

E. Classifying peace movements

Similar difficulties attend the attempt to provide a precise way of *distinguishing* peace movements one from another. A number of classifications and typologies have been put forward. For example, Bob Overy, in a pioneering effort, develops the initially plausible idea that it should be possible to classify peace movements according to their ends or goals – are they against all wars, against some wars, against some aspects of wars or weapons?[5] But since movements and their members pursue so many different goals, often shifting priorities within their groups in the process, the typology seems problematic. They also often pursue overlapping goals. For example, many movements have had as a central goal the *prevention* of a war (Overy seems to miss this in his typology) – most notably, between 1918 and 1989, a major war between the West and the Soviet Union.[6] The same preventative goal existed with respect to wars in Central America, and, early in peace movement history, with respect to a potential war between Norway and Sweden at the time of Norway's secession.

Let us develop the first of these points a little more fully. Most peace movements have included multiple goals and issues. I will give two examples. First, we have the anti-Vietnam War coalitions of 1964–1973, mentioned earlier, in which *all* of Overy's goals are apparent. Another example is the nuclear disarmament movement after 1958, which also pursued multiple goals. Despite its adherence to unilateral nuclear disarmament (in Europe at least), the ND coalition in fact campaigned for multilateral goals, agreements to ban nuclear tests, and later, nuclear-free zones. Many of its organizations and groups opposed all nuclear weapons East and West; some just certain missiles such as Thor, or weapons like Polaris, or US bases. Some opposed deterrence or the threat of using nuclear weapons, while others did not. There were some who campaigned against manufacture as well as testing and use and linked this with economic conversion. Later on, others fused this together in opposition to nuclear power. By the 1980s the campaigns had involved feminist and ecological issues. Some adhered to civil disobedience, others did not. In the early years this was as divisive an issue as pacifism or political alignment. In the 1980s, feminism became contentious, especially in a separatist camp like Greenham. Nuclear disarmament became linked to issues as diverse as human rights or world hunger. In the 1960s the movement campaigned for prison reform and against the Greek military junta, and in the 1980s for the Helsinki process in Eastern Europe and the autonomy of Pacific islands.

It becomes clear, therefore, that to distinguish peace movements by goals is inappropriate. The problem is the same problem Max Weber found in defining the state by its ends: there are few ends or goals which peace movements, like states, do *not* pursue. Consequently, defining the means specific to them and their relations with states – as April Carter also stresses— become more significant.[7] Peace movements are part of society and culture. In terms of goals, what I would argue (and will develop more fully later on) is that the unifying idea of creating a peace culture or consciousness at a global level has become a latent, if not always manifest, goal and function of these social movements. But, as suggested, this is a goal that unifies (or may unify) peace movements, not one that enables us to distinguish between them.

It should be noted that Overy has also distinguished in his scheme between (a) movements which are lobbies or pressure groups, (b) movements which are mass movements, and (c) movements which are revolutionary (violent or nonviolent), and (d) the permanent or prophetic *minorities* which may aspire to become (b) or (c).[8] But while useful for some purposes, this scheme also fails to do justice to the complexity of the facts. In fact, movements usually involve elements from all of (a) to (d). For example, one of the best forms of creating leverage for a political lobby is to back it with mass protest. In England the Campaign for Nuclear

Disarmament (CND) was envisaged in 1958 as a short, sharp pressuring lobby. Ideally it would be led by political and intellectual elites, not the grassroots mass *movement* of public protest which did in fact evolve spontaneously in the next three years. Indeed many of the CND leaders were dismayed by the populist turn of events, especially when this Frankenstein monster demanded democratic structures for its campaign and was also permissive towards its direct action wing.

How then should peace movements be classified? A chronological approach which I have used, and which has been developed further by other scholars, particularly for the Japanese and European movements, is called *periodization*. This scheme chronicles the phases when a *mass* peace movement existed and others when it did not. The phases are measured by the degree of support, of mass activity on peace issues. It is an attempt to establish periods (though these are admittedly difficult to delimit).

For example: certainly a widespread, it diffuse and nationally separated, surge of support for peace developed in the two decades before 1915. This movement arose simultaneously and in the face of the opposing rise of a militarist-nationalist and imperialist groundswell. It arose again in reaction to World War I and its aftermath, in the 1920s. Mass peace protest emerged once more, though deeply divided, in the face of the arms race and war-fears of the 1930s and again in the late 1950s, lasting into the 1960s. This latter resurfacing encompassed two overlapping (but in many ways separate) peace movements and shifting issues and (to some extent) memberships in the mid-1960s. The latter, anti-Vietnam War protest, faded during the early 1970s. And then again a peace movement developed, initiated late in the decade, drawing on the same prophetic minorities and growing to a peak in North America and Western Europe in the early 1980s and in Eastern/Central Europe in the later 1980s.

If one concludes – and I believe one should – that the great nonviolent campaigns are peace movements, then the Gandhian movement of 1917–21, in the 1930s, and again in the 1940s should be included. So should the Civil Rights movement in the USA (1956–65) and the "people's power" movements of resistance in Eastern Europe in the 1980s – and there are countless other examples

As can be seen, periodization emphasises ebb and flow of support in its classification of peace movements. One should not, however, infer from these very real distinctions that participation in peace movements is entirely discontinuous. Indeed, studies like Sidney Tarrow's have shown the recidivism of activists in several different movements – even on the same issues, even in different countries.[9] In the discussion of "why peace movements fail," too little is made of the issue *of political generations*. There are, as we might say, cycles of protest. It is only a few remarkable individuals who can sustain high levels of movement activity over more than a few years, especially if imprisonment, injury or failure to achieve immediate goals occur. Social involvement tends therefore to have life-cycles, possibly three to five years long when participation is intense. Peace movements are no exception, which creates problems in sustaining an ongoing collective identity for such a movement. Nevertheless, there is plenty of evidence that people return to movement activity, albeit in a different way. For example, someone may be active in her or his student years (16–24), when ties and responsibilities are few. They may return in their mid-40s or 50s when middle life security has been achieved. And they may return yet again when retirement liberates them from regular work routines. To call these episodic involvements *failures*, as some do, is perhaps to miss the point that social movements do not encompass all of life.

We must expect peace movements to arise in different forms, in different places, and at different times. The anti-atomic survivors in Japan – the *Hibakusha* – were active earlier than the anti-nuclear testing lobbies of the later 1950s in the West and elsewhere. Moreover, even where the collapse of a peace movement is most dramatically evident, prophetic minorities remain. Within a few years of the 1914 debacle, for example, important new peace organizations like the War Resisters' International (WRI), the Women's International League for Peace and Freedom (WILPF), and others had been created. In 1940 the story was different and more surprising, The peace or pacifist movement did not collapse, even in the face of fascism and what appeared to many to be a "just war." Indeed, outside the dictatorships, and against all predictions – and contrary to many accounts by historians – the pacifist movement maintained considerable strength. From 1940–45 there were many more COs (Conscientious Objectors) than in 1914–18, and important voices spoke out against the bombing of mass civilian targets. By 1945, however, this movement had dissipated, and except among some scientists and religious leaders, it took some years for a public outcry against nuclear arms to emerge. Only the permanent minorities or peace sects or prophetic individuals tended to maintain a peace stance or witness in the post-war and post-holocaust wreckage of 1945. It seemed that peace, like poetry, had been dealt an almost mortal blow by World War II and the Holocaust.

F. Peace movements, peace traditions, peace coalitions

Recognizing that peace movements begin and end, ebb and flow, we can not only distinguish them one from another, but distinguish the notion of a peace movement from that of peace traditions.[10] Peace traditions in themselves are not movements. I have argued that most traditions, unlike movements, survive over time and are cumulative and evolutionary. They are often connected to particular issues – compulsory military service, for example – or outstanding individuals like Thoreau, Cobden, Tolstoy, Gandhi, and Rolland. They may be linked to ideas or political ideologies, such as *anarchism*, or to particular constituencies; the peace mobilization of women provides the major example since 1915, but the Japanese *Hibakusha* would be another. Though they are not movements as such, peace traditions may develop strong organizational expressions and engage in public activity. Sometimes these organizational manifestations are ephemeral, at other times long lasting.

The first peace societies, while certainly linked to traditions, cannot properly be called social movements. This is so even though they generally supported abolitionism and in some cases supported the issues of liberal, labour, and anarchist movements. Like the peace churches, they may be described as prophetic minorities. They have tended to survive the ebb and flow of larger public supported, mass peace movements and organizations. This has been so even in the face of appalling or daunting persecution, not least in the USA, from 1917–21.

Until the early twentieth century these permanent minorities were almost entirely rooted in religious faith. The Dutch leader, Domela Niewenhuis, was a Protestant pastor as well as a militant anti-war orator at the meetings of the Socialist Internationals. In later years Lord Donald Soper, a Methodist preacher, played a similar role in England, linking himself to the political left. There are countless similar examples; Dorothy Day, A.J. Muste, Martin Niemoller, the Berrigans, Bruce Kent, and indeed Gandhi and King.

Secular traditions such as internationalism in its liberal and socialist variants flowered in the later nineteenth century, having their roots in eighteenth-century cosmopolitanism and a belief in progress. Free trade, global communication, and peace institutions, including international law, characterized the liberal variant. The radical links of all working people across national boundaries and opposition to the war-making, arms-manufacturing, capitalist elites of all the imperial countries, were the bonds which linked many socialists, anarchists, and Marxists against war.

There is also a grey area in which pacifists and anti-militarists tried to synthesize these liberal, radical, and socialist ideas. However, as public movements, they rarely combined. The link between economic waste of resources in war and arms races was an issue monopolized by the left until the more recent emergence of ecological and Green movements within peace coalitions

Eventually from the latter variant of Socialist Internationalism a Communist Internationalism emerged. At first, in 1915 and at Zimmerwald, it was anti-war, without a state base, and with Leninist and Luxemburgist variants. But after 1917, or more properly after the founding of the Comintern (the Communist International), it tried to succeed the socialist internationals broken by World War I. The Communist peace tradition then had a base in the new Soviet state. After 1945 this evolved into a new, broader-based phase – the most successful, and arguably genuine, of all Communist-inspired or initiated projects: the Stockholm Peace Appeal of the early 1950s.

Many of these traditions did not work together or even see themselves as part of a common movement. However, at different times and in different places, broad coalitions did emerge, including many mentioned above. As one would expect, they usually formed or emerged around a specific issue *or goal*, or lowest common denominator. (This is where the typology spelled out by Overy may be helpful.) Illustrations might include a specific war like Algeria or Vietnam; particular weapons such as the atomic bomb, or napalm; or an issue like opposition to the draft in the US in the 1960s.

G. Resisting war: supporting peace?

Anti-conscriptionism has been mentioned and is sometimes linked with peace movements, but it presents a different problem. War resistance, refusal or evasion has often been highly individualized or self-preservatory, and certainly much of it is not pacifist. In point of fact, often it is not part of a peace movement. It is frequently localized, or community-based. Refusal to serve has involved a diverse set of sects or groups from Jehovah's Witnesses to "left-wing" Leninists and Maoists and "right-wing" Libertarians. Even so it did, as in the USA in 1917, often raise important general issues of civil liberties. Moreover, in places like West Germany, where 20 per cent of the conscriptable population became conscientious objectors, a natural constituency for a peace movement was created. I am convinced this helps explain the strength of the Greens and the growth of peace culture and *memory* in Germany since the 1980s, including de-nazification at a deeper level.

Anti-conscriptionist agitation for conscientious objection as a legal right and for alternatives to military service has spread dramatically in the past three decades. Agitation around these specific issues has more often become linked with peace organizations. Eventually these linked across national borders after World War I in such bodies as the War Resisters International (in the USA, War Resisters League). Very often, however, young men (but rarely young women) have merely voted with their feet to avoid serving in a war. And they continue doing so at the time of this writing. For a whole variety of reasons they have migrated, gone underground, deserted, or voluntarily gone to jail or even execution. Establishing the boundaries of peace movement activity, when confronted with such acts of individual or communal refusal, is again problematic.

H. From peace movement to peace culture

As mentioned earlier, one way of finding, or creating, unity within the many forms of peace activity I have outlined (and as I shall go on to argue, between them and Peace Studies) involves the idea of a *peace culture, or consciousness* at a global level. I would argue that emergent peace communities and networks, which are not necessarily yet a movement, are part of this project – a project that includes, but extends beyond, the opposition to war (that includes the idea of negative peace, but extends beyond it to positive peace). They make up the plural constitution of a peace culture as opposed to a war culture. This project is a conscious human endeavour with many manifestations, requiring great political will, cultural imagination, and scientific research. It demands as much funding as a war, or the preparations for war. Such an enterprise requires creating a transformatory consciousness, including a new peace history and a whole range of institutions. Many of these agencies will be in their infancy, and many others are yet to be born. In one sense such a project returns to the dreams and visions of a century ago, to images of world law, universal rights, and global institutions. It is with such an imaginative concept that I will conclude, since it relates very much to peace movement identity.

There is a convergence at the end of the twentieth century in the realm of the construction of peace culture and peace memory. Both peace action and peace theory and research are part of a slow transformation of consciousness. The so-called "just wars" of democracies against dictatorships – Spain in 1936 and Europe in 1939 – brought a new public legitimation of war. Yet one must weigh not only the cost of 80 million direct deaths as a result, but the clear and demonstrable connection between war and genocide from Armenia in 1915, through the Central European Holocaust, 1942–45, on to the Cambodian, Rwandan, and Bosnian killing fields. These horrors suggest that war has become barbarism, and that total war means more civilian than military casualties, as in World War II, Korea, Vietnam and in many of the wars of Africa. For a time it was said that anti-colonial wars of national liberation also gave a new legitimation to war or armed struggle. Yet the legacy of Algeria and Vietnam is a dubious one. Nationalism, as well as statism and alignment, have been as deeply divisive of peace culture as the use of violence, either by proxy or by protestors and activists

At the centre of this problem is the reconstruction of historical memory. I speak here of both a war memory, which looks at the inhuman toll beyond deaths in war, and a peace memory, which sustains the idea of a new public history and with it a firmer human global identity. This creation of culture has become more of a conscious effort as the century has progressed. One can multiply the examples indefinitely, but they might include a peace museum, a Peace Studies department, a peace-keeping force of the UN, a peace park, a centre for mediating disputes, a peace education text or a manual for nonviolent action, and a peace community or peace library. Such projects sustain identity just as many movements do.

A century ago some such projects were balanced between the positive creation of globalizing institutions and communications and "negative" war-prevention activities and propaganda. Others were ameliorative in nature, like the Red Cross and its attempts to deal with the aftermath of war. Participants were divided between scepticism of existing institutions and a willingness to work through them. The issue tended to be reductionist – for example, *the* problem could be reduced to that of economic inequality, or the lack of international law.

In a sense we have returned to that juncture with a more holistic and plural emphasis. This has been immensely expanded in past decades by the rise of such tendencies as ecological pacifism and feminist nonviolence, linking a range of issues such as patriarchy, violence, and socialization for war. Moreover, the revolution in global communications has made transnational linkages much more practical than a century ago. While these forms can be used by terrorists as much as by nonviolent activists, the sense of a world village, and the growth of multiple forms of English as a shared world-language, strengthen the forces for a peace movement in this wider sense. It allows a peace movement to sustain an identity of its own that is flexible and evolutionary rather than orthodox and dogmatic.

In part this culture has always been an anti-war culture. The truth of this is illustrated in a novel like Remarque's *All Quiet on the Western Front*, in films like *J'Accuse*, or *Shoah*, or a poem like Owen's *Dulce et Decorum Est*. All of these works of art remain in parts of the public memory longer than the so often ephemeral peace speech or pamphlet. Some peace prose, especially by women, retains a longer lasting quality simply because it is experiential and reflective and less rooted in the heat of conflict. One thinks, for example, of Rosa Luxemburg's letters from prison, Vera Britain's "testaments," Pat Barker's late twentieth-century novels, and Virginia Wolf's essays. The peace culture is inclusive in this and many other ways. There is, in addition, a positive and often more widely accessible and *popular* peace culture. Such celebratory expressions of life and hope include John Lennon's song "Imagine," the graffiti on the Berlin Wall, the glorification of life with personal objects placed on fences of the Greenham nuclear missile base, or the woven banners of the women's peace movement. The peace symbol itself is part of this still progressing cultural change. It was designed in 1958, in part an anti-nuclear "negative symbol" – N and D in semaphore – and was adopted by the positively creative counter culture in the 1960s as part of a linking of peace and love.

One of the abiding weaknesses of this peace movement, however, is a lack of material resources. While it campaigns for the diversion of funds from the arms trade and war into peaceful production and economic development, it rarely suggests the diversion of military taxation into a massive peace tax. The building of peace culture is hampered by this under-funding of peace institutions. From the United Nations to the local peace library, this is as serious a limitation as is the failure to sustain masses in protest movements. Indeed, if the latter is seen as simply part of the episodic character of peace movements, the issue of resources becomes most crucial. Even great works of anti-war art and literature – Otto Dix's astounding 1920s war etchings and Remarque's best-selling novel are good examples – were produced and a success because they paid. There was an economic market for them, and to create such a market is in large part an educational task.

In the 1960s, the phrase "the long march through the institutions" was used, and although this remains one strategic possibility for peace, the relative failure to promote the OSCE/CSCE (Organization for Security and Cooperation in Europe) after 1989 suggests its limitations. The longer march to create the *peace* institutions and culture I have described seems to me more plausible (of course, the two may not be incompatible). The Helsinki process was an interesting example of how governmental and non-governmental strategies can complement each other. It was one of the failures of the post-Cold War era that a military alliance (NATO) should be able to claim "victory" at the end of it all. The real victors were the peoples who emerged from the shadow of nuclear threat and bureaucratic oppression, largely through peaceful means. Part of peace culture is to reclaim that history.

Notes

1 In making my arguments I wish to acknowledge the use of certain sources not otherwise noted in the following endnotes: Peter Brock, *20th Century Pacifism* (New York: Van Nostrand, 1970). A revised, expanded and updated edition of this book is now available. See Peter Brock and Nigel Young, *Pacifism in the 20th Century* (Syracuse, NY: Syracuse University Press, 1999). I refer, further, to much of my research on war resistance which remains unpublished.

2 April Carter, *Peace Movements: International Protest and World Politics Since 1945* (London and New York: Longman, 1992) 14–25.

3 Carter; Bob Overy, *How Effective are Peace Movements?* (Montreal: Harvest Books, 1982).

4 R. Taylor and Nigel Young, eds., *Campaigns for Peace: British Peace Movements in the 20th Century* (Manchester, UK: Manchester University Press, 1987), Chapters 2 and 3.

5 Overy.

6 Overy.
7 Carter, See especially Chapter 1 and Conclusion.
8 Overy.
9 Sidney Tarrow's work has been released in new editions. See *Power in Movement: Social Movements, Collective Action and Politics* (Cambridge, MA: Cambridge University Press, 1998) and Sidney Tarrow and David Meyer, eds., *The Social Movement Society* (Totowa. NJ: Rowman and Littlefield, 1998).
10 See Nigel Young's chapter, *Towards a Comparative Analysis of Peace Movements*, eds. Katsuya Kodama and Unto Vesa (Brookfield, VT: Gower Publishers, 1990).

PART 2: PEACE THEORIES AND PEACE MOVEMENTS

Part II Suggestions for further reading

Brock, Peter and Nigel Young (1999). *Pacifism in the 20th Century*. Syracuse: Syracuse University Press.

Carter, April (1992). *Peace Movements: International Protest and World Politics Since 1945*. New York: Longman.

Einstein, Albert (not dated). *Ideas and Opinions*. New York: Wing Books.

Fahey, Joseph (1970). *War and the Christian Conscience*. Maryknoll, NY: Orbis Books.

Glover, Jonathan (2000). *Humanity A Moral History of the Twentieth Century*. New Haven: Yale University Press.

Howard, Michael (1978). *War and the Liberal Conscience*. London: Temple Smith.

Mayer, Peter, ed. (1966). *The Pacifist Conscience*. Harmondsworth: Penguin.

Somerville, John (2007). *The Philosophy of Peace*. Whitefish, MT: Kessinger Publishing.

Tarrow, Sidney (1998). *Power in Movement: Social Movements, Collective Action and Politics*. Cambridge: Cambridge University Press.

Walzer, Michael (1992). *Just and Unjust Wars: A Moral Argument with Historical Illustrations*. New York: Basic Books.

Journals

Interface: a journal for and about social movements: http://www.interfacejournal.net/
Mobilization: http://www.mobilization.sdsu.edu/
Pambazuka News: http://www.pambazuka.org/en/

Websites

International Alert: http://www.international-alert.org/
Peace History Society: http://www.peacehistorysociety.org/
Peace and Justice Studies Association: http://www.peacejusticestudies.org/
Peace and Collaborative Development Network: www.internationalpeaceandconflict.org/
Bibliography on Islam, Peace, and Nonviolence: www.nonviolenceinternational.net/islambib_001.htm

Questions for reflection and discussion

1   Take a philosophical view (Kant, William James, etc.) of peace/war and assess its strengths and weaknesses.
2   Take a spiritual/religious view (Tolstoy, Dalai Lama, etc.) of peace/war and assess its strengths and weaknesses.
3   Take scientific/ethical view (The Russell--Einstein Manifesto, etc.) of peace/war in the nuclear age and assess its strengths and weaknesses.
4   Pick a peace movement after 1900 and assess its strengths and weaknesses.
5   How do assess the strengths and weaknesses of pacifism, both 'pragmatic' and 'absolute'?

Part 3

The meanings and nature of conflict

SUMMARY

What is a conflict? Is conflict always undesirable? What is the range of human conflicts? What are the reasons for conflicts? And when conflicts arise, how should one optimally deal with them?

The English word 'conflict' derives from the Latin word *confligere*, to 'strike together'. For example, because it is physically impossible for two objects, such as billiard balls, to occupy the same place, if one is in motion toward the other and strikes it, then it collides or conflicts with it and displaces it. Conflict is inevitable and may or may not be destructive.

Within the human realm, a conflict may occur within a person, between two or more individuals or groups, or within or between large social organizations, most notably nation states. Hence there is a variety of kinds of conflicts, ranging from the intra-psychic to the international.

Conflicts within and between individuals may occur for a number of reasons. For Sigmund Freud, we are torn between our innate drives for love and self-preservation on the one hand, and aggression and destruction on the other hand. Such contemporary conflict theorists as Johan Galtung tend to eschew such overarching explanations and instead claim that human conflicts are largely due to a real or perceived incompatibility, or contradiction, between conflicting parties' attitudes, behaviours, interests, needs, positions and/or values.

If conflicts are not addressed, or 'managed' at an early stage in the dispute, they may escalate, and the conflict parties may employ whatever means they have available, including threats, legal reprisals, and direct or indirect violence, to 'defeat' the other and 'win' the conflict. This happens frequently between such parties as couples in the process of a nasty divorce, as well as between nations (India and Pakistan, for example), existing states and nascent nation-states (Israel and Palestine), and states and non-state adversaries (the United States and Al-Qaeda).

Parties in conflict may resort to three basic types of behaviour: persuasion, coercion and reward. If arguments fail, the force of arms often intercedes. If and when the opponents tire of threats and/or violence, one or both parties may be induced by positive and/or negative sanctions to cease hostilities.

Conflicts have different outcomes. One side may 'win' and the other 'lose' (but not be eliminated), as in divorce settlements involving contested assets or child custody, or in many international disputes. Both sides may withdraw temporarily from the conflict, but because one or both parties may not believe its interests/needs were satisfactorily addressed, they might resume the conflict later.

Many international conflicts fit this profile, and historians argue that World War II resulted in part from the failure to address successfully long-simmering resentments on the part of Germany against the 'victors' of World War I. Israel's ongoing conflicts with its Arab neighbours, and many insurrections and 'terrorist' actions against governments, especially against occupying powers, also conform to this model.

A conflict may infrequently result in the real or perceived total elimination of the 'enemy'. The Sri Lankan government, for example, claims to have 'eliminated' the Tamil Tigers; the Allies 'destroyed' the Nazi regime; and the 'Free World', led by the United States, 'won' the Cold War once the Soviet Union collapsed.

But in the nuclear era, it is possible that a conflict involving the significant use of weapons of mass destruction would conclude with the elimination not only of the conflicting parties, but with the end of humanity and possibly of life on Earth.

Accordingly, we must devise and implement efficacious and enduring modes of conflict analysis, prevention, management, resolution and transformation. There are two dominant, and sometimes 'conflicting', models of addressing conflicts. From a 'realist', 'security-oriented' perspective, actions taken to address conflicts include such bellicose measures as wars, espionage and sanctions, often in tandem with diplomacy. The goal is to defend one's perceived interests and to defeat or 'neutralize' the 'enemy', preferably by 'managing' a conflict so that it does not spiral out of control, and by 'resolving' it through a mixture of violent and nonviolent means, such as mediation, arbitration, ceasefires and treaties. The Cuban missile crisis is a classic example of international conflict management. But since the underlying reasons for the conflict are not addressed or resolved, hostilities may resume at a later time.

A peace-oriented perspective, in contrast, stresses the prevention rather than the management of conflicts, and nonviolent conflict transformation as the preferred means of conflict resolution. Since violence rarely works to control violence, nonviolent strategies and tactics must be utilized if conflicting parties are to transform their attitudes and behaviour from enmity to tolerance. Gandhi's campaign for Indian independence, Martin Luther King's struggle for civil rights in the U.S., and the 'Velvet Revolution' of 1989 are examples of nonviolent conflict resolution.

Conflict appears to be inherent in human relations and is therefore unlikely to be eliminated. Hence the mission of conflict transformers and peace-workers is not to end conflict, but as Kenneth Boulding said, to 'make the world safe for conflict'. This means to reduce the likelihood that social conflict erupts into violent combat and war.

Violence: its nature, costs and perceived benefits

Violence may be the worst injury, the most traumatic act, human beings inflict on each other. If a peaceful alien species were to observe human behaviour, perhaps the conduct that would most perplex them would be the deliberate infliction of pain, suffering and death by members of the same species against others of their species, especially when survival is not at stake.

Identifying violence appears simple – we know it when we see or feel it. But defining violence is tricky. The noted political philosopher C.A.J. (Tony) Coady, appropriating the *Oxford English Dictionary*, offers a 'restricted' definition of violence in purely physical terms: 'The exercise of physical force so as to inflict injury on or damage to persons or property; action or conduct characterised by this.'[1] Johan Galtung, on the other hand, has a 'wide' definition: Galtung's definition is one that includes 'direct', 'structural' and 'cultural' violence, in addition to physical and psychological violence. And violence and nonviolence are not absolutes – they lie on a continuum.

The World Health Organization (WHO), in its 'World Report on Violence and Health' (2002), has also adopted an expansive definition of violence as:

> The intentional use of physical force, threatened or actual, against oneself, another person, or against a group or community, that either results in or has a high likelihood of resulting in injury, death, psychological harm, maldevelopment or deprivation.
>
> (WHO, 'An Internationally Accepted Definition of Violence', Chapter 17)

The WHO further provides a typology, subdividing violence into self-directed violence, interpersonal violence and collective violence, each of which may be 'physical, sexual, psychological, and involving deprivation or neglect'.

The Geneva Declaration on Armed Violence and Development is a diplomatic initiative aimed at addressing the interrelations between armed violence and development. Although the incidence of armed conflict has declined in recent years, the number of people killed by armed violence has not. More than 740,000 men, women and children die each year as a result of armed violence. The majority of these deaths – 490,000 – occur in countries that are not affected by armed conflicts.

The Geneva Declaration is designed to support states and civil society actors to achieve measurable reductions in the global burden of armed violence in conflict and non-conflict settings by 2015 (and beyond). The Geneva Declaration was first adopted by 42 nations in 2006 during a Ministerial Summit in Geneva. The Ministerial Summit reflected a political will by both representatives from affluent donor nations and from countries directly affected by armed violence to develop measures to reduce political and criminal armed violence in order to enhance sustainable development at global, regional and national levels. The Geneva Declaration is now endorsed by over 100 nations and is the strongest political statement to date that addresses the impact of armed violence within a development context.

According to the Geneva Declaration, most violent deaths occur in non-war situations, due to small or large-scale criminally or politically motivated violence. And weapons matter, with approximately 60% of all homicides committed with firearms. Unsurprisingly, the consequences of armed violence are felt hardest by the poor and most vulnerable people, particularly in Latin America, Asia, Africa and the Middle East. But armed violence is preventable, and the Geneva Declaration emphasizes the role of early intervention in saving lives.

The WHO concurs, and in 'Violence prevention: the evidence', lists seven specific violence-prevention strategies. These include:

> developing safe, stable and nurturing relationships between children and their parents and caregivers; . . . reducing access to guns, knives and pesticides; . . . changing cultural and social norms that support violence; [and] victim identification, care and support programmes.
>
> (WHO, Violence Prevention: The Evidence, Overview, Chapter 18)

Finally, one of the twentieth century's most eminent political thinkers, Hannah Arendt, offers her own reflections 'On Violence'. Arendt writes against the background of a century (the twentieth), which was 'a century of wars and revolutions . . . a century of that violence which is believed to be their common denominator' (Arendt, Chapter 15). Arendt claims that 'warfare has lost much of its effectiveness and nearly all its glamour' because of the 'technical development of the instruments of violence', especially nuclear and biological weapons. And she argues that 'the chief reason warfare is with us . . . [is] the simple fact that no substitute for this final arbiter in international affairs has yet appeared on the political scene'. Finally, although some violence, such as rage, may have 'beastly' and or 'irrational' sources, political violence in general and revolutionary violence in general may sometimes be 'deliberate' and even 'rational', because it 'is the only way to set the scales of justice right again'. Arendt claims that violence may be 'effective', and 'life itself, the immortal life of the species, nourished . . . by the . . . dying of its individual members . . . is actualised in the practice of violence.'

We invite you to analyse the actual costs and perceived benefits of violence in all its dimensions.

The reasons for violent conflicts and terrorism

People have been speculating about the reasons for war and other types of political and non-political violence for millennia. More recently, in part due to the horrific carnage of World Wars I and II, social scientists, philosophers and psychoanalysts have begun systematically, as well as speculatively, to propose causal explanations for belligerent behaviour. In this section, we present a few of these speculations and analyses.

Albert Einstein and Sigmund Freud engaged in one of the twentieth century's most famous epistolary exchanges, commencing on July 30, 1932, when Einstein addressed 'the most insistent of all problems civilisation has to face . . .: Is there any way of delivering mankind from the menace of war?' (Einstein, Chapter 19). Einstein argues that the principal reasons for war (aka international conflict) lie in the minds and deeds of 'the political power-hungry . . . composed of individuals, who regard warfare, the manufacture and sale of arms, simply as an occasion to advance their personal interests and enlarge their personal authority'. To counteract this, Einstein sees 'a simple way of dealing with . . . the problem: the setting up, but international consensus, of a legislative and judicial body to settle every conflict arising between nations.' But Einstein does not appear optimistic that even this step (which eventuated about a decade later in the creation of the United Nations) will end war 'because man has within him a lust for hatred and destruction'. He asks Freud 'to present the problem of world peace in the light of [Freud's] most recent discoveries.'

In his letter written to Einstein in September 1932, Freud concurred with much of Einstein's analysis but substituted 'the balder and harsher term violence' for Einstein's word 'might' in assessing the origins of conflict. To Freud, human history is in large part the history of human violence, with the human race having exchanged 'numerous, and indeed unending, minor wars for wars on a grand scale that are rare but all the more destructive' (Freud, Chapter 20). Freud postulates the existence of 'the death' or 'destructive instinct' (calling it by the ancient Greek term, *thanatos*) as the ultimate, but largely hidden, core of the problem. But in opposition to *thanatos*, Freud poses a 'life' (or erotic) 'instinct', Eros, which may 'encourage the growth of emotional ties between men [and] must operate against war.' Like Einstein, Freud argues that:

> Wars will only be prevented . . . if mankind unites in setting up a central authority to which the right of giving judgment upon all conflicts of interest shall be handed over. There are clearly two separate requirements..: the creation of a supreme authority and its endowment with the necessary power. One without the other would be useless.
>
> (Ibid.)

At end of World War II, a little more than a decade after Einstein and Freud pleaded for a supranational authority, the United Nations was created (but without 'supreme authority' over its member states and lacking 'the necessary power' to impose its will over belligerent nations). UNESCO, the United Nations Educational, Scientific and Cultural Organization, in part to scientifically refute the existence and importance of a 'death instinct', convened a group of distinguished social and biological scientists in 1986 in Seville, Spain. They issued a 'Statement on Violence' that rejected claims that 'we have inherited a tendency to make war from our animal ancestors'; 'that war or any other violent behaviour is genetically programmed into our human nature'; 'that in . . . human evolution there has been a selection for aggressive behaviour more than for other kinds of behaviour'; 'that humans have a violent brain'; and 'that war is caused by "instinct" or any single motivation'. The authors of the Seville Statement concluded that 'biology does not condemn humanity to war . . . [and] just as "wars begin in the minds of men", peace also begins in our minds. The same species who invented war is capable of inventing peace.'

Charles Webel and Viera Sotakova summarize important empirical and theoretical psychological contributions to understanding peace and conflict. They present and assess psychological theories and findings regarding the roots of violence, aggression and personality; the importance of social situations, groups, prejudice, images of the enemy and human needs; the significance of attributions, intergroup relations and just world theories of behaviour; and the relevance of altruism and reconciliation for diminishing violence and building peace. They suggest possible future directions for peace psychology and peace research more generally.

Noam Chomsky, the eminent linguistics scholar and political analyst, argues – by appropriating and inverting former U.S. President Ronald Reagan's phase 'the evil scourge of terrorism' – that the real 'plague of the modern age' is not 'their' terrorism 'against us', but 'our' (American) 'state-directed international terrorism' against 'them' (nations and peoples that resist 'us'). Chomsky claims that 'state-directed international terrorism is considered an appropriate tool of diplomacy across the [U.S.] political spectrum.' He provides numerous examples to support his contention, including the U.S. bombing of Libya; funding of the Afghan *jihadi* movement and dictators in Pakistan; attacks on socialist governments in Cuba, Nicaragua and Chile; and support for terrorist regimes in El Salvador, Brazil and Argentina, inter alia. Chomsky dissects 'the good war' being conducted by the U.S. (and its allies) in Afghanistan since October 2001 and concludes that this invasion and occupation, like the American invasion and occupation of Iraq, did not confront 'the evil scourge of terrorism' but instead 'caused a seven-fold increase in terror'. From these experiences, Chomsky concludes that 'violence engenders violence, while sympathy and concern cool passions and can evoke compassion and empathy'. To attempt to end the plague of terrorism, Chomsky recommends that 'we' 'end our own role as perpetrators. . . . Attend to the grievances [of those we brand as "terrorists"]. . . . [and] deal with it [an act of terror against us] as a criminal act.' These nonviolent measures of confronting terrorism work, as in the case of Northern Ireland, in contrast with the ongoing 'war on terror'.

We now invite you to reach your own conclusions once you've studied the range of analyses and recommendations presented in the texts that follow.

Note

1 C.A.J. Coady, 'The Idea of Violence', in *Violence and its Alternatives*, Manfred B. Steger and Nancy S. Lind, eds (New York: St. Martin's Press, 1999), 25.

15 On violence

Hannah Arendt

These reflections were provoked by the events and debates of the last few years as seen against the background of the twentieth century, which has become indeed, as Lenin predicted, a century of wars and revolutions, hence a century of that violence which is currently believed to be their common denominator. There is, however, another factor in the present situation which, though-predicted by nobody, is of at least equal importance. The technical development of the implements of violence has now reached the point where no political goal could conceivably correspond to their destructive potential or justify their actual use in armed conflict. Hence, warfare – from time immemorial the final merciless arbiter in international disputes – has lost much of its effectiveness and nearly all its glamour. The "apocalyptic" chess game between the superpowers, that is, between those that move on the highest plane of our civilization, is being played according to the rule "if either 'wins' it is the end of both";[1] it is a game that bears no resemblance to whatever war games preceded it. Its "rational" goal is deterrence, not victory, and the arms race, no longer a preparation for war, can now be justified only on the grounds that more and more deterrence is the best guarantee of peace. To the question how shall we ever be able to extricate ourselves from the obvious insanity of this position, there is no answer.

Since violence – as distinct from power, force, or strength – always needs *implements* (as Engels pointed out long ago),[2] the revolution of technology, a revolution in tool-making, was especially marked in warfare. The very substance of violent action is ruled by the means-end category, whose chief characteristic; if applied to human affairs, has always been that the end is in danger of being overwhelmed by the means which it justifies and which are needed to reach it. Since the end of human action, as distinct from the end products of fabrication, can never be reliably predicted, the means used to achieve political goals are more often than not of greater relevance to the future world than the intended goals.

Moreover, while the results of men's actions are beyond the actors' control, violence harbors within itself an additional element of arbitrariness; nowhere does Fortuna, good or ill luck, play a more fateful role in human affairs than on the battlefield, and this intrusion of the utterly unexpected does not disappear when people call it a "random event" and find it scientifically suspect; nor can it be eliminated by simulations, scenarios, game theories, and the like. There is no certainty in these matters, not even an ultimate certainty of mutual destruction under certain calculated circumstances. The very fact that those engaged in the perfection of the means of destruction have finally reached a level of technical development where their aim, namely, warfare, is on the point of disappearing altogether by virtue of the means at its disposal[3] is like an ironical reminder of this all-pervading unpredictability, which we encounter the moment we approach the realm of violence. The chief reason warfare is still with us is neither a secret death wish of the human species, nor an irrepressible instinct of aggression, nor, finally and more plausibly, the serious economic and social dangers inherent in disarmament,[4] but the simple fact that no substitute for this final arbiter in international affairs has yet appeared on the political scene. Was not Hobbes right when he said: "Covenants, without the sword, are but words"?

Nor is a substitute likely to appear so long as national independence, namely, freedom from foreign rule, and the sovereignty of the state, namely, the claim to unchecked and unlimited power in foreign affairs, are identified. (The United States of America is among the few countries where a proper separation of freedom and sovereignty is at least theoretically possible.) That war is still the *ultima ratio*, the old continuation of politics by means of violence, in the foreign affairs of the underdeveloped countries is no argument against its obsoleteness, and the fact that only small countries without nuclear and biological weapons can still afford it is no consolation. It is a secret from nobody that the famous random event is most likely to arise from those parts of the world where the old adage "There is no alternative to victory" retains a high degree of plausibility.

Under these circumstances, there are, indeed, few things that are more frightening than the steadily increasing prestige of scientifically minded brain trusters in the councils of government during the last decades. The trouble is not that they are cold-blooded enough to "think the unthinkable," but that they do not *think*. Instead of indulging in such an old-fashioned, uncomputerizable activity, they reckon with the consequences of certain hypothetically assumed constellations without, however, being able to test their hypotheses against actual occurrences. The logical flaw in these hypothetical constructions of future events is always the same: what first appears as a hypothesis – with or without its implied alternatives, according to the level of sophistication – turns immediately, usually after a few paragraphs, into a "fact," which then gives birth to a whole string of similar non-facts, with the result that the purely speculative character of the whole enterprise is forgotten. Needless to say, this is not science but pseudo-science, "the desperate attempt of the social and behavioral sciences," in the words of Noam Chomsky, "to imitate the surface features of sciences that really have significant intellectual content." And the most obvious and "most profound objection to this kind of strategic theory is not its limited usefulness but its danger, for it can lead us to believe we have an understanding of events and control over their flow which we do not have," as Richard N. Goodwin recently pointed out in a review article that had the rare virtue of detecting the "unconscious humor" characteristic of many of these pompous pseudo-scientific theories.[5]

No one engaged in thought about history and politics can remain unaware of the enormous role violence has always played in human affairs, and it is at first glance rather surprising that violence has been singled out so seldom for special consideration.[6] [. . .] This shows to what an extent violence and its arbitrariness were taken for granted and therefore neglected; no one questions or examines what is obvious to all. Those who saw nothing but violence in human affairs, convinced that they were "always haphazard, not serious, not precise" (Renan) or that God was forever with the bigger battalions, had nothing more to say about either violence or history. Anybody looking for some kind of sense in the records of the past was almost bound to see violence as a marginal phenomenon. Whether it is Clausewitz calling war "the continuation of politics by other means," or Engels defining violence as the accelerator of economic development,[7] the emphasis is on political or economic continuity, on the continuity of a process that remains determined by what preceded violent action. Hence, students of international relations have held until recently that "it was a maxim that a military resolution in discord with the deeper cultural sources of national power could not be stable," or that, in Engels' words, "wherever the power structure of a country contradicts its economic development" it is political power with its means of violence that will suffer defeat.[8]

Today all these old verities about the relation between war and politics or about violence and power have become inapplicable. The Second World War was not followed by peace but by a cold war and the establishment of the military-industrial-labor complex. To speak of "the priority of war-making potential as the principal structuring force in society," to maintain that "economic systems, political philosophies, and corpora juris serve and extend the war system, not vice versa," to conclude that "war itself is the basic social system, within which other secondary modes of social organization conflict or conspire" – all this sounds much more plausible than Engels' or Clausewitz's nineteenth-century formulas. Even more conclusive than this simple reversal proposed by the anonymous author of the *Report from Iron Mountain* – instead of war being "an extension of diplomacy (or of politics, or of the pursuit of economic objectives)," peace is the continuation of war by other means – is the actual development in the techniques of warfare. In the words of the Russian physicist Sakharov, "A thermonuclear war cannot be considered a continuation of politics by other means (according to the formula of Clausewitz). It would be a means of universal suicide."[9]

Moreover, we know that "a few weapons could wipe out all other sources of national power in a few moments,"[10] that biological weapons have been devised which would enable "small groups of individuals . . . to upset the strategic balance" and would be cheap enough to be produced by "nations unable to develop nuclear striking forces,"[11] that "within a very few years" robot soldiers will have made "human soldiers completely obsolete,"[12] and that, finally, in conventional warfare the poor countries are much less vulnerable than the great powers precisely because they are "underdeveloped," and because technical superiority can "be much more of a liability than an asset" in guerrilla wars.[13] What all these uncomfortable novelties add up to is a complete reversal in the relationship between power and violence, foreshadowing another reversal in the future relationship between small and great powers. The amount of violence at the disposal of any given country may soon not be a reliable indication of the country's strength or a reliable guarantee against destruction by a substantially smaller and weaker power. And this bears an ominous similarity to one of political science's oldest insights, namely that power cannot be measured in terms of wealth, that an abundance of wealth may erode power, that riches are particularly dangerous to the power and well-being of republics [. . .]

[. . .]

To speak about the nature and causes of violence in these terms must appear presumptuous. [. . .]

First, while I find much of the work of the zoologists fascinating, I fail to see how it can possibly apply to our problem. In order to know that people will fight for their homeland we hardly had to discover instincts of "group territorialism" in ants, fish, and apes; and in order to learn that overcrowding results in irritation and aggressiveness, we hardly needed to experiment with rats. One day spent in the slums of any big city should have sufficed. I am surprised and often delighted to see that some animals behave like men; I cannot see how this could either justify or condemn human behavior. I fail to understand why we are asked "to recognize that man behaves very much like a group territorial species," rather than the other way round – that certain animal species behave very much like men.[14]

Second, the research results of both the social and the natural sciences tend to make violent behavior even more of a "natural" reaction than we would have been prepared to grant without them. Aggressiveness, defined as an instinctual drive, is said to play the same functional role in the household of nature as the nutritive and sexual instincts in the life process of the individual and the species. But unlike these instincts, which are activated by compelling bodily needs on one side, by outside stimulants on the other, aggressive instincts in the animal kingdom seem to be independent of such provocation; on the contrary, lack of provocation apparently leads to instinct frustration, to "repressed" aggressiveness, which according to psychologists causes a damming up of "energy" whose eventual explosion will be all the more dangerous. (It is as though the *sensation* of hunger in man would increase with the decrease of hungry people.)[15] In this interpretation, violence without provocation is "natural"; if it has lost its *rationale*, basically its function in self-preservation, it becomes "irrational," and this is allegedly the reason why men can be more "beastly" than other animals. [. . .]

Quite apart from the misleading transposition of physical terms such as "energy" and "force" to biological and zoological data, where they do not make sense because they cannot be measured,[16] I fear there lurks behind these newest "discoveries" the oldest definition of the nature of man – the definition of man as the *animal rationale*, according to which we are distinct from other animal species in nothing but the additional attribute of reason. Modern science, starting uncritically from this old assumption, has gone far in "proving" that men share all other properties with some species of the animal kingdom – except that the additional gift of "reason" makes man a more dangerous beast. It is the use of reason that makes us dangerously "irrational," because this reason is the property of an "aboriginally instinctual being."[17] The scientists know, of course, that it is man the tool maker who has invented those long-range weapons that free him from the "natural" restraints we find in the animal kingdom, and that tool-making is a highly complex *mental* activity.[18] Hence science is called upon to cure us of the side effects of reason by manipulating and controlling our instincts, usually by finding harmless outlets for them after their "life-promoting function" has disappeared. The standard of behavior is again derived from other animal species, in which the function of the life instincts has not been destroyed through the intervention of human reason. And the specific distinction between man and beast is now, strictly speaking, no longer reason (the *lumen naturale* of the human animal) but science, the knowledge of these standards and the techniques applying them. According to this view, man acts irrationally and like a beast if he refuses to listen to the scientists or is ignorant of their latest findings. As against these theories and their implications, I shall argue in what follows that violence is neither beastly nor irrational – whether we understand these terms in the ordinary language of the humanists or in accordance with scientific theories.

That violence often springs from rage is a commonplace, and rage can indeed be irrational and pathological, but so can every other human affect. It is no doubt possible to create conditions under which men are dehumanized – such as concentration camps, torture, famine – but this does not mean that they become animal-like; and under such conditions, not rage and violence, but their conspicuous absence is the clearest sign of dehumanization. Rage is by no means an automatic reaction to misery and suffering as such; no one reacts with rage to an incurable disease or to an earthquake or, for that matter, to social conditions that seem to be unchangeable. Only where there is reason to suspect that conditions could be changed and are not does rage arise. Only when our sense of justice is offended do we react with rage, and this reaction by no means necessarily reflects personal injury, as is demonstrated by the whole history of revolution, where invariably members of the upper classes touched off and then led the rebellions of the oppressed and downtrodden. To resort to violence when confronted with outrageous events or conditions is enormously tempting because of its inherent immediacy and swiftness. To act with *deliberate* speed goes against the grain of rage and violence, but this does not make them irrational. On the contrary, in private as well as public life there are situations in which the very swiftness of a violent act may be the only appropriate remedy. The point is not that, this permits us to let off steam – which indeed can be equally well done by pounding the table or slamming the door. The point is that under certain circumstances violence – acting without argument or speech and without counting the consequences – is the only way to set the scales of justice right again. (Billy Budd, striking dead the man who bore false witness against him, is the classical example.) In this sense, rage and the violence that sometimes – not always – goes with it belong among the "natural" *human* emotions, and to cure man of them would mean nothing less than to dehumanize or emasculate him. That such acts, in which men take the law into their own hands for justice's sake, are in conflict with the constitutions of civilized communities is undeniable; but their antipolitical character, so manifest in Melville's great story, does not mean that they are inhuman or "merely" emotional.

Absence of emotions neither causes nor promotes rationality. "Detachment and equanimity" in view of "unbearable tragedy" can indeed be "terrifying,"[19] namely, when they are not the result of control but an evident manifestation of incomprehension. In order to respond reasonably one must first of all be "moved," and the opposite of emotional is not "rational," whatever that may mean, but either the inability to be moved, usually a pathological phenomenon, or sentimentality, which is a perversion of feeling. Rage and violence turn irrational only when they are directed against substitutes, and this, I am afraid, is precisely what the psychiatrists and polemologists concerned with human aggressiveness recommend, and what corresponds, alas, to certain moods and unreflecting attitudes in society at large. [. . .]

Moreover, if we inquire historically into the causes likely to transform *engagés* into *enragés*, it is not injustice that ranks first, but hypocrisy. Its momentous role in the later stages of the French Revolution, when Robespierre's war on hypocrisy transformed the "despotism of liberty" into the Reign of Terror, is too well known to be discussed here; but it is important to remember that this war had been declared long before by the French moralists who saw in hypocrisy the vice of all vices and found it ruling supreme in "good society," which somewhat later was called bourgeois society. Not many authors of rank glorified violence for violence's sake; but these few – Sorel, Pareto, Fanon – were motivated by a much deeper hatred of bourgeois society and were led to a much more radical break with its moral standards than the conventional Left, which was chiefly inspired by compassion and a burning desire for justice. [. . .]

And this violence again is not irrational. Since men live in a world of appearances and, in their dealing with it, depend on manifestation, hypocrisy's conceits – as distinguished from expedient ruses, followed by disclosure in due time – cannot be met by so-called reasonable behavior. Words can be relied on only if one is sure that their function is to reveal and not to conceal. It is the semblance of rationality, much more than the interests behind it, that provokes rage. To use reason when reason is used as a trap is not "rational"; just as to use a gun in self-defense is not "irrational." This violent reaction against hypocrisy, however justifiable in its own terms, loses its *raison d'être* when it tries to develop a strategy of its own with specific goals; it becomes "irrational" the moment it is "rationalized," that is, the moment the reaction in the course of a contest turns into an action, and the hunt for suspects, accompanied by the psychological hunt for ulterior motives, begins.

Although the effectiveness of violence does not depend on numbers – one machine gunner can hold hundreds of well-organized people at bay – nonetheless in collective violence its most dangerously attractive features come to the fore, and this by no means because there is safety in numbers. It is perfectly true that in military as well as revolutionary action "individualism is the first [value] to disappear";[20] in its stead, we find a kind of group coherence which is more intensely felt and proves to be a much stronger, though less lasting, bond than all the varieties of friendship, civil or private.[21] To be sure, in all illegal enterprises, criminal or political, the group, for the sake of its own safety, will require "that each individual perform an irrevocable action" in order to burn his bridges to respectable society before he is admitted into the community of violence. But once a man is admitted, he will fall under the intoxicating spell of "the practice of violence [which] binds men together as a whole, since each individual forms a violent link in the great chain, a part of the great organism of violence which has surged upward."[22]

Fanon's words point to the well-known phenomenon of brotherhood on the battlefield, where the noblest, most selfless deeds are often daily occurrences. Of all equalizers, death seems to be the most potent, at least in the few extraordinary situations where it is permitted to play a political role. Death, whether faced in actual dying or in the inner awareness of one's own mortality, is perhaps the most antipolitical experience there is. It signifies that we shall disappear from the world of appearances and shall leave the company of our fellowmen, which are the conditions of all politics. As far as human experience is concerned, death indicates an extreme of loneliness and impotence. But faced collectively and in action, death changes its countenance; now nothing seems more likely to intensify our vitality than its proximity. Something we are usually hardly aware of, namely, that our own death is accompanied by the potential immortality of the group we belong to and, in the final analysis, of the species, moves into the center of our experience. It is as though life itself, the immortal life of the species, nourished, as it were, by the sempiternal dying of its individual members, is "surging upward," is actualized in the practice of violence.

It would be wrong, I think, to speak here of mere sentiments. After all, one of the outstanding properties of the human condition is here finding an adequate experience. In our context, however, the point of the matter is that these experiences, whose elementary force is beyond doubt, have never found an institutional, political expression, and that death as an equalizer plays hardly any role in political philosophy, although human mortality – the fact that men are "mortals," as the Greeks used to say – was understood as the strongest motive for political action in prephilosophic political thought. It was the certainty of death that made men seek immortal fame in deed and word and that prompted them to establish a body politic which was potentially immortal. Hence, politics was precisely a means by which to escape from the equality before death into a distinction assuring some measure of deathlessness. (Hobbes is the only political philosopher in whose work death, in the form of fear of violent death, plays a crucial role. But it is not equality before death that is decisive for Hobbes; it is the equality of fear resulting from the equal ability to kill possessed by everyone that persuades men in the state of nature to bind themselves into a commonwealth.) At any event, no body politic I know of was ever founded on equality before death and its actualization in violence; the suicide squads in history, which were indeed organized on this principle and therefore often called themselves "brotherhoods," can hardly be counted among political organizations. But it is true that the strong fraternal sentiments collective violence engenders have misled many good people into the hope that a new community together with a "new man" will arise out of it. The hope is an illusion for the simple reason that no human relationship is more transitory than this kind of brotherhood, which can be actualized only under conditions of immediate danger to life and limb.

That, however, is but one side of the matter. Fanon concludes his praise of the practice of violence by remarking that in this kind of struggle the people realize "that life is an unending contest," that violence is an element of life. And does that not sound plausible? Have not men always equated death with "eternal rest," and does it not follow that where we have life we have struggle and unrest? Is not quiet a clear manifestation of lifelessness or decay? Is not violent action a prerogative of the young – those who presumably are fully alive? Therefore are not praise of life and praise of violence the same? [. . .]

Notes

1 Harvey Wheeler, "The Strategic Calculators," in Nigel Calder, *Unless Peace Comes*, New York, 1968, p. 109.

2 *Herrn Eugen Dührings Umwälzung der Wissenschaft* (1878), Part II, ch. 3.

3 As General André Beaufre, in "Battlefields of the 1980s," points out: Only "in those parts of the world not covered by nuclear deterrence" is war still possible, and even this "conventional warfare," despite its horrors, is actually already limited by the ever-present threat of escalation into nuclear war. (In Calder, *op. cit.*, P.3.)

4 *Report from Iron Mountain*, New York, 1967, the satire on the Rand Corporation's and other think tanks' way of thinking, is probably closer to reality, with its "timid glance over the brink of peace," than most "serious" studies. Its chief argument, that war is so essential to the functioning of our society that we dare not abolish it unless we discover even more murderous ways of dealing with our problems, will shock only those who have forgotten to what an extent the unemployment crisis of the Great Depression was solved only through the outbreak of World War II, or those who conveniently neglect or argue away the extent of present latent unemployment behind various forms of featherbedding.

5 Noam Chomsky in *American Power and the New Mandarins*, New York, 1969; Richard N. Goodwin's review of Thomas C. Schelling's *Arms and Influence*, Yale, 1966, in *The New Yorker*, February 17, 1968.

6 There exists, of course, a large literature on war and warfare, but it deals with the implements of violence, not with violence as such.

7 See Engels, *op, cit.*, Part II, ch. 4.

8 Wheeler, *op. cit.*, p. 107; Engels, *ibidem*.

9 Andrei D. Sakharov, *Progress, Coexistence, and Intellectual Freedom*, New York, 1968, p. 36.

10 Wheeler, *ibidem*.

11 Nigel Calder, "The New Weapons," in *op. cit.*, p. 239.

12 M. W. Thring, "Robots on the March," in Calder, *op. cit.*, p. 169.

13 Vladimir Dedijer, "The Poor Man's Power," in Calder, *op. cit.*, p. 29.

14 Nikolas Tinbergen, "On War and Peace in Animals and Man," in *Science*, 160: 1411 (June 28, 1968).

15 To counter the absurdity of this conclusion a distinction is made between endogenous, spontaneous instincts, for instance, aggression, and reactive drives such as hunger. But a distinction between spontaneity and reactivity makes no sense in a discussion of innate impulses. In the world of nature there is no spontaneity, properly speaking, and instincts or drives only manifest the highly complex way in which all living organisms, including man, are adapted to its processes.

16 The hypothetical character of Konrad Lorenz's *On Aggression* (New York, 1966) is clarified in the interesting collection of essays on aggression and adaptation edited by Alexander Mitscherlich under the title *Bis hierher und nicht weiter. Ist die menschliche Aggression unbefriedbar?*, München, 1968.

17 von Holst, *op. cit.*, p. 283: "*Nicht, weil wir Verstandeswesen, sondern weil wir ausserdem ganz urtümliche Triebwesen sind, ist unser Dasein im Zeitalter der Technik gefährdet.*"

18 Long-range weapons, seen by the polemologists as having freed man's aggressive instincts to the point where the controls safeguarding the species do not work any longer (see Tinbergen, *op. cit.*), are taken by Otto Klineberg ("Fears of a Psychologist," in Calder, *op. cit.*, p. 208) rather as an indication "that personal aggressiveness played [no] important role as a motive for war." Soldiers, one would like to continue the argument, are not killers, and killers – those with "personal aggressiveness" – are probably not even good soldiers.

19 I am paraphrasing a sentence of Noam Chomsky (*op. cit.*, p. 371), who is very good in exposing the "facade of toughmindedness and pseudoscience" and the intellectual "vacuity" behind it, especially in the debates about the war in Vietnam.

20 Fanon, *op. cit.* p. 47

21 J. Glenn Gray, *The Warriors* (New York, 1959; now available in paperback), is most perceptive and instructive on this point. It should be read by everyone interested in the practice of violence.

22 Fanon, *op. cit.*, pp. 85 and 93, respectively.

16 Geneva declaration on armed violence and development

Armed violence destroys lives and livelihoods, breeds insecurity, fear and terror, and has a profoundly negative impact on human development. Whether in situations of conflict or crime, it imposes enormous costs on states, communities and individuals.

Armed violence closes schools, empties markets, burdens health services, destroys families, weakens the rule of law, and prevents humanitarian assistance from reaching people in need. Armed violence kills – directly and indirectly – hundreds of thousands of people each year and injures countless more, often with lifelong consequences. It threatens permanently the respect of human rights.

Living free from the threat of armed violence is a basic human need. It is a precondition for human development, dignity and well-being. Providing for the human security of their citizens is a core responsibility of governments.

In the 2005 World Summit Outcome document, global leaders recognized the strong linkage and mutual reinforcement between development, peace, security and human rights. They stressed the right of people to live in dignity, free from fear and from want.

The international community has acknowledged that armed violence and conflict impede realization of the Millennium Development Goals, and that conflict prevention and resolution, violence reduction, human rights, good governance and peace-building are key steps towards reducing poverty, promoting economic growth and improving people's lives.

The Peacebuilding Commission, by establishing an institutional link between security and development, will also promote an integrated approach to post-conflict peace building and play a central role in addressing the problem of armed violence.

Recognizing these realities, we, Ministers and representatives from 42 countries, representing all the world's regions, have gathered in Geneva and have resolved to promote sustainable security and a culture of peace by taking action to reduce armed violence and its negative impact on socio-economic and human development.

We will strengthen our efforts to integrate armed violence reduction and conflict prevention programmes into national, regional and multilateral development frameworks, institutions and strategies, as well as into humanitarian assistance, emergency, and crisis management initiatives.

We will work individually and together, at national, regional and multilateral levels, on practical measures that:

- promote conflict prevention, resolution and reconciliation, and support post-conflict peace-building and reconstruction;
- stem the proliferation, illegal trafficking and misuse of small arms and light weapons and ammunition, and lead to effective weapons reduction, post-conflict disarmament, demo-

bilization and reintegration, and small arms control, including control of arms transfers and of illicit brokering;

- uphold full respect for human rights, promote the peaceful settlement of conflicts based on justice and the rule of law, and address a climate of impunity;
- foster effective and accountable public security institutions;
- promote a comprehensive approach to armed violence reduction issues, recognizing the different situations, needs and resources of men and women, boys and girls, as reflected in the provisions of UN Security Council Resolutions 1325 and 1612;
- ensure that armed violence prevention and reduction initiatives target specific risk factors and groups, and are linked to programmes providing non-violent alternative livelihoods for individuals and communities.

We will take further action to deal effectively both with the supply of, and the demand for, small arms and light weapons. This includes implementing fully existing instruments, in particular the UN Programme of Action to Prevent, Combat and Eradicate the Illicit Trade in Small Arms and Light Weapons in All Its Aspects, and promoting the development of further international instruments, including legally binding ones.

We commit to enhancing the financial, technical and human resources devoted to addressing armed violence issues in a cooperative, comprehensive and coordinated manner, including working *inter alia* to advance this issue within the United Nations, the Organization for Economic Cooperation and Development and other relevant organizations.

We will support initiatives to measure the human, social and economic costs of armed violence, to assess risks and vulnerabilities, to evaluate the effectiveness of armed violence reduction programmes, and to disseminate knowledge of best practices. We will work with affected states and communities, and with the donor community, to promote solutions, including capacity-building, at the local, national, regional and global level.

We will strive to achieve, by 2015, measurable reductions in the global burden of armed violence and tangible improvements in human security worldwide.

We will work in partnership with the development, peace and security-building, public health, humanitarian, human rights and criminal justice communities, and, recognizing the important role civil society has to play in reducing armed violence, promote active partnerships between governments, international organizations and civil society.

We will present this declaration to the upcoming UN conference to review the Programme of Action to Prevent, Combat and Eradicate the Illicit Trade in Small Arms and Light Weapons in All Its Aspects.

We commit ourselves to pursuing this initiative and to meeting again no later than 2008 to assess our progress in achieving these goals.

Geneva, 7 June 2006

17 Preventing violence and reducing its impact

How development agencies can help

World Health Organization

An internationally accepted definition of violence

Since the launch of the *World report on violence and health* in October 2002, an increasing number of global and national agencies have adopted the World Health Organization definition of violence:

> The intentional use of physical force or power, threatened or actual, against oneself, another person, or against a group or community, that either results in or has a high likelihood of resulting in injury, death, psychological harm, maldevelopment or deprivation.

This definition covers a broad range of outcomes, going beyond physical acts. The definition reflects a growing recognition of the need to address violence that does not necessarily result in injury or death, but that nonetheless imposes a substantial burden on individuals, families, communities, and health care systems worldwide.

Accompanying the definition is a typology that subdivides violence into three broad categories according to who commits the violent act:

- Self-directed violence is subdivided into suicidal behaviours including suicidal thoughts, attempted suicide, and completed suicide; and self-abuse including acts such as self-mutilation.
- Interpersonal violence is subdivided into family violence (including child abuse and neglect, intimate partner violence, and elder abuse) and community violence (including youth violence, rape or sexual assault involving strangers, and violence in institutional settings such as schools, workplaces, prisons, and nursing homes).
- Collective violence is subdivided into social violence including crimes of hate or terrorist acts committed to advance a social agenda; political violence including war and related violent conflicts, state violence and similar acts carried out by larger groups; and economic violence including attacks by larger groups motivated by economic gain.

Cross-cutting each of these categories is the nature of the violent acts, which can be physical, sexual, psychological, and involving deprivation or neglect.

18 Violence prevention

The evidence

World Health Organization

As noted in the *World report on violence and health*,[1] violence has always been part of the human experience. Today, violence results in more than 1.5 million people being killed each year, and many more suffer non-fatal injuries and chronic, non-injury health consequences as a result of suicide attempts, interpersonal violence (youth violence, intimate partner violence, child maltreatment, elder abuse and sexual violence) and collective violence (war and other forms of armed conflict). Overall, violence is among the leading causes of death worldwide for people aged 15–44 years.

> Despite the fact that violence has always been present, the world does not have to accept it as an inevitable part of the human condition. As long as there has been violence, there have also been systems – religious, philosophical, legal and communal – that have grown up to prevent or limit it. None has been completely successful, but all have made their contribution to this defining mark of civilization. Since the early 1980s, the field of public health has been a growing asset in this response. A wide range of public health practitioners, researchers and systems have set themselves the tasks of understanding the roots of violence and preventing its occurrence.[1]

Their experience and the scientific studies they have conducted clearly demonstrate that violence can be prevented and its impact reduced, in the same way that public health efforts have prevented and reduced pregnancy-related complications, workplace injuries, infectious diseases and illness resulting from contaminated food and water in many parts of the world. The factors that contribute to violent responses – whether they are factors of attitude and behaviour or related to larger social, economic, political and cultural conditions – can be changed.

Violence can be prevented. This is not an article of faith, but a statement based on evidence. *Violence prevention: the evidence* is a set of seven briefings based on rigorous reviews of the literature which examines scientific evidence for the effectiveness of interventions to prevent interpersonal and self-directed violence.[2] Each briefing focuses on a broad strategy for preventing violence, and under that umbrella reviews the evidence for the effectiveness of specific interventions. The violence prevention strategies covered in the seven briefings are:

1. Developing safe, stable and nurturing relationships between children and their parents and caregivers;
2. Developing life skills in children and adolescents;
3. Reducing the availability and harmful use of alcohol;
4. Reducing access to guns, knives and pesticides;

5. Promoting gender equality to prevent violence against women;
6. Changing cultural and social norms that support violence;
7. Victim identification, care and support programmes.

This document summarizes the headline findings from each of the seven briefings and spotlights the specific interventions within each strategy that have the strongest evidence for preventing violence. Table 1 presents the overview, indicating for each intervention the strength of the evidence for its effectiveness and the types of violence it has been found to prevent.

The interventions

The seven briefing documents themselves provide more detail about these and other interventions, additional examples of their implementation and a full discussion of the strengths and limitations of the evidence for their effectiveness.

Table 1 Overview of violence prevention interventions with some evidence of effectiveness by types of violence prevented

Intervention	Type of violence					
	CM	IPV	SV	YV	EA	S
1 Developing safe, stable and nurturing relationships between children and their parents and caregivers						
Parent training, including nurse home visitation	●			○		
Parent-child programmes	○			○		
2 Developing life skills in children and adolescents						
Preschool enrichment programmes				○		
Social development programmes				●		
3 Reducing the availability and harmful use of alcohol						
Regulating sales of alcohol				○		
Raising alcohol prices				○		
Interventions for problem drinkers		●				
Improving drinking environments				○		
4 Reducing access to guns, knives and pesticides						
Restrictive firearm licensing and purchase policies				○		○
Enforced bans on carrying firearms in public				○		
Policies to restrict or ban toxic substances						○
5 Promoting gender equality to prevent violence against women						
School-based programmes to address gender norms and attitudes		●	○			
Microfinance combined with gender equity training		○				
Life-skills interventions		○				
6 Changing cultural and social norms that support violence						
Social marketing to modify social norms		○	○			
7 Victim identification, care and support programmes						
Screening and referral		○				
Advocacy support programmes		●				
Psychosocial interventions				○		
Protection orders		○				

KEY
● Well supported by evidence (multiple randomized controlled trials with different populations)
○ Emerging evidence
CM – Child maltreatment; IPV – Intimate partner violence; SV – Sexual violence; YV – Youth violence; EA – Elder Abuse; S – Suicide and other forms of self-directed violence

1. Developing safe, stable and nurturing relationships between children and their parents and caregivers

Some interventions that encourage nurturing relationships between parents (or caregivers) and children in their early years have been shown to prevent child maltreatment and reduce childhood aggression. These types of interventions also have the potential to prevent the life-long negative consequences of child maltreatment for mental and physical health, social and occupational functioning, human capital and security and, ultimately, for social and economic development. There is also emerging evidence that they reduce convictions and violent acts in adolescence and early adulthood, and probably help decrease intimate partner violence and self-directed violence in later life.

High-quality trials in the United States of America and other developed countries have shown that both the Nurse Family Partnership home-visiting programme and the Positive Parenting Programme (Triple P) reduce child maltreatment. In home-visiting programmes, trained personnel visit parents and children in their homes and provide health advice, support, child development education and life coaching for parents to improve child health, foster parental care-giving abilities and prevent child maltreatment. Parenting education programmes, such as the Triple P, are usually centre-based and delivered in groups and aim to prevent child maltreatment by improving parents' child-rearing skills, increasing parental knowledge of child development and encouraging positive child management strategies. Evidence also suggests that parent and child programmes – which typically incorporate parenting education along with child education, social support and other services – may prevent child maltreatment and youth violence later in life.

As evidence for the effectiveness of these parenting and parent-child programmes in high-income countries continues to expand, the time is ripe to initiate their large-scale implementation and outcome evaluation in low-income and middle-income countries.

2. Developing life skills in children and adolescents

Evidence shows that the life-skills acquired in social development programmes (which are aimed at building social, emotional and behavioural competencies) can prevent youth violence, while preschool enrichment programmes (which provide children with academic and social skills at an early age) appear promising. Life skills help children and adolescents effectively deal with the challenges of everyday life. Such programmes that target children early in life can prevent aggression, reduce involvement in violence, improve social skills, boost educational achievement and improve job prospects. These effects are most pronounced in children from poor families and neighbourhoods. The benefits of high-quality programmes which invest early in an individual's life have the potential to last into adulthood.

Most of the research on life skills programmes has been conducted in high-income countries, particularly the United States. More evidence is needed on the impacts of preschool enrichment and social development programmes in low-income and middle-income countries.

3. Reducing the availability and harmful use of alcohol

Evidence is emerging that violence may be prevented by reducing the availability of alcohol, through brief interventions and longer-term treatment for problem drinkers and by improving the management of environments where alcohol is served. Currently, evidence for the effectiveness of such interventions is rarely from randomized controlled trials and comes chiefly from developed countries and some parts of Latin America.

Alcohol availability can be regulated by restricting the hours or days it can be sold and by reducing the number of alcohol retail outlets. Reduced sales hours have generally been found to be associated with reduced violence and higher outlet densities with higher levels of violence. Economic modelling strongly suggests that raising alcohol prices (e.g. through increased taxes, state controlled monopolies and minimum price policies) can lower consumption and, hence, reduce violence.

Brief interventions and longer-term treatment for problem drinkers – using, for instance, cognitive behavioural therapy – have been shown in several trials to reduce various forms of violence such as child maltreatment, intimate partner violence and suicide.

Some evidence is beginning to support interventions in and around drinking establishments that target factors such as crowding, comfort levels, physical design, staff training and access to late night transport.

4. *Reducing access to guns, knives and pesticides*

Evidence emerging suggests that limiting access to firearms and pesticides can prevent homicides (most of which occur between young males between 15–29-years-old), suicides and injuries and reduce the costs of these forms of violence to society. More rigorous studies are, however, needed.

There is some evidence, for example, to suggest that jurisdictions with restrictive firearms legislation and lower firearms ownership tend to have lower levels of gun violence. Restrictive firearm licensing and purchasing policies – including bans, licensing schemes, minimum ages for buyers, background checks – have been implemented and appear to be effective in countries such as Australia, Austria, Brazil and New Zealand. Studies in Colombia and El Salvador indicate that enforced bans on carrying firearms in public may reduce homicide rates.

Safer storage of pesticides, bans and replacement by less toxic alternatives could prevent many of the estimated 370,000 suicides caused by ingestion of pesticides every year. International conventions attempt to manage hazardous substances; however, many highly toxic pesticides are still widely used. Research suggests, however, that bans must be accompanied by evaluations of agricultural needs and replacement with low-risk alternatives for pest control.

5. *Promoting gender equality to prevent violence against women*

Though further research is needed, some evidence shows that school and community interventions can promote gender equality and prevent violence against women by challenging stereotypes and cultural norms that give men power and control over women.

School-based programmes can address gender norms and attitudes before they become deeply engrained in children and youth. Trials of the Safe Dates programme in the United States and the Youth Relationship Project in Canada, which also addresses dating violence, have reported positive results.

Outcome evaluation studies are beginning to support community interventions that aim to prevent violence against women by promoting gender equality. Evidence suggests that programmes that combine microfinance with gender equity training can reduce intimate partner violence. Some of the strongest evidence is for the IMAGE initiative in South Africa which combines microloans and gender equity training. Another intervention for which evidence of effectiveness is building up is the Stepping Stones programme in Africa and Asia which is a life-skills training programme which addresses gender-based violence, relationship skills, assertiveness training and communication about HIV.

6. Changing cultural and social norms that support violence

Rules or expectations of behaviour-norms-within a cultural or social group can encourage violence. Interventions that challenge cultural and social norms supportive of violence can prevent acts of violence and have been widely used, but the evidence base for their effectiveness is currently weak. Further rigorous evaluations of such interventions are required.

The effectiveness of interventions addressing dating violence and sexual abuse among teenagers and young adults by challenging social and cultural norms related to gender is supported by some evidence. Other interventions appear promising, including those targeting youth violence and education through entertainment ("edutainment") aimed at reducing intimate partner violence.

7. Victim identification, care and support programmes

Interventions to identify victims of interpersonal violence and provide effective care and support are critical for protecting health and breaking cycles of violence from one generation to the next.[3]

Evidence of effectiveness is emerging for the following interventions: screening tools to identify victims of intimate partner violence and refer them to appropriate services; psychosocial interventions – such as trauma-focused cognitive behavioural therapy – to reduce mental health problems associated with violence, including post-traumatic stress disorder; and protection orders, which prohibit a perpetrator from contacting the victim, to reduce repeat victimization among victims of intimate partner violence. Several trials have shown that advocacy support programmes – which offer services such as advice, counselling, safety planning and referral to other agencies – increase victims' safety behaviours and reduce further harm.

Harnessing policies that address social determinants of violence

Interpersonal violence is strongly associated with such macro-level social factors as unemployment, income inequality, rapid social change and access to education. Any comprehensive violence prevention strategy must not only address those risk factors targeted by the interventions outlined in these briefings, but must also be integrated with policies directed at these macro-level social factors and harness their potential to reduce the inequities which fuel interpersonal violence.

Next steps

The last decades have seen a rapid growth in the awareness that violence can be prevented. In high-income countries, in particular, there has been a clear increase in the number of governments actively developing violence prevention policies and implementing programmes informed by the kinds of evidence reviewed in this document and the seven briefings. However, the challenge of scaling up violence prevention investments in low-income and middle-income countries remains. This requires encouraging wealthy donor countries to devote more development aid to the issue. Just as importantly, it also calls for getting governments to shift more of their budget from caring for victims of violence and from detecting, prosecuting and punishing its perpetrators to preventing violence. Based on these reflections, the following next steps, if implemented, would do much to help advance the violence prevention agenda, and with it the safety, security and well being of people everywhere.

- The need to expand the evidence base in no way precludes taking action now and implementing interventions, guided by the evidence base described in these briefings, to prevent interpersonal and self-directed violence in all countries.
- Intensify and expand violence prevention awareness among decision makers in low-income andmiddle-income countries and leaders of high-income countries and international donor agencies.
- Increase the flow to low-income and middle-income countries of financial resources and technical support for violence prevention. Currently, the international community, through bodies such as the Global Fund to Fight AIDS, Malaria and Tuberculosis, supports disease prevention in developing countries; it could also contribute to the start-up costs of national violence prevention initiatives.
- Strengthen evidence-based, prevention-oriented collaborative work between public health and criminal justice agencies, these being the two arms of government most directly impacted by violence and with the highest stakes in its prevention.
- Enhance investment in research on violence and violence prevention, especially in low-incomeand middle-income countries, and particularly with a view to expanding the number of outcome evaluation studies.

Violence prevention: the evidence can help advocates, policy makers and programme designers and implementers to reduce the heavy burden of death and injury caused by violence. It can contribute towards reducing the far-reaching impact violence has on mental and physical health, school and job performance, people's ability to successfully relate to others, the safety of communities and, ultimately, the social and economic development of countries.

Notes

1 Krug EG et al., eds. *World report on violence and health.* Geneva, World Health Organization 2002.
2 While these briefings and this overview draw on a wide range of literature, the are particularly indebted to the following two previous publications: (1) Rosenberg ML et al. Interpersonal violence. In Jamison DT et al. (eds.) *Disease Control Priorities in Developing Countries,* 2nd Edition. Washington, D.C.: Oxford University Press and The World Bank, 2006: 755–770; (2) Mercy JA et al. Preventing violence in developing countries: a framework for action. *International Journal of Injury Control and Safety Promotion* 2008, 15(4): 197–208.
3 The briefing does not cover the area of pre-hospital and emergency medical care since this is already addressed by the following guidelines: Mock C. et al. *Guidelines for trauma quality improvement.* Geneva, World Health Organization, 2009; Sasser S. et al. *Prehospital trauma care systems.* Geneva, World Health Organization, 2005; Mock C. et al. *Guidelines for essential trauma care.* Geneva, World Health Organization, 2004.

19 Letter to Sigmund Freud, 30 July 1932

Albert Einstein

The proposal of the League of Nations and its International Institute of Intellectual Co-operation at Paris that I should invite a person, to be chosen by myself, to a frank exchange of views on any problem that I might select affords me a very welcome opportunity of conferring with you upon a question which, as things now are, seems the most insistent of all the problems civilisation has to face. This is the problem: Is there any way of delivering mankind from the menace of war? It is common knowledge that, with the advance of modern science, this issue has come to mean a matter of life and death for civilisation as we know it; nevertheless, for all the zeal displayed, every attempt at its solution has ended in a lamentable breakdown.

I believe, moreover, that those whose duty it is to tackle the problem professionally and practically are growing only too aware of their impotence to deal with it, and have now a very lively desire to learn the views of men who, absorbed in the pursuit of science, can see world problems in the perspective distance lends. As for me, the normal objective of my thought affords no insight into the dark places of human will and feeling. Thus, in the enquiry now proposed, I can do little more than to seek to clarify the question at issue and, clearing the ground of the more obvious solutions, enable you to bring the light of your far-reaching knowledge of man's instinctive life to bear upon the problem. There are certain psychological obstacles whose existence a layman in the mental sciences may dimly surmise, but whose interrelations and vagaries he is incompetent to fathom; you, I am convinced, will be able to suggest educative methods, lying more or less outside the scope of politics, which will eliminate these obstacles.

As one immune from nationalist bias, I personally see a simple way of dealing with the superficial (i.e., administrative) aspect of the problem: the setting up, by international consent, of a legislative and judicial body to settle every conflict arising between nations. Each nation would undertake to abide by the orders issued by this legislative body, to invoke its decision in every dispute, to accept its judgments unreservedly and to carry out every measure the tribunal deems necessary for the execution of its decrees. But here, at the outset, I come up against a difficulty; a tribunal is a human institution which, in proportion as the power at its disposal is inadequate to enforce its verdicts, is all the more prone to suffer these to be deflected by extrajudicial pressure. This is a fact with which we have to reckon; law and might inevitably go hand in hand, and juridical decisions approach more nearly the ideal justice demanded by the community (in whose name and interests these verdicts are pronounced) in so far as the community has effective power to compel respect of its juridical ideal. But at present we are far from possessing any supranational organisation competent to render verdicts of incontestable authority and enforce absolute submission to the execution of its verdicts. Thus I am led to my first axiom: The quest of international security involves the unconditional surrender by every nation, in a certain measure, of its liberty of action, its sovereignty that is to say, and it is clear beyond all doubt that no other road can lead to such security.

The ill-success, despite their obvious sincerity, of all the efforts made during the last decade to reach this goal leaves us no room to doubt that strong psychological factors are at work, which paralyse these efforts. Some of these factors are not far to seek. The craving for power which characterises the governing class in every nation is hostile to any limitation of the national sovereignty. This political power-hunger is wont to batten on the activities of another group, whose aspirations are on purely mercenary, economic lines. I have specially in mind that small but determined group, active in every nation, composed of individuals who, indifferent to social considerations and restraints, regard warfare, the manufacture and sale of arms, simply as an occasion to advance their personal interests and enlarge their personal authority.

But recognition of this obvious fact is merely the first step toward an appreciation of the actual state of affairs. Another question follows hard upon it: How is it possible for this small clique to bend the will of the majority, who stand to lose and suffer by a state of war, to the service of their ambitions? (In speaking of the majority, I do not exclude soldiers of every rank who have chosen war as their profession, in the belief that they are serving to defend the highest interests of their race, and that attack is often the best method of defence.) An obvious answer to this question would seem to be that the minority, the ruling class at present has the schools and press, usually the Church as well, under its thumb. This enables it to organise and sway the emotions of the masses, and make its tool of them.

Yet even this answer does not provide a complete solution. Another question arises from it: How is it these devices succeed so well in rousing men to such wild enthusiasm, even to sacrifice their lives? Only one answer is possible. Because man has within him a lust for hatred and destruction. In normal times this passion exists in a latent state, it emerges only in unusual circumstances; but it is a comparatively easy task to call it into play and raise it to the power of a collective psychosis. Here lies, perhaps, the crux of all the complex of factors we are considering, an enigma that only the expert in the lore of human instincts can resolve.

And so we come to our last question. Is it possible to control man's mental evolution so as to make him proof against the psychoses of hate and destructiveness? Here I am thinking by no means only of the so-called uncultured masses. Experience proves that it is rather the so-called "Intelligentsia" that is most apt to yield to these disastrous collective suggestions, since the intellectual has no direct contact with life in the raw, but encounters it in its easiest, synthetic form—upon the printed page.

To conclude: I have so far been speaking only of wars between nations; what are known as international conflicts. But I am well aware that the aggressive instinct operates under other forms and in other circumstances. (I am thinking of civil wars, for instance, due in earlier days to religious zeal, but nowadays to social factors; or, again, the persecution of racial minorities.) But my insistence on what is the most typical, most cruel and extravagant form of conflict between man and man was deliberate, for here we have the best occasion of discovering ways and means to render all armed conflicts impossible.

I know that in your writings we may find answers, explicit or implied, to all the issues of this urgent and absorbing problem. But it would be of the greatest service to us all were you to present the problem of world peace in the light of your most recent discoveries, for such a presentation well might blaze the trail for new and fruitful modes of action.

20 Why war?[1]

Sigmund Freud

Dear Professor Einstein,

When I heard that you intended to invite me to an exchange of views on some subject that interested you and that seemed to deserve the interest of others besides yourself, I readily agreed, I expected you to choose a problem on the frontiers of what is knowable today, a problem to which each of us, a physicist and a psychologist, might have our own particular angle of approach and where we might come together from different directions upon the same ground. You have taken me by surprise, however, by posing the question of what can be done to protect mankind from the curse of war. I was scared at first by the thought of my – I had almost written 'our' – incapacity for dealing with what seemed to be a practical problem, a concern for statesmen. But I then realized that you had raised the question not as a natural scientist and physicist but as a philanthropist. [. . .] I reflected, moreover, that I was not being asked to make practical proposals but only to set out the problem of avoiding war as it appears to a psychological observer. Here again you yourself have said almost all there is to say on the subject. But though you have taken the wind out of my sails I shall be glad to follow in your wake and content myself with confirming all you have said by amplifying it to the best of my knowledge – or conjecture.

You begin with the relation between Right and Might.[2] There can be no doubt that that is the correct starting-point for our investigation. But may I replace the word 'might' by the balder and harsher word 'violence'? Today right and violence appear to us as antitheses. It can easily be shown, however, that the one has developed out of the other; and if we go back to the earliest beginnings and see how that first came about, the problem is easily solved. [. . .]

It is a general principle, then, that conflicts of interest between men are settled by the use of violence. This is true of the whole animal kingdom, from which men have no business to exclude themselves. In the case of men, no doubt, conflicts of *opinion* occur as well which may reach the highest pitch of abstraction and which seem to demand some other technique for their settlement. That, however, is a later complication. To begin with, in a small human horde,[3] it was superior muscular strength which decided who owned things or whose will should prevail. Muscular strength was soon supplemented and replaced by the use of tools: the winner was the one who had the better weapons or who used them the more skilfully. From the moment at which weapons were introduced, intellectual superiority already began to replace brute muscular strength; but the final purpose of the fight remained the same – one side or the other was to be compelled to abandon his claim or his objection by the damage inflicted on him and by the crippling of his strength. That purpose was most completely achieved if the victor's violence eliminated his opponent permanently, that is to say, killed him. This had two advantages: he could not renew his opposition, and his fate deterred others from following his example. In addition to this, killing an enemy satisfied an instinctual inclination which I shall have to mention later. The intention to kill might be countered by a reflection that the enemy could be employed in performing useful services if he were left alive in an intimidated condition. In that case the victor's violence was content to subjugate him instead of killing him. This was a first beginning of the idea of sparing an enemy's life, but thereafter the victor had to reckon with his defeated opponent's lurking thirst for revenge and sacrificed some of his own security.

Such, then, was the original state of things: domination by whoever had the greater might – domination by brute violence or by violence supported by intellect. As we know, this regime was altered in the course of evolution. There was a path that led from violence to right or law. What was that path? It is my belief that there was only one: the path which led by way of the fact that the superior strength of a single individual could be rivalled by the union of several weak ones. '*L'union fait la force.*' Violence could be broken by union, and the power of those who were united now represented law in contrast to the violence of the single individual. Thus we see that right is the might of a community. It is still violence, ready to be directed against any individual who resists it; it works by the same methods and follows the same purposes. The only real difference lies in the fact that what prevails is no longer the violence of an individual but that of a community. But in order that the transition from violence to this new right or justice may be effected, one psychological condition must be fulfilled. The union of the majority must be a stable and lasting one. If it were only brought about for the purpose of combating a single domineering individual and were dissolved after his defeat, nothing would have been accomplished. The next person who found himself superior in strength would once more seek to set up a dominion by violence and the game would be repeated *ad infinitum*. The community must be maintained permanently, must be organized, must draw up regulations to anticipate the risk of rebellion and must institute authorities to see that those regulations – the laws – are respected and to superintend the execution of legal acts of violence. The recognition of a community of interests such as these leads to the growth of emotional ties between the members of a united group of people – feelings of unity which are the true source of its strength.

Here, I believe, we already have all the essentials: violence overcome by the transference of power to a larger unity, which is held together by emotional ties between its members. [. . .]

Thus we see that the violent solution of conflicts of interest is not avoided even inside a community. But the everyday necessities and common concerns that are inevitable where people live together in one place tend to bring such struggles to a swift conclusion and under such conditions there is an increasing probability that a peaceful solution will be found. But a glance at the history of the human race reveals an endless series of conflicts between one community and another or several others, between larger and smaller units – between cities, provinces, races, nations, empires – which have almost always been settled by force of arms. Wars of this kind end either in the spoliation or in the complete overthrow and conquest of one of the parties. It is impossible to make any sweeping judgement upon wars of conquest.

Paradoxical as it may sound, it must be admitted that war might be a far from inappropriate means of establishing the eagerly desired reign of 'everlasting' peace, since it is in a position to create the large units within which a powerful central government makes further wars impossible. Nevertheless it fails in this purpose, for the results of conquest are as a rule short-lived: the newly created units fall apart once again, usually owing to a lack of cohesion between the portions that have been united by violence. Hitherto, moreover, the unifications created by conquest, though of considerable extent, have only been *partial*, and the conflicts between these have cried out for violent solution. Thus the result of all these warlike efforts has only been that the human race has exchanged numerous, and indeed unending, minor wars for wars on a grand scale that are rare but all the more destructive.

If we turn to our own times, we arrive at the same conclusion which you have reached by a shorter path. Wars will only be prevented with certainty if mankind unites in setting up a central authority to which the right of giving judgement upon all conflicts of interest shall be handed over. There are clearly two separate requirements involved in this: the creation of a supreme authority and its endowment with the necessary power. One without the other would be useless. [. . .]

We have heard that a community is held together by two things: the compelling force of violence and the emotional ties (identifications is the technical name) between its members. If one of the factors is absent, the community may possibly be held together by the other. The ideas that are appealed to can, of course, only have any significance if they give expression to important concerns that are common to the members, and the question arises of how much strength they can exert.

A lust for aggression and destruction is certainly among them: the countless cruelties in history and in our everyday lives vouch for its existence and its strength. The gratification of these destructive impulses is of course facilitated by their admixture with others of an erotic and idealistic kind. When we read of the atrocities of the past, it sometimes seems as though the idealistic motives served only as an excuse for the destructive appetites; and sometimes – in the case, for instance, of the cruelties of the Inquisition – it seems as though the idealistic motives had pushed themselves forward in consciousness, while the destructive ones lent them an unconscious reinforcement. Both may be true.

I fear I may be abusing your interest, which is after all concerned with the prevention of war and not with our theories. Nevertheless I should like to linger for a moment over our destructive instinct, whose popularity is by no means equal to its importance. As a result of a little speculation, we have come to suppose that this instinct is at work in every living being and is striving to bring it to ruin and to reduce life to its original condition of inanimate matter. Thus it quite seriously deserves to be called a death instinct, while the erotic instincts represent the effort to live. The death instinct turns into the destructive instinct if, with the help of special organs, it is directed outwards, on to objects. The living creature preserves its own life, so to say, by destroying an extraneous one. Some portion of the death instinct, however, remains operative *within* the living being, and we have sought to trace quite a number of normal and pathological phenomena to this internalization of the destructive instinct. We have even been guilty of the heresy of attributing the origin of conscience to this diversion inwards of aggressiveness. You will notice that it is by no means a trivial matter if this process is carried too far: it is positively unhealthy. On the other hand if these forces are turned to destruction in the external world, the living creature will be relieved and the effect must be beneficial. This would serve as a biological justification for all the ugly and dangerous impulses against which we are struggling. It must be admitted that they stand nearer to Nature than does our resistance to them, for which an explanation also needs to be found. [. . .]

For our immediate purpose then, this much follows from what has been said: there is no use in trying to get rid of men's aggressive inclinations. We are told that in certain happy regions of the earth, where nature provides in abundance everything that man requires, there are races whose life is passed in tranquillity and who know neither compulsion nor aggressiveness. I can scarcely believe it and I should be glad to hear more of these fortunate beings. [. . .] In any case, as you yourself have remarked, there is no question of getting rid entirely of human aggressive impulses; it is enough to try to divert them to such an extent that they need not find expression in war.

Our mythological theory of instincts makes it easy for us to find a formula for *indirect* methods of combating war. If willingness to engage in war is an effect of the destructive instinct, the most obvious plan will be to bring Eros, its antagonist, into play against it. Anything that encourages the growth of emotional ties between men must operate against war. These ties may be of two kinds. In the first place they may be relations resembling those towards a loved object, though without having a sexual aim. There is no need for psychoanalysis to be ashamed to speak of love in this connection, for religion itself uses the same words: 'Thou shalt love thy neighbour as thyself.' This, however, is more easily said than done. The second kind of emotional tie is by means of identification. Whatever leads men to share important interests produces this community of feeling, these identifications. And the structure of human society is to a large extent based on them.

A complaint which you make about the abuse of authority brings me to another suggestion for the indirect combating of the propensity to war. One instance of the innate and ineradicable inequality of men is their tendency to fall into the two classes of leaders and followers. The latter constitute the vast majority; they stand in need of an authority which will make decisions for them and to which they for the most part offer an unqualified submission. This suggests that more care should be taken than hitherto to educate an upper stratum of men with independent minds, not open to intimidation and eager in the pursuit of truth, whose business it would be to give direction to the dependent masses. [. . .] The ideal condition of things would of course be a community of men who had subordinated their instinctual life to the dictatorship of reason. Nothing else could unite men so completely and so tenaciously, even if there were no emotional ties between them. But in all probability that is a Utopian expectation. No doubt the other indirect methods of preventing war are more practicable, though they promise no rapid success. An unpleasant picture comes to one's mind of mills that grind so slowly that people may starve before they get their flour.

I should like, however, to discuss one more question, which you do not mention in your letter but which specially interests me. Why do you and I and so many other people rebel so violently against war? Why do we not accept it as another of the many painful calamities of life? After all, it seems quite a natural thing, no doubt it has a good biological basis and in practice it is scarcely avoidable. There is no need to be shocked at my raising this question. For the purpose of an investigation such as this, one may perhaps be allowed to wear a mask of assumed detachment. The answer to my question will be that we react to war in this way because everyone has a right to his own life, because war puts an end to human lives that are full of hope, because it brings individual men into humiliating situations, because it compels them against their will to murder other men, and because it destroys precious material objects which have been produced by the labours of humanity. Other reasons besides might be given, such as that in its present-day form war is no longer an opportunity for achieving the old ideals of heroism and that owing to the perfection of instruments of destruction a future war might involve the extermination of one or perhaps both of the antagonists. All this is true, and so incontestably true that one can only feel astonished that the waging of war has not yet been unanimously repudiated. No doubt debate is possible upon one or two of these points. It may be questioned whether a community ought not to have a right to dispose of individual lives; every war is not open to condemnation to an equal degree; so long as there exist countries and nations that are prepared for the ruthless destruction of others, those others must be armed for war. But I will not linger over any of these issues; they are not what you want to discuss with me, and I have something different in mind. It is my opinion that the main reason why we rebel against war is that we cannot help doing so. We are pacifists because we are obliged to be for organic reasons. And we then find no difficulty in producing arguments to justify our attitude.

No doubt this requires some explanation. My belief is this. For incalculable ages mankind has been passing through a process of evolution of culture. (Some people, I know, prefer to use the term 'civilization'.) We owe to that process the best of what we have become, as well as a good part of what we suffer from. Though its causes and beginnings are obscure and its outcome uncertain, some of its characteristics are easy to perceive. It may perhaps be leading to the extinction of the human race, for in more than one way it impairs the sexual function; uncultivated races and backward strata of the population are already multiplying more rapidly than highly cultivated ones. The process is perhaps comparable to the domestication of certain species of animals and it is undoubtedly accompanied by physical alterations; but we are still unfamiliar with the notion that the evolution of culture is an organic process of this kind. The psychical modifications that go along with the cultural process are striking and unambiguous. They consist in a progressive displacement of instinctual aims and a restriction of instinctual impulses. Sensations which were pleasurable to our ancestors have become indifferent or even intolerable to ourselves; there are organic grounds for the changes in our ethical and aesthetic ideals. Of the psychological characteristics of culture two appear to be the most important: a strengthening of the intellect, which is beginning to govern instinctual life, and an internalization of the aggressive impulses, with all its consequent advantages and perils. Now war is in the crassest opposition to the psychical attitude imposed on us by the cultural process, and for that reason we are bound to rebel against it; we simply cannot any longer put up with it. This is not merely an intellectual and emotional repudiation; we pacifists have a constitutional intolerance of war, an idiosyncracy magnified, as it were, to the highest degree. It seems, indeed, as though the lowering of aesthetic standards in war plays a scarcely smaller part in our rebellion than do its cruelties.

And how long shall we have to wait before the rest of mankind become pacifists too? There is no telling. But it may not be Utopian to hope that these two factors, the cultural attitude and the justified dread of the consequences of a future war, may result within a measurable time in putting an end to the waging of war. By what paths or by what side-tracks this will come about we cannot guess. But one thing we *can* say: whatever fosters the growth of culture works at the same time against war.

I trust you will forgive me if what I have said has disappointed you, and I remain, with kindest regards,

Yours sincerely,
Sigm. Freud

Notes

1 *Warum Krieg?* was the title of an interchange of open letters between Professor Albert Einstein and Freud. This formed one of a series of similar interchanges arranged by the International Institute of Intellectual Co-operation under the auspices of the League of Nations, and was first published simultaneously in German, French and English in Paris in 1933, Freud's letter was reprinted *Ges. Schr.*, 12, 347, and *Ges. W.*, 16. Professor Einstein's, which preceded it, was a short one setting out the problems to be discussed. Present translation by James Strachey.

2 In the original the words '*Recht*' and '*Macht*' are used throughout the essay. It has unfortunately been necessary to sacrifice this stylistic unity in the translation. '*Recht*' has been rendered indifferently by 'right', 'law' and 'justice'; and '*Macht*' by 'might', 'force' and 'power'.

3 Freud uses the word 'horde' to denote a comparatively small group.

21 UNESCO

The Seville statement

Introduction

Believing that it is our responsibility to address from our particular disciplines the most dangerous and destructive activities of our species, violence and war; recognising that science is a human cultural product which cannot be definitive or all encompassing; and gratefully acknowledging the support of the authorities of Seville and representatives of the Spanish UNESCO, we, the undersigned scholars from around the world and from relevant sciences, have met and arrived at the following Statement on Violence. In it, we challenge a number of alleged biological findings that have been used, even by some in our disciplines, to justify violence and war. Because the alleged findings have contributed to an atmosphere of pessimism in our time, we submit that the open, considered rejection of these misstatements can contribute significantly to the International Year of Peace.

Misuse of scientific theories and data to justify violence and war is not new but has been made since the advent of modern science. For example, the theory of evolution has been used to justify not only war, but also genocide, colonialism, and suppression of the weak.

We state our position in the form of five propositions. We are aware that there are many other issues about violence and war that could be fruitfully addressed from the standpoint of our disciplines, but we restrict ourselves here to what we consider a most important first step.

First proposition

It is Scientifically Incorrect to say that we have inherited a tendency to make war from our animal ancestors. Although fighting occurs widely throughout animal species, only a few cases of destructive intraspecies fighting between organised groups have ever been reported among naturally living species, and none of these involve the use of tools designed to be weapons. Normal predatory feeding upon other species cannot be equated with intraspecies violence. Warfare is a peculiarly human phenomenon and does not occur in other animals.

The fact that warfare has changed so radically over time indicates that it is a product of culture. Its biological connection is primarily through language which makes possible the co-ordination of groups, the transmission of technology, and the use of tools. War is biologically possible, but it is not inevitable, as evidenced by its variation in occurrence and nature over time and space. There are cultures which have not engaged in war for centuries, and there are cultures which have engaged in war frequently at some times and not at others.

Second proposition

It is Scientifically Incorrect to say that war or any other violent behaviour is genetically programmed into our human nature. While genes are involved at all levels of nervous system function, they provide a developmental potential that can be actualised only in conjunction with the ecological and social environment. While individuals vary in their predispositions to be affected by their experience, it is the interaction between their genetic endowment and conditions of nurturance that determines their personalities. Except for rare pathologies, the genes do not produce individuals necessarily predisposed to violence. Neither do they determine the opposite. While genes are co-involved in establishing our behavioural capacities, they do not by themselves specify the outcome.

Third proposition

It is Scientifically Incorrect to say that in the course of human evolution there has been a selection for aggressive behaviour more than for other kinds of behaviour. In all well-studied species, status within the group is achieved by the ability to co-operate and to fulfil social functions relevant to the structure of that group. 'Dominance' involves social bondings and affiliations: it is not simply a matter of the possession and use of superior physical power, although it does involve aggressive behaviours. Where genetic selection for aggressive behaviour has been artificially instituted in animals, it has rapidly succeeded in producing hyperaggressive individuals; this indicates that aggression was not maximally selected under natural conditions. When such experimentally-created hyperaggressive animals are present in a social group, they either disrupt its social structure or are driven out. Violence is neither in our evolutionary legacy nor in our genes.

Fourth proposition

It is Scientifically Incorrect to say that humans have a 'violent brain.' While we do have the neural apparatus to act violently, it is not automatically activated by internal or external stimuli. Like higher primates and unlike other animals, our higher neural processes filter such stimuli before they can be acted upon. How we act is shaped by how we have been conditioned and socialised. There is nothing in our neurophysiology that compels us to react violently.

Fifth proposition

It is Scientifically Incorrect to say that war is caused by 'instinct' or any single motivation. The emergence of modern warfare has been a journey from the primacy of emotional and motivational factors, sometimes called 'instincts,' to the primacy of cognitive factors. Modern war involves institutional use of personal characteristics such as obedience, suggestibility, and idealism, social skills such as language, and rational considerations such as cost-calculation, planning, and information processing. The technology of modern war has exaggerated traits associated with violence both in the training of actual combatants and in the preparation of support for war in the general population. As a result of this exaggeration, such traits are often mistaken to be the causes rather than the consequences of the process.

Conclusion

We conclude that biology does not condemn humanity to war, and that humanity can be freed from the bondage of biological pessimism and empowered with confidence to undertake the transformative tasks needed in this International Year of Peace and in the years to come. Although these tasks are mainly institutional and collective, they also rest upon the consciousness of individual participants for whom pessimism and optimism are crucial factors. Just as 'wars begin in the minds of men', peace also begins in our minds. The same species who invented war is capable of inventing peace. The responsibility lies with each of us.

22 Psychological contributions to understanding peace and conflict

Charles P. Webel and Viera Sotakova

Individual reflections about 'the nature of human nature' and the reasons for peace and war date back to ancient times. But what is now known as 'peace psychology' – the branch of academic psychology that investigates individual and collective determinants of irenic and belligerent behaviour – is, like peace and conflict studies, a product of the Cold War and its termination, when the perceived threat to global peace posed by nuclear weapons was at its peak.

Forerunners of contemporary psychological investigations of peace and conflict include such distinguished researchers as William James, Sigmund Freud, Konrad Lorenz and Stanley Milgram, who have focused on inner and outer *aggression and conflict*, not on inner and outer *peace*. It is only relatively recently that peace studies has examined the roots of peace and peaceful societies, in addition to the reasons for war and violent conflict.

Psychology is used for the investigation of the causes of war and peace, and psychological contributions to peace and conflict research are numerous and noteworthy. Only a few can be mentioned here (for more comprehensive overviews, see Barash and Webel, 2009, Chapters 5 and 6; and Christie, Wagner and Winter, 2001). They range from philosophical and meta-psychological reflections on war, peace and the human condition as a whole, to empirical studies of the behaviour of individuals and groups in stress-inducing circumstances. And psychological explanations of belligerent and irenic behaviour operate on a number of occasionally isolated and often intersecting levels – ranging from the intra-psychic and individual, through the interpersonal and small group, and extending to the socio-political and cultural dimensions of human belief, motivation and interaction. While we acknowledge the limitations of a Western-centred approach, our focus here is mainly on some North American and European psychological contributions.

The roots of violence, aggression and personality; the importance of social situations

In 1910, William James, referred to by Morton Deutsch as the first peace psychologist, published his classic article, 'The moral equivalent of war'. There, James noted the 'militant enthusiasm' of humans to rally around the military flag, and he challenged the simplistic view that war was an inevitable result of human nature. He argued for 'the moral equivalent of war' because he claimed that war gives people an opportunity to express their spiritual inclinations towards self-sacrifice and personal honor, and to create peace it is necessary to express these sentiments in another, less bellicose way.

From 1915 until 1932, Sigmund Freud published a serious of reflections on aggression, war and civilization. Like Albert Einstein, with whom he corresponded, Freud was a pacifist.

But he postulated the existence of a 'death drive' (*thanatos*) that is ultimately responsible for the deplorable state of the human condition. And while *thanatos* could not be extinguished, Freud, foreshadowing Lorenz, claimed that aggression might be rechannelled, or sublimated, into non-destructive activities. While Freud was of course better known for his understanding of *inner* conflict, he also contributed significantly to assessing how outer conflicts might be mollified if humanity's destructive propensities could be redirected. In this lay the hope of human civilization, according to Freud.

Konrad Lorenz (1966) agreed with Freud that aggression is instinctive. However, he believed that fighting within a species (including humanity) performs species-preserving functions, and he emphasized the role of inhibitions, which control aggression and deter us from killing fellow animals. Paradoxically, Lorenz believed that the same unique characteristics that elevate humanity above the rest of nature – conceptual thinking and verbal speech – may also cause its extinction. However, many reductionistic theories regard violence as an inherent human (and animal) tendency and ignore its social and cultural roots.

Investigators after Lorenz argued that significant cultural variations in humans' propensity to violence necessitate the reconsideration of theories of biological determinism of violence. And the data from cross-cultural studies have tended to favour theories of cultural constructivism.

For example, the 'Seville Statement' of 1986, by a distinguished group of social and biological scientists, provided a list of objections to biological determinism. And the growing realization that both the theories of biological determinism and cultural constructivism are too reductionistic, led to the development of interactionist perspectives on violent behaviour, combining such multiple factors as personality, motivation and situational variables. According to Zillmann's 'excitation transfer model' (1979), the violent expression of individual aggression is a function of learned behaviour, a personal expression of an aroused state, and it is based on excitation by another, external source.

The German philosopher T. Adorno and the American social psychologist N. Sanford approached individual inclinations toward violence from a more political perspective. In *The Authoritarian Personality* (1950) they connected anti-Semitism, proto-fascism and other anti-democratic practices with a set of personal traits that predisposes one to act in these ways. The 'authoritarian personality' was negatively associated with peace-supportiveness. Similarly, the 'Machiavellian personality', as described by R. Christie and F. Geis in their *Studies in Machiavellianism* (1970), is likely to be supportive of unjust and violent behaviour, if it is profitable for the person. In opposition to the Machiavellian personality stands the altruistic personality – emphatic, moral and highly peace-supportive.

In 1939, Dollard, in contrast, assumed that it was individuals' frustration with their environment that causes people to turn violent. According to the frustration–aggression hypothesis, when circumstances disallow people from achieving their goals, individuals are likely to engage in aggressive behaviour. Subsequent studies by Milgram in the 1960s showed the importance of situational factors; so Dollard's causal hyptheis has been shown to be too far-reaching, because, according to Bandura, subjectivity and the possibility of social learning were downplayed. Milgram, in contrast, connected violence with individual obedience to perceived authority figures. His classic experiments demonstrated that specific situations often elicit compliance and aggression.

Groups, prejudice, images of the enemy and human needs

In *Victims of Groupthink* (1972), Irving Janis focused on the failures of group decision-making. He found that groups sometimes make irrational decisions and authorize extremely dehumanizing activities, such as large-scale bombing, because the core concern is to reach group consensus, not the quality of the decision. Janis named this phenomenon 'groupthink' and claimed that it may result in the group's illusion of invulnerability, while viewing the opponent as weak and stupid.

In *The Nature of Prejudice* (1954) Gordon Allport argued that prejudice is founded on igno-rance of others; therefore, less ignorance would mean less prejudice. Allport claimed that conflicts escalate due to ignorance of one's adversaries. According to Allport's 'contact hypothesis', an increase in social interaction between members of in- and out-groups could reduce intergroup prejudice.

Jerome Frank, in *Sanity and Survival: Psychological Aspects of War and Peace* (1968) and Ralph White, in *Fearful Warriors* (1984) and *Psychology and the Prevention of Nuclear War* (1986), empha-sized the dangers of developing diabolical enemy images, which people tend to create, espe-cially when they feel threatened. White developed U. Bronfenbrenner's theory of mirror images (1961) and emphasized their destructive consequences.

Charles Osgood, in *An Alternative to War or Surrender* (1962), proposed 'Graduated and Recip-rocated Initiatives in Tension-reduction' (GRIT), a method of defusing international tensions by having each side take turns at initiating tension-reducing actions. President Kennedy and Soviet premier Khrushchev engaged in GRIT when they took a series of initiatives that cul-minated in a nuclear arms-control treaty in the early 1960s.

John Burton, in *Conflict Resolution and Prevention* (1990), claimed that human needs, values and interests are relevant for understanding the causes of conflicts. Many violent conflicts result from the suppression of human needs. Basic needs, such as security, and core values are not negotiable, unlike interests, which are negotiable and depend on circumstances.

Johan Galtung, perhaps the dean of peace studies, for several decades has also been stress-ing the primacy of human needs – especially our needs for security and identity, which, if frustrated, may engender intrastate and destructive identity conflicts. He argues that sustain-able peace requires the satisfaction of our needs for security, identity, well-being and self-determination. For Galtung, psychology has much to say about the causes of intolerance and the way to increase peace and tolerance.

Attribution, intergroup relations and just world theories of behaviour

Attributions refer to the causal explanations that people devise in order rationalize both phys-ical events and human behaviour, especially acts perceived as successes or failures and that benefit or harm oneself and others. Attribution theory is especially relevant for understanding behaviour that is based on cognitive errors and biases, and that may often lead to interper-sonal and group conflict.

According to Brewer's 'optimal distinctiveness theory' (1991), humans are characterized by two opposing needs – a need to belong and the need for differentiation – and we seek to maintain some balance between them. Later, Brewer (2007) argued that a major consequence of in-group identification is that individuals modify their social behaviour depending whether they are interacting with an in-group or an out-group; groups promote trust and cooperation within the group, and caution, wariness and constraint in intergroup interactions. Thus stere-otypical and ethnocentric intergroup attributions are necessary consequences of in-group/out-group differences.

These attributions are governed by such attribution biases as 'the illusion of control'. This is an idea put forward by contemporary 'just-world theory', according to which there is a (deterministic) tendency of people to believe that the world is a just place, one in which people get what they deserve – 'good things happen to good people and bad things happen to bad people'. Therefore, we tend to blame the victim for his/her misfortune, and not the society/culture/economy/environment. (Lerner, 1977; Lerner & Miller, 1978). If our thinking is 'self-serving' and 'other-blaming', then it's easy to valorize one's 'own' group and demean or demonize others and to rationalize 'our' good fortune and the misfortune of others.

According to Tajfel (1981), social groups may activate or accentuate existing stereotypes for the purpose of anxiety reduction. For example, racists, Nazis and other anti-Semites attribute large-scale distressing events – such as economic recessions – to the actions of specific outgroups, e.g. to blacks, Jews and 'gypsies'. They do this to relieve themselves of any blame or guilt for antisocial beliefs and to rationalize and justify violent and discriminatory actions committed or planned against out-groups.

This dynamic could be malevolent because the social-psychological process of categorizing individuals into in-groups and out-groups may lead to depersonalization: individuals are perceived as without distinctive features and as anonymous members of a 'mass'. And 'they' may no longer viewed as (fully) human, especially when the language of dehumanization is at play (Brennan, 1995).

According to Brennan, crimes against humanity share a common language of dehumanization. Labelling people as more or less human facilitates or makes possible denying them their basic and essential dignity as fully fledged human beings. To Brennan, an important part of the solution to human oppression would be to change from dehumanizing, 'toxic' rhetoric to life-affirming rhetoric. Brennan speaks of an 'expansive definition of humanity', one that embraces all human persons regardless of their physical characteristics or stage of life.

The discourse of dehumanization motivates and activates stereotypical and ethnocentric thinking and behaviour; once viewed as 'sub-human', other groups and individuals are easily stripped of their dignity, and their humanity is denied. Discriminatory, belligerent and even genocidal behaviour against 'non-persons' may therefore be 'justifiable'.

Biased attributions may also be present at the level of larger-scale societal, class, religious, cultural and even civilizational attributions. For example, many Westerners, especially affluent ones, tend make more dispositional attributions ('individuals make their own destinies'), based on shared cultural assumptions of Western individualism; whereas people in non-Western cultures may attribute beneficial or harmful events and actions to fate, nature, collectivity or the 'will of God'. This provides an ideological and motivational basis for a 'clash of civilizations' and a 'war between cultures', with all participants in the conflict believing they are 'good', their adversaries are 'evil' and 'God is on our side'.

Goal compatibility and group interdependence

Based on his studies of boys' camps, Sherif (1966) claimed that group dynamics depend on the compatibility or incompatibility of goals – the higher the perceived incompatibility of intergroup goals, the greater the likelihood of conflict, and vice versa. And according to 'relative deprivation theory' (Berkowitz, 1962), under conditions of relative deprivation –when people believe that they have less than what they feel entitled to – humans feel frustrated; and in the presence of aversive and aggressive stimuli, collective violence happens.

Brewer (2000) argued that perceptions of common goals and common threats may promote intergroup conflict and hostility, because positive interdependence threatens intergroup differentiation. Volkan (1985) had reached a similar conclusion 15 years earlier, arguing that groups have a need for a bipolar relation – us versus them – with their enemies, and this need becomes exaggerated and possibly accompanied by violence if a group's identity is threatened. Another group is perceived as a 'container' of unacceptable psychic content previously built into unconscious mechanisms. According to Volkan, the perception of an 'enemy' is formulated in a way to protect oneself from contamination by the possible boomeranging of psychic content.

Altruism, aggression and reconciliation

In sharp contract to the paradigm that human behaviour is primarily egoistic, altruism denotes activities that are costly to individuals themselves but benefit others. According to the empirically well-supported 'empathy-altruism hypothesis', formulated by Batson et al. (2003), empathic concern (an emotional reaction brought about by the act of perspective-taking, and characterized by such feelings as compassion, tenderness, soft-heartedness and sympathy for another) leads to truly selfless motivation to help the other person.

De Waal (1990) argues against the allegedly antisocial character of aggression and instead proposes a 'reconciliation hypothesis', according to which aggression is a well-integrated part of social life. By examining the dynamics of social interactions among non-human primates, de Waal argues that confrontation should not be viewed as a barrier to sociality but rather as an unavoidable element, upon which social relationships can be built and strengthened through reconciliation. Social animals, including humans, seek contact with former opponents and engage in post-conflict reunion practices like kissing, embracing, sexual intercourse, grooming, etc. Reconciliation serves to decrease aggression and socially destabilizing anxiety. Reconciliation occurs especially after a conflict between parties whose possible partnership may have a high socially reproductive value.

De Waal's demonstration of reconciliation in both monkeys and apes supports his idea that forgiveness and peacemaking are widespread among non-human primates. The evolutionary advantages of reconciliation are obvious for animals that survive through mutual aid, i.e., the continuation of cooperation among parties with partially conflicting interests. De Waal's findings regarding non-human primates (especially among the young) may have significant potential applications for understanding human conflict resolution: to him, reconciliation behaviour must be seen as a shared heritage of the primate order.

Conclusion and directions for future research

Peace and conflict studies in general, and peace psychology in particular, have come very far in a relatively brief period. But they have a great deal more to offer – both for studying and for making peace.

For example, by focusing less on 'terrorists', and more on the victims of all forms of political violence, especially that perpetrated by states, we might transform the current, constrained terrorism discussion in the West. By developing a cross-cultural political psychology of terrorism, peace psychology might contribute to negotiations between adversaries, instead of violent confrontation, and to reconciliation rather than revenge.

Psychology might also contribute to peacemaking and war prevention by investigating the inner and intersubjective factors that facilitate or block peace. Minds at peace, and families, small groups and organizations that practise equitable and nonviolent modes of conflict resolution, are less predisposed to violence.

Peace psychology is indispensable – both to peace and conflict studies, and to peace.

References

Barash, D.P. and C.P. Webel (2009). *Peace and Conflict Studies*. Second edition. London: Sage.

Batson, C. D., P.A.M. Van Lange, N. Ahmad and D.A. Lishner (2003). 'Altruism and Helping Behavior', in M. A. Hogg and J. Cooper, eds., *Sage Handbook of Social Psychology*. London: Sage Publications, 279–295.

Berkowitz, L. (1962). *Aggression: A Social Psychological Analysis*. New York: McGraw-Hill.

Bercovich, J., V. Kremenjuk and I.W. Zartman, eds. (2009). *The Sage Handbook of Conflict Resolution*. London: Sage.

Brennan, W. (1995). *Dehumanizing the Vulnerable: When Word Games Take Lives*. Chicago: Loyola University Press.

Brewer, M.B. (1991). 'The Social Self – On Being the Same and Different at the Same Time', *Personality and Social Psychology Bulletin*, 17(5), 475–482.

Brewer, M.B. (2000). 'Superordinate Goals versus Superordinate Identity as Bases for Intergroup Cooperation', in D. Capozza and R. Brown, eds., *Social Identity Processes*. London: Sage, 117–132.

Brewer, M.B. (2007). 'The Importance of Being We: Human Nature and Intergroup Relations', *American Psychologist*, 62, 728–738.

Christie, D.J. (2006). 'What is Peace Psychology the Psychology of?', *Journal of Social Issues*, Volume 62, Number 1, Oxford: Blackwell Publishing, 1–17.

Christie, D.J., R.V. Wagner and D.D. Winter (2001). *Peace, Conflict, and Violence: Peace Psychology for the 21st Century*. Upper Saddle River, New Jersey: Prentice-Hall.

de Waal, F. (1990). *Peacemaking Among Primates*. Cambridge, MA: Harvard University Press.

Jeong, Ho-Wen (2000). *Peace and Conflict Studies: An Introduction*. Aldershot: Ashgate.

Lerner, M.J. (1977). 'The Justice Motive: Some Hypotheses as to its Origins and Forms', *Journal of Personality*, 45, 1–52.

Lerner, M.J. and D.T. Miller (1978). 'Just World Research and the Attribution Process: Looking Back and Ahead', *Psychological Bulletin*, 85, 1030–1051

MacNair, R.M. (2003). *The Psychology of Peace: An Introduction*. Westport, CT: Praeger.

Sherif, M. (1966). *In Common Predicament: Social Psychology of Intergroup Conflict and Cooperation*. Boston: Houghton Mifflin.

Tajfel, H. (1981). 'Social Stereotypes and Social Groups', in J.C. Turner and H. Giles, eds., *Intergroup Behavior*. Oxford: Blackwell Publishing, 144–167.

UNESCO (1986) Seville Statement on Violence, Spain: http://portal.unesco.org/education/en/ev.php-URL_ID=3247&URL_DO=DO_TOPIC&URL_SECTION=201.html

Volkan, V.D. (1985). 'The Need to Have Enemies and Allies: A Developmental Approach', *Political Psychology*, 6(2), 219–247.

Webel, C. and J. Galtung, eds. (2009). *Handbook of Peace and Conflict Studies*. London & New York: Routledge.

Additional resources

Reflections on the History and Status of Peace Research: http://www.wcfia.harvard.edu/node/867

Peace Psychology History: http://www.rachelmacnair.com/peace-psych-history

The American Psychology Association, Division of Peace Psychology: http://www.webster.edu/peacepsychology/

23 "The evil scourge of terrorism"

Reality, construction, remedy

Noam Chomsky (Erich Fromm Lecture, April 3, 2010)

The president could not have been more justified when he condemned "the evil scourge of terrorism." I am quoting Ronald Reagan, who came into office in 1981, declaring that a focus of his foreign policy would be state-directed international terrorism, "the plague of the modern age" and "a return to barbarism in our time," to sample some of the rhetoric of his administration.

When George W. Bush declared a "war on terror" 20 years later, he was *re*-declaring the war, an important fact that is worth exhuming from Orwell's memory hole if we hope to understand the nature of the evil scourge of terrorism, or more importantly, if we hope to understand ourselves. We do not need the famous Delphi inscription to recognize that there can be no more important task. Just as a personal aside, that critical necessity was forcefully brought home to me almost 70 years ago in my first encounter with Erich Fromm's work, in his classic essay on the escape to freedom in the modern world, and the grim paths that the modern free individual was tempted to choose in the effort to escape the loneliness and anguish that accompanied the newly discovered freedom – matters all too pertinent today, unfortunately.

The reasons why Reagan's war on terror has been dispatched to the repository of unwelcome facts are understandable and informative – about ourselves. Instantly, Reagan's war on terror became a savage terrorist war, leaving hundreds of thousands of tortured and mutilated corpses in the wreckage of Central America, tens of thousands more in the Middle East, and an estimated 1.5 million killed by South African terror that was strongly supported by the Reagan administration in violation of congressional sanctions. All of these murderous exercises of course had pretexts. The resort to violence always does. In the Middle East, Reagan's decisive support for Israel's 1982 invasion of Lebanon, which killed some 15–20,000 people and destroyed much of southern Lebanon and Beirut, was based on the pretense that it was in self-defense against PLO rocketing of the Galilee, a brazen fabrication: Israel recognized at once that the threat was PLO diplomacy, which might have undermined Israel's illegal takeover of the occupied territories. In Africa, support for the marauding of the apartheid state was officially justified within the framework of the war on terror: It was necessary to protect white South Africa from one of the world's "more notorious terrorist groups," Nelson Mandela's African National Congress, so Washington determined in 1988. The pretexts in the other cases were no more impressive.

For the most part, the victims of Reaganite terror were defenseless civilians, but in one case the victim was a state, Nicaragua, which could respond through legal channels. Nicaragua brought its charges to the World Court, which condemned the US for "unlawful use of force" – in lay terms, international terrorism – in its attack on Nicaragua from its Honduran bases, and ordered the US to terminate the assault and pay substantial reparations. The aftermath is instructive.

Congress responded to the Court judgment by increasing aid to the US-run mercenary army attacking Nicaragua, while the press condemned the Court as a "hostile forum" and therefore irrelevant. The same Court had been highly relevant a few years earlier when it ruled in favor of the US against Iran. Washington dismissed the Court judgment with contempt. In doing so, it joined the distinguished company of Libya's Qaddafi and Albania's Enver Hoxha. Libya and Albania have since joined the world of law-abiding states in this respect, so now the US stands in splendid isolation. Nicaragua then brought the matter to the UN Security Council, which passed two resolutions calling on all states to observe international law. The resolutions were vetoed by the US, with the assistance of Britain and France, which abstained. All of this passed virtually without notice, and has been expunged from history.

Also forgotten – or rather, never noticed – is the fact that the "hostile forum" had bent over backwards to accommodate Washington. The Court rejected almost all of Nicaragua's case, presented by a distinguished Harvard University international lawyer, on the grounds that when the US had accepted World Court jurisdiction in 1946, it added a reservation exempting itself from charges under international treaties, specifically the Charters of the United Nations and the Organization of American States. Accordingly, the US is self-entitled to carry out aggression and other crimes that are far more serious than international terrorism. The Court correctly recognized this exemption, one aspect of much broader issues of sovereignty and global dominance that I will put aside.

Such thoughts as these should be uppermost in our minds when we consider the evil scourge of terrorism. We should also recall that although the Reagan years do constitute a chapter of unusual extremism in the annals of terrorism, they are not some strange departure from the norm. We find much the same at the opposite end of the political spectrum as well: the Kennedy administration. One illustration is Cuba. According to long-standing myth, thoroughly dismantled by recent scholarship, the US intervened in Cuba in 1898 to secure its liberation from Spain. In reality, the intervention was designed to *prevent* Cuba's imminent liberation from Spain, turning it into a virtual colony of the United States. In 1959, Cuba finally did liberate itself, causing consternation in Washington. Within months, the Eisenhower administration planned in secret to overthrow the government, and initiated bombing and economic sanctions. The basic thinking was expressed by a high State Department official: Castro would be removed "through disenchantment and disaffection based on economic dissatisfaction and hardship [so] every possible means should be undertaken promptly to weaken the economic life of Cuba [in order to] bring about hunger, desperation and [the] overthrow of the government."

The incoming Kennedy administration took over and escalated these programs. The reasons are frankly explained in the internal record, since declassified. Violence and economic strangulation were undertaken in response to Cuba's "successful defiance" of US policies going back 150 years; no Russians, but rather the Monroe Doctrine, which established Washington's right to dominate the hemisphere.

The concerns of the Kennedy administration went beyond the need to punish successful defiance. The administration feared that the Cuban example might infect others with the thought of "taking matters into their own hands," an idea with great appeal throughout the continent because "the distribution of land and other forms of national wealth greatly favors the propertied classes and the poor and underprivileged, stimulated by the example of the Cuban revolution, are now demanding opportunities for a decent living." That was the warning conveyed to incoming President Kennedy by his Latin America advisor, liberal historian Arthur Schlesinger. The analysis was soon confirmed by the CIA, which observed that "Castro's shadow looms large because social and economic conditions throughout Latin

America invite opposition to ruling authority and encourage agitation for radical change," for which Castro's Cuba might provide a model.

Ongoing plans for invasion were soon implemented. When the invasion failed at the Bay of Pigs, Washington turned to a major terrorist war. The president assigned responsibility for the war to his brother, Robert Kennedy, whose highest priority was to bring "the terrors of the earth" to Cuba, in the words of his biographer, Arthur Schlesinger. The terrorist war was no slight affair; it was also a major factor in bringing the world to the verge of nuclear war in 1962, and was resumed as soon as the missile crisis ended. The terrorist war continued through the century from US territory, though in later years Washington no longer undertook terrorist attacks against Cuba, but only provided the base for them, and continues to provide haven to some of the most notorious international terrorists, with a long record of these and other crimes: Orlando Bosch, Luis Posada Carriles, and numerous others whose names would be well-known in the West if the concerns about terrorism were principled. Commentators are polite enough not to recall the Bush doctrine declared when he attacked Afghanistan: those who harbor terrorists are as guilty as the terrorists themselves, and must be treated accordingly, by bombing and invasion.

Perhaps this is enough to illustrate that state-directed international terrorism is considered an appropriate tool of diplomacy across the political spectrum. Nevertheless, Reagan was the first modern president to employ the audacious device of concealing his resort to "the evil scourge of terrorism" under the cloak of a "war on terror."

The audacity of Reaganite terrorism was as impressive as its scale. To select only one example, for which events in Germany provided a pretext, in April 1986 the US Air Force bombed Libya, killing dozens of civilians. To add a personal note, on the day of the bombing, at about 6:30pm, I received a phone call from Tripoli from the Mideast correspondent of ABC TV, Charles Glass, an old friend. He advised me to watch the 7pm TV news. In 1986, all the TV channels ran their major news programs at 7pm. I did so, and exactly at 7, agitated news anchors switched to their facilities in Libya so that they could present, live, the US bombing of Tripoli and Benghazi, the first bombing in history enacted for prime time TV – no slight logistical feat: the bombers were denied the right to cross France and had to take a long detour over the Atlantic to arrive just in time for the evening news. After showing the exciting scenes of the cities in flames, the TV channels switched to Washington, for sober discussion of how the US was defending itself against Libyan terror, under the newly devised doctrine of "self-defense against future attack." Officials informed the country that they had certain knowledge that Libya had carried out a bombing of a disco in Berlin a few days earlier in which a US soldier had been killed. The certainty reduced to zero shortly after, as quietly conceded well after its purpose had been served. And it would have been hard to find even a raised eyebrow about the idea that the disco bombing would have justified the murderous assault on Libyan civilians.

The media were also polite enough not to notice the curious timing. Commentators were entranced by the solidity of the non-existent evidence and Washington's dedication to law. In a typical reaction, the *New York Times* editors explained that "even the most scrupulous citizen can only approve and applaud the American attacks on Libya . . . the United States has prosecuted [Qaddafi] carefully, proportionately – and justly," the evidence for Libyan responsibility for the disco bombing has been "now laid out clearly to the public," and "then came the jury, the European governments to which the United States went out of its way to send emissaries to share evidence and urge concerted action against the Libyan leader." Entirely irrelevant is that no credible evidence was laid out and that the "jury" was quite skeptical, particularly in Germany itself, where intensive investigation had found no evidence at all; or that the jury was calling on the executioner to refrain from any action.

The bombing of Libya was neatly timed for a congressional vote on aid to the US-run terrorist force attacking Nicaragua. To ensure that the timing would not be missed, Reagan made the connection explicit. In an address the day after the bombing Reagan said:

> I would remind the House [of Representatives] voting this week that this arch-terrorist [Qaddafi] has sent $400 million and an arsenal of weapons and advisers into Nicaragua to bring his war home to the United States. He has bragged that he is helping the Nicaraguans because they fight America on its own ground.

Namely America's own ground in Nicaragua. The idea that the "mad dog" was bringing his war home to us by providing arms to a country we were attacking with a CIA-run terrorist army based in our Honduran dependency was a nice touch, which did not go unnoticed. As the national press explained, the bombing of Libya should "strengthen President Reagan's hand in dealing with Congress on issues like the military budget and aid to Nicaraguan 'contras'."

This is only a small sample of Reagan's contributions to international terrorism. The most lasting among them was his enthusiastic organization of the *jihadi* movement in Afghanistan. The reasons were explained by the CIA station chief in Islamabad, who directed the project. In his words, the goal was to "kill Soviet Soldiers," a "noble goal" that he "loved," as did his boss in Washington. He also emphasized that "the mission was not to liberate Afghanistan" – and in fact it may have delayed Soviet withdrawal, some specialists believe. With his unerring instinct for favoring the most violent criminals, Reagan selected for lavish aid Gulbuddin Hekmatyar, famous for throwing acid in the faces of young women in Kabul and now a leader of the insurgents in Afghanistan, though perhaps he may soon join the other warlords of the Western-backed government, current reports suggest. Reagan also lent strong support to the worst of Pakistan's dictators, Zia ul-Haq, helping him to develop his nuclear weapons program and to carry out his Saudi-funded project of radical Islamization of Pakistan. There is no need to dwell on the legacy for these tortured countries and the world.

Apart from Cuba, the plague of state terror in the Western hemisphere was initiated with the Brazilian coup in 1964, installing the first of a series of neo-Nazi National Security States and initiating a plague of repression without precedent in the hemisphere, always strongly backed by Washington, hence a particularly violent form of state-directed international terrorism. The campaign was in substantial measure a war against the Church. It was more than symbolic that it culminated in the assassination of six leading Latin American intellectuals, Jesuit priests, in November 1989, a few days after the fall of the Berlin wall. They were murdered by an elite Salvadoran battalion, fresh from renewed training at the John F. Kennedy Special Forces School in North Carolina. As was learned in November 2008, but apparently aroused no interest, the order for the assassination was signed by the chief of staff and his associates, all of them so closely connected to the Pentagon and the US Embassy that it becomes even harder to imagine that Washington was unaware of the plans of its model battalion. This elite force had already left a trail of blood of the usual victims through the hideous decade of the 1980s in El Salvador, which opened with the assassination of Archbishop Romero, "the voice of the voiceless," by many of the same hands.

The murder of the Jesuit priests was a crushing blow to liberation theology, the remarkable revival of Christianity initiated by Pope John XXIII at Vatican II, which he opened in 1962, an event that "ushered in a new era in the history of the Catholic Church," in the words of the distinguished theologian and historian of Christianity, Hans Küng. Inspired by Vatican II, Latin American bishops adopted "the preferential option for the poor," renewing the radical pacifism of the Gospels that had been put to rest when the Emperor Constantine established Christianity as the religion of the Roman Empire – "a revolution" that converted "the persecuted church" to a "persecuting church," in Küng's words. In the post-Vatican II attempt to revive the Christianity of the pre-Constantine period, priests, nuns, and laypersons took the message of the Gospels to the poor and the persecuted, brought them together in "base communities," and encouraged them to take their fate into their own hands and to work together to overcome the misery of survival in the brutal realms of US power.

The reaction to this grave heresy was not long in coming. The first salvo was the Kennedy-initiated military coup in Brazil in 1964, overthrowing a mildly social democratic government and instituting a reign of torture and violence. The campaign ended with the murder of the Jesuit intellectuals 20 years ago. There has been much debate about who deserves the credit for the fall of the Berlin wall, but there is none about the responsibility for the brutal demolition of the attempt to revive the church of the Gospels. Washington's School of the Americas, famous for its training of Latin American killers, proudly announced as one of its "talking points" that liberation theology was "defeated with the assistance of the US army" – given a helping hand, to be sure, by the Vatican, using the gentler means of expulsion and suppression.

November 2009 was dedicated to celebration of the 20th anniversary of the liberation of Eastern Europe from Russian tyranny, a victory of the forces of "love, tolerance, nonviolence, the human spirit and forgiveness," as Vaclav Havel declared. Less attention – in fact, virtually zero – was devoted to the brutal assassination of his Salvadoran counterparts a few days after the Berlin wall fell. And I doubt that one could even find an allusion to what that brutal assassination signified: the end of a decade of vicious terror in Central America, and the final triumph of the "return to barbarism in our time" that opened with the 1964 Brazilian coup, leaving many religious martyrs in its wake and ending the heresy initiated in Vatican II – not exactly an era of "love, tolerance, nonviolence, the human spirit and forgiveness."

We can wait until tomorrow to see how much attention will be given to the 30th anniversary of the assassination of the Voice of the Voiceless while he was reading mass, a few days after he wrote a letter to President Carter pleading with him – in vain – not to send aid to the military junta, who "know only how to repress the people and defend the interests of the Salvadorean oligarchy" and will use the aid "to destroy the people's organizations fighting to defend their fundamental human rights." As happened. And we can learn a good bit from what we are unlikely to see tomorrow.

The contrast between the celebration in November 2009 of the fall of the tyranny of the enemy, and the silence about the culmination of the hideous atrocities in our own domains, is so glaring that it takes real dedication to miss it. It sheds a somber light on our moral and intellectual culture. The same is true of the retrospective assessments of the Reagan era. We can put aside the mythology about his achievements, which would have impressed Kim il-Sung. What he actually did has virtually disappeared. President Obama hails him as a "transformative figure." At Stanford University's prestigious Hoover Institution, Reagan is revered as a colossus whose "spirit seems to stride the country, watching us like a warm and friendly ghost." We arrive by plane in Washington at Reagan international airport – or if we prefer, at John Foster Dulles international airport, honoring another prominent terrorist commander, whose exploits include overthrowing Iranian and Guatemalan democracy, and installing the terror and torture state of the Shah and the most vicious of the terrorist states of Central America. The terrorist exploits of Washington's Guatemalan clients reached true genocide in the highlands in the 1980s while Reagan praised the worst of the killers, Rioss Montt, as "a man of great personal integrity" who was "totally dedicated to democracy" and was receiving a "bum rap" from human rights organizations.

I have been writing about international terrorism ever since Reagan declared a war on terror in 1981. In doing so, I have kept to the official definitions of "terrorism" in US and British law and in army manuals, all approximately the same. To take one succinct official definition, terrorism is "the calculated use of violence or threat of violence to attain goals that are political, religious, or ideological in nature . . . through intimidation, coercion, or instilling fear." Everything I have just described, and a great deal more like it, falls within the category of terrorism, in fact state-directed international terrorism, in the technical sense of US-British law.

For exactly that reason, the official definitions are unusable. They fail to make a crucial distinction: the concept of "terrorism" must somehow be crafted to include *their* terrorism against *us*, while excluding *our* terrorism against *them*, often far more extreme. To devise such a definition is a challenging task. Accordingly, from the 1980s there have been many scholarly conferences, academic publications, and international symposia devoted to the task of defining "terrorism." In public discourse the problem does not arise. Well-educated circles have internalized the special sense of "terrorism" required for justification of state action and control of domestic populations, and departure from the canon is generally ignored, or if noticed, elicits impressive tantrums.

Let us keep, then, to convention, and restrict attention to the terror *they* commit against *us*. It is no laughing matter, and sometimes reaches extreme levels. Probably the most egregious single crime of international terrorism in the modern era was the destruction of the World Trade Center on 9/11, killing almost 3,000 people, a "crime against humanity" carried out with "wickedness and awesome cruelty," as Robert Fisk reported. It is widely agreed that 9/11 changed the world.

Awful as the crime was, one can imagine worse. Suppose that al-Qaeda had been supported by an awesome superpower intent on overthrowing the government of the United States. Suppose that the attack had succeeded: al-Qaeda had bombed the White House, killed the president, and installed a vicious military dictatorship, which killed some 50–100,000 people, brutally tortured 700,000, set up a major center of terror and subversion that carried out assassinations throughout the world, and helped establish "National Security States" elsewhere that tortured and murdered with abandon. Suppose further that the dictator brought in economic advisers who within a few years drove the economy to one of the worst disasters in its history while their proud mentors collected Nobel Prizes and received other accolades. That would have been vastly more horrendous even than 9/11.

And as we all should know, it is not necessary to imagine, because it in fact did happen: in Chile, on the date that Latin Americans sometimes call "the first 9/11," September 11, 1973. The only change I have made is to per capita equivalents, an appropriate measure. But the first 9/11 did not change history, for good reasons: the events were too normal. In fact the installation of the Pinochet regime was just one event in the plague that began with the military coup in Brazil in 1964, spreading with similar or even worse horrors in other countries and reaching Central America in the 1980s under Reagan – whose South American favorite was the regime of the Argentine generals, the most savage of them all, consistent with his general stance on state violence.

Putting all of this inconvenient reality aside, let us continue to follow convention and imagine that the war on terror re-declared by George W. Bush on 9/11 2001 was directed to ending the plague of international terrorism, properly restricted in scope to satisfy doctrinal needs. There were sensible steps that could have been undertaken to achieve that goal. The murderous acts of 9/11 were bitterly condemned even within the *jihadi* movements. One constructive step would have been to isolate al-Qaeda, and unify opposition to it even among those attracted to its project. Nothing of the sort ever seems to have been considered. Instead, the Bush administration and its allies chose to unify the *jihadi* movement in support of Bin Laden and to mobilize many others to his cause by confirming his charge that the West is at war with Islam: invading Afghanistan and then Iraq, resorting to torture and rendition, and in general, choosing violence for the purposes of state power. With good reason, the hawkish Michael Scheuer, who was in charge of tracking Bin Laden for the CIA for many years, concludes that "the United States of America remains Bin Laden's only indispensable ally."

The same conclusion was drawn by US Major Matthew Alexander, perhaps the most respected of US interrogators, who elicited the information that led to the capture of Abu Musab al-Zarqawi, the head of al-Qaeda in Iraq. Alexander has only contempt for the harsh interrogation methods demanded by the Bush administration. Like FBI interrogators, he believes that the Rumsfeld–Cheney preference for torture elicits no useful information, in contrast with more humane forms of interrogation that have even succeeded in converting the targets and enlisting them as reliable informants and collaborators. He singles out Indonesia for its successes in civilized forms of interrogation, and urges the US to follow its methods. Not only does Rumsfeld–Cheney torture elicit no useful information: it also creates terrorists. From hundreds of interrogations, Alexander discovered that many foreign fighters came to Iraq in reaction to the abuses at Guantánamo and Abu Ghraib, and that they and their domestic allies turned to suicide bombing and other terrorist acts for the same reason. He believes that the use of torture may have led to the death of more US soldiers than the toll of the 9/11 terrorist attack. The most significant revelation in the released Torture Memos is that interrogators were under "relentless pressure" from Cheney and Rumsfeld to resort to harsher methods to find evidence for their fantastic claim that Saddam Hussein was cooperating with al-Qaeda.

The attack on Afghanistan in October 2001 is called "the good war," no questions asked, a justifiable act of self-defense with the noble aim of protecting human rights from the evil Taliban. There are a few problems with that near-universal contention. For one thing, the goal was not to remove the Taliban. Rather, Bush informed the people of Afghanistan that they would be bombed unless the Taliban turned Bin Laden over to the US, as they might have done, had the US agreed to their request to provide some evidence of his responsibility for 9/11. The request was dismissed with contempt, for good reasons. As the head of the FBI conceded eight months later, after the most intensive international investigation in history they still had no evidence, and certainly had none the preceding October. The most he could say is that the FBI "believed" that the plot had been hatched in Afghanistan and had been implemented in the Gulf Emirates and Germany.

Three weeks after the bombing began, war aims shifted to overthrow of the regime. British Admiral Sir Michael Boyce announced that the bombing would continue until "the people of the country . . . get the leadership changed" – a textbook case of international terrorism. It is also not true that there were no objections to the attack. With virtual unanimity, international aid organizations vociferously objected because it terminated their aid efforts, which were desperately needed. At the time it was estimated that some 5 million people were relying on aid for survival, and that an additional 2.5 million would be put at risk of starvation by the US–UK attack. The bombing was therefore an example of extreme criminality, whether or not the anticipated consequences took place.

Furthermore, the bombing was bitterly condemned by leading anti-Taliban Afghans, including the US favorite, Abdul Haq, who was given special praise as a martyr after the war by President Hamid Karzai. Just before he entered Afghanistan, and was captured and killed, he condemned the bombing that was then underway and criticized the US for refusing to support efforts of his and others "to create a revolt within the Taliban." The bombing was "a big setback for these efforts," he said, outlining them and calling on the US to assist them with funding and other support instead of undermining them with bombs. The US, he said, "is trying to show its muscle, score a victory and scare everyone in the world. They don't care about the suffering of the Afghans or how many people we will lose."

Shortly after, 1000 Afghan leaders gathered in Peshawar, some of them exiles, some coming from within Afghanistan, all committed to overthrowing the Taliban regime. It was "a rare display of unity among tribal elders, Islamic scholars, fractious politicians, and former guerrilla commanders," the press reported. They had many disagreements, but unanimously "urged the US to stop the air raids" and appealed to the international media to call for an end to the "bombing of innocent people." They urged that other means be adopted to overthrow the hated Taliban regime, a goal they believed could be achieved without further death and destruction. The bombing was also harshly condemned by the prominent women's organization RAWA – which received some belated recognition when it became ideologically serviceable to express concern (briefly) about the fate of women in Afghanistan.

In short, the unquestionably "good war" does not look so good when we pay some attention to unacceptable facts.

It should not be necessary to tarry on the invasion of Iraq. Keeping solely to the effect on *jihadi* terror, the invasion was undertaken with the expectation that it would lead to an increase in terrorism, as it did, far beyond what was anticipated. It caused a seven-fold increase in terror, according to analyses by US terrorism experts.

One may ask why these attacks were undertaken, but it is reasonably clear that confronting the evil scourge of terrorism was not a high priority, if it was even a consideration.

If that had been the goal, there were options to pursue. Some I have already mentioned. More generally, the US and Britain could have followed the proper procedures for dealing with a major crime: determine who is responsible, apprehend the suspects (with international cooperation if necessary; easy to obtain), and bring them to a fair trial. Furthermore, attention would be paid to the roots of terror. That can be extremely effective, as the US and UK had just learned in Northern Ireland. IRA terror was a very serious matter. As long as London reacted by violence, terror, and torture, it was the "indispensable ally" of the more violent elements of the IRA, and the cycle of terror escalated. By the late '90s, London began to attend to the grievances that lay at the roots of the terror, and to deal with those that were legitimate – as should be done irrespective of terror. Within a few years terror virtually disappeared. I happened to be in Belfast in 1993. It was a war zone. I was there again last fall. There are tensions, but at a level that is barely detectable to a visitor. There are important lessons here. Even without this experience we should know that violence engenders violence, while sympathy and concern cool passions and can evoke cooperation and empathy.

If we seriously want to end the plague of terrorism, we know how to do it. First, end our own role as perpetrators. That alone will have a substantial effect. Second, attend to the grievances that are typically in the background, and if they are legitimate, do something about them. Third, if an act of terror occurs, deal with it as a criminal act: identify and apprehend the suspects and carry out an honest judicial process. That actually works. In contrast, the techniques that are employed enhance the threat of terror. The evidence is fairly strong, and falls together with much else.

This is not the only case where the approaches that might well reduce a serious threat are systematically avoided, and those that are unlikely to do so are adopted instead. One such case is the so-called "war on drugs." Over almost 40 years, the war has failed to curtail drug use or even the street price of drugs. It has been established by many studies, including those of the US government, that by far the most cost-effective approach to drug abuse is prevention and treatment. But that approach is consistently avoided in state policy, which prefers far more expensive, violent measures that have barely any impact on drug use, though they have other consistent consequences.

In cases like these, the only rational conclusion is that the declared goals are not the real ones, and that if we want to learn about the real goals, we should adopt an approach that is familiar in the law: relying on predictable outcome as evidence for intent. I think the approach leads to quite plausible conclusions, for the "war on drugs," the "war on terror," and much else. That, however, is work for another day.

PART 3: THE MEANINGS AND NATURE OF CONFLICT

Suggestions for further reading

Blumberg, Herbert H., A. Paul Hare and Anna Costin (2006). *Peace Psychology: A Comprehensive Introduction*. Cambridge: Cambridge University Press.
Brown, Michael E., Owen R. Cole, Jr., Sean M. Lynn-Jones and Steven E. Miller, eds. (1999). *Theories of War and Peace*. Cambridge, M.A. and London: MIT Press.
Brown, Seyom (2001). *The Causes and Prevention of War*. New York: Macmillan.
Camus, Albert (1972). *Neither Victims nor Executioners*. Chicago: World Without War Publications.
Christie, Daniel J., Richard V. Wagner and Deborah DuNann Winter, eds. (2001). *Peace, Conflict, and Violence Peace Psychology for the 21st Century*. Upper Saddle River, N.J.: Prentice Hall.
Frank, Jerome (1968). *Sanity and Survival Psychological Aspects of War and Peace*. New York: Vintage Books.
Fromm, Erich (1973). *The Anatomy of Human Destructiveness*. New York: Henry Holt.
Howard, Michael (1983). *The Causes of War*. Cambridge, M.A.: Harvard University Press.
Lutz, James, M. and Brenda J. Lutz (2005). *Terrorism: Origins and Evolution*. New York: Palgrave Macmillan.
Rapaport, Anatol (1997). *The Origins of Violence Approaches to the Study of Conflict*. New Brunswick, N.J. and London: Transaction.
Richardson, Louise (2007). *What Terrorists Want*. New York: Random House.
Manfred B. Steger and Nancy S. Lind, eds. (1999). *Violence and its Alternatives*. New York: St. Martin's Press.
Webel, Charles (2007). *Terror, Terrorism, and the Human Condition*. New York: Palgrave-Macmillan.
Webel, Charles and John Arnaldi, eds. (2011). *The Ethics and Efficacy of the Global War on Terror*. New York: Palgrave-Macmillan.

Journals

Critical Studies on Terrorism: http://www.tandf.co.uk/journals/titles/17539153.asp
Security Studies: http://www.tandf.co.uk/journals/titles/09636412.asp
Security Dialog: http://sdi.sagepub.com/

Websites

Transnational Foundation for Peace and Future Studies (TFF): http://transnational.org/
Alternative to Violence: http://www.avpusa.org/
Resources from United Nations Educational, Scientific and Cultural Organization (UNESCO): www.unesco.org/new/en/unesco/resources/
'Executive Summary' in The Global Burden of Armed Violence. Geneva: The Geneva Declaration Secretariat, 2008, 1–8: http://www.genevadeclaration.org/fileadmin/docs/Global-Burden-of-Armed-Violence-full-report.pdf

Questions for reflection and discussion

1   Consider the various meanings and definitions of violence. Which one(s) do you prefer and why?

2   From what you've now read about the origins of and reasons for war and other forms of violent human conflict, what would you consider to be the most and least plausible explanations? Why and why not?

3   If you were to design a violence-prevention programme for your community, what would you include and why?

4   Assess the strengths and weaknesses of such empirical tools as the Geneva Declaration and World Heath Organization documents.

5   Do you think the end of war, or of terrorism, is achievable in your lifetime? Why/why not?

Part 4

Conflict analysis, transformation and prevention

SUMMARY

Scientific studies of conflicts have developed enormously since pioneers like Quincy Wright published *A Study of War*[1] in 1942 and Lewis Fry Richardson published *Statistics of Deadly Quarrels*[2] in 1960. The sophisticated models of conflicts used today are based on theoretical accounts combined with case studies and years of practical work in the field. Insights into the dynamics and complexities of conflicts have led to a terminology reflecting the new understanding of conflicts as well as different views on what conflicts actually are. In the contemporary conflict analysis literature, concepts like *conflict resolution, conflict management, conflict transformation* and *conflict prevention* are used for specific understandings of how conflicts should be handled.

Even if many of the pioneers of what came to be named 'peace and conflict studies' were driven by the personal conviction that war is not the best way to respond to a conflict it was important for them to present their result in an unbiased and scientific way. Discussions about the ethical issues involved, 'neutrality', and 'normativity' are still going on.[3]

Over the years, many researchers and activists have argued that conflicts as such are not the problem. Some say conflicts are an integrated and natural part of everyday life and can be a good pedagogical resource. Almost all forms of human development, at individual and societal levels, include conflicts. Children have conflicts with their parents in the process of becoming independent adults; when societies based on agricultural production became industrialized, there were a number of necessary conflicts, just to mention two well-known illustrative cases. In the development of democratic rights and freedoms there are numerous conflicts with the old power-holders.

These processes still continue in Western societies; democracy is more a process than a system. It is when one or more of the stakeholders use violence that problems occur. When nonviolent means dominate, we are mainly pleased with the processes. When deaths and violence are the most visible consequences of conflicts, we often condemn them. The uprisings in Tunisia and Libya in early 2011 illustrate the differences between violent and nonviolent means. This is not to blame any actor in particular or to claim that it is easy to decide what to do in such complex processes, but we can observe the different consequences and reflect on what is happening.

Studies of conflicts are not limited to the confrontational peaks. The history prior to an escalation and the future after a violent phase are just as important. Reconciliation, Truth Commissions, courts and other processes of justice and/or healing are a growing field of studies and practices. Without wise actions after a war, the next war can come soon. The treatment of Germany in the Treaty of Versailles after World War I gave Hitler an easier way to power than if the winners had not humiliated the Germans.

Arms control and disarmament are important fields for students of peace and conflicts. Since Henry Dunant travelled through war-torn Normandy in June 1859, saw the horrors of war at the battle of Solferino and came up with the idea of the Red Cross, laws and conventions have become one of the main ways to reduce the suffering caused by war.[4] Starting with the Geneva Convention of 1864, which laid the foundation for contemporary humanitarian law, today we have hundreds of conventions and laws aiming to regulate warfare (*jus in bello*) and to decide when it is legal to use war as a means to address a conflict (*jus ad bellum*). Some argue that these laws, rules and conventions are of little value because they are violated in every war. But just as with criminal laws, which are also violated frequently, there are strong arguments for keeping them and for doing our best to create respect for them.

We have seen a growing number of institutions set up to respond when humanitarian law, laws of war, and international conventions are violated. Former political leaders are arrested and taken to court and sanctions of different kinds are imposed on states that do not respect these laws. Part of the work has been to reduce and limit the number of weapons. Extremely cruel and inhumane weapons systems, such as anti-personnel mines, have been made illegal (even if not all nations are decommissioning them). New initiatives aiming to regulate small arms transfers are in the process of being established.[5] Some states with nuclear weapons and other forms of weapons of mass destruction have agreed to reduce their arsenals. At the same time, many states do not accept the regulations of arms and the legal systems created to establish respect for these institutions. Some of those who refuse to join are among the largest nations in the world. They care more about their own domestic situation than about international agreements.

One problem with arguing against war as an instrument to handle conflicts has been the lack of apparent alternatives. In the last two decades, a number of initiatives posed as alternatives to war have been presented. Parts of the peace movement have moved their activities from traditional demonstrations outside parliaments and embassies to the war zones. They have developed new techniques and strategies for civilian interventions. One of them, the Nonviolent Peaceforce, has published an impressive feasibility study that provides a thorough record of the practices of different kinds of peace teams in the field.[6]

Parts of these projects are based on the idea that by observing and reporting atrocities and human right violations the perpetrators will, over time, behave better. It is like when you have guests in your house, you are prone to behave more decently with other family members than you otherwise may have done. One of these initiatives, Peace Brigades International, was founded 1981 and has been working in war zones like Nicaragua, Colombia, Nepal, Mexico, the Balkans, El Salvador, Guatemala, Sri Lanka and Haiti. Their work as 'unarmed bodyguards' has been greatly appreciated by threatened civilians.

One problem with all types of interventions, whether using military or nonviolent tools, is that it is difficult to measure the impact, because we will never know what would have happened without the intervention. Are they able to prevent or reduce violence? Are they doing more harm than good? Here there are needs for many more case studies and more comparative studies.

Conflict dynamics, resistance and democracy

A serious problem in many early analyses of conflicts was created by over-simplifications. A common one was that a war has only two actors. Anyone living in a war zone for some time understands that reality is so much more complex. Louis Kriesberg and Gearoid Millar understand this complexity fully and see it as an advantage. In their chapter 'Protagonist

Strategies that Help End Violence', based on concrete examples they map the main actors and the strategies these actors adopt as they escalate and de-escalate the conflicts. In many cases a number of armed actors are not part of a state structure, but their role in conflicts is not very different. There are overlaps and blurred borders between armed actors in conflicts. Many groups can have some sense of shared identity even if they belong to adversarial camps. Whether we look at proactive or reactive strategies, escalation or de-escalation, multiple relations between protagonists have an impact on the process. This complexity is very important to bear in mind for anyone who either wants to understand or act in a conflict, and Kriesberg and Millar help us to better understand the multifaceted processes in wars.

While nonviolence is usually regarded as one of the tools for civil society, Richard Falk in his chapter discusses the implications of nonviolent geopolitics. He sees military tools and their tragic consequences as 'pointless from every perspective'. For the U.S., hard-power solutions have led to a series of failures, acknowledged and unacknowledged, from the war in Vietnam to the United States' reactions to the attacks on the Twin Towers and Pentagon on 9/11/2001. The sensible Spanish responses to the Madrid attacks of 11 March 2004, prove that other options are possible. The Spanish withdrew from the war in Iraq and contributed to attempts to reduce tension between Islam and the West. Spain moved from military means to the use of police, the criminal law and courts.

Falk concludes that the right lesson to learn is that what can be achieved with military means is extremely limited in a post-colonial world. There is a need to think outside the military box and rely more on an array of soft-power instruments, like diplomacy and 'lawfare', nonviolent coercive boycotts or divestment campaigns, and a variety of civil society initiatives.

Steven Zunes discusses the present wave of nonviolent uprisings in Northern Africa and the Middle East from two perspectives: the role of the U.S. government and the long, but not well-known, tradition of the use of nonviolent techniques and strategies in Muslim countries. The lip service President Obama and his predecessors played to democracy is not compatible with their support for authoritarian and brutal regimes in the region. As long as the U.S. has good relations with and can benefit from friendly ties with dictators, they do not question this form of rule. In dictatorships like Saudi Arabia and Bahrain, there is virtually no American support for the democratic forces.

Zunes presents a number of historical cases of nonviolent movements, which help us to understand the events in early 2011. Although some activists and academics with experiences and knowledge of nonviolence conducted workshops in recent years, external actors had limited impact on these events. Zunes concludes:

> The fundamental reality is that democracy will not come to the Middle East through foreign intervention, sanctimonious statements from Washington, voluntary reforms by autocrats, or armed struggle by a self-selected vanguard. It will only come through the power of massive non-cooperation with illegitimate authority and the strategic application of nonviolent action by Middle Eastern peoples themselves.

Reconciliation

If the cycles of violence are to be broken, there is a need to change direction and move on. In the expanding field of reconciliation research, there are many schools and practices. Andrew Rigby provides a basic introduction to the field.

Conflicts do not end with a ceasefire; after fighting has ceased, tensions, disagreements and, more importantly, the wounds from committed atrocities are still very much alive. His thesis is that there is a close relation between types of settlements and the strategy most likely to be adopted in terms of dealing with the past. Like all other social processes, reconciliation cannot be painted in black and white. Rigby brings up a critique by David Crocker of the South African Truth and Reconciliation Commission. It may be wrong to expect ideal social harmony after decades of brutal apartheid. In South Africa, they prioritized 'the truth' over 'justice'. In courts dealing with war crimes, they focused more on 'justice' (very often as justice is understood by the winners). Rigby concludes that we must learn from how wars start and try to avoid repetitions; but there are no easy ways to deal with the past.

Disarmament and alternatives to militarization

Marc Pilisuk argues for disarmament with the statement: 'War is hell!' Many years of disarmament efforts have clearly limited the number of some weapons, and several agreements have been signed. Still there are wars that kill humans and destroy societies in many regions around the world. Some will argue that it is not a question of the actual weapons but of human behaviour. The slaughters in Rwanda 1994[7] were carried out with machetes and knives. Evil human behaviour will always find tools to be used for attacks.

At the same time, we see the very existence of weapons of mass destruction as a threat to all human beings. They can be used on purpose, as in August 1945, or stolen and used by actors outside the state system. There have been many documented cases of misunderstandings, accidents and technical errors leading to the near launch of such weapons.[8]

A well-known argument against disarmament is that arms are necessary for self defence. That is the starting point for the cycle of deterrence, which has led nations to have stockpiles of enough nuclear arms to destroy all life on Earth. Pilisuk argues that the risks of disarmament can be greatly limited by solid and enforceable universal agreements.

The Soviet Union and the U.S. had several rounds of negotiations during the Cold War. Several of them resulted in agreements to dismantle certain weapon systems, but then new missile technologies that fell outside the agreement were already under production. Bans on specific types of weapons have been successful, and the opening for inspections of each other's facilities is another important example of progress.

Pilisuk reminds us that financial factors must not be forgotten in these discussions. Wars are costly and some actors make huge profits from arms. As millions of humans are dying from easily curable diseases and lack of drinkable water, the billions spent for arms and wars are difficult to justify.

What are the alternatives to war and more specifically to the institution of war? Christine Schweitzer presents an overview of some concrete ideas of how to act in large-scale social conflicts other than by deploying massive military force. For the national defence of a nation-state, there are some historical examples of civilian-based defence with positive consequences, and there are books published on how it could work today. So far no state has adopted these ideas in a serious way. There is no country with the political will to explore these ideas.

More has been done when it comes to nonviolent conflict transformation and civilian peacekeeping. Civil-society actors have taken on tasks to start reducing levels of violence, building peace and creating a stable future. Organizations like the Nonviolent Peaceforce have set themselves the goal of developing into large-scale organizations with a structure and membership to be able to deploy large groups of civilian peacekeepers to a conflict zone. Their tasks can be many and varied. Some of them are: observing and reporting on human rights violations; supporting local activists to build solid and effective organizations; training and education; building bridges between adversaries; and helping build the type of massive mobilizations of skilled nonviolent activists we have seen in peaceful revolutions since the 1980s.

Notes

1 Wright, Quincy (1942). *A Study of War*. Chicago, I.L.: University of Chicago Press.
2 Richardson, L.F. (1960). *Statistics of Deadly Quarrels*. Pacific Grove, CA: Boxwood Press.
3 According to human rights activist Caroline Cox and philosopher Roger Scruton, 'Their curricula are "intellectually incoherent, riddled with bias and unworthy of academic status".' Source: Barbara Kay, *National Post*, 18 February 2009.
4 Dunant, Henri (1986). *A Memory of Solferino*. New edition. Geneva: International Committee of the Red Cross.
5 Norwegian Initiative on Small Arms Transfers: http://www.prio.no/NISAT
6 http://www.nonviolentpeaceforce.org/nonviolent-peaceforce-feasibility-study
7 Hatzfeld, Jean (2005). *A Time for Machetes. The Rwandan Genocide: The Killers Speak*. London: Serpent's Tail.
8 Sagan, Scott Douglas (1993). *The Limits of Safety: Organizations, Accidents, and Nuclear Weapons*. Princeton Studies in International History and Politics. Princeton, N.J.: Princeton University Press.

24 Protagonist strategies that help end violence

Louis Kriesberg and Gearoid Millar

We examine the choices that particular organizations make as they contend against each other. We examine the various goals adversaries set, the strategies they adopt to progress toward them, and how and why such choices are made. Because the choice of objectives and the means to attain them impact each other, both are discussed. The focus throughout is on non-violent strategic choices.

Conflict circumstances

Resource asymmetry is evident in most conflicts and profoundly affects the equity of their resolution (Mitchell 1995). Asymmetry is often discussed as the relative capacity to exercise coercion, particularly violence, and although this is important in many struggles, it is never all important. Noncoercive capacities also can be decisive, such as the commitment to a struggle, as evident in the Vietnam War. Conflicting partisans have access to and actualize different resources as group capacities, which then impact each side's choice of strategies. Adversary groups therefore differ in their capacities to use both noncoercive and coercive inducements to affect each other's conduct.

The resources available to a party in any particular conflict environment are social, economic and demographic. Social resources may include relationships with allies and external powers, strong leadership, cohesive identity, or perceived legitimacy. Such resources affect the conflict when actualized as organizational capacities, but may be used either for violent or non-violent strategies. Strong leadership, for example, may influence the capacity to conduct long and costly military operations, such was the leadership of George Washington, but it may also be required, as in the case of Mohandas Gandhi or Martin Luther King, for a campaign of non-violence.

Likewise, economic resources can be utilized to purchase weapons, hire mercenaries, train troops, or to build defensive or offensive infrastructure. Alternatively they can be used to import supplies during a boycott, support striking workers, bold anti-war rallies, or build monument to peace.

Finally, demographic resources can be actualized to struggle for various ends. The character of a population, whether large or small, well or badly educated, homogenous or heterogeneous, young or old, is influential; but it does not dictate a particular strategy of conflict. A large, young population may be turned to peaceful protest just as it is to violent rioting.

Most conflict resources persist over time, but some change significantly and quickly. Thus, states that regard as criminals the leaders of a challenging organization may kill or imprison them, depriving that organization of a critical resource. In 1992, for example, the Peruvian government captured Abimel Guzman, the primary leader of the Shining Path

(Sendero Luminosa), greatly diminishing the capacities of that organization (Thomas and Casebeer 2004: 49). In 1999, the Turkish government imprisoned Abdullah Õcalan, leader of the Kurdistan Workers Party (PKK), which contributed to modifying their conflict (Radu 2001).

Similarly, many partisans throughout the world suddenly lost important external support when the Cold War ended, staunching the flow of arms and money from the US and the Soviet Union. What might previously have been considered long term resources in these environments were suddenly eliminated, and affected parties were forced to change strategies or even goals.

Significantly, perceptions of relative resources and the anticipation of future changes can also have large effects on a party's goals and strategies. White South Africans, anticipating becoming a smaller proportion of the population, had reason to move toward an accommodation sooner rather than later. Similarly, many Jewish Israelis, foreseeing a growing Palestinian population, favored a territorial separation that could preserve a predominantly Jewish Israel.

It is therefore insufficient to view power differences only in terms of relative coercive capabilities and the ability to exercise them (negative sanctions). Power is also based on non-coercive inducements (Boulding 1989). One set of such inducements result from a capacity to promise benefits to reward desired conduct (positive sanctions). Noncoercive inducements can also be based on persuasive arguments derived from shared norms and values or on shared identities based on ideology or religion. In actually, power is exercised in various combinations of these inducements, depending in part upon organizational capacities and characteristics.

Organizational characteristics

For qualities characterizing contending organizations are particularly relevant for the materials analyzed in this volume. They are: structure, ideology, relations with other organizations, and attachments to violence. The internal and external factors affecting these features will be discussed, taking into account the effect of resource availability and decisions regarding their actualization.

Structural features

The distinction between state and non-state entities is often based on their structural differences, but this can be exaggerated. States are often regarded as having clear boundaries, clearly defined members (citizens), and clearly recognized decision-making procedures, yet they vary in these regards. Conversely, while non-state entities may tend to have fewer of such attributes, many have them to a significant degree.

Both differ in the extend to which rank-and-file members follow the directions of their official leaders, the degree to which particular groups of supporters influence or direct the official leaders, and the degree to which rivals can mobilize and direct people they regard as their constituents. Both state and non-state actors may sometimes incorporate armed groups, functioning somewhat autonomously, and leaders of both tend to make broad claims about who they represent and can control. For example, government officials, who may or may not have been acting independently of their official leaders, have been known to operate in cooperation with armed militia groups in South Africa, Colombia, and Gautemala. Such failures of command structures within state hierarchies are similar to splits within non-state armed groups such as Hamas.

The internal structure of the adversaries may also vary greatly over time as the circumstances of the conflict change. Thus, the increase in international governmental and non-governmental organizations increasingly affects the structure of contending parties through the provision or restriction of resources that influence their strategies. For example, the Organization for Security and Co-operation in Europe (OSCE) contributed to the largely peaceful transitions and transformations among and within the countries in Eastern Europe and the former Soviet republics (McMahon 2007; Möller 2007). Similarly, expanding transnational linkages can strengthen some groups in particular countries, affecting the structure of societal and organizational political processes and relative influence. Expanding diaspora communities, which sustain relations in their former homelands, may provide economic and social resources that further influence the group's structural characteristics there.

Ideologies

The diverse groups in each adversary camp often have some sense of shared identity. Members of each group try to define both themselves and the other. They may define themselves exclusively and believe they have certain rights relative to other persons within or outside their own camp. These identities may not be precisely formulated and articulated, or be contradictory and shifting as circumstances change. Yet some aspects of these identities can become dominant within an ideology and drive the choice of violent strategies.

Some ideologies are highly institutionalized, incorporated in legislation and with special agencies dedicated to their maintenance. This is the case, for example, in states that are constituted to embody or to serve a particular religion, ethnicity, or political ideology. They also may be vigorously challenged by minority groups who object to the subordinate treatment they suffer. Alternatively, secular democratic governments may be challenged by organizations to establish a state that gives priority to an exclusive religious, ethnic, or political ideology. Such matters are prone to conflicts that are waged violently, such as in Afghanistan during the 1980s, but can also be waged peacefully, such as the Hizbut Tahrir movement for a global Caliphate, active in over 40 countries (Cornell 2002).

Additionally, changes in major ideologies, norms, and belief systems can significantly impact the ideologies of local organizations. The breakup of the Soviet Union not only ended Soviet material assistance to Marxist governments and revolutionary movements, it also reduced the adherence to Marxist ideologies and the concern among others about their threat. Conflicts became more frequently couched in ethnic and religious terms. In this way different ideological characteristics became salient, as one ideological resource was replaced by another.

Relations with other organizations

As highlighted above, each organization in a conflict is affected by its interaction with other organizations in the conflict environment, including its primary adversaries, organizations allied with the adversaries, and non-engaged third parties. Furthermore, each side usually consists of a coalition of organizations, each with internal factions and sub-groups. It is useful to keep this complexity in mind, even if a particular subunit is the primary one in the choice and employment of strategies.

The autonomy or dependency, for example, of a particular conflict unit in relation to supporting, allying, and ruling organizations affects its leader's options. An adversary may be highly dependent upon an outside government for material support and adhere to the goals and interests of that outside government in order to maintain its assistance. This was evident during the Cold War for the organizations relying greatly on American or Soviet support. Global economic and technological developments have greatly contributed to increasing inter-dependence and transnational linkages. For example, the increasing scope of international trade and investment, combined with increased capital mobility, enhances governmental interdependence, while also increasing vulnerability to policies of major corporate actors and particular IGOs, such as the International Monetary Fund (IMF).

Attachment to violence

The capability and readiness to use violent methods by various contending groups must receive special attention. Factions and groups who prepare for and carry out violent actions are significant components of most major conflict organizations. The army, police, and other armed units may be highly influential components of larger organizations. In many societies membership in such armed groups is attractive because alternative ways of earning a living are few. These factors both increase the chances of escalation and hamper the de-escalation and settlement of conflict.

In addition, various beliefs serve to sustain an attachment to violence. There is often little popular knowledge or faith in alternative means of struggle and the enemy is often regarded as "only understanding force." Indeed, channels for non-violent pressure, influence, and persuasive efforts are often closed by the opposing party or competing internal factious, cutting off potential alternative choices.

Outside actors and influences also sometimes contribute to local reliance upon violent methods. For example, during the 1960s some leaders and interpreters of war of national liberation and revolutionary change influentially argued that violence could help establish conditions needed for a successful revolution (Fanon 1966; Debray 1967). Recourse to violence was romanticized and those ready to commit violent deeds celebrated. This glorification of violence was a resource for partisan actors, but one that could only be actualized in strategies utilizing violence, thus it restricted strategic options. Such influences contributed to the adoption of violent strategies by the Palestine Liberation Organization.

Currently, some strands of Islamic religious beliefs are used to legitimate such violence against civilians deemed enemies of Islam. Terrorist attacks with transnational support have some novel features, but terrorism has a long history, and is an important means of struggle at particular times. Strategies within the Liberation Tigers of Tamil Eelam (LTTE) in Sri Lanka are prominent examples.

Interestingly, however, in recent years, non-violent methods of struggle also have gained adherents through their successful application in the Philippines, Poland, the Ukraine and many other countries and through external actors' encouragement of non-violent methods and provision of training and counseling. For example, El Servicio de Paz y Justicia (SER-PAJ), a non-violent human rights organization, resisted military dictatorships in many Latin American countries, in the 1970s and 1980s (Pagnucco and McCarthy 1992; Pagnucco 1997). Gene Sharp's analyses of, and his prescriptions for, non-violent action have also been translated into many languages and organizations in many countries consider adopting those strategies (Sharp 1973).

Each of the four partisan characteristics we highlight here is a function of available resources and decisions regarding their actualization. In each case the characteristic's development is influenced not only by group leadership decisions, but by the impact of external third parties, allies, internal divisions, and the contending party. Having analyzed both conflict circumstances and organizational characteristics, we now turn to protagonists' strategic choices.

Strategies of protagonists

Partisan strategies differ in many ways: by time frames and in the combination of inducements used; by who is undertaking them and toward whom they are directed: and by the stage of the conflict in which they are undertaken. This discussion is organized in terms of the latter, the major conflict stages in which strategies are employed: (a) escalation; (b) de-escalation and settlement; and (c) post-violence recovery. We stress the de-escalation and settlement stage but highlight those strategies at each stage that may best allow for a later transition to non-violent struggle. For each stage we examine partisan strategies directed internally, toward various members of the protagonists' own side, and externally, towards members of the opposing side.

This discussion is not limited to carefully considered strategies, consciously selected after comparing many alternatives. Actions may be taken with little reflection, being regarded as the only possible choice under the circumstances. In such cases we sometimes note alternatives that were not considered or were rejected by the protagonists. We infer a strategy and its objectives from the sequence of actions undertaken by contending groups and by the reasons that they give for their conduct. Admittedly, the reasons may be misleading, as the actors seek to justify their goals and how they strive to achieve them, and do so in ways that they think will win them support from other people. Further complicating matters, goals and strategies are often re-formulated, after the fact in order to justify past actions or to claim success.

We focus on strategies, both proactive and reactive, employed by each side, and intended, presumably, to affect the conduct of the other. However, it should be recognized that actions directed toward the adversary may be chosen for their effects on the perpetrator's own side. Thus they may be intended to reassure constituents that "something is being done," or to satisfy the desire to "get even." Alternatively, they may provide benefits to some members of the acting group, ranging from looted goods, control of resources, or constituents' rewards such as increased regard. Such considerations should not be ignored, since they frequently affect the choice of strategy and also the targeted adversary's responses. Furthermore, such considerations often account for the selection of strategies ill-suited to influence the external opponent.

Additionally, strategies that may be effective at one stage may be ineffective or even counter productive at the next and the transitions between stages are fraught with difficulties. Some of the goals and strategies of the Palestine Liberation Organization (PLO) illustrate this. The PLO leadership had great difficulties in building an independent Palestinian organization after 1948, and these difficulties increased after the 1967 war. Rashid Khalidi observes of the PLO that "the deviousness and subterfuge that were indispensable for a weak PLO in dealing with the predatory more of the states that dominated Arab politics were much less well adapted to . . . other arenas" (Khalidi 2006: 174). Most notably, he observes, such strategies were ill-suited to dealing with the Western powers and were a major contributing factor in the failure of the PLO to develop the infrastructure for a Palestinian state.

Finally, it is also important to recognize that strategies directed internally, at the various constituent elements and individual members of the organization, shape what strategy choices are available for waging the external conflict. The strategic choices of protagonists, therefore, are not only directed in two directions, internally and externally, and vary depending on the conflict stage, but are also temporally and casually related, with the external conflict strategy chosen by each protagonist being reliant on previous internally directed capacity building strategies.

Escalation

The strategies adopted by an organization as it begins to escalate a conflict have great import for the violent or non-violent trajectory of the conflict. Conflict escalation is often regarded as necessarily involving the use of violence, but it is important to consider the many non-violent ways partisans can increase a conflict's scope and intensity. We note the choice of policies that are conducive to non-violent escalations as well as violent ones.

Directed internally

Escalation generally requires the devotion of increased resources to the struggle. This usually necessitates greater mobilization of people. One strategy to achieve this is to arouse emotions of fear and hatred, forming a negative identity for the enemy relative to the group's own members. By depicting the enemy as subhuman or evil, leaders justify extreme methods of struggle. Such a strategy, however, tends to make de-escalation, settlement and recovery very difficult because the creation of polar identities limits future strategic options.

A contrary policy would be for leaders to stress differences within the opposing side. Constituents may be assured that not everyone in the adversary camp is an enemy, that many share important values and concerns with them. This has the effect of isolating the enemy within the opposing side, providing the opportunity later to revert to peaceful, or at least nonviolent, relations with the bulk of the adversary's population.

Unfortunately, one internally directed strategy is to attack internal factions that are considered rivals; dissenters are threatened, intimidated and killed. This may be the result of seeking greater power, ideological purity, or unity about goals and means. For such reasons the LTTE leadership has suppressed rival Tamil groups in Sri Lanka and in the diaspora, as discussed by Orjuela in this volume. As a result, consideration of alternative strategies hardly occurs and Tamils are relatively isolated. Other options then might be available to the group if additional resources were available; alternative leadership, knowledge, identity; have been denied them because of the internally directed strategy of factional elimination.

Since conflicts are interlocked, acts of violence may occur on many fronts at the same time. Wars of national liberation and civil wars often incorporate fights among clans, tribes, and families. Leaders of one sub-group may exploit the larger conflict to defeat a rival. As the number of parties increases and their interrelationships become more knotted and entangled, the odds of the two main parties clearly communicating their readiness to de-escalate become less favorable.

In many cases, however, some factions and elements within the adversarial camps have interests, values, or beliefs that tend to constrain violent escalation or to foster non-violent goals and strategies. This occurs when business, religious, educational, and other leaders cooperate with similar people in the opposing camp. Such connections potentially limit escalation in order to protect those relationships.

Directed at the external adversary

Many contending groups initially escalate their conflict through non-violent means such as petitions or demonstrations. However, if they believe that these efforts have been ignored or forcibly repressed, some resort to violent means. This has been true in South Africa, Sri Lanka, Northern Ireland, and elsewhere. Alternatively, a government's response recognizing that the challengers feel aggrieved and offering some concessions may avert violent escalations. This was the case in Belgium, Malaysia, and Canada, where protests did not escalate into destructive, protracted violence.

An obstacle to such accommodating responses is that challengers are often protesting policies the government deems to be appropriate or even essential. In such situations government officials are limited in how responsive they can be. Furthermore, they may believe that any concession is a sign of weakness inviting greater demands, or feel constrained by the expectations of their constituents. Consequently, they resort to violent suppression.

In many conflicts, this dynamic results in each side claiming that it is the aggrieved party, threatened by the other side. Both sides claim to be acting defensively and become locked into violent reciprocating escalation, with both internally and externally directed strategies of confrontation channeling the party's options ever more narrowly in the direction of greater violence.

The dynamics of violent conflict escalation can be a trap for both sides. A challenging group may use violence to provoke government overreactions, which serve to isolate government leaders (Debray 1967). This seems to have occurred in Cuba in the 1950s when Fidel Castro's small group of revolutionaries conducted attacks against the government. In response, Fulgencio Batista, the self-appointed president, undertook increasingly harsh and indiscriminate countermeasures, antagonizing many segments of the population. The government became isolated and fell in January 1959. Che Guevara considered this strategy to be an effective way to foment revolution and he and many others attempted to follow the strategy in several countries. These efforts failed when countermeasures were limited, and sometimes handled as police, rather than military matters. In these situations the government proved effective by not responding too aggressively against challenging parties. Overreaction is a severe risk in responding to challenges, often proving to be counterproductive (Mueller 2006). As discussed below, relying on violence can entrap the initiating challengers.

The goals set by the opposing sides greatly affect the likelihood of destructive escalations. Some group goals threaten the existence of the opposing side but more often groups seek changes, not elimination. In many cases the opposing groups contend over the control of particular territories or of other valued resources, such as in the case of ETA.

These varying goals provide an important context for choosing the means of struggle, and their effects on the opponent. The goals and strategies adopted by the ANC in its conflict with the South African government illustrate their importance in reaching a non-violent and negotiated settlement. Nelson Mandela and other ANC leaders consistently proclaimed the non-racist character of their party and the South African society they sought. They reassured the whites of South African that they were viewed as another people enjoying equal protection under the law in the new rainbow nation.

In addition, early decisions regarding organizational goals fostered the possibility of non-violent conflict and de-escalation in the future. At the beginning of the struggle the ANC relied on non-violent methods, in the tradition of Mohandas Gandhi as a young lawyer in South Africa. The decision to use violence, but also the kind of violence chosen, had implications for turning away from it at a later time. This was recognized, for example, in the explicit decision by ANG leaders to eschew terrorism in order to negotiate later (Mandela 1994).

Using particular violent methods requires specific human capabilities and non-human materials. The development of such resources then creates a vested interest in continuing to rely on those methods. Members and leaders gain status and other rewards as fighters. Yielding benefits in a peaceful accommodation with the adversary may not be attractive. In addition, committing violent acts binds fighters to their organizations, and armed fighters and their leaders develop skills for combat and may lack the skills needed for alternative means of making a living. Because the skills needed for non-violent governance are not developed, if a peaceful accommodation is reached, implementation is difficult.

When the fighters are only one wing of a broader entity some difficulties in transitioning into non-violent relations with an opponent may be alleviated. Organizations with open, democratic structures are more likely than authoritarian organizations to avoid such limitations and to make the transformation from relying on violence to struggling non-violently (Wanis-St. John and Kew 2006; Pace and Kew 2008; Kew forthcoming). The social resources provided by such structures provide for the development of non-violent capacities that can then be utilized in later conflict stages.

Finally, we discuss escalating actions taken at the grass roots and mid-elite levels within adversary camps. Forming connections between particular groups or persons who are members of opposing sides not only adds resources but weakens the solidarity of the opposition. This was true in the US during the civil rights movement where blacks and whites together formed CORE. Similarly, religious organizations and trade unions have often provided channels for mobilizing people across ethnic or class lines in escalating struggles for improved conditions for particular groups (Rose 2000).

In short, carefully controlled strategies may escalate conflicts in ways that set the stage for de-escalation and sustainable mutual accommodations. This was the case as opposition against apartheid surged across the black townships of South Africa in 1985. Nationally the United Democratic Front (UDF) undertook low-key acts of defiance, such as rent boycotts, labor strikes, and school stayaways. The blacks of Port Elizabeth launched an economic boycott of the city's white-owned businesses. The country was becoming ungovernable under apartheid. Such acts escalated the conflict between whites and blacks, between the ANC and the National Party, but it also developed the capacity for non-violent conflict and set the stage for later de-escalation and settlement.

A comparison of the first and second Palestinian intifadas is also illuminating (Hammami and Tamara 2001). During the first intifada, beginning in 1987, the Palestinians engaged in various forms of non-violent resistance including boycotts of Israeli goods. Lethal weapons were eschewed and the image of stone-throwing youths pursued by heavily armed Israeli soldiers won widespread sympathy for Palestinians. The second intifada, which erupted in 2000, was conducted by armed Palestinian militias and security forces, with relatively little popular engagement. The Israeli military suppression of the armed struggle was widely seen as justified. The chosen strategies of the first intifada contributed to the Israeli belief that a negotiated two-state resolution was desirable, whereas those of the second convinced many Israelis that negotiation was not feasible (Kriesberg 2002).

De-escalation and settlement

The stage of primary interest is that of de-escalation and settlement. Even the most intractable violent conflicts eventually become tractable or otherwise terminated. Often militias and other armed groups abandon violence because they are defeated, and they submit to the other side, suffer separation, or even disappear as an organized entity. However we are particularly interested here in the transformation of conflicts and the adoption of non-violent means of contention.

Internally directed

Because persistent conflicts generate strong feelings of fear and hatred, as well as a strength-ened commitment to winning in order to justify accrued losses, compromising with the enemy is very difficult. Leaders at all levels must prepare their constituents to accept some unpleasant realities. Preparing for a settlement, and therefore broadening strategic options can help ensure successful implementation of later accommodations. The ANC was thought-ful in this regard, encouraging higher ranking persons to become educated in ways relevant to governance, thus ensuring that they added a resource necessary for the capacity to govern, and developed new strategic options. Interestingly, some of the ANC leaders carried out such studies while imprisoned on Robben Island.

Reaching a sustained accommodation is often obstructed by factionalism and spoilers on each side of a conflict, including governments. The partisans in any large-scale conflict consist of varyingly autonomous subgroups and coalition partners, some of which may not accept the de-escalation movement. They may take covert or overt actions that undermine the reaching and implementing of any joint agreement. For example, when the negotiations for ending apartheid were underway a third force, some elements within the South African security agency, supported black South African groups that attached the ANC. How con-tending groups on a de-escalating course handle challenges to that process is critical. If they are able to demonstrate increased commitment, they may be able to prevent the breakdown of the de-escalation movement. In South Africa, winning a general referendum helped isolate and marginalize the would-be spoilers (Kydd and Walter 2002).

Subversion is another complication that must be dealt with handily. Leaders of the de-escalating adversaries may make concessions to some members or factions of their constitu-encies and coalition partners in order to keep their support. The concessions may however be viewed by the opposition as evidence of unwillingness or inability to take the necessary steps to reach a mutually acceptable accommodation. This was evident in the Israeli-PLO peace process of the 1990s during which Jewish settlements were expanded in the occupied territories and episodes of terrorist attacks by Palestinians recurred. Strategies that take these matters into account can contribute to maintaining de-escalating momentum. It may be helpful to make such considerations explicit.

And finally, just as they can promote non-violent strategies of escalation, grass roots and mid-level leaders sometimes campaign to pressure their own official leaders to de-escalate. Finding their interests harmed by the diversion of resources to a destructive escalation, they pressure their own leaders to end the fight. This has played a role in the transformation of many international conflicts, including the US-Soviet Cold War (Suri 2003). Peace Now is a good example in Israel.

Directed externally

At some point particular members of one or more sides employ strategies directed at the adversary that promote a joint de-escalation (Evangelista 1999). These strategies range from tentative signals and probes to bold unilateral de-escalating gestures. The adoption of one or another strategy arises from the convergence of several sets of conditions. A positive response to a unilateral de-escalatory action, so that joint moves are made, requires the convergence of even more developments. This may require the shared perception of a hurting stalemate and a feasible better option.

Several developments within and between adversaries, as well as external to them, affect the belief that better options than painful stalemate are possible. Formerly impossible options become credible when one side can demonstrate the existence of its internal differences or can act on the recognition of differences within the other side. One strategy is for at least one side to initiate gestures that convey that it desires de-escalation and it can be trusted to deliver what it is promising (Mitchell 2000; Kriesberg 2007). Once de-escalation has been initiated additional strategies are useful in consolidating the early progress. Tools such as confidence-building measures (CBMs) proved successful during the Cold War.

Calling upon and utilizing external actors can also help undertake and consolidate de-escalation steps. One adversary may attract allies and so increase its resources relative to its opponent. This may enhance coercive strength, but it may also provide increased moral suasion for its side, a powerful social resource that opens up new strategic options. Undoubtedly, the ANC's success in winning widespread condemnation of apartheid undermined the conviction of many white South Africans that apartheid was morally defensible, thus promoting alternate strategies. Outside parties may also be drawn into a conflict as mediators, as guarantors of agreement and as providers of joint benefits for the antagonists.

De-escalating initiatives are sometimes undertaken by grass roots and mid-level leaders from the opposing camps. When the violence in Northern Ireland was high in 1976, Máiread Corrigan Maguire and Betty Williams organized weekly peace marches and demonstrations. Very quickly over half a million people throughout Northern Ireland, as well as in England and the Republic of Ireland, came out on marches. The women co-founded the Community of the Peace People to continue their peace-making initiatives and were later awarded the Nobel Peace Prize. Such strategies break down bi-polar conceptions of group identities and promote the choice of non-violent strategies.

Academics and various NGOs can initiate and facilitate meetings, workshops, and exercises in dialogue which accomplish similar outcomes. For example, in December 1984 an Afrikaner sociologist, Hendrik W. van der Merwe, organized a series of meetings between ANC officials and Afrikaner newspaper editors (Van der Merwe 1989; Van der Merwe 2000) which contributed to the recognition that the different peoples in South Africa were all South Africans, thus promoting de-escalation.

An additional strategy practiced by some NGO and grass roots organizations is the establishment of "Zones of Peace." This has been accomplished in both the Philippines and in Colombia (Hancock and Mitchell 2007). Such zones enable people in a particular locality to opt out of the fighting, demonstrating that security can be achieved without complying with the demands of any armed party.

Post-settlement and recovery

Establishing secure and equitable relations between former enemies and avoiding a recurrence of violence has become a matter of high concern since the 1980s. Increased recognition is being given to the value of positive peace (Paris 2004; Mac Ginty 2006). Many analyses of peacebuilding focus on external intervention, but the partisans themselves bear the greatest burden in building a stable and just peace.

Directed internally

One method of consolidating peacebuilding is for leaders of formerly contending groups to secure access to education, employment, and social welfare for their followers. Such assurances of well-being help ensure that not only the leadership but their constituents commit to a non-violent future. Additionally, competence in governance is necessary for transformation to endure. Moving from reliance on violence to active governance is very difficult and some organizations simply fail to make the transition. The PLO is one such example.

Another strategy is for the leaders of each group to undo the damage caused by the creation of polar identities. Just as leaders painted the other as evil or subhuman, it is also possible for them to reaffirm the similarities and shared humanness of the antagonists (Boudreau and Polkinghorn 2008). Religious and civic leaders have important roles to play in this process and at times actively engage their constituencies in this redefinition of the self and the other. Closely related to this is the need for leaders to promote the acceptance of what cannot be changed. Leaders can help their constituents accept unpleasant realities, since some compromises usually have to be made. Of course, the more sober the group's initial goals, the easier this process will be.

Directed externally

Reaching out to former enemies and demonstrating at least minimal respect for them are fundamental elements of many strategies to establish enduring peace. This is often expressed in policies and laws ensuring basic human rights for all. One common strategy in post-violence environments is the creation of Human Rights Commissions, Commissions of Inquiry, War Crimes Tribunals, and other official bodies tasked with ensuring the rule of law. Additionally, resources are very often provided for the restructuring and retraining of military and police forces inorder to ensure their purging of rogue factional elements or war criminals. These policies often contribute to building confidence between the former antagonists.

Other strategies are geared toward the construction of a shared identity by creating common symbols such as new anthems, flags, and monuments. Such symbols can blend elements from old symbols of the formerly contending groups, signifying their unity and shared future (Ross 2007).

Reconciliation is receiving growing attention and is an important aspect of post-violence recovery. But reconciliation is not a single condition that does or does not exist: rather, it is multidimensional and varies over time for different members of the previously antagonistic sides (Kriesberg 1999). Considerable attention has been given to the establishment of various forms of truth commissions in order to foster reconciliation, most notably the Truth and Reconciliation Commission of South Africa. They are thought to contribute to managing resentments between members of the formerly antagonistic sides.

Grass roots and local level accommodations are also important, since it is at the grass roots level that relationships are built and communities are restored after violence (Pouligny *et al.* 2007). A stable peace is fostered by small acts between individuals, such as friendships or marriages across lines of division. Groups that foster mutual understanding may be established in neighborhoods and cities such as dialogue circles, neighborhood redevelopment schemes and economic cooperatives.

Finally, for agreed-upon settlements to endure, it is important to build institutions, both to handle conflicts, and to deliver mutual gains (Paris 2004). Such institutions can help ensure an equitable distribution of resources among the parties. The failure to adopt such a strategy risks a return to violence in the future by those who feel newly aggrieved by the post-conflict disposition of resources.

Conclusion

Adversaries in a violent conflict can use a wide variety of strategies to transform their struggle and continue to engage each other without relying on the threat or commission of violence. The process of transformation, however, is usually very lengthy and requires different strategies at various conflict stages. Important strategies are directed both internally and externally, but sometimes inconsistently in regard to advancing conflict transformation.

The strategies are joined together in complex, sometimes contradictory, sometimes complementary ways, and often constituting campaigns that change over time with externally directed strategies being reliant on prior internally directed and capacity creating strategic decisions. Adding to the complexity, different persons and groups within each adversary camp enact particular strategies, consistent with or contrary to the primary campaign.

Some general patterns regarding the choices and the consequences of different strategies and their combinations were suggested. Certainly much more research is needed to verify, correct, amplify and specify them. However, since every conflict has unique features, no body of theory and research can prescribe the precise set of strategies that will maximize the diverse set of goals which members of one or another side in a conflict seek to advance. Recognition of many possible alternative strategies and likely responses to them nevertheless can improve the chances of avoiding destructive conflict escalations. Thinking ahead about possible responses and subsequent counter-responses to a chosen strategy is a sound principle for policy making.

Finally, we wish to acknowledge that people rarely regard the resort to violence as the worst possible means of struggle. People often assert that there are some goals for which it is worth both dying and killing to advance. In retrospect, however, after periods of extreme violence, many people come to believe they were mistaken. These considerations are important, but they go beyond this chapter's parameters.

References

Boudreau, T. E. and B. Polkinghorn (2008). "Changing an Enemy into a Friend: A Model for Reframing Narratives in Protracted Social Conflict through Identity Affirmation," in R. Fleishman, R. O'Leary and C. Gerard (eds.) *Pushing the Boundaries: New Frontiers in Conflict Resolution and Collaboration*, Bingley, UK, Emerald Press.

Boulding, K. E. (1989). *Three Faces of Power*, Newbury Park, Sage.

Cornell, S. E. and R. A. Spector (2002). "Central Asia: More than Islamic Extremists," *Washington Quarterly* 25 (1): 193–206.

Debray, R. (1967). *Revolution in the Revolution?* New York, Grove Press.

Evangelista, M. (1999). *Unarmed Forces: The Transnational Movement to End the Cold War*, Ithaca and London, Cornell University Press.

Fanon, F. (1966). *The Wretched of the Earth*, New York, Grove Press.

Hammami, R. and S. Tamara. (2001). "The Second Uprising: End or New Beginning?" *Journal of Palestine Studies* 30 (2) (118): 5–25.

Hancock, L. E. and C. Mitchell, (eds.) (2007). *Zones of Peace*, Bloomfield, CT, Kumarian.

Kew, D. (Forthcoming). *Classrooms for Democracy: Civil Society, Conflict Resolution, and Building Democracy in Nigeria*, Syracuse, Syracuse University Press.

Khalidi, R. (2006). *The Iron Cage: The Story of the Palestinian Struggle for Statehood*, Boston, Beacon Press.

Kriesberg, L. (1999). "Paths to Varieties of Inter-Communal Reconcilliation," in H. W. Jeong (ed.) *Conflict Resolution: Dynamics, Process and Structure*, Fitchburg, MD, Dartmouth, 105–129.

Kriesberg, L. (2002). "The Relevance of Reconciliation Actions in the Breakdown of Israeli-Palestinian Negotiations, 2000," *Peace & Change* 27 (4): 546–571.

Kriesberg, L. (2007). *Constructive Conflicts: From Escalation to Resolution*, 3rd edn., Lanham, MD, Rowman & Littlefield.

Kydd, A. and B. F. Walter. (2002). "Sabotaging the Peace: The Politics of Extremist Violence," *International Organization* 56 (2): 263–296.

Mac Ginty, R. (2006). *No War, No Peace: The Rejuvenuation of Stalled Peace Process and Peace Accounts*, New York, Palgrave Macmillan.

McMahon, P. C. (2007). *Ethnic Cooperation and Transnational Networks in Eastern Europe*, Syracuse, Syracuse University Press.

Mandela, N. (1994). *Long Walk to Freedom*. Boston, Little, Brown.

Merwe, H. W. van der (1989). *Pursuing Justice and Peace in South Africa*. London and New York, Routledge.

Merwe, H. W. van der (2000). *Peacemaking in South Africa: A Life in Conflict Resolution*. Cape Town, Tafelberg.

Mitchell, C. R. (1995). Asymmetry and Strategies of Regional Conflict Reduction. In I. W. Zartman and V. A. Kremenyuk (eds.) *Cooperative Security: Reducing Third World Wars*, Syracuse, NY, Syracuse University Press: 25–57.

Mitchell, C. R. (2000). *Gestures of Conciliation: Factors Contributing to Successful Olive Branches*. New York, St. Martin's Press.

Möller, F. (2007). *Thinking Peaceful Change: Baltic Security Policies and Security Community Building*, Syracuse, Syracuse University Press.

Mueller, J. E. (2006). *Overblown: How Politicians and the Terrorism Industry Inflate National Security Threats, and Why we Believe Them*, New York, Free Press.

Pace, M. and D. Kew (2008). "Catalysts of Change Applying New Forms of Practice to the Context of Nigeria's Democratic Development," in R. Fleishmann, R. O'Leary and C. Gerard (eds.) *Pushing Boundaries: New Frontiers in Conflict Resolution and Collaboration*, Bingley, UK, Emerald Press.

Pagnucco, R. (1997). "The Transnational Strategies of the Service for Peace and Justice in Latin America," in J. Smith, C. Chatfield and R. Pagnucco (eds.) *Transnational Social Movements and Global Politics*, Syracuse, Syracuse University Press: 123–138.

Pagnucco, R. and J. D. McCarthy (1992). "Advocating Nonviolent Direct Action in Latin America: The Antecedents and Emergence of SERPAJ," in B. Misztal and A. Shupe (eds.) *Religion and Politics in Comparative Perspective*, Westport, CN, Praeger: 125–147.

Paris, R. (2004). *At War's End: Building Peace After Civil Conflict*, Cambridge, UK, Cambridge University Press.

Pouligny, B., S. Chesterman and A. Schnabel, (eds.) (2007). *After Mass Crime: Rebuilding States and Communities*, Tokyo, United Nations University Press.

Radu, M. (2001). "The Rise and Fall of the PKK," *Orbis* 45 (1): 47–63.

Rose, F. (2000). *Coalitions across the Class Divide: Lessons from the Labor, Peace, and Environmental Movements*, Ithaca, NY, Cornell University Press.

Ross, M. H. (2007). *Cultural Contestation in Ethnic Conflict*, Cambridge, UK, Cambridge University Press.

Sharp, G. (1973). *The Politics of Nonviolent Action*, Boston, Porter Sargent.

Suri, J. (2003). *Power and Protest: Global Revolution and the Rise of Detente*, Cambridge, MA and London, Harvard University Press.

Thomas, T. S. and W. D. Casebeer (2004). *Violent Systems: Defeating Terrorists, Insurgents, and Other Non-State Adversaries*, USAF Academy, CO, USAF Institute for National Security Studies: 1–108.

Wanis-St. John, A. and D. Kew (2006). "The Missing Link? Civil Society and Peace Negotiations: Contributions to Sustained Peace," *Annual Convention of the International Studies Association*, San Diego, CA.

25 Nonviolent geopolitics

Rationality and resistance

Richard Falk

In this short essay, my attempt will be to articulate a Galtungian conception of a world order premised on nonviolent geopolitics, as well as to consider some obstacles to its realisation. By focusing on "geopolitics" the intention is to consider the role played by dominant political actors on the global stage. It challenges the main premise of realism that security, leadership and influence in the 21st century continue to rest primarily on military power, or what is sometimes described as "hard power" capabilities.[1] The contrasting argument presented here is that political outcomes since the end of World War II have been primarily shaped by soft power ingenuity that has rather consistently overcome a condition of military inferiority to achieve its desired political outcomes. The United States completely controlled land, air, and sea throughout the Vietnam War, winning every battle, and yet eventually losing the war, killing as many as 4 million Vietnamese on the road to the failure of its military intervention. Ironically, the US government went on to engage the victorious Vietnam government, and currently enjoys a friendly and productive diplomatic and economic relationship. In this sense, the strategic difference between defeat and victory is almost unnoticeable, making the wartime casualties and devastation even more tragic, as being pointless from every perspective. Nevertheless, US militarists labelled the impact of this defeat as a kind of geopolitical disease, the "Vietnam syndrome", thereby drawing the wrong lesson, implying that the outcome was the exception rather than the rule.[2]

A second demonstration of the anachronistic reliance on a violence-based system of security was associated with the response to the 9/11 attacks on the Twin Towers and the Pentagon, the dual symbols of the US imperium. A feature of this event was the exposure of the extreme vulnerability of the most militarily dominant state in the whole of human history to attack by a non-state actor without significant weaponry and lacking in major resources. In the aftermath it became clear that the enormous US investment in achieving "full spectrum dominance" had not brought enhanced security, but the most acute sense of insecurity in the history of the country. Once again the wrong lesson was drawn, namely, that the way to restore security was to wage war regardless of the distinctive nature of this new kind of threat, to make mindless use of the military machine abroad and the curtailment of liberties at home despite the absence of a territorial adversary or any plausible means/ends relationship between recourse to war and reduction of the threat.[3] The appropriate lesson, borne out by experience, is that such a security threat can best be addressed by a combination of transnational law enforcement and through addressing the *legitimate* grievances of the political extremists who launched the attacks. As Galtung has argued, the Spanish response to the Madrid attacks of 11 March 11 2004 seemed sensitive to the new realities: withdraw from involvement in the Iraq war, enhance police efforts to identify and arrest violent extremists, and join in the dialogic attempts to lessen tension between Islam and the West.[4] In another setting, the former British prime minister, John Major, has observed that he only began to make progress in ending the violence in Northern Ireland when he stopped thinking of the IRA as a terrorist organisation and began treating it a political actor with real grievances and its own motivations in reaching accommodation and peace.

The right lesson is to recognise the extremely limited utility of military power in conflict situations within the postcolonial world, grasping the extent to which popular struggle has exerted historical agency during the last 60 years. It has shaped numerous outcomes of conflicts that could not be understood if assessed only through a hard power lens that interprets history as almost always determined by wars being won by the stronger military side that then gets to shape the peace.[5] Every anticolonial war in the latter half of the 20th century was won by the militarily weaker side, which prevailed in the end despite suffering disproportionate losses along its way to victory. It won because the people were mobilised on behalf of independence against foreign colonial forces, and their resistance included gaining complete control of the high moral ground. It won because of the political truth embodied in the Afghan saying: "You have the watches, we have the time." Gaining the high moral ground both delegitimised colonial rule and legitimised anti-colonial struggle; in the end even the state-centric and initially empire-friendly UN was induced to endorse anticolonial struggles by reference to the right of self-determination, which was proclaimed to be an inalienable right of all peoples.

This ascendancy of soft power capabilities in political struggles was not always the case. Throughout the colonial era, and until the mid-20th century, hard power was generally effective and efficient, as expressed by the colonial conquests of the Western hemisphere with small numbers of well-armed troops, British control of India with a few thousand soldiers or the success of "gunboat diplomacy" in supporting US economic imperialism in Central America and the Caribbean. What turned the historical tide against militarism was the rise of national and cultural self-consciousness in the countries of the South, most dramatically in India under the inspired leadership of Gandhi, where coercive nonviolent forms of soft power first revealed their potency. More recently, abetted by the communications revolution, resistance to oppressive regimes based on human rights has demonstrated the limits of hard power governance in a globalised world. The anti-apartheid campaign extended the struggle against the racist regime that governed South Africa to a symbolic global battlefield where the weapons were coercive nonviolent reliance on boycotts, divestment, and sanctions. The collapse of apartheid in South Africa was largely achieved by developments outside of the sovereign territory, a pattern that is now being repeated in the Palestinian "legitimacy war" being waged against Israel. The outcome is not assured, and it is possible for the legitimacy war to be won, and yet the oppressive conditions sustained, as seems to be currently the case with respect to Tibet.

Against this background, it is notable, and even bewildering, that geopolitics continues to be driven by a realist consensus that ahistorically believes that history continues to be determined by the grand strategy of hard power dominant state actors.[6] In effect, realists have lost touch with reality. It seems correct to acknowledge that there remains a rational role for hard power, as a defensive hedge against residual statist militarism, but even here the economic and political gains of demilitarisation would seem to far outweigh the benefits of an anachronistic dependence on hard power forms of self-defence, especially those that risk wars fought with weaponry of mass destruction. With respect to non-state political violence, hard power capabilities are of little or no relevance, and security can be best achieved by accommodation, intelligence and transnational law enforcement. The US recourse to war in addressing the Al Qaeda threat, as in Iraq and Afghanistan, has proved to be costly, and misdirected.[7] Just as the US defeat in Vietnam reproduced the French defeats in their colonial wars waged in Indochina and Algeria, the cycle of failure is being renewed in the post-9/11 global setting. Why do such lessons bearing on the changing balance between hard and soft power remain unlearned in the imperial centre of geopolitical manoeuvre?

It is of great importance to pose this question even if no definitive answer can be forthcoming at this time. There are some suggestive leads that relate to both material and ideological explanations. On the materialist side, there are deeply embedded governmental and societal structures whose identity and narrow self-interests are bound up with a maximal reliance upon and projection of hard power. These structures have been identified in various ways in the US setting: "national security state", "military-industrial complex", "military Keynesianism", and "the war system". It was Dwight Eisenhower who more than 50 years ago warned of the military-industrial complex in his farewell speech, notably making the observation after he no longer was able to exert influence on governmental policy.[8] In 2010 there seems to be a more deeply rooted structure of support for militarism that extends to the mainstream media, conservative think tanks, an army of highly paid lobbyists, and a deeply compromised Congress whose majority of members have substituted money for conscience. This politically entrenched paradigm linking realism and militarism makes it virtually impossible to challenge a military budget even at a time of fiscal deficits that are acknowledged by conservative observers to endanger the viability of the US empire (Ferguson 2010). The scale of the military budget, combined with navies in every ocean, more than 700 foreign military bases, and a huge investment in the militarisation of space exhibit the self-fulfilling inability to acknowledge the dysfunctionality of such a global posture.[9] The US spends almost as much as the entire world put together on its military machine, and more than double what the next 10 leading states spend. And for what benefit to either the national or global interest?

The most that can be expected by way of adjustment of the realist consensus under these conditions is a certain softening of the hard power emphasis. In this respect, one notes that several influential adherents of the realist consensus have recently called attention to the rising importance of non-military elements of power in the rational pursuit of a grand strategy that continues to frame geopolitics by reference to presumed hard power "realities", but are at the same time critical of arch militarism attributed to neoconservatives (see Nye 1990; Gelb 2009; Walt 2005).[10] This same tone pervades the speech of Barack Obama at the 2009 Nobel Peace Prize ceremony. This realist refusal to comprehend a *largely* post-militarist global setting is exceedingly dangerous given the continuing hold of realism on the shaping of policy by governmental and market/finance forces.[11] Such an outmoded realism not only engages in imprudent military undertakings; it tends also to overlook a range of deeper issues bearing on security, survival and human wellbeing, including climate change, peak oil, water scarcities, fiscal fragility and market freefall. As such, this kind of policy orientation is incapable of formulating the priorities associated with sustainable and benevolent forms of global governance.

In addition to the structural rigidity that results from the entrenched militarist paradigm, there arises a systemic learning disability that is incapable of analysing the main causes of past failures. As a practical matter, this leads policy options to be too often shaped by unimaginative thinking trapped within a militarist box. In recent international policy experience, thinking mainly confined to the military box has led the Obama administration to escalate US involvement in an internal struggle for the future of Afghanistan and to leave the so-called military option on the table for dealing with the prospect of Iran's acquisition of nuclear weapons. An attractive alternative policy approach in Afghanistan would be based on the recognition that the Taliban is a movement seeking nationalist objectives amid raging ethnic conflict. As a result it would tend towards a conclusion that the US security interests would benefit from an end of combat operations, followed by the phased withdrawal of NATO forces, a major increase in developmental assistance that avoids channelling funds through a corrupted Kabul government, and a genuine shift in US foreign policy towards respect for the politics of self-determination. Similarly, in relation to Iran, instead of threatening a military strike and advocating punitive measures, a call for regional denuclearisation, which insisted on the inclusion of Israel, would be expressive of both thinking outside the militarist box, and the existence of more hopeful non-military responses to admittedly genuine security concerns.

In conclusion, some form of geopolitics is almost bound to occur, given the gross inequality of states and the weakness of the United Nations as the institutional expression of unified governance for the planet.

Especially since the collapse of the Soviet Union the primacy of the United States has resulted inevitably in its geopolitical ascendancy. Unfortunately, this position has been premised upon an unreconstructed confidence in the hard power paradigm, which combines militarism and realism, producing violent geopolitics in relation to critical unresolved conflicts. The experience of the past 60 years shows clearly that this paradigm is untenable from both pragmatic and principled perspectives. It fails to achieve its goals at acceptable costs, if at all. It relies on immoral practices that involve massive killing of innocent persons and colossal waste of resources.

Those relying on the alternative of nonviolent practices and principles, in contrast, have shown the capacity to achieve political goals and a willingness to pursue their goals by ethical means. The Gandhi movement resulting in Indian independence, the Mandela-led transformation of apartheid South Africa, people power in the Philippines and the soft revolutions of Eastern Europe in the late 1980s are exemplary instances of domestic transformations based on nonviolent struggle. None of these soft power victories produced entirely just societies or addressed the entire agenda of social and political concerns, often leaving untouched exploitative class relations and bitter societal tensions, but they did overcome the immediate situation of oppressive state/society relations without significant reliance on violence. Turning to the global setting, there exist analogous opportunities for the application of nonviolent geopolitics. These opportunities are grounded in an acceptance of the self-constraining discipline of international law as reinforced by widely endorsed moral principles embodied in the great religions and world civilisations. Certainly a first step would be the repudiation of weaponry of mass destruction, starting with an announced declaration of no first use of nuclear weaponry, and moving on to an immediate and urgent negotiation of a nuclear disarmament treaty that posits as a *non-utopian* goal "a world without nuclear weapons" (Krieger 2009). The essential second step is liberating the moral and political imagination from the confines of militarism, and consequent thinking within that dysfunctional box.

Notes

1 A mainstream exception is Rosecrance 2002.
2 Significantly, every US leader after Nixon did his best to eliminate the Vietnam syndrome, which was perceived by the Pentagon as an unwanted inhibitor of the use of aggressive force in world politics. After the end of the Gulf war in 2001, the first words of President George H. W. Bush were

"We have finally kicked the Vietnam syndrome," meaning, of course, that the United States was again able to fight 'wars of choice'.

3 Well depicted in Cole and Lobel 2007; see also my own attempt, Falk 2003.

4 This comparison is so analysed in Galtung 2008.

5 Significantly documented in Schell 2003.

6 It is notable that the changes in the global geopolitical landscape associated with the rise of China, India, Brazil and Russia are largely to do with their economic rise, and not at all with their military capabilities, which remain trivial compared to those of the United States.

7 As interventionary struggles go on year after year with inconclusive results, but mounting costs in lives and resources, the intervening sides contradicts their own war rationale, searching for compromises, and even inviting the participation of the enemy in the governing process. This has been attempted in both Iraq and Afghanistan, but only after inflicting huge damage, and enduring major loss of life among their own troops and incurring great expense.

8 Among the valuable studies are Barnet 1972 and Lewin 1968.

9 Most convincingly demonstrated in a series of books by Chalmers Johnson. See especially the first of his three books on the theme (2004).

10 For a progressive critique of American imperial militarism see Kolko 2006.

11 Johan Galtung has long been sensitive to this disconnect that separates even relatively prudent realists from reality. For a still relevant major work see Galtung 1980. For other recent perceptive studies along these lines see Booth 2007, especially the section on 'emancipatory realism', pp. 87–91; Camilleri and Falk 2009; Mittelman 2010.

References

Barnet, Richard J., 1972, *The Roots of War*, New York: Atheneum.

Booth, Ken, 2007, *Theory of World Security*, Cambridge, UK: Cambridge University Press.

Camilleri, Joe and Jim Falk, 2009, *Worlds in Transition: Evolving Governance Across a Stressed Planet*, Cheltenham: Edward Elgar.

Cole, David and Julius Lobel, eds, 2007, *Less Safe, Less Free: Why America is Losing the War on Terror*, New York: New Press.

Falk, Richard, 2003, *The Great Terror War*, Northampton, MA: Olive Branch Press.

Ferguson, Niall, 2010, "The fragile empire. Here today, gone tomorrow – could the United States fall fast?", *LA Times*, 28 February.

Galtung, Johan, 1980, *The True Worlds: A Transnational Perspective*, New York: Free Press.

Galtung, Johan, 1996, *Peace by Peaceful Means: Peace and Conflict, Development and Civilization*, London: Sage.

Galtung, Johan, 2004, *Transcend and Transform: An Introduction to Conflict Work*, Boulder, CO: Paradigm.

Galtung, Johan, 2008, "Searching for peace in a world of terrorism and state terrorism", in Shin Chiba and Thomas J. Schoenbaum, eds, *Peace Movements and Pacifism after September 11*, Cheltenham: Edward Elgar, pp. 32–48.

Gelb, Leslie H., 2009, *Power Rules: How Common Sense can Rescue American Foreign Policy*, New York: Harper-Collins.

Johnson, Chalmers, 2004, *The Sorrows of Empire: Militarism, Secrecy, and the End of the Republic*, New York: Metropolitan.

Kolko, Gabriel, 2006, *The Age of War: The United States Confronts the World*, Boulder, CO: Lynne Rienner.

Krieger, David, ed., 2009, *The Challenge of Abolishing Nuclear Weapons*, New Brunswick, NJ: Transaction.

Lewin, Leonard C, 1968, *Report from Iron Mountain on the Possibility and Desirability of Peace* (for Special Study Group), London: Macdonald.

Mittelman, James H., 2010, *Hyperconflict: Globalization and Insecurity*, Stanford, CA: Stanford University Press.

Nye, Joseph S., 1990, *Bound to Lead: The Changing Nature of American Power*, New York: Basic Books.

Nye, Joseph S., 2004, *Soft Power: The Means to Success in World Politics*, New York: Public Affairs.

Rosecrance, Richard, 2002, *The Rise of the Virtual State: Wealth and Power in the Coming Century*, New York: Basic.

Schell, Jonathan, 2003, *The Unconquerable World: Power, Nonviolence, and the Will of the People*, New York: Henry Holt.

Walt, Stephen M., 2005, *Taming American Power: The Global Response to American power*, New York: Norton.

26 The United States and pro-democracy revolutions in the Middle East

Stephen Zunes

The unarmed insurrection that overthrew the Ben Ali regime in Tunisia and the Mubarak regime in Egypt in early 2011 – which inspired largely nonviolent uprisings in Yemen, Bahrain, Syria and other countries – has opened up debate regarding prospects for democratization in Arab and other predominately Muslim countries. Many in the West are familiar with the way unarmed pro-democracy insurrections have helped bring democracy to Eastern Europe, Latin America, and parts of Asia and Africa, but discounted the chances of such movements in Islamic countries. Meanwhile, the United States – despite giving lip service in support for democracy – continues to actively support authoritarian governments in the Middle East, along with the Israeli and Moroccan occupations.

There is serious debate regarding what kind of role the United States should play regarding nonviolent struggles for democracy in the greater Middle East. President Barack Obama was correctly cautious about offering more overt support for the 2009 pro-democracy uprising in Iran. He was aware that the history of U.S. intervention, explicit threats of 'regime change' by the previous administration, the overthrow of Iran's last democratic by the CIA in 1953, support for the repressive regime under the Shah, and the U.S. invasion of two neighbouring countries in the name of democracy had resulted in such strong anti-Americanism in Iran that the Islamic regime could use such support to discredit the pro-democracy movement.

Obama's continuation of the Bush administration's policy of arming and training security forces in Saudi Arabia, Oman, Bahrain, Morocco, Jordan and other dictatorial regimes in the region is much harder to defend.

The Obama administration, in rejecting the dangerous neo-conservative ideology of its predecessor, essentially fell back onto the *realpolitik* of previous administrations by continuing to support repressive regimes through unconditional arms transfers and other security assistance. Indeed, Obama's understandable scepticism of externally mandated, top-down approaches to democratization through 'regime change' is no excuse for his policy of further arming these regimes, which then use these instruments of repression to subjugate popular indigenous bottom-up struggles for democratization. (Ironically, this authoritarianism is then used to justify the large-scale, unconditional support of Israel on the grounds that it's 'the sole democracy in the Middle East'.)

President George W. Bush's high-profile and highly suspect 'democracy promotion' agenda provided repressive regimes and their apologists an excuse to label any popular pro-democracy movement that challenges them as foreign agents, even when led by independent grassroots nonviolent activists. It is presumably no coincidence that the only autocratic regimes that the Bush administration seriously pressed for reform were those that traditionally opposed American hegemonic goals. Bush called for spreading democracy 'from Damascus to Teheran'. Yet, while Syria and Iran could certainly use more democracy, it is striking he did not similarly call for spreading democracy from Tunis to Cairo – or to Sanaa or Manama or Rabat or other capitals of U.S.-backed autocracies. In many respects, Bush did for the cause of democracy what Stalin did for the cause of socialism: he used an idealistic principle to justify war, repression and hegemony, and gave the concept a band name in certain quarters.

Furthermore, in recent years the United States has promoted 'economic freedom' – a neo-liberal capitalist economic model that emphasizes open markets and free trade – as at least as important as political freedom. It is noteworthy that, according to 2007 figures, the largest single recipient of funding from the National Endowment for Democracy for the Middle East was the Center for International Private Enterprise (CIPE). Even during the height of U.S. assistance to Egypt and Algeria, the two most populous Arab countries, CIPE received three times as much NED funding as all human rights, development, legal and civil society organizations combined. While liberalizing the economy from stifling state control can some-times encourage political liberalization, the more extreme neo-liberal model of the so-called 'Washington consensus' has tended to concentrate economic and political power in the hands of elites, particularly under authoritarian regimes, where the result is often crony capitalism rather than a truly free market, which weakens civil society rather than strengthens it.

The use of democracy as a disingenuous means of promoting U.S. hegemony was appar-ent in the way the Bush administration largely focused its attention on autocratic govern-ments that opposed U.S. interests in the region. It criticized the human rights record of such countries as Syria and Iran and drew attention to the plight of certain suppressed minori-ties, dissident organizations and individuals, while ignoring similar or worse abuses by pro-Western dictatorships. Even worse, at the request of the Bush administration in October 2002, a large bipartisan majority of the U.S. Congress supported the Iraq War resolution, asserting the right of the United States to invade Middle Eastern countries on the grounds of 'promoting democracy'.

In a report released in 2008, polls showed that while the majority of Middle Easterners sup-ported greater democracy in their countries, there was a decidedly negative attitude toward the stated goal of the Bush administration for 'democracy promotion'. Only 19 percent thought such efforts had a positive effect on their overall opinion of the United States while 58 percent stating it had a negative effect.[1] Another revealing poll indicated that although two-thirds of Americans surveyed believed Muslim nations cannot be democratic, an even larger majority of Muslims in predominantly Muslim countries believe they can and should.

To Obama's credit, there was a subtle but important shift in the U.S. government's dis-course on human rights. The Bush administration pushed a rather superficial structuralist view. It focused, for instance, on elections – which can easily be rigged and manipulated in many cases – in order to change certain governments for purposes of expanding U.S. power and influence. Obama embraced more of an agency view of human rights, emphasizing such rights as freedom of expression and the right to protest, recognizing that human rights reform can only come from below and not imposed from above. Although in practice this proved to be more in rhetoric only and did not alter Washington's propensity to provide security assistance to repressive regimes, it is this very right of protest that is key to the promotion of democracy in Islamic countries.

How change occurs

Throughout the world in recent years there has been a dramatic growth of the use of stra-tegic nonviolent action. In contrast to armed struggles, these nonviolent insurrections are movements of organized popular resistance to government authority. Either consciously or by necessity, they eschew the use of weapons of modern warfare. Unlike conventional political movements, nonviolent campaigns usually employ tactics outside the mainstream political processes of electioneering and lobbying. These tactics may include strikes, boycotts, mass demonstrations, the popular contestation of public space, tax refusal, destruction of symbols of government authority (such as official identification cards), refusal to obey official orders (such as curfew restrictions), and the creation of alternative institutions for political legitimacy and social organization.

Freedom House recently produced a study that, after examining the 67 transitions from authoritarian regimes to varying degrees of democratic governments over the past few decades, concluded that they came overwhelmingly through democratic civil society organizations using nonviolent action and other forms of civil resistance.[2] Such transitions did not result from foreign invasion and came about only rarely through armed revolt or voluntary, elite-driven reforms. In another study on civil resistance of more than 300 struggles for self-determination against colonialism, military occupation and colonial rule over the past century, Maria Stephan and Erica Chenoweth noted that nonviolent struggles were more than twice as likely to succeed as armed struggles.[3]

Islamic countries have experienced this phenomenon at least as often as any place else in the world. In Iran, the tobacco strike in the 1890s and the constitutional revolution in 1906 were both cases of mass nonviolent resistance against neo-colonialism and authoritarian rule. In Egypt, the 1919 Revolution, consisting of many months of civil disobedience and strikes, eventually led to independence from Britain.

In addition to the recent waves up uprising in North Africa and the Middle East, there have been other recent successful unarmed insurrections in the Islamic world. Civil insurrections in Sudan in 1964 and 1985 overthrew dictatorial regimes and led to brief periods of democratic governance. A popular nonviolent uprising toppled Mali's repressive Traore regime in 1991, resulting in 20 years of stable democracy in that West African country.

In Iran, the largely unarmed insurrection against the Shah toppled the monarchy in 1979 and brought a brief hope for freedom prior to hard-line Islamists consolidating their power; the aborted 2009 uprising may mark the beginning of a more complete democratic revolution. Strikes and other forms of mass resistance forced the resignation of Bangladesh's General Ershad and the restoration of democracy in 1990. A student-led movement in 1998 forced the resignation of Suharto, one of the world's most brutal dictators, after 33 years in power in Indonesia.

In Lebanon, the 2004 Cedar Revolution forced Syria to withdraw its troops and end its domination of Lebanese government. The largely nonviolent 2006 Tulip Revolution ousted the corrupt and autocratic regime of Askar Akeyev in Kyrgystan. Years of protests against the 30-year Gayoum dictatorship regime led to free elections in the Maldives in 2008, resulting in the autocrat's defeat. And in Pakistan, a movement led by lawyers and other civil society organizations resulted in the resignation of U.S.-backed military ruler Pervez Musharraf in 2009.

And, even prior to the wave or protests beginning in 2011, there were ongoing nonviolent popular struggles against foreign military occupation, including those by Palestinians in the West Bank, Syrian Druze in the Golan Heights, and Sahrawis in Western Sahara as well as significant pro-democracy protests in such countries as Kuwait, Bahrain, Niger, Azerbaijan and elsewhere. While these have been chronicled in such books as *Civilian Jihad: Nonviolent Struggle, Democratization and Governance in the Middle East*, there is little appreciation of this history in the West.[4]

Despite Western stereotypes to the contrary, Islamic countries have been at least as prone to large-scale nonviolent struggles as other societies. One of the great strengths of Islamic culture, which makes unarmed insurrections possible, is the implied social contract between a ruler and subject. Prophet Muhammad's successor, Abu Bakr al-Siddiq, stated this explicitly: 'Obey me as long as I obey God in my rule. If I disobey him, you will owe me no obedience.' Such a pledge was reiterated by successive caliphs, including Imam Ali, who said, 'No obedience is allowed to any creature in his disobedience of the Creator.' Indeed, most Islamic scholars have firmly supported the right of the people to depose an unjust ruler. The decision to refuse cooperation is a crucial step in building a nonviolent movement. Massive non-cooperation with illegitimate authority is critical for any successful pro-democracy struggle.

From the poorest nations of Africa to the relatively affluent countries of Eastern Europe; from communist regimes to right-wing military dictatorships; from across the cultural, geographic and ideological spectrum, democratic and progressive forces have recognized the power of nonviolent action to free them from oppression. This has not come, in most cases, from a moral or spiritual commitment to nonviolence, but simply because it works.

The case of Egypt

As one of the largest and most important countries to have its government ousted by an unarmed insurrection, the overthrow of Hosni Mubarak in Egypt in February 2011, despite subsequent struggles to transform that country into a real democracy, captured the attention of the world as millions of ordinary Egyptians – men and women, Christian and Muslim, young and old, workers and intellectuals, poor and middle class, secular and religious – faced down the truncheons, tear gas, water cannons, bullets and goon squads for their freedom.

It was not the military that was responsible for Mubarak's downfall. While some top army officers belatedly eased Mubarak aside on February 11, it was more of a coup de grace and than a coup d'état. It was clear to the military brass, watching the popular reaction following his non-resignation speech the previous day, who recognized that if they did not ease him out, they would be taken down with him. The army's refusal to engage in a Tiananmen Square-style massacre in Tahrir Square came not because the generals were on the protesters' side – indeed, they had long been the bedrock of Mubarak's regime – but because they could not trust their own soldiers, disproportionately from the poor and disenfranchised sectors of society, to obey orders to fire on their own people.

It was not the United States, long the primary foreign backer of the Mubarak regime. The Obama administration played catch-up for most of the 18-day uprising, initially calling only for reforms within the regime. To Obama's credit, he did push for an end to attacks on protesters and the shutting down of the Internet, and reportedly threatened a cut-off of military aid and strategic cooperation if U.S. weapons were used in a massacre or other major repression. Though Obama eventually called for a speedy transition to democracy, however, he never explicitly called on Mubarak to step down. His strongest and most eloquent words in support for the pro-democracy struggle came only after Mubarak's departure, giving a sense that it came more from a desire to not be on the wrong side of history than his desire to play the role as a catalyst.

Some U.S. Embassy staffers had had sporadic contacts with pro-democracy activists in recent years and, through such Congressionally funded foundations as the National Endowment for Democracy (NED), there was some limited financial assistance to a number of civil society organizations. This small amount of US 'democracy' assistance did not include any support for training in strategic nonviolent action or other kinds of grassroots mobilization that proved decisive in the struggle, and the key groups that organized the protests resisted U.S. funding on principle. In any case, the amount of U.S. funding for NED and related programmes in Egypt paled in comparison with the billions of dollars worth of military and economic assistance to the Mubarak regime and the close and regular interaction among U.S. officials and leading Egyptian political and military leaders. In addition, most of this limited 'pro-democracy' funding had been eliminated altogether a couple of years previously, following Obama's inauguration.

Nor was it the Internet. Social media helped expose the abuses of the regime and get around censorship prior to the uprising and, during the revolt, at times helped with tactical coordination for the protests. It is important to note, however, that less than 15 percent of the Egyptian population had access to the Internet (mostly through cafes heavily policed by the regime) and, for a number of key days early in the struggle, it was shut down completely. (Ironically, it may have helped the movement in some cases, as a number of residents in Cairo, Alexandria and other cities decided to come out onto the streets to see what was happening first hand since they could not learn it from the Internet.) While, on balance, the Internet was certainly helpful, it was probably not necessary for the movement's success. The Eastern European revolutions of 1989 and other successful pro-democracy civil insurrections in Latin America, Southeast Asia and Africa took place without access to Internet technology. In Mali – an impoverished landlocked West African nation – word of the eventually victorious 1991 pro-democracy struggle against the Traore dictatorship was spread through *griots*, the traditional singing storytellers, who would wander from village to village. When a people are committed to a struggle, they will find ways to communicate.

Nor was the successful, large-scale application of nonviolent tactics that succeeded in bringing down the dictator a result of assistance or training by outsiders. There were a couple of seminars organized by Egyptian pro-democracy groups that brought in veterans of popular unarmed insurrections in Serbia, South Africa, Palestine and other countries along with some Western academics who had studied the phenomenon, but these seminars focused on generic information about the history and dynamics of strategic nonviolent action, not on how to overthrow Mubarak. Neither the foreign speakers nor their affiliated institutions provided any training, advice, money or anything tangible to the small number of Egyptian activists that attended. (As one of the academics who lectured at one of these seminars, I can vouch that the Egyptians present were already very knowledgeable and sophisticated in terms of strategic thinking about their struggle. None of us foreigners can take credit for what later transpired.) The writings of Gene Sharp, the noted American academic who brought the study of strategic nonviolent action into the realm of serious social science, was studied by Egyptian activists, along with other theorists, but its application to the Egyptian situation was of their own making.[5]

Nor was it a spontaneous reaction to the Tunisian revolution, which had emerged victorious in its largely nonviolent uprising against the Ben Ali dictatorship two weeks earlier. While the unarmed insurrection in Tunisia certainly inspired and empowered many Egyptians who had long been sunk in fear, cynicism and apathy, the Egyptian revolution had been a long time coming. There had been a dramatic growth in Egyptian civil society during the preceding years, with an increasing number of labour strikes and small, but ever-larger, demonstrations led by such youthful, secular pro-democracy groups as Kefaya (meaning 'Enough!') and the April 6 Movement (named after a nationwide strike and protest on that date in 2008.) Increasing government repression, worsening economic conditions and parliamentary elections in November 2010, which were even more transparently fraudulent than most, led many of us to suspect that it was only a matter of time before Mubarak would be ousted in a popular uprising. (Indeed, my visits to Egypt and meetings with pro-democracy activists led me to predict in an article posted in early December that 'Egypt could very well be where the next unarmed popular pro-democracy insurrection takes place of the kind that brought down Marcos in the Philippines, Milosevic in Serbia and scores of other autocratic regimes in recent decades.'[6])

The victories against the Mubarak and Ben Ali regimes struck a serious blow to the two extremes in the nearly decade-long battle between Islamist extremists and U.S. imperialists. Al-Qaeda's first attack against U.S. interests was in 1995 against a residential compound in Riyadh used by U.S. soldiers responsible for training the Saudi National Guard, the branch of the Saudi military used primarily for internal repression. The line put forward by Osama bin Laden and like-minded self-styled *jihadists* has long been that U.S.-backed dictatorships can only be defeated through terrorism and adherence to a reactionary and chauvinistic interpretation of Islam. At the other extreme, the line put forward by American neo-conservatives and their supporters had long been that democracy could only come to the Middle East through U.S. military intervention, as with the U.S. invasion and occupation of Iraq.

The people of Egypt and Tunisia powerfully demonstrated that both of these violent militaristic ideologies are wrong.

It is noteworthy that the Libyan uprising scored its most dramatic victories during the first week, when it was overwhelmingly nonviolent, only to suffer a series of losses when the opposition took up arms, prompting NATO military intervention. It is hard to speculate whether a better organized, strategically savvy and persistent nonviolent movement could have toppled the regime and avoided the costly civil war and foreign intervention that resulted, but leaders at least as brutal as Gaddafi have been toppled when pro-democracy activists have leveraged the regime's repression to gain greater sympathy within the population and greater defections among security forces.

The role of the United States

What can the United States and other Western nations do to help build democracy in the Middle East? External support for nonviolent struggles in the Middle East can be a double-edged sword. Most struggles against a repressive regime would normally welcome international solidarity. But if the outside support is seen as coming from forces that don't hold the best interest of the country's people in mind, it can harm the chances of such a movement succeeding in its goals. At the same time, external actors have played an important role in supporting nonviolent struggles in the past. And thanks to enhanced international mobility and communication, such actors will likely play an increasingly important role in the future.

Aid for democracy assistance should be provided very carefully to avoid backlash. Such aid worked in Eastern Europe in the 1980s, where the United States was seen as an ally to democracy. In most Islamic countries, however, the United States has been seen as an ally to dictatorship and foreign military occupation. So if Washington embraced opposition groups too warmly, this could work against the public acceptance of these groups. At the same time, given the serious challenges facing pro-democracy groups struggling against the powerful autocratic regimes in the region, many activists will likely continue to look to the United States and other Western powers for, at minimum, moral and diplomatic support. The United States can apply diplomatic pressure to free political prisoners, promote the right to free assembly, and support other means of creating the political space for nonviolent pro-democracy movements to grow. Western leaders who avoid messianic and self-righteous rhetoric when talking about democracy, pursue policies that neither practise nor condone violations of international humanitarian law, and directly communicate with and respect the wishes of nonviolent activists struggling against their autocratic rulers could help to rectify the historically counter-productive policies that have for so long hurt the cause of democracy in the region.

Unfortunately, it's not clear that the United States even wants greater democracy in the Islamic world. Tear gas canisters lobbed at pro-democracy demonstrators were inscribed with the words 'Made in USA', a reminder of whose side Washington was on in the struggle against the dictatorship. Despite severe repression against pro-democracy demonstrators in Bahrain and Yemen subsequent to the Egyptian revolution, U.S. support for these dictatorships continued. In Tunisia and Egypt, U.S. policy evolved from support for the regime, to calls for modest reforms from within the regime, to statements for 'restraint' from 'both sides', to more explicit support for a democratic transition, to – following the dictators' departure – eloquent statements from President Obama lauding the pro-democracy struggle.

There has long been a sense of fatalism in the Arab world; that they are simply passive victims of outside forces. Although it is easy to dismiss Obama's comments as merely a last-minute show of support to the winning side, this shift indicates the significance of what happened in Tunisia and Egypt: rather than Washington controlling the course of events influencing the 'Arab street', the 'Arab street' is influencing policies emanating from Washington.

Indeed, at the point where a movement embarks upon a strategy of large-scale, nonviolent action, there is little foreign governments can do to help or hinder its chances of success, other than pressure the regime to limit its repression. Large bureaucratic governments accustomed to projecting political power through military force or elite diplomatic channels tend to have little understanding of, or appreciation for, nonviolent action or any other kind of mass popular struggle or the complex, internal political dynamics of a given country necessary to create the broad coalition capable of ousting the incumbent authoritarian government.

Unlike changes of regime historically promoted by foreign governments during the colonial and much of the post-colonial period, which have tended to be violent seizures of power that install an undemocratic minority, nonviolent 'people power' movements make change through empowering pro-democratic majorities. (This serves as yet another reason why the Iranian regime's claims that the United States is somehow responsible for the Green Revolution are so ludicrous.) Every successful nonviolent insurrection has been a homegrown movement rooted in the realization by the masses that their rulers were illegitimate and that the current political system was incapable of redressing injustice.

The fundamental reality is that democracy will not come to the Middle East through foreign intervention, sanctimonious statements from Washington, voluntary reforms by autocrats, or armed struggle by a self-selected vanguard. It will only come through the power of massive non-cooperation with illegitimate authority and the strategic application of nonviolent action by Middle Eastern peoples themselves.

Notes

1 David DeBartolo, 'Perceptions of U.S. Democracy Promotion: Middle Eastern and American Views,' Project on Middle East Democracy Report, May 2008.
2 Adrian Karatnycky, *How Freedom is Won*, Washington, DC: Freedom House, 2005.
3 Maria J. Stephan and Erica Chenoweth, 'Why Civil Resistance Works: The Logic of Strategic Nonviolent Conflict,' *International Security*, Volume 33, Number 1, Summer 2008, 7–44.
4 Maria J. Stephan, *Civilian Jihad: Nonviolent Struggle, Democratization and Governance in the Middle East*, New York: Palgrave MacMillan, 2009.
5 See, for example, Gene Sharp, *From Dictatorship to Democracy*, Boston: Albert Einstein Institution, 1992.
6 Stephen Zunes, 'Fraudulent Egyptian Election' (Washington, DC: Foreign Policy In Focus, December 7, 2010).

27 How do post-conflict societies deal with a traumatic past and promote national unity and reconciliation?

Andrew Rigby

Introductory observations

'How do societies deal with the legacy of violent and destructive conflict in the attempt to promote national unity and reconciliation?'

Let us start off with the concept of 'post-conflict societies'. It seems very clear that a conflict does not end with a ceasefire and a peace settlement. Rather it takes on different forms, which hopefully include an end to the more-or-less organized and intentional killing and other extreme forms of physical violence. This means that strategies and policies relating to dealing with the past do not emerge in a political vacuum. They reflect to a significant degree the lines of political contention and the balance of political forces prevalent during the relevant post-ceasefire period.

The power ratios in turn relate very closely to the manner in which the peace agreement has been brought about. Three ideal-typical forms of transition from violent to nonviolent conflict can be identified.

1   A negotiated settlement reached between parties that are more or less exhausted and do not see any realistic chance of outright victory of one over the other.
2   A negotiated settlement between asymmetric forces, in which the weaker still controls sufficient resources to exercise a veto power.
3   The victory of one party over the other.

My thesis is that there is a close link between types of settlement, the consequent power relationships during the post-settlement period, and the likely strategy to be adopted in terms of dealing with the past.

But before going on to illustrate this thesis, let us first look briefly at the other terms in the title – 'national unity and reconciliation'. 'National unity' refers to some form of coexistence between those actors/parties that were divided by violence and destructive conflict. In this context it is worth bearing in mind that we can have different levels of coexistence, different degrees of national unity.

The concept of reconciliation can be used to refer to a process and a condition. As David Bloomfield has observed, reconciliation is both a *goal* – something to achieve – and a *process* – a means to achieve that goal.[1] How to recognize when that goal or condition of reconciliation has been achieved is somewhat problematic. Johan Galtung, for example, has defined reconciliation as 'closure plus healing; closure in the sense of not reopening hostilities, healing in the sense of being rehabilitated.'[2] For others, however, reconciliation refers primarily to a process. Thus, for Louis Kriesberg reconciliation 'refers to the processes by which parties that have experienced an oppressive relationship or a destructive conflict with each other move to attain or to restore a relationship that they believe will be minimally acceptable.'[3] Such processes can be initiated at any point during a destructive conflict, as people seek to establish bridges across the conflict lines, but it is an activity more commonly encountered during the post-settlement phase of a conflict when the space available for such activities becomes broader.

Reconciliation as a process leading to coexistence

In attempting to sketch out the features of different types of coexistence as forms or degrees of reconciliation, a number of models are available to be drawn upon. David Crocker has suggested a three-fold typology of levels or degrees of coexistence.[4] Crocker challenged the appropriateness and relevance of Archbishop Desmond Tutu's calls for forgiveness in the context of the South African Truth and Reconciliation Commission. One aspect of his critique was that Tutu's formulation of reconciliation as *ubuntu*, an ideal of social harmony within which the well-being of the whole community depended on the restoration of broken relationships between its members, was unrealistic and unrealizable. Crocker also argued that *ubuntu* subordinated other values such as individual freedom, including the freedom to withhold forgiveness. As against Tutu's concept of reconciliation, Crocker offered two other versions of social cooperation, which he labelled as 'non-lethal coexistence' and 'democratic reciprocity'.

In the case of 'non-lethal coexistence', according to Crocker, 'former enemies no longer kill each other or routinely violate each other's basic rights.' He continues:

> This thin sense of reconciliation, attained when cease fires, peace accords, and negotiated settlements begin to take hold, can be a momentous achievement. . . . Reconciliation as non-lethal coexistence – however difficult to achieve – demands significantly less and is easier to realise than Tutu's much 'thicker' ideal that requires mutuality and forgiveness.[5]

'Democratic reciprocity' constitutes a more robust form of coexistence:

> In this conception, former enemies or former perpetrators, victims, and bystanders are reconciled insofar as they respect each other as fellow citizens. Further, all parties play a role in deliberations concerning the past, present, and future of their country. A still-divided society will surely find this ideal of democratic reciprocity difficult enough to attain – although much easier than an ideal defined by mutual compassion and the *requirement* of forgiveness.[6]

Any agency seeking the restoration of relationships between those who have become estranged must commence with an analysis of the nature of the pre-fractured relationship and the nature of the process of fracture or estrangement. As David Crocker has phrased it, 'it matters what a given transition is from and what it is to.'[7] That is, in envisaging the type of coexistence – the goal – of any particular reconciliation process, due consideration must be given to the types of relationships pertaining prior to the fracture and, of course, to the nature of the process of fracture itself. Furthermore, it is very important that those tasked with healing damaged relationships should be sensitive to the feelings and perceptions of those that have been divided from each other. For example, in some research carried out in Northern

Ireland during 2004, six years after the signing of the Good Friday Agreement, which set the terms for the continuing ceasefire and associated peace process, it was found that a number of people who were engaged in what they considered to be peace-building work were very hesitant to use the term 'reconciliation'. They felt that the word had the potential to frighten off those with whom they wished to engage. Talk of reconciliation was perceived as 'utopian or idealistic, demanding a process of coming together for which they were not ready.'[8] These peace-builders preferred to talk about developing 'good relations' or 'community relations' rather than promoting 'reconciliation'.[9] As Chayes and Minow have remarked, 'reconciliation may remain elusive or even an insulting notion to people still reeling from the murder of their loved ones or their own torture or rape. . . . Clumsy, premature attempts at reconciliation may do more harm than good.'[10]

Accordingly, 'realistic reconciliation workers' might find it useful to work towards one of three ideal types of coexistence:[11]

1. *Surface coexistence of separate lives*, where those that have been and remain divided continue to *live apart from each other* in a form of social apartheid, informed by the general ethos of 'You leave us alone and we shall leave you alone'. In such circumstances, interaction between the two is often by arrangement, with very little casual social interaction. As Michael Ignatieff concluded on the basis of his observations of the workings of the South African Truth and Reconciliation Commission,

> You can have coexistence without any heart-to-heart reconciliation at all. Political enemies, historical antagonists, do not have to be reconciled before they can sit in the same room. You can coexist with people you cheerfully detest. You can coexist with people without forgetting or forgiving their crimes against you. Cold peace of many kinds does not require reconciliation of a personal kind.[12]

2. *Shallow coexistence of parallel lives*, where people *live alongside each other* and cross-community interaction tends to be quite role-specific (as in the exchange of various types of goods and services) with only a limited amount of casual social interaction, although the spaces and occasions for cross-community conviviality are generally recognized and respected.

3. *Deep coexistence of community*, where people from different identity groups and networks *live with and amongst each other*, and where everyday interaction is rich and multi-textured.

Reconciliation *to* as a necessary precondition for reconciliation *with* one's former enemies?

Considering reconciliation as a process intended to promote forms of coexistence between those that have been divided by destructive conflict, it is possible to distinguish at the analytical level between two dimensions of such processes according to their time-orientation: *reconciliation to* the pain and loss of the past, and *reconciliation with* former enemies for the sake of future coexistence. For reconciliation *with and between* former enemies to take place, one or more of the parties has to become reconciled *to* past loss and the frustration of their maximalist goals, and thereby reconciled *to* carrying some of the cost of moving forward towards future coexistence alongside those from whom they have been divided.

Different levels of coexistence (*reconciliation with*) require different degrees of *reconciliation to* past loss. Thus, surface forms of coexistence can go on without people being reconciled to their past loss and suffering, although they do require people to acknowledge the new 'post-settlement reality' in the sense of a preparedness to cooperate within the institutional framework that constitutes the infrastructure of their collective lives. As Ignatieff has observed, 'Many South African whites may coexist with blacks because they have no choice but not because they fundamentally accept or are reconciled to their change of status.'[13] Richer forms of coexistence, however, do require deeper levels of *reconciliation to* past loss, particularly insofar as these involve the relinquishment of any significant desire to avenge past loss.

Dealing with the past

Becoming reconciled to past loss is one way in which people 'deal with the past'. As such it involves what we might term 'memory work'. That is, for people to become *reconciled to* past loss it is necessary for them to reinterpret that past. They must look backwards through time with a different lens, one that enables them to create a new narrative, a new story brought about through the reconstruction or reframing of their memories in such a manner that eases the intensity of feelings of hatred and bitterness that used to be occasioned when they revisited the past.[14] Susan Dwyer has conceptualized the core process of reconciliation as 'bringing apparently incompatible descriptions of events into narrative equilibrium', a process involving the articulation of a range of interpretations of those events and the attempt by the parties 'to choose from this range of interpretations some subset that allows them each to accommodate the disruptive event into their ongoing narratives.'[15]

A number of factors impact on people's capacity to reframe or reinterpret the past in such a manner as to enable them to become reconciled to past loss and anticipate the possibility of some level of coexistence with former enemies:

1   Security: A necessary condition for people to become reconciled to past loss is the experience of a break with the past in the form of an identifiable end to the wrongs perpetrated sufficient for the survivors to enjoy a degree of personal and collective security and thereby be reassured about the future actions of former wrong-doers.
2   Truth: The capacity of communities to create new collective memories that allow for the relinquishment of the desire for revenge will be enhanced to the degree that former enemies acknowledge the wrongs perpetrated in the past.[16]
3   Justice: The capacity of the survivors to relinquish the desire for revenge fed by feelings of bitterness towards former perpetrators is enhanced to the extent that they feel genuine efforts have been made to 'make things right' – either in terms of punishing the perpetrators or making reparations to their victims.
4   Time: Dealing constructively with the past, whether at the interpersonal or collective level, requires time. The length of time necessary for new memories to be formed that allow for new relationships between those that were divided will vary from person to person and community to community according to the particular circumstances. It will also depend on the degree to which the conditions or values of security, truth and justice have been realized.
5   Culture: Different cultures have different approaches to dealing with the past. In some cultures, to acknowledge culpability would involve an unconscionable degree of shame and loss of face.[17] Other societies seem to have an unbelievable capacity for forgiveness and letting go of any desire for retribution.[18] Furthermore, in many cultures in Africa and parts of Asia, the spirits of the dead are believed to play a role in the healing of interpersonal and social wounds.[19]

When individuals apologize and express remorse for past actions, and when they occupy public positions which enable them to claim with some legitimacy that they represent a particular community or broader entity, then they can act as significant agents in promoting reconciliation between such collectivities. As Michael Ignatieff has remarked, 'Leaders give their societies permission to say the unsayable, to think the unthinkable, to rise to gestures of reconciliation that people, individually, cannot imagine.'[20] Such 'prophetic acts of witness', which can also be represented in public memorials and other symbolic spaces, have the power to touch people in such a manner that they feel more willing to become reconciled to past loss and anticipate reconciliation with former enemies. As Fanie du Toit has observed in the South African context, 'Processes of reconciliation need champions . . . In practically every reconciliation story there are individuals tirelessly driving the twin processes of dialogue and development.'[21]

Just as there are those who might insist on pursuing convivial relationships with those from across the 'divide', within any community or collectivity there will also be others who refuse to 'let go' of the past and insist on ever more 'truth' and ever more 'justice' before they are prepared to consider future coexistence of any depth. Those seeking to promote reconciliation between divided communities must never assume homogeneity or group uniformity with regard to attitudes towards future coexistence with former enemies. Moreover, in certain circumstances different factions can succeed in mobilizing others around their 'cause', with the result that social movements emerge, each championing different orientations towards the past and the future. This means that whatever level or depth of coexistence achieved between former enemies, it must always be considered conditional, as an ongoing process that is not necessarily a linear one.

Institutional approaches to dealing with past

The most problematic dimension of any reconciliation process in the aftermath of a civil war or a period of gross human rights abuse is balancing the tension between the three values that most observers agree are pre-conditions for movement along the coexistence axis: peace/security, truth and justice. Most state-directed efforts to deal with the legacy of past abuses are variants of three standard approaches: amnesties and official amnesia, truth commissions, and purges and prosecutions. To a significant degree the approach adopted reflects the interests and the balance of power of relevant state and non-state actors during the process of transition. This relationship is presented in the table below.

Mode of transition to peace settlement	Power relationship between parties to peace settlement	Prime value sought in dealing with past	Institutional means of dealing with past
Negotiated settlement (Mozambique)	Balance of power	Peace/security	Amnesty & official amnesia
Power settlement (South Africa)	Asymmetry of power	Truth	Truth commission
Imposed settlement (Rwanda)	Victory/defeat	Justice	Prosecutions & purges

Amnesia and amnesty – the prioritizing of peace and security

In 1975, the Spanish dictator Franco died. He came to power through a military rebellion and subsequent civil war, and after his victory in 1939 his regime became infamous for its brutal treatment of the defeated Republicans and the repression of all perceived foes. Yet after Franco's death and the transition to democratic rule, there was no purge of those responsible for the abuses of Franco's era, but rather an exercise in collective amnesia. This 'pact of oblivion' was made by the post-Franco political elite in order to ensure political stability. There were good grounds for believing that any attempt to sully the reputation of Franco and purge the military and security forces would lead to a coup attempt. Everything was subordinated to the peaceful transition to democratic rule – and this exercise in letting bygones be bygones would appear to have worked; the roots of democracy in Spain have deepened.

The desire to cover up the past can also be the wish of people at the grassroots level in addition to political elites. For people who have been involved in mass violence such as can happen in a civil war, it can certainly seem as if the past is best left where it belongs, in the past. To introduce it into the present might lead to further bloodshed, conflict and pain.

An example of such an approach to dealing with the past was the case of Mozambique where, after 15 years of civil war, there was a peace accord agreed in 1992. Following the settlement there were no trials, no official truth commissions. Those ex-combatants who returned to their villages were 'cleansed' of their past sins by local healers and welcomed back into the fold of their community, putting the war behind them. There were many reasons this approach was adopted, but particularly important was the recognition that war pollutes everyone and the prime value should be the restoration of community cohesion, peace and security.[22]

Prioritizing truth, but whose truth?

Typically the truth commission approach to dealing with the past is adopted in situations where there is an asymmetry of power but where the weaker partner still possesses sufficient resources to threaten the national reconstruction project.

The prime concern of the truth commission approach to addressing the pains of the past is with the victims. The aim is to identify them and to uncover and formally acknowledge the wrongs done to them. In a number of cases this exercise is implemented not only in pursuit of the value of truth but also as a necessary step towards the establishment of some system of compensation for victims.

The pattern was set by the National Commission on the Disappeared, established in Argentina in 1983, which tried to uncover the secrecy surrounding the torture, killing and disappearance of the thousands of victims of the military regime. Chile followed Argentina's example in 1991. A few years later there was the South African Truth and Reconciliation Commission, and more recently there was the Sierra Leone commission Nw there is one in Liberia.

At times it can seem as if there is a virtual 'fashion' for truth commissions, and there is a great danger that too many people will conclude that all one has to do to sow the seeds of national unity and reconciliation is to have a truth commission. Such an assumption needs to be tempered by the following considerations.

1. The history that is revealed by truth commissions can only be a partial truth. The very process of uncovering a part of the truth and granting it the status of official, public and authoritative record can serve to cover up other aspects of the past. For instance, in the cases of the Latin American truth commissions there was no identification of the actual individuals responsible for abuses. From the perspective of those that survived this meant that the perpetrators continued to enjoy impunity and justice was forfeited.

It was because of such criticisms that the South Africans introduced the element of *conditional* amnesty into their model. To be free from the fear of prosecution, perpetrators were required to confess their crimes and convince the Amnesty Committee that these had been 'political' in nature and were not committed out of personal malice or for private gain.

2. Another way in which a truth commission can serve to cover up certain 'truths' is by limiting its terms of reference to a particular time period. For example, if there was to be a truth commission in Cambodia and its scope was confined to the period 1975–79 when the Khmer Rouge regime of Pol Pot held power and created the conditions for genocide amongst the Cambodian people, then there would be no reference to the United States' bombing of Cambodia prior to 1975 as part of its pursuance of the Vietnam War and which caused so much suffering and helped pave the way to power of the Khmer Rouge.

3. Amongst some advocates of truth commissions as an institutional mode of dealing with the past there is a rhetoric about their 'healing power' that should be viewed with caution. There is some evidence, particularly from the South African experience, that victims who testified to the truth commission experienced a kind of 're-traumatization' insofar as the experience brought back to the surface their past pain and suffering. Moreover, those concerned with promoting reconciliation processes in the aftermath of collective violence and division should be careful about assuming that 'therapeutic truth-telling' is always the most appropriate means of healing the personal and collective wounds of the past. They should be aware that different cultures have their own methods of dealing with the legacy of a painful past, and should be wary of those who seem to believe that 'one method fits all' when dealing with individual and collective trauma. Thus, in a report on the truth and reconciliation process in Sierra Leone, Rosalind Shaw noted the widespread appeal of a 'forgive and forget' approach amongst many Sierra Leoneans, an approach based in part on local indigenous strategies of recovery and reintegration. By contrast, the Sierra Leone Truth and Reconciliation Commission, modelled on the South African process, was guided by the assumption that truth-telling, the public recounting of memories of violence, was the appropriate way to promote individual and collective healing. Shaw concluded:

> Where a TRC is initiated, it will be more effective if it builds upon established practices of healing and reconciliation. In Sierra Leone, the TRC set itself in opposition to widespread local practices of social reconstruction as forgetting by valorizing verbally discursive remembering as the only road to reconciliation and peace.[23]

Purges and prosecutions: the prioritization of justice

In general one can say that the path of prosecutions and purges is likely to be followed when the new regime has come to power as a result of a comprehensive victory over those who are the potential targets of such a purge.

There is something appealing about the idea of holding people to account for their misdeeds, and the advocates of retributive justice put forward a number of points to support their case.

1   The individualization of guilt: The German philosopher Karl Jaspers said of the Nuremberg trials in 1946, 'For us Germans this trial has the advantage that it distinguished between the particular crimes of the leaders and that it does not condemn the Germans collectively.'[24]

2   Symbolizing due process and the rule of law: The punishment of perpetrators through due legal process helps prevent the incidence of private acts of revenge and 'self-help justice', and demonstrates that there are ways of coping with difference other than resorting to violence.[25]

3   Challenging a culture of impunity: By prosecuting and punishing those who abused the rights of others, new regimes affirm the fundamental axiom at the heart of common-sense notions of justice that people should face the consequences of their actions.

4   Deterrence: Linked with the challenge to any culture of impunity, punishment is defended as a deterrent to potential perpetrators in the future.

Such are the arguments made by those who advocate the punishment of all those guilty of perpetrating crimes and human rights abuses during periods of destructive conflict. However, critics of the strategy of trials and purges as a mode of dealing with the past can cite five main problem areas:

1   Victor's justice: The debate over the Nuremberg trials after the Second World War is still ongoing. Was it due process or revenge? The accused were not prosecuted by their peers but by their conquerors, and as such many believe that it was a perverted 'victor's justice' that was served there. After all, if the German leaders were tried for war crimes, what about those responsible for the bombing of Dresden, Hiroshima and Nagasaki? Were they not also war crimes?

2   The multi-dimensionality of guilt: The prosecution of those who have violated other people's human rights exercises a strong appeal for those who are convinced that there is a clear division between guilty and innocent, perpetrators and victims. But this Manichean paradigm does not reflect the complexity and the 'messiness' of life under repression. It was for this reason that President Vaclav Havel of the Czech Republic was initially reluctant to endorse any kind of purge following the Velvet Revolution of 1989. He was too aware of the manner in which the machinery of the old regime could colonize people, turning them into unwitting accomplices of the repressive apparatuses of the state.[26]

Even in the most violent of situations, such as that which prevailed in Cambodia between 1975 and 1979, one has to acknowledge that many of those guilty of horrendous abuses were themselves poor, uneducated conscripts, overwhelmed by the culture of violence that permeated the Khmer Rouge. Moreover, they faced summary and extreme punishment if they refused to carry out orders. Clearly they were guilty of perpetrating terrible acts, but were they not also victims?[27] Karl Jaspers, reflecting on the Holocaust, distinguished between four types of guilt:

i)   The criminal guilt of those who actually committed the crimes;

ii)   The political guilt of those who helped such people get to power;

iii) The moral guilt of those who stood by doing nothing as the crimes were being committed; and finally;

iv)   The metaphysical guilt of those who survived whilst others were killed, thereby failing in their responsibility to do all that they might have done to preserve the standards of civilised humanity.[28]

Trials might be valid processes for determining criminal guilt, but they are not best suited to coping with all the different forms, shades and degrees of culpability and complicity characteristic of people living under repressive regimes or in violent and destructive conflicts.[29]

3   Trials and the manipulation of history: Trials can have their limitations when it comes to unveiling the truth about the past. They are combative encounters where defendant

and prosecutor compete to get their version of the truth accepted as authoritative. In this process both sides are engaged in what we might term the manipulation of history, insofar as they each have an interest in concealing some aspects of the past and highlighting others.

As part of this process trials can serve as morality plays, where good triumphs over evil and the guilty are made to pay the price for their misdeeds. As such they might function as symbolic history lessons, but they are not the best means for dealing with all the subtleties of the past.

4   Prosecutions are very expensive and due process is slow: Writing in 2007, Helena Cobban estimated that the 26 cases completed by the International Criminal Tribunal for Rwanda since its establishment in 1994 had cost one billion dollars. One has to ask if that has been the best use of such an amount of money. Furthermore, it has been estimated that prior to the establishment of the community based *gacaca* courts, it would have taken up to 200 years to deal with the 140,000 prisoners who were detained in camps by the late 1990s.[30]

5   Prosecutions and trials are only one type of justice: The notion of restorative justice proclaims the idea that true justice involves the restoration of right relationships within the community and the broader human household, and this is more important than to prosecute and punish individuals.

People who have been affected by violence frequently say that they would like 'justice'. But we should not assume that by 'justice' they mean the punishment of perpetrators. They might be seeking proper compensation for their suffering in the form of some kind of socio-economic justice – the satisfaction of basic needs such as housing, health care and employment.

National reconciliation projects: rhetoric and theatre

Whichever of the above variants is pursued as a means of 'dealing with the past', the dominant concern of all new regimes is to promote the necessary degree of social order to ensure regime security and legitimacy. This is the *national reconciliation project*. Unfortunately such state-driven projects can appear distant and irrelevant to many victims of violence and abuse. The evidence from South Africa would seem to indicate that too many victims experienced the truth and reconciliation process almost as a piece of theatre taking place on a public stage far removed from their own lives and experiences. As one respondent in a survey conducted in the rural community of Grabouw in the Western Cape complained, 'We have seen reconciliation on television with the TRC, but here in Grabouw we have not had anything like that.'[31] Furthermore, there is some evidence that whilst the South African truth commission was 'therapeutic' at the national level, many of those who gave evidence and bore witness were (re-) traumatized by the experience.[32]

In similar vein, Rosalind Shaw has delivered some cautionary advice to those that share the faith in the South African approach to national reconciliation that informed the architects of the Sierra Leone experiment, 'Nations . . . do not have psyches that can be healed. Nor can it be assumed that truth telling is healing on a personal level: truth commissions do not constitute therapy.'[33]

Observers and third parties seeking to intervene to promote and deepen reconciliation should be wary of being deluded by the rhetoric and the theatre that are a significant dimension of national reconciliation projects. In particular attention needs to be paid to addressing the emotional challenges faced by those tasked with establishing some form of social coexistence in the aftermath of violence and divisive conflict.

Security, trust and hope: the emotional requirements for coexistence

The focus above has been on the institutional approaches to 'dealing with the past' that constitute what we have termed the national reconciliation project. Such approaches have been an integral component of the dominant state-building approach to post-conflict peace-building in recent years.[34] Theorists and practitioners within this approach have focused on the primacy of institution-building and infrastructural reconstruction, and have paid very little overt attention to the 'subjective' dimension of peace-building; they fail to resonate with people at the community level. In particular they fail to take account of the emotional challenges faced by those seeking to come to terms with loss in the context of post-conflict life. In the remainder of this paper some of these emotional challenges will be examined. The pivotal role of emotions in influencing patterns of political and social life has been recognized more clearly by social scientists in recent years.[35] Unfortunately this awareness and associated theorising has not spread to the peace-building field. As Neta Crawford observed, 'post-conflict peacebuilding efforts too frequently fail . . . because peace settlements and peacebuilding policies play with emotional fire that practitioners scarcely understand but nevertheless seek to manipulate.'[36] An understanding of the emotional dynamics of societies emerging out of violent and destructive conflict will allow theorists and practitioners of conflict transformation to comprehend more clearly the challenges of post-war reconstruction and related efforts to promote coexistence.

Whilst acknowledging the importance of creating the necessary institutional and infrastructural foundations for people to recreate 'normal' lives for themselves, I think it needs to be recognized that 'negative' emotions, especially rage, fear and the desire for revenge, are central to processes of destructive conflict and to 'post-conflict' reconciliation and peace-building.

The challenge facing those seeking to promote sustainable peace processes in the aftermath of civil war and other forms of divisive collective violence is to erode the basis for negative emotion generated by the conflict whilst laying the foundation for the growth of more positive emotions such as compassion, forgiveness, trust and hope. What this means in practice is that however committed peace-builders might be to some model of a harmonious future, it is imperative that they take seriously the emotions of the survivors of conflict.[37] People have to deal with their ghosts from the past before they can be expected to embrace a new future.

At the most superficial level of coexistence the dominant emotion remains that of fear – fear about the return of the violence, the generalized fear that the past is not past, such that the violence and abuse of the war continue to cast their long shadow over the present, and feed the fear of what the future might bring.[38] So long as people's emotional lives are dominated by this fear they cannot develop the trust necessary for social reconstruction and coexistence in the present. It is the growth of this second emotion, trust, that helps undermine and accompanies the erosion of the fear of 'the returning past' – trust in one's fellow citizens and in the institutions that constitute the context for everyday life. This restoration of trust requires some experience of 'normality' in everyday life, a level of predictability that is dependent upon people sharing a similar interpretive scheme for making sense of and acting in the world, making compatible judgements about the appropriateness of particular forms of behaviour. This is the type of *horizontal trust* between people that is a precondition for 'normal everyday life'.[39] But the experience of normality and predictability as a basis for developing trust also requires an institutional infrastructure that facilitates levels of security and thereby helps generate what De Grieff has characterized as the *vertical trust* between citizens and their institutions.

Mneesha Gellman, exploring the inter-relationship in Cambodia between the 'national reconciliation project' orchestrated by the political elite at the central state level and grass-roots initiatives to promote constructive coexistence, has highlighted the inter-relationship between the different 'levels', and in the process has emphasized the importance of developing horizontal and vertical trust as a means of loosening the appeal of victimhood and promoting hope for the future. She writes,

> Improved democratic capacity at the national level might assist in rebuilding trust and enthusiasm at the local levels . . . Conversely, building trust at the community level will give government the much needed social capital to implement peacebuilding agendas . . . . competent leadership and democratic organizations that encourage public input and participation can *motivate people to develop a positive vision of the future rather than cling to past grievances.*[40]

A key indicator of deeper forms of coexistence is when people start sharing their hopes for the future, when they start imagining a shared future together, and when they start to believe that they have grounds for such hope. Of course, to hope for something indicates a recognition that what is desired may be beyond our present capacity to bring about. But to 'hope well' is to experience ourselves as agents of potential, confronting our limitations and seeking to move beyond them. As such, there is a strong relationship between hope and social change. But hope cannot survive without the conditions to sustain it.

One factor that can contribute to keeping hope alive is being amongst others who share and support our hopes – being a member of a community of hope. But the creation and maintenance of such a community depends in turn upon there being recognizable grounds for hope. As such there is a very powerful positive relationship between social change and hope – evidence of constructive change on the ground reinforces one's sense of agency and hence one's capacity to hope.[41] From this perspective a major challenge for peace-builders is to help create the grounds for hope in societies emerging out of the trauma of collective violence. Whilst in certain circumstances such initiatives can come from external actors and agencies, people can create their own grounds for hope within their own communities through different community development and socio-economic regeneration initiatives. The successful implementation of community development projects can act as symbols of what the future might hold, serving as symbols of the efficacy of local people as agents of social change, and thereby functioning as emotional joggers, enhancing individual and collective capacities for hope.

In conclusion, it would appear that peace-builders seeking to harness the emotional dynamics of a population in the process of post-conflict reconstruction should be sensitive to the following questions:

i)   Do the initiatives anticipated help strengthen the sense of personal and collective security and reduce the fear of a return of the violence?
ii) Will the initiatives help foster trust – the horizontal trust in others and the vertical trust in the 'system' – necessary for sustainable coexistence?
iii) Will the initiatives help establish the grounds for people to have a shared hope for the future?

Notes

1 D. Bloomfield, in D. Bloomfield et al, eds., *Reconciliation After Violent Conflict: A Handbook*, Stockholm: International IDEA, 2003, p. 12.

2 J. Galtung, 'After violence, reconstruction, reconciliation, and resolution', pp. 3–23 in M. Abu-Nimer, ed., *Reconciliation, Justice and Coexistence*, Lanham, MD: Lexington, 2001, p. 4

3 L. Kriesberg, 'Changing forms of coexistence', pp. 47–64 in M. Abu-Nimer (2001), p. 48.

4 See D. A. Crocker, 'Punishment, reconciliation, and democratic deliberation', *Buffalo Criminal Law Review*, v. 5:509, 2002, pp. 509–549. See also D. Crocker, 'Retribution and reconciliation', Institute for Philosophy & Public Policy, available at www.puasf.umd.edu/IPPP/Winter-Spring00?retribution_and_ reconciliation.htm.

5 Crocker (2002), p. 528.

6 Crocker, (2002), pp. 528–529.

7 D. Crocker, 'Reckoning with past wrongs', pp. 39–63 in C.A. Prager & T. Govier, eds., *Dilemmas of Reconciliation*, Waterloo, Ontario: Wilfred Laurier University Press, 2003, p. 57.

8 G. Kelly & B. Hamber, 'Coherent, contested or confused? Views in Northern Ireland', pp. 21–35 in G. Kelly & B. Hamber, eds., *Reconciliation: Rhetoric or Relevant?*, Belfast: Democratic Dialogue, 2005, p. 24.

9 Except in their funding applications to the European Union! As one respondent replied to the question 'what is reconciliation?': 'It's what you have to put down on a form to get the money. It is funder-speak and it doesn't mean much to people.' Kelly & Hamber, p. 25.

10 Antonia Chayes & Martha Minow, eds., *Imagine Coexistence: Restoring humanity after violent ethnic conflict*, eds., San Francisco: Jossey-Bass, 2003, p. XX.

11 The choice of three is just that – a choice that seems to be an adequate balance between clarity, simplicity and utility. Carolos Sluzki suggests five categories: coexistence, collaboration, cooperation, interdependence and integration. C. Sluzki, 'The process toward reconciliation', in Chayes & Minow (2003), pp. 21–31.

12 M. Ignatieff, 'Afterword' in Chayes & Minow, p. 326.

13 Ignatieff, in Chayes & Minow, p. 327.

14 Hannah Arendt, quoting the novelist Isak Deneson, remarked, ' "All sorrows can be borne if you put them into a story or tell a story about them." The story reveals the meaning of what otherwise would remain an unbearable sequence of sheer happenings.' Quoted in E. Skaar et al, eds., *Roads to Reconciliation*, Lanham, MD: Lexington Books, 2005, p. 8.

15 S. Dwyer, 'Reconciliation for realists', pp. 91–110 in C. Prager & T. Govier, eds., *Dilemmas of reconciliation: Cases and concepts*, Waterloo, Ontario: Wilfred Laurier University Press, 2003, p. 100.

16 For an interesting discussion of the significance of acknowledgement to victims, see T. Govier, 'What is acknowledgement and why is it important?' in Prager & Govier (2003), pp. 65–89. Commenting on the manner in which our sense of self is formed with and through other people, Govier observes 'If those other people deny or ignore events and harms that have been fundamental in shaping our experience, we will be unable to stand in an honest and constructive relationship with them. Acknowledgement offers soothing, relief, and a basis for open, comfortable, and more trusting relationships.' (p. 86).

17 This is one of the dilemmas of promoting reconciliation in a society like Cambodia.

18 This is an observation that has been made to me on a number of occasions by people who have spent time in Sierra Leone.

19 See, for example, Honwana's account of social reintegration in Mozambique and Angola in Skaar et al (2005).

20 M. Ignatieff, *The Warrior's Honor*, London: Chatto & Windus, 1998, p. 188.

21 F. du Toit, ed., *Learning to Live Together*, Cape Town: Institute for Justice and Reconciliation, 2003, p. 141.

22 See H. Cobban, *Amnesty after atrocity? Healing nations after genocide and war crimes*, Boulder, CO.: Paradigm, 2007. Especially pp. 161–182.

23 R. Shaw, *Rethinking Truth and Reconciliation Commissions: Lessons from Sierra Leone*, Washington, D.C.: United States Institute of Peace Special Report 130, 2005. Accessible at www.usip.org/pubs/specialreports/sr130.html

24 Quoted in M. Ignatieff (1998), p. 178

25 See T. Rosenberg, 'Overcoming the legacies of dictatorship', *Foreign Affairs*, May/June 1995, v.74, n. 3, pp. 134–152.

26 See, for example, his essay 'The power of the powerless', in which he analyses the manner in which 'individuals confirm the system, fulfil the system, make the system, are the system', in V. Havel, *Living In Truth*, London: Faber & Faber, 1989, p. 45.

27 See Meng Try Ea, *Victims and Perpetrators*, Phnom Penh: Documentation Centre of Cambodia, 2002.

28 Jaspers' friend Hannah Arendt wrote to him that the scale of the Nazi crimes revealed the limits of the law, for no punishment could match the enormity of what had been done. Cited in M. Minow, *Between Vengeance and Forgiveness*, Boston: Beacon Press, 1998, p.47.

29 The contrast between Rwanda and South Africa illustrates the complexity of determining degrees of guilt and complicity. Thus, in South Africa there were very few perpetrators (criminally guilty) but very many beneficiaries of the apartheid system (politically, morally and metaphysically guilty). In Rwanda, by contrast, there were many who were criminally guilty of killing and other acts of violence, but very few beneficiaries of the genocide – indeed it is possible to conclude from a review of the history of Rwanda that many of the direct victims of the genocide shared different degrees of political and moral guilt for the circumstances within which the genocide became possible. See Mahmood Mamdani, *When Victims Become Killers: Colonialism, Nativism and the Genocide in Rwanda*, Oxford: James Currey, 2001.

30 Cobban, pp. 18–24.

31 Quoted in C. Spies, 'A safe space: How local leaders can make room for reconciliation', in *Track Two*, v. 6, n. 3–4, December 1997, pp.11–15, p. 15.

32 See A. Allan, 'Truth and reconciliation: a psycho-legal perspective', in *Ethnicity and Health*, v.5, nos.3–4, Aug/Nov. 2000, pp. 191–204, p. 197.

33 R. Shaw, *Rethinking Truth and Reconciliation Commissions: Lessons from Sierra Leone*, Washington, D.C.: United States Institute of Peace Special Report 130, 2005. Accessible at www.usip.org/pubs/specialreports/sr130.html

34 Recent publications in this 'genre' include C. Call & V. Wyeth, eds., *Building states to build peace*, Boulder, CO.: Lynne Rienner, 2008; R. Paris & T. Sisk, eds., *The dilemmas of statebuilding: Confronting the contradictions of postwar peace operations*, Abingdon: Routledge, 2009.

35 See for example, J. Goodwin et al, eds., *Passionate politics: Emotions and social movements*, Chicago: University of Chicago Press, 2001.

36 Neta Crawford, 'The passion of world politics: Propositions of emotion and emotional relationships', *International Security*, v. 24, n. 4 (Spring 2000), pp. 116–156, p. 116.

37 A. Obeidi, K. Hipel and D. Kilgour, 'The role of emotions in envisioning outcomes in conflict analysis', *Group Decision and Negotiation*, Vol. 14, 2005, p.482

38 One should also acknowledge that accompanying the emotion of fear there can also be the kindred desire for revenge against those deemed responsible for causing the pain, the suffering and the fear.

39 P. de Greiff, 'The role of apologies in national reconciliation processes: On making trustworthy institutions trusted' in M. Gibney & R. Howard-Hassman, eds., *The Age of Apology*, Philadelphia, PA: University of Pennsylvania Press, 2008. He defines reconciliation as 'the condition under which citizens can trust one another as citizens again (or anew). That means that they are sufficiently committed to the norms and values that motivate their ruling institutions, sufficiently confident that those who operate those institutions do so also on the basis of those norms and values, and sufficiently secure about their fellow citizens' commitment to abide by these basic norms and values.'

40 M. Gellman, 'No justice, no peace? National reconciliation and local conflict resolution in Cambodia', *Asian Perspective*, v. 32, n. 2, 2008, pp. 37–57, p. 47. (Emphasis added.)

41 On the concept of hoping well, see V. McGeer, 'The art of good hope', *Annals*, AAPSS, 592, March 2004, pp. 100–127.

28 Disarmament and survival

Marc Pilisuk

The importance of the quest for disarmament seems obvious. War is hell. While war is glorified in history, revered in memory as a moment of absolute life and death involvement and of camaraderie, and used as a rallying point by political leaders in calls for unity and sacrifice, the actual human consequences of armed conflict, and its aftermath, are devastating and growing worse. War has apparently caused more than three times the number of casualties in the last 90 years than in the previous 500. Upwards of 250 major wars have occurred in the post World War II era, taking over 50 million lives and leaving tens of millions of homeless (Peace Pledge Union Website, 2005). Rarely considered in the costs are the displaced refugees, mostly children and women, and the soldiers who return with enduring disability and traumatic disorders that diminish their lives and those of their families.

War is also expensive (Sivard, 1996). The ability to make war and the extent of destruction in warfare depend upon the availability of weapons. Though patterns in arms transfers have shifted since the Cold War era, weapon sales and distribution remain concentrated on developing nations (Shanker, 2005). This extensive world market in weapons trade provides the means by which ethno-political wars are being fought (Greider, 1998, Renner, 1998). Resources that might otherwise improve life are consumed in war (Piven, 2004).

"Hawks" suggest that an overwhelming superiority of weapons will deter all potential enemies, a suggestion clearly not borne out historically. There are numerous examples in which disarmament referred to the maintaining of weapons by the winning side and the forced elimination of weapons in the conquered countries. Such imposed restrictions on the armed forces of defeated countries have a long history. In classical antiquity, the Romans tried to disarm Carthage, their long-standing rival. After military victories, Napoleon also dictated limits on the size of the Prussian and Austrian military. In the twentieth century, the peace settlement that ended World War I, placed limits set by the victorious nations on the German army and navy. The intent was to prevent Germany's military from posing a serious offensive threat to its neighbors. At the end of WW 2, both Germany and Japan were disarmed. Although more than 60 years have elapsed since the end of World War II, both countries still observe important limitations on their armed forces. Neither country has tried to reassert its independent status as a great power by developing nuclear weapons. The converse of enforced disarmament by countries with large and victorious military establishments can also be seen. Tsar Nicholas II of Russia, for example, called for the convening of the Hague Conference, in 1899, to prevent wealthier great powers from modernizing their armed forces (Maurer, 2005; Towle, 1997).

Controlling and limiting weapons

More "dovish" proposals include arms control and disarmament. These terms encompass a spectrum of alternatives from partial to complete elimination of weapons, from phased reductions to immediately enforced elimination of certain weapon categories, from unilateral to multilateral efforts, the latter often requiring tools for inspection and enforcement, and including the concept of global disarmament.

The word *disarmament* is sometimes used interchangeably with *arms control*. Actually the two terms represent somewhat different concepts. Agreements among nation states to limit or even to reduce particular weapons occur in a pragmatic context. This context does not address directly the somewhat anarchic international environment in which autonomous nation states are assumed to compete for interests as defined by their governments. Military might is seen in this context as a tool to expand such interests and as a way of protecting against the aggression by other states. With the advent of highly destructive biochemical and nuclear weapons, the costs of waging war can grow to be incommensurate with any possible gains. Arms control does not aim to eliminate the competitive assumptions that drive nation states, or even to eliminate violent conflict. The objectives of arms control are better viewed as efforts to promote international stability and to reduce the likelihood of war. Other objectives are to reduce the costs of weaponry and the damage that follows once violent conflict occurs. Major states give consideration to arms control as part of their security policy. The U.S. Congress, for example, established the Arms Control and Disarmament Agency (ACDA) in 1961 to provide a bureaucratic institution for dealing with arms control issues (Institute for Defense and Disarmament Studies, 2005).

Examples of arms control date back to twelfth-century Europe. The church at that time strived to ban crossbows in warfare among Christians. This attempt at arms control was not successful and crossbows remained in widespread use throughout Europe. During the past century, arms control negotiations played a major role in international relations. After the First World War, the major naval powers of the world made a serious effort to negotiate the relative force levels among them. The Washington Conference (1921–1922) and the London Conference (1930) succeeded for a time in limiting naval armaments. Efforts by the League of Nations to advance international disarmament culminated in the Geneva Conference (1932–1934). There an attempt was made to distinguish between "defensive" and "offensive" weapons and then to eliminate the offensive ones. That is often a difficult distinction since perceptions of intention can play a major role. In what psychologists have called the *attribution error*, armaments in an opponent are typically viewed as an indication of aggressive intent, while one's own arms are seen as a defensive response to a situation presented by the behavior of others. With the rise of German, Italian, and Japanese imperialism during the 1930s, the Western liberal democracies felt threatened and this important effort at arms control came to an end (Maurer, 2005).

There are more successful stories of the disarming of borders between neighboring states. The Rush-Bagot Agreement (1817), led to the successful demilitarization of the border between Canada and the United States. This has served as an illustration of the way disarmament between modern democracies can be achieved. The European Union has taken important steps in this direction. Such agreements do not actually call for the participating nations to reduce their weapons or the size of their military. But they affirm a non-military and collaborative relationship among the parties (Institute for Defense and Disarmament Studies, 2005).

The pursuit of disarmament

The goal of general disarmament is more far reaching and speaks to the need for a world in which competing states no longer have the responsibility to promote their own security in an international environment in which might makes right. The dream of disarmament envisions a world in which conflicts still occur but the rules for their resolution preclude the possible use of lethal weapons. It prescribes a world in which enforceable restrictions on the massing of armaments, and armed forces, are in place with a universal transparency and openness for early detection of violations. Disarmament calls for the support of institutions like the International Court of Justice that might be called upon to make binding judgments in disputes and for police functions available to monitor outbreaks of violence.

At present, most countries are unlikely to disarm voluntarily. In fact their leaders would consider such actions as suicidal as long as other nations did not also renounce war and armaments. Moreover, disarmament has a psychological or perhaps cultural component. It requires not only laws and institutions to make it happen but also a willingness of people to respect those laws and institutions as just and to consider the goal of pursuing peace by peaceful means to be a universal value on which the survival of life depends. Hence, disarmament is often considered a long-range goal that is associated with a fundamental reordering of the international political environment. That change aims at ending the law of the jungle among nations by establishing some form of world government or an effective system of collective security (Myrdal, 1982; Institute for Defense and Disarmament Studies, 2005).

The ideal of a world in which access to weapons of great destructive capability is banned, is often countered by the argument that weapons are needed to prevent a potential Adolph Hitler from dominating the world, that there will always be such crazed enemies, and that to disarm is to give an upper hand to those with evil intent. The responses to this are complex. The risks of disarmament may be greatly limited by strong and enforceable, universal agreements. The willingness to undertake such risks makes sense only in comparison to the risks incurred by allowing the current and costly patchwork of efforts at security to grow worse as the number of parties with access to weapons of mass destruction increases. Moreover, the core reasons for violent conflict remain with the use of weapons to deter adversaries. To address theses reasons, the world will need to deal with gross inequality and exploitation of people and of habitats, to promote effective forms of non-violent resolution of conflict, including tools to convert rather than to confront potential enemies, and to increase resources for those committed to building cultures of peace. When resources are instead devoted to preparing for war, we continue a caste of military and corporate professionals whose life work is to find enemies and to fight them.

In the western world, the origins of the idea of disarmament arose with the nineteenth-century development of liberal doctrines about international politics. Advocates of disarmament believed that wars occurred because of the competition among major powers in armaments. The outbreak of WW1 was precipitated by an assassination of one leader and was rapidly escalated by the involvement of heavily armed states. This appeared to confirm the explanation that major increases in armaments were fundamental factors in the conflict. Sir Edward Grey, Great Britain's foreign secretary (1906–1916), observed, "The enormous growth of armaments in Europe, the sense of insecurity and fear caused by them—it was these that made war inevitable." This theory of why violent conflicts occur had an implication for subsequent policy. Disarmament could provide a way to reduce international tension and to prevent war.

In an attempt to promote a humane international order, President Woodrow Wilson called for disarmament as part of his peace program known as the Fourteen Points. The disarmament called for did not actually happen and the failure of other powers to disarm after World War I was used as an excuse by the Hitler regime for German rearmament of Germany in the 1930s (Hyde, 1988; Institute for Defense and Disarmament Studies, 2005).

Bans on particular weapons

Efforts to ban particular types of weapons have had some success. The horrible consequences of poison gas used in the First World War led to the acceptance of the Geneva Protocol in June of 1925. Eventually 132 nations signed the protocol. The Protocol bans the use of chemical and "bacteriological" weapons (UNIDC, 2005). The United Nations created a forum for discussion of disarmament related issues. One product of its deliberations has been the Chemical Weapon Convention. One hundred and thirty countries signed the original agreement in 1993 (OPCW 2005).

In August 1992, The International Conference on Disarmament's Ad Hoc Committee on Chemical Weapons completed an effort to draft a ban on chemical weapons (CW). 130 states signed the Chemical Weapons Convention in 1993. The CWC went into force in 1997, when the Organization for the Prohibition of Chemical Weapons (OPCW), the treaty's implementing organization, came into operation.

Under the treaty, each signatory nation agrees never "to develop, produce, otherwise acquire, stockpile or retain chemical weapons." It agrees as well not to use or prepare to use CW and not to assist others in acting against any of the prohibitions of the convention. The convention also requires states to destroy any CW in their possession, to destroy any of their own CW abandoned on the territory of another state, and to dismantle their CW production facilities (UNOPDW, 2005; UNIDC, 2005). One problem in restricting the use of chemical weapons is that the range of products produced is quite wide and most of the research and production activity is done secretly (Barnaby, 1999).

Antipersonnel landmines are a particularly insidious source of death and disability that continue long after actual combat has ended. Landmines kill or injure civilians, soldiers, peacekeepers and aid workers alike. Children are particularly susceptible. Mine deaths and injuries total in the hundreds of thousands. Estimates of 15,000 and 20,000 new casualties are caused by landmines and unexploded ordnance each year, some 1,500 new casualties each month, more than 40 new casualties a day. The numbers are an underestimate since some countries with mines, such as Myanmar (Burma), India, and Pakistan, fail to provide public information about the extent of the problem (International Campaign, 2005, a).

By 2005, 154 countries signed on to the 1997 Convention on the Prohibition of the Use, Stockpiling, Production and Transfer or Anti-Personnel Mines and on Their Destruction. Forty countries, including Russia, China and the United States, have not signed on. Some antipersonnel landmines are from earlier conflicts. They claim victims in many parts of the world. Antipersonnel landmines are still being planted and minefields dating back decades claim innocent victims. Vast stockpiles of landmines remain in warehouses around the world and a handful of countries still produce the weapon (International Campaign (2005, b; Human Rights Watch, 2003).

The impact of nuclear weapons

The advent of atomic weapons during World War II gave further impetus to advocates of disarmament. Many prominent writers, intellectuals, and policy activists supported efforts to "ban the bomb," even if this entailed unilateral disarmament. Nuclear disarmament became for many a moral imperative for the stakes seemed nothing less than the extinction of the human species. Movies and television popularized an apocalyptic vision, helping to garner significant support for the disarmament movement.

The leaders of the superpowers paid considerable attention to arms control during the Cold War. A relaxation of tensions in superpower relations, or detente, was widely viewed to coincide with arms control agreements, such as the conclusion of the first round of SALT (Strategic Arms Limitation Talks) in 1972, the INF (intermediate nuclear forces) agreement in 1987, and START (Strategic Arms Reduction Talks) in 1991. To many analysts of international relations, the superpower experience showed that arms control could play a useful (if modest) role in helping rival states to manage the uncertainty of their armaments competitions.

Nuclear weapons add a new dimension to discussions of disarmament. Their level of potential destructiveness far outweighs any gain from their use. A major exchange of nuclear weapons might so totally destroy places and people and so contaminate the earth's capacity to provide uncontaminated food and water as to leave the planet unsuited to support life. But for many political leaders, these weapons are considered a requirement for deterring a attack from other countries.

After the Cold War

The end of the Cold War has not dampened interest in disarmament and arms control. In the liberal democracies, organizations promoting disarmament retain some clout in the domestic political arena. A current view holds that modern liberal democracies can achieve effective disarmament among themselves, because they seem less prone to make war on one another. The spread of democracy, then, conceivably advances the cause of disarmament Maurer, 2005). The US government has been the primary advocate of the theory that democracies are, at least, not sources of aggression. However, its own record has one been of military support for either democracies or dictatorial police states depending only upon the favorability of their policies to corporate economic interests in the US (Chomsky, 2004; Pilisuk and Zassi, 2005).

Recent attempts to limit the geographical spread of nuclear weapons and ballistic missiles, and to eliminate the use of chemical and biological agents as weapons of mass destruction, have also emerged as important policy concerns. Disarmament has even been used as a justification for resorting to war. The coalition that fought Iraq in 1991, for instance, aimed not only at restoring Kuwait as an independent, sovereign state, but also at eliminating Iraq's ability to manufacture and use nuclear, chemical, and biological weapons. The prospect for a major war in northeast Asia, brought about by North Korea's desire to build a nuclear arsenal, and the determination of the United States and South Korea to prevent this development, is also part of an attempt to further international disarmament on a selective basis. The establishment of a neo-liberal world order could therefore entail the paradox of fighting wars for the sake of disarmament. Hence the claim of disarmament advocates—namely, that weapons themselves cause war—might come to have a new, more ominous meaning. Arms and their use might be justified as instruments for disarming other countries by attacking them (Maurer, 2005).

The world owes much to the United Nations for whatever progress toward disarmament has occurred. UN responsibility falls upon the First Committee of the UN General Assembly, which is responsible for disarmament and security matters. All 191 member states are included.

The more specialized UN Conference on Disarmament (CD), currently with 66 members, meets in Geneva to produce multilateral agreements. It is the only group given authority to negotiate actual treaties. This group sets its own agenda, taking into account recommendations from the UN General Assembly (UNGA). Its work has been slow, reflecting wide differences among members on what should be discussed. The dividing issue frequently is linkage. Some nations will refuse to participate in discussions limiting one type of weapon or the weapons in one particular area unless weapons threats from other sources are also up for consideration. For example, the US might wish to mobilize international support for disarming what it considers "rogue states," while others will only agree to such discussion if they include attention to US weapons that threaten other nations. The United States opposed any negotiating mandate on general nuclear disarmament, while China, at the same time, opposed negotiating a fissile material cut-off treaty in the absence of negotiations on general nuclear disarmament. Egypt has urged Arab states not to sign the Chemical Weapons Treaty until Israel signs the Nuclear Proliferation treaty (The United Nations and Disarmament, 1988; The United Nations and Disarmament Since 1945, 1996; INIDC, 2005).

The UN disarmament agenda in 2005 had the following priorities: Cessation of the nuclear arms race and nuclear disarmament, prevention of nuclear war, including all related matters, prevention of an arms race in outer pace, effective international arrangements to assure non nuclear weapon states against the use or threat of use of nuclear weapons (negative security assurances), new types of weapons of mass destruction and new systems of such weapons, radiological weapons, comprehensive program of disarmament, transparency in armaments, and landmines (UNIDC, 2005). But little significant progress was achieved on any of these items. To understand why, it is important to place the issues of disarmament in a larger, economic, political and psychosocial context.

Profits from weapons

Arms make money. Small weapon transfers, for example, are a business in which independent entrepreneurs are often involved. Arms brokers have engaged in disturbing weapons transfers to highly abusive armed groups and to countries that are under U.N. arms embargoes. One well-known arms broker Victor Bout, has been implicated in violating or contributing to violate U.N. arms embargoes in Sierra Leone, Angola, Liberia, and the Democratic Republic of Congo.

Armed groups wreak havoc on innocent civilians. Yet, many arms brokers remain free and continue to traffic arms to human rights abusers outside the purview of international regulations. Arms brokers were reported to have shipped 3,117 surplus assault rifles from Nicaragua to Panama. The weapons were diverted to Colombia's paramilitary Autodefensas Unidas de Colombia (AUC). At the time, the AUC was accused of killing thousands of civilians and was on the U.S. Department of State list of terrorist organizations (Institute for Defense and Disarmament Studies, 2005).

There have been U.S. and international efforts to stem such arms transfers. The U.S. government adopted a law on arms brokering in 1996. The law covers a wide range of activities, including transporting and financing. It requires arms brokers to both register and to apply for a license for each activity. The US used this law to prosecute a British citizen for attempting to sell shoulder-fired missiles in the United States to a group intending to use the missiles to shoot down a commercial airliner. Many governments, however, have no law, or only very weak law, on arms brokering. For example, Irish law does not restrict brokers who arrange weapons supplies from foreign countries. Hence Ireland was unable to prosecute an arms broker who was reportedly involved in 2004 in efforts to supply 50 T72 tanks from Ukraine to the Sudanese military. Because mall arms transfers are quite important in abuses of human rights, Amnesty International has called for an international agreement to prevent arms brokering activity, such as transfers to governments and groups with consistent records of gross human rights violations (Institute for Defense and Disarmament Studies, 2005; Multilateral Arms Regulation and Disarmament Agreements, 2005).

Weapons of mass destruction

With the Cold war long past, one might have expected that the United States would be a leader in the effort to fulfill its 30-year-old promise, embodied in Article VI of The Nuclear Non-proliferation Treaty, "to pursue negotiations in good faith on effective measures relating to cessation of the nuclear arms race at an early date and to nuclear disarmament." There has been a dramatic change in the last decade regarding the words used to describe US nuclear and missile development programs, especially by President Obama, an avowed nuclear abolitionist. But the content of these programs speaks to escalation in the efforts to produce new, high technology weapons.

In preparation for the transition to the use of space for warfare, the Air Force science and technology community has doubled its commitments in "space only" technologies from 13% in FY 1999 to 32% by FY 2005. This activity jeopardizes the modest stability afforded by the ABM Treaty. The Department of Energy's nuclear weapons research facilities at Livermore, Los Alamos and Sandia have long been the advocates and the producers of new nuclear weapons. The National Ignition Facility, which will house a laser forty times more powerful than any yet in existence, will have many nuclear weapon applications. Space-based laser weapons are viewed as a means to destroy chemical or biological weapons that might be launched against the US.

Weapons have created incentives for other countries to develop their arsenals and have caused severe damage to human health and the environment (Bertell, 2004; Boly, 1989 & 1990). And there continues to be a diversion of public funds from needed programs in health, education, housing and renewable energy development. Even funds for peace-keeping activities that might provide greater security have suffered.

It is important to note that the weapons laboratories operate in relative secrecy. They employ bright scientists and provide them with unparalleled support and facilities. They provide lucrative contracts to defense industries, which in turn provide extensive consultation to government. Behind closed doors, weapons are conceived, justified, funded and developed (Pilisuk, 1989).

The US and disarmament

Nation states in general are poorly designed for the responsibilities of disarmament. They sometimes operate as vehicles for the expansion of the interests of rulers. Many exist as the vassals for large corporate interests (Korten, 1996; Johnson, 2004; Pilisuk, 2001), but even those professing to do what is best for their own citizens find the lure of weapons to be great and are cautious about agreements that might weaken military forces or weapons. True progress toward disarmament may require the development of some form of world government with the policing authority to limit weapons and the moral authority to require mediated or judicial resolution of disputes. The role of the US is particularly important to progress in moving toward disarmament.

After two world wars, may European nations were ready to forgo the weapons and policies that had create such devastation. The animosity of governments in capitalist economies to the communist experiment in the Soviet Union remained, but primarily as a battle to prevent the colonized world from developing socialist governments and controlling their own resources. The US, as the first atomic power, assumed this role of containment primarily through military superiority. Efforts by Stalin and later by Khrushchev to offer the unification of Germany in exchange for substantial mutual reductions and controls in armaments were dismissed and US won the competition to become the most heavily armed state. It is the US, then, that will have to modify its policies if movement toward disarmament is to occur (Chomsky, 2004).

Between WW II and the end of the last century the US led 73 military interventions around the world, almost double the total from the preceding fifty-five year period (Grossman, 1999). If we include all covert operations in which casualties occurred, the figure rises to 196 (Ferraro, 2005). The Pentagon has an ever-expanding empire of over 6,000 domestic bases, and 725 overseas. The USA's $455 billion military expenditure in 2004 was larger than the combined amount the 32 next-most-powerful nations spent on their militaries (Engelhardt, 2005).

United States policy has often been guided by an assumption that interests defined by the United States take precedence over international agreements. This has occurred first in matters that might constrain United States military activities. In August 2001, the United States withdrew from a major arms control accord, the 1972 Antiballistic Missile Treaty. In July 2001, the United States walked out of a conference to discuss adding on-site inspectors to strengthen the 1972 Biological and Toxic Weapons Convention, which was ratified by 144 nations, including the United States (DuBoff, 2001). Meanwhile, United States' preparations to use chemical and biological weapons at Fort Dietrich and other sites have been extensive (Barnaby, 1999). The United States was the only nation to oppose the UN Agreement to Curb the International Flow of Illicit Small Arms. The Land Mine Treaty (banning mines) was signed in 1997 by 122 nations, but the United States refused to sign, along with Russia, China, India, Pakistan, Iran, Iraq, Vietnam, Egypt, and Turkey. In February 2001, the United States refused to join 123 nations pledged to ban the use and production of anti-personnel bombs (DuBoff, 2001).

Preparedness for war has been costly

The US spent $10.5 trillion dollars on the military during the Cold War (Markusen & Yukden, 1992). The nuclear powers of that time spent an estimated $8 trillion on their nuclear weapons (Sivard 1996). If annual US expenditures for such weapons were instead invested into global life-saving measures, the result could have covered *all* of the following—the elimination of starvation and malnutrition, basic shelter for every family, universal health care— the control of AIDS, relief for displaced refugees and the removal of land mines (World Game Institute, 1997). The U.S. is pouring more than a billion dollars a week into its current wars, money that could otherwise be spent on health care, schools and infrastructure at home. The money goes largely to contractors, specialized in the production not only of weapons but in the marketing of strategies in which such weapons appear to be needed and the support of officials sharing their views.

US plans for the future are no more promising. These involve nuclear weapons and their use in outer space. The National Missile Defense proposal (previously referred to as "Star Wars") poses the greatest threat to the erosion of existing arms control agreements. In preparation for the transition to the use of space for warfare, the Air Force science and technology community has doubled its commitments in "space only" technologies from 13% in FY 1999 to 32% in FY 2005. This activity jeopardizes the modest stability afforded by the ABM Treaty. Yet major lobbies for the defense industries, like the Missile Defense Advocacy Alliance, provide constant pressure for continued development of space weapons.

In addition, The Pentagon has launched programs for research and testing of a missile defense system. While technically dubious, this expensive program has been viewed by other nations with alarm as a signal that the US is working toward being able to attack other nations with the security that it could intercept missiles sent in retaliation. Such planning has the consequence of provoking other nations to develop their own arsenals, a process already taking place. Russia and China have responded with plans for new or updated development for nuclear weapons. Without enforceable controls, nuclear weapons technology is spreading (Roche, 2002).

Disarmament is more than a set of formal agreements. It is also a commitment to a worldview that differs from the dominant view in developed countries. If one envisions the world as a place in which mutual cooperation can provide more benefits to all parties than violent conflict, then the possibilities for disarmament become more promising.

The reliance upon weapons to provide security has been outmoded by technology. It is clear to many psychologists that the threatened use of force typically begets retaliatory force. Retribution continues a cycle of animosity and violence. Conversely, a proposal for graduated reciprocation in tension reduction (GRIT) suggests that a series of small unilateral moves toward conciliation, announced in advance, are likely to be gradually reciprocated and move the adversaries to more trustful and less threatening relations (Osgood, 1962).

For examples, in 1961, President Kennedy called for a reappraisal of the Cold War, for new modes of cooperation and suspending nuclear weapons tests in the atmosphere. The USSR broadcast the Kennedy speech intact and premier Khrushchev responded with a conciliatory speech. The USSR stopped production of strategic bombers and removed objections to the presence of UN observers in Yemen. The US then removed objections to restoration of the full recognition of the Hungarian delegation to the United Nations. A limited nuclear weapons test ban was signed. The Soviet Foreign Minister Gromyko called for a non-aggression treaty between NATO and the Warsaw Pact. Kennedy called for joint efforts to "explore the stars together." The US agreed to the sale of wheat to the USSR. Gromyko called for a pact outlawing nuclear weapons in outer space. Kennedy responded favorably and an agreement was reached on the exchange of captured spies (Etzioni, 1967).

Studies in the laboratory provide confirming evidence that humans in conflict situations can use the GRIT strategy to reduce the distrust that keeps them armed and start a process toward mutually beneficial disarmament (Pilisuk & Skolnick, 1968; Pilisuk, 1984). To understand why such a conciliatory strategy is not more actively pursued it is important to examine the stakes of powerful decision makers. The perceived short-term benefits to certain beneficiaries of war often dominate the policy process. The small group of persons obsessed with weapons development and with military support for corporate expansion unduly influences a potentially dangerous direction for American policy (Pilisuk & Zazzi, 2005). It is a policy that blurs the lines of reality between video game dueling and the actual domination of space by lethal weapons. The public has not been told this story, and has surely not been asked if this should be the national direction.

The survival of the planet will require progress toward disarmament. Public demand for, and involvement in, a culture of peace appears necessary if leaders are to respond to the challenge.

References

Barnaby, W. (1999) *The plague makers: The secret world of biological warfare.* London: Vision.

Bertell, R. (2004). *Health and Environmental Costs of Militarism.* Presented in Barcelona, Thursday, 24 June, 2004.

Boly, W. (1989). Behind the nuclear curtain. *Public Citizen*, 9(1), 12–16.

Boly, W. (1990). Downwind. *In Health*, July/August, 58–69.

Chomsky, N. (2004) *Hegemony or survival: Americas quest for global dominance*. New York: Holt and Co.

Englehart, T. (2005). Bases, bases everywhere: It's a Pentagon world and welcome to it. (online) http://www.commondreams.org/views05/0602-28.htm. Retrieved 11/2/05

Etzioni, A. (1967) The Kennedy experiment. *Western Political Quarterly* 20 (June) 361–380.

Greider, W. (1998). *Fortress America: The American military and the consequences of peace*. New York: Public Affairs.

Human Rights Watch (2003) Landmine Monitor Report: August 2003 http://www.icbl.org/lm/2003/

Hyde, H. A. (1988) *Scraps of paper: the disarmament treaties between the world wars*. 1st ed. Lincoln, Neb.: Media Pub.

Institute for Defense and Disarmament Studies (2005) disarm//Institute//for//Defense&Disarmament//Studies.html http://www.idds.org/

International Campaign to Ban Landmines (a), http://www.icbl.org/treaty retrieved 9/11/05

International Campaign to Ban Landmines (b), http://www.icbl.org/problem/what retrieved 9/11/05

Johnson, C. (2004) *The Sorrows of empire: Militarism, secrecy, and the end of the republic*. New York: Metropolitan Books.

Korten, D.C. (1998) *Globalizing civil society*. NY: Seven stories Press

Landmine Monitor Report 2003: Toward a Mine-Free World. International Committee to Ban Landmines http://www.icbl.org/lm/2003/findings.html

Markusen, A & Yukden, J (1992) *Dismantling the War economy*. New York: Basic Books.

Maurer, J.H. (2005) *Reader's Companion to Military History* Houghton Mifflin College Division file:///history/readerscomp/mil/html/mh_000101_publicationd.htm retrieved 12/3/05 Multilateral Arms Regulation and Disarmament Agreements (2005) http://disarmament.un.org/TreatyStatus.nsf, retrieved 11/10/05

Myrdal, A. R., (1982) The game of disarmament: how the United States & Russia run the arms race. New York: Pantheon Books.

OPCW (2005) Organization For The Prohibition Of Chemical Weapons 'Chemical weapons' http://www.opcw.org/retrieved 12/02/05

Osgood, C. (1962) An alternative to war or surrender. Urbana, IL: Univ. of Illinois Press.

Peace Pledge Union (2005) War and peace: What's it all about? http://www.ppu.org.uk/war/war_peace-modernwar.html retrieved 11/20/05

Pilisuk, M., & Skolnick, P. (1968). Inducing trust: A test of the Osgood proposal. *Journal of Personality and Social Psychology*. 8(2), 121–133.

Pilisuk, M. (1984) Experimenting with the arms race. *Journal of Conflict Resolution*, 28(2), 296–315.

Pilisuk, M. (1999) Addictive rewards in nuclear weapons development. *Peace Review* 11:4, 597–602

Pilisuk, M. (2001) Globalism and structural violence. In Christie, D., Wagner, R., and Winter, D. (eds) *Peace, Conflict, and Violence: Peace Psychology for the 21st Century 2001*. Englewood, NJ: Prentice Hall. 149–160.

Pilisuk, M and Joanne Zazzi, J. (2005) Toward a Psychosocial Theory of Military and Economic Violence in the Era of Globalization. *Journal of Social Issues* Vol. 62, No. 1.

Piven, F.F.(2004) *The War at home: The domestic costs of Bush's militarism*. New York: The New Press. Potyarkin, Ye and S. Kortunov, S. (1986). *The USSR proposes disarmament, 1920s–1980s* [translated from the Russian.]. Moscow: Progress Publishers.

Rapoport, A. (1960) *Fights games and debates*. Ann Arbor, ML: University of Michigan Press.

Rapoport, A.(1 965) Chicken a la Kahn *Virginia Quarterly Review* 41 (summer) 370–389.

Renner, M. (1998). *Curbing the proliferation of small arms*. In L.R. Brown, C. Flavin & H. French (Eds.), *State of the World 1998*. New York: Norton, 131–148.

Roche, D (2002) Rethink the Unthinkable. *Globe and Mail*. (Canada's "national" newspaper): Tuesday, March 12, 2002 – Print Edition, Page A19.

Shanker, T. (2005) Weapons Sales Worldwide Rise to Highest Level Since 2000. *New York Times*. http://www.nytimes.com/2005/08/30/politics/30weapons.html

Sivard, L. (1996) *World Military and social expenditures*. Washington, DC: World Priorities

Towle, P. (1997) *Enforced disarmament: from the Napoleonic campaigns to the Gulf War*. Oxford: Clarendon Press: New York: Oxford University Press,

The United Nations and Disarmament: A short history (1988). New York: United Nations Department for Disarmament Affairs.

The United Nations and disarmament since 1945. (1996) New York: United Nations, updated ed. New York: Pantheon Books

UNIDC (2005) United Nations Institute for Disarmament Research, Geneva, Switzerland. (http://disarmament.un.org/TreatyStatus.nsf.2005).

29 Overcoming war

The importance of constructive alternatives

Christine Schweitzer

Although organised group violence has probably accompanied most of the history of human-kind (see Otterbein 2005), this is not true for standing armies and weapons of mass destruc-tion, which have defined warfare since Napoleonic times and the American Civil War (see Krippendorff 1985 and Dougherty and Pfaltzgraff 1997: 18). Modern warfare has "evolved" to such a point that today it actually threatens the continued survival of humankind. But war remains an instrument of politics. Often it is not even seen as the means of last resort but as one of the first options, as exemplified not only by numerous civil wars but also by the so-called War on Terror, with its international aggression against Iraq and Afghanistan. Those speaking up and fighting against war, those who want to see disarmament and a fundamen-tally different way of dealing with conflicts, seem to be on the defensive at the beginning of the new millenium. But there have been other institutions, considered immortal until quite recently, which have indeed been largely abolished – slavery being the best example. There is no reason, therefore, to believe that war cannot be overcome as well.

My focus is what I call the "constructive" approach (see Ebert 1981) – the various concepts of alternatives to war and the military. I will present here three basic concepts which have developed, or at least come to the forefront of attention, in a historical sequence: civilian-based (or social) defence, civil (or nonviolent) conflict transformation and civilian (unarmed) peacekeeping. I will conclude with the statement that the "constructive approach" is not a complete solution as such, but that its pursuit will help to overcome war for three reasons. First, it deals with the legitimisation of war and the military, taking away much of the argument that "there is no other means". Second, the implementation of these approaches, whenever suitable, demonstrates the power of nonviolence. And third, its determined pursuit would contribute to the removal of a number of other factors that favour war.

Why is there war?

How to abolish war is not a new question. Many philosophers of the Enlightenment asked this question, including Erasmus, Crucé, Penn, Voltaire, Rousseau, Kant and Bentham. The strategies of course are highly dependent on the particular analysis of the causes of war. Unfortunately, there is no consensus as to why and how wars come about. Different theories and approaches have been offered by the social sciences: genetic and evolutionist theories (aggression as a genetically based function to maximise survival); behaviourist theories (war as learned behaviour); rational theories (maximisation of profit); various economic theories (greed, relative deprivation, bad economic situation, the interests of the arms industry); vari-ous political theories (power imbalances, the institution of the state per se, repressive political systems especially when there is rapid change, lack of access to power, cycles of peace and war, the institution of the military, etc.); ecological theories (worsening ecological conditions and availability of resources); cultural theories (ethnicity or nationalism as causes of war); and cognitive theories (attitudes and belief systems) (see Dougherty and Pfaltzgraff 1997, Smith 2004). The only "almost-consensus" is that it is wrong to assume that war has only one cause, and that there is therefore only one remedy that would do away with it. Dan Smith (2004) argues that it is obvious that there are "very few necessary conditions" that need to be fulfilled in order for a war to develop, and

> very many sufficient conditions, of which only a few . . . may apply, in any single conflict. War is possible as soon as weapons are available with which to fight it and as long as there is a dispute between two or more parties. What makes war probable, however, is a far more complicated question
>
> (Smith 2004: 4).

He proposes distinguishing between background causes (for example, the exclusion of groups from power), mobilisation strategies (how key actors seek to achieve their goals), triggers (factors that influence the timing when an armed conflict starts) and catalysts (factors influencing the intensity and duration of a conflict).

There is even less agreement on how to overcome or abolish war. Those considering economics the root cause – either concretely in the form of the arms industry and other war profiteers, or as a result of the capitalist and consumerist system in general – see the solution as lying in a changed world-wide economic system. Those who consider the psyche of the individual human being and its shortcomings the beginning of the problem all argue that, first, the individual must change, that attitudes towards violence and towards life must change, and everything else will follow. Those coming from a *realpolitik* position point out that democracies have more or less stopped fighting each other, and therefore suggest working on international governance with democratic rules (for a scientific argument, see Senghaas 2004). Those who believe that the ultimate power rests with the people, not with any government, go for peoples' uprisings and civilian disobedience (see Sharp 1973). And a constructive "school" works through the creation of "alternatives". What such alternatives may be has changed over the time. Before 1989, when the threat of an international conflict between West and East seemed the predominant parameter, it was social (or civilian-based) defence that was promoted. After 1989 when it seemed that international conflicts might die out and be replaced by internal (civil) wars as the main threat, "civil conflict resolution" (or "transformation", or whatever terms are used) became the new key concept and still is. What mainly characterises this approach is the discussing of conflicts that other people have, and seeing one's own (usually the Western) world as an impartial "third party". Moreover, in recent years, the issue of protection has come to the forefront of many discussions (as in the doctrine of the Responsibility to Protect), and the concept of civilian (or unarmed) peacekeeping has been proposed as an alternative to military peacekeeping.

Social defence

Social defence (or civilian-based defence) is a concept of nonviolent resistance for very particular situations of large-group conflict which allows a clear distinction between aggressor and defender. It was developed on the basis of a particular scenario, that of a military attack by the Warsaw Pact countries on Western Europe – a war to bring about regime change, as it would be called today. Later, social defence was broadened to cover other scenarios, such as coups d'états or interventions by (former) allies. The starting point for social defence is that in most cases of (international) war the occupying forces depend on the cooperation of the population of the occupied country, just as putschists replace only the people at the top of the bureaucracy and rely on ruling over the others. The basic idea is that this cooperation can be refused or withdrawn, and that if the population is willing to accept the sanctions that are sure to follow, the aggressor is eventually bound to fail because he cannot govern the territory he occupied with his troops (see Sharp 1985, Martin 1993).

In the 1990s the interest in social defence waned with the breakdown of the Warsaw Pact and the consequent new security threats perceived. In fact, social defence has few answers to offer in scenarios of civil war or international terrorism. However, the concept has survived, and entered both into training and advising of civil rights movements in other places (see Sharp 1992, Huxley 1992), and also remains a valid concept for whatever future constellations might bring the threat of international war closer to our doorsteps again.

Nonviolent conflict transformation

Nonviolent conflict transformation as a practice is of course as old as conflict itself, as countless examples from history as well as so-called traditional mechanisms of dealing with conflict show. As a concept presented as an alternative to military interventions and mediation backed by military force it is, however, much younger. Most of the peace research literature-with the exception of the field of mediation – stems from the 1990s onwards. Generally speaking, the task of conflict transformation is to prevent wars and, where conflicts do escalate into violence, to end them, restore security and remove the causes and the consequences of violence successfully and in a sustainable manner (see Galtung 1976). Today, states have created a number of instruments for this purpose. On the side of civil society the number of actors, programmes and projects has similarly increased. In addition, conflict sensitivity is considered more and more a general issue in aid, development cooperation and human rights work.

Conflict transformation has three main functions or tasks. Johan Galtung (1976) called them peace strategies, and the former UN secretary general, Boutros Boutros-Ghali (1992), used them in his "Agenda for Peace" (see Schweitzer 2009a and 2009b for an overview).

The first is peacemaking, the task of finding an agreement about the visible aspects of the conflict, which usually happens in negotiations. Peacemaking refers to the search for a solution to the visible, explicit aspects of the conflict between the parties. There are three basic types:

- Peacemaking by law. This quite rare type could mean for example that the conflict is taken to an international court whose rulings are considered binding for the parties in conflict. The precondition of course is that all parties are willing to respect the authority of the court.
- Peacemaking by negotiation. Very often external parties play the role of mediators. These mediators are usually representatives of international organisations (such as the UN or its regional organisations) or governments. Comparatively rare are so-called "elder statesmen". NGOs are even rarer since they usually lack the access to this highest level of decision-makers. A small number of them nevertheless have established themselves in this field, usually in the role of mediators that prepare formal negotiations through various "good offices".
- The enforcement of an agreement by external powers through power and violence, for example through sanctions or the use of military power. It is difficult to separate this type of peacemaking from the second since "coercive diplomacy" is often used in negotiation.

Peacekeeping is the task of using controls to prevent violence and restore security. This task will be discussed further below.

Peacebuilding is the task of dealing with the causes as well as the consequences of the violent conflict. It consists of a combination of different tasks that all aim to reduce the causes of violent conflict and work to undo its destructive consequences. These destructive consequences are destitution, material destruction, the breakdown of social relations, hatred of the "other", who is perceived as the "enemy", traumatisation, and often also the weakening or total breakdown of state functions and of civil society. Peacebuilding also includes activities aiming openly at inducing social change. It is often placed in the post-war stage of a conflict. But the majority of the tasks and functions of peacebuilding also take place in the "hot" phases of a conflict. So it needs to be emphasised that this is not about the description of a certain phase of conflict, but about certain tasks or functions. In two another publications (Schweitzer 2009a and 2009b) I have tried to formulate 10 categories of peacebuilding objectives and tasks:

1   To help people to survive: humanitarian aid.
2   To reduce the number of weapons and warriors: disarmament generally (arms control), disarmament, demobilisation and reintegration of soldiers (DDR) after a peace agreement, and removal of land mines.
3   To repair the damage and enable people to return: reconstruction and refugee return.
4   To strengthen social behaviour and social relations, empower people and help them to overcome the wounds of war: social and psycho-social work.
5   To support economic recovery.
6   To create justice: transitional justice, dealing with the past.
7   To build a functioning state: state-building and democratisation.
8   To support civil society.
9   To support the capacity for peace and reconciliation: peace work.
10 Normalisation of relationships and cooperation in further sectors of society: support and exchange in science, culture and sports.

Conflict transformation must not be equated with what external actors (so-called third parties) – international organisations, third countries and NGOs working on a world-wide scope – are doing. Much more decisive is what state and non-state actors are doing in the country concerned. It is they who have the key to war or peace, while intervention by external parties is often useful, sometimes essential but sometimes also harmful, namely if it leads to marginalisation and disempowerment of these local actors.

Civilian peacekeeping

Peacekeeping is one component in the total picture of functions and strategies that are needed when seeking to transform conflict and eventually overcome war. In many cases peacekeeping has proven to be essential in

*   monitoring ceasefire agreements and, in doing so, building the trust necessary to overcome the conflict in the post-war stage;
*   controlling buffer zones, disarmament and demobilisation;
*   protecting the civilian population in general and vulnerable groups in particular (for example, minorities, internally displaced people) in all phases of a conflict;

- preventing violence in critical moments like elections, referendums or the implementation of other agreements.

The by now almost traditional picture of the lightly armed Blue Helmet soldier standing on some street surrounded by curious children has today, due to these developments, and due to wars like those in Afghanistan and Iraq which are falsely presented to the international public as "humanitarian", been replaced by the picture of a NATO soldier in combat dress sitting in an armoured vehicle, driving around in fear of a suicide attack by terrorists.

But at the same time as what I would call the militarisation of peacekeeping has occurred, the concept of alternative peacekeeping undertaken by unarmed civilians has also won ground. Why is the military often used? Of course it has the short-term enforcement capacity that unarmed missions lack. But often more important is that it has the material resources available or easy access to them (equipment and money), that it has the necessary personnel resources both in terms of a large standing army and institutions for training, that it can therefore always be deployed at short notice, that it has expert knowledge relevant for moving in areas recently affected by war, and that it has a professional attitude towards risks. All these points could easily be transferred to a civilian organisation (or organisations) if the political will was there to do so.

Civilian peacekeeping I have defined elsewhere (Schweitzer 2010) as "the prevention of direct violence through influence or control of the behaviour of potential perpetrators by unarmed civilians who are deployed on the ground". Compared to other fields in peace and conflict research, civilian peacekeeping has so far received very little attention.

Civilian peacekeeping as it presents itself today has five different manifestations:

1   Activities that could be summarised under the heading of civilian peacekeeping have a history that goes back at least to the 1930s, certainly with earlier cases yet to be discovered in the history books (see Weber 2000, Schweitzer et al 2001), and with Gandhi's concept of a Shanti Sena as model.
2   Different peace team organisations, with quite different approaches, methods and philosophies. At one end of the spectrum there is Peace Brigades International (PBI). This was founded in 1981 and has specialised in non-partisan protective accompaniment of human rights activists, and been very successful in this work in many countries (Guatemala, El Salvador, Colombia, Sri Lanka, Nepal, Indonesia). At the other end there are groups – often of fundamentalist Christian orientation – engaging in solidarity work with groups or peoples they perceive as being oppressed, in particular in countries in which the United States (where most of these groups hail from) are involved in the conflicts (see Moser-Puangsuwan and Weber 2000).
3   The 1990s saw the first larger civilian missions with protection mandates deployed by governments or international organisations: the European Community (later, Union) Monitoring Mission (ECMM) and the OSCE Kosovo Verification Mission (KVM) in the former Yugoslavia and the Truce/Peace Monitoring Group in Bougainville are examples (see Schweitzer et al 2001), as are today's EU observers in Georgia.
4   In the last 10 years relief, development (and human rights) organisations have increasingly started to realise that humanitarian protection is a task they must take into account in their programming and work in the field.
5   The fifth has yet to come to completion: larger-scale unarmed civilian peacekeeping by NGOs. The NGO, Nonviolent Peace-force, has (as did many earlier organisations) set itself the goal of growing sufficiently to enable it to deploy civilian peacekeepers in

numbers that would allow comparison with governmental peacekeeping missions, but in spite of fast progress over the last years and growing recognition by a number of governments who fund its activities it has yet to achieve this aim (see www.nonviolentpeace-force.org).

Many people, used to the predominant framework where violence is considered the only source of protection, find it hard to understand what an unarmed peacekeeper can achieve in a violent environment. It is true that unarmed civilians do not have means for direct enforcement – they cannot shoot and kill attacking perpetrators, as military peacekeepers nowadays are usually mandated and equipped for. Unarmed peacekeepers however, have their own sources of power (see Mahony and Eguren 1997, Schirch 2006, Schweitzer (ed.) 2010):

- Foreign nationals often are protected – at least to a certain degree which may vary from place to place – from violence because they are respected per se or because the countries or organisations they come from enjoy such respect. This is particularly true in countries of the global South where past and present power disparities protect those coming from the global North or representing the international community (UN). Being protected themselves they can help protect individuals, groups and communities they are accompanying because a potential perpetrator, if he attacks, risks hurting or killing foreign nationals.
- In addition the potential perpetrator runs the risk that the foreign nationals will report the misdeed to the international world, which may lead directly or indirectly to repercussions for them, for example in the form of pressure by supporters of the perpetrators who find themselves vulnerable to international discredit or sanctions. "The world is watching" has often proved a powerful deterrent.
- Foreign nationals and locals may be protected because of the standing they have within the local community (for example, in the latter case, as village elders), and again transmit this standing to the community as a whole.

All these sources of protection of course are relative – perpetrators may be aware of these factors but dismiss them, or there may be countries and areas where foreign nationals are hated rather than protected by their status as outsiders – our Western countries unfortunately tending to be such places.

Nevertheless, when one takes a step back and looks at the efficiency of nonviolence as such, it must be recognised that the nonviolent means are very powerful means (see the bibliography on people power by Carter, Clark and Randle 2006 for references). "People power" movements have without use of any organised violence overthrown numerous dictatorships (as in the Philippines and the Federal Republic of Yugoslavia), have liberated countries from colonial rule (India, Zambia) and have made very powerful countries withdraw their armies from foreign places they have invaded (Vietnam). Even under the Nazi regime, which was not known for its leniency regarding civil society protest, civil society in Germany as well as the countries occupied by the German forces in World War II was able to protect Jews or other threatened groups when they tried. Famous examples are the teachers in Norway refusing to submit to the implementation of a fascist school curriculum, and the "women of Rosen Street" – women married to Jews who, when their husbands were arrested in 1942, protested in front of the prison on Rosen Street, Berlin, until their husbands were released (see Semelin 1995).

Conclusions

I have briefly presented three generations of concepts that are part of the "constructive approach". Their pursuit alone would of course not be enough to overcome the institution of war, or lead countries to disarm and abolish their armies. There are other factors at work which are relevant when looking at the causes of war. In particular, war profiteering by private and governmental actors, strategic interests to control the world (or large parts of it) and strong ideological barriers cannot be overcome simply as a result of pointing out that it is not necessary to send in the military or to resort to arms, and that there are other ways to solve conflict and to make a living without exploiting one's neighbour. The three constructive alternatives presented here do not present a full solution, but their pursuit will help to overcome war for three reasons. First, these alternatives deal with the legitimisation of war and military, taking away much of the argument, "but there are no other means". This goes both for the conservative legitimisation of the military as a means of defence against the evil neighbour and for military interventions.

Second, the implementation of these approaches, wherever suitable, demonstrates the power of nonviolence. A good example is the wave of people power movements that have gone around the world since the Philippine uprising against Marcos in 1986. People see that nonviolence can be efficient and effective, and that does positively influence other movements trying to work out how to achieve their goals. To use Dan Smith's terminology, mobilisation strategies, which are one factor in how war comes about, may be affected positively.

And third, pursuing these determinedly would contribute to the removal of certain other factors that favour war, in the area of triggers as well as root causes. If the threat of the use of arms is removed so too is one powerful potential trigger of the actual outbreak of violence. And the different means described as those areas where conflict transformation may be active deal with many of the root causes there may be.

In other words, social defence, nonviolent conflict transformation and civilian peacekeeping work on all the three angles of Johan Galtung's famous triangle: They have the potential to change attitudes, they constitute a different form of behaviour and are thereby a catalyst for further nonviolent action, and they have the potential to tackle the root causes – the contents or contradiction – of the conflict.

References

Boutros-Ghali, Boutros, 1992, *An Agenda For Peace: Preventive Diplomacy, Peacemaking and Peacekeeping: Report of the Secretary-General pursuant to the statement adopted by the Summit Meeting of the Security Council on 31 January 1992*, New York: United Nations.

Carter, April, Howard Clark and Michael Randle, 2006, *People Power and Protest Since 1945: A Bibliography of Nonviolent Action*, London: Housmans, http://www.civilresistance.info/bibliography, accessed on 5.4.2009.

Dougherty, James E. and Robert L. Pfaltzgraff, Jr, 1997 (4th edition), *Contending Theories of International Relations: A Comprehensive Survey*, New York: Addison-Wesley Educational Publishers.

Ebert, Theodor, 1981, *Gewaltfreier Aufstand: Alternative zum Bürgerkrieg*, Waldkirch: Wald-kircher Verlagsgesellschaft.

Galtung, Johan, 1976, "Three Approaches to Peace: Peacekeeping, Peacemaking and Peace-building", in Johan Galtung, *Peace, War and Defence – Essays in Peace Research*, Vol. 1, Copenhagen: Christian Ejlers, pp. 282–304.

Galtung, Johan, 1996, *Peace by Peaceful Means: Peace and Conflict, Development and Civilization*, London: Sage Publications.

Huxley, Steven, 1992, "Lessons from the Baltics", *Civilian-based Defense: News and Opinion*, Vol. 7, No. 6.

Krippendorff, Ekkehart, 1985, *Staat und Krieg: Die historische Logik politischer Unvernunft*, Frankfurt am Main: Edition Suhrkamp.

Mahony, Liam, 2006, *Proactive Presence: Field Strategies For Civilian Protection*, Geneva: Henry Dunant Centre for Humanitarian Dialogue, http://www.hdcentre.org/publications, accessed on 10.9.2008.

Martin, Brian, 1993, *Social Defence: Social Change*, London: Freedom Press.

Moser-Puangsuwan, Yeshua and Thomas Weber, eds, 2000, *Nonviolent Intervention Across Borders: A Recurrent Vision*, Honolulu: Spark M. Matsunaga Institute for Peace.

Otterbein, Keith F., 2005, *How War Began*, College Station: Texas A&M University Press.

Schirch, Lisa, 2006, *Civilian Peacekeeping: Preventing Violence and Making Space for Democracy*, Uppsala: Life and Peace Institute.

Schweitzer, Christine, 2009a, *Erfolgreich gewaltfrei: Professionelle Praxis in ziviler Friedens-forderung*, Ed. IFA, http://www.erfolgreich-gewaltfrei.de.

Schweitzer, Christine, 2009b, *Strategies of Intervention in Protracted Violent Conflicts by Civil Society Actors: The Example of Interventions in the Violent Conflicts in the Area of Former Yugoslavia*, 1990–2002, http://www.ifgk.de/oben/publikationen_all.htm, accessed on 6.2.2010.

Schweitzer, Christine, ed., 2010, "Civilian Peacekeeping – A Barely Tapped Resource", *Working Paper No. 23*, Institute for Peace Work and Nonviolent Conflict Transformation, Vehrte: Sozio-Publishing, http://www.ifgk.de/oben/publikationen_all8.htm, accessed on 6.2.2010.

Schweitzer, Christine, Donna Howard, Mareike Junge, Corey Levine, Carl Stieren and Tim Wallis, 2001, *Nonviolent Peaceforce Feasibility Study*, Minneapolis, http://www.nonvio-lentpeaceforce.org/en/feasibilitystudy, accessed on 2.3.2009.

Semelin, Jacques, 1995, *Ohne Waffen gegen Hitler: Eine Studie zum zivilen Widerstand in Europa*, Frankfurt am Main: dipa Verlag.

Sharp, Gene, 1973, *The Politics of Nonviolent Action*, Boston: Porter Sargent Publisher.

Sharp, Gene, 1985, *Making Europe Unconquerable: The Potential of Civilian-based Deterrence and Defence*, London: Taylor & Francis.

Sharp, Gene, 1992, *Self-Reliant Defense: Without Bankruptcy or War*, Cambridge: The Albert Einstein Institution.

Smith, Dan, 2004, "Trends and Causes of Armed Conflicts", in Hrsg. David Bloomfield, Martina Fischer and Beatrix Schmelzle, eds, *Berghof Handbook of Conflict Transformation*, Berlin: Berghof Research Center for Constructive Conflict Management, http://www.berghof-handbook.net, accessed on 17 September 2008.

Weber, Thomas, 2000, "A History of Nonviolent Interposition and Accompaniment", in Yeshua Moser-Puangsuwan and Thomas Weber, eds, *Nonviolent Intervention Across Borders: A Recurrent Vision*, Honolulu: Spark M. Matsunaga Institute for Peace, pp. 45–72.

PART 4: CONFLICT ANALYSIS, TRANSFORMATION AND PREVENTION

Suggestions for further reading

Clark, Howard (2009). *People Power: Unarmed Resistance on Global Solidarity*. London, New York: Pluto Press.

Galtung, Johan (1996). *Peace by Peaceful Means: Peace and Conflict, Development and Civilization*. London: Sage Publications.

Galtung, Johan (2000). *Conflict Transformation by Peaceful Means (the Transcend Method)*. Geneva: United Nations Disaster Management Training Programme.

Galtung, Johan and Paul D. Scott (2008). *Democracy, Peace, Development*. Oslo: Kolofon.

Kelleher, Catherine McArdle and Judith Reppy (2011). *Getting to Zero: The Path to Nuclear Disarmament?* Stanford, CA: Stanford University Press.

Mahony, Liam and Luis Enrique Eguren (1997). *Unarmed Bodyguards: International Accompaniment for the Protection of Human Rights*. West Hartford, CT: Kumarian Press.

Rigby, Andrew (2001). *Justice and Reconciliation: After the Violence*. Boulder, CO: L. Rienner.
Sharp, Gene and Bruce Jenkins (1990). *Civilian-Based Defense: A Post-Military Weapons System*. Princeton, NJ: Princeton University Press.

Websites

The Berghof Handbook for Conflict Transformation: http://www.berghof-handbook.net/
Christian Peacemaker Teams: http://www.cpt.org/
Nonviolent Peaceforce: http://www.nonviolentpeaceforce.org/
SIPRI's Databases: http://www.sipri.org/databases
South African Truth and Reconciliation Commission: http://www.justice.gov.za/trc/

Questions for reflection and discussion

1   What are some of the main challenges in building a stable democratic state after the end of a war?
2   What are the most important arguments in favour of and against the view presented by Richard Falk in 'Nonviolent Geopolitics: Rationality and Resistance'?
3   What can be done to reduce the dominant role of the winners in courts for war crimes and commissions for reconciliation?
4   What is the role of disarmament negotiations when an increasing number of wars are fought by non-state actors?
5   Why have the alternatives to war less clout among most politicians and academics than do the military measures used to try to reduce or end conflicts?

Part 5

Nonviolent action and political change

SUMMARY

Ideas about peace and nonviolence can be found in all religions and many philosophical traditions.[1] As we've previously noted, religions have been used to justify violence but also been important inspirations for peaceful actions throughout history. For those who today use nonviolent means in their struggles for justice against authoritarian regimes, the inspirations can also be traced to people like Henry David Thoreau, Mohandas Karamchand Gandhi and Martin Luther King, Jr. Their theories and practices of nonviolence are still important, especially for oppressed peoples around the world.

For some, nonviolence is seen as a way of life, one lived according to one's philosophy and ethical principles. When Gandhi established his first communities, called Ashrams, in South Africa, and later in India, it was as a way of constructing a society as a model for how he wanted the whole country to be in the future.[2] The hope was to multiply these 'islands' of peaceful, self-sufficient and disciplined societies, and to create an archipelago of similar villages. For Gandhi, life in the community was an integrated part of his active struggle for a better world. He often labelled this strategy the 'constructive program'.[3]

Far from isolating himself and his colleagues in the Ashram, Gandhi argued that it was very important to combine the life in the Ashram with actions against the evil parts of society outside. The main idea for the nonviolent struggle against the racism in South Africa and later the British colonization of India was that any political power was based on 'support from below'. He developed several ways of non-cooperation to undermine and remove the support for the British rule in India.

Nonviolent action, in the form of non-cooperation or otherwise, is very far from being passive; it neither avoids confrontation, nor is it inactive. Nonviolent action is the use of non-violent means against violence, oppression and other forms of injustices. Boycotts, strikes and protests are just a few of many techniques. Gene Sharp has listed 198, and there are many more.[4]

The use of nonviolent techniques and strategies is probably as old as humans themselves. But when it comes to documentation, they are far less historically documented than the uses of violence. This has resulted in serious consequences both for those who are engaged in the use on nonviolence as tools for change and those who want to study these ways of acting in conflicts. When a case is not documented, it has a tendency to be forgotten and disappear from our history. The result is that they are not recognized. Any university library is living proof of the overwhelming documentations of wars, violence, massacres and other atrocities, and the lack of good books and articles on peaceful ways to act in conflicts.

One very important exception is Gene Sharp and his colleagues at the Albert Einstein Institute. They have for years studied and published extensively on nonviolent alternatives to national defence and for revolutionary changes in a society.

Very recently, the number of case studies, handbooks, theoretical developments and policy documents on nonviolent resistance has grown. Academic studies of civil societies, the actors involved and the role they play in shaping our societies have opened up a new field for researching nonviolence as means to influence the policies of states, companies and other social constituencies. Social movements working with environmental questions, gender issues, political conflicts, racist issues, animal rights, etc., have almost without exception used nonviolent means in their social activism programmes.

When it comes to revolutionary movements that aim to change the entire political leadership of a state, the use of nonviolent strategies has been dominant during the past 30 years. While most of the armed liberation movements around the world have achieved close to nothing of lasting significance, the unarmed uprisings in Eastern Europe in the late 80s, the 'coloured' revolutions in the early part of this century, and the recent developments in Northern Africa and the Middle East are just the tip of the iceberg of successful nonviolent political revolutions around the world.

In future history books, the waves of nonviolent movements of our time should have a central place. Every student who wants to understand the world today needs to study the nonviolent changes taking place in our increasingly globalized world.

Nonviolent philosophy

Most philosophies of nonviolence are based on religious interpretations of what is right and what is wrong. That is not to say that they could not be pragmatic and realistic. Both M.K. Gandhi and M.L. King are good examples of practical nonviolent activists who had firm convictions based on religion. They were both open-minded and tolerant of other religions, but for Gandhi the Hindu scriptures in the Bhagavad Gita, and for King the Christian Bible provided the foundations upon which they built their movements for a liberated India and a desegregated United States.

In the book *Hind Swaraj*, Gandhi describes in detail how he would like society to be. 'Hind Swaraj' means 'Home Rule', and he saw the realization of his ideas as a liberated India. The book was written on his return from London in 1908 and published as a series of articles in the newspaper *Indian Opinion*, which Gandhi edited. During the hundredth anniversary of the first publication of this book, several seminars were held to discuss its relevance has for our time. A number of people claimed that it could still be used as a 'handbook' for liberation. Others argued that *Hind Swaraj* is mainly a historical document and at best could function as an inspiration today.

Martin Luther King, Jr., in the essay 'Pilgrimage to Nonviolence', points to the academic influences that have led him to see nonviolence as 'a way of life'. King's studies of theology and philosophy had an impact on his view of God as well. God was no longer a 'metaphysical category' but 'a living reality that has been validated in the experiences of everyday life.' The combination of philosophical inspiration from people like David Hume, Immanuel Kant, Søren Kierkegaard, Friedrich Nietzsche, and Martin Heidegger and his deep religious conviction, impelled King to stand up against segregation and injustices. His saw imperfect human beings as having the potential to act in many different ways. Everyone has a choice, and it is important to make the right one. Dr. King's 'Pilgrimage' was very much inspired by the 'Experiments with Truth' Gandhi made during his life.

Nonviolence as a political tool

The pragmatic use of nonviolent techniques is widespread. As the Australian researcher Brian Martin demonstrates, nonviolent theories and techniques were used long before people actually could explain how they worked. When Richard Gregg wrote the book *The Power of Nonviolence*[5] in 1935, he was among the first to explore the actual function of nonviolent techniques in social conflicts. Gregg focused on psychological processes. Later Gene Sharp came with the concept of 'political jiu-jitsu'[6] when he described how a nonviolent actor could use the force of an opponent against him/herself. Martin has taken this idea one step further in what he calls 'the backfire process'; the use of violence against unarmed people has a certain tendency to backfire on the violent actor.[7] Martin presents several cases of this phenomenon, explains the theory in detail, and urges more research and development of nonviolent strategies beyond Gandhi.

When Gene Sharp published the booklet *From Dictatorship to Democracy* in 1993, he could hardly have predicted the impact it would have all over the world. It was meant to be a helpful handbook for the opposition in Burma. Almost 20 years later, it has been translated into at least 26 languages and is often referred to as a most useful tool by those who have carried out peaceful revolutions in many countries. In 2009, Sharp came out with a new handbook: *Self-Liberation: A Guide to Strategic Planning for Action to End a Dictatorship or Other Oppression.*[8] When the people of Tunisia and Egypt took to the streets in January 2011, the works of Gene Sharp were well known and cited by many of the activists.

Even if the international media cover mainly the 'spectacular events' of people occupying central squares in main cities, it is more the rule than the exception that revolutionary movements use nonviolent techniques. As Jørgen Johansen shows in his piece, the most successful mass social movements in recent years have removed authoritarian regimes much more effectively without the use of arms than by armed struggle. He identifies wave after wave of cases of nonviolent movements successfully dismantling dictators and unpopular political leaders. Johansen also raises questions about the lack of preparation by these activists for running a country after the old regimes have been removed.

Notes

1 Johansen, Jørgen (2007). 'Nonviolence: More Than the Absence of Violence', in Charles Webel and Johan Galtung, eds., *Handbook of Peace and Conflict Studies*. London, New York: Routledge, 143–159
2 Gandhi, M.K. (1955). *Ashram Observances in Action*. Ahmedabad: Navajivan Pub. House.
3 Gandhi, M.K. (1941). *Constructive Programme, Its Meaning and Place*. First edition. Ahmedabad: Navajivan Press.
4 Sharp, Gene (1973). *The Politics of Nonviolent Action*. Boston: P. Sargent Publisher.
5 Gregg, Richard B. (1966). *The Power of Nonviolence*. New York: Schocken.
6 Sharp, Gene (1973). *The Politics of Nonviolent Action*. Boston: Porter Sargent.
7 Brian Martin (2007). *Justice Ignited: The Dynamics of Backfire*. Lanham, MD: Rowman & Littlefield.
8 Available for downloading at: http://www.aeinstein.org/selfLiberation.html.

30 Home rule

M. K. Gandhi

What is Swaraj?

READER: I have now learnt what the Congress has done to make India one nation, how the Partition has caused an awakening, and how discontent and unrest have spread through the land. I would now like to know your views on Swaraj. I fear that our interpretation is not the same as yours.

EDITOR: It is quite possible that we do not attach the same meaning to the term. You and I and all Indians are impatient to obtain Swaraj, but we are certainly not decided as to what it is. To drive the English out of India is a thought heard from many mouths, but it does not seem that many have properly considered why it should be so. I must ask you a question. Do you think that it is necessary to drive away the English, if we get all we want?

READER: I should ask of them only one thing, that is: "Please leave our country." If, after they have complied with this request, their withdrawal from India means that they are still in India, I should have no objection. Then we would understand that, in their language, the word "gone" is equivalent to "remained".

EDITOR: Well then, let us suppose that the English have retired. What will you do then?

READER: That question cannot be answered at this stage. The state after withdrawal will depend largely upon the manner of it. If as you assume they retire, it seems to me we shall still keep their constitution and shall carry on the Government. If they simply retire for the asking, we should have an army, etc., ready at hand. We should, therefore, have no difficulty in carrying on the Government.

EDITOR: You may think so; I do not. But I will not discuss the matter just now. I have to answer your question, and that I can do well by asking you several questions. Why do you want to drive away the English?

READER: Because India has become impoverished by their Government. They take away our money from year to year. The most important posts are reserved for themselves. We are kept in a state of slavery. They behave insolently towards us and disregard our feelings.

EDITOR: If they do not take our money away, become gentle, and give us responsible posts, would you still consider their presence to be harmful?

READER: That question is useless. It is similar to the question whether there is any harm in associating with a tiger if he changes his nature. Such a question is sheer waste of time. When a tiger changes his nature, Englishmen will change theirs. This is not possible, and to believe it to be possible is contrary to human experience.

EDITOR: Supposing we get Self-Government similar to what the Canadians and the South Africans have, will it be good enough?

READER: That question also is useless. We may get it when we have the same powers; we shall then hoist our own flag. As is Japan, so must India be. We must own our navy, our army, and we must have our own splendour, and then will India's voice ring through the world.

EDITOR: You have drawn the picture well. In effect it means this: that we want English rule without the Englishman. You want the tiger's nature, but not the tiger; that is to say, you would make India English. And when it becomes English, it will be called not Hindustan but *Englishtan*. This is not the Swaraj that I want.

READER: I have placed before you my idea of Swaraj as I think it should be. If the education we have received be of any use, if the works of Spencer, Mill and others be of any importance, and if the English Parliament be the Mother of Parliaments, I certainly think that we should copy the English people, and this to such an extent that, just as they do not allow others to obtain a footing in their country, so we should not allow them or others to obtain it in ours. What they have done in their own country has not been done in any other country. It is, therefore, proper for us to import their institutions. But now I want to know your views.

EDITOR: There is need for patience. My views will develop of themselves in the course of this discourse. It is as difficult for me to understand the true nature of Swaraj as it seems to you to be easy. I shall, therefore, for the time being, content myself with endeavouring to show that what you call Swaraj is not truly Swaraj.

Civilization

READER: Now you will have to explain what you mean by civilization.

EDITOR: It is not a question of what I mean. Several English writers refuse to call that civilization which passes under that name. Many books have been written upon that subject. Societies have been formed to cure the nation of the evils of civilization. A great English writer has written a work called *Civilization: Its Cause and Cure*. Therein he has called it a disease.

READER: Why do we not know this generally?

EDITOR: The answer is very simple. We rarely find people arguing against themselves. Those who are intoxicated by modern civilization are not likely to write against it. Their care will be to find out facts and arguments in support of it, and this they do unconsciously believing it to be true. A man whilst he is dreaming, believes in his dream; he is undeceived only when he is awakened from his sleep. A man labouring under the bane of civilization is like a dreaming man. What we usually read are the works of defenders of modern civilization, which undoubtedly claims among its votaries very brilliant and even some very good men. Their writings hypnotize us. And so, one by one, we are drawn into the vortex.

READER: This seems to be very plausible. Now will you tell me something of what you have read and thought of this civilization?

EDITOR: Let us first consider what state of things is described by the word "civilization". Its true test lies in the fact that people living in it make bodily welfare the object of life. We will take some examples. The people of Europe today live in better-built houses than they did a hundred years ago. This is considered an emblem of civilization, and this is also a matter to promote bodily happiness. Formerly, they wore skins, and used spears as their weapons. Now, they wear long trousers, and, for embellishing their bodies, they wear a variety of clothing, and, instead of spears, they carry with them revolvers containing five or more chambers. If people of a certain country, who have hitherto not been in the habit of wearing much clothing, boots, etc., adopt European clothing, they are supposed to have become civilized out of savagery. Formerly, in Europe, people ploughed their lands mainly by manual labour. Now, one man can plough a vast tract by means of steam engines and can thus amass great wealth. This is called a sign of civilization. Formerly, only a few men wrote valuable books. Now, anybody writes and prints anything he likes and poisons people's minds. Formerly, men travelled in waggons. Now, they fly through the air in trains at the rate of four hundred and more miles per day. This is considered the height of civilization. It has been stated that, as men progress, they shall be able to travel in airship and reach any part of the world in a few hours. Men will not need the use of their hands and feet. They will press a button, and they will have their clothing by their side. They will press another button, and they will have their newspapers. A third, and a motor-car will be in waiting for them. They will have a variety of delicately dished up food. Everything will be done by machinery. Formerly, when people wanted to fight with one another, they measured between them their bodily strength; now it is possible to take away thousands of lives by one man working behind a gun from a hill. This is civilization. Formerly, men worked in the open air only as much as they liked. Now thousands of workmen meet together and for the sake of maintenance work in factories or mines. Their condition is worse than that of beasts. They are obliged to work, at the risk of their lives, at most dangerous occupations, for the sake of millionaires. Formerly, men were made slaves under physical compulsion. Now they are enslaved by temptation of money and of the luxuries that money can buy. There are now diseases of which people never dreamt before, and an army of doctors is engaged in finding out their cures, and so hospitals have increased. This is a test of civilization. Formerly, special messengers were required and much expense was incurred in order to send letters; today, anyone can abuse his fellow by means of a letter for one penny. True, at the same cost, one can send one's thanks also. Formerly, people had two or three meals consisting of home-made bread and vegetables; now, they require something to eat every two hours so that they have hardly leisure for anything else. What more need I say? All this you can ascertain from several authoritative books. These are all true tests of civilization. And if anyone speaks to the contrary, know that he is ignorant. This civilization takes note neither of morality nor of religion. Its votaries calmly state that their business is not to teach religion. Some even consider it to be a superstitious growth. Others put on the cloak of religion, and prate about morality. But, after twenty years' experience, I have come to the conclusion that immorality is often taught in the name of morality. Even a child can understand that in all I have described above there can be no inducement to morality. Civilization seeks to increase bodily comforts, and it fails miserably even in doing so. This civilization is irreligion, and it has taken such a hold on the people in Europe that those who are in it appear to be half mad. They lack real physical strength or courage. They keep up their energy by intoxication. They can hardly be happy in solitude. Women, who should be the queens of households, wander in the streets or they slave away in factories. For the sake of a pittance, half a million women in England alone are labouring under trying circumstances in factories or similar institutions. This awful fact is one of the causes of the daily growing suffragette movement.

This civilization is such that one has only to be patient and it will be self-destroyed. According to the teaching of Mahomed this would be considered a Satanic Civilization. Hinduism calls it the Black Age. I cannot give you an adequate conception of it. It is eating into the vitals of the English nation. It must be shunned. Parliaments are really emblems of slavery. If you will sufficiently think over this, you will entertain the same opinion and cease to blame the English. They rather deserve our sympathy. They are a shrewd nation and I therefore believe that they will cast off the evil. They are enterprising and industrious, and their mode of thought is not inherently immoral. Neither are they bad at heart. I therefore respect them. Civilization is not an incurable disease, but it should never be forgotten that the English people are at present afflicted by it.

Why was India lost?

READER: You have said much about civilization – enough to make me ponder over it. I do not now know what I should adopt and what I should avoid from the nations of Europe, but one question comes to my lips immediately. If civilization is a disease and if it has attacked England, why has she been able to take India and why is she able to retain it?

EDITOR: Your question is not very difficult to answer, and we shall presently be able to examine the true nature of Swaraj; for I am aware that I have still to answer that question. I will, however, take up your previous question. The English have not taken India; we have given it to them. They are not in India because of their strength, but because we keep them. Let us now see whether these propositions can be sustained. They came to our country originally for purposes of trade. Recall the Company Bahadur. Who made it Bahadur? They had not the slightest intention at the time of establishing a kingdom. Who assisted the Company's officers? Who was tempted at the sight of their silver? Who bought their goods? History testifies that we did all this. In order to become rich all at once we welcomed the Company's officers with open arms. We assisted them. If I am in the habit of drinking *bhang* and a seller thereof sells it to me, am I to blame him or myself? By blaming the seller, shall I be able to avoid the habit? And, if a particular retailer is driven away will not another take his place? A true servant of India will have to go to the root of the matter. If an excess of food has caused me indigestion, I shall certainly not avoid it by blaming water. He is a true physician who probes the cause of disease, and if you pose as a physician for the disease of India, you will have to find out its true cause.

READER: You are right. Now I think you will not have to argue much with me to drive your conclusions home. I am impatient to know your further views. We are now on a most interesting topic. I shall, therefore, endeavour to follow your thought, and stop you when I am in doubt.

EDITOR: I am afraid that, in spite of your enthusiasm, as we proceed further, we shall have differences of opinion. Nevertheless, I shall argue only when you stop me. We have already seen that the English merchants were able to get a footing in India because we encouraged them. When our princes fought among themselves, they sought the assistance of Company Bahadur. That corporation was versed alike in commerce and war. It was unhampered by questions of morality. Its object was to increase its commerce and to make money. It accepted our assistance, and increased the number of its warehouses. To protect the latter it employed an army which was utilized by us also. Is it not then useless to blame the English for what we did at that time? The Hindus and the Mahomedans were at daggers drawn. This, too, gave the Company its opportunity and thus we created the circumstances that gave the Company its control over India. Hence it is true to say that we gave India to the English than that India was lost.

READER: Will you now tell me how they are able to retain India?

EDITOR: The causes that gave them India enable them to retain it. Some Englishmen state that they took and they hold India by the sword. Both these statements are wrong. The sword is entirely useless for holding India. We alone keep them. Napoleon is said to have described the English as a nation of shopkeepers. It is a fitting description. They hold whatever dominions they have for the sake of their commerce. Their army and their navy are intended to protect it. When the Transvaal offered no such attractions, the late Mr. Gladstone discovered that it was not right for the English to hold it. When it became a paying proposition, resistance led to war. Mr. Chamberlain soon discovered that English enjoyed a suzerainty over the Transvaal. It is related that someone asked the late President Kruger whether there was gold in the moon. He replied that it was highly unlikely because, if there were, the English would have annexed it. Many problems can be solved by remembering that money is their God. Then it follows that we keep the English in India for our base self-interest. We like their commerce; they please us by their subtle methods and get what they want from us. To blame them for this is to perpetuate their power. We further strengthen their hold by quarrelling amongst ourselves. If you accept the above statements it is proved that the English entered India for the purpose of trade. They remain in it for the same purpose and we help them to do so. Their arms and ammunition are perfectly useless. In this connection I remind you that it is the British flag which is waving in Japan and not the Japanese. The English have a treaty with Japan for the sake of their commerce, and you will see that if they can manage it their commerce will greatly expand in that country. They wish to convert the whole world into a vast market for their goods. That they cannot do so is true, but the blame will not be theirs. They will leave no stone unturned to reach the goal.

What is true civilization?

READER: You have denounced railways, lawyers and doctors. I can see that you will discard all machinery. What, then, is civilization?

EDITOR: The answer to that question is not difficult. I believe that the civilization India has evolved is not to be beaten in the world. Nothing can equal the seeds sown by our ancestors. Rome went, Greece shared the same fate; the might of the Pharaohs was broken; Japan has become westernized; of China nothing can be said; but India is still, somehow or other, sound at the foundation. The people of Europe learn their lessons from the writings of the men of Greece or Rome, which exist no longer in their former glory. In trying to learn from them, the Europeans imagine that they will avoid the mistakes of Greece and Rome. Such is their pitiable condition. In the midst of all this India remains immovable and that is her glory. It is a charge against India that her people are so uncivilized, ignorant and stolid, that it is not possible to induce them to adopt any changes. It is a charge really against our merit. What we have tested and found true on the anvil of experience, we dare not change. Many thrust their advice upon India, and she remains steady. This is her beauty: it is the sheet-anchor of our hope.

Civilization is that mode of conduct which points out to man the path of duty. Performance of duty and observance of morality are convertible terms. To observe morality is to attain mastery over our mind and our passions. So doing, we know ourselves. The Gujarati equivalent for civilization means "good conduct".

If this definition be correct, then India, as so many writers have shown, has nothing to learn from anybody else, and this is as it should be. We notice that the mind is a restless bird; the more it gets the more it wants, and still remains unsatisfied. The more we indulge in our passions the more unbridled they become. Our ancestors, therefore, set a limit to our indulgences. They saw that happiness was largely a mental condition. A man is not necessarily happy because he is rich, or unhappy because he is poor. The rich are often seen to be unhappy, the poor to be happy. Millions will always remain poor. Observing all this, our ancestors dissuaded us from luxuries and pleasures. We have managed with the same kind of plough as existed thousands of years ago. We have retained the same kind of cottages that we had in former times and our indigenous education remains the same as before. We have had no system of life-corroding competition. Each followed his own occupation or trade and charged a regulation wage. It was not that we did not know how to invent machinery, but our forefathers knew that, if we set our hearts after such things, we would become slaves and lose our moral fibre. They, therefore, after due deliberation decided that we should only do what we could with our hands and feet. They saw that our real happiness and health consisted in a proper use of our hands and feet. They further reasoned that large cities were a snare and a useless encumbrance and that people would not be happy in them, that there would be gangs of thieves and robbers, prostitution and vice flourishing in them and that poor men would be robbed by rich men. They were, therefore, satisfied with small villages. They saw that kings and their swords were inferior to the sword of ethics, and they, therefore, held the sovereigns of the earth to be inferior to the Rishis and the Fakirs. A nation with a constitution like this is fitter to teach others than to learn from others. This nation had courts, lawyers and doctors, but they were all within bounds. Everybody knew that these professions were not particularly superior; moreover, these vakils [Indian ambassadors] and vaids [Ayurvedic physicians] did not rob people; they were considered people's dependants, not their masters. Justice was tolerably fair. The ordinary rule was to avoid courts. There were no touts to lure people into them. This evil, too, was noticeable only in and around capitals. The common people lived independently and followed their agricultural occupation. They enjoyed true Home Rule.

And where this cursed modern civilization has not reached, India remains as it was before. The inhabitants of that part of India will very properly laugh at your new-fangled notions. The English do not rule over them, nor will you ever rule over them. Those in whose name we speak we do not know, nor do they know us. I would certainly advise you and those like you who love the motherland to go into the interior that has yet been not polluted by the railways and to live there for six months; you might then be patriotic and speak of Home Rule.

Now you see what I consider to be real civilization. Those who want to change conditions such as I have described are enemies of the country and are sinners.

READER: It would be all right if India were exactly as you have described it, but it is also India where there are hundreds of child widows, where two-year old babies are married, where twelve-year old girls are mothers and housewives, where women practise polyandry, where the practice of Niyoga obtains, where, in the name of religion, girls dedicate themselves to prostitution, and in the name of religion sheep and goats are killed. Do you consider these also symbols of the civilization that you have described?

EDITOR: You make a mistake. The defects that you have shown are defects. Nobody mistakes them for ancient civilization. They remain in spite of it. Attempts have always been made and will be made to remove them. We may utilize the new spirit that is born in us for purging ourselves of these evils. But what I have described to you as emblems of modern civilization are accepted as such by its votaries. The Indian civilization, as described by me, has been so described by its votaries. In no part of the world, and under no civilization, have all men attained perfection. The tendency of the Indian civilization is to elevate the moral being, that of the Western civilization is to propagate immorality. The latter is godless, the former is based on a belief in God. So understanding and so believing, it behoves every lover of India to cling to the old Indian civilization even as a child clings to the mother's breast.

Brute force

READER: This is a new doctrine, that what is gained through fear is retained only while the fear lasts. Surely, what is given will not be withdrawn?

EDITOR: Not so. The Proclamation of 1857 was given at the end of a revolt, and for the purpose of preserving peace. When peace was secured and people became simple-minded its full effect was toned down. If I cease stealing for fear of punishment, I would recommence the operation as soon as the fear is withdrawn from me. This is almost a universal experience. We have assumed that we can get men to do things by force and, therefore, we use force.

READER: Will you not admit that you are arguing against yourself? You know that what the English obtained in their own country they obtained by using brute force. I know you have argued that what they have obtained is useless, but that does not affect my argument. They wanted useless things and they got them. My point is that their desire was fulfilled. What does it matter what means they adopted? Why should we not obtain our goal, which is good, by any means whatsoever, even by using violence? Shall I think of the means when I have to deal with a thief in the house? My duty is to drive him out anyhow. You seem to admit that we have received nothing, and that we shall receive nothing by petitioning. Why, then, may we not do so by using brute force? And, to retain what we may receive we shall keep up the fear by using the same force to the extent that it may be necessary. You will not find fault with a continuance of force to prevent a child from thrusting its foot into fire. Somehow or other we have to gain our end.

EDITOR: Your reasoning is plausible. It has deluded many. I have used similar arguments before now. But I think I know better now, and I shall endeavour to undeceive you. Let us first take the agreement that we are justified in gaining our end by using brute force because the English gained theirs by using similar means. It is perfectly true that they used brute force and that it is possible for us to do likewise, but by using similar means we can get only the same thing that they got. You will admit that we do not want that. Your belief that there is no connection between the means and the end is a great mistake. Through that mistake even men who have been considered religious have committed grievous crimes. Your reasoning is the same as saying that we can get a rose through planting a noxious weed. If I want to cross the ocean, I can do so only by means of a vessel; if I were to use a cart for that purpose, both the cart and I would soon find the bottom, "As is the God, so is the votary," is a maxim worth considering. Its meaning has been distorted and men have gone astray. The means may be likened to a seed, the end to a tree; and there is just the same inviolable connection between the means and the end as there is between the seed and the tree. I am not likely to obtain the result flowing from the worship of God by laying myself prostrate before Satan. If, therefore, anyone were to say: "I want to worship God; it does not matter that I do so by means of Satan," it would be set down as ignorant folly. We reap exactly as we sow. The English in 1833 obtained greater voting power by violence. Did they by using brute force better appreciate their duty? They wanted the right of voting, which they obtained by using physical force. But real rights are a result of performance of duty; these rights they have not obtained. We, therefore, have before us in England the force of everybody wanting and insisting on his rights, nobody thinking of his duty. And where everybody wants rights, who shall give them to whom? I do not wish to imply that they do no duties. They don't perform the duties corresponding to those rights; and as they do not perform that particular duty, namely, acquire fitness, their rights have proved a burden to them. In other words, what they have obtained is an exact result of the means they adopted. They used the means corresponding to the end. If I want to deprive you of your watch, I shall certainly have to fight for it; if I want to buy your watch, I shall have to pay you for it; and if I want a gift I shall have to plead for it; and, according to the means I employ, the watch is stolen property, my own property, or a donation. Thus we see three different results from three different means. Will you still say that means do not matter?

Now we shall take the example given by you of the thief to be driven out. I do not agree with you that the thief may be driven out by any means. If it is my father who has come to steal I shall use one kind of means. If it is an acquaintance I shall use another; and in the case of a perfect stranger I shall use a third. If it is a white man, you will perhaps say you will use means different from those you will adopt with an Indian thief. If it is a weakling, the means will be different from those to be adopted for dealing with an equal in physical strength; and if the thief is armed from top to toe, I shall simply remain quiet. Thus we have a variety of means between the father and the armed man. Again, I fancy that I should pretend to be sleeping whether the thief was my father or that strong armed man. The reason for this is that my father would also be armed and I should succumb to the strength possessed by either and allow my things to be stolen. The strength of my father would make me weep with pity; the strength of the armed man would rouse in me anger and we should become enemies. Such is the curious situation. From these examples we may not be able to agree as to the means to be adopted in each case. I myself seem clearly to see what should be done in all these cases, but the remedy may frighten you. I therefore hesitate to place it before you. For the time being I will leave you to guess it, and if you cannot, it is clear you will have to adopt different means in each case. You will also have seen that any means will not avail to drive away the thief. You will have to adopt means to fit each case. Hence it follows that your duty is *not* to drive away the thief by any means you like.

Let us proceed a little further. That well-armed man has stolen your property; you have harboured the thought of his act; you are filled with anger; you argue that you want to punish that rogue, not for your own sake, but for the good of your neighbours; you have collected a number of armed men, you want to take his house by assault; he is duly informed of it, he runs away; he too is incensed. He collects his brother robbers, and sends you a defiant message that he will commit robbery in broad daylight. You are strong, you do not fear him, you are prepared to receive him. Meanwhile, the robber pesters your neighbours. They complain before you. You reply that you are doing all for their sake, you do not mind that your own goods have been stolen. Your neighbours reply that the robber never pestered them before, and that he commenced his depredations only after you declared hostilities against him. You are between Scylla and Charybdis. You are full of pity for the poor men. What they say is true. What are you to do? You will be disgraced if you now leave the robber alone. You, therefore, tell the poor men: "Never mind. Come, my wealth is yours, I will give you arms, I will teach you how to use them; you should belabour the rogue; don't you leave him alone." And so the battle grows; the robbers increase in numbers; your neighbours have deliberately put themselves to inconvenience. Thus the result of wanting to take revenge upon the robber is that you have disturbed your own peace; you are in perpetual fear of being robbed and assaulted; your courage has given place to cowardice. If you will patiently examine the argument, you will see that I have not overdrawn the picture. This is one of the means. Now let us examine the other. You set this armed robber down as an ignorant brother; you intend to reason with him at a suitable opportunity; you argue that he is, after all, a fellow-man; you do not know what prompted him to steal. You, therefore, decide that, when you can, you will destroy the man's motive for stealing. Whilst you are thus reasoning with yourself the man comes again to steal. Instead of being angry with him you take pity on him. You think that this stealing habit must be a disease with him. Henceforth, you, therefore, keep your doors and windows open, you change your sleeping-place, and you keep your things in a manner most accessible to him. The robber comes again and is confused as all this is new to him; nevertheless, he takes away your things. But his mind is agitated. He inquires about you in the village, he comes to learn about your broad and loving heart, he repents, he begs your pardon, returns you your things and leaves off the stealing habit. He becomes your servant, and you find for him honourable employment. This is the second method. Thus, you see, different means have brought about totally different results. I do not wish to deduce from this that robbers will act in the above manner or that all will have the same pity and love like you, but I only wish to show that fair means alone can produce fair results, and that, at least in the majority of cases, if not indeed in all, the force of love and pity is infinitely greater than the force of arms. There is harm in the exercise of brute force, never in that of pity.

Now we will take the question of petitioning. It is a fact beyond dispute that a petition, without the backing of force, is useless. However, the late Justice Ranade used to say that petitions served a useful purpose because they were a means of educating people. They give the latter an idea of their condition and warn the rulers. From this point of view, they are not altogether useless. A petition of an equal is a sign of courtesy; a petition from a slave is a symbol of his slavery. A petition backed by force is a petition from an equal and, when he transmits his demand in the form of a petition, it testifies to his nobility. Two kinds of force can back petitions. "We shall hurt if you do not give this," is one kind of force; it is the force of arms, whose evil results we have already examined. The second kind of force can thus be stated: "If you do not concede our demand, we shall be no longer your petitioners. You can govern us only so long as we remain the governed; we shall no longer have any dealings with you." The force implied in this may be described as love-force, soul-force, or, more popularly but less accurately, passive resistance. This force is indestructible. He who uses it perfectly understands his position. We have an ancient proverb which literally means: "One negative cures thirty-six diseases." The force of arms is powerless when matched against the force of love or the soul.

Now we shall take your last illustration, that of the child thrusting its foot into fire. It will not avail you. What do you really do to the child? Supposing that it can exert so much physical force that it renders you powerless and rushes into fire, then you cannot prevent it. There are only two remedies open to you – either you must kill it in order to prevent it from perishing in the flames, or you must give your own life because you do not wish to see it perish before your very eyes. You will not kill it. If your heart is not quite full of pity, it is possible that you will not surrender yourself by preceding the child and going into the fire yourself. You, therefore, helplessly allow it to go into the flames. Thus, at any rate, you are not using physical force. I hope you will not consider that it is still physical force, though of a low order, when you would forcibly prevent the child from rushing towards the fire if you could. That force is of a different order and we have to understand what it is.

Remember that, in thus preventing the child, you are minding entirely its own interest, you are exercising authority for its sole benefit. Your example does not apply to the English. In using brute force against the English you consult entirely your own, that is the national, interest. There is no question here either of pity or of love. If you say that the actions of the English, being evil, represent fire, and that they proceed to their actions through ignorance, and that therefore they occupy the position of a child and that you want to protect such a child, then you will have to overtake every evil action of that kind by whomsoever committed and, as in the case of the evil child, you will have to sacrifice yourself. If you are capable of such immeasurable pity, I wish you well in its exercise.

Passive resistance

READER: Is there any historical evidence as to the success of what you have called soul-force or truth-force? No instance seems to have happened of any nation having risen through soul-force. I still think that the evil-doers will not cease doing evil without physical punishment.

EDITOR: The poet Tulsidas has said: "Of religion, pity, or love, is the root, as egotism of the body. Therefore, we should not abandon pity so long as we are alive." This appears to me to be a scientific truth. I believe in it as much as I believe in two and two being four. The force of love is the same as the force of the soul or truth. We have evidence of its working at every step. The universe would disappear without the existence of that force. But you ask for historical evidence. It is, therefore, necessary to know what history means. The Gujarati equivalent means: "It so happened". If that is the meaning of history, it is possible to give copious evidence. But, if it means the doings of kings and emperors, there can be no evidence of soul-force or passive resistance in such history. You cannot expect silver ore in a tin mine. History, as we know it, is a record of the wars of the world, and so there is a proverb among Englishmen that a nation which has no history, that is, no wars, is a happy nation. How kings played, how they became enemies of one another, how they murdered one another, is found accurately recorded in history, and if this were all that had happened in the world, it would have been ended long ago. If the story of the universe had commenced with wars, not a man would have been found alive today. Those people who have been warred against have disappeared as, for instance, the natives of Australia of whom hardly a man was left alive by the intruders. Mark, please, that these natives did not use soul-force in self-defence, and it does not require much foresight to know that the Australians will share the same fate as their victims. "Those that take the sword shall perish by the sword." With us the proverb is that professional swimmers will find a watery grave.

The fact that there are so many men still alive in the world shows that it is based not on the force of arms but on the force of truth or love. Therefore, the greatest and most unimpeachable evidence of the success of this force is to be found in the fact that, in spite of the wars of the world, it still lives on.

Thousands, indeed tens of thousands, depend for their existence on a very active working of this force. Little quarrels of millions of families in their daily lives disappear before the exercise of this force. Hundreds of nations live in peace. History does not and cannot take note of this fact. History is really a record of every interruption of the even working of the force of love or of the soul. Two brothers quarrel; one of them repents and re-awakens the love that was lying dormant in him; the two again begin to live in peace; nobody takes note of this. But if the two brothers, through the intervention of solicitors or some other reason take up arms or go to law – which is another form of the exhibition of brute force, – their doings would be immediately noticed in the press, they would be the talk of their neighbours and would probably go down to history. And what is true of families and communities is true of nations. There is no reason to believe that there is one law for families and another for nations. History, then, is a record of an interruption of the course of nature. Soul-force, being natural, is not noted in history.

READER: According to what you say, it is plain that instances of this kind of passive resistance are not to be found in history. It is necessary to understand this passive resistance more fully. It will be better, therefore, if you enlarge upon it.

EDITOR: Passive resistance is a method of securing rights by personal suffering; it is the reverse of resistance by arms. When I refuse to do a thing that is repugnant to my conscience, I use soul-force. For instance, the Government of the day has passed a law which is applicable to me. I do not like it. If by using violence I force the Government to repeal the law, I am employing what may be termed body-force. If I do not obey the law and accept the penalty for its breach, I use soul-force. It involves sacrifice of self.

Everybody admits that sacrifice of self is infinitely superior to sacrifice of others. Moreover, if this kind of force is used in a cause that is unjust, only the person using it suffers. He does not make others suffer for his mistakes. Men have before now done many things which were subsequently found to have been wrong. No man can claim that he is absolutely in the right or that a particular thing is wrong because he thinks so, but it is wrong for him so long as that is his deliberate judgement. It is therefore meet that he should not do that which he knows to be wrong, and suffer the consequence whatever it may be. This is the key to the use of soul-force.

READER: You would then disregard laws – this is rank disloyalty. We have always been considered a law-abiding nation. You seem to be going even beyond the extremists. They say that we must obey the laws that have been passed, but that if the laws be bad, we must drive out the law-givers even by force.

EDITOR: Whether I go beyond them or whether I do not is a matter of no consequence to either of us. We simply want to find out what is right and to act accordingly. The real meaning of the statement that we are a law-abiding nation is that we are passive resisters. When we do not like certain laws, we do not break the heads of law-givers but we suffer and do not submit to the laws. That we should obey laws whether good or bad is a new-fangled notion. There was no such thing in former days. The people disregarded those laws they did not like and suffered the penalties for their breach. It is contrary to our manhood if we obey laws repugnant to our conscience. Such teaching is opposed to religion and means slavery. If the Government were to ask us to go about without any clothing, should we do so? If I were a passive resister, I would say to them that I would have nothing to do with their law. But we have so forgotten ourselves and become so compliant that we do not mind any degrading law.

A man who has realized his manhood, who fears only God, will fear no one else. Man-made laws are not necessarily binding on him. Even the Government does not expect any such thing from us. They do not say: "You must do such and such a thing," but they say "If you do not do it, we will punish you." We are sunk so low that we fancy that it is our duty and our religion to do what the law lays down. If man will only realize that it is unmanly to obey laws that are unjust, no man's tyranny will enslave him. This is the key to self-rule or home-rule.

It is a superstition and ungodly thing to believe that an act of a majority binds a minority. Many examples can be given in which acts of majorities will be found to have been wrong and those of minorities to have been right. All reforms owe their origin to the initiation of minorities in opposition to majorities. If among a band of robbers a knowledge of robbing is obligatory, is a pious man to accept the obligation? So long as the superstition that men should obey unjust laws exists, so long will their slavery exist. And a passive resister alone can remove such a superstition.

To use brute-force, to use gunpowder, is contrary to passive resistance, for it means that we want our opponent to do by force that which we desire but he does not. And if such a use of force is justifiable, surely he is entitled to do likewise by us. And so we should never come to an agreement. We may simply fancy, like the blind horse moving in a circle round a mill, that we are making progress. Those who believe that they are not bound to obey laws which are repugnant to their conscience have only the remedy of passive resistance open to them. Any other must lead to disaster.

READER: From what you say I deduce that passive resistance is a splendid weapon of the weak, but that when they are strong they may take up arms.

EDITOR: This is gross ignorance. Passive resistance, that is, soul-force, is matchless. It is superior to the force of arms. How, then, can it be considered only a weapon of the weak? Physical-force men are strangers to the courage that is requisite in a passive resister. Do you believe that a coward can ever disobey a law that he dislikes? Extremists are considered to be advocates of brute force. Why do they, then, talk about obeying laws? I do not blame them. They can say nothing else. When they succeed in driving out the English and they themselves become governors, they will want you and me to obey their laws. And that is a fitting thing for their constitution. But a passive resister will say he will not obey a law that is against his conscience, even though he may be blown to pieces at the mouth of a cannon.

What do you think? Wherein is courage required – in blowing others to pieces from behind a cannon, or with a smiling face to approach a cannon and be blown to pieces? Who is the true warrior – he who keeps death always as a bosom-friend, or he who controls the death of others? Believe me that a man devoid of courage and manhood can never be a passive resister.

This however, I will admit: that even a man weak in body is capable of suffering this resistance. One man can offer it just as well as millions. Both men and women can indulge in it. It does not require the training of an army; it needs no jiu-jitsu. Control over the mind is alone necessary, and when that is attained, man is free like the king of the forest and his very glance withers the enemy.

Passive resistance is an all-sided sword, it can be used anyhow; it blesses him who uses it and him against whom it is used. Without drawing a drop of blood it produces far-reaching results. It never rusts and cannot be stolen. Competition between passive resisters does not exhaust. The sword of passive resistance does not require a scabbard. It is strange indeed that you should consider such a weapon to be a weapon merely of the weak.

READER: You have said that passive resistance is a speciality of India. Have cannons never been used in India?

EDITOR: Evidently, in your opinion India means its few princes. To me it means its teeming millions on whom depends the existence of its princes and our own.

Kings will always use their kingly weapons. To use force is bred in them. They want to command, but those who have to obey commands do not want guns; and these are in a majority throughout the world. They have to learn either body-force or soul-force. Where they learn the former, both the rulers and the ruled become like so many madmen; but where they learn soul-force the commands of the rulers do not go beyond the point of their swords, for true men disregard unjust commands. Peasants have never been subdued by the sword, and never will be. They do not know the use of the sword, and they are not frightened by the use of it by others. That nation is great which rests its head upon death as its pillow. Those who defy death are free from all fear. For those who are labouring under the delusive charms of brute-force, this picture is not overdrawn. The fact is that, in India, the nation at large has generally used passive resistance in all departments of life. We cease to co-operate with our rulers when they displease us. This is passive resistance.

I remember an instance when, in a small principality, the villagers were offended by some command issued by the prince. The former immediately began vacating the village. The prince became nervous, apologized to his subjects and withdrew his command. Many such instances can be found in India. Real Home Rule is possible only where passive resistance is the guiding force of the people. Any other rule is foreign rule.

READER: Then you will say that it is not at all necessary for us to train the body?

EDITOR: I will certainly not say any such thing. It is difficult to become a passive resister unless the body is trained. As a rule, the mind, residing in a body that has become weakened by pampering, is also weak, and where there is no strength of mind there can be no strength of soul. We shall have to improve our physique by getting rid of infant marriages and luxurious living. If I were to ask a man with a shattered body to face a cannon's mouth I should make a laughing-stock of my self.

READER: From what you say, then, it would appear that it is not a small thing to become a passive resister and, if that is so, I should like you to explain how a man may become one.

EDITOR: To become a passive resister is easy enough but it is also equally difficult. I have known a lad of fourteen years become a passive resister; I have known also sick people do likewise; and I have also known physically strong and otherwise happy people unable to take up passive resistance. After a great deal of experience it seems to me that those who want to become passive resisters for the service of the country have to observe perfect chastity, adopt poverty, follow truth, and cultivate fearlessness.

Chastity is one of the greatest disciplines without which the mind cannot attain requisite firmness. A man who is unchaste loses stamina, becomes emasculated and cowardly. He whose mind is given over to animal passions is not capable of any great effort. This can be proved by innumerable instances. What, then, is a married person to do is the question that arises naturally; and yet it need not. When a husband and wife gratify the passions, it is no less an animal indulgence on that account. Such an indulgence, except for perpetuating the race, is strictly prohibited. But a passive resister has to avoid even that very limited indulgence because he can have no desire for progeny. A married man, therefore, can observe perfect chastity. This subject is not capable of being treated at greater length. Several questions arise: How is one to carry one's wife with one, what are her rights, and other similar questions. Yet those who wish to take part in a great work are bound to solve these puzzles.

Just as there is necessity for chastity, so is there for poverty. Pecuniary ambition and passive resistance cannot well go together. Those who have money are not expected to throw it away, but they *are* expected to be indifferent about it. They must be prepared to lose every penny rather than give up passive resistance.

Passive resistance has been described in the course of our discussion as truth-force. Truth, therefore, has necessarily to be followed and that at any cost. In this connection, academic questions such as whether a man may not lie in order to save a life, etc., arise, but these questions occur only to those who wish to justify lying. Those who want to follow truth every time are not placed in such a quandary; and if they are, they are still saved from a false position.

Passive resistance cannot proceed a step without fearlessness. Those alone can follow the path of passive resistance who are free from fear, whether as to their possessions, false honour, their relatives, the government, bodily injuries or death.

These observances are not to be abandoned in the belief that they are difficult. Nature has implanted in the human breast ability to cope with any difficulty or suffering that may come to man unprovoked. These qualities are worth having, even for those who do not wish to serve the country. Let there be no mistake, as those who want to train themselves in the use of arms are also obliged to have these qualities more or less. Everybody does not become a warrior for the wish. A would-be warrior will have to observe chastity and to be satisfied with poverty as his lot. A warrior without fearlessness cannot be conceived of. It may be thought that he would not need to be exactly truthful, but that quality follows real fearlessness. When a man abandons truth, he does so owing to fear in some shape or form. The above four attributes, then, need not frighten anyone. It may be as well here to note that a physical-force man has to have many other useless qualities which a passive resister never needs. And you will find that whatever extra effort a swordsman needs is due to lack of fearlessness. If he is an embodiment of the latter, the sword will drop from his hand that very moment. He does not need its support. One who is free from hatred requires no sword. A man with a stick suddenly came face to face with a lion and instinctively raised his weapon in self-defence. The man saw that he had only prated about fearlessness when there was none in him. That moment he dropped the stick and found himself free from all fear.

31 Pilgrimage to nonviolence

Martin Luther King, Jr.

Ten years ago I was just entering my senior year in theological seminary. Like most theological students I was engaged in the exciting job of studying various theological theories. Having been raised in a rather strict fundamentalistic tradition, I was occasionally shocked as my intellectual journey carried me through new and sometimes complex doctrinal lands. But despite the shock, the pilgrimage was always stimulating, and it gave me a new appreciation for objective appraisal and critical analysis. My early theological training did the same for me as the reading of Hume did for Kant: it knocked me out of my dogmatic slumber.

At this stage of my development I was a thoroughgoing liberal. Liberalism provided me with an intellectual satisfaction that I could never find in fundamentalism. I became so enamored of the insights of liberalism that I almost fell into the trap of accepting uncritically everything that came under its name. I was absolutely convinced of the natural goodness of man and the natural power of human reason.

I

The basic change in my thinking came when I began to question some of the theories that had been associated with so-called liberal theology. Of course there is one phase of liberalism that I hope to cherish always: its devotion to the search for truth, its insistence on an open and analytical mind, its refusal to abandon the best light of reason. Liberalism's contribution to the philological-historical criticism of biblical literature has been of immeasurable value and should be defended with religious and scientific passion.

It was mainly the liberal doctrine of man that I began to question. The more I observed the tragedies of history and man's shameful inclination to choose the low road, the more I came to see the depths and strength of sin. My reading of the works of Reinhold Niebuhr made me aware of the complexity of human motives and the reality of sin on every level of man's existence. Moreover, I came to recognize the complexity of man's social involvement and the glaring reality of collective evil. I came to feel that liberalism had been all too sentimental concerning human nature and that it leaned toward a false idealism.

I also came to see that liberalism's superficial optimism concerning human nature caused it to overlook the fact that reason is darkened by sin. The more I thought about human nature the more I saw how our tragic inclination for sin causes us to use our minds to rationalize our actions. Liberalism failed to see that reason by itself is little more than an instrument to justify man's defensive ways of thinking. Reason, devoid of purifying power of faith, can never free itself from distortions and rationalizations.

In spite of the fact that I had to reject some aspects of liberalism, I never came to an all-out acceptance of neo-orthodoxy. While I saw neo-orthodoxy as a helpful corrective for a liberalism that had become all too sentimental, I never felt that it provided an adequate answer to the basic questions. If liberalism was too optimistic concerning human nature, neo-orthodoxy was too pessimistic. Not only on the question of man but also on other vital issues neo-orthodoxy went too far in its revolt. In its attempt to preserve the transcendence of God, which had been neglected by liberalism's overstress of his immanence, neo-orthodoxy went to the extreme of stressing a God who was hidden, unknown and "wholly other." In its revolt against liberalism's overemphasis on the power of reason, neo-orthodoxy fell into a mood of antirationalism and semifundamentalism, stressing a narrow, uncritical biblicism. This approach, I felt, was inadequate both for the church and for personal life.

So although liberalism left me unsatisfied on the question of the nature of man, I found no refuge in neo-orthodoxy. I am now convinced that the truth about man is found neither in liberalism nor in neo-orthodoxy. Each represents a partial truth. A large segment of Protestant liberalism defined man only in terms of his essential nature, his capacity for good. Neo-orthodoxy tended to define man only in terms of his existential nature, his capacity for evil. An adequate understanding of man is found neither in the thesis of liberalism nor in the antithesis of neo-orthodoxy, but in a synthesis which reconciles the truths of both.

During the past decade I also gained a new appreciation for the philosophy of existentialism. My first contact with this philosophy came through my reading of Kierkegaard and Nietzsche. Later I turned study of Jaspers, Heidegger and Sartre. All of these thinkers stimulated my thinking; while finding things to question in each, I nevertheless learned a great deal from study of them. When I finally turned to a serious study of the works of Paul Tillich I became convinced that existentialism, in spite of the fact that it had become all too fashionable, had grasped certain basic truths about man and his condition that could not be permanently overlooked.

Its understanding of the "finite freedom" of man is one of existentialism's most lasting contributions, and its perception of the anxiety and conflict produced in man's personal and social life as a result of the perilous and ambiguous structure of existence is especially meaningful for our time. The common point in all existentialism, whether it is atheistic or theistic, is that man's existential situation is a state of estrangement from his essential nature. In their revolt against Hegel's essentialism, all existentialists contend that the world is fragmented. History is a series of unreconciled conflicts and man's existence is filled with anxiety and threatened with meaninglessness. While the ultimate Christian answer is not found in any of these existential assertions, there is much here that the theologian can use to describe the true state of man's existence.

Although most of my formal study during this decade has been in systematic theology and philosophy. I have become more and more interested in social ethics. Of course my concern for social problems was already substantial before the beginning of this decade. From my early teens in Atlanta I was deeply concerned about the problem of racial injustice. I grew up abhorring segregation, considering it both rationally inexplicable and morally unjustifiable. I could never accept the fact of having to go to the back of a bus or sit in the segregated section of a train. The first time that I was seated behind a curtain in a dining car I felt as if the curtain had been dropped on my selfhood. I had also learned that the inseparable twin of racial injustice is economic injustice. I saw how the systems of segregation ended up in the exploitation of the Negro as well as the poor whites. Through these early experiences I grew up deeply conscious of the varieties of injustice in our society.

II

Not until I entered theological seminary, however, did I begin a serious intellectual quest for a method to eliminate social evil. I was immediately influenced by the social gospel. In the early fifties I read Rauschenbusch's *Christianity and the Social Crisis*, a book which left an indelible imprint on my thinking. Of course there were points at which I differed with Rauschenbusch. I felt that he had fallen victim to the nineteenth century "cult of inevitable progress," which led him to an unwarranted optimism concerning human nature. Moreover, he came perilously close to identifying the kingdom of God with a particular social and economic system – a temptation which the church should never give in to. But in spite of these shortcomings Rauschenbusch gave to American Protestantism a sense of social responsibility that it should never lose. The gospel at its best deals with the whole man, not only his soul but his body, not only his spiritual well-being, but his material well-being. Any religion that professes to be concerned about the souls of men and is not concerned about the slums that damn them, the economic conditions that strangle them and the social conditions that cripple them is a spiritually moribund religion awaiting burial.

After reading Rauschenbusch I turned to a serious study of the social and ethical theories of the great philosophers. During this period I had almost despaired of the power of love in solving social problems. The "turn the other cheek" philosophy and the "love your enemies" philosophy are only valid, I felt, when individuals are in conflict with other individuals; when racial groups and nations are in conflict a more realistic approach is necessary. Then I came upon the life and teachings of Mahatma Gandhi. As I read his works I became deeply fascinated by his campaigns of nonviolent resistance. The whole Gandhian concept of *satyagraha* (*satya* is truth which equals love, and *graha* is force; *satyagraha*, thus means truth-force or love-force) was profoundly significant to me. As I delved deeper into the philosophy of Gandhi my skepticism concerning the power of love gradually diminished, and I came to see for the first time that the Christian doctrine of love operating through the Gandhian method of nonviolence was one of the most potent weapons available to oppressed people in their struggle for freedom. At this time, however, I had a merely intellectual understanding and appreciation of the position, with no firm determination to organize it in a socially effective situation.

When I went to Montgomery, Alabama, as a pastor in 1954, I had not the slightest idea that I would later become involved in a crisis in which nonviolent resistance would be applicable. After I had lived in the community about a year, the bus boycott began. The Negro people of Montgomery, exhausted by the humiliating experiences that they had constantly faced on the buses, expressed in a massive act of noncooperation their determination to be free. They came to see that it was ultimately more honorable to walk the streets in dignity than to ride the buses in humiliation. At the beginning of the protest the people called on me to serve as their spokesman. In accepting this responsibility my mind, consciously or unconsciously, was driven back to the Sermon on the Mouth and the Gandhian method of nonviolent resistance. This principle became the guiding light of our movement. Christ furnished the spirit and motivation while Gandhi furnished the method.

The experience in Montgomery did more to clarify my thinking on the question of nonviolence than all of the books that I had read. As the days unfolded I became more and more convinced of the power of nonviolence. Living through the actual experience of the protest, nonviolence became more than a method to which I gave intellectual assent: it became a commitment to a way of life. Many issues I had not cleared up intellectually concerning nonviolence were now solved in the sphere of practical action.

A few months ago 1 had the privilege of traveling to India. The trip had a great impact on me personally and left me even more convinced of the power of nonviolence. It was a marvelous thing to see the amazing results of a nonviolent struggle. India won her independence, but without violence on the part of Indians. The aftermath of hatred and bitterness that usually follows a violent campaign is found nowhere in India. Today a mutual friendship based on complete equality exists between the Indian and British people within the commonwealth.

I do not want to give the impression that nonviolence will work miracles overnight. Men are not easily moved from their mental ruts or purged of their prejudiced and irrational feelings. When the underprivileged demand freedom, the privileged first react with bitterness and resistance. Even when the demands are couched in nonviolent terms, the initial response is the same. I am sure that many of our white brothers in Montgomery and across the South are still bitter toward Negro leaders, even though these leaders have sought to follow a way of love and nonviolence. So the nonviolent approach does not immediately change the heart of the oppressor. It first does something to the hearts and souls of those committed to it. It gives them new self-respect; it calls up resources of strength and courage that they did not know they had. Finally, it reaches the opponent and so stirs his conscience that reconciliation becomes a reality.

III

During recent months I have come to see more and more the need for the method of nonviolence in international relations. While I was convinced during my student days of the power of nonviolence in group conflicts within nations, I was not yet convinced of its efficacy in conflicts between nations. I felt that while war could never be a positive or absolute good, it could serve as a negative good in the sense of preventing the spread and growth of an evil force. War, I felt, horrible as it is, might be preferable to surrender to a totalitarian system. But more and more I have come to the conclusion that the potential destructiveness of modern weapons of war totally rules out the possibility of war ever serving again as a negative good. If we assume that mankind has a right to survive then we must find an alternative to war and destruction. In a day when sputniks dash through outer space and guided ballistic missiles are carving highways of death through the stratosphere, nobody can win a war. The choice today is no longer between violence and nonviolence. It is either nonviolence or nonexistence.

I am no doctrinaire pacifist. I have tried to embrace a realistic pacifism. Moreover, I see the pacifist position not as sinless but as the lesser evil in the circumstances. Therefore I do not claim to be free from the moral dilemmas that the Christian nonpacifist confronts. But I am convinced that the church cannot remain silent while mankind faces the threat of being plunged into the abyss of nuclear annihilation. If the church is true to its mission it must call for an end to the arms race.

[. . .]

The past decade has been a most exciting one. In spite of the tensions and uncertainties of our age something profoundly meaningful has begun. Old systems of exploitation and oppression are passing away and new systems of justice and equality are being born. In a real sense ours is a great time in which to be alive. Therefore I am not yet discouraged about the future. Granted that the easygoing optimism of yesterday is impossible. Granted that we face a world crisis which often leaves us standing amid the surging murmur of life's restless sea. But every crisis has both its dangers and its opportunities. Each can spell either salvation or doom. In a dark, confused world the spirit of God may yet reign supreme.

32 How nonviolence works

Brian Martin

There is ample evidence from historical examples that nonviolent action can be an effective method of social action. Examples from recent decades include the toppling of Philippines dictator Ferdinand Marcos in 1986 through 'people power', the collapse of communist regimes in Eastern Europe in 1989, the thwarting of a coup in the Soviet Union in 1991, the ending of apartheid in South Africa in the early 1990s, the resignation of President Suharto due to popular pressure in Indonesia in 1998, and the overthrow of Serbian ruler Milosevic in 2000 (Ackerman and DuVall 2000).

There are also examples of nonviolent campaigns that have been less successful, such as the repression of the Chinese pro-democracy movement in 1989 and failure of the movement, led by Aung San Suu Kyi, to overthrow the Burmese military regime (Schock 2005). Yet the track record for nonviolence seems quite a bit better than for violence: it is hard to think of a single recent success by an armed liberation struggle against a powerful state. In South Africa, the anti-apartheid movement made much more progress after armed struggle was subordinated to nonviolent action (Zunes 1999). In East Timor, nonviolent protests in urban areas were far more successful in building international support than guerrilla warfare in the interior (Fukuda 2000). In Palestine, the first intifada, from 1987–1993, which was largely unarmed, was much more successful in winning popular support in Palestine and internationally than the earlier terrorist campaigns by the Palestinian Liberation Organisation and than the more violent tactics used in the second intifada from 2000.

Despite the many successes of nonviolent action, the mechanism by which nonviolent action works has received relatively little attention.

Critics often say that nonviolence only works against opponents who are less than ruthless, citing the example of the British in India. Yet this claim does not stand up to scrutiny, given the many instances of success against dictators, including the Nazis (Semelin 1993). For example, during the Nazi occupation of Norway during World War II, the Norwegian government led by Quisling directed the teaching of Nazi doctrine in schools. But the teachers refused, even though many were sent to remote prison camps. Eventually, worried about angering the population too much, the Quisling government backed down: Nazi doctrine was never taught in Norway. In the heart of Berlin in 1943, non-Jewish wives protested against the arrest of their Jewish husbands. After several days of protests, the Nazi government released the Jewish prisoners (Stoltzfus 1996).

Nor should it be thought that British were always polite and gentle as colonialists. They were quite capable of brutality. For example, in putting down the Mau Mau rebellion in Kenya, the British suspended civil liberties, imprisoned thousands in special camps, used torture systematically, executed over a thousand prisoners, and killed tens of thousands of civilians (Elkins 2005).

It is important to go beyond debates with critics of nonviolence and to probe the dynamics of nonviolent action, because the insights gained may be useful for making campaigns more effective. Here I examine a series of perspectives on the operation of nonviolence, beginning with Gandhi and his interpreter Richard Gregg. Then I turn to nonviolence researcher Gene Sharp, who expanded on Gregg's ideas. Finally I present an expanded perspective on Sharp's ideas. As a test bed for the discussion, I use the example of the salt march; in particular the beatings at Dharasana, drawing especially on Weber (1997).

Gandhi on nonviolence

In 1930, Gandhi developed the idea of making salt as a challenge to British rule in India. The British had imposed a monopoly on salt manufacture and put a tax on salt. Given salt's role as a basic commodity, this had the capacity to cause resentment and thus was a potential issue for mobilizing opposition to the British. Gandhi's idea was to make salt from the sea as a symbolic form of defiance to the government. To increase the impact of this civil disobedience, Gandhi and his supporters organized a march to the coastal town of Dandi over 24 days. The march permitted speeches and recruitment along the way and a crescendo of anticipation and publicity before the actual violation of the salt laws.

The salt march illustrates Gandhi's methods perfectly. By exploring various ideas for campaigns, he hit upon a topic and opportunity that seemed promising. He announced the campaign with an open letter to Lord Irwin, the Viceroy, in which he politely but assertively requested acquiescence to his reasonable demands for making salt, and described the civil disobedience that would follow otherwise. Polite dialogue with the opponent was a key part of Gandhi's method. He considered the opponent to be a partner in his quest for 'truth'. At a pragmatic level, this approach put Irwin in an awkward situation. If he acquiesced to Gandhi's demands, he would appear weak and open the way for further demands. But if he came down on Gandhi too heavily, he would appear to be unreasonable and unjust and thus increase the level of opposition (Dalton, 1993).

What Gandhi realized as much as anyone was the importance of winning support. It is easy to assume that the British were united in imposing their rule on India and that the Indian masses felt oppressed but afraid to act due to the likely consequences. Neither assumption is correct. Among the British, especially in Britain, there was opposition to colonial rule in India. A false step by Irwin could easily increase the level of opposition. Within India, there was active opposition to British rule from only a tiny minority of the people. The Indian population was divided by gender, caste, class and religion, making it quite a challenge to mobilize support for any campaign. Gandhi knew the importance of choosing and executing a campaign that triggered the popular imagination.

The defining images of the salt march derive from the salt raids at Dharasana, in the weeks after the march reached the sea. In what can be described as a battlefront, activists moved forward and were met by native police, who beat them ruthlessly using wooden batons called *lathis*. Many of the activists were severely injured and taken away to hospital. This was a stern test of nonviolent discipline. The confrontations at Dharasana were dramatically portrayed in the film *Gandhi*.

How exactly did this acquiescence to brutal beatings help to undermine British rule? Some hints are available from Gandhi's comments at the time.

In his letter to Lord Irwin, 2 March 1930, Gandhi expounded on the British exploitation of India and said that 'the conviction is growing deeper and deeper in me that nothing but unadulterated non-violence can check the organized violence of the British Government.' He explained that 'my ambition is no less than to convert the British people through non-violence, and thus make them see the wrong they have done to India.' (Gandhi 1971: 6). Gandhi thus believed that nonviolence worked by converting the opponent.

Gandhi was also quite aware that violent attacks on nonviolent protesters could arouse widespread condemnation. In an interview with Associated Press of India on 10 April 1930, he said:

> In order to avoid needless injury, I advised the people to take only a handful of salt which could be contained in their closed fists and invited even women and children, if they had the courage to take part in the battle, and challenged the police to lay their hands upon women and children. If the police laid their hands upon women and children, I said that the whole of India would become inflamed, and resent the insult by inviting suffering of the same kind as they. The manner in which I expected Indians to respond to such an insult was by taking up other methods of civil resistance, and by students boycotting schools and Government servants giving up service by way of protest. There is no departure from my creed of non-violence, and I regard this snatching of salt from the civil resisters as a piece of barbarity. The greater the barbarity of the Government, the greater will be my call for self-suffering.
>
> (Gandhi 1971: 235–236).

Here Gandhi is committed to nonviolence and self-suffering, but with a powerful outcome if the British use violence: the 'inflaming' of India. Thus nonviolence, when met by violence, also worked by mobilizing the masses.

Gandhi was in no doubt that adherence to nonviolence was necessary for the struggle to be effective: 'In my humble opinion, a struggle so free from violence has a message far beyond the borders of India' (Gandhi 1971: 336). One of the dangers for the independence struggle, in his view, was violence by opponents of the British. Following 'disturbances' in Calcutta and Karachi, Gandhi wrote on 21 April 1930 that these were

> . . . most regrettable and interfere with the growth of the movement which is otherwise shaping itself marvellously well and gaining fresh momentum from day to day. . . . Violence is bound to impede the progress towards independence. I am unable to demonstrate how it will impede. Those who survive the struggle will know how.
>
> (Gandhi 1971: 296).

Gandhi thus knew that British violence, if used against nonviolent resisters, could arouse the masses, but violence by Indians would neutralize the effect. Therefore, for Gandhi 'popular violence is as much an obstruction in our path as the Government violence' (Gandhi 1971: 296).

I have selected quotes from Gandhi, during the period of the salt march, to suggest his views about how nonviolence works. In doing so, I have added more coherence to his ideas than are readily apparent in his prolific writings, which cover a vast range of topics. Gandhi was eloquent and emphatic in his commitment to nonviolence as a principled method of struggle, but he was not a systematic theorist. Nor was he a scholar who kept abreast of research findings.

At the level of practice, Gandhi saw himself as an experimentalist with nonviolence (Gandhi 1927/1929). In today's terms, this might be called a type of action research. But Gandhi did not report his findings in any organized way.

Gregg on nonviolence

In addition to probing Gandhi's writings and actions for insight into how nonviolence works, it is fruitful to turn to Gandhi's interpreters. One of the earliest and best was Richard Gregg, who closely studied Gandhi's campaigns. In his 1934 book *The Power of Nonviolence*, Gregg presented Gandhi's ideas in a way suited for Western audiences, in a systematic form backed up with references.

Gregg developed the concept of 'moral jiu-jitsu' to explain the core mechanism by which nonviolent action brings about change. In Gregg's view, using violence in response to violence was no challenge to moral values, but instead offered 'reassurance and moral support' (Gregg 1966: 43). Using nonviolence in response to violence, on the other hand, made the attacker lose moral balance, while the defender maintained moral balance. The term 'moral jiu-jitsu', by analogy with the sport of jiu-jitsu in which the energy of the opponent is turned against them, captured this dynamic. Moral jiu-jitsu is largely a psychological process which works by the nonviolent activist taking the initiative morally, not being surprised, avoiding anger and not being suggestible, causing opponents to become more suggestible. Gregg also noted that nonviolence, because it shows respect for the opponent's integrity, wins over onlookers. I will return to this important observation.

In Gregg's view, nonviolence worked primarily by affecting the psychology of the attacker. He said that nonviolence induced shame in the attacker. To induce this effect on the psychology of the attacker, activists had to adopt particular psychological states themselves: they had to suffer voluntarily, thereby demonstrating sincerity and deep commitment, and yet love their opponent. Loving the opponent was a central theme of Gandhi's. Gregg's genius was in capturing the essence of Gandhi's view, packaging it in a logical framework readily understandable to Western audiences.

The trouble with Gregg's formulation is that there was no evidence to back it up. Moral jiu-jitsu was a plausible explanation of the effectiveness of nonviolent action, but not the only possible explanation. More than half a century later, Thomas Weber (1993) examined the dynamics of the Dharasana salt raids and found that Gregg's explanation was inadequate. Weber noted that the Indian police wielding *lathis* against the nonresisting *satyagrahis* did not lose their moral balance. Or rather, even if they lost their moral balance, this did not affect their behaviour. Few of the police declined to carry out the repulsive job of beating the protesters. Indeed, a number of the police became angry at the lack of resistance and became even more energetic in their beatings.

Weber said that the impact of the salt raids largely came from their effect on third parties. A key to this was the reporting by U.S. journalist Webb Miller, who eloquently described the situation and the horrific beatings in stories that were published in hundreds of newspapers. Here are a few paragraphs from one of his key stories:

> Suddenly, at a word of command, scores of native police rushed upon the advancing marchers and rained blows on their heads with their steel-shod lathis. Not one of the marchers even raised an arm to fend off the blows. They went down like ten-pins. From where I stood I heard the sickening whacks of the clubs on unprotected skulls. The waiting crowd of watchers groaned and sucked in their breaths in sympathetic pain at every blow.
>
> Then another column formed while the leaders pleaded with them to retain their self-control. They marched slowly towards the police. Although every one knew that within a few minutes he would be beaten down, perhaps killed, I could detect no signs of waver-

ing or fear. They marched steadily with heads up, without the encouragement of music or cheering or any possibility that they might escape serious injury or death. The police rushed out and methodically and mechanically beat down the second column. There was no fight, no struggle: the marchers simply walked forward until struck down. There were no outcries, only groans after they fell. There were not enough stretcher-bearers to carry off the wounded; I saw eighteen injured being carried off simultaneously, while forty-two still lay bleeding on the ground awaiting stretcher-bearers. The blankets used as stretchers were sodden with blood.

At times the spectacle of unresisting men being methodically bashed into a bloody pulp sickened me so much that I had to turn away. The Western mind finds it difficult to grasp the idea of non-resistance. I felt an indefinable sense of helpless rage and loathing, almost as much against the men who were submitting unresistingly to being beaten as against the police wielding the clubs, and this despite the fact that when I came to India I sympathised with the Gandhi cause.

(Weber 1997: 444–445).

Weber noted the significant effect of the beatings on observers, both the immediate observer Miller and the readers of his eloquent prose. Nonviolence works through a psychological process, to be sure, but not quite in the way that Gandhi or Gregg believed. According to Weber's analysis, affecting audiences was the key to the success of the salt march. Gregg had noted the influence on onlookers, though he did not think this was the main effect.

Sharp on nonviolence

One of the many individuals inspired by Gandhi was Gene Sharp, a U.S. pacifist and researcher. Sharp systematized the study of nonviolent action. He looked at hundreds of cases and observed patterns. In his epic work *The Politics of Nonviolent Action* (1973), Sharp listed 198 methods of nonviolent action, from leaflets to parallel government, and classified them into three main types: protest and persuasion; noncooperation; and intervention. By examining numerous campaigns, he observed that they usually went through a series of stages which he called the 'dynamics of nonviolent action'. One of the stages he called 'political jiu-jitsu', a generalization of Gregg's moral jiu-jitsu.

The basic idea of political jiu-jitsu is that nonviolent action can work in several domains: the psychological domain (as postulated by Gregg) but also political, social and economic domains. Furthermore, nonviolent action works not just on opponents but also on the grievance group (the group of potential supporters of activists) and third parties.

In presenting political jiu-jitsu and documenting the effects of nonviolent action on opponents, the grievance group and third parties, Sharp used several historical examples, including 'Bloody Sunday' in St. Petersburg, Russia in 1905, the Russian revolution, resistance to the Nazis, and the East German revolt of 1953. In this context, Sharp commented on the salt raids as follows:

The nonviolent raids on the salt works at Dharasana . . . were deliberately planned by Gandhi with the knowledge that they would provoke extreme repression. He expected such repression to put the British *Raj* in a very bad light, strengthening the Indian position while weakening the British. Concerning this instance, J. C. Kumarappa has written: 'Dharasana raid was decided upon not to get salt, which was only the means. Our expectation was that the Government would open fire on unarmed crowds. . . . Our primary object was to show to the world at large the fangs and claws of the Government in all its ugliness and ferocity. In this we have succeeded beyond measure.'

(Sharp 1973: 687).

Sharp also referred to the 1919 Amritsar shootings as seriously counterproductive for the British.

Sharp's concept of political jiu-jitsu is valuable in pointing to the power of disciplined nonviolent action to cause a violent attack to rebound against the attacker through a variety of mechanisms, including influences on third parties and members of the grievance group. Weber's (1993) analysis of the salt march showed these mechanisms at work.

On the other hand, though the concept of political jiu-jitsu is more comprehensive than Gregg's moral jiu-jitsu, this comprehensiveness has a negative side: a lack of precision. In much of his work, Sharp was inclined to list lots of factors that could be involved, for example listing six sources of power and nine effects of nonviolent action on the nonviolent group. This approach is valuable for classificatory purposes but lacks the cogency and insight that can come with a more structured model.

Backfire and nonviolence

Inspired by the concept of political jiu-jitsu, I have sought to expand its range and power. The first step is to look at essential conditions for political jiu-jitsu. One of these is that people react with outrage to something. In the case of the Dharasana beatings, the outrage was over the injustice of brutal assaults on nonresisting protesters. Indeed, violent attacks against peaceful protesters, or against innocent victims generally, are a potent cause of outrage. This is why maintaining nonviolent discipline is such an important requirement for the effectiveness of nonviolent action: if even a little violence is used in response, this diffuses the outrage response. This condition is implicit in most discussions of nonviolent action.

A second essential condition for political jiu-jitsu is that information about the event be communicated to relevant audiences. [On communication and nonviolence, see Martin and Varney (2003).] This seems obvious enough, but in reality there are many cases where brutal assaults occur but few people know about them. Webb Miller's news reports about the Dharasana beatings were essential for political jiu-jitsu to occur.

Noting these two essential conditions, it is then possible to generalize the concept of political jiu-jitsu to events that do not involve nonviolent action. For example, censorship sometimes rebounds against the censors, generating more attention to the forbidden object, such as the *fatwa* against Salman Rushdie's book *The Satanic Verses*, which stimulated enormous interest in the book and mobilized many anti-censorship constituencies. Censorship involves violation of free speech, something that is valued in many societies. If information about the censorship is communicated to relevant audiences, a sort of jiu-jitsu process can occur.

To refer to this more general social jiu-jitsu process, I use the term 'backfire', to distinguish it from political jiu-jitsu, which refers to cases of violence against peaceful protesters. Backfire can be observed in censorship (Jansen and Martin 2003, 2004), defamation (Martin and Gray 2005), attacks on whistleblowers (Martin 2005a; Martin with Rifkin 2004), dismissal of academics (Martin 2004b, 2005b), police beatings (Martin 2005c), torture (Martin and Wright 2003), the attack on Iraq (Martin 2004a) and social movements (Hess and Martin 2006).

The second step in expanding the concept of political jiu-jitsu starts with the observation that some violent attacks on peaceful protesters do not cause outrage. For example, many massacres occurred in East Timor after the 1975 Indonesian occupation, but few led to repercussions for the occupiers. In other words, political jiu-jitsu is a contingent phenomenon rather than an automatic one. To find out why, it is useful to look at methods used by attackers that inhibit outrage. Examination of a wide range of cases reveals a diversity of methods, which for convenience can be grouped into five categories:

> Cover up the attack, hiding it from observers.
> Devalue the target.
> Reinterpret the attack, describing it as something else or as someone else's responsibility.
> Use official channels, such as authoritative pronouncements or official inquiries, that give the appearance of justice.
> Intimidate or bribe participants, thereby discouraging action against those responsible for the attack.

For example, torture is usually hidden. Torture victims may be labelled criminals or terrorists. The torture process may be said to be routine interrogation that does not harm the victim. Official investigations into judicial processes can be initiated to dampen concern. Threats to torturers, victims and witnesses discourage action.

Attention to methods that inhibit outrage naturally leads to attention to ways of overcoming these methods or, in other words, amplifying backfire. There are five obvious categories:

> Expose the attack.
> Validate the target.
> Interpret the attack as an injustice.
> Avoid or discredit official channels.
> Resist intimidation and bribery.

By examining methods of inhibiting or amplifying outrage, attention is drawn to backfire as a *process*, not just a potential outcome. Backfires are socially constructed, not inevitable consequences of injustice. By examining the construction processes, it is possible to learn how to be more effective in mobilizing action against injustice.

Sharp, in developing the concept of political jiu-jitsu as well as his other concepts for understanding the dynamics of nonviolent action, used a pragmatic approach, in which nonviolence is the method of choice because it is more effective than violence. This contrasted with Gandhi's approach of principled nonviolence. The concept of backfire builds on Sharp's pragmatic approach, probing the effectiveness of techniques used by parties in a struggle. But this is seldom a process of cool calculation, because it revolves around outrage, namely anger directed outwards against injustice. The sense of injustice is what also drives those who adhere to nonviolence for principled reasons.

It is now fruitful to return to the Dharasana salt raids using the lens of backfire. The two essential conditions for backfire were present. The first was perceived injustice, initially over the British salt monopoly but more acutely over the savage beatings of nonresisting protesters. The second condition was communication to relevant audiences, which was achieved internationally through Webb Miller's stories.

Next consider each of the five methods that attackers can use to inhibit outrage. The British attempted to *cover up* the beatings by imposition of press censorship throughout India. During the salt raids, they chased away journalists. They also tried to prevent Miller's stories getting out of the country, even though censorship laws did not apply to foreign correspondents. A Gandhi supporter alerted Miller that one of his cables had not been sent. Only after repeated protests was Miller able to have his story transmitted.

British officials *devalued* the protesters, for example by commenting that some of them requested a 'tap or two on the back of the legs' in order to obtain meal tickets and go home (Weber 1997: 453).

British *reinterpretation* of the events amounted to blatant lies: they claimed that there was no brutality by the police, that few protesters were hurt and that they were faking their injuries.

Official channels were involved when Gandhi and other independence leaders were arrested. The courts gave the appearance of justice, though the rules had been established by the British. The British government held a conference in London to seek a settlement with the independence movement, but, according to Weber (1997: 461), 'The negotiations yielded no tangible gains to the nationalist cause'.

Finally, the beatings and arrests served as a form of *intimidation* of those who might potentially join the protest. *Bribery* was implicit: those police and other officials who performed according to British requirements could expect to maintain their jobs and possibly obtain additional rewards.

The British thus used every one of the five methods for inhibiting outrage. But their efforts were unsuccessful, most importantly because Miller's stories breached the cover-up and communicated to a huge audience of potential sympathizers. British efforts to devalue the protesters had little success because of their nonviolent discipline. British lies about the beatings had little credibility in the face of Miller's stories. The use of the legal system to arrest and try Gandhi and others had little credibility to those with sympathy for the struggle. Indeed, the arrests were seen as an additional injustice. Intimidation and bribery undoubtedly reduced participation in the salt raids, but they had no impact on the readers of Miller's stories.

Conclusion

Gandhi showed through his campaigns that nonviolence could work to challenge injustice, but understanding how the process operates is complicated. Richard Gregg focused on conversion of attackers through direct psychological processes, but this is not backed up by observations. But Gregg came up with the concept of moral jiu-jitsu, which inspired Gene Sharp to develop his expanded concept of political jiu-jitsu. The key idea is that violence against peaceful protesters can be counterproductive as a result of support mobilized from opponents, the grievance group and third parties.

The next step of conceptual expansion is to look at the same jiu-jitsu process outside violence-vs-nonviolence scenarios, with a new frame: backfire. Backfires are contingent: attackers often act to prevent them and the opponents try to amplify them. This struggle over outcomes can be a social version of the struggles within an individual over how to respond to information about an unjust event (Bandura 1986: 375–389).

It should not be surprising that there is still much to learn by studying Gandhi's campaigns. In refining his approach over decades, and through his leadership of the Indian independence struggle, he and his team were able to mount campaigns that have a structural clarity that is ideal for research purposes. Furthermore, Gandhi's commitment to openness means there is ample material for investigation, at least on the side of the *satyagrahis*.

It is common to study Gandhi's campaigns, and other nonviolence struggles, either using their own terms or by using concepts from social science and psychology, such as social movement theory. But it is also possible to move in the other direction, namely to develop concepts inspired by study of nonviolent action and, by generalizing them, apply them to arenas outside of the nonviolence sphere. If people can understand personal experiences and world events through frames informed by nonviolence theory, then there is a much greater prospect for expanding the use of nonviolent action itself.

Acknowledgements

I thank Tom Weber for helpful discussions and Truda Gray for comments on a first draft of this paper. An earlier version of this paper was presented at the conference on Gandhi, Non-Violence and Modernity, 1–3 September 2004, Humanities Research Centre, Australian National University. This work is supported by the Australian Research Council.

References

Ackerman, Peter and Jack DuVall (2000), *A Force More Powerful: A Century of Nonviolent Conflict*, New York: St. Martin's Press.

Bandura, Albert (1986), *Social Foundations of Thought and Action: A Social Cognitive Theory*, Englewood Cliffs, NJ: Prentice Hall.

Dalton, Dennis (1993), *Mahatma Gandhi: Nonviolent Power in Action*, New York: Columbia University Press.

Elkins, Caroline (2005), *Imperial Reckoning: The Untold Story of Britain's Gulag in Kenya*, New York: Henry Holt.

Fukuda, Chisako M. (2000), 'Peace through nonviolent action: the East Timorese resistance movement's strategy for engagement', *Pacifica Review*, Vol. 12, No. 1, pp. 17–31.

Gandhi, M. K. (1927/1929), *An Autobiography or the Story of My Experiments with Truth*, Ahmedabad: Navajivan.

Gandhi, M. K. (1971), *The Collected Works of Mahatma Gandhi*, XLIII (March–June 1930), New Delhi: Publications Division, Ministry of Information and Broadcasting, Government of India.

Gregg, Richard B. (1966), *The Power of Nonviolence*, New York: Schocken.

Hess, David and Brian Martin (2006), 'Backfire, repression, and the theory of transformative events', *Mobilization*, in press.

Jansen, Sue Curry and Brian Martin (2003), 'Making censorship backfire', *Counterpoise*, Vol. 7, No. 3, pp. 5–15.

Jansen, Sue Curry and Brian Martin (2004), 'Exposing and opposing censorship: backfire dynamics in freedom-of-speech struggles', *Pacific Journalism Review*, Vol. 10, No. 1, pp. 29–45.

Martin, Brian (2004a), 'Iraq attack backfire', *Economic and Political Weekly*, Vol. 39, No. 16, 17–23 April, pp. 1577–1583.

Martin, Brian (2004b), 'The Richardson dismissal as an academic boomerang', in Kenneth Westhues (ed.), *Workplace Mobbing in Academe* (Lewiston, NY: Edwin Mellen Press), pp. 317–330.

Martin, Brian (2005a), 'Bucking the system: Andrew Wilkie and the difficult task of the whistleblower', *Overland*, No. 180 (Spring), pp. 45–48.

Martin, Brian (2005b), 'Boomerangs of academic freedom', *Workplace: A Journal for Academic Labor*, Vol. 6, No. 2.

Martin, Brian (2005c), 'The beating of Rodney King: the dynamics of backfire', *Critical Criminology*, in press.

Martin, Brian and Truda Gray (2005), 'How to make defamation threats and actions backfire', *Australian Journalism Review*, Vol. 27, No. 1, pp. 157–166.

Martin, Brian with Will Rifkin (2004), 'The dynamics of employee dissent: whistleblowers and organizational jiu-jitsu', *Public Organization Review*, Vol. 4, pp. 221–238.

Martin, Brian and Wendy Varney (2003), *Nonviolence Speaks: Communicating against Repression*, Cresskill, NJ: Hampton Press.

Martin, Brian and Steve Wright (2003), 'Countershock: mobilising resistance to electroshock weapons', *Medicine, Conflict and Survival*, Vol. 19, No. 3, July–September, pp. 205–222.

Schock, Kurt (2005), *Unarmed Insurrections: People Power Movements in Nondemocracies*, Minneapolis, MN: University of Minnesota Press.

Semelin, Jacques (1993), *Unarmed Against Hitler: Civilian Resistance in Europe 1939–1943*, Westport, CT: Praeger.

Sharp, Gene (1973), *The Politics of Nonviolent Action*, Boston: Porter Sargent.

Stoltzfus, Nathan (1996), *Resistance of the Heart: Intermarriage and the Rosenstrasse Protest in Nazi Germany*, New York: Norton.

Weber, Thomas (1993), '"The marchers simply walked forward until struck down": nonviolent suffering and conversion', *Peace and Change* 18, 267–289.

Weber, Thomas (1997), *On the Salt March: The Historiography of Gandhi's March to Dandi*, New Delhi: HarperCollins.

Zunes, Stephen (1999), 'The role of non-violent action in the downfall of apartheid', *Journal of Modern African Studies*, Vol. 37, No. 1, pp. 137–169.

33 From dictatorship to democracy

A conceptual framework for liberation

Gene Sharp

Dictatorships usually exist primarily because of the internal power distribution in the home country. The population and society are too weak to cause the dictatorship serious problems, wealth and power are concentrated in too few hands. Although dictatorships may benefit from or be somewhat weakened by international actions, their continuation is dependent primarily on internal factors.

International pressures can be very useful, however, when they are supporting a powerful internal resistance movement. Then, for example, international economic boycotts, embargoes, the breaking of diplomatic relations, expulsion from international organizations, condemnation by United Nations bodies, and the like can assist greatly. However, in the absence of a strong internal resistance movement such actions by others are unlikely to happen.

Facing the hard truth

The conclusion is a hard one. When one wants to bring down a dictatorship most effectively and with the least cost then one has four immediate tasks:

- One must strengthen the oppressed population themselves in their determination, self-confidence, and resistance skills;
- One must strengthen the independent social groups and institutions of the oppressed people;
- One must create a powerful internal resistance force; and
- One must develop a wise grand strategic plan for liberation and implement it skillfully.

A liberation struggle is a time for self-reliance and internal strengthening of the struggle group. As Charles Stewart Parnell called out during the Irish rent strike campaign in 1879 and 1880:

> It is no use relying on the Government . . . You must only rely upon your own determination . . . [H]elp yourselves by standing together . . . strengthen those amongst yourselves who are weak . . ., band yourselves together, organize yourselves . . . and you must win . . .
>
> When you have made this question ripe for settlement, then and not till then will it be settled.[1]

Against a strong self-reliant force, given wise strategy, disciplined and courageous action, and genuine strength, the dictatorship will eventually crumble. Minimally, however, the above four requirements must be fulfilled.

As the above discussion indicates, liberation from dictatorships ultimately depends on the people's ability to liberate themselves. The cases of successful political defiance – or nonviolent struggle for political ends – cited above indicate that the means do exist for populations to free themselves, but that option has remained undeveloped. [. . .]

"Agreeable" dictators

Dictators may have a variety of motives and objectives underlying their domination: power, position, wealth, reshaping the society, and the like. One should remember that none of these will be served if they abandon their control positions. In the event of negotiations dictators will try to preserve their goals.

Whatever promises offered by dictators in any negotiated settlement, no one should ever forget that the dictators may promise anything to secure submission from their democratic opponents, and then brazenly violate those same agreements.

If the democrats agree to halt resistance in order to gain a reprieve from repression, they may be very disappointed. A halt to resistance rarely brings reduced repression. Once the restraining force of internal and international opposition has been removed, dictators may even make their oppression and violence more brutal than before. The collapse of popular resistance often removes the countervailing force that has limited the control and brutality of the dictatorship. The tyrants can then move ahead against whomever: they wish. "For the tyrant has the power to inflict only that which we lack the strength to resist," wrote Krishnalal Shridharani.[2]

Resistance, not negotiations, is essential for change in conflicts where fundamental issues are at stake. In nearly all cases, resistance must continue to drive dictators out of power. Success is most often determined not by negotiating a settlement but through the wise use of the most appropriate and powerful means of resistance available. It is our contention, that political defiance, or nonviolent struggle, is the most powerful means available to those struggling for freedom.

What kind of peace?

If dictators and democrats are to talk about peace at all, extremely clear thinking is needed because of the dangers involved. Not everyone who uses the word "peace" wants peace with freedom and justice. Submission to cruel oppression and passive acquiescence to ruthless dictators who have perpetrated atrocities on hundreds of thousands of people is no real peace. Hitler often called for peace, by which he meant submission to his will. A dictators' peace is often no more than the peace of the prison or of the grave.

There are other dangers. Well-intended negotiators sometimes confuse the objectives of the negotiations and the negotiation process itself. Further, democratic negotiators, or foreign negotiation specialists accepted to assist in the negotiations, may in a single stroke provide the dictators with the domestic and international legitimacy that they had been previously denied because of their seizure of the state, human rights violations, and brutalities. Without that desperately needed legitimacy, the dictators cannot continue to rule indefinitely. Exponents of peace should not provide them legitimacy.

Reasons for hope

As stated earlier, opposition leaders may feel forced to pursue negotiations out of a sense of hopelessness of the democratic struggle. However, that sense of powerlessness can be changed.

Dictatorships are not permanent. People living under dictatorships need not remain weak, and dictators need not be allowed to remain powerful indefinitely. Aristotle noted long ago, ". . . [O]ligarchy and tyranny are shorter-lived than any other constitution . . . [A]ll round, tyrannies have not lasted long."[3] Modern dictatorships are also vulnerable. Their weaknesses can be aggravated and the dictators' power can be disintegrated.

Recent history shows the vulnerability of dictatorships, and reveals that they can crumble in a relatively short time span: whereas ten years – 1980–1990 – were required to bring down the Communist dictatorship in Poland, in East Germany and Czechoslovakia in 1989 it occurred within weeks. In El Salvador and Guatemala in 1944 the struggles against the entrenched brutal military dictators required approximately two weeks each. The militarily powerful regime of the Shah in Iran was undermined in a few months. The Marcos dictatorship in the Philippines fell before people power within weeks in 1986: the United States government quickly abandoned President Marcos when the strength of the opposition became apparent. The attempted hard-line coup in the Soviet Union in August 1991 was blocked in days by political defiance. Thereafter, many of its long dominated constituent nations in only days, weeks, and months regained their independence.

The old preconception that violent means always work quickly and nonviolent means always require vast time is clearly not valid. Although much time may be required for changes in the underlying situation and society, the actual fight against a dictatorship sometimes occurs relatively quickly by nonviolent struggle. [. . .]

Niccolo Machiavelli had much earlier argued that the prince ". . . who has the public as a whole for his enemy can never make himself secure; and the greater his cruelty, the weaker does his regime become."[4]

The practical political application of these insights was demonstrated by the heroic Norwegian resisters against the Nazi occupation, and by the brave Poles, Germans, Czechs, Slovaks, and many others who resisted Communist aggression and dictatorship, and finally helped produce the collapse of Communist rule in Europe. This, of course, is no new phenomenon: cases of nonviolent resistance go back at least to 494 B.C. when plebeians withdrew cooperation from their Roman patrician masters.[5] Nonviolent struggle has been employed at various times by peoples throughout Asia, Africa, the Americas, Australasia, and the Pacific islands, as well as Europe.

Three of the most important factors in determining to what degree a government's power will be controlled or uncontrolled therefore are: (1) the relative *desire* of the populace to impose limits on the government's power; (2) the relative *strength* of the subjects' independent organizations and institutions to withdraw collectively the sources of power; and (3) the population's relative *ability* to withhold their consent and assistance.

The workings of nonviolent struggle

Like military capabilities, political defiance can be employed for a variety of purposes, ranging from efforts to influence the opponents to take different actions, to create conditions for a peaceful resolution of conflict, or to disintegrate the opponents' regime. However, political defiance operates in quite different ways from violence. Although both techniques are means to wage struggle, they do so with very different means and with different consequences. The ways and results of violent conflict are well known. Physical weapons are used to intimidate, injure, kill, and destroy.

Nonviolent struggle is a much more complex and varied means of struggle than is violence. Instead, the struggle is fought by psychological, social, economic, and political weapons applied by the population and the institutions of the society. These have been known under various names of protests, strikes, noncooperation, boycotts, disaffection, and people power. All governments can rule only as long as they receive replenishment of the needed sources of their power from the cooperation, submission, and obedience of the population and the institutions of the society. Political defiance, unlike violence, is uniquely suited to severing those sources of power.

Nonviolent weapons and discipline

The common error of past improvised political defiance campaigns is the reliance on only one or two methods, such as strikes and mass demonstrations. In fact, a multitude of methods exist that allow resistance strategists to concentrate and disperse resistance as required.

About two hundred specific methods of nonviolent action have been identified, and there are certainly scores more. These methods are classified under three broad categories: protest and persuasion, noncooperation, and intervention. Methods of nonviolent protest and persuasion are largely symbolic demonstrations, including parades, marches, and vigils (54 methods). Noncooperation is divided into three sub-categories: (a) social noncooperation (16 methods), (b) economic noncooperation, including boycotts (26 methods) and strikes (23 methods), and (c) political noncooperation (38 methods). Nonviolent intervention, by psychological, physical, social, economic, or political means, such as the fast, nonviolent occupation, and parallel government (41 methods), is the final group. A list of 198 of these methods is included as the Appendix to this publication.

The use of a considerable number of these methods – carefully chosen, applied persistently and on a large scale, wielded in the context of a wise strategy and appropriate tactics, by trained civilians – is likely to cause any illegitimate regime severe problems. This applies to all dictatorships.

In contrast to military means, the methods of nonviolent struggle can be focused directly on the issues at stake. For example, since the issue of dictatorship is primarily political, then political forms of nonviolent struggle would be crucial. These would include denial of legitimacy to the dictators and noncooperation with their regime. Noncooperation would also be applied against specific policies. At times stalling and procrastination may be quietly and even secretly practiced, while at other times open disobedience and defiant public demonstrations and strikes may be visible to all.

On the other hand, if the dictatorship is vulnerable to economic pressures or if many of the popular grievances against it are economic, then economic action, such as boycotts or strikes, may be appropriate resistance methods. The dictators' efforts to exploit the economic system might be met with limited general strikes, slowdowns, and refusal of assistance by (or disappearance of) indispensable experts. Selective use of various types of strikes may be conducted at key points in manufacturing, in transport in the supply of raw materials, and in the distribution of products.

Some methods of nonviolent struggle require people to perform acts unrelated to their normal lives, such as distributing leaflets, operating an underground press, going on hunger strike, or sitting down in the streets. These methods may be difficult for some people to undertake except in very extreme situations.

Other methods of nonviolent struggle instead require people to continue approximately their normal lives, though in somewhat different ways. For example, people may report for work, instead of striking, but then deliberately work more slowly or inefficiently than usual. "Mistakes" may be consciously made more frequently. One may become "sick" and "unable" to work at certain times. Or, one may simply refuse to work. One might go to religious services when the act expresses not only religious but also political convictions. One may act to protect children from the attackers' propaganda by education at home or in illegal classes. One might refuse to join certain "recommended" or required organizations that one would not have joined freely in earlier times. The similarity of such types of action to people's usual activities and the limited degree of departure from their normal lives may make participation in the national liberation struggle much easier for many people.

Since nonviolent struggle and violence operate in fundamentally different ways, even limited resistance violence during a political defiance campaign will be counterproductive, for it will shift the struggle to one in which the dictators have an overwhelming advantage (military warfare). Nonviolent discipline is a key to success and must be maintained despite provocations and brutalities by the dictators and their agents.

The maintenance of nonviolent discipline against violent opponents facilitates the workings of the four mechanisms of change in nonviolent struggle. Nonviolent discipline is also extremely important in the process of political jiu-jitsu. In this process the stark brutality of the regime against the clearly nonviolent actionists politically rebounds against the dictators' position, causing dissention in their own ranks as well as fomenting support for the resisters among the general population, the regime's usual supporters, and third parties.

In some cases, however, limited violence against the dictatorship may be inevitable. Frustration and hatred of the regime may explode into violence. Or, certain groups may be unwilling to abandon violent means even though they recognize the important role of nonviolent struggle. In these cases, political defiance does not need to be abandoned. However, it will be necessary to separate the violent action as far as possible from the nonviolent action. This should be done in terms of geography, population groups, timing, and issues. Otherwise the violence could have a disastrous effect on the potentially much more powerful and successful use of political defiance.

The historical record indicates that while casualties in dead and wounded must be expected in political defiance, they will be far fewer than the casualties in military warfare. Furthermore, this type of struggle does not contribute to the endless cycle of killing and brutality.

Nonviolent struggle both requires and tends to produce a loss (or greater control) of fear of the government and its violent repression. That abandonment or control of fear is a key element in destroying the power of the dictators over the general population.

[...]

Four mechanisms of change

Nonviolent struggle produces change in four ways. The first mechanism is the least likely, though it has occurred. When members of the opponent group are emotionally moved by the suffering of repression imposed on courageous nonviolent resisters or are rationally persuaded that the resisters' cause is just, they may come to accept the resisters' aims. This mechanism is called conversion. Though cases of *conversion* in nonviolent action do sometimes happen, they are rare, and in most conflicts this does not occur at all or at least not on a significant scale.

Far more often, nonviolent struggle operates by changing the conflict situation and the society so that the opponents simply cannot do as they like. It is this change that produces the other three mechanisms: accommodation, nonviolent coercion, and disintegration. Which of these occurs depends on the degree to which the relative and absolute power relations are shifted in favor of the democrats.

If the issues are not fundamental ones, the demands of the opposition in a limited campaign are not considered threatening, and the contest of forces has altered the power relationships to some degree, the immediate conflict may be ended by reaching an agreement, a splitting of differences or compromise. This mechanism is called *accommodation*. Many strikes are settled in this manner, for example, with both sides attaining some of their objectives but neither achieving all it wanted. A government may perceive such a settlement to have some positive benefits, such as defusing tension, creating an impression of "fairness," or polishing the international image of the regime. It is important, therefore, that great care be exercised in selecting the issues on which a settlement by accommodation is acceptable. A struggle to bring down a dictatorship is not one of these.

Nonviolent struggle can be much more powerful than indicated by the mechanisms of conversion or accommodation. Mass noncooperation and defiance can so change social and political situations, especially power relationships, that the dictators' ability to control the economic, social, and political processes of government and the society is in fact taken away. The opponents' military forces may become so unreliable that they no longer simply obey orders to repress resisters. Although the opponents' leaders remain in their positions, and adhere to their original goals, their ability to act effectively has been taken away from them. That is called *nonviolent coercion*.

In some extreme situations, the conditions producing nonviolent coercion are carried still further. The opponents' leadership in fact loses all ability to act and their own structure of power collapses. The resisters' self-direction, noncooperation, and defiance become so complete that the opponents now lack even a semblance of control over them. The opponents' bureaucracy refuses to obey its own leadership. The opponents' troops and police mutiny. The opponents' usual supporters or population repudiate their former leadership, denying that they have any right to rule at all. Hence, their former assistance and obedience falls away. The fourth mechanism of change, *disintegration* of the opponents' system, is so complete that they do not even have sufficient power to surrender. The regime simply falls to pieces.

In planning liberation strategies, these four mechanisms should be kept in mind. They sometimes operate essentially by chance. However, the selection of one or more of these as the intended mechanism of change in a conflict will make it possible to formulate specific and mutually reinforcing strategies. Which mechanism (or mechanisms) to select will depend on numerous factors, including the absolute and relative power of the contending groups and the attitudes and objectives of the nonviolent struggle group.

Appendix One

The methods of nonviolent action

The methods of nonviolent protest and persuasion

Formal statements

1. Public speeches
2. Letters of opposition or support
3. Declarations by organizations and institutions
4. Signed public statements
5. Declarations of indictment and intention
6. Group or mass petitions

Communications with a wider audience

7. Slogans, caricatures, and symbols
8. Banners, posters, and displayed communications
9. Leaflets, pamphlets, and books
10. Newspapers and journals
11. Records, radio, and television
12. Skywriting and earthwriting

Group representations

13. Deputations
14. Mock awards
15. Group lobbying
16. Picketing
17. Mock elections

Symbolic public acts

18. Display of flags and symbolic colors
19. Wearing of symbols
20. Prayer and worship
21. Delivering symbolic objects
22. Protest disrobings
23. Destruction of own property
24. Symbolic lights
25. Displays of portraits
26. Paint as protest
27. New signs and names
28. Symbolic sounds
29. Symbolic reclamations
30. Rude gestures

Pressures on individuals

31. "Haunting" officials
32. Taunting officials
33. Fraternization
34. Vigils

Drama and music

35. Humorous skits and pranks
36. Performance of plays and music
37. Singing

Processions

38. Marches
39. Parades

40. Religious processions
41. Pilgrimages
42. Motorcades

Honoring the dead

43. Political mourning
44. Mock funerals
45. Demonstrative funerals
46. Homage at burial places

Public assemblies

47. Assemblies of protest or support
48. Protest meetings
49. Camouflaged meetings of protest
50. Teach-ins

Withdrawal and renunciation

51. Walk-outs
52. Silence
53. Renouncing honors
54. Turning one's back

The methods of social noncooperation

Ostracism of persons

55. Social boycott
56. Selective social boycott
57. Lysistratic nonaction
58. Excommunication
59. Interdict

Noncooperation with social events, customs, and institutions

60. Suspension of social and sports activities
61. Boycott of social affairs
62. Student strike
63. Social disobedience
64. Withdrawal from social institutions

Withdrawal from the social system

65. Stay-at-home
66. Total personal noncooperation
67. Flight of workers

68. Sanctuary
69. Collective disappearance
70. Protest emigration *(hijrat)*

The methods of economic noncooperation: (1) economic boycotts

Action by consumers

71. Consumers' boycott
72. Nonconsumption of boycotted goods
73. Policy of austerity
74. Rent withholding
75. Refusal to rent
76. National consumers' boycott
77. International consumers' boycott

Action by workers and producers

78. Workmen's boycott
79. Producers' boycott

Action by middlemen

80. Suppliers' and handlers' boycott

Action by owners and management

81. Traders' boycott
82. Refusal to let or sell property
83. Lockout
84. Refusal of industrial assistance
85. Merchants' "general strike"

Action by holders of financial resources

86. Withdrawal of bank deposits
87. Refusal to pay fees, dues, and assessments
88. Refusal to pay debts or interest
89. Severance of funds and credit
90. Revenue refusal
91. Refusal of a government's money

Action by governments

92. Domestic embargo
93. Blacklisting of traders
94. International sellers' embargo

   95. International buyers' embargo
   96. International trade embargo

The methods of economic noncooperation: (2) the strike

Symbolic strikes

   97. Protest strike
   98. Quickie walkout (lightning strike)

Agricultural strikes

   99. Peasant strike
100. Farm workers' strike

Strikes by special groups

101. Refusal of impressed labor
102. Prisoners' strike
103. Craft strike
104. Professional strike

Ordinary industrial strikes

105. Establishment strike
106. Industry strike
107. Sympathetic strike

Restricted strikes

108. Detailed strike
109. Bumper strike
110. Slowdown strike
111. Working-to-rule strike
112. Reporting "sick" (sick-in)
113. Strike by resignation
114. Limited strike
115. Selective strike

Multi-industry strikes

116. Generalized strike
117. General strike

Combinations of strikes and economic closures

118. Hartal
119. Economic shutdown

The methods of political noncooperation

Rejection of authority

120. Withholding or withdrawal of allegiance
121. Refusal of public support
122. Literature and speeches advocating resistance

Citizens' noncooperation with government

123. Boycott of legislative bodies
124. Boycott of elections
125. Boycott of government employment and positions
126. Boycott of government departments, agencies and other bodies
127. Withdrawal from government educational institutions
128. Boycott of government-supported organizations
129. Refusal of assistance to enforcement agents
130. Removal of own signs and placemarks
131. Refusal to accept appointed officials
132. Refusal to dissolve existing institutions

Citizens' alternatives to obedience

133. Reluctant and slow compliance
134. Nonobedience in absence of direct supervision
135. Popular nonobedience
136. Disguised disobedience
137. Refusal of an assemblage or meeting to disperse
138. Sitdown
139. Noncooperation with conscription and deportation
140. Hiding, escape and false identities
141. Civil disobedience of "illegitimate" laws

Action by government personnel

142. Selective refusal of assistance by government aides
143. Blocking of lines of command and information
144. Stalling and obstruction
145. General administrative noncooperation
146. Judicial noncooperation
147. Deliberate inefficiency and selective noncooperation by enforcement agents
148. Mutiny

Domestic governmental action

149. Quasi-legal evasions and delays
150. Noncooperation by constituent governmental units

International governmental action

151. Changes in diplomatic and other representation
152. Delay and cancellation of diplomatic events
153. Withholding of diplomatic recognition
154. Severance of diplomatic relations
155. Withdrawal from international organizations
156. Refusal of membership in international bodies
157. Expulsion from international organizations

The methods of nonviolent intervention

Psychological intervention

158. Self-exposure to the elements
159. The fast

    (a) Fast of moral pressure
    (b) Hunger strike
    (c) Satyagrahic fast

160. Reverse trial
161. Nonviolent harassment

Physical intervention

162. Sit-in
163. Stand-in
164. Ride-in
165. Wade-in
166. Mill-in
167. Pray-in
168. Nonviolent raids
169. Nonviolent air raids
170. Nonviolent invasion
171. Nonviolent interjection
172. Nonviolent obstruction
173. Nonviolent occupation

Social intervention

174. Establishing new social patterns
175. Overloading of facilities
176. Stall-in
177. Speak-in
178. Guerrilla theater
179. Alternative social institutions
180. Alternative communication system

Economic intervention

181. Reverse strike
182. Stay-in strike
183. Nonviolent land seizure
184. Defiance of blockades
185. Politically motivated counterfeiting
186. Preclusive purchasing
187. Seizure of assets
188. Dumping
189. Selective patronage
190. Alternative markets
191. Alternative transportation systems
192. Alternative economic institutions

Political intervention

193. Overloading of administrative systems
194. Disclosing identities of secret agents
195. Seeking imprisonment
196. Civil disobedience of "neutral" laws
197. Work-on without collaboration
198. Dual sovereignty and parallel government

Notes

1 Patrick Sarsfield O'Hegarty, *A History of Ireland Under the Union, 1880–1922* (London: Methuen, 1952), pp. 490–491.
2 Krishnalal Shridharani, *War Without Violence: A Study of Gandhi's Method and Its Accomplishments* (New York: Harcourt, Brace, 1939, and reprint New York and London: Garland Publishing, 1972), p. 260.
3 Aristotle, *The Politics,* transl. by T. A. Sinclair (Harmondsworth, Middlesex, England and Baltimore, Maryland: Penguin Books 1976 [1962]), Book V, Chapter 12, pp. 231 and 232.
4 Niccolo Machiavelli, "The Discourses on the First Ten Books of Livy," in *The Discourses of Niccolo Machiavelli* (London: Routledge and Kegan Paul, 1950), Vol. I, p. 254.
5 See Gene Sharp, *The Politics of Nonviolent Action* (Boston: Porter Sargent, 1973), p. 75 and passim for other historical examples.

34 Nonviolent revolutionary movements

Jørgen Johansen

The history of nonviolence goes back hundreds if not thousands of years. Several philosophical, political and religious traditions have strong elements of nonviolence in their theories and practice.[1] Library shelves are filled with books on the wars in our history, yet it is close to impossible to find books on the history of peace. Historians seem to regard peace as something that can be found between wars, but barely a topic in itself. In the modern media we all 'know' that a story is not worth covering if it doesn't involve violence. Most journalists and academics lack interest in and understanding of nonviolence. The result is meagre coverage and a focus on nonviolence.

Nonviolent revolution

My focus is on some of those movements that have confronted governments and parliaments and demanded changes in leadership. These movements have gotten different labels depending on who they are and who is using the terminology, from 'terrorists' to 'democratic movements'. Between those extremes we find terms like 'paramilitaries', 'rebels', 'freedom fighters', 'guerrillas' and 'opposition'. Often the same movement receives many of these labels at the same time from different quarters. This labelling is part of the political rhetoric included in the conflicts.

I focus on movements that do not use violent means in their struggle and that have been successful in toppling the leadership of a country.

I am not evaluating the consequences of changing the leadership in a country. Cases are included only because the former regime resigned; I do not judge what replaced them. To include short- and long-term consequences will be an important follow-up of the present research.

I exclude all movements that follow constitutional procedures. Cases where movements have used ordinary channels such as elections, referendums or other conventional political tools within the system of law are consequently excluded. I also exclude all forms of coups d'état by elitist groups, which is the most common type of non-constitutional regime change. Most coups d'état are even carried out with few or no casualties.[2]

Nonviolence

There is little agreement on the definition of the concept 'nonviolent revolution'. Both 'revolution' and 'nonviolence' are controversial terms, separately, and, of course, when they are used together. Dave Dellinger wrote in his 1965 essay, 'The Future of Nonviolence', that 'the theory and practice of active nonviolence are roughly at the stage of development today as those of electricity in the early days of Marconi and Edison' (Dellinger, 1971, p. 368).[3]

In the framework I am using here, 'nonviolence' is used as a political tool. It is not primarily a philosophy or lifestyle but a number of activities used by individuals and groups in order to influence a conflict. This form of nonviolence could be seen in Poland from 1980 to 1989, when the trade union Solidarity challenged the role of the Communist Party and its leadership. Solidarity's strategy did not include the use of violence against other human beings. They decided for strategic reasons to use nonviolence. If they took up arms, they knew the state was stronger and could easily justify the use of massive force against armed rebellions.

There is a widespread view that in most conflicts there are only two or three actors. Typical examples are the conflicts in Kashmir, Colombia and the Middle East. Seen from a distance or through the lens of the mainstream media, it is indeed difficult to recognize more than a few actors. Kashmir is presented as a conflict between India and Pakistan. The war in Colombia is described as the government against Marxist drug-financed guerrillas. In Palestine, the mainstream media often explain the situation as a conflict between Israel and Palestine. But anyone who spends time in these areas will easily identify many more actors.[4] By 'actor' I mean an individual or a group that influences the conflict and that has its own distinct agenda.[5] In most micro-, and all meso-, macro- and mega-scale conflicts, the majority of actors and activities/means are not violent. Even in the midst of the most violent conflict, one will always find nonviolent actors and nonviolent activities. It is not exceptional to find that the numbers of actors is more than 20 in such conflicts, and most do not use violence. The tendency to limit the number of actors when describing a conflict creates a number of difficulties for those who want to understand or act in the conflict. All important actors need to be recognized in order to understand the process in the conflicts.

Most political actors never use violent means, and those who do also have a number of nonviolent means in their toolbox.[6] Should a few actors using violent means on some occasions be enough to label the whole movement violent? Or does it depend on who is using the violent means? I argue that those actors with wide popular support who are opposing the present situation should be the ones to determine whether the conflict is violent or not. Even in these bloodspattered conflicts, most successful acts by non-state actors should be labelled nonviolent.[7]

The situations where the opposition has access to arms but has promised not to use them are more complicated. That was the situation in Serbia when Milosevic was forced to step down in October 2000.

Revolution

The main difference between a political revolution and a social one is that the victorious forces in the first achieve their political goals by taking over state power, while in the second, the winners take power as a means to either achieve or secure broader socio-economic goals. Peralta argues that for a socio-political change to be labelled revolutionary it must be comprehensive, thorough and deep within the society. It is not enough to have an insurgency that ends after minimal changes have been achieved, like a government that resigns or a change of a law. A social revolution is dependent on a political revolution, but a political revolution does not require a social revolution (Peralta, 1990).[8]

Here, revolution means a non-constitutional process of changing the political leadership of a country; this is a typical political revolution that does not necessarily include significant social change. The process is relatively quick, and it is not part of a constitutional process. The changes at the top of the political pyramid may influence the rest of society; the possible changes may be intentional or not. And they may come as an immediate result of the new leadership or as a delayed consequence.

Complexity

Revolutionary conflicts are, like most societal conflicts, extremely complex.[9] The number of factors influencing their outcome is very high. Some factors and actors are external, while others are internal. Some factors are necessary, while others are not that important to the outcome. Probably none of them are sufficient by themselves for a change to occur. Grix discusses different factors and their importance (Grix, 2000),[10] and his analysis of East Germany has a general relevance for similar cases. He discusses the collapse of the GDR (the former German Democratic Republic), and categorizes changes in five broad, interlinked groups, to which he gives the following labels:

- Foreign policy-based approach/external factors
- Economic/systemic approach
- Elite intransigence approach
- Revolution or no revolution?
- Legitimacy deficit/opposition

Each of these approaches produces a distinct set of questions. To get a fuller picture of the revolutionary process and to understand the entire process and its results, each of these approaches is important. Together these approaches may produce a more comprehensive picture of the complete process of political change.

The use of nonviolence is certainly one aspect that plays an important role. In some cases, that may have been the only factor that was required for a regime change to take place. If that is the case, then one must examine the reasons that masses of people were willing to mobilize. In other words, there is a need to explain why large groups of people take to the streets with common demands and goals. Here the answers will be almost as complex as the revolutions themselves.

The waves of nonviolence

The types of revolutions described and discussed here have grown in numbers in the last 30 years.[11]

In the last 30 years we have seen six waves of such revolutions.

1   Poland, Bolivia, Uruguay and the Philippines
2   Czechoslovakia, DDR, Hungary, Bulgaria, Latvia, Estonia, Lithuania, Russia
3   Francophone Sub-Saharan Africa: Benin, Burkina Faso, Guinea, Senegal, Mali, Malawi, Madagascar
4   Serbia, Georgia, Ukraine, Kyrgyzstan, Lebanon
5   Iceland, Latvia, Hungary, . . .
6   Tunisia, Egypt, . . .

This list is not complete but gives an indication of how frequent such revolutions are. In the first wave the Catholic Church played an important role. In the next, the former East European block collapsed. The third started in Benin, as former French colonies celebrated the 300th anniversary of 1789. Then followed what was labelled the 'Coloured Revolutions'. Wave number five was a direct result of ordinary peoples' reactions to the financial crisis and the speculative collapsing economy. The last wave started in Tunis and is still going on as this text is being written.

Some of the cases were in the headlines for days when the escalation of the conflict reached its peak, but most of them were hardly mentioned, and none were described in such a way that the reader, listener or viewer of newspapers, radios, websites or TV news could get more than a superficial understanding of what was going on. In some of these cases, good research was done. Most of the cases, however, still have not been examined and studied systematically and methodically enough to get a good understanding of what happened. English-language publications on the nonviolent revolution in Benin 1990 and the other earlier French colonies to follow are typically few in number.

The following are a few illustrative cases and a more complete list can be found in 'Waves of Nonviolence and the New Revolutionary Movements'.[12]

Poland 1980–1989

After two centuries of armed uprising, Polish workers tried to fight the regime in 1980 with unarmed means (Garton Ash, 1991; Karpinski, 1982; Lukowski and Zawadzki, 2006).[13]

After the turmoil in 1956 in Poland and Hungary, the workers movement was just waiting for an opportunity to resurface. Jacek Kuron's 1964 'Open Letter to the Members of the Polish United Workers Party' challenged the system and influenced underground discussions (Weber and Brust, 1989, pp. 57–90).[14] In both December 1970 and June 1976, revolutionary attempts were made, but without the necessary momentum. The Committee in Defence of Workers (KOR) was one important result of the discussion. (Blumsztajn et al., 1986, pp. 73–91).[15] What Jane Leftwich Curry calls 'Poland's permanent revolution' changed its strategy in 1980 and went public with strikes (Curry and Fajfer, 1996).[16] After many discussions, a network of groups and organizations became better structured. The Catholic Church and the Polish pope, John Paul II, played crucial roles in inspiring individuals in the years ahead. The visit by the Pope to Poland in June 1979 mobilized some of the largest gatherings ever in Poland. None doubted the Pope's critical view of communism.

Solidarity was also famous for its use of symbols in its struggle. Not only the flag and the Catholic cross but also a number of monuments and historic dates were used to express Solidarity's views in times of censorship.[17] On July 1, 1980, localized strikes broke out all over Poland due to a government decree that raised meat prices by almost 100 percent.[18] In August 1980, the Gdansk Strike Committee (MKS) formed and 21 demands were presented. By early September, agreements were signed in three cities, giving workers the right to form trade unions and to strike.[19]

On September 21, Sunday Mass was on national radio for the first time since World War II. The autumn strikes and court cases were augmented with dialogue between Solidarity and the Communist regime. A nationwide one-hour warning strike was held on October 3. The Supreme Court officially registered Solidarity on November 10. On December 5, Warsaw Pact members met for a summit in Moscow; four days later, the Soviets initiated military exercises all around Poland, and many feared that an invasion like the one in Hungary in 1956 or Prague in 1968 was approaching. A week later, leading cultural, religious, governmental and Solidarity figures attended a dedication of a memorial in Gdansk commemorating workers martyred in the 1970 strike. By early February 1981, General Jaruzelski was named prime minister, and he asked for a three-month 'ceasefire'. Industrial and general strikes occurred throughout 1981 in several parts of the country. Starting in the shipyards in Gdansk, the strikes spread to many sectors and cities. The scope of the protests and the lack of violence created a situation in which the government was forced to start negotiations with the newly formed free trade unions. By the end of autumn, close to 10 million people of a total population of 35 million had joined the protests.

The unions created a multitude of diverse forums for free expression of opinions. An Independent Student Union was also recognized by the government, and farmers began to form independent organizations; 1981 continued with strikes and recognition of more organizations. The peak came on December 13, when PM Jaruzelski declared a state of war, and a number of Solidarity leaders and activists were arrested. In the spring of 1982, Solidarity started to organize underground and formed a Temporary Coordinating Commission (TKK). In the following 12 months, a number of demonstrations took place, but without large numbers of participants. In October a new law dissolved independent self-governing trade unions, and by January 1983, martial law was suspended. The visit by the Pope in June 1983 resulted in the lifting of martial law, and in October Lech Walesa was awarded the Nobel Peace Prize. The struggle continued, and Solidarity asked people to boycott the 1984 local government elections. In 1985, a major shift started in the Soviet Union, with the election of Gorbachev as the General Secretary of the Communist Party. In 1989, Solidarity got 35 percent of the seats in Sejm[20] and 99 out of 100 seats in the new upper house, the Senate. After almost a decade of nonviolent action, Walesa was elected president on December 9, 1999.

The GDR 1989

After the important changes in Poland, many opposition movements in other East European countries were energized and inspired in their struggles. East Germany was one of the first of these countries to see the opportunity for change.[21]

There has been excellent research done on the nonviolent fall of the German Democratic Republic.[22] Many nonviolent activists were involved in what happened in the autumn of 1989 in East Germany, not all of them in public. Open files have made these events seem a little more transparent today, and the decisions to set up investigations and publicize material from these days have been important.[23] When the first people managed to get permission to leave East Germany by train via Czechoslovakia in 1989, the communist leadership thought that it would get rid of the 'troublemakers'. More and more people took the opportunity to leave. At the same time, protests grew in several cities around the country. In Leipzig, protests and other actions in 1989 were led by the Protestant church (Bartee, 2000; Bohse and Neues Forum Leipzig, 1990; Burgess, 1997).[24]

It would be a misinterpretation of what happened to focus only on civil resistance and nonviolence. These are important and necessary elements, but they are not sufficient to explain what happened, although the means used had an important impact on the process as well as on the outcome of the revolutions in Eastern and Central Europe. To what degree and in what way the means influenced how the revolutions took place and their outcomes is still to be investigated.

Estonia 1991

By 1988, the bloodless 'Singing Revolution' was about to make history: a series of singing mass demonstrations eventually led to one that saw 300,000 Estonians (more than one-fifth of the population) in Tallinn singing national songs played by rock musicians. And on August 23, 1989, about two million people from Estonia, Latvia and Lithuania stood on the Vilnius–Tallinn road holding hands. The unprecedented living chain measured nearly 600 kilometres.[25]

This period was the peak of a movement that gained more room for manoeuvre during *glasnost*[26] and *perestroika*[27] in the Soviet Union under the liberalization led by Gorbachev. The

Estonian Communist Party (ECP) lost members as well as credibility, and several networks and organizations filled the vacuum that it left. The Estonian Popular Front was one major part of the new civil society. Created in 1988, it was joined by the dissident Estonian National Independence Party and the Green Party. By 1988, the Estonian Supreme Soviet was transformed into a regional law-making body, and soon afterward Estonia achieved economic independence from the Soviet Union and recognition of Estonian as the official language.

A grassroots Estonian Citizens' Committees Movement was launched in 1989, with the objective of registering all pre-war citizens of the Republic of Estonia and their descendants in order to convene a Congress. The ECCM emphasized what it deemed the illegal nature of the Soviet system and the fact that hundreds of thousands of inhabitants of Estonia had not ceased to be citizens of the Estonian Republic, which still legally existed and was recognized by the majority of Western nations. Despite the hostility of the mainstream official press and intimidation by Soviet Estonian authorities, dozens of local citizens' committees were elected by popular initiative nationwide. These quickly organized into a coordinated body, and by the beginning of 1990, more than 900,000 persons had registered themselves as citizens of the Republic of Estonia.

Two free elections and two alternative legislatures developed in Estonia in 1990. On February 24, 1990, the 464-member Congress of Estonia (including 35 delegates of refugee communities abroad) was elected by the registered citizens of the republic. The Congress of Estonia convened for the first time in Tallinn on March 11–12, 1990, passing 14 declarations and resolutions.[28] This was a democratically elected but informal body without its base in the constitution or any other law. The Congress represented a broad array of civic groups, and functioned as an alternative to the formal structure.

Despite having 50,000 Soviet troops and a large percentage of Russian-speaking Soviet-era immigrants, Estonia managed to gain its independence without the violent incidents that occurred in its sister republics Latvia and Lithuania.

Sweden put a lot of energy into diplomatic efforts to support an independent Estonia and to gain international support for it. When Estonia declared its formal independence on August 20, 1991, a number of Western countries recognized it quickly, and the U.S. and the Soviet Union, which was disintegrating, followed in early September.

Russia 1991

The collapse of the Soviet Union left Russia as the main political power in the region. Inside Russia, the struggle over power escalated in August 1991. A group calling itself the Emergency Committee arrested President Gorbachev on August 19 while he was on vacation. The arrest was covered up by reports that Gorbachev was ill. The coup plotters were against *perestroika* and *glasnost*, but most of all opposed the process to give the republics independence. A treaty to make them independent in a federation with a common president, foreign policy and military was to be signed on August 20. The plotters included the vice president, the defence minister and the head of the KGB. They banned all forms of public demonstrations, protests and strikes. Orders were given for military units to enter Moscow and protect vital buildings. The men behind the coup expected popular support for their actions, but the majority of the population in the capital turned against them. Many realized that the news about Gorbachev being sick was a ploy. Large crowds came to the 'White House' to protest the coup. More people met at other central places in Moscow. Boris Yeltsin became famous when he climbed on a military vehicle and urged people to use civil disobedience against the coup makers. That event was shown on TV and resulted in many more citizens joining the protesters.

Other cities also held large-scale demonstrations, which included the intelligentsia, middle classes and workers. In Leningrad more than 100,000 protested in Palace Square.

Serbia 2000

The first successful nonviolent revolution in this century took place in the former Yugoslavia. NATO tried to remove Slobodan Milosevic with three months of intensive bombing in 1999, but they were more successful in destroying the opposition than in removing Milosevic. When external troops are bombing a country, the population has a tendency to forget internal disagreements and stand together against the enemy. Serbs stood hand-in-hand on the bridges in Novia Sad and Belgrade to prevent the external aggressor from destroying their cities.

The student movement Otpor,[29] created in October 1998 to oppose a new university law, soon became the main organization opposing the government. The first leader of a state to be removed by a peaceful revolution in the new century was Milosevic. Otpor focused on three demands: Free and fair elections in Serbia, a free university and guarantees for independent media (Sharp, 2005, p. 317). The students had some early discussions on strategies and means, but decided early on to use nonviolence. This was not due to philosophical or moral arguments, but basically because armed struggle would be much easier for Milosevic to handle than nonviolent actions.[30] The main demand was a call for early elections. The students expected to win and remove Milosevic and his people from power.

Otpor, the Center for Civic Initiatives, and other opposition movements got a lot of financial support from foreign sources. The National Democratic Institute and the International Republican Institute, two U.S.-based institutions, were among those who gave at least 40 million dollars prior to the elections in 2000, which was used to run the opposition groups' campaigns.

Georgia 2003

In 2003, Georgia's 'Rose Revolution' dethroned Eduard Shevardnadze. Here the student movement 'Kmara'[31] was the main organizer of demonstrations and protests. Kmara began organizing civilian groups of mainly students as election observers, and was vocal about the need for fair elections prior to the November 2003 elections. Its work garnered much attention from Shevardnadze, who complained that the Russian government and George Soros' Open Society Institute (OSI) had been funding an opposition movement meant to remove Shevardnadze from power. Links to the Russian government have never been proven, although the OSI is well known to have funded training for Kmara. The Belgrade-based Center for Nonviolent Resistance was also key in training Kmara, and several other Western organizations were involved in supporting the group. After international observers condemned Shevardnadze's conduct of the November 2003 parliamentary elections, Kmara led the protests that led to his downfall. Kmara also received training and inspiration from Otpor, which had led the overthrow of Slobodan Milosevic in Serbia in 2000. Kmara also used Gene Sharp's handbook *From Dictatorship to Democracy* as a basis for its campaigns.[32]

People encircled the parliament for weeks before the old regime gave up in 2005.

Conclusion

The nonviolent revolutions on five continents in the last 30 years demonstrate that the trend of nonviolent resistance to oppression has grown to a global force more powerful than many people could have imagined. Countries in all parts of the world, with many different cultural, religious and political backgrounds, have recently changed leadership through massive, organized and nonviolent revolutions. These occurred outside the framework of constitutional rules, and were often a surprise to most of the involved parties.

These cases of nonviolent political revolutions are all based on an understanding of political power as being dependent on cooperation from below. It is like an old Greek temple whose roof support is based on pillars and columns. When Mohandas Gandhi developed his strategy against the British Empire he understood that the colonial power was completely dependent on Indians supporting the 'occupiers'. By means of non-cooperation he wanted all Indians to remove the support and hence the control over India to collapse. By weakening and removing the supporting pillars he reduced and challenged the political power. Refusal to pay salt tax, strikes, massive civil disobedience, and bureaucrats refusing to do their jobs were all parts of this strategy of removing the support the British rulers were dependent on.

Later, Gene Sharp and other scholars studied the case of Gandhi and the Indian liberation struggle and they developed the strategy further. In the books *The Politics of Nonviolent Action*,[33] *Gandhi as a Political Strategist*,[34] *Social Power and Political Freedom*[35] and *Waging Nonviolent Struggle*[36] Sharp has, step by step, developed an advanced understanding of political power and a nonviolent strategy to utilize such power. His latest contributions are *From Dictatorship to Democracy*[37] and *Self Liberation*,[38] which are frequently used as manuals for oppositional groups all around the world.

In each case the situation and context are different and hence it is not possible to just copy what was successfully done in other situations. The basic strategy can be similar, but the implementation and the techniques need to be adopted according to the local context. What Solidarity did successfully in Poland in the eighties would probably not function in Egypt in 2011. At the same time we can recognize similarities like strikes, religious ceremonies, the use of media to spread the message, and phases of negotiations with the opponent.

Most media report such events as surprising news, and most politicians around the world seem to be taken by surprise as well. The only people who may be less astonished when old regimes are toppled are those actors who have done the preparation and training for such events. There are a number of actors who have taken on the responsibility for strategizing, planning and financing some of these movements. Preparation is probably the most important ingredient in these processes. They cannot happen completely spontaneously. Even if much of the planning and training includes relatively small circles of people and gets little or no attention outside the inner circle, the case studies carried out later show the role of preparations in almost every case.

Governments, politicians, dictators and militaries worldwide are faced with a new phenomenon – massive, popularly supported nonviolent oppositional movements for progressive political change. Will they be able to control these movements? If so, what sort of control will they achieve and by what means? Will new movements learn from recent history? Serious studies of the cases we have witnessed so far are only the first steps for such developments to take place. It is clear, however, that despite neoliberal control and attempts at maintaining empire, new revolutionary movements – ones strategically centred around nonviolent methods – are a crucial part of the contemporary political landscape.

Since the use of cellphones and text messages in nonviolent revolution in the Philippines in 2001, the role of electronic media has been discussed and developed in most revolutionary movements. The relatively easy and cheap ways to communicate, inform others, mobilize people, document what is going on, and counter false rumours have been facilitated by Facebook, Twitter and other social media. At the same time these means of communication also add to the vulnerability of the movement. The web can easily be monitored, cellphone users can be identified and state authorities can both manipulate and shut down these systems.

It is not possible to give a general answer as to why some movements are successful and others are still struggling. Like all other political means, nonviolence has no guarantee for success. Some victories are won within months; others take decades. The liberation of India took at least 50 years. For Solidarity in Poland it was nine years from the first strike to free elections. The fall of the Berlin wall was a matter of months, and in Tunisia, Ben Ali was forced out of power in a few weeks.

In countries like Belarus, Burma, China and Zimbabwe the democratic opposition has tried for years to remove the authoritarian leaders. If or when the opposition will be in a position to succeed in these countries is not possible to predict. But recent history tells us that most recent victories come with nonviolent means.

Notes

1 See Vogele, William B., 'Nonviolence, Theory and Practice of' in Nagler (ed) *The Oxford International Encyclopedia of Peace*, Vol 3, pp. 168–173, Oxford, 2010; Johansen, J., 'Nonviolence, More than Absence of Violence' in Webel & Galtung, eds., *Handbook of Peace and Conflict Studies*, London: Routledge, 2007.
2 For data up to 1995 see Frank R. Pfetsch and Christoph Rohloff, *National and International Conflicts, 1945–1995: New Empirical and Theoretical Approaches*, Routledge advances in international relations and politics, London, New York: Routledge, 2000.
3 Dellinger, Dave. *Revolutionary Nonviolence: Essays*, Garden City, NY: Anchor Books, 1971.
4 When I was teaching an MA course in Jerusalem with students from Palestine, Israel and Europe some years ago, I gave the students the task of identifying actors in the Middle East. They never came back after a 40-minute session of group work with fewer than 40 actors.
5 More on the number of actors is discussed in the later section called 'Complexity'.
6 The number of political actors in the world will depend on definition. But even with a limited definition like 'political parties, parliaments, and organizations' they far outnumber armies and military unites.
7 Stephan, M.J. and E. Chenoweth. 'Why Civil Resistance Works: The Strategic Logic of Nonviolent Conflict', *International Security* 33, 2008, 7–44.
8 Peralta, A. '. . . med andra medel. Från Clausewitz till Guevara – krig revolution och politik i en marxistisk idétradition', Göteborg: Daidalos, 1990, 35–36.
9 Few authors have dealt with the complexity of conflicts. Sandole, in his book *Capturing the Complexity of Conflict*, London: Pinter, 1999, developed a multilevel theory for analysing violent ethnic conflicts in postwar situations. Parts of his model are also useful for the types of conflicts we deal with in this article.
10 Grix, J. *The Role of the Masses in the Collapse of the GDR*, Hampshire: Macmillan Press, 2000.
11 Johansen, Jørgen. 'Gewaltfrei erfolgreicher als bewaffneter Kampf', *Wissenschaft und Frieden* 22, no. 2, 2004.
12 ———. 'Waves of Nonviolence and the New Revolutionary Movements', in Matt Meyer and Elavie D. Ouédraogo, eds., *Seeds of New Hope, Pan-African Peace Studies for the Twenty-First Century*. Asmara: African World Press, 2009.
13 Garton Ash, Timothy. *The Polish Revolution: Solidarity*, rev. and updated ed., London: Granta Books, 1991; Karpinski, Jakub. *Countdown: The Polish Upheavals of 1956, 1968, 1970, 1976, 1980*. New York: Karz-Cohl, 1982; Lukowski, Jerzy and W.H. Zawadzki. *A Concise History of Poland*. Second ed., Cambridge Concise Histories, Cambridge, UK; New York: Cambridge University Press, 2006.
14 Weber, Wolfgang and Bill Brust. *Solidarity in Poland, 1980–1981 and the Perspective of Political Revolution*. Detroit: Labor Publications, 1989.
15 Blumsztajn, Seweryn et al., *Från röda scouterna till Solidarnosc*, Stockholm: Ordfront, 1986.
16 Curry, Jane Leftwich and Luba Fajfer. *Poland's Permanent Revolution: People vs. elites, 1956 to the present*. Washington, D.C.: American University Press, 1996.
17 J. Kubik, in his 1994 book *The Power of Symbols against the Symbols of Power*, gives the reader an excellent and sophisticated cultural understanding of these nonviolent means.

18 One major reason for this price rise was the demand from Russia to send large quantities of meat to Moscow before the Olympics Games started. They wanted to prove false rumours from the West that there was a lack of meat in Russia.

19 It was explicitly written that they had to acknowledge the directive role of the Communist Party.

20 That was the maximum agreed to in the Round Table discussions.

21 Opposition was not as well known there as in other countries, but as Fricke, Steinbach and Tuchel (Fricke, 1984), Raschka (Raschke, Kuhrt, et al., 2001), Torpey (1995), Herrmann (Herrmann and Petzold, 2002) and Neubert (1997) have shown, there was a long tradition of opposition, although it was less organized than in countries like Czechoslovakia and Hungary.

22 Opp, Karl-Dieter, Peter Voss and Christiane Gern, *Origins of a Spontaneous Revolution: East Germany.* 1989. Economics, cognition, and society. Ann Arbor: University of Michigan Press, 1995.

23 The Enquete-Kommission has published internal discussions from many about how they reacted to the large-scale peaceful demonstrations (Enquete-Kommission, 'Aufarbeitung von Geschichte und Folgen der SED-Diktatur in Deutschland', 1999). The collection of internal documents from Germany from 1989–1990, edited by Küsters and Hofmann (1998), is also important in order to understand how the leaders in the U.S. and the Soviet Union reacted when the Berlin wall was removed. Maier (1997) has also written an excellent study on the crises of communism and the end of East Germany. For a good chronology of the background and events in East Germany, see Philipsen (1993) and Childs (2001).

24 Bartee, Wayne C. *A time to speak out: The Leipzig citizen protests and the fall of East Germany.* Westport, CT: Praeger, 2000; Bohse, Reinhard and Neues Forum Leipzig. *Jetzt oder nie – Demokratie: Leipziger Herbst '89.* First ed. München: Bertelsmann, 1990; Burgess, John P. *The East German Church and the End of Communism.* New York: Oxford University Press, 1997.

25 The many oppositional meetings at the end of the 1980s are described in detail by Ignats in his 1989 book *Estland: Den Sjungande Revolutionen,* as well as the movie: *The Singing Revolution*

26 *Glasnost* means 'openness'.

27 *Perestroika* means 'reform'.

28 http://en.wikipedia.org/wiki/History_of_Estonia. Accessed 2010-12-06.

29 *Otpor* means 'Resistance'.

30 Parts of the discussions in Otpor can be found at http://www.otpor.net. Accessed 2010-12-06.

31 Kmara means 'Enough'.

32 http://en.wikipedia.org/wiki/GeneSharp

33 Sharp, Gene. *The Politics of Nonviolent Action.* Boston: P. Sargent Publishers, 1973.

34 ——, *Gandhi as a Political Strategist: With essays on ethics and politics.* Boston: Extending Horizons Books, Boston: P. Sargent Publishers, 1979.

35 ——, *Social Power and Political Freedom.* Boston: P. Sargent Publishers, 1980.

36 ——, *Waging Nonviolent Struggle,* 20th Century Practice and 21th Century Potential. Boston: Extending Horizon Books, 2005.

37 Sharp, Gene and Albert Einstein Institution (Cambridge, MA), *From Dictatorship to Democracy: A conceptual framework for liberation,* 3rd U.S. ed. East Boston, MA: Albert Einstein Institution, 2008.

38 Available to download from http://www.aeinstein.org/

Bibliography

Bartee, Wayne C. *A Time to Speak Out : The Leipzig Citizen Protests and the Fall of East Germany.* Westport, CT: Praeger, 2000.

Blumsztajn, Seweryn, Patrick Michel, Georges Mink and Anders Bodegård. *Från Röda Scouterna Till Solidarnosc.* Stockholm: Ordfront, 1986.

Bohse, Reinhard and Neues Forum Leipzig. *Jetzt Oder Nie – Demokratie: Leipziger Herbst '89.* First ed. München: Bertelsmann, 1990.

Burgess, John P. *The East German Church and the End of Communism.* New York: Oxford University Press, 1997.

Childs, David. *The Fall of the GDR: Germany's Road to Unity.* Themes in Modern German History Series. Harlow, England; New York: Longman, 2001.

Curry, Jane Leftwich and Luba Fajfer. *Poland's Permanent Revolution: People vs. Elites, 1956 to the Present.* Washinton, D.C.: American University Press, 1996.

Dellinger, Dave. *Revolutionary Nonviolence : Essays*, 787. Garden City, NY: Anchor Books, 1971.

Fricke, Karl Wilhelm. *Opposition Und Widerstand in Der DDR: Ein Politischer Report*. Köln: Verlag Wissenschaft und Politik, 1984.

Garton Ash, Timothy. *The Polish Revolution: Solidarity*. Rev. and updated ed. London: Granta Books, 1991.

Germany. Enquete-Kommission 'Aufarbeitung von Geschichte und Folgen der SED-Diktatur in Deutschland', and Germany. Bundestag. Materialien Der Enquete-Kommission 'Überwindung Der Folgen Der Sed-Diktatur Im Prozess Der Deutschen Einheit' (13. Wahlperiode Des Deutschen Bundestages). First ed. Baden-Baden, Frankfurt am Main: Nomos; Suhrkamp, 1999.

Grix, J. *The Role of the Masses in the Collapse of the GDR*. Hampshire: Macmillan Press, 2000.

Herrmann, Ulrich, and Joachim Petzold. *Protestierende Jugend: Jugendopposition Und Politischer Protest in Der Deutschen Nachkriegsgeschichte*, Materialien Zur Historischen Jugendforschung. Weinheim: Juventa, 2002.

Hofmann, Daniel, Hanns Jürgen Küsters, and Förbundsrepubliken Västtyskland. Bundesministerium für innerdeutsche Beziehungen. *Dokumente Zur Deutschlandpolitik*. Frankfurt am Main: Metzner, 1998.

Ignats, Ülo. *Estland: Den Sjungande Revolutionen*. First ed. Göteborg: MH Publishing, 1989.

Johansen, Jørgen. 'Gewaltfrei Erfolgreicher Als Bewaffneter Kampf'. *Wissenschaft und Frieden* 22, no. 2 (2004), 12–15.

——. 'Waves of Nonviolence and the New Revolutionary Movements' in Matt Meyer and Elavie D. Ouédraogo, eds., *Seeds of New Hope, Pan-African Peace Studies for the Twenty-First Century*. Asmara: African World Press, 2009, 69–124.

——. 'Nonviolence, More than Absence of Violence' in Webel & Galtung, eds., *Handbook of Peace and Conflict Studies*, London: Routledge, 2007.

Karpinski, Jakub. *Countdown: the Polish Upheavals of 1956, 1968, 1970, 1976, 1980*. New York: Karz-Cohl, 1982.

Kubik, Jan. *The Power of Symbols Against the Symbols of Power: The Rise of Solidarity and the Fall of State Socialism in Poland*. University Park, PA: Pennsylvania State University Press, 1994.

Lukowski, Jerzy and W. H. Zawadzki. *A Concise History of Poland*. Second ed. Cambridge Concise Histories. Cambridge, UK; New York: Cambridge University Press, 2006.

Maier, Charles S. *Dissolution: The Crisis of Communism and the End of East Germany*. Princeton, NJ: Princeton University Press, 1997.

Neubert, Ehrhart. *Geschichte Der Opposition in Der DDR 1949–1989*. 2. Durchgesehene und erw. sowie korrigierte Aufl. ed. Bonn: Bundeszentrale für politische Bildung, 1997.

Opp, Karl-Dieter, Peter Voss and Christiane Gern. *Origins of a Spontaneous Revolution: East Germany, 1989, Economics, Cognition, and Society*. Ann Arbor: University of Michigan Press, 1995.

Peralta, A. '. . . med andra medel. Från Clausewitz till Guevara – krig revolution och politik i en marxistisk idétradition', Göteborg: Daidalos, 1990.

Pfetsch, Frank R., and Christoph Rohloff. *National and International Conflicts, 1945–1995: New empirical and theoretical approaches*, Routledge advances in international relations and politics, London, New York: Routledge, 2000.

Philipsen, Dirk. *We Were the People: Voices from East Germany's Revolutionary Autumn of 1989*. Durham: Duke University Press, 1993.

Raschka, Johannes, Eberhard Kuhrt, Hannsjörg F. Buck, Gunter Holzweissig and Germany. Bundesministerium des Innern. *Zwischen Überwachung Und Repression: Politische Verfolgung in Der DDR 1971 Bis 1989, Am Ende Des Realen Sozialismus*. Bd. 5. Opladen: Leske + Budrich, 2001.

Sharp, Gene. *The Politics of Nonviolent Action*. Boston: P. Sargent Publishers, 1973.

——. *Gandhi as a Political Strategist : With Essays on Ethics and Politics*. Extending Horizons Books. Boston: P. Sargent Publishers, 1979.

——. *Social Power and Political Freedom*. Boston: P. Sargent Publishers, 1980.

——. *Waging Nonviolent Struggle, 20th Century Practice and 21th Century Potential*. Boston: Extending Horizons Books, 2005.

——. *From Dictatorship to Democracy: A Conceptual Framework for Liberation.* 3rd U.S. ed. East Boston, MA: Albert Einstein Institution, 2008.

Stephan, M.J. and E. Chenoweth. 'Why Civil Resistance Works: The Strategic Logic of Nonviolent Conflict'. *International Security* 33 (2008), 7–44.

Torpey, John C. *Intellectuals, Socialism, and Dissent: The East German Opposition and Its Legacy, Contradictions of Modernity.* Vol. 4. Minneapolis: University of Minnesota Press, 1995.

Vogele, William B. 'Nonviolence, Theory and Practice of' in Nagler, ed. *The Oxford International Encyclopedia of Peace.* Vol. 3. Oxford, 2010, 168–173.

Weber, Wolfgang and Bill Brust. *Solidarity in Poland, 1980–1981 and the Perspective of Political Revolution.* Detroit: Labor Publications, 1989.

PART 5: NONVIOLENT ACTION AND POLITICAL CHANGE

Suggestions for further reading

Gandhi, Mohandas Karamchand (1960). *All Men Are Brothers.* First Indian edition. Ahmedabad: Navajivan Pub. House.

King, Martin Luther and James Melvin Washington. *A Testament of Hope: The Essential Writings and Speeches of Martin Luther King, Jr. (*1991) First HarperCollins publication. ed. San Francisco: HarperSanFrancisco.

Martin, Brian and Wendy Varney (2003). *Nonviolence Speaks: Communicating against Repression,* The Hampton Press Communication Series. Cresskill, NJ: Hampton Press.

Schock, Kurt (2005). *Unarmed Insurrections: People Power Movements in Nondemocracies, Social Movements, Protest, and Contention,* Volume 22. Minneapolis: University of Minnesota Press.

Sharp, Gene, (1973). *The Politics of Nonviolent Action.* Boston: P. Sargent Publisher.

Sharp, Gene and Joshua Paulson (2005). *Waging Nonviolent Struggle: 20th Century Practice and 21st Century Potential.* Boston: Extending Horizons Books.

Stephan, M.J. and E. Chenoweth (2008). 'Why Civil Resistance Works: The Strategic Logic of Nonviolent Conflict', *International Security* 33, 7–44.

Stephan, Maria J. (2009). *Civilian Jihad: Nonviolent Struggle, Democratization, and Governance in the Middle East.* New York: Palgrave Macmillan.

Websites with online resources

International Center on Nonviolent Conflict: http://www.nonviolent-conflict.org/
Bibliography for texts on Civil Resistance: http://www.civilresistance.info/
The Albert Einstein Institute: http://www.aeinstein.org/

Questions for reflection and discussion

1 Reflect on the role religions have had in justifying the means (violent and nonviolent) of engaging in social and political conflicts.

2 How are nonviolent movements able to successfully confront armed police and militaries?

3 Why do you think the history of nonviolent movements has fared so poorly in history books and academic studies of conflicts?

4 What do you think is the impact of having charismatic leaders, like Gandhi in India and Lech Walesa in Poland, in nonviolent movements, compared with the apparent lack of such figures in Egypt in 2011 or in Serbia in 2000?

5 How do you regard the role of domestic and international media in large-scale nonviolent conflicts?

Part 6

Building institutions and cultures of peace

SUMMARY

The end of the Cold War has presented new challenges and there was perceived to be a need to reform the traditional UN Blue Helmet Peacekeeping forces. When Secretary-General of the United Nations Boutros Boutros-Ghali presented *An Agenda for Peace* in 1992, his intention was to develop new ways for utilizing the 'UN toolbox'. It was no longer sufficient in some conflicts for the Blue Helmets to wait for invitations from the parties in conflict and then 'stand in the middle' in order to prevent further clashes. And as a result of the genocide in Rwanda in 1994, when around 800,000 people were slaughtered, it appeared justifiable for external actors to intervene in states by force. The sovereignty of states was challenged, and in the years to come there were several cases of *peace enforcement* when the UNSC or other actors argued that if the government in a country did not prevent, or itself committed, crimes against humanity, then war crimes were being committed inside their territory and outside intervention became justifiable. When NATO decided to use military means against the Federal Republic of Yugoslavia for crimes against the Kosovo-Albanians, it acted without the consent from the UNSC, and this challenged international law. Some argued that the military operation was illegal but still legitimate.

The discussion of who, how and when to intervene, is ongoing. Questions arise like: Is it justified? Can it be done without a UNSC resolution? And who decides when and where to intervene? Superpowers, with their own agendas, have a tendency to act when it is in their interests to do so. New and more sophisticated models for international interventions are developed, tested and evaluated. Just like the continuous development of new weapon systems, ways to act in so-called humanitarian interventions are also in the process of continually being evaluated. But research on military means has a huge advantage when it comes to such resources as financial and political support.

During the years after interventions, it became clear that there was a need to develop tools to reconstruct war zones and reconcile conflict parties after the cessation of violent hostilities. As ceasefire agreements were signed, it was obvious that the task of rebuilding the war-torn societies needed new efforts, resources and skills. Modern warfare results in destroyed societies on many levels; social relations, infrastructures and institutions needed to be restored. Peacebuilding became a contested concept for this.

Within the different schools of peacebuilding, we find those who argue that peoples' minds are the most important part, while others say we need to build a democratic structure for a sustainable state. Rebuilding societies has been a growing and profitable area for businesses as well as civil society actors. Peacebuilding can start in any phase of a conflict – before, during or after a violent peak. Each phase requires a specific type of peacebuilding.

Wars have traditionally been seen as a 'male thing' – male soldiers shooting other men. In modern wars, violence against women has become an escalating part of the atrocities. It became obvious that analysis of wars needs to include a gender perspective. Systematic and organized rapes on a large scale became a tool for many armies. UN Security Council resolution (SCR) 1325 in 2000 was the first to link women to the peace and security agenda. The gender perspective is of growing importance in all aspects on conflicts.

One side of the gender debate focuses on the question of peacefulness. Are men more aggressive than women? And the larger question: Are human beings aggressive by nature? The discussion has not concluded with a consensus, but there are a growing number of studies showing that even if humans are born with an aggressive potential, our cultural training has an immense impact on how we behave in conflicts.

There are peaceful societies of different kinds, and in some cultures humans accept violence as a way to behave in conflicts. Even if there are biological elements in our way of acting in conflicts, much can be done to control our allegedly 'natural' dispositions. If violence and aggressiveness dominated our behaviour, we would most probably never have been able to build advanced societies based on many levels of cooperation.

To change attitudes in a culture is an immense task. Peace education developed from studying the impact of wars and weapons to teaching skills for building peaceful relations and transforming conflicts in a positive direction. Studies of the links between individual behaviour and group behaviour became an important tool for raising new generations.

Peacekeeping, peace-building and peacemaking

Thierry Tardy of the Geneva Centre for Security Policy discusses the problems faced by contemporary peace operations. During the massacres in 1994 in Rwanda, and in July 1995 in Srebrenica, the passivity of the UN and other actors raised questions about the capacities and robustness of available international interventions. Tardy argues there is need for something between traditional peacekeeping and invasion by a full military force – so called *peace enforcement*. He concludes that there has not only been a lack of robustness, but also that interventions pushed by states in the North and implemented in the South is problematic. A more advanced strategy and more robust forces backed by the UN Security Council may be a solution for some of the problems.

Praszkier, Nowak and Coleman, as psychologists, argue against traditional conflict-resolution models like John Burton's – namely, that conflicts are mainly related to the aggregation of the needs of individuals. They present arguments as to why we must also look at social dynamics in order to understand and act wisely in conflicts. A society is much more than the sum of its individuals. The constructive changes they want to see would create positive 'islands' of hope that can circumvent conflicts. By removing the focus and attention from the individuals and letting social entrepreneurs build new collective goods, these researchers hope that the grounds for the conflict will be reduced or disappear. Without denying more traditional view such as Burton's, they want to add the structural and social elements to conflict resolution. The theory is supported by several empirical studies.

Peter Haldén has done research on state-building and security in African and Central Asian societies; these are both regions of the world with failed states. Based on his studies of Somalia, Namibia and Afghanistan, he argues that states cannot be built by supporting internal processes and institutions alone. Haldén does not find sufficient understanding of the underlying problems in the contemporary IR literature and concludes that it is important for successful nation-building to have a wider perspective. Without regional stability and constitutional settlements for wider contexts than the failed state itself, it is very difficult to establish sustainable and stable states. In unstable regions, the problems of building states have been underestimated. Every state interacts with its neighbours, and in the process of establishing states, these relations are particularly important.

Jenkins and Reardon present significant gender perspectives on peace issues. They give examples ranging from the classical Greek drama *Lysistrata*, whose eponymous protagonist encouraged her sisters to refuse to have sex with their men until they ended the war, to the modern Greenham Common Women who encamped around a U.S. military base in the UK in the 1980s. The documentation of women actively working against war is important to highlight. What they call the 'patriarchal paradigm' is a problem for studies of peace and human security. If future generations are more aware of the consequences of a male-dominated world, there are possibilities for the development of a better world order. Norms, conventions and global institutions all have their role to play in the creation of a world with more human security and equality, and with less violence and fewer oppressive social structures.

From cultures of violence to cultures of sustainable peace

Majken Jul Sørensen discusses the competing discourses on aggression and peacefulness. The claim that *Homo sapiens* is 'innately' aggressive does not seem compatible with the fact that some societies are very peaceful. Using the examples of the Semai Senoi, an indigenous people in Malaysia, and the Inuits, the original inhabitants of Greenland, northern Canada and Siberia, Sørensen illustrates this. Sørensen makes a point of separating aggression and violence. Then it is easier to understand that aggression does not necessarily lead to violent behaviour, but if it is handled in a different way, there can be a certain level of aggression even in a peaceful society. The Semai Senoi regard all strong emotions as dangerous, as something to fear. And fear is the only acceptable emotion. Children are socialized to fear all other emotions, which leads to fear of conflicts. They do all they can to avoid conflicts. Similarly, the Inuits are raised to control anger to a degree traditional Western people would call extreme. Feelings like anger and jealousy are strongly disapproved of in this culture. Sørensen concludes that it is meaningless to try to copy these cultures, but they can serve as inspirations to develop new ways to handle aggressiveness.

Maja Korac describes identities and conflicts in the former Yugoslavia from a gender perspective. The wars in the Balkans in the 1990s were made possible by destroying social networks and creating new identities. The complexity of ethnic identities in Yugoslavia was not of major concern until political elites and nationalistic parties orchestrated individual fear and social tension. This resulted in violent clashes, wars resulting in many refugees, and rapes on an organized scale. Korac describes how and why women played an important role in rebuilding trust and restoring social networks. Civil society groups like Women in Black and Autonomous Women´s Centre Belgrade created a social space for women to meet and start building trust across ethnic division lines. Women's organizations started before the armed conflicts broke out, and they were active both in opposing the wars and in reconciliation efforts after ceasefires were reached. These groups brought together women from different classes, countries and ethnic groups and acted against the propaganda of the nationalistic forces.

The late Elise Boulding see conflicts as ubiquitous and reminds us not to confuse *conflicts* with *violence*. There are a number of ways to act during a conflict, not all of which include violence. All societies can be placed somewhere on a continuum between *war* on the one side and *integration* and *union* on the other. Where we end up on that spectrum is decided neither by coincidence nor by nature. Since the days when Boulding acted as one of the core people who established peace studies, she has emphasized the roles of education and research on a society's ability to handle conflicts wisely. Based on studies of ethnic, religious, philosophically based groups with a much lower level of violence than others, Boulding concludes that there are lessons to be learned and inspiration to be found for those who want to be part of the creation of a more peaceful future.

35 A critique of robust peacekeeping in contemporary peace operations

Thierry Tardy

The concept of robust peacekeeping emerged in the late 1990s as a response to the tragedies of Rwanda and Srebrenica, where UN peacekeepers failed to stop massive violations of human rights, allegedly because they were not sufficiently robust. In 2000 the Brahimi Report referred several times to the necessity of 'robust peacekeeping forces',[1] as a lesson from past experiences. Subsequently, the mandates of new operations increasingly included the idea that UN peacekeepers must be given the political and operational means to successfully implement their mandate. In particular, the simultaneous attention given to the protection of civilians in peace missions led the Security Council to instil a vocabulary of robustness in its resolutions.[2] In the majority of the mandates in the last decade, resolutions have authorized peacekeepers to use all 'necessary means to protect civilians when under imminent threat of physical violence'. In these various cases, robustness is understood to give an operation a degree of credibility, in particular vis-à-vis 'spoilers'. Robustness is designed to allow a peacekeeping force to protect itself, to provide freedom of manoeuvre, and to prevent situations where the implementation of the mandate, or more broadly the peace process, is 'taken hostage' by spoilers.

Although 'robust peacekeeping' is not a new concept and has been partially implemented in some operations (Sierra Leone, Democratic Republic of Congo [DRC], Haiti, Lebanon),[3] it attracted renewed attention in 2008–10 arising from conceptual developments. Several policy documents issued by different units of the UN Department of Peacekeeping Operations (DPKO) – 'UN Peacekeeping Operations. Principles and Guidelines', the 'New Horizon' non-paper, and a 'Concept Note on Robust Peacekeeping' – provided definitions of the term, partly in response to critiques of confusion and lack of clarity about the operational implications of robustness.[4] Subsequently, robust peacekeeping was discussed at the 2010 session of the Special Committee for Peacekeeping Operations' (known as the C-34). The debates revealed the high degree of politicization that has characterized the C-34 (with its 144 members) over the last decade, as well as the sensitivity of the idea of robustness, particularly among countries of the Non-Aligned Movement (NAM).

Here I challenge the coherence and feasibility of the concept of robust peacekeeping. While recognizing the necessity and virtue of a robust approach as a protection mechanism for peacekeepers, I question the extent to which robust peacekeeping is politically acceptable and operationally viable. Beyond the doctrinal difficulty of ensuring the compatibility of robustness with the principles of peace operations, robust peacekeeping is directly challenged by some enduring constraints of contemporary peace operations, such as weak political support, erratic availability and quality of troops, and reticence of troop contributors to embrace a robust approach. Thus, while robustness is presented as a solution to the 'credibility gap' confronting the UN, it leads to so many interrelated problems that the relevance of robustness is questionable.

My argument consists of three parts. First, it examines the different meanings of 'robust peacekeeping' and some of the issues deriving from definitional ambiguities. Second, it considers the broader peacekeeping environment and explores how robustness relates to other political issues that, in turn, affect the politics of robust peacekeeping. This leads to the third part and the question of the feasibility of robustness. How likely is it that troop contributors will meet the requirements for robust peacekeeping? What are the implications and possible unintended consequences of robustness and the use of force that it implies? How feasible is robustness in the broad implementation of peace operations mandates, say, beyond the mere protection of peacekeepers?

What is robust peacekeeping?

The UN has always had difficulty in reconciling its central role in the maintenance of international peace and security with the idea of coercion.[5] The use of force is not absent from UN prerogatives, but the nature of the organization, its broad composition, and the politics within its main organs have made coercion conceptually and practically ambiguous. Robust peacekeeping was at the heart of what, in the early 1990s, was referred to as the 'grey area' of peacekeeping, an ill-defined activity situated between traditional peacekeeping and peace enforcement.[6] The UN and its member states have faced great difficulty in handling this grey area, in terms of both doctrine and operations.[7] At the core of the matter is the use of force by the military in situations that are not wars. This implies a doctrinal and cultural shift that the UN, states, and their military institutions have long resisted. This was epitomized in the 1990s in both Somalia and Bosnia and Herzegovina, where peacekeepers either resorted to excessive force (Somalia) or refused military confrontation (Srebrenica), but in each case acted in a conceptual vacuum – as well as in the absence of political will in the Balkans case.

Meanwhile, the implications of more intrusive interventions for host countries' sovereignty have been largely overlooked. Host states consent to the presence of a UN operation, yet they are placed de facto in a situation of dependence that affects the nature of the relationship with the interveners (see the article by Ian Johnstone in *International Peacekeeping*). The idea that peacekeepers can resort to force on the territory of a sovereign country is not an anodyne issue. It carries a meaning that goes beyond the framework of a given operation and touches on international politics and the principles that regulate it. In this context, peacekeeping practices have evolved over the last two decades in a somewhat improvised manner, and with little reflection on the broad implications of these changing practices. Robust peacekeeping is presented as a response to standing weaknesses of UN operations, and, although it may well be part of the solution in some cases, it also reflects the ambiguities of UN and state policies in the management of international and intrastate crises. Moreover, it confirms the inherent difficulty in reconciling UN multilateralism and politics with coercion.

Narrow versus broad approaches to robust peacekeeping

There is a consensus that robust peacekeeping is an ill-defined concept and that it is, as a consequence, difficult to operationalize. What does it mean for an operation to be robust? What does it entail for the Security Council, for peacekeepers, for the local authorities? Two conceptions – narrow and broad – of robust peacekeeping can be distinguished. The narrow approach is about enabling peacekeepers to implement their mandate by relying on their robustness – in posture, equipment, and their ability to resort to force. This approach is narrow in the sense that it focuses on the robustness of peacekeepers. This definition is in keeping with the 2008 'Principles and Guidelines' that, in its glossary of terms, defines 'robust peace-keeping' as 'the use of force by a United Nations peacekeeping operation at the tactical level, with the authorization of the Security Council, to defend its mandate against spoilers whose activities pose a threat to civilians or risk undermining the peace process'.[8] In this context, robust peacekeeping is also defined by what it is not: peace enforcement. Two key elements distinguish robust peacekeeping from peace enforcement: the level of force (tactical for robust peacekeeping, strategic for peace enforcement); and host state consent (required for robust peacekeeping but not in the case of peace enforcement).

The 'Principles and Guidelines' clarifies the distinction as follows:

> robust peacekeeping should not be confused with peace enforcement, as envisaged under Chapter VII of the Charter. Robust peacekeeping involves the use of force at the tactical level with the authorization of the Security Council and consent of the host nation and/or the main parties to the conflict. By contrast, peace enforcement does not require the consent of the main parties and may involve the use of military force at the strategic or international level, which is normally prohibited for Member States under Article 2(4) of the Charter, unless authorized by the Security Council.[9]

By contrast, the broad approach considers robust peacekeeping in more political terms. It is defined in the 2009 UN 'New Horizon' non-paper as a 'robust approach to peacekeeping', which is a 'political and operational strategy to signal the intention of a UN mission to implement its mandate and to deter threats to an existing peace process in the face of resistance from spoilers'.[10] While recognizing that at the tactical level a 'robust approach means that contingents may be required to use force in defence of the mandate', it emphasizes that 'it should be driven by a clear political strategy' (p.21), and that a 'successful robust approach depends on the commitment of the Security Council and the willingness of troop and police contributors to implement it'. This approach significantly broadens that of the 'Principles and Guidelines'. It recognizes that robustness cannot be confined to the peacekeepers and their ability to use force in defence of their mandate, but needs to be embedded in a broader framework that combines operational and political parameters. More than the robustness of the force, the firm stance adopted at all levels of the management of the mission is essential to the credibility and success of an operation. Ultimately, the use of force may be necessary, but as a means to an end that needs to be clearly identified.

In 2009 the Office of Military Affairs of DPKO/DFS (Department of Field Support) issued a 'Concept Note on Robust Peacekeeping' aimed at clarifying the 'key issues surrounding robust peacekeeping'.[11] Its interim definition of robust peacekeeping is as 'a posture by a peacekeeping operation that demonstrates willingness, capacity and capability to deter and confront, including through the use of force when necessary, an obstruction to the implementation of its mandate'. The document emphasizes that robust peacekeeping is a 'posture' rather 'than a specific activity', meaning that 'robustness . . . can be demonstrated in many ways, including the use of political dialogue' but also 'targeted sanctions against identified spoilers . . . support and incentives to national reconciliation efforts and [even] the initiation of early peacebuilding activities to help deliver a tangible peace dividend to local populations'.[12] This 'posture' issue is underlined by Under-Secretary-General for Peacekeeping Operations Alain Le Roy at the 2010 C-34 session in very similar terms.[13] The Concept Note further reiterates that robust peacekeeping is not peace enforcement, and that 'large scale violence or one where the major parties are engaged in violent conflict is no longer a robust peacekeeping context'.

To a certain extent, the Concept Note tries to reconcile the narrow and broad approaches. It states that 'robust peacekeeping is not only a military or police posture but also a political and operational approach that signals the determination of a peacekeeping operation to implement its mandate and to deter threats to an existing peace process'. In the same vein, robust peacekeeping does not necessarily entail the use of force, as deterrence 'based on the readiness to use force' is presented as 'the most effective approach'.[14] However, its focus tends to be more on the military/peacekeeping dimension of the operation rather than on its political element. Robustness seems to derive from the possibility to resort to force more than from the existence of a political strategy or from the triangular dialogue between the Security Council, the Secretariat, and the troop-contributing countries (TCCs).

Overall, these documents help clarify what robust peacekeeping is and what it is not. However, it is worth noting that none of them has been endorsed by the member states, and therefore they can hardly be considered UN policy.[15] Many Western states would no doubt support the general effort at conceptualizing robustness and would subscribe to the spirit of the DPKO/DFS documents; the same is not true, however, for many countries of the NAM that contest the terms of the debate as it is advanced by the UN Secretariat (see below).

Definitional ambiguities: robustness or effectiveness?

Contemporary peace operations do not lend themselves easily to a piecemeal analysis. Some activities of multidimensional operations might be more important than others. Yet the overall effectiveness of peace operations requires a holistic approach that simultaneously addresses key issues and that does not, by definition, compartmentalize them. Activities that are dependent upon a high degree of political engagement can hardly be analysed without examining the political setting. The narrow approach to robust peacekeeping is problematic precisely because it tends to single out one requirement of effectiveness without embedding it into a broader framework.

In other words, there is little point in promoting robustness in the field if no political process underlies it, if the host country is lukewarm about it, or if a large number of key states deliberately stay away from UN operations and are not therefore engaged in the implementation of the concept. Yet, within the C-34, robustness seems to have been singled out by Western states as if it were a solution to the generic problems of effectiveness in peace operations. A large presence in UN operations (including from Western countries) and the existence of a political process backed by the Security Council and other important stakeholders, while presumably equally important to the overall success of peace missions, have not received the same level of attention.

The limits of the narrow approach would seem to make more attractive the broader vision proposed by the New Partnership Agenda. This favours going beyond the robustness of the force and adopting a more political approach to robustness. In other words, robustness at the field level works only if it is backed by robustness at the political level: in the Security Council, in dialogue with local actors, and in the constant and unified support that TCCs get from the Security Council. However, this approach runs the risk of diluting the concept of robustness. The rhetoric of robust peacekeeping/strategy/doctrine/ peacebuilding[16] overlooks the very meaning of the adjective 'robust' and the flaws in associating it with a variety of terms that are not intuitively close to the idea of robustness. What Western states and the DPKO wish to promote is peacekeeping with the appropriate mandate, support, and capabilities to fulfil the mission assigned by the Security Council. Quite simply the idea is fundamentally about effectiveness, not robustness.

This leads to a terminological debate about the use of the term 'robust'. As shown in the following section, debates at the UN in general and at the C-34 in particular are highly politicized, shaped by divergent objectives as well as by subjective positions. In this context, for an idea to be accepted it needs to be carefully calibrated and communicated. Yet the concept of robust peacekeeping has not been promoted effectively. For many countries of the South, the term 'robust' implies a degree of intrusiveness in the internal affairs of states and the possibility of coercion. In the end, one wonders if the reference to robustness in UN documents has actually been counterproductive, by dividing countries along a North-South axis over terminology rather than bringing them together on the operational necessity of robustness.

Indeed, several countries, including ones in the NAM, accept that peacekeeping forces need to be able to ensure their security and implement their mandate, potentially through a firm posture that may imply the resort to force, and do perform robust peacekeeping in the field.[17] In 2005, the Report of the C-34 acknowledged the 'need for an appropriately strong military and civilian police presence, backed by adequate support resources throughout the peacekeeping operation, in order to deter spoilers and establish the credibility of the United Nations'.[18] For example, Indian units have been regularly involved in robust operations, including during the Cold War.[19] Robustness is therefore not a priori rejected. Yet many NAM countries disagree with the way the term is being framed. Ultimately, while clarification on the meaning of 'robust peacekeeping' is important, over-conceptualization has also attenuated the strength of the concept, to the extent that the use of the term itself is being questioned.[20]

Robustness in the broader peacekeeping context

The 'New Horizon' non-paper insists on the necessity of going beyond the robustness of the force to include that of political actors – the Security Council, member states, and regional partners in particular. This is indeed crucial, as it is the nature of the political environment underlying an operation that determines the chances of success. Ideally, a firm stance at the political level would even make robustness in the field unnecessary. Yet, the politics of peacekeeping is complex, and robustness can hardly work as a substitute for a missing strategy.

Politicization of robust peacekeeping and substantive divergence

The very concept of robust peacekeeping is extremely contentious. Within the UN, debates on robust peacekeeping are intensely politicized, reflecting strong divergences on the meaning and implications of the concept. Politicization has been evident in the C-34. At the 2010 session, debates pitted the EU group pushing for robustness against the NAM that expressed concerns about the concept and its implications.[21] For European states, robustness has been a response to a lack of effectiveness of peace operations, and is aimed at enabling peacekeepers to properly protect themselves and to have the freedom of manoeuvre to implement a mandate. A link is also established between robustness and the protection of civilians, which may require a robust posture and, if need be, the capacity to use force. By contrast, robustness is perceived by many NAM countries as deviating from the key principles of peacekeeping and as a potential threat to the sovereignty of host countries. A parallel is implicitly made between robustness, understood as a new instrument of domination over countries of the South, and a form of neo-colonialism. The fact that DPKO has developed a narrative that is very similar to that of Western countries adds to the perception of the UN as Western dominated. Within DPKO, units in charge of policy development are predominantly composed of nationals from Western countries, and their ability to truly reflect the diversity of views of the member states is questioned.[22]

Some countries even see a continuum between the 'responsibility to protect' and robustness within peacekeeping missions in the protection of civilians. In both cases, critics are concerned that external forces will infringe state sovereignty by coercive means.[23] Several Security Council resolutions, including resolution 1674 (2006) on the protection of civilians in armed conflict, and many resolutions on Sudan,[24] explicitly refer to the 2005 'UN World Summit Outcome' document and its provisions on the responsibility to protect, which adds to suspicion of a continuum between the two levels of coercion.

Equally problematic, the risk of abuse of a robust posture is invoked. Critics question the ability of crisis management actors to ensure that what begins as robust peacekeeping does not end as peace enforcement.

This leads to the question of compatibility of robust peacekeeping with the key principles of peace operations: impartiality, consent of the host state, and non-resort to force. For some NAM countries the use of force, other than in self-defence, is a direct challenge to the principle of non-resort to force, and therefore to the very nature of UN peace operations. Although the C-34 added the possibility of resorting to force 'in defence of the mandate'[25] to the principle of non-resort to force except in self-defence (a possibility incorporated in the 'Principles and Guidelines'), this evolution is still resisted and sometimes perceived as a deviation. Overall, there is an apparent tension between the conservatism of the key principles of peace operations, on the one hand, and the practical evolutions that have been endorsed by the Security Council, on the other, in particular the protection of civilians and the implied possible resort to force.

The impact of the 'commitment gap' on robust peacekeeping

The North–South divisions over peacekeeping issues have been further shaped by some of the trends in peace operations. Debates on contemporary peacekeeping cannot ignore some of its tangible characteristics, and in particular who is doing what in peace operations. In fact, while Western states are the main financial contributors to the peacekeeping budget, they have been largely absent in terms of troop contributions since the mid-1990s.[26] Conversely, the developing countries have shouldered the largest troop contributions, and to a large extent have thus shaped the politics of peacekeeping in the field.[27] At the same time, the peacekeeping decision-making process remains dominated by the Security Council and its permanent members, to the detriment and chagrin of the main TCCs. This division of labour feeds the divide and the politicization of debates, particularly when, as is the case with robust peacekeeping, a concept is pushed by countries that are unlikely to actually implement it. Furthermore, the commitment gap raises questions about the abilities of TCCs to be 'robust' militarily. Former Under-Secretary-General for Peacekeeping Operations Jean-Marie Guéhenno identifies three negative consequences of this paradox. First, there is 'much less willingness among troop contributors to take risks if the risks that they are expected to take are not shared by those who make the decisions'; second, the 'capacities available in the armed forces of the richer nations (intelligence, mobility, targeted firepower) mitigate the risks of robust peacekeeping and would make it more effective'; third, robust peacekeeping can work

> only if it is embedded in a broader political strategy. While developed countries can give political support to a UN mission through non-military means, their systematic absence in UN military deployments undermines and weakens the message of universal

commitment that such deployments should convey, and can be construed as a lack of strategic commitment to the success of the mission.[28]

These points illustrate the difficulty of confining the debate to the issue of robustness when it is one element among many influencing the effectiveness of peacekeeping. The mere idea that robustness requires some sort of collegiality and burden-sharing among member states is hard to contest and undermines the Western position accordingly. For some troop contributors, this leads to the possible role of Western countries in financing and equipping the TCCs to enable them to implement robustness. 'If the countries that push for robustness do not want to send their own troops, let them finance and/or equip the countries that are doing the job,' is an argument often heard in New York.[29]

These divergences led some NAM members to contest the term 'robust peacekeeping' at the C-34's 2010 session to propose an 'effective peacekeeping' instead, objecting to the idea that robustness can be presented as the solution to what they see as much broader problems.[30] Eventually, the C-34 Report mentioned neither 'robust peacekeeping' nor the use of force. However, it

> recognizes the necessity to intensify dialogue among Member States and the Secretariat, including in this forum, on ways and means to enhance the effectiveness of peacekeeping missions, including by addressing the requirement for peacekeeping missions to be able to deter, through the posture they adopt and actions they take, threats to the implementation of mandates, safety and security of peacekeeping personnel, and ongoing peace processes, in accordance with the Charter of the United Nations.[31]

The wording may seem disappointing for proponents of an explicit reference to robust peacekeeping. Given the divergences expressed in the debates, however, the language has the merit of characterizing robustness by periphrases. That peacekeepers should be able to deter threats to peace processes, through their posture, recalls the vocabulary used for robustness. Moreover, the reference to peace processes goes much further than robustness confined to force protection, indicating a need to be firm at the political level, for example against the host state.

How feasible is robustness?

Any realistic approach to the reform of UN peacekeeping must reconcile what is needed and what is possible, and must therefore account for the enduring constraints of multidimensional peace operations. These constraints relate to the existence of a political process that underlies the deployment of a peace operation, the extent to which the Security Council is backing this process, the durability of a ceasefire or peace agreement, the nature of host state consent, the number and quality of troops available, and their propensity to take risks in the implementation of the mandate. Robustness needs to be approached in relation to these constraints, to which it is closely linked and that directly impact its feasibility. Three issues require special attention: the requirements of robust peacekeeping, its unintended consequences, and the varied degrees of its feasibility.

Requirements of robust peacekeeping

Robust peacekeeping implies a suite of political and operational requirements. Both the DPKO/DFS 'Concept Note on Robust Peacekeeping' and the 'New Horizon' non-paper provide lists of such requirements. The Concept Note refers to 'clear and achievable mandates', 'improved consultation', 'better logistics and support', 'enhanced capacities and structures', 'enhanced training and readiness standards', a 'comprehensive communication strategy', and 'strong leadership'.[32] In the same vein, the 'New Horizon' non-paper states that robust peacekeeping requires 'agreed minimum standards among contributing countries', a 'high degree of mobility . . . and the willingness and capacity to operate at a high tempo for sustained periods, night and day', 'effective mission command and control structures and units that can work together in larger formations', 'regular joint training and exercises', 'enhanced situational awareness and risk analysis', 'scenario-based planning and reliable contingency arrangements', 'modern technology, responsive logistics support and delegated authority to take difficult decisions in the field', to which the document adds 'the commitment of the Security Council and the willingness of troop and police contributors to implement [a resolution]'.[33]

The UN Secretariat plays its part when it pushes for the improvement of state capabilities and practices, and the setting of standards in the peacekeeping domain. However, the list of requirements is very ambitious, and difficult to square with the constraints of contemporary peace operations, not to mention the financial implications of acquiring modern equipment.

With a few exceptions the main TCCs fall well short on most of the listed requirements. The last ten years of UN involvement in peace operations have amply demonstrated this in relation to UN overstretch, deployment and logistical problems, level of equipment, and performance of troop and police suppliers.[34] Whether NATO members would meet the requirements is far from certain, and the average level of equipment and training within NATO is significantly higher than that within the main UN TCCs. Once again the meaning and feasibility of robust peacekeeping in the absence of the countries that are best equipped and trained for it must be interrogated.

Also integral to robustness is a strong and lasting commitment by the Security Council and personnel contributors. Although robust peacekeeping is explicitly mandated by the Security Council, its unity and full support of peacekeepers' actions on the ground is never guaranteed over time. The level of commitment of contributors is equally erratic. For personnel contributors, robustness requires preparation, a sound knowledge of what robustness means politically and operationally and how robustness is distinguished from peace enforcement (in rules of engagement), awareness of the potential risks of robust action (see below), and the readiness to take casualties. A brief survey of UN operations and state policies over the last decade reveals a scarcity of countries displaying such a level of preparedness. Whether in relation to robustness or to the protection of civilians, troop contributors have little expertise in operationalizing Security Council resolutions.[35]

Furthermore, to produce results, robust action also necessitates consecutive longer-term measures (police deployment, rule of law, disarmament) in order to consolidate the outcomes of robustness. Referencing the British operation in Sierra Leone (2000) and the French/EU operation in the DRC (2003), Mats Berdal concludes that the 'strategic impact' of 'coercive military action' 'depends crucially on what follows the short-term tactical engagement'.[36] Unless follow-up actions are present, 'it is not clear that the occasional robust foray will do the trick'.[37] This cautionary note relates not only to the need for a political objective that is served by robustness, but also to the impossibility of singling out robustness from other peacekeeping and peacebuilding activities. Most importantly, while robustness would be an option in operations that are perceived as falling within the strategic interests of the intervening countries (as in Afghanistan), the nature of UN peacekeeping makes it difficult to determine the tong-term commitment of TCCs to robustness. This is true simply because troop contributors frequently have little strategic interest at stake in the operation's host state. In other words, what is the 'strategic value' of the place where they intervene that would justify risking escalation of violence and fatalities?[38]

In summary, robust peacekeeping faces 'conceptual overstretch', reflected by the mismatch between doctrinal development and the political and operational capacity of the UN and its member states to implement the concept.[39]

Unintended consequences

The narrative in favour of robust peacekeeping generally assumes that robustness comes as a solution to some of the difficulties that peace operations face. Although this may be true in some circumstances, robustness also carries unintended consequences that may challenge its relevance. The DPKO/DFS Concept Note identifies the following risks of robust peacekeeping:[40]

- 'loss or perception of loss of impartiality by a peacekeeping operation providing robust support to a government that is party to an ongoing conflict';
- risk deriving from 'collateral damage and civilian casualties as a result of robust military/police operations';
- 'conflict escalation by spoilers in reaction to a robust mandate implementation';
- perception by host authorities and population of 'infringement on national sovereignty';
- 'greater insecurity and retaliation either against peacekeepers or "soft" targets such as humanitarian actors and the local population, as well as the possibility of population displacement and its associated consequences'.

The Concept Note adds that the Security Council 'should be clearly informed of the risks before the decision [on the use of force] is taken'.

The risk of conflict escalation requires particular attention because it may imply an undesired shift from the use of force at the tactical level (which falls within robust peacekeeping) to the use of force at the strategic level (which characterizes peace enforcement). Ensuring that the use of force indeed remains at the tactical level is a complex issue for peacekeepers. The blurring gives credence to the argument put forward by some NAM countries that posits that the distinction between robust peacekeeping and peace enforcement is impossible to guarantee in practice. In the DRC, for example, some robust operations conducted by the UN operation against militias in the Ituri district in 2005 were close to war-fighting, leading the UN to comment on the nature of its 'peacekeeping' engagement.[41]

The management of the risk of conflict escalation has to do with the command and control structure of the operation. A critique by Western states of the UN system is its decentralized nature, with a high degree of devolution to the field in the persons of the special representative of the secretary-general (SRSG) and the force commander, and the risk that decisions taken at field level have consequences well beyond the mission itself. This decentralized command and control model is contrary to the more centralized approach of the EU or NATO, where strategic control remains at headquarters level. According to Guéhenno, the 'objective should be to strengthen the grip of UN Headquarters on missions, above all for peacekeeping missions with robust mandates, without losing the flexibility of a decentralized approach'.[42]

Appropriate command and control arrangements are all the more important when robustness requires a degree of expertise that most troop contributors do not have. At the field level, this expertise is closer to that of police forces than to the military, especially in urban environments where proximity to local populations is high and where escalation prevention cannot be improvised. The role played by the UN mission in Haiti (MINUSTAH) attests to this specificity of a robust posture within cities. Brazilian peacekeepers acted quite robustly on several occasions in the slums of Port-au-Prince at the request of the Haitian government, and they were indeed effective in trouncing some of the criminal groups. However, the operations were conducted by military – not police – units that had very limited training in urban modes of action, and therefore carried the risk of massive collateral damage, for example by the extensive use of automatic weapons in the high-density area of Cité-Soleil in July 2005. Indeed, in this particular case, allegations of excessive use of force and even human rights violations by the MINUSTAH were made by several human rights organizations. [43]

At the political level, the risk of loss of impartiality and legitimacy is exacerbated by the intrusive and coercive nature of robust peacekeeping. Robustness is supposed to provide credibility to a mission, and may also enhance the host state's sovereignty by confronting non-state spoilers,[44] but the chance that the consequent use of force will damage its impartiality and legitimacy is high. The problem reinforces the need to embed robust peacekeeping in a political framework that robustness is supposed to serve.[45] The effectiveness and legitimacy of robust peacekeeping are dependent on the level of political backing that it gets from the Security Council members, the main personnel contributors, and the host state.

The full backing of the host state is crucial, in particular when confronting so-called spoilers.[46] But when consent is weak and tenuous as in Sudan and the DRC, when the spoilers are backed by the government as in Darfur, or when spoilers are either the state itself or resistance groups such as Hezbollah, then the very feasibility of robustness is at stake. Here again the tension between what is required and what is possible comes to the surface. In most UN peace missions, the level of political support and the character of the political process are issues of constant concern. The extent to which robustness is possible in these circumstances is highly debateable.

Finally, altering the nature of peace operations through the adoption of a more openly robust posture is likely to lead to unpredictable counter-reactions – concerning host acceptance, spoilers' behaviour, impacts on local actors, and even TCC motives and behaviour. Robustness may deter some spoilers, but it may also induce reactions or new forms of disruption that would not have appeared in the absence of robustness. Faced with a robust military force, politically motivated groups may change tactics or areas of operations in a way that will further complicate the robust approach. As Richard Gowan and Benjamin Tortolani argue, robustness creates new vulnerabilities that have not been clearly identified and that vary from one mission to the other,[47] A robust approach can also directly impact on the level of integration (when risks of retaliation against non-military components of the operation increase), the unity among contributors (that may diverge on the virtues of robustness), and the level of cooperation with external partners. It follows that, although robustness is presented as a solution, there may be cases where it is part of the problem.

Varying degrees of feasibility according to the meaning of robustness

Finally, the several meanings of 'robust peacekeeping' lead to a typology of activities that can be significantly different, therefore necessitating different types of requirements. First, the generic term of 'robust peacekeeping' embraces both the idea of robustness in protection of the force and robustness in defence of the mandate, which in most cases includes protecting civilians. This amalgam is problematic, as these two activities are fundamentally different. Robust peacekeeping for the protection of the force is aimed at ensuring a certain level of security for the peacekeepers and at deterring intermittent or continuous harassment from spoilers. It is peacekeeper centred and is regarded by many potential and actual contributors as a condition of their commitment. By contrast, robust peacekeeping in defence of the mandate and in the protection of civilians is mandate centred and is far more ambitious. The two approaches entail different postures, operational capabilities, and levels of political commitment from the Security Council, TCCs and host authorities. In Darfur, for example, where peacekeepers face attacks on a daily basis, few would contest the necessity of guaranteeing their protection. This vision of robustness is broadly accepted, including by a majority of NAM states. Yet robustness in confronting the spoilers in a coercive way or in implementing the mandate is far less acceptable, in particular to the TCCs, some of which neighbour Sudan and would be reluctant to engage in a confrontation with state-backed spoilers.

Robustness in defence of the mandate places the operation in a very different situation. First, it increases the degree of intrusiveness into the internal affairs of the host state as well as the risk of moving from the use of force at the tactical level to that at the strategic level. Second, the above-mentioned changes directly impact on the nature of motives and the degree of commitment from the contributing states. Leaving aside the capabilities issue, the key question is whether current TCCs would indeed consider robustness beyond their own protection. Are they ready to assume the above-identified risks? Does their conceptualization of their role in UN peace operations allow them to contemplate a long-term confrontation with potential spoilers that are at times backed by the host state? If we do not confine the debate to current TCCs, would Western states be ready and/or willing to commit to a possible and repeated use of force against spoilers in a UN peace mission? Not many examples come to mind to demonstrate such willingness. When the UK and France did take the risks of defeating spoilers, respectively in Sierra Leone (Operation *Palliser)* and the DRC in 2003 (EU-led Operation *Artemis)*, the operations were limited in time and space, in contrast to usual operations by the UN.[48]

Furthermore, to what extent are host states ready to accept robust peacekeeping operations and the associated threat to their sovereignty? The cases of Sudan and Lebanon are telling examples. In the case of Sudan, President Omar al-Bashir made sure that any troop contributor inclined to act robustly would not participate. In the case of Lebanon, the government refused to accept any explicit reference to Chapter VII of the UN Charter though resolution 1701 (2006) authorized 'UNIFIL [UN Interim Force in Lebanon] to take all necessary action in areas of deployment of its forces and as it deems within its capabilities, to ensure that its area of operations is not utilized for hostile activities of any kind, to resist attempts by forceful means to prevent it from discharging its duties under the mandate of the Security Council'.[49] And, despite Western states' initial insistence on the robustness of UNIFIL II, such robustness is in practice peacekeeper centred rather than mandate centred, and Western states are extremely reluctant to take any action that could lead to escalation. In both cases, potential spoilers are powerful and/or state-backed and therefore alter the nature of robustness.

In general terms, while the peacekeeper-centred approach to robustness is broadly accepted, there is little indication of readiness among UN member states to embrace the robust peacekeeping approach in all its dimensions. On the contrary, the majority of current operations evince a strong reluctance to do so. In some cases, as in the DRC with Indian and Pakistani contingents, or in Haiti with Brazilian peacekeepers, robust action has been taken. Yet very few countries are ready to assume the consequences of this type of action over a long period. It follows that a distinction between robustness in protection of the force and robustness in defence of the mandate may be justified. Thus far, it appears that housing the two notions under the same conceptual umbrella is counterproductive.

Conclusion

Contemporary peace operations face a wide range of difficulties which sometimes leads them to overall failure. Addressing those difficulties is critical and requires long-term efforts that target different actors and activities. Guaranteeing that UN peace operations are given the means to implement mandates, including through the use of force in some cases, is a pivotal issue. Rwanda and Srebrenica are cases in point where peacekeepers remained passive while massive violations of human rights were perpetrated. In the same vein, letting criminal groups and other militias harass UN units is unacceptable. Consequently, robustness does have some merits that need to be developed. At the same time, I have argued that robustness poses a host of conceptual as well as operational difficulties that undermine its coherence and feasibility.

Conceptually, the idea of robustness places peacekeepers in the grey area between peace-keeping and peace enforcement, and therefore challenges the key principles of peacekeeping. Understandably this creates resistance. At the operational level, the sense of common effort that robust peacekeeping implies is undermined by the commitment gap in troop contributions and the absence of Western states from UN operations. Robustness pushed by the North and implemented by the South has clearly been problematic. Finally, and most importantly, while robustness needs to be part of a broader political strategy (more than does 'non-robust' peacekeeping), backed by the Security Council, the main TCCs, and even the host state, this has not been observed to date. It follows that the conditions for effectively implementing robustness do not seem to be met. The worst scenario would be robust peacekeeping as a substitute for a lack of strategy.

Notes

1 The Brahimi Report mentions a 'robust doctrine' (p.ix), 'sufficiently robust rules of engagement' (p.x), 'robust peacekeeping forces' (p.xi), 'robust force posture' (p.1), and 'robust rules of engagement' (pp. 10, 54). 'Report of the Panel on United Nations Peace Operations', UN doc., A/55/305, S/2000/809, 21 Aug. 2000.
2 See Victoria Holt and Glyn Taylor, 'Protecting Civilians in the Context of UN Peace keeping Operations. Successes, Setbacks and Remaining Challenges', independent study, DPKO and Office for the Coordination of Humanitarian Assistance (OCHA), New York, 2009.
3 See Ian Johnstone, 'Dilemmas of Robust Peace Operations', *Annual Review of Global Peace Operations 2006*, New York: Center on International Cooperation, New York University/ Boulder, CO: Lynne Rienner 2006, pp. 1–17.
4 'United Nations Peacekeeping Operations. Principles and Guidelines' ('Capstone Doctrine'), DPKO/DFS, New York, 2008; 'A New Partnership Agenda. Charting a New Horizon for UN Peacekeeping', DPKO/DFS, non-paper, New York, 2009; 'DPKO/DFS Concept Note on Robust Peacekeeping', Office of Military Affairs, DPKO, New York, 2009.
5 Thierry Tardy, 'The UN and the Use of force. A Marriage against Nature', *Security Dialogue* Vol. 38, No. 1, 2007, pp. 49–70,
6 See John Ruggie, 'Wandering in the Void. Charting the UN's New Strategic Role', *Foreign Affairs*, Vol. 72, No. 5, 1993, p. 28; Marrack Goulding, 'The Evolution of United Nations Peacekeeping', *International Affairs*, Vol. 69, No. 3, 1993, p. 461.
7 See Peter Viggo Jakobsen, 'The Emerging Consensus on Grey Area Peace Operations Doctrine: Will It Last and Enhance Operational Effectiveness?', *International Peacekeeping*, Vol. 7, No. 3, 2000, pp. 36–56.

8 'Principles and Guidelines' (see n.4 above), p. 98.

9 Ibid., pp. 34–5.

10 'A New Partnership Agenda' (see n.4 above), p. 21.

11 'DPKO/DFS Concept Note' (see n.4 above), p. 1.

12 Ibid., p. 3.

13 See Proceedings of the C-34 debates, UN doc, GA/PK/203, 22 Feb. 2010.

14 'DPKO/DFS Concept Note' (see n.4 above), p. 2.

15 DPKO's 'Principles and Guidelines' states in a footnote that 'the list [of terms of its glossary] does not provide authoritative UN definitions', and that 'official UN definitions are being considered in the context of the ongoing terminology deliberations of the General Assembly's Special Committee on Peacekeeping Operations' (see n.4 above), p. 100.

16 The 'DPKO/DFS Concept Note' also mentions 'robust support' (see n.4 above), p. 3.

17 For example, the representative of South Africa at the C-34 session spoke about robust peacekeeping using the same terms as those of the 'New Horizon' non-paper. Declaration of the Representative of South Africa, UN doc, GA/PK/203 [see n.13 above].

18 'Report of the Special Committee on Peacekeeping Operations and Its Working Group', UN doc, A/59/19, 1 March 2005, §46.

19 See Statement of the Representative of India in the Security Council, 5 Aug. 2009: 'India is not unfamiliar with the concept of "robust" peacekeeping', as it contributed in a major way to the UN operation in Congo in the 1960s that was 'the first UN "robust" peacekeeping operation' (at: www.un.int/india/2009/ind1585.pdf).

20 Several experts have proposed that DPKO reframe its approach and even abandon the term 'robust'. See Cedric de Coning, Andreas O. Stensland, and Thierry Tardy (eds), *Beyond the 'New Horizon'*, Oslo: NUPI and GCSP, 2010.

21 See Proceedings of the C-34 debates (n.13 above) and UN doc, GA/PK/204, 23 Feb. 2010.

22 Author's interviews at Missions to the UN, New York, June 2010.

23 Author's interviews with NAM country representatives, New York, June 2010; see also Philip Cunliffe (ed.), *Critical Perspectives on the Responsibility to Protect: Interrogating Theory and Practice*, London: Routledge, forthcoming.

24 See UN Security Council resolutions 1706 (2006); 1784 (2007); 1812 (2008); 1828 (2008); 1870 (2009); 1881 (2009); 1919 (2010); 1935 (2010).

25 See 'Report of the Special Committee' (n.18 above), §30.

26 Alex Bellamy and Paul Williams, 'The West and Contemporary Peace Operations', *Journal of Peace Research*, Vol. 46, No. 1, 2009, pp. 39–57; Thierry Tardy, *Gestion de crise, maintien et consolidation de la paix. Acteurs, activités, défis* [Crisis Management, Peacekeeping and Peacebuilding. Actors, Activities, Challenges], Louvain-la-Neuve: De Boeck, 2009, pp.] 83–5.

27 As of July 2010, the top ten troop contributors were Pakistan, Bangladesh, India, Nigeria, Egypt, Nepal, Ghana, Rwanda, Jordan, and Uruguay (UN website at: www.un.org/en/peacekeeping/contributors/2010/june10_2.pdf).

28 Jean-Marie Guéhenno, 'Robust Peacekeeping: Building Political Consensus and Strengthening Command and Control', in *Robust Peacekeeping: The Politics of Force*, New York: Center on International Cooperation, New York University, 2009, p. 9.

29 Author's interviews at Missions to the UN, New York, June 2010.

30 Cf. Declaration of the Representative of Morocco on behalf of the NAM at the C-34, UN doc, GA/PK/203, 22 Feb. 2010.

31 'Report of the Special Committee' (see n.18 above), § 65.

32 'DPKO/DFS Concept Note' (see n.4 above), pp. 4–5.

33 'New Horizon Report' (see n.4 above), p. 21.

34 Cf. Richard Gowan and Benjamin Tortolani, 'Robust Peacekeeping and its Limitations', in *Robust Peacekeeping* (see n.28 above), p.52.

35 On the difficulty of operationalizing the mandate on protection of civilians, see Holt and Taylor (n. 2 above).

36 Mats Berdal, *Building Peace after War*, London: International Institute for Security Studies, 2009, p. 111.

37 Maciek Hawrylak and David Malone, 'Haiti, Again! A Tough Peacebuilding Task', *Policy Options*, Sept. 2005, p. 36, cited in Berdal (see n.36 above), p. 111.

38 See Sarjoh Bah, 'Understanding the Political Dimensions of Robust Peacekeeping', presentation at

seminar on 'Robust Peacekeeping: Principles and Practical Guidelines', French Ministry of Defence and Research Network on Peacekeeping Operations (Montreal), Paris, 12–13 April 2010.

39 See Stian Kjeksrud, 'Matching Robust Ambitions with Robust Action in UN Peace Operations. Towards a Conceptual Overstretch?', Norwegian Defence Research Establishment, Oslo, April 2009.

40 'DPKO/DFS Concept Note' (see n.4 above), p. 3.

41 See Denis Tull, 'Peacekeeping in the Democratic Republic of Congo: Waging Peace and Fighting War', *International Peacekeeping*, Vol. 16, No. 2, 2009, pp. 224–5. Tull also notes the inconsistency of the MONUC's action in not applying the same level of robustness throughout the DRC.

42 Guéhenno (see n.28 above), p. 11.

43 Following the events in Haiti in July 2005, the UN Commission of Human Rights' Special Rapporteur on Extrajudicial, Summary or Arbitrary Executions asked MINUSTAH for clarifications regarding 'allegations of serious human rights violations' committed by the blue helmets. In his report to the Commission on 27 March 2006, the Special Rapporteur described MINUSTAH's response as 'broadly satisfactory'. See 'Report of the Special Rapporteur, Commission on Human Rights', UN doc, E/CN.4/2006/53/Add.1, 27 March 2006; 'Report of the Secretary-General on the UN Stabilization Mission in Haiti', UN doc, S/2006/592, 28 July 2006. In parallel, a complaint against Brazil was submitted to the Inter-American Commission on Human Rights by human rights activists, but was eventually rejected by the Commission.

44 In Haiti, notwithstanding the controversy over some of its methods, MINUSTAH's action against criminal groups in Port-au-Prince was clearly aimed at enhancing the government's own authority. Also see Johnstone (n.3 above), pp. 5, 13.

45 See Berdal (n.36 above), pp. 100–121.

46 See Bah (n.38 above).

47 Gowan and Tortolani (see n.34 above), p. 53.

48 Berdal (see n.36 above), pp. 102–15.

49 UN Security Council resolution 1701, 11 Aug. 2006; see also Alexandra Novosseloff and Richard Gowan, 'Security Council Diplomacy and the New UNIFIL', in Efrat Elron and Joe Soeters (eds), *Multiple Perspectives on UNIFIL*, New York: International Peace Institute, 2011.

36 Social entrepreneurs and constructive change

The wisdom of circumventing conflict

Ryszard Praszkier, Andrzej Nowak and Peter T. Coleman

Ashoka Fellows – social entrepreneurs – often operate in a context of conflict as they challenge critical social problems that are seemingly hopeless and unsolvable. We present the strategies they employ, such as building new positive attractors (i.e., social capital) outside the field of influence of the conflict attractors; as a next step, they build a feedback loop between the success of their initiatives and reinforcement of social capital. Through subsequent positive experiences, they introduce constructive change outside of the field of conflict in a manner that modifies the societal balance based on higher levels of trust and tendencies to cooperate. Through this strategy, they make conflict less relevant and less salient. Several case studies are presented as illustrations of this approach, and general principles are identified.

Our aim is to compare and contrast two distinct ways of tackling seemingly intractable conflicts. The traditional approach is to attack the conflict directly, focusing on issues that divide the parties and attempting to find common ground. The alternative approach is to circumvent the conflict altogether, focusing effort instead on creating a cooperative setting "somewhere else," away from the gravity of the conflict. The fact that conflicts seem intractable suggests that the traditional approach may be missing some important points. However, from a positive perspective, there is a compelling theoretical rationale for favoring the alternative approach to conflict resolution. We develop this rationale and, more important, illustrate the feasibility and utility of this approach by contrasting it with the traditional approach in the context of a specific (and seemingly intractable) conflict.

A traditional approach

A conflict-resolution and peace-building group arrived at a Palestinian school in Israel to work on its planned initiative. The group defined its mission as "to promote peaceful coexistence among Muslims, Christians, and Jews in Israel/Palestine" exclusively through an intensive educational program in peace and conflict resolution. The program comprised a series of workshops that featured various exercises designed to develop participants' conflict-resolution skills and to change their perspective on the subject of conflict itself. It soon became clear that this intervention evoked negative feelings and attitudes among the local Palestinians. Some complained that the interveners simply did not have sufficient understanding of their circumstances; others expressed the opinion that by making the Palestinians the focus of the program, the interveners were implying that they, the Palestinians, were the source of the problem. Resentments built, and the result was that the school authorities were forced to terminate the program long before its completion.

An alternative approach

In the second instance, a group of activists, who worked closely with local residents and were familiar with the specific needs of the community, decided to focus their work on an area that crossed cultural lines and was a shared interest of both groups: information technology (IT). The group proceeded to establish an IT school for Arab and Jewish students. As they had intuited, the study of computer science proved to be a "bonding agent" among the students, without regard to religious and ethnic differences. The long-term outcome resulted in alumni starting their own IT businesses and becoming outstanding models of Arab-Jewish cooperation. The leaders of the program, when asked to add peace-building courses to the curriculum, respectfully declined, declaring that doing so would polarize and antagonize the participants in the well-oiled system they had built.

Why were there such significantly different results between the two well-intentioned interventions? We have observed that behind some of these highly effective methodologies are the passionate and creative individuals known as *social entrepreneurs*. Because of the nature of their work – meeting the challenge of solving "the unsolvable" and ultimately bringing about change and innovation – social entrepreneurs usually find themselves in conflict with a rigid and inflexible society.

What are the methods they use to circumvent potential conflict situations and make constructive improvements in communities? We explore this question beginning with the introduction of the theoretical framework based on dynamical systems theory, followed by an analysis of social entrepreneurship, then sharing insights gleaned from five case studies that define the core principles of this "anti-conflict-resolution" approach to peace-building. We conclude with a discussion of the implications of this model for research and practice on changing the dynamics of difficult, long-term conflicts.

Theoretical framework: dynamical social psychology

Critical social problems in communities are sometimes long-lasting and intractable *because* the societies that embody them have over decades developed their own stable equilibriums associated with the problems (De Rosnay, 1997) that, in effect, tend to disable or disperse any movement for change. There are usually "good" and "rational" reasons for striking specific balance points with regard to such problems, so one should not blame societies for being resistant to change. On the contrary, according to O'Toole (1996), resistance may be a healthy symptom indicating cohesiveness, shared values, bonds, and a common symbolic capital. However, there are some social problems that cry out for change, such as unemployment, economically disenfranchised communities, illiteracy, discrimination against women in the job market, gaps in educational achievement, lack of inclusiveness of the disabled, environmental threats, domestic violence, child abuse, and many more. Yet, imposing change and challenging the societal equilibrium in settings struggling with such challenges is usually a recipe for creating conflict.

Through its analysis of the stable states toward which social systems are ultimately drawn, the paradigm of dynamical social psychology offers us insight into this phenomenon. As described by Nowak and Lewenstein (1994) and Vallacher and Nowak (2005), social systems have a tendency to drift back toward a previously established stable state regardless of actions taken to introduce a change in direction. This stable state is called an attractor. According to dynamical social psychology, real change is created by building new attractors toward which the system will naturally tend to drift, rather than by temporarily disrupting the state of a system within its old equilibrium.

One strategy for developing new attractors in social systems is by initiating small changes in basic rules of interactions between people and groups, which can result in significant changes on the macro level over time. For example, in many places around the world, cross-ethnic, cross-religious, and cross-cultural conflicts are impeding economic development. Krzysztof Czyzewski, a social entrepreneur from Poland,[1] demonstrated that the attempt to overcome deeply ingrained cross-border and cross-religious prejudices can be far more effective when addressed through a variety of small, community-based initiatives rather than tackling the issues head-on (e.g., through lecturing or training members of the society). On the Polish-Lithuanian-Belarus border, a previously economically disadvantaged area, Krzysztof encouraged children to publish a local chronicle, publicizing their efforts in collecting and exhibiting old postcards and photos, and tracing the multi-ethnic history of the area. The historic Catholic, Jewish, Orthodox, and Protestant roots in the region are thereby rescued from obscurity and disseminated throughout the community. Other initiatives involve teaching multi-traditional crafts and cross-cultural music lessons. Also, local youth who in the past were living lives dominated by a spirit of hopelessness and depression, are now involved in reviving the Indigenous Jewish folk music, even founding a Klezmer Orchestra, which performs locally at home, as well as abroad. By transforming young people's perceptions and roles within communities scarred by historical divides, Krzysztof is creating a new vision for the future. His brand of entrepreneurship shows how many small initiatives can accumulate and foster a shift in the collective mindset of a community, which eventually engenders social and economic development.[2] If it is possible that such seemingly irrelevant and unrelated initiatives could lead to the emergence of a new, more constructive attractor within a community, then this approach may offer an important alternative and rationale for circumventing conflict.

From the Palestinian-Israeli cases cited in the introduction, we can conclude that in highly polarized settings, rather than approaching the conflict head-on, it can be far more effective to address it indirectly. The first case may be characterized as challenging the conflict situation with the direct force of a bulldozer, which led to the disruption of the system and yielded a setback. The second narrative demonstrates that creating situations where the attention is focused on an external common interest, one that requires interacting cooperatively and without mutual antagonism, in time renders the conflict less relevant. In other words, this case is also about building cooperation and trust around "something else" (i.e., IT), other than the conflict, resulting in an emergent positive attractor.

Social activists working from a conflict-resolution paradigm often tend to address situations directly, disrupting the *status quo* through their actions. In situations of protracted social conflict, the result is often neutral (the system, over time, drifts back to the old attractor) or negative (the dynamics of the system may backfire, leaving damage in its wake). Moving the focus away from the central conflict may strike some as improbable. For instance, in one of the lethargic and underdeveloped Polish communities with skyrocketing juvenile delinquency, including the prevalence of bullying as a lifestyle, there was a growing conflict between various groups of troubled youth and the community. Traditional approaches (i.e., addressing the problem directly) failed; instead, the conflict was resolved through introducing dance lessons for the boys. The idea was based on the observation that, during community parties, the boys who did not dance usually were the ones who drank and instigated fights, whereas the boys who took part in the dancing behaved properly. As a result of the boys' participation in the dance lessons – as far-fetched as it may have seemed at first glance – dancing became trendy and, indirectly, alleviated the conflict.

According to Martin and Osberg (2007), "the (social) entrepreneur is inspired to alter the unpleasant equilibrium" (p. 33). In other words, it is the social entrepreneurs who are focused on changing the attractors. The genius of social entrepreneurs may, therefore, be related to modifying the regulatory parameters of trust and cooperation instead of addressing the conflict situation directly.

Social entrepreneurs

According to Drayton (2000), Hammonds (2005), and Bornstein (1998, 2004), social entrepreneurs are a rich source of new and creative ideas on how to solve the pressing social problems of the day. Made of distinguished ethical fiber, their impact is far-reaching.

We define *social entrepreneurs* here according to the selection criteria used by the international association Ashoka, Innovators for the Public.[3] These include the following:

- Having a new idea for solving a critical social problem.
- Being creative (as a personality trait).
- Having an entrepreneurial personality.
- Envisioning the broad social impact of the idea.
- Possessing an unquestionable ethical fiber.[4]

Since 1980, Ashoka has had unprecedented worldwide experience in identifying and selecting leading social entrepreneurs. The founder and Chief Executive Officer of Ashoka, Bill Drayton, was the first to introduce the concept of social entrepreneurship as a method for effecting social change. Drayton (2002) claimed that there is no social entrepreneur without a powerful, system-changing idea and that social entrepreneurs "envisage a systemic change, identifying the jiu-jitsu points that allow them to tip the whole society into the new path and then persist and persist until the job is done" (p. 123).

Social entrepreneurs are selected to be Ashoka Fellows through a rigorous, multi-stage selection process.[5] Currently 2,200 Fellows from 70 countries have been selected and supported by this organization.[6] The following case studies illustrate the way social entrepreneurs are approaching conflict situations. We attempt to glean from these cases a few basic principles for working constructively *with* conflict by working *away from* conflict.

Case studies

The five cases we explore here (involving 6 Ashoka Fellows, as 1 is a joint case) (a) represent several continents and cultures, (b) address a diverse set of critical social problems, and (c) occur in situations of seemingly intractable and protracted conflicts. In addition, the cases were chosen based on the accessibility of information and materials. The cohort comprises 4 men and 2 women, 40 to 45 years old, who exemplify diverse walks of life, and who started out as professionals in several fields such as architecture, sociology, religion, management, and education. They all chose social entrepreneurship as the next step in their personal and professional development. The projects discussed here were implemented between 1999 and 2004 – 4 had total communities in their sights, and 2 focused on specific problems. All of the changes are still operational and are gradually being replicated. Each of the cases is characterized in the following way:

1. The critical issues addressed.
2. A description of the conflict along two dimensions:

- Structured-unstructured: Some conflicts are well-structured: The parties involved are well-defined, as are the issues involved in the conflict. In other cases, the conflict may be hard to capture and specify, despite the existence of interpersonal and intergroup tension.
- Manifest-latent: Some conflicts are fully developed and obvious to all involved. However, in many situations, the conflict lurks below the surface, not yet revealed and not yet defined. Detecting and addressing the early indicators of those potential conflicts may help to defuse them.

3. The social entrepreneur's approach (descriptive) and the way the conflict was circumvented through building a new attractor.
4. Results of the initiative.

David Kuria, Kenya[7]

A high potential for conflict existed for years around the Nairobi-Kibera slums, the biggest slum in Nairobi and the second largest in Africa, after Soweto. It is home to 800,000 people, about one-third of the entire population of Nairobi, squeezed into a territory occupying one square mile. Added to the overcrowding, these populations live in squalid conditions. Due to the absence of government services, Kibera relies on a privately run, largely inadequate water supply. It is estimated that the 800,000 residents have to share 600 toilets. The result is indiscriminate disposal of waste; ancient, stinking latrines; open sewers; no proper drainage; no rubbish collection; and widespread disease. The critical issue is sanitation. Top-down solutions failed (e.g., the efforts of the United Nations Children's Fund), as they violated the taboos and prejudices of the local people. Furthermore, they resulted in growing resistance and elicited a "they want to impose things on us against our will" response. These conditions contributed to a sense of hopelessness among the youth, leading to an increase in crimes, drug use, and dropouts.

Kiberia's decades-old status as a health threat to the region created a seemingly insurmountable and protracted conflict with the government over sanitation issues. The community objected to top-down solutions, vandalized the facilities, and continued to maintain an unsanitary disaster area. The conflict dimensions are as follows:

- Sanitation issues: a well-structured and manifest conflict.
- Juvenile crime: unstructured and potentially volatile.
- Cross-tribal violence: unstructured and latent, with a strong potential to become manifest, with well-identified tribal membership.

Approach. David Kuria became part of the community and, in doing so, developed a deeper understanding of local beliefs and habits. An architect by profession and a social entrepreneur by spirit, he then initiated many small-group discussions accompanied by actual illustrations drawn by members of the group depicting the way they would envision a public toilet "of their own." This process engaged the community and led to associating the idea with the people. From all the drawings, David put together realistic plans.

With some seed money that he raised, along with the volunteer work of the community members, David built the toilets. Each featured a variety of add-on services: shoe and boot polishing, soda machines, and cafeterias; one wall was reserved for advertising. The human waste was transformed into bio-gas, making it easier for women to cook. Clean and shining, the toilets became a focal social point. This soon became a draw for the media, which, for example, covered the "very important people" of Kenya visiting and getting their shoes polished. The communities imposed some fees on the use of the toilets and showers, with a 1-month family discount. Using those facilities became trendy, made people proud of the place, and triggered many other business initiatives, highlighting the positive impact of this success by strengthening and empowering the social capacity of the community.

Circumventing conflict through building a new attractor. David stepped away from the conflict between the community and the authorities and avoided direct confrontation over the issues of sanitation; instead, he redirected the energy into discussing and imagining their "dream toilets." The important component of this approach was reframing the symbolic understanding of the toilets into clean, modern, social centers associated with "cleaning." By doing this, he triggered a high-potential commitment and energy, which yielded cooperation and consequently social capital through which the toilets appeared as a natural outcome. As a result, there emerged a process of community business development. Establishing a positive feedback loop, the new initiatives became a constructive example of the power of enterprising actions, which triggered self-esteem and an openness to new initiatives and to cooperation.

Results. In 2003, David constructed the first three toilets in Kibera. The facility was maintained by a management committee elected by the slum community. The committee manages the facility through collection of user fees and by keeping the facility clean and in good working order. David's role at this point is to provide technical support and management advice to the committee. Each of the toilets was designed to serve 200 people, but currently serves 500. Because the facilities are kept clean, many residents have abandoned their own toilets and opted to pay for the cleaner facilities. After the building of the first three toilets proved a huge success in improving the hygiene and dignity of the residents of the Kibera slum, David is now concentrating on duplicating the facilities in the other 198 slums around Kenya. The finances generated from these enterprises go back to the management committee on an agreement to reduce the user fees. Even the human waste is collected and turned into gas, which is pumped back into the facility for lighting and heating water. The urine harvested is donated to community groups engaged in composting. David has convinced Safaricom, Kenya's largest telecommunications company, and Royal Gate, a local real estate firm, to purchase advertising spots at the facility; and Kiwi, Kenya's leading manufacturer of shoe polish, has also bought into the idea and is renting all the shoeshine spots. With these income streams plus user fees, the balance sheet is impressive.

Dagmara Bienkowska, Poland[8]

This project took place in an economically and socially disadvantaged region of southern Poland. Several top-down attempts at addressing the society's plight had failed, evoking frustration and resistance to outside experts who had little knowledge of the population. As a result of growing frustration, the society split into two distinct parts – Trzciana, which took possession of all the economic assets; and Zegocina, which was left without any financial capital. The inhabitants of the latter developed a lack-of-power attitude combined with distrust, aggression, and lowered self-esteem. The conflict between the two communities was apparently growing in strength and becoming virtually intractable. Also, the society split into several isolated and conflicting groups, such as youth and senior citizens. The conflict dimension is as follows:

• Conflict between the two split communities: structured and manifest.

Approach. Dagmara started her intervention in Zegocina by learning about the community from within: She lived there for 1 month, shared stories and lifestyles, spent time with youth groups, and so forth. She soon learned that, in the community, there is a strong identification with the region and dreams for its development. She noticed, however, that excluded from this shared sentiment were two groups: senior citizens and aggressive, wayward young people. On the other hand, she understood that both groups played significant roles in the community: the first through the ability to exert their influence, albeit from behind the scenes; the latter by occupying a prominent place on the list of negative stories that traveled through the community's gossip mill and acted as a magnet for shared frustrations.

Dagmara's first move was to involve both groups in a joint undertaking. While sharing a beer with some young people, she suggested they visit the senior citizens and gather some recipes of regional dishes. This worked out perfectly, as the senior citizens were more than eager to share their traditional recipes, and the young people felt that they were doing something new and important. The image of local bullies and senior citizens working on a project together, although inconceivable, was intriguing. The local authorities saw this as an opportunity and proceeded to print an unedited edition of the Cookbook of Zegocina County, distributing it at conferences as a local product that they could be proud of. The second edition was published professionally and sold out, and the income was channeled into community educational projects.

The success of the project transformed the youth group into a major entrepreneurial force, as they saw that cooperation yielded an immense payback. They launched several new ventures, triggering an entrepreneurial movement among other community members. For instance, during a time of national disaster, when the region was heavily affected by floods, it turned out that the Zegocina community was the best organized and coped the best with the disaster. Capitalizing on this development, a Zegocina Flood Book was published and sold as a manual for other communities to cope with natural disasters. The income again was channeled into the community's social projects. Eventually, through their bottom-up approach, Zegocina County experienced unforeseen economic development, surpassing all the neighboring communities (including the one that originally appropriated all the resources).

Circumventing conflict through building a new attractor. Dagmara circumvented the regular field of confrontation, which was the conflict between the two split communities. Primarily, she addressed the two most marginalized groups – the semi-bullying youth and the senior citizens – by creating a new field for their cooperation. She intuited that, by joining forces, the two groups could have a strong impact on the community. Dagmara prompted them to cooperate over a neutral topic (cooking recipes), far away from the conflict. Through this process, a new positive attractor appeared – the tendency toward cooperation and entrepreneurial behavior. The success of the consecutive undertakings proliferated in a positive feedback loop, reinforcing the new positive attractors of trust and cooperation.

Results. The Zegocina community, initially deprived of economic resources, through building social capital, triggered the growth of financial capital. The feeling of being a victim and an underdog in the conflict between the two communities died out over time and, as a result, the cooperation and partnership between Trzciana and Zegocina was revived (e.g., sport and education), opening prospects for reunification.

Pastor James Wuye and Imam Mohammed Ashafa, Nigeria[9]

The first layer of this case is the Christian-Muslim conflict *per se,* which is traditionally and historically well-grounded in Nigeria. In between violent episodes between these groups, there is typically a form of peaceful coexistence and cooperation. However, during periods of peace, the conflict is always lurking. For generations, the society has gone through repetitive cycles of violent clashes and peaceful coexistence. Over time, violence becomes internalized as a way of solving problems; for instance, there was an outburst of violence during the elections. In addition, young people are taught from early childhood that the source of all problems is the other religious community. Attempts to include peaceful education usually fail as the religious influence remains immensely more powerful.

Thus, this community evidenced a deeply ingrained, intractable religious conflict, fueled by hate and an eagerness to shed blood. This was seen in a wide variety of lurking and conspicuous conflicts, including the burning of mosques, churches, killings, refugees, and so forth. These multiple conflicts over power and control decreased the region's ability to develop and prosper. The conflict dimensions are as follows:

- Conflict around religious differences: unstructured and manifest.
- Conflict around building peace through education: unstructured and latent.

Approach. Pastor James Wuye, a Christian priest, and Imam Mohammed Ashafa, a Muslim cleric, are today bringing peace and peace-building education to Nigeria. In the past, they were both members of militant youth groups, chasing, hating, and harming each other (e.g., James Wuye lost his arm in a clash with Mohammed Ashafa's group). At some point, in a moment of mutual enlightenment, they understood that by operating together they could bring peace and understanding between their respective religions.

The original idea was to organize Christian-Muslim camps, building new mindsets among youth and influencing the schools' curriculum. The camps prompted a spirit of cooperation for handling many practical issues in a natural way. They also heavily influenced the educational system through introducing the Ethical Code for Religious Instructions in Schools. They are now using the power of their faith and the example of interfaith cooperation to prevent and intervene in religious and politically motivated conflicts in Nigeria, and especially to educate youth in building avenues to peaceful cooperation. Through TV programs and a portfolio of educational projects, they are changing the model of reacting to any stimulus with violence into a model of dialogue and understanding. They also have published a book comparing how such issues as forgiveness, love, and "expiation" are understood in Islam, Christianity, and Judaism.

Circumventing conflict through building a new attractor. Pastor James Wuye and Imam Mohammed Ashafa were transforming religions from sources of hatred and violence into vehicles for peace, redefining the social role of religion. Their focus on the positive messages of the Koran, Bible, and Torah is mutually reinforced by the living example of their own story of hate converted into partnership and cooperation. By operating together, the pastor and the imam are becoming new role models for cooperation and interfaith dialogue. Other trials failed. Only the two of them telling their story of hatred and willingness to kill each other were successful because they were able to redirect people's focus from differences to similarities. In other words, they successfully changed the concept of "mortal enemy" into "partner," and that shift provided the opportunity for creating a new attractor by influencing people's mindsets.

Results. The original initiative has resulted in other techniques, including "deprogramming" of violent youth through Christian and Islamic instruction, which teaches forgiveness and nonviolence. They also help communities identify and use traditionally accepted peace-building methods that may have been forgotten or abandoned. In addition, to ensure that their ideas are passed on to the next generation, they have set up peace clubs in preschool, primary, secondary, and tertiary institutions. Each child who goes through the training is encouraged to plant a tree to symbolize their commitment to building, and not destroying, their communities. They have also developed a peace-education curriculum, which is used in schools and by other organizations interested in peace-building, as well as the Ethical Code for Religious Instructions in Schools.

As for prevention, they have developed an early-warning mechanism, which alerts the communities to signs of trouble and ways to immediately defuse whatever is provoking the tension. For instance, the most recent anti-Muslim cartoon riots did not spread to many parts of the north because Ashafa and Wuye immediately asked the head of the Christian Association of Nigeria in the states they work in to go on the radio to condemn the explosive matter of the cartoons, and asked the chief imams to accept the condemnation and appeal for calm.

To sustain their initiatives in the states where they practice, Wuye and Ashafa have set up committees and advisory councils comprising religious leaders and community heads to monitor peace-building efforts and provide feedback. Their initiatives have also been sustained through support from international donors, governments, and religious organizations.

Steve Bigari, United States[10]

This conflict took place in the Seattle McDonald's enterprises. Steep challenges faced by newly hired, low-income workers (especially Hispanic), vis-à-vis their inability to deal with life's normal obstacles, resulted in high absenteeism and created a conflict between them and their employers. This usually resulted in a cycle of firing, hiring new staff, and significantly high staff turnover and high costs of constantly training new staff. On the one hand, the firm was losing money; on the other, the fired workers were entering the vicious cycle of unemployment, with devastating effects on their families, especially their children, who were prone to becoming dropouts, juvenile delinquents, and drug addicts. Attempts to convince employers to retain low-income workers were met with negative responses: "What? I received too many calls from this guy saying that he is not coming to work because his car is broken or his kid is sick!" In this setting, high dropout rates and high staff turnover were perceived as normal and treated as routine.

This resulted in a seemingly intractable conflict between managers and low-income workers in the community. Low-income workers tend to have poor resources and coping skills so, faced with problems with their children's health or a malfunctioning car, they simply leave their workplace, leading to their termination and subjecting the entire family to the hardships of unemployment. Such scenarios can lead to serious dysfunction within the family. The conflict dimensions are as follows:

- Conflict around the harsh and multi-pronged results of unemployment of low-income dropouts: unstructured and latent.
- Conflict around company's expectations and firing of employees: structured and manifest.

Approach. Steve Bigari saw that "low-wage workers in the United States are often one crisis away from dropping out." A highly valued and promising management employee at McDonald's,

Steve observed firsthand the consequences of firing low-income workers. On the one hand, he could not agree with exposing people and their families to the endless cycle of unemployment; on the other hand, as a manager, he had seen the money wasted on acquiring and training new staff. Therefore, he took it upon himself to reverse the way the workers were handled when they called in and reported problems. When someone called with car problems, for example, saying he or she could not report to work, the call was transferred to the owner, who said, "Great, this is a fabulous learning opportunity. I am going to send someone right away who will help you fix the problem with your car and teach you how to do it in the future." Similarly, when someone called in sick, Steve turned this into a positive learning opportunity, having organized a system of local nongovernmental organizations to train people to handle such situations. He also made deals with car-repair shops, arranging discounts for low-income workers. The major change, however, was in the radical reversal of the way the manager responded to the calls.

The result of this change in the system was two-pronged: First, the workers easily adopted the coping techniques, and the absentee rate rapidly decreased; second, the long-term retention of staff resulted in increased profits for the firm. The win-win strategy motivated others in the organization to pursue this approach. A more far-reaching result was that many of those "one crisis away from dropping out" became valued managers for the company, and advanced rapidly. The relatively small amount of positive reinforcement provided at the beginning of their employment, plus minimal training, were enough to spur on these employees to study and advance professionally. In the end, they became the company's most loyal and dedicated employees.

As a manager, Steve demonstrated the positive financial results of such an approach, and encouraged many other firms in the United States to duplicate this system. The idea resulted in employers taking a lead role in addressing the problems that make workers vulnerable, thus helping to break the cycle of persistent poverty by assisting workers to achieve personal stability and develop the skills they need to get a foothold on the ladder to the middle class.

Circumventing conflict through building a new attractor. Steve initiated a totally new approach by turning failures, which previously were arguments for firing the employees, into opportunities for learning and growth. By doing so, he brought dignity to low-income workers and increased their motivation to grow and be committed to their work. This initiative opened a new path to learning and advancement. Transforming the new attractor from failures into opportunities was mutually reinforced by the generation of profit for companies through retaining staff, and companies also gained more committed and loyal staff.

Results. Steve has since founded a nonprofit organization, America's Family, and has created an innovative plan to provide health care to low-wage workers. He persuaded Community Health Centers, a provider of high-cost emergency care, to create the Healthy Workforce program, with an emphasis on disease prevention and health education. To pay for the program, he instituted a payroll deduction-employer match system. In this way, employees gained access to affordable health care while Community Health Centers gained a new source of revenue. Furthermore, because the Community Health Centers program emphasizes the prevention of illness and maintenance of wellness, it dramatically lowers workers' dependence on costly emergency services.

Through their work with Steve and his organization, hundreds of workers obtain computers, affordable child care and housing, reliable transportation, and online access to education. Clients of America's Family can purchase low-cost computers through a payroll deduction program; they receive their computers when they pay 50% of the cost, and get free Internet service as a bonus. America's Family recently partnered with citizen groups and a government housing provider to create a 100-unit hotel that provides its clients with low-cost transitional housing. America's Family also works with car dealers and banks to help employees establish credit and qualify for loans, and trains employees to manage these loans through an online course on personal finance. By 2006, 100% of the 1,200 clients of America's Family had access to affordable housing, child care, cars, and e-mail. Many have progressed from subsidized to private health insurance. After 1 year under the America's Family program, the profits in four companies improved by $300,000. Turnover rates were 63% lower after 1 year and an additional 29% lower after 2 years. America's Family has already expanded from Seattle to Dallas and is now launching programs in Denver.

Helena Balabanova, Czech Republic[11]

In the Czech Republic, there was an open conflict between the Roma and Czech population. The Roma were traditionally objects of discrimination in this region. In the early 1990s, 800 acts of racial violence were recorded, but the number of attacks was substantially higher than statistical reports revealed. It became such a pervasive social problem that there was a massive exodus of the Roma from the Czech Republic, primarily to Canada and Great Britain.

One of the dramatic aspects of anti-Roma discrimination sprang up in the school system, where Roma kids were abused and often punished physically. At the same time, the Roma's perception of the state-run school system was negative, perceived as impersonal and unjust, and alien to their cultural sensitivities or traditions. The Roma system of education is traditionally based in the community, whereas outside the Roma community, kids feel disempowered and paralyzed. Teachers misinterpret these reactions as hostile and problematic. Many Roma children are merely labeled "mentally retarded" and shipped off to schools for the disabled.

Helena Balabanova came from a family labeled by the Communist system as "politically unreliable" and, hence, after graduating from the university, was sent to teach at a special school in Ostrava to which the Communist regime sentenced people as a form of punishment. Not unlike a prison to the teachers and the students, this school was a hardship post. Helena, a young woman, found herself in the middle of the nightmare, crying through the first night and the second night vowing that she would change this school into a model place with a humane policy. The conflict dimensions are as follows:

*   Conflict between the Czech and the Roma populations: structured and manifest.
*   Conflict around mandatory and non-inclusive education as a focal point of the conflict in schools: structured and manifest.

Approach. As the first step, Helena introduced the practice of incorporating Roma adults as teaching assistants in the classroom, which was a shocking innovation in the Czech educational system still embedded in 19th-century practices. The Roma assistants were dedicated and perceived as moral authorities in the Roma community. Their presence made Roma kids feel that they were in a familiar setting and, therefore, enabled them to open up.

The problem that Helena faced at the beginning was the negative stereotypes of the Roma people held by the teachers and the school authorities. They were convinced that nothing else could be done to address the behavior of the Roma children other than discipline and punishment. Helena noticed that teachers complained about the "heavy burden" imposed on

them; therefore, in her strategic thinking, the idea for introducing the Roma assistants into the classroom was a sort of Trojan Horse: It was presented as a way to ease teachers' burdens and, as such, was well-received by the teachers and school authorities.

The Roma teaching assistants served as more than just tutors: They became mentors for the children, helping them to better focus on success in the classroom by encouraging and supporting their individual development. This proved to be successful because the teaching assistants became, first of all, important role models and also because they were more easily accepted and trusted by the Roma parents and children, who shared the same ethnicity.

As the next step, Helena created a new model of social work through community centers that were affiliated with the schools. The Roma pedagogical assistants worked in the centers as "social assistants"; besides participating actively with the schools, they served as a bridge with other public institutions, such as the police. As a result, communication developed between the school and the community, and a mutual learning process broke down the mental stereotypes between the non-Roma teachers and the Roma children. This created a family- and community-like atmosphere both in the classroom and in the community centers. As the next step, Helena initiated the publication of new textbooks and teaching materials that widened the curriculum to include studies of the Roma culture, including history, music, and art.

Circumventing conflict through building a new attractor. Instead of addressing, head-on, the problems of the rigidity among the teachers and within the school system, and of the stereotyping based on prejudices, Helena presented a solution that, on one hand, was an incentive for the teachers and, on the other, indirectly changed their attitudes, as they observed the children thriving. In addition, in the course of partnering with the Roma assistant, they learned in a natural, informal way about the Roma populations and traditions. This built a new attractor for cooperation and mutual understanding, especially with the Roma assistants extending their role into the community centers.

The problem of the Roma perception of the Czech education system was also addressed in an indirect way (after many direct, more patronizing attempts failed): The Roma assistants understood and accepted the importance of education and children's intellectual development, and conveyed this to the Roma community. This was done through a natural process instead of, for instance, addressing this issue in a direct way by lecturing the Roma community.

Results. Helena's school has since become the living laboratory for her innovative approaches to multicultural education in the Czech Republic. In a concerted effort to redefine race relations in the Czech Republic, she spread a palette of educational and cultural programs and festivals across the country, which enabled Roma and non-Roma people to respect and recognize the validity of Roma culture and identity. Helena continues to spread her methods, materials, and programs throughout the Czech Republic and beyond. She opened a training program for school principals and teachers to use her teaching methodology to train teachers, teaching assistants, and social workers. She also succeeded in influencing federal education law, so that the idea became institutionalized and supported by governmental resources. In addition, Helena created a course on "Romaology," which has been adopted as part of the teacher-training curriculum at Charles University in Prague, the leading university in the country. This will ensure that instructors will be qualified to teach Roma culture and history.

Discussion

The five case studies presented here reveal that many of the traditional attempts to transform societal problems and conflicts fail when the interveners pursue change within the existing societal equilibrium, meeting the resistance of the old attractors head-on. Various top-down United Nations and governmental projects failed in the Kibera slums; the rural Polish community resisted being pushed by various activists and local authorities to behave cooperatively; patronizing peace advocacy in Nigeria (e.g., by requiring peace programs in the schools) failed, and so did attempts to put pressure on managers to care more for low-income workers; finally, pressing and patronizing both the Czech and Roma populations to change attitudes not only failed, but also created more tensions.

However, the social entrepreneurs chose different strategies, with their abilities to think creatively, to demonstrate the value of achieving mutually beneficial goals while at the same time circumventing the basic conflict by doing "something different somewhere else." David Kuria organized groups that had fun drawing and fantasizing schemes for public toilets. This fun and drawing time built participants' identification with the idea of unbelievably fantastic toilets. Dagmara Bienkowska initiated a simple process that connected the bullying youth with the senior citizens in a joint venture to produce the regional cookbook and, by so doing, brought success and pride to the previously underperforming community. Pastor Wuye's and Imam Mohammed's life stories were so inspiring that they had an immediate and profound influence on others. Steve Bigari gave respect to low-income workers and turned their problem situations into an educational opportunity. Helena Balabanova introduced the idea of Roma teachers' assistants, which changed the mindsets of all parties involved.

In most of these cases, the alternative approach was pursued through building social capital, which involved facilitating the development of a higher level of trust and cooperation. Outside the toxic field of conflict, new cooperative and trusting attractors emerged, becoming gateways to further constructive developments. Following this path, social entrepreneurs, as the next step, succeeded in building a positive feedback loop between their initial success and reinforcement of social capital, which, in turn, strengthened the new attractor. The dream public toilet facility in the Nairobi slums was built by people who then cared for its sustainability, renting space for advertisements and imposing small user fees; the dreaming process continued, and they added a shoeshine booth plus a cafeteria; and the success released an entrepreneurial trend in the community. The cookbook opened a process of communication and cooperation, and released an enterprising attitude in a feedback loop enhancing trust and cooperation in the community. The impact of the living example of the pastor and the imam led to such initiatives as Christian-Muslim camps or peace clubs in pre-, primary, and secondary schools. Retaining low-income workers resulted in their accelerated professional development and higher level of loyalty, which yielded better performance and generated innovative projects; in turn, the projects gave the company an immense financial payback, raising in a feedback loop the position of the low-income workers. The Roma assistants in the schools triggered a process of mutual identification and co-ownership of the educational system and empowered the Roma community; in return, the children thrived and performed excellently, pursuing their mainstream education and becoming role models themselves. This process immensely influenced the mindsets of the Czech teachers and general population, and opened channels for cooperation.

This strategy leads to decreasing the pull of previous attractors for destructive relationships while new attractors for well-being are being developed and strengthened. The conflicts, without being directly addressed, become less important, less rage-filled, less relevant, and ultimately dissipate.

Principles and recommendations

The question is, "What are the lessons to be derived from these case studies?" The answer to this question can be summarized using the following principles and guidelines:

- Constructive change involves creating a new psychosocial dynamic defined by mutual reinforcement among new initiatives and social capital.
- The constructive-change approach works best if the new initiative is embedded in the society's latent needs, tendencies, and potentials. In effect, this approach releases energies and desires that are dormant in the system.
- This approach requires an ability to identify latent societal tendencies and potentials, which, in turn, requires deep intuition or a psychological "radar set" for detecting potential dynamics that can be amplified to foster "something new somewhere else." Such insight, called "ethno- empathy" by Bar-Tal (2009), is impossible without immersion in the everyday life of the society, developing a feel or instinct for what is possible.
- The new structures must meld with the society's Indigenous cultures, beliefs, and rituals. Therefore, in searching for a new attractor, it is of utmost importance to identify one that is embedded in the society's culture, so that it will be naturally sustained.
- Social entrepreneurs usually reframe the conflict situation so that the new epistemology does not refer to the factors of the conflict. To the contrary, it is promotive: built on positive messages and positive prospects (such as projects and economic development), thereby fostering hope and the desire to grow.
- One successful action in isolation does not guarantee the construction of a strong (deep and stable), positive attractor. Such change is built on a chain of initiatives, each logically derived from those that preceded it.
- In most of the cases, social entrepreneurs do not act as charismatic leaders (except the pastor and the imam, which, in this case, was pivotal). Their primary function, instead, is to trigger a self-perpetuating process that empowers the community. Indeed, it is often advisable to operate from behind the scenes – not an easy role to enact if one is concerned with garnering attention and gaining "ego benefits."
- Personal excitement, rather than ego enhancement, is the reward for promoting constructive change. The sense of excitement functions as the barometer or indicator that one has facilitated the development of a new and positive attractor. The pleasure of observing a positive dynamic unfolding on its own, without further intervention, is immeasurable.

Conclusion

The "anti-conflict resolution" approach described here clearly differs from traditional conflict-resolution models. For instance, John Burton's (1998) approach, based on Human Needs Theory, assumes that conflicts are lurking in areas where basic human needs are neglected – a condition that can incite and prolong violence. According to Burton (1993), these needs include distributive justice, safety, security, belongingness, love, self-esteem, personal fulfillment, identity, cultural security, freedom, and participation. Burton argued that the conflict-resolution approach should focus on securing those needs. Although the importance of human needs cannot be denied, this approach is problematic because it is based on a simple aggregation of individual needs. Societal dynamics represent more than the simple sum of individual dynamics. A society as a whole, for instance, may decide to deprive itself from fulfilling some individual needs, acting instead for the common good.[12] The constructive-change approach, in contrast, focuses on altering societal dynamics. It does so by creating positive "islands" that do not initially intersect with the "mainland" of conflict. Over time, these islands may expand and become connected, thereby creating a new land of promise and hope.

Notes

Correspondence should be addressed to Ryszard Praszkier, Kopernika 11 m. 25, 00–359 Warszawa, Poland. E-mail: ryszardpr@gmail.com

1 Krzysztof Czyzewski is an Ashoka Fellow, elected in 2003 (see http://www.ashoka.org/node/2917), and a founder of The Borderland Foundation (see http://www.pogranicze.sejny.pl/?s=flash&lang=eng).
2 Krzysztof disseminated The Borderline Foundation's approach to many regions of conflict in central and eastern Europe, the Caucasus, and central Asia.
3 See www.ashoka.org
4 See more on the selection criteria at http://www.ashoka.org/support/criteria
5 See http://www.ashoka.org/support/sands and www.ashoka.org/files/5StageSelection%20Process_0.jpg
6 The support comes through a palette of programs helping Ashoka Fellows to scale-up, as well as through a global platform for cooperation; in addition, there is a stipend program helping Fellows to fully commit to their ideas.
7 See http://www.ashoka.org/node/4356
8 See http://www.ashoka.org/node/2871
9 See http://www.ashoka.org/node/3875, http://www.ashoka.org/node/3874
10 See http://www.ashoka.org/node/3170
11 See http://www.ashoka.org/node/2895
12 See, for instance, the Polish Underground Solidarity in the decade of the 1980s; nearly all actors and TV presenters boycotted the governmental media and went on driving taxis and working at other, alternative jobs.

References

Bar-Tal, D. (2009). Peace education in societies involved in intractable conflicts: Direct and indirect models. *Review of Educational Research, 79*, 557–575.

Bornstein, D. (1998). Changing the world on a shoestring. *Atlantic Monthly, 281*, 34–39.

Bornstein, D. (2004). *How to change the world: Social entrepreneurs and the power of new ideas.* New York: Oxford University Press.

Burton, J. W. (1993). *Conflict: Human Needs Theory.* New York: Palgrave Macmillan.

Burton, J. W. (1998). Conflict resolution: The human dimension. *The International Journal of Peace Studies, 5*(1). Retrieved March 16, 2010, from http://www.gmu.edu/programs/icar/ijps/vol3-l/burton.htm

De Rosnay, J. (1997). *Homeostasis: Resistance to change.* Principia Cybernetica Web. Retrieved March 16, 2010, from http://pespmc1.vub.ac.be/HOMEOSTA.html

Drayton, W. (2000). *Selecting leading social entrepreneurs.* Arlington, VA: Ashoka.

Drayton, W. (2002). The citizen sector: Becoming as entrepreneurial and competitive as business. *California Management Review, 44*, 119–131.

Hammonds, K. (2005). A lever long enough to move the world. *Fast Company, 90*. Retrieved March 16, 2010, from http://www.fastcompany.com/magazine/90/open_ashoka.html

Martin, R. L., & Osberg, S. (2007). Social entrepreneurship: The case for definition. *Stanford Social Innovation Review*, 29–39. Retrieved March 16, 2010, from http://www.ssireview.org/articles/entry/social_entreprenuership_the_case_for_definition/

Nowak, A., & Lewenstein, M. (1994). Dynamical systems: A tool for social psychology? In R. Vallacher & A. Nowak (Eds.), *Dynamical systems in social psychology* (pp. 17–53). San Diego, CA: Academic.

O'Toole, J. (1996). *Leading change.* New York: Ballantine.

Vallacher, R. R., & Nowak, A. (2005). Dynamical social psychology: Finding order in the flow of human experience. In A. Kruglanski & E. T. Higgins (Eds.), *Social psychology: Handbook of basic principles.* New York: Guilford Press, 734–758.

37 Systems-building before State-building

On the systemic preconditions of state-building

Peter Haldén

Introduction

State-building is a highly prioritised practice in contemporary international security. The implicit or explicit rationale for state-building is to increase regional inter-state security, to prevent threats with potential global reach like terrorism, organised crime and proliferation of weapons of mass destruction. I will re-evaluate the possibilities of state-building by emphasising the need to take the systemic context into account. Debate and research on state failure/state-building tend to focus on endogenous causes of state fragility or failure. Correspondingly, policy solutions have often focused on endogenous solutions, in other words building viable institutions within the target country. While these measures are important, the idea that state-building can be conceived of only as an internal exercise, i.e. the idea that a state can be created inside-out, as it were, is misguided judging from historical processes of state formation and contemporary examples. The external preconditions of state-building and the negative as well as positive feedback loops between building strong states and regional stability have to be taken into account. I will illustrate this point with examples from historical processes of state formation and analysis of three contemporary countries and regions: Namibia/southwestern Africa, Somalia/the Horn of Africa and Afghanistan/Central Asia.

Contemporary evidence shows that we are in many cases facing failed regions. Historical evidence shows that state formation was a region-wide process and was preceded by the formation of the elements of a state system. Although internal causes, factors and flaws are important to address, such efforts could come to nothing unless problems originating in the wider context are dealt with. The tendency to focus only on the particular state that is identified to have 'failed' has led to the obscuring of three factors: one, effective stateness as well as sustainable regional security, which is expressed on an inter-state as well as a sub-state level, requires a region-wide creation of effective structures of state; two, effective states as well as effective inter-state security require well-functioning states systems; and three, the building of effective states require regional acceptance of the process of state-building.

Some previous writers have called attention to the importance of taking a regional perspective on state failure/state-building,[1] as well as on security relations in general.[2] Many more have stressed the difficulties originating in the conflicting interests of external, intervening actors and local, receiving ones.[3] Building on these advances, I hope to contribute to the debate by making explicit connections to European history and to the considerable literature on state formation which enables the argument that the difficulties in contemporary state-building are similar to the difficulties in the much longer period of European state formation.

Not only are effective state structures dependent on functioning state structures in neighbouring countries, but stability also requires the creation of a stable inter-state system in the region in question. By a stable inter-state system I mean a system in which explicit and commonly agreed upon norms and rules exist between the actors that limit conflict, which provides mutual recognition of the legitimacy of other actors and lays down elementary rules of *ius ad bellum* as well as *ius in bello*. A complete absence of armed conflict is, however, in many regions of the world a goal that can only be achieved in the long term.

The idea in the current debates on state-building that effective state-structures in a country where these are lacking can be established only by focusing on that selfsame country is unrealistic considering how the European states were established in the early modern era. Rather we must have a contextual understanding of the 'social ecology',[4] understood as the wider international context in which state-building is to take place. Indeed, since the historical formation of states was intertwined with the process of forming a system of states, it may be misleading to talk about 'state formation' as if the formation of each state took place independently from that of others. Likewise, we maybe misled if we believe that the currently urgent tasks of state-building can be accomplished without a systemic perspective.

State formation and state-building do not automatically lead to regional stability, but in many cases to increased regional tensions and instability. Historically, creating strong states out of weak ones was seen as controversial in the international system: firstly, since a strong state might become a rival in the balance of power and, secondly, since a vital intermediary body – one without the capacity to threaten its neighbours – might be lost and thereby upset the system. Balance of power politics do not characterise the international system of the contemporary Western world and hence there is no need to retain weak states as buffers or insulators between great powers. This is however not the case everywhere in today's world; in some regions weak states serve buffer functions and, more importantly, because of regional power relations surrounding actors perceive that they stand to lose if weaker powers would be strengthened and turned into potential allies of their adversaries. Such regional perspectives must be taken into account in Western strategic thinking since state-building may be in our security interests but not in the interests of the regions in which we operate.

My argument is structured according to the following: the next section argues that policies on 'failed states' as well as the state-building literature are often one-sidedly focused on building state structures only within states identified as 'failed' and 'fragile'. The section after that demonstrates that historical state formation took place in a systemic context. This systemic context is understood as the synergy effects of co-formation, the establishment of an international system and of regional acceptance of state formation. I do not claim that these factors are perennial laws of state-building. Rather, they are salient tendencies found in some cases in European history as well as in some, not all, contemporary cases of state-building. The following section illustrates the relevance of a systemic perspective on state-building by studies of Namibia, Somalia and Afghanistan. I do not see these cases nomothetically, as instances of universal laws or phenomena, but rather ideographically, as specific countries which theoretical perspective sheds new light on. Afghanistan and Somalia were chosen because of their importance to regional and international security and because both represent what could be said are extremes of state failure. Namibia, on the other hand, provides an elucidating comparison/contrast through its relative state density and stability (e.g. absence of large-scale violence).

The final section outlines implications of the argument for projects of state-building. It focuses on the conflict between achieving effective state structures in a target country and strengthening regional security. This conflict entails in the short run that we may have to limit the ambitions of achieving both international stability and effective state structures. However, avoiding this conflict is likely to lead to sub-optimal outcomes in the long run in terms of international and national development. Indeed they may give rise to what Spruyt has called 'low-level equilibrium traps'.[5]

The endogenous bias in state failure and state-building debates

There can be no doubt that state-building is high on the international agenda. This is attested by the proliferation of academic publishing on the subjects of 'state-building', as well as on the problem that it sets out to address, 'failed states'. A survey of white papers by major and medium Western powers demonstrates that most accord a high importance to the task of state-building. While some countries deal extensively with the issue such as Canada, Finland, Germany and the United Kingdom,[6] others pay more passing regard to the issue.[7] Although the countries that mention state failure and state-building as a security task differ with regard to details, they emphasise its urgency. This goes for the United States and the European Union.[8]

The surveyed white papers agree on why failed or fragile states are security issues: firstly, they may pose a threat to international, but primarily regional, security;[9] secondly, they may become havens for terrorism or organised crime;[10] thirdly, they may assist the proliferation of CBRN or WMD;[11] and fourthly, state failure leads to movements of migrants and refugees, which destabilise regional security.[12] All the surveyed papers describe the security threats connected to failed states in an inside-out fashion: the failed state threatens the surrounding region. An exception is that regional conflicts are sometimes seen as a cause of state failure.[13] Although these factors are important, none of the surveyed white papers discuss either the structural regional causes of state failure or that regional remedies may be necessary to come to terms with the problems of failed states, regardless of whether these are mainly endogenous or exogenous in origin.

From a perspective that ascribes state failure only to internal causes, state-building efforts will appear as a solution that addresses all these problems. On the other hand, if state failure – as well as state-building – is recognised as having significant external as well as internal dimensions one can begin to identify contradictions in state-building as a strategy to counter these threats. For example, state-building could, if successful, be an effective tool in countering organised crime as well as the establishment of terrorist groups and actually increase regional instability.

Previous research is divided over the causes of state failure. The majority of works stress internal causes: that state collapse is driven by political decisions, by the sequence of events and that political actors are responsible for squandering the riches of their countries, opportunities for stability and the legitimacy of their governments. Critical approaches, however, point out that it is sometimes in the interest of many actors to maintain a condition of state weakness which the West labels, 'state failure'.[14] The endogenous perspective takes the state for granted, an approach that is mirrored in political documents. Against this position, structural approaches paint a more sombre picture as to the possibility of creating state structures in certain parts of the world.

Herbst stresses the continuities in the difficulties that many African countries have had in projecting power throughout their territories from the pre-colonial era to our age.[15] Similarly, Clapham stresses that certain states may be inherently unviable and only owe their existence to legal recognition by the international community.[16] This argument has also been raised by Jackson who claims that 'quasi-states' are only sustained by 'negative sovereignty', which is bestowed by the international system.[17] Hence quasi-states are states only in a de jure sense and are sustained by external economic, legal and political factors. These positions share a combination of an analysis of local political contexts with international systemic factors to explain, not primarily 'state failure' but in fact why Weberian-Western states have never been established in certain locations. By a Western-Weberian state, I mean a form of rule with a single centre capable of legitimate violence, final authority and with a routinised bureaucracy.[18]

Building on these insights, I argue that the regional context and its dynamics must be weighted in. Some quasi-states, which often tend to be the ones that 'fail', cluster in groups. In such a grouping, not all are quasi-states but many show weaknesses in terms of administration, infrastructural power and economic progress. It is beyond the scope of my argument to trace the histories of such clusters in detail. However, the empirical observation serves to open up new avenues of analysis. These factors contribute to the difficulties in establishing Weberian-Western stateness in certain countries, in particular at a central level. Recognising that some countries have never had 'real' state structures, but have nevertheless been treated as such by the international community, puts the discourse on 'state failure' in a different light. In the case of quasi-states we do not face the task of 'rebuilding' or 'reconstruction' but rather a deep transformation of the social and political structures of the country. The fact that we have to assist in the formation of a unitary state tout court makes it necessary to consider the historical preconditions more closely than if the idea of resuscitation, strengthening or rebuilding had been correct.

Failed states are often presented as problems to regional security. While this is true, regarding the security problems with failed states as a one-way relation may obscure the fact that regional conditions in some cases may sustain the state of 'failure'. To a certain extent, the sustainment of failed states can be understood on an actor level, as part of divide and rule strategies. A deeper problem is that structural factors in the regional subsystem may be perpetuating weak states. Neighbouring countries are often included in efforts of conflict resolution/mediation and in post-conflict reconstruction projects. Their role in facilitating or managing peace treaties is widely recognised.

While this is important, it does not go far enough if state-building is the aim, since the problems of state-building cannot be reduced to a particular conflict or to factors internal to the country. Since 'failed states' often have neighbours that also are quasi-state or at least do not conform to the Western pattern, there needs to be an agreement on the building of state structures throughout the region. Since some failed states are found in regions without functioning states systems, or indeed functioning constitutional institutions of any kind, the entire region would need a constitutional settlement, not just the country being focused on. Since state-building entails fundamental transformation of polities, this is likely to be problematic and can lead to more conflict in the short run. In the long run, however, it may be the only way out of a low-level equilibrium trap and towards stability in the long term.

Historical state formation as systems formation

The systemic context of state formation is recognised in the historical sociological literature. However, the literature on state-building has generally only discussed one dimension of the historical process – military competition as a driver of state formation. Many discussions of contemporary efforts of state-building start out with a reference to the works of Tilly,[19] often invoking the dictum that 'war made states, and states made war'.[20] The quote captures the systemic nature of European state formation by pointing to the necessity of creating strong state structures in order to survive in Europe's militarily competitive environment.[21] Herbst seized upon this insight from European history in order to highlight the differences between the formation of states as well as the form of states in Europe and Africa.[22] Military inter-state competition has been weaker in pre- as well as post-colonial Africa due to a combination of geography and international politics after decolonisation. Consequently, this particular systemic imperative to modernise has been much weaker in post-colonial Africa than it was in Europe's history. Recent studies have also argued that organising for and waging war are not conducive to contemporary state formation, rather the opposite.[23]

These insights inform us that the conditions of state-building are radically different in the developing world today than in Europe's past. Since it is neither possible nor desirable to reproduce the military inter-state rivalry as a driver of state formation in developing parts of the world, we must look to other ways of encouraging state formation. Herbst's conclusion is no argument against but rather in favour of comparisons. However, we must also consider other systemic aspects of the historical processes of state formation than military competition, in particular, ones that are more analogous to the situations that we face in the contemporary environment.

I will advance three propositions regarding systemic context as a precondition of state formation based on examples from European history. This systemic context is understood as the synergy effects of co-development, the establishment of an international system and of regional acceptance of state formation. The first focuses on the growth and transmission of state institutions. A precondition of successful state formation was the transmission of institutional innovation across regions. State formation in Europe benefited not only from military competition between units but also from the synergetic effects that arose from several states modernising at the same time.

The second argues that the creation of a system in which European realms interacted according to generally accepted organisational logics or constitutional principles preceded the formation of modern state structures within them. Only after an inter-state system, that defined and regulated the physical borders and legal boundaries between the realms as well as codes of conduct between them, had been established could the processes of broadening and deepening the state take place.

One of the problems with some cases of contemporary state-building is that the reverse is being attempted: building broad and deep states without an accepted system that regulates inter-unit relations being in place. This highlights the third proposition that regional acceptance of a state was in many cases necessary for it to develop strong state structures. Current discourse tends to emphasise democratic norms and institutions as a precondition of peaceful co-existence and the acceptance of state-building. A more important factor might be to take the security interests of regional actors into account when fundamental changes are being wrought in their neighbouring countries. Acceptance of the consolidation of a weak state does not only hinge upon choices made by political actors in isolation but it rather depended on the character of relations between states in the region. Hence gaining regional acceptance for externally aided state-building may require structural transformation rather than persuasion of actors.

State formation requires synergies

State formation in Europe was aided by synergetic effects in terms of economic and administrative developments. As effective state structures were developed in one country, other countries imitated the forerunners and learned from their mistakes. Growth of state structures in a sub-region lowered transaction costs for diplomatic as well as economic interactions.[24] This concerns not only economic synergies but also the effectiveness of state institutions. For example, the Austro-Prussian rivalry in the eighteenth century led to a 'reform race' in which both powers were spurred in their efforts by the progress made by the other.[25] Consequently, the growth in state efficiency in Europe from the Renaissance onwards can be understood as due to regional synergies. Even though it lies beyond the current inquiry, one may wonder whether Europe is not a more appropriate unit of analysis than individual states in the study of the modernisation of administrative technologies, i.e. state formation.[26]

Furthermore, institutional likeness was encouraged by the actors of the European system.[27] Since transaction costs were lower in dealings between like units, sovereign or semi-sovereign states preferred to deal with other sovereign units over dealing with city-states or city-leagues. Hence it can be assumed that state formation will be more effective in a region with co-evolving units than in a region where the majority of countries are not developing state structures. The argument that international stability and economic growth is fostered in strong regions is not new. Rather it was a central part of the neo-functionalist school of regional integration.[28] My argument differs from the neo-functionalist one, since it does not claim that integration is a necessary, let alone realistic, condition of state-building. State formation was not only characterised by the system-wide spread of institutional innovation but also by the establishment of constitutional rules regulating relations and by regional consensus on which and what kind of states were acceptable in the system. It is to these factors that I now turn.

State formation requires an international system

Many writings on state failure emphasise the need to bolster the sovereignty of fragile or failed states. However, sovereignty cannot be said to be the property either of the unitary state or the states system since, as Walker has pointed out, the 'international' and the 'national' presuppose and mutually support one another.[29] Sovereignty is rather an institution in the states system and inter-state and intra-state politics are different practices that both presuppose this institution. Of course, sovereignty is an internationally accepted basic norm of the contemporary international system. We see this in the inability to recognise instances when sovereignty does not function in a de facto sense. Nevertheless sovereignty in practice is not the property of certain regional sub-systems, as we shall see below.

Historically, the concept of sovereignty was a creation of the monarchs of European realms who first accepted it as a basic norm between them, and then it began to regulate actions. It spread because it was of tremendous benefit to the monarchs, vis-à-vis internal rivals like Dukes and Counts, as well as vis-à-vis external ones because it provided clearer rules of the game. The European states system was formed over a very long period of time. The Peace of Augsburg in 1555 stipulated that each ruler had the right to decide the religion of his subjects. Sovereignty in its recognisably modern form was first formulated by Jean Bodin in 1578 after the wars of religion in France and substantially reinforced philosophically a century later by Thomas Hobbes after the English Civil War. Sovereignty is but one of the constitutive institutions of the modern states system.[30]

The norms of diplomacy were formalised in a succession of treaties from the Peace of Westphalia in 1648, the peace of Nijmegen in 1679 and Utrecht in 1714. It is perhaps only after the latter peace that the states system begins to take on a more modern character as the *Ius Publicum Europeum* or the Public International Law of Europe. During this long period the character of large wars changed from being conflicts over the constitutive rules of the states system to being conflicts fought according to them.[31] Some of the key peace treaties in

European history did not only end a conflict but were also contractual agreements in which the parties agreed to constitutional principles concerning their relations. The peace of Augsburg in 1555 and the peace of Utrecht in 1713 are two examples. Others were combinations of constitutional settlements for certain areas, a general peace and consensus regarding constitutional institutions. The peace of Westphalia in 1648 and the Vienna Congress in 1815 are two examples.[32] Another example is the peace of the Pyrenees in 1659 between France and Spain, which was the first to establish a modern conception of an inter-state border. Before that, the boundaries between realms were understood not only as physically permeable but in essence as indistinct zones.

This venture into the history of the international system serves one point. All these innovations, too summarily dealt with here, were preconditions for the solidification of realms like France and Spain – to take two examples. The Europe-wide processes of broadening the purview of the state from its original core aimed at internal subjugation and external conquest, as well as deepening its influence, did not follow for at least half a century after the Peace of Utrecht. The capacity of states to patrol and enforce their borders did not become truly effective until the nineteenth century, but a precondition thereof was not only the conceptual innovation itself but also the inter-state consensus on the border as a meaningful category.

State formation requires regional acceptance

The processes of state formation during the eighteenth and nineteenth centuries in Europe within states created international tensions. For example, attempts to transform the sprawling Holy Roman Empire into a more efficient entity, more unified and with greater capabilities, were consciously resisted not only by local princes who risked losing power but also by other European powers, like France and Sweden, who feared that it would upset the balance in the European system. Another example is Poland in the eighteenth century, at the time an anarchic confederation of noblemen each holding the *liberum veto* in parliament, which enabled each noble to block reforms and decisions.[33] In short, the country had retained its medieval characteristics and a unified Weberian state had not been formed. Attempts at constitutional reform began in the 1770s and 1780s, which would have allowed Poland to modernise its ossified and outdated institutions. The process was short-circuited by its neighbours – and aided by internal spoilers – who resisted a more effective Poland since they would no longer be able to influence it.[34]

It was only after the Congress of Vienna in 1815 that the great powers of the European sub-system were ready, willing and able to agree in concert on modernisation measures in the smaller European states, like the Netherlands and the German states. Under the aegis of the great powers, these entities received constitutions that allowed greater state effectiveness. This greater regional responsibility was in turn due to a change in the states system of Europe after Napoleon. Historical research has demonstrated that states systems vary with regard to organisational logics and constitutional norms.[35] Hence not only is a states system per se a necessary precondition for the formation of states but a particular kind of states system is necessary in order for regional great powers to accept that smaller and/or weaker states develop and modernise. After 1815 the balance of power rivalry and thinking about security as 'divisible' gave way to systemic co-management and thinking about security between the European realms in 'indivisible' terms.[36] This change was a precondition for the growth in internal strength of several of the weaker states, like the Southern German ones.

Earlier, the states system had a precondition of the formation of the first unitary states like Brandenburg and France. However, the consolidation of weaker states that had failed to coalesce at this earlier stage depended on changes in the perception of security among the major powers. Such changes in the regional sub-system may be the necessary prerequisite that provides powers with incentives to support state transformation in a weak neighbour. This has less to do with an increased acceptance of democratic or humanitarian norms and more to do with incentives of state security and state survival.[37] As long as states in a certain region perceive the primary threats to their survival as coming from other states then they will find weak states useful as buffers, intermediary bodies, pawns or bargaining chips. In such a system, the threats emanating from a weak state can be absorbed and/or be seen as 'afford-able' because they are preferable to the full-scale military threats that could be forthcoming if the failed state were to become a strong one.

Furthermore, the properties of units influence which kind of threat is dominant. It could be argued that the threats which weak states may create in contemporary international poli-tics (e.g., organised crime and terrorism) are more problematic to well-developed countries, where the state is broad as well as deep and hence has a responsibility and accountability vis-à-vis its population. In contrast, states which have more the character of 'regimes' than polities are not as vulnerable to attacks on civilian targets or to organised economic crime.[38] Indeed, it might be easier for the leadership of such states to work with criminal economic actors than it would be for well-integrated and democratically accountable states. Hence, in a region composed of such state regimes the acceptance of or even need for weak states increases.

To summarise, state-building in cases of quasi-states entails a fundamental transformation of political institutions in the country and hence the process is likely to become a political concern in the wider region. In a peaceful system, like today's Europe, strengthening weak states or creating states out of non-states (speaking de facto) is seen as beneficial. In a bel-licose one, the process might be seen as threatening instead. Enhancing state effectiveness in lesser powers in the sub-system is facilitated by a more co-operative states system in the region. Reasoning by analogy it seems that contemporary state-building requires a co-ordi-nated transformation of state institutions in the entire region as well as a transformation of the systemic relations between the countries of the region. Consequently, seen in this light, the task grows far beyond that of 'rebuilding' individual states.

The problem is not that the sovereign state as a formal category of rule is unpopular. In fact, de jure recognition and formal legal equality, and the protection it offers, are much sought after. Nevertheless, this does not amount to de facto state character or capacity – which numerous writers, Robert Jackson being the most prominent one, point out. This is particularly the case if we consider state structures, functions and purposes in terms of what Michael Mann calls 'infrastructural power'. On close inspection, we find that international legal recognition has often been used as an external source of power augmentation to bolster what Mann calls 'despotic power'.[39]

Country studies: Namibia, Somalia and Afghanistan

The three countries analysed in this section have had seriously deficient state structures and on different occasions been the recipients of substantial amounts of international aid and state-building efforts. The difference in the success of state-building is quite substantial. Namibia is still facing many economical, political and social problems but has made consider-able progress on its way to greater state efficiency and expansion. By contrast, Afghanistan and Somalia are still far from having modern state and security institutions. Naturally, the three differ with respect to internal contexts, state structures, conflict histories, cultures and the context of external intervention. Recognising the importance of such factors, differences in the states system of the surrounding region also have to be weighed into our understanding of the possibilities of success for state-building. The three countries are analysed in relation to: (1) Synergetic development; (2) a functioning states system; and (3) regional acceptance.

Namibia and south-western Africa

The first case, Namibia, is a country where state-building prevented state failure. It gained independence in 1990 after 23 years of civil war that also involved the South African Defence Forces. It had also been implicated in another regional conflict, the war in Angola between guerrilla movements, Cuba and South Africa. At the time of independence Namibia had no democratic traditions and faced several security challenges. During the two decades after independence the state has remained stable and secure and has enjoyed comparatively robust democratic institutions. Hence it can be seen as a successful case of state-building. Internal factors have contributed to the success; for example, a functioning civil service and infrastructure,[40] and not lacking the heritage of a neo-patrimonial regime but rather that of a 'settler oligarchy' with established institutions.[41] Yet stability and security were far from evident, given the extent of atrocities and abuses during the war.[42] Although there have been signs of increased one-party dominance, human rights abuses and infringement of democratic norms,[43] as a state, Namibia remains stable.

The three systemic dimensions of state formation help us understand this. Firstly, Namibia is well placed with regard to synergetic development. Two of its neighbours, Botswana and South Africa, are Africa's most stable and economically well-developed states. This provides opportunities for economic development, institutional emulation and stable co-operation. Namibia is also a member of SADC, which provides an institutional forum for co-operation and regional stability.

Secondly, Namibia's independence was embedded in international and regional consensus. It is widely recognised that the help from South Africa and Angola as well as from the United Nations was important in ending the conflict and facilitating the transition to majority rule. A reading of the 'New York Accords' from 1988 between Angola, Cuba and South Africa demonstrates a point of deeper significance. The agreement stated that the powers of the region accepted that the fundamental institutions of the international system would be constitutive of politics in, as the document explicitly states, 'south-western Africa'.[44] This agreement preceded the development of democratic institutions of Namibia. In what looks like a text-book reiteration of the principles of the modern international system, the parties affirmed the 'sovereignty, sovereign equality and independence of all states of south-western Africa'. Thereby the agreement is comparable to the historical peace treaties in Europe – which established the system of states – wherein the parties also agreed on the constitutional principles of the whole region. The 1988 agreement is analogous to the Vienna settlement of 1815 whereby the constitutions of intermediary bodies (like the German Confederation) were embedded in and guaranteed by a regional constitution. As we shall see, such agreements on constitutional principles in general and on the international system in particular are glaringly lacking with regard to Somalia/the Horn of Africa as well as Afghanistan/Central Asia.

Thirdly, the regional acceptability of a viable or even strong Namibia from a security perspective has been significant. One factor that may have sustained Namibia as a viable state is the preponderance of South Africa in economic and security matters. South Africa is so much more powerful than its neighbours that it does not have to fear the establishment of viable and even strong states on its borders. In contrast to Pakistan it is not engaged in a balance of power struggle with any other power in its neighbourhood and hence does not need buffers or weak intermediary states.

The second and third case studies, the Horn of Africa/Somalia and Central Asia/Afghanistan, respectively, are regions where neither the unitary state nor an international system has been fully established. A part of the problem is that no other stable regional constitutional order has been created. Hence conflicts tend to be carried out over, rather than according to, constitutive rules.[45] Somalia today is reminiscent of a system of autonomous polities but is not recognised as such by the outside world or by all of the Somali actors. Instead, the international community insists on treating Somalia as a state, regardless of the facts on the ground. A large portion of the political violence can be traced to the lack of consensus about the basic organising principles of politics between the different power-holders. The situation in Central Asia appears the converse, but is structurally similar. Central Asia, including Afghanistan and Pakistan, are treated by the Western world as a states system. However, on closer examination the label does not quite fit. The component states are not Western-Weberian states and the relations of political elites with each other are not quite of the international type. If we consider the systemic context the situation in Afghanistan/Central Asia may be an even more difficult case of state-building than Somalia.

Somalia and the Horn of Africa

Somalia is arguably the paradigmatic example of a failed state. But advocates of this view would have to argue for a starting point to this failure. It could be traced further back in time than the final overthrow of Siad Barré in 1991. It could be argued that Somalia began to display the signs associated with state failure after the Ogaden war in 1977–78, 18 years after the formal independence of Somalia in 1960. Then again, a close study of the elections of 1964 and 1969 demonstrate that extreme factionalism, fragmentation and predation upon the state were prevalent already in the first decade of independence.[46] The unitary state in Somalia, then, seems more like an evanescent and highly contested project than a permanent structure that was brought to collapse. There are several important reasons why a unitary state was never established in Somalia. One of them is the clan system which some argue prevents the establishment of a unitary polity.[47] Here I will however focus on the systemic context.

Firstly, if we consider Somalia's neighbours, the changes of positive synergies of state formation are low. Ethiopia has recovered from a period of disintegration and now has greater means of power projection at home and abroad. The 'infrastructural power' of the state, i.e. its capacity to penetrate and engage society,[48] remains weak. In many ways, it is reminiscent of a 'quasi-empire' whose distinct parts are ruled from a centre but not included into the polity. Kenya, despite the appearances of calm, erupted into violence and political turmoil after the elections in 2008.

Secondly, political conditions inside Somalia resemble a proto-states system of its own.[49] In the north, Somaliland has declared independence and achieved substantial stability. In the east, Puntland is a distinct entity whose leadership wavers between trying to dominate a future unified Somalia and using Puntland as an autonomous entity. In the south 'a loose constellation of city-states and villages separated by pastoral statelessness' has been established.[50] Other regional state formation projects, like the Riverine state of the Rahanwein people, have been attempted but failed.[51] Thus, although a de facto polycentric order can be discerned there is no consensus among Somali or non-Somali actors on the legitimacy of this order, let alone its fundamental institutions. The situation is thus analogous to sixteenth century Europe which was riddled with wars and uncertainty over the constitutive rules of the system as well as conflicts over the legitimacy of different actors. As Menkhaus observes, the political violence in Somalia is fuelled by attempts to establish a unitary state by rival actors which are supported by regional powers and encouraged by the international community determined to maintain Somalia as a state. A possible solution would rather be to encourage the development of Somalia as a states system, trying to steer it into a 'Lockean' direction rather than forcing it into the mould of a 'Hobbesian' state. Such a venture would require that external actors also are embedded in a common constitutional settlement.

Thirdly, even if the substantial hurdles to creating a strong or at least viable state in Somalia were to be overcome, it is doubtful whether it would contribute to regional stability. Although Somalia's current condition is worrying to Ethiopia, a unitary state could also cause problems. The aim of uniting all ethnic Somalis in a single state has been a strong discourse in Somalia since 1960. Ethiopia's eastern region, Ogaden, is inhabited by Somalis and is hence a latent target for pan-Somalism, particularly since it harbours a secessionist guerrilla movement. Since Ethiopia is a multinational and multi-faith country, Ogadeni secession and terrorism or secessionism among the country's Muslims are two major security threats. Consequently, any unified Somali state acceptable to Ethiopia would have to foreswear irredentism and pan-Somali ideology in a credible way and give guarantees that no other movement would try to mobilise political support using pan-Somalism.

This would be very difficult to achieve: firstly, since pan-Somalism and anti-Ethiopian sentiment are effective ways of bolstering or achieving political support; and secondly, since the persistent Eritrean-Ethiopian rivalry means that Eritrea will be interested in supporting any and all Somali groups laying claim to Ogaden.[52] Hence risk aversion rather than a positive idea of order is likely to play a role in external actors' involvement in any processes for a future order in Somalia. The current peace process, the Djibouti process, is deemed by many to have a better chance of success than previous attempts. However, it does not take account of the regional dimensions of conflicts in Somalia. Firstly, it does not recognise the security concerns of Ethiopia. Secondly, the self-proclaimed republic of Somaliland is not addressed and included in the settlement.[53] Hence even though actors in the region are involved, the Djibouti process is very far from the kind of constitutional settlement the Horn of Africa needs.

Afghanistan and Central Asia

Afghanistan is even more complicated than Namibia and Somalia. A series of wars have raged on its territory from the Soviet invasion in 1979 to the current conflict since 2001. To call Afghanistan a failed state, caused by conflicts between internal and external actors, is misleading. As with Somalia, it has been a quasi-state since its inception. Modern Afghanistan is an externally-driven project created in the early 1880s as a buffer between the British and Russian empires.[54] Foreign capital, primarily civilian and military aid from the Soviet Union and Iran, built and sustained Afghanistan between the 1920s and 1990s.[55] As Suhrke argues, this pattern continues under the present Western-driven process of state-building.[56] From its creation to the current situation, Afghanistan has been shaped by the projection of power by modern empires and states in its surroundings and several of its problems can be traced to structural problems in these realms, in other words, to the systemic context.

Firstly, the potential for synergies is weak since many of its neighbours are economically underdeveloped and structurally weak. Some of the Central Asian republics are rich in oil and natural gas but this wealth is creating rentier states rather than boosting overall development. Concerning state structures, the countries of Central Asia (Kazakhstan, Kyrgyzstan, Tajikistan, Turkmenistan and Uzbekistan) display strong continuities with pre-Soviet forms of organisation such as tribal and clan networks taking precedence of Western-type state structures.[57] Pakistan's economy is also faltering and, as we shall see, its state institutions are defective. Hence, little synergy is available in terms of economic co-development or institutional emulation.

Secondly, the states system is rudimentary. This does not mean an absence of cross-border politics; on the contrary, the region is characterised by a high degree of intertwining of many of its polities. Worse still, it is characterised by uncertainty and non-consensus as to the constitutive principles in general. Thirdly the region is marked by imperial geo-strategies pursued by the major powers. Afghanistan and the Central Asian republics are caught in and shaped by this crossfire. Afghanistan is intertwined with several of its neighbours as many of its ethnic groups also live in other states, e.g. Tajiks, Turkmen and Uzbeks live in Tajikistan, Turkmenistan and Uzbekistan respectively. The most significant intertwining is however with Pakistan.

The official as well as unofficial economies of Afghanistan and Pakistan have become increasingly connected. This is partly due to Pakistani attempts to control Afghanistan, which have resulted in more and more of the Pakistani economy becoming a part of Afghanistan's illegal economy and partly due to the increasing strength of transnational mafias operating in both countries. This process has severely undermined Pakistan's stability.[58] Intertwining also concerns ethnic groups since Afghanistan's largest, the Pashtuns, also live in Pakistan's north-western provinces. This led to Afghanistan raising territorial claims on the frontier areas when Pakistan became independent.[59] Since 1979 the flow of refugees from the Afghan civil war into Pakistan has immensely increased the intermingling of Pashtuns in Afghanistan and in Pakistan's hinterlands.[60] Many Taliban have been raised and educated on the Pakistani side of the border and, with the help of the Pakistani security forces, the Inter-Services Intelligence Directorate (ISI), has been able to use Pakistani territory as a place to regroup and train.

This predicament must not be confused with irredentism in nineteenth and twentieth century Europe when consolidating nation states claimed overlordship over ethnic 'kin' living in another country. Although the disagreements between Afghanistan and Pakistan over the 'Pashtun belt' on both sides of the border might seem like a case of irredentism, it is not. In nineteenth and twentieth century Europe, the constitutive structure of the units was clear and accepted by all participants, the nation state was the norm. Similarly, the rules of interaction were also agreed upon. This enabled the reciprocal actions of territorial seizure, 'repatriation' and ethnic cleansing or extermination of foreign elements within the nation-state. This is not the case in Central Asia. No such firm consensus on the nature of the constituent units – and hence of their relations – exists within or between the states of the region. Since its inception Pakistan has been fundamentally unclear about what is usually called its 'identity' but what I would identify – using a stronger term – as its organising or constitutional principle.

Pakistan is not a polity with Weberian state institutions. Since its creation it has been controlled by the military whose main focus has been survival in the rivalry with India as well as economic self-enrichment. A multinational country without past traditions on which it can draw legitimacy, Pakistan has sought to build its raison d'être on its character as an Islamic state.[61] Its vacillation between a territorial and a religious principle of organisation has created uncertainty in its foreign policy as well as in the region. Pakistan's quest to control Afghanistan has been linked to its ambitions to project power into Central Asia which would strengthen it strategically, economically and ideologically as a leader of other Muslim countries. Pakistan is not alone in attempting to use different Afghan factions in order to control the country. Iran, Saudi Arabia, Russia and now the Western powers have also employed strategies that bear resemblances to imperial geo-strategies.[62]

Consequently, Afghanistan is less of a 'failed state' than, along with its northern neighbours, a classic example of an imperial frontier zone.[63] Perhaps one could even see the region as a transfrontier one, beyond the reach of rival empires but dotted with different kinds of satrapies. It is well known that this is Central Asia's historical predicament but there are strong continuities into the present in this respect. Not only is Afghanistan very little of a state, understood in the Western-Weberian sense, but so are its neighbours. This includes not only the impoverished and weak states of Central Asia but also the comparatively powerful and nuclear-armed Pakistan to the south. The region suffers not only from a collective deficit of stateness but also of state system institutions. It is characterised by imperial strategies but without imperial structures that would provide predictability, 'rules of the game' and stability.

The 2002 Afghan Constitution has been described as a step forward,[64] but what is really required is a constitutional settlement for the entire region in which all powers agree upon the rules that will govern their relations. Central Asia, Afghanistan and Pakistan would require their own Peace of Westphalia, or at least a settlement like the New York Accords that settled south-western Africa. Probably an attempt to impose a states system on the region would be very difficult. The analogy with the Peace of Westphalia, as interpreted by Osiander and Teschke, is perhaps more appropriate: a constitutional arrangement for an entire subsystem that embeds the different units but nevertheless grants them far-reaching autonomy.[65]

Thirdly, due to the configuration of the regional system in security terms, certain powers resist a viable Afghanistan, let alone a strong one. Foremost among these is Pakistan. Because of its strategic rivalry with India the Pakistani military establishment and the ISI have cultivated the idea that Afghan territory could be used as 'strategic depth' in case of a conflict with India.[66] The ISI has used Afghanistan as a training ground for its proxy war with India in Kashmir. Consequently, as long as Pakistan's dominant threat perception is a conventional conflict with India it will pursue a risk averse strategy of either maintaining Afghanistan in a state of weakness or trying to install a friendly regime in Kabul. It will try to avoid a strong Afghanistan, since a hostile government might ally itself with India or Iran. Within this strategic paradigm, the negative security effects that a weak Afghanistan brings are likely to be seen as affordable side effects of a strategy for inter-state security.

Unfortunately, the problem is not limited to Afghanistan or even to the role or worldview of the ISI. The relations between Iran and Pakistan are also tense and characterised by mutual perceptions of threats. Buffers or weak intermediary states fill an important structural role between states in a security dilemma.[67] This assertion is by no means a prediction and it makes no claims to universal validity. However, the situations we face in Afghanistan and in Somalia are consistent with a pattern, a 'generative grammar' that we are familiar with from earlier historical periods.

Strategic consequences of goal conflicts

The section above demonstrated that there is a tension, and in some cases a direct conflict, between state-building and regional stability. Some studies have shown that wars in the contemporary developing world do not support dynamics of state formation. Nevertheless, state-building in these regions may lead to armed conflicts. From the viewpoint of the contemporary West, the state seems like an ideal solution to problems of organised crime, development and regional security. Historically, however, processes of state formation led to a proliferation of conflicts. Hence we should be aware that our programmes of state-building may in fact be drivers of conflicts, within as well as between countries.

The fall of large-scale empires and the process of decolonisation during the twentieth century left many regions of the world without functioning constitutional settlements for establishing consensus on fundamental institutions of inter-units relations. Exceptions, like south-western Africa, do exist. Although changes to the current situation may entail conflicts, we should be clear that the current situation in places like the Horn of Africa and Central Asia is a 'low-level equilibrium trap',[68] where human development and security suffer. I have tried to make the case that we should tread gingerly when trying to change these situations. However, prudence does not mean passivity. Although I won't go into this here, we should perhaps begin to question whether the state would be the solution to the security problems in the Horn of Africa or in Central Asia. It is fully possible that other constitutive paradigms would be possible or even more stable than the current situation. As Watson has argued, orders that combine some kind of hierarchy with autonomy for the constituent units may be more stable than international systems normatively oriented towards 'anarchy'.[69]

An inquiry into alternative paradigms has to be self-reflexive and lead to a questioning of our own motives. The assumption that state-building is a way to solve several different security problems in synergy is valid primarily from a Western perspective. The dependence on a certain perspective does not make it less valid but it has to be tempered by the possibility that attempts to establish viable Western-Weberian states will not solve all the security problems of regions that today are highly problematic. Some, like organised crime, might be solved while others, like internal and international security, may actually be worsened. My findings lend credence to arguments that state-building is a strongly 'donor-driven' exercise since it primarily addresses Western security concerns, not those of the regions we purportedly try to help.[70]

From an operative perspective, the findings of this article suggest that programmes of state-building have to be seriously regional in character. The European Union is indeed pursuing such a course of action in the Western Balkans. This situation, however, differs greatly from the situation facing Western state-builders in Africa and Asia for two reasons. Firstly, the EU has substantial clout and resources in relation to the Balkan countries, even amounting to a kind of informal suzerainty. Secondly, these countries also have strong interests in compliance since joining the EU is a major political objective. Regional foci outside of Europe, which would facilitate state-building, already exist but they have to be reinforced. In contrast to the EU's 'near abroad', such programmes face greater challenges since Western countries lack the advantages of the EU in relation to the Western Balkans.

Conclusions

Three main conclusions can be drawn. Firstly, the challenges of state-building are greater than usually imagined in much of the literature and strategic documents. Secondly, the exercise of state-building sometimes stands in direct conflict with achieving regional stability/security. Thirdly, in order to create conditions for regional stability, as well as state-building, we must strive to achieve constitutional settlements for wider regions than just the state identified as the most 'failed' one. With such 'ground rules' in place concerning legitimate units, inter-unit relations and codes of war, the formation of states or other kinds of viable polities could follow. The conclusions are borne out by historical evidence and the contemporary studies. In the successful case a regional settlement preceded the independence and deepening of Namibia. In the unsuccessful cases, the problems of state formation are bound up with the absence of a states system or indeed of any constitutional settlement for the wider region. Somalia and Afghanistan are different in many ways but they share some traits. Both are part of 'failed regions' rather than simply failed states. Somalia is unusual since it resembles a not fully-formed and institutionalised region in itself. By contrast, Afghanistan is only a part of a similar area.

I have argued that the challenges of state-building are greater than usually assumed since we do not only face 'failed states' but in fact 'failed regions'. To be precise, these areas have not become inter-national regions, which has inhibited the growth of Western-Weberian states. This paper has only surveyed three regions, but further studies might show a correlation between successful state-building and successful regions. In two of the studied regions, the process of creating unitary states has generated conflict both within and beyond the boundaries of de jure states. A characteristic of the two problematic regions studied here is that they are characterised not only by post-imperial but also by quasi-imperial strategies and structures.[71] This characterises Central Asia to a much greater extent than the Horn of Africa. I am not claiming that the security dynamics of these regions are only or even primarily constituted by imperial or imperialist policies. It is far from my intention to substitute a one-sided emphasis on endogenous factors with an equally one-sided emphasis on exogenous factors. Both sides must be weighed in. Doing so prompts the conclusion that, given the deep-seated structural nature of the preconditions of the formation of viable and strong states, there is a need to have more realistic assessment of the possibilities of state-building.

A key to bringing about change in terms of regional acceptance (the more material factors of economy and administration would still remain to be solved) lies in changing dominant conceptions of security (e.g. in terms of what type of actor is seen as constituting the main threat as well as the nature and gravity of that threat) in the region.[72] This point, undoubtedly a substantial one, cannot be addressed to the full merit that it deserves within the scope of a single piece. Hence it is an urgent task for future research.

Drawing upon the historical background as well as contemporary cases, the difficulties in state-building are often underestimated, as are the direct conflicts between some of the goals that state-building efforts set out to achieve. This underestimation is not only one of degree, for example in terms of the time, money and manpower required, but one of kind. These are the conflicts between the basic policy goals of Western actors in relation to troublesome regions in the world, for example between creating stable states and maintaining regional stability. As suggested by policy and strategy documents these goals are doubtlessly mutually supportive in the long term. In the short term, however, building strong states may actually beget instability in certain vulnerable regions, like the Horn of Africa, a conundrum that policymakers and military strategists have yet to address. Analysing the systemic context with a historical perspective has highlighted the goal-conflicts that state-building entails. Historical knowledge can never give blueprints but it can offer suggestions for ways out of the current predicament. One has already been mentioned, the need for systems-building to take precedence over state-building. Another has only been suggested, namely that some regions may be in need of another kind of constitutional settlement than the national/international paradigm. What such orders have looked like in the past or may look like in the future has to be the subject and challenge of further research.

Notes

1 Armstrong and Rubin, 'The Great Lakes'.
2 Buzan and Wsever, *Regions and Powers*.
3 This literature is large but see, for example, Chandler, 'Problems of Nation-Building'; and Orford, 'Jurisdiction without Territory'.
4 Scott, *Organizations*, 117–120.
5 Spruyt, *Sovereign State*.
6 Canada, *Canada's International Policy Statement*, ii, 1, 11, 13–15; Finland, *Finnish Security*, 19, 22, 26, 48, 75; Germany, *German White Paper*, 5, 14–15, 19, 25, 35, 48–49; UK, *National Security Strategy*, 3, 7, 13–14, 31, 33–41.
7 France, *French White Paper*, 6; Italy, *Il Concetto Strategico*, 3; Netherlands, *National Security Strategy*, 18; Norway, *Relevant Force*, 27–28; Poland, *National Security Strategy*, 7.
8 US, *National Security Strategy*, 15, 44; EU, *A Secure Europe*, 6, 7.
9 UK, *National Security Strategy*, 14; Canada, *Canada's International Policy Statement*, 13; Germany, *German White Paper*, 19; EU, *A Secure Europe*, 4; Australia, *Defending Australia*, 15; Norway, *Relevant Force*, 28; Finland, *Finnish Security*, 19.
10 UK, *National Security Strategy*, 14; Canada, *Canada's International Policy Statement*, 13; Germany, *German White Paper*, 18; Australia, *Defending Australia*, 15; Norway, *Relevant Force*, 28; Poland, *National Security Strategy*, 7; Finland, *Finnish Security*, 26; EU, *A Secure Europe*, 4, 7.
11 UK, *National Security Strategy*, 31; Australia, *Defending Australia*, 18.
12 Canada, *Canada's International Policy Statement*, 1; Norway, *Relevant Force*, 28.
13 EU, *A Secure Europe*, 4; US, *National Security Strategy*, 15.
14 Bøås and Dunn, 'African Guerrilla Polities', 19.
15 Herbst, *States and Power*.
16 Clapham, *Africa and the International System*.
17 Jackson, *Quasi-States*
18 Poggi, *Development of the Modern State*.
19 Tilly, *Formation of National States and Coercion, Capital and European States*.
20 Tilly, *Formation of National States*.
21 See also Hintze, 'Wesen und Wandlung'.
22 Herbst, *States and Power*.
23 See, for example, Eriksen, 'Congo War'.
24 North, 'Transaction Cost Theory' and 'Institutions'; North and Weingast, 'Order, Disorder and Economic Change'.
25 Link, 'Die Habsburgischen Erblände', 519.
26 C.f. North, *Rise of the Western World*; Jones, *European Miracle*.
27 Spruyt, *Sovereign State*.
28 Mitrany, *Functional Theory*.
29 Walker, *Inside/Outside*.
30 Reus-Smit, 'Constitutional Structure'.
31 Wendt, *Social Theory*, 270.
32 Aretin, *Das Altes Reich*, 160; Wilson, *Holy Roman Empire*, 30.
33 Grześkowiak-Rwawicz, 'Anti-monarchism'.
34 Schroeder, *Transformation of European Politics*.
35 Watson, *Evolution of International Society*; Reus-Smit, 'Constitutional Structure'.
36 C.f. Adler, 'Seeds of peaceful change', 119, 122.
37 Deudney, 'Publius before Kant'.
38 Buzan and Wæver, *Regions and Powers*, 226–227.
39 Mann, *Sources of Social Power*.
40 Dobbins et al., *UN's Role*, 32–33.
41 Bratton and van de Walle, in Bauer, 'Namibia in the First Decade', 34–35.
42 Parlevliet, 'Truth Commissions in Africa', 100–101.
43 Lamb, 'Debasing Democracy'.
44 Agreement Among the People's Republic of Angola, the Republic of Cuba and the Republic of South Africa. Available at: http://www.usip.org/library/pa/angola/angola_cuba_sa_12221988.html [Accessed 5 February 2009].
45 Wendt, *Social Theory*, 165.

46 For an overview, see Lyons and Samatar, *Somalia*.
47 There have been vigorous debates among Somali specialists about the relative importance of clans. See Besteman, 'Violent Polities'; Helender, 'Emperor's New Clothes Removed'; Besteman, 'Primordialist Blinders'; Besteman, 'Response to Helander's Critique'; and Lewis, 'Visible and Invisible Differences'.
48 Mann, *Sources of Social Power*, 59.
49 The following paragraph is based on Haldén, *Somalia*.
50 Menkhaus, 'Crisis in Somalia', 86.
51 Brons, *Society, Security, Sovereignty*, 260ff.
52 For a recent update on the Ethiopian-Eritrean conflict, see ICG, 'Beyond the Fragile Peace'.
53 Institute for Security Studies, 'Somalia'.
54 Rubin, *Fragmentation of Afghanistan*, 48–52.
55 Rubin, *Fragmentation of Afghanistan*.
56 Suhrke, 'When More is Less'.
57 Egnell and Haldén, 'Laudable, Ahistorical and Over-ambitious', 43–44.
58 Rashid, *Taliban*, 193–195.
59 Rubin, *Fragmentation of Afghanistan*, 62–64.
60 Rashid, *Taliban*, 185.
61 Rashid, *Descent into Chaos*, 34–36.
62 See Akbarzadeh, 'Keeping Central Asia stable', 699–703.
63 C.f. Browning and Joeniemi, 'Geostrategies'.
64 Rashid, *Descent into Chaos*, 211–218. For a somewhat contrary point, see Simonsen, 'Ethnicising Afghanistan'.
65 Osiander, *States System of Europe*; Teschke, *Myth of 1648*.
66 Rashid, *Descent into Chaos*, 186–187; Rubin, 'Afghanistan under the Taliban', 84.
67 Schroeder, 'Lost Intermediaries'.
68 C.f. Spruyt, *Sovereign State*.
69 Watson, *Limits of Independence*.
70 Chandler, *Empire in Denial*.
71 C.f. Shaw, 'Post-Imperial and Quasi-Imperial', 335.
72 These problems have been discussed by, among others, Wendt, *Social Theory*; and Adler, 'Seeds of Peaceful Change'.

References

Adler, Emanuel, 1998. 'Seeds of Peaceful Change: The OSCE's Security-Community Building Model', in Emanuel Adler and Michael Barnett, (eds), *Security Communities*. Cambridge University Press, Cambridge, 119–161.

Akbarzadeh, Shahram, 2004. 'Keeping Central Asia Stable'. *Third World Quarterly* 25(4), 689–705.

Aretin, Karl Otmar Fh.V, 1997. *Das Altes Reich 1648–1806 Bd. 1 Föderalistische oder Hierarchische Ordnung (1648–1684)* [The Old Realm: Federal or Hierarchical Order]. Klett-Cotta, Stuttgart.

Armstrong, Andrea and Barnett R. Rubin, 2005. 'The Great Lakes and South Central Asia', in S. Chesterman, M. Ignatieff and R. C. Thakur, (eds), *Making States Work: State Failure and the Crisis of Governance*. United Nations University Press, Tokyo, 79–101.

Australia, 2009. *Defending Australia in the Asia Pacific Century: Force 2030*. Australian Government Department of Defence. Available at: http://www.apo.org.au/research/defending-australia-asia-pacific-century-force-2030 [Accessed 12 December 2009].

Bauer, Gretchen, 2001. 'Namibia in the First Decade of Independence: How Democratic?'. *Journal of Southern African Studies* 27(1), 33–55.

Besteman, Catherine, 1996. 'Violent Politics and the Politics of Violence: The Dissolution of the Somali Nation-State'. *American Ethnologist* 23(3), 579–596.

Besteman, Catherine, 1998. 'A Response to Helander's Critique of "Violence Politics and the Politics of Violence"'. *American Ethnologist* 26(4), 981–983.

Besteman, Catherine, 1998. 'Primordialist Blinders: A Reply to I. M. Lewis'. *Cultural Anthropology* 13(1), 109–120.

Bøås, Morten and Kevin C. Dunn, 2007. 'African Guerrilla Politics: Raging Against the Machine?', in Morten Bøås and Kevin C. Dunn, (eds), *African Guerrillas: Raging Against the Machine*. Lynne Rienner, Boulder, CO, 9–37.

Brons, Maria H., 2001. *Society, Security, Sovereignty and the State: Somalia. From Statelessness to Statelessness?* International Books, Utrecht.

Browning, Christopher S. and Pertti Joenniemi, 2008. 'Geostrategies of the European Neighbourhood Policy'. *European Journal of International Relations* 14(3), 519–551.

Buzan, Barry and Ole Wæver, 2004. *Regions and Powers: The Structure of International Security*. Cambridge University Press, Cambridge.

Canada, 2005. *Canada's International Policy Statement: The Role of Pride and Influence in the World*. Department of Foreign Affairs and International Trade, Ottawa, Ontario.

Chandler, David, 2004. 'The Problems of Nation-Building: Imposing Bureaucratic Rule from Above'. *Cambridge Review of International Affairs* 17(3), 577–591.

Chandler, David, 2006. *Empire in Denial: The Politics of State-Building*. Pluto, London.

Clapham, Christopher, 1996. *Africa and the International System: The Politics of State Survival*. Cambridge University Press, Cambridge.

Deudney, Daniel H., 2004. 'Publius before Kant: Federal-Republican Security and Democratic Peace'. *European Journal of International Relations* 10(3), 315–356.

Dobbins, James, Seth G. Jones, Keith Crane, Andrew Rathmell, Brett Steele, Richard Teltshick and Anga Timilsina, 2005. *The UN's Role in Nation-Building. From the Congo to Iraq*. RAND, Santa Monica, CA.

Egnell, Robert and Peter Haldén, 2009. 'Laudable, Ahistorical and Overambitious: Security Sector Reform Meets State Formation Theory'. *Conflict, Security and Development* 9(1), 27–54.

Eriksen, Stein Sundstøl, 2005. 'The Congo War and the Prospects of State Formation: Rwanda and Uganda compared'. NUPI Working paper, no. 675. Norwegian Institute of International Affairs, Oslo.

EU, 2003. *A Secure Europe in a Better World: European Security Strategy*. EU, Brussels.

Finland, 2009. *Finnish Security and Defence Policy*. Prime Minister's Office Publications, Helsinki.

France, 2008. *The French White Paper on Defence and National Security*. Présidence de la République, Paris. Available at: http://merln.ndu.edu/whitepapers/France_English2008.pdf [Accessed 12 December 2009].

Germany, 2006. *German White Paper on German Security Policy and the Future of the Bundeswehr*. Federal Ministry of Defence, http://merln.ndu.edu/whitepapers/Germany_White_Paper_2006.pdf [Accessed 20 July 2006].

Grześkowiak-Rwawicz, Anna, 2000. 'Anti-monarchism in Polish Republicanism in the Seventeenth and Eighteenth Centuries', in Martin van Gelderen and Quentin Skinner, (eds), *Republicanism: A Shared European Heritage Volume II*. Cambridge University Press, Cambridge, 43–59.

Haldén, Peter, 2008. *Somalia: Failed State or Nascent States-System?* Swedish Defence Research Agency, Stockholm. Available at: http://www.foi.se/upload/projects/Africa/FOI-R-2598.pdf [Accessed 10 December 2009].

Helander, Bernhard, 1998. 'The Emperor's New Clothes Removed: A Critique of Besteman's "Violent Politics and the Politics of Violence"'. *American Ethnologist* 25(3), 489–501.

Herbst, Jeffery, 2000. *States and Power in Africa. Comparative Lessons in Authority and Control*. Princeton University Press, Princeton.

Hintze, Otto, 1970. 'Wesen und Wandlung des Modernen Staats', in Gerhard Oestrich Otto, (ed.), *Staat und Verfassung Gesammelte Abhandlungen zur Allgemeinen Verfassungsgeschichte* [Nature and Transformation of the Modern State in State and Constitution. Collected Works on general Constitutional History] *Bd I*. Vandenhoeck & Ruprecht, Göttingen, 470–496.

Italy, 2004. *Il Concetto Strategico del Capo del SMD Stato Maggiore della Difesa*. [The Strategic Concept of the General Staff] Rome. Available at: http://merln.ndu.edu/whitepapers.html [Accessed 12 December 2009].

International Crisis Group (ICG), 2008. 'Beyond the Fragile Peace between Ethiopia and Eritrea:

Averting New War'. Africa Report no. 141. ICG, 17 June. Available at: http://www.crisisgroup.
org/library/documents/africa/horn_of_africa/nd_the_fragile_peace_between_ethiopia_and_ eri-
trea_averting_new_war.pdf [Accessed 9 February 2009].

Institute for Security Studies, 2009. 'Somalia: The Djibouti Process Has a Better Chance of Success'.
Institute for Security Studies, 29 January. Available at: http://www.issafrica.org/index.php?link_
id=14&slink_id=7229&link_type=12&slink_type=12&tmpl_id=3 [Accessed 5 February 2009].

Jackson, Robert H., 1996. *Quasi-states: Sovereignty, International Relations, and the Third World.* Cambridge
University Press, Cambridge.

Jones, Eric, 2003. *The European Miracle. Environments, Economies and Geopolitics in the History of Europe and
Asia.* Cambridge University Press, Cambridge.

Lamb, Guy, 2002. 'Debasing Democracy: Security Forces and Human Rights Abuses in Post-Libera-
tion Namibia and South Africa', in Yul Derek Davids and Henning Melber, (eds), *Measuring Democracy
and Human Rights in Southern Africa.* Nordic Africa Institute, Uppsala.

Lewis, I. M., 2004. 'Visible and Invisible Differences: The Somali Paradox'. *Africa* 74(4), 489–515.

Link, Christoph, 1983. 'Die Habsburgischen Erblände, Die Böhmischen Länder und Salzburg', [The
Hereditary Lands of the Hapsburgs, the Bohemian Lands and Salzburg] in Kurt G. A. Jeserich,
Hans Pohl and Georg-Christoph von Unruh, (eds), *Deutsche Verwaltungs-geschichte Band I Vom Spätmit-
telalter bis zum Ende des Reiches.* [German Administrative History Vol. 1 From the Late Middle Ages to
the End of the Empire.] Deutsche Verlags-Anstalt, Stuttgart.

Lyons, Terrence and Ahmed I. Samatar, 1995. *Somalia. State Collapse, Multilateral Intervention and Strategies
for Political Reconstruction.* Brookings Institution, Washington DC.

Mann, Michael, 1993. *The Sources of Social Power, Vol. 2: The Rise of Classes and Nation-States, 1760–1914.*
Cambridge University Press, Cambridge.

Menkhaus, Ken, 2007. 'The Crisis in Somalia: Tragedy in Five Acts'. *African Affairs* 106(204),
357–390.

Mitrany, David, 1975. *The Functional Theory of Politics.* Martin Robertson for the LSE, London.

The Netherlands, 2007. *National Security Strategy and Work Programme 2007–2008.* Ministry of the Interior
and Kingdom Relations, Breda.

North, Douglass C, 1973. *The Rise of the Western World: A New Economic History.* Cambridge University
Press, Cambridge.

North, Douglass C, 1990. 'Transaction Cost Theory of Politics'. *Journal of Theoretical Politics* 2(4),
355–367.

North, Douglass C, 1991. 'Institutions'. *Journal of Economic Perspectives* 5(1), 97–112.

North, Douglass C, William Summerhill and Barry R. Weingast, 2000. 'Order, Disorder and Economic Change: Latin America vs. North America', in Bruce Bueno de Mesquita and Hilton Root,
(eds), *Governing for Prosperity.* Yale University Press, New Haven, 17–59.

Norway, 2004. *Relevant Force: Strategic Concept of the Norwegian Armed Forces.* Ministry of Defence. Available at: http://www.regjeringen.no/upload/FD/Dokumenter/Relevant_force.pdf [Accessed 12
December 2009].

Orford, Anne, 2009. 'Jurisdiction without Territory From the Holy Roman Empire to the Responsibility to Protect'. *Michigan Journal of International Law* 30(3), 981–1015.

Osiander, Andreas, 1994. *The States System of Europe, 1640–1990: Peacemaking and the Conditions of International Stability.* Clarendon Press, Oxford.

Parlevliet, Michelle, 2000. 'Truth Commissions in Africa: The Non-Case of Namibia and the Emerging
Case of Sierra Leone'. *International Law Forum Du Droit International* 2(2), 98–111.

Poggi, Gianfranco, 1978. *The Development of the Modern State A Sociological Introduction.* Stanford University
Press, Stanford.

Poland, 2007. *National Security Strategy of the Republic of Poland.* Warsaw.

Rashid, Ahmed, 2001. *Taliban: Militant Islam, Oil, and Fundamentalism in Central Asia.* Yale Nota Bene,
New Haven.

Rashid, Ahmed, 2008. *Descent into Chaos: How the War against Islamic Extremism is being Lost in Pakistan,
Afghanistan and Central Asia,* Allen Lane, London.

Reus-Smit, Christian, 1997. 'The Constitutional Structure of International Society and the Nature of Fundamental Institutions'. *International Organization* 51(4), 55–89.

Rubin, Barnett R., 1995. *The Fragmentation of Afghanistan: State Formation and Collapse in the International System.* Yale University Press, New Haven.

Rubin, Barnett R., 1999. 'Afghanistan under the Taliban'. *Current History* 98(625), 79–91. Schroeder, Paul, 1994. *The Transformation of European Politics 1763–1848.* Oxford University Press, Oxford.

Schroeder, Paul, 2004. 'The Lost Intermediaries: The Impact of 1870 on the International System', in Paul W. Schroeder, (ed.), *Systems, Stability and Statecraft.* Palgrave, Basingstoke, 77–95.

Scott, W. Richard, 2003. *Organizations, Rational, Natural and Open Systems.* Prentice-Hall, Upper Saddle River, NJ.

Shaw, Martin, 2002. 'Post-Imperial and Quasi-Imperial: State and Empire in the Global Era'. *Millennium* 31(2), 327–336.

Simonsen, Sven Gunnar, 2004. 'Ethnicising Afghanistan? Inclusion and Exclusion in Post-Bonn Institution Building'. *Third World Quarterly* 25(4), 707–729.

Spruyt, Henrik, 1994. *The Sovereign State and its Competitors.* Princeton University Press, Princeton.

Suhrke, Astri, 2006. 'When More is Less: Aiding Statebuilding in Afghanistan', Fundacion para las Relaciones Internacionales y el Dialogo Exterior (FRIDE) Working paper, no. 26. FRIDE, Madrid.

Teschke, Benno, 2003. *The Myth of 1648 Class, Geopolitics and the Making of Modern International Relations.* Verso, London.

Tilly, Charles, 1975. *The Formation of National States in Western Europe.* Princeton University Press, Princeton.

Tilly, Charles, 1995. *Coercion, Capital and European States 992–1992.* Blackwell, Oxford.

UK, 2008. *The National Security Strategy of the United Kingdom: Security in an Interdependent World.* Cabinet Office, London.

US, 2006. *The National Security Strategy of the United States of America.* The White House, Washington D.C.

Walker, R. B. J., 1993. *Inside/Outside International Relations as Political Theory.* Cambridge University Press, Cambridge.

Watson, Adam, 1992. *The Evolution of International Society.* Routledge, London.

Watson, Adam, 1997. *The Limits of Independence. Relations Between States in the Modern World.* Routledge, London.

Wendt, Alexander, 1999. *Social Theory of International Relations.* Cambridge University Press, Cambridge.

Wilson, Peter, 1999. *The Holy Roman Empire, 1495–1806.* MacMillan.

38 Gender and peace

Towards a gender-inclusive, holistic perspective

Tony Jenkins and Betty A. Reardon

Introduction: toward a new phase of the enquiry into gender and peace

We are peace educators who believe that peace knowledge in all its forms constitutes one field from which multiple forms of learning relevant to the tasks of educating and acting for peace can be gleaned. We have drawn upon all of them, the fruits of peace research, the substance of university peace studies, the methodologies of peace education and practical peace action in the development of the pedagogies we practise. We adhere to educational methods consistent with the values of justice and nonviolence that inform the pursuit of peace knowledge. These are built upon a verifiable knowledge base, informed by sound theories, and directed toward developing the capacities of learners to make normative judgements based on the values, to apply the knowledge and verify or refute the theories through enquiry and communal learning. These methods imbue the approach we take to gender and peace. They reflect adherence to principles of holism in enquiry into problems and in exploration of possible resolutions of or means to transcend the problems of peace that we take in sum to be the problematic of violence.

These are the premises that underlie the following discussions, which will reflect upon the possibility that gender, the social roles of and social distinctions between men and women, when fully perceived, is not only as the United Nations refers to it, a cross-cutting issue, affecting most problems and areas of concern to peace knowledge, but also one possible core of a holistic study of the central problematic of violence. Because of this cross-cutting character and the universality of gender concerns, might not gender also serve as an organizing concept around which to build studies not only of gender equality and peace, but as the potential core of a systematic enquiry into the possibilities for the transformation of the present violent world order? We also ask whether such a transformation is possible without recognizing, dismantling and forswearing various institutions and habits of patriarchy that we perceive as integral to the present global culture of violence, a major factor affecting such problems as denial of human rights, economic inequity, ecological deterioration and armed conflict. Taken as a whole these problems comprise all that we have come to consider as the war system – those pervasive habits and institutions of political, economic, social and cultural violence that are a major impediment to peace and human security. We hope that others concerned with the role of gender in the creation and dissemination of peace knowledge would join in an enquiry into the illumination of contemporary forms of patriarchy as a complement and extension to what has gone before in the evolution of the field of gender and peace. We define patriarchy, as does Joshua Goldstein, as the 'social organization of men's control of power'.[1] The topic is classified as knowledge supporting peace; we, however, ask is not this problematic of gender as constitutive to peace knowledge as are conflict studies or any of the other topics here categorized as central to the substance of peace studies?

Overview of some significant developments in the field

The field of gender and peace has evolved through various phases, each with a perspective based on the concerns of its time. All phases, however, found some roots in the problematic of patriarchy, a social and cultural construct that has not only privileged men over women, but can be seen as a paradigm for other forms of authoritarianism, hierarchy and inequality. It is precisely the 'patriarchal privilege' as it is termed by Michael Kaufman,[2] that is the common thread that runs through the development of the field as it does through women's and men's struggles for gender justice. Through this century we see the field as evolving over the following chronology on which scholarship responds to and influences social movements for gender equality.

This chronology is developmental rather than uniquely event based. It underlies an organic view of the evolution of the field in which all realms of peace knowledge interact around the 'cross-cutting issue' of gender. Peace action, research and education on the subject of gender evolved in a process of reciprocal influence that illustrates the holistic nature of peace knowledge that informs our approach to peace education. The periods delineated below are not discrete, nor do the developments, even when viewed from a global perspective, evolve simultaneously in all areas of the world. We offer them here as a general framework for the narrative which will, by nature of the topics addressed, weave in and out of the various developmental phases we designate as follows.

The years 1900–45 were decades of the articulation of the problematic of women's subordinate social and political status, and, in the years preceding both world wars, of the articulation of intuitions regarding women's lack of political power as an obstacle to peace. Women's primary political activities were devoted to achieving suffrage. From 1945–70, attention was focused on the ongoing subordination of women and the limitations on their legal rights that existed, in some cases, even where women had the vote. The United Nations established a Commission on the Status of Women and later a more proactive agency, the Division for the Advancement of Women. A number of foundational works in modern feminism were published.

From 1970–85, the activism of women directed toward the realization of equality in all spheres, both public and private, energized the United Nations to launch efforts to set standards and goals for women's equality. These efforts were significantly advanced by two international decades on women and three international conferences, held in 1975, 1980 and 1985, organized around the themes of 'Equality, Development and Peace'. A major landmark of the period was the adoption of the Convention on the Elimination of All Forms of Discrimination against Women (CEDAW). These were also the years of the first academic enquiries into women and peace and the emergence of what was to become a significant body of literature on the topic.

The final developmental phase of the century occurred from 1985–2000. There was intense interest and activity around the denial of the human rights of women, resulting in campaigns to implement and augment CEDAW, one result of which was the Declaration on the Elimination of All Forms of Violence against Women. The 1995 Beijing Fourth World Conference on Women set a range of standards to assure that women's rights were recognized and implemented as universal human rights. Feminist theory on women and peace was further developed and was complemented in the 1990s by the initiation of masculinities studies, making an actual gender perspective on the peace problematic possible. The culminating development of this phase was the adoption of Security Council Resolution 1325 on 'Women, Peace and Security'. The first decade of the twenty-first century saw the beginning of enquiry and action around the vestiges of traditional patriarchy that continue to pose significant obstacles not only to gender equality but to a range of problems addressed by the fields of peace knowledge. The Patriarchy Project we describe in the last section of the essay was launched at the UN Conference on Racism held in 2002 in Durban, South Africa and carried to global civil society at the World Social Forum held in Rio de Janeiro, Brazil in 2004. It is carried on by a worldwide network of scholars and activists, committed to the achievement of universal gender justice and an end to war.

In the first sections of our essay we offer a selective account from our own particular perspective of issues and developments in action, research and education that have influenced the place of gender in the realms of peace knowledge. Starting with some consideration of women's resistance to war, we will move to noting how taking a political perspective on women's secondary status in most societies led feminists to proposing integral links between women's exclusion from policy-making and the continued recourse to war as a mechanism for the conduct of international conflict. Next, we will observe how international attention to the status of women led to the development of international agreements intended to achieve gender equality. Then, we take note of how the international cooperation among women that produced the agreements bought about an even wider view of the relationship between gender inequality and gender violence and a more holistic gender analysis of the problematic of the global culture of violence currently being informed by masculinities studies. These sections serve as a preface to a statement of the new more inclusive dimension we hope to see integrated into this essential field of enquiry into the conditions of peace as a means to more fully illuminate the problematic of patriarchy.

We place our account in the framework of the twentieth-century international women's movement and peace actions interacting with scholarship on gender and peace. While taking this international view, we acknowledge that our own experiences, knowledge and interpretations derive primarily from developments in the United Nations, the United States and various international civil society initiatives. The global movement that contributes to knowledge about gender and peace we know to be far wider and more varied than our limited account. We see this as an invitation to exchanges with others that might broaden and deepen gender and peace knowledge so that we may be more effective enquirers into the conditions and consequences of patriarchy and some alternative approaches to transcending them.

From the mid-twentieth century to the last decade, the academic field evolved primarily out of the theoretical frameworks of feminist scholarship introduced into international relations, peace studies and peace research, and United Nations policies. The earlier phases (1945–70) were focused on legal and political and later economic equality of women, dealing with the manifestations more than the causes of women's subordination, and seeing remedy primarily in the changing of women's legal status. Feminist perspectives that focused more on the underlying structural and cultural causes came in the later decades of the century as the term gender came to replace woman and the descriptor of the problematic. The recent addition of masculinities studies, addressing the consequences of men's socialization for peace issues and the consequences to men of the expectations and responsibilities that devolve to them in the war system, now gives validity to 'gender and peace' as the designator of a field, still referred to in some cases as 'women and peace' or 'women and world order'.[3] The roots of the field lie, as noted, in women's experience of and response to war, documented in literature and history as the experience of loss, mourning, heroic maternal sacrifice and – most important to the field – dissent and resistance. Study of these universal experiences and responses came out of concern with women's secondary position in human society, noted as a problematic since the outset of Western democratic experiments with representative government.

The relevance of the status of women to peace was somewhat acknowledged when raising the status of women was undertaken as a task for international society in the mid-twentieth century by the United Nations, largely at the behest of a few women diplomats, such as Helvi Sippila of Finland, who became chair of the first UN World Conference on Women in 1975 and Margaret Bruce of the UK, who served in the 1970s as director of the UN Division for the Advancement of Women and women's NGOs. Feminist discourse around the connections between women's political status and war, however, dates to the early decades of the century in Europe and the United States, and while neither vigorous nor prominent, it laid the foundation for the scholarship that gained attention with the new mid-century interest in the status of women. This interest inspired an outpouring of critiques of the gender blindness of the established field of international relations and the emerging field of peace knowledge, comprising research, studies, education and action.[4]

The gender blindness was first attributed to the limited participation of women in these fields, in policy-making, scholarship and, especially from the lack of women's perspectives in the research and teaching of the two interrelated but distinct fields, international relations and peace studies. Largely as a consequence of the two UN-declared International Women's Decades (1975–95), these critiques brought about attempts to remedy gender bias through a set of international standards set forth by the United Nations. These standards were introduced into the substance of a growing body of research and courses in women's studies, some of them including issues related to women, war and peace and violence against women. While it was in the area of human rights scholarship that this body of normative standards – including references to violence against women and women in armed conflict – received most academic attention, some scholars began to integrate feminist theories and peace theories in work that ultimately became a sub-field in peace studies and a major pedagogical influence on peace education. These standards are an essential component of the inclusive, integrative approach to gender and peace that we, the authors, now take in our research and teaching.

Feminist arguments, bolstered by international human rights norms, gave public validation to assertions concerning the negative effects of women's exclusion from analysis and policy-making on matters of peace and security. Taken up by scholars who explored the ways in which gender arrangements contributed to the perpetuation of the social and political uses of violence and the rationalization of war as an instrument of national policy, the links among women's secondary status, war and gender violence became more widely accepted as a given of the problematic of war, and a body of literature on these connections began to emerge and continues to grow. However, there was at first only minimal integration of the work done by feminist scholars and activists working on peace with that of those focusing on human rights. The mainstream women's studies, for the most part, perceived these particular enquiries as somewhat more specialized than their own more general study of women's issues and women's history.[5]

One of the most politically effective aspects of the international women's movement focused on the human rights of women and the use of the international standards to defend and implement them. Efforts were led by the Rutgers University Center for Women's Global Leadership and its executive director, Charlotte Bunch. It was from these efforts, mainly on the part of women scholar-activists, that intensive public attention was brought to violence against women.[6] Enquiry into issues of pervasive social and cultural gender violence and later into the effects of armed conflict on women by feminist scholar-activists in the human rights movement contributed to the articulation of a more general theory of violence, encompassing multiple forms and arenas of violence from interpersonal and domestic violence to organized warfare. The gendered aspects of violence became an important area of enquiry for a number of feminist scholars who sought to develop theories addressing male aggression as a factor in cultures of violence and the inclination toward war. Some argued that male aggressivity was socially and culturally cultivated in men and problematized male dominance in science – among them, Brian Easlea and Evelyn Fox Keller – as well as politics as a major causal factor in the origins and continuation of the arms race.[7]

Enquiries into social and gender violence, a significant aspect of the emerging field of the study of masculinities, have increased the number of male scholars in the field and led to the conceptualization of an inclusive gender perspective now taking hold. Recent developments have deepened and extended the arguments advanced on the issue of gender violence by feminist scholarship through the twentieth century to the present day in which institutionalized patriarchy itself is becoming more widely viewed as a central problematic.

We see this latest development to be infusing new possibilities for the transformational learning pursued by the education realm of peace knowledge. We would suggest that this currently developing phase of the field could integrate masculinities studies with human rights norms and concepts in a framework of enquiry into patriarchy. We have a particular interest in issues of gender enquiry of this type because of its relevance to the fundamental elements in the puzzle of peace as well as the transformative learning possibilities it offers. The gender issue itself is at once challenging, comprehensive and, we believe, highly amenable to positive change through learning facilitated by the critical and reflective pedagogies practised in peace education.

Gender refers to the culturally defined and socially sanctioned roles in human affairs played by men and women and the characteristics attributed to each that have rationalized these roles. Gender here is construed as it has been defined by the United Nations in the Beijing Platform for Action, the Swedish report on patriarchal violence quoted below, and in such documents as those calling for gender mainstreaming – including a gender perspective in the consideration of all issues and in all programmes addressed and conducted by the world body. We believe that the systematic nature of patriarchal gender designations and roles constitutes a highly significant and much neglected aspect of the study of gender and peace. Because we perceive gender aspects in virtually every issue and problem addressed by peace and conflict studies, we are attempting to integrate elements of these issues into all our work in peace education.[8]

This concept of gender and our assumptions about the connections of gender violence and patriarchy were articulated by the government of Sweden. In a 2005 report of a survey 'Patriarchal violence – an attack on human security', identified as a major global issue, they define gender as:

> The totality of ideas and actions that combine to create social gender identity in individuals. A cultural process that collectively attributes traditionally male/masculine or female/feminine qualities to individuals. Also used in queer theory, which to a greater extent emphasizes gender as a diverse concept in which heterosexuality is seen as the basis of the gender order.[9]

Lysistrata to Greenham Common and Okinawa: women's resistance to war and militarism

The Lysistrata phenomenon, our designation of women's resistance to war – taken from the classical work by the Greek playwright, Aristophanes – gave rise to discussion of some gender concepts that have been largely repudiated as essentialism, the notion that there are essences or essential characteristics within each sex that significantly influence how they respectively view the world and behave in it. Women's purported tendency to avoid or prevent violence is one such characteristic, sometimes attributed to the perception that women have less physical strength than men, and are therefore more timid and fearful of violence. As recent experiences of the men of the Christian Peacemakers Team held hostage in Iraq in 2005 attest, nonviolence is not an exclusively 'womanly' behaviour.[10]

Women's resistance has involved a range of strategies of active nonviolence, which while not intended to harm those whose power, policies or ideas are being resisted, involves significant risks on the part of the resisters.[11] Withholding sexual access in a patriarchal society risks the wrath of the patriarchs who control the destinies of the women resisting. The strategy is largely based on the essentialist assumption that men cannot or will not live without sexual gratification. While this strategy is said to have been employed by pre-colonial Native American women, and maybe others in addition to women of ancient Greece, it is not credited with ending any particular war and certainly has not limited or weakened the institution of war. However, such actions have helped to feed the essentialist notion that women are more 'civilized' or morally developed than men, and that this quality rather than a considered judgement on the political efficacy of war has accounted for women's resistance.[12]

Resistance as a strategy to avoid or end war has continued to be practised in other forms by women peace activists, often in highly visible forms such as the Greenham Common Women, encamped around the US military bases in the UK during the early 1980s to demonstrate their opposition to the presence of the bases, and to the nuclear weapons stored beneath the common. Within this particular initiative there were strong separatist elements that rejected men's participation in the resistance. There were elements of radical feminism, one school of which, articulated by Andrea Dworkin, held that misogyny and the binary gender designations that came from the assumption of heterosexuality as 'normal' served to perpetuate patriarchal control over women and children as it oppressed and repressed all other forms of sexuality and gender identities.[13] Those who held these views insisted that women's actions should be separated from men's actions (indeed, that it was the behaviours of men that formed the problematic) in various women's acts of resistance to war. This position was reinforced by women's relegation to secondary or auxiliary roles in many peace movement activities by the lack of acknowledgement of women's taking primary responsibility in the organizing of major peace campaigns and actions, and by the exploitation of women's efforts by some men in the peace movement – such as the major anti-base manifestations in Okinawa, and one of the largest peace marches in history in New York on 12 June 1982 – and by instances of sexual harassment experienced by some women in the movement.

The experience of the marginalization, even the exclusion, of women was not unknown in the other realms of peace knowledge and peace action. While the first efforts to introduce the question of the relationship of women's status to peace into the International Peace Research Association (IPRA) were undertaken in 1975, it was not until a decade later that the Women and Peace Commission was established, officially recognizing the topic as a field of peace research. In Okinawa, women who sought to call attention to the gender security problems posed by the long-term presence of US military on that island were rebuffed as distracting from the goal of base removal by male activists who could not understand the repeated gender violence against women committed by US service personnel as another argument to place before the Japanese government to induce it to request base closings. These women organized Okinawa Women Act Against Military Violence (OWAAM) in 1995 in launching protests about the rape of a 12-year-old girl by three US servicemen. This and subsequent actions of resistance and opposition were taken within an analytic framework that placed this gender violence, which OWAAM termed military violence – violence committed by the military against civilians or outside the realm of combat – within a framework of patriarchal militarization. A similar analysis of the militarization of society informed the resistance efforts of the Israeli women who organized New Profile.[14] Both groups continue to resist as the Israeli occupation of Palestinian territory continues, and US bases, while somewhat changed by moving forces from one base to another, still occupy large, formerly agricultural areas of Okinawa.[15] New Profile also facilitates men's nonviolent resistance in its support of conscientious objectors' refusal of service in the occupied territories of Palestine.

Accounts of Greenham Common and similar encampments in other countries were widely admired by the international women's peace movement that proliferated along with the proliferation of nuclear weapons during the Cold War, and so were included in some peace studies as well women's studies courses. These actions along with the 'gender gap', a phrase used to describe the purported tendency of women to vote for more peace-oriented candidates and policies while men tended to support policies of 'strength' and armed force, were included among other such types of evidence to explore the sources of these differences. The notion that women's experience as mothers, if not their reproductive biology per se, accounted for these manifestations of resistance, or that women were by nature more peaceful than men was, as noted, rejected by most feminists as essentialism, reducing the phenomenon to the reproductive difference between the sexes. Some, such as Christine Sylvester, argued that women had warrior capacity and inclination equal to that of men.[16] These manifestations took on political forms such as the women's delegation to European leaders on the eve of the First World War, which attempted to persuade them to continue to follow the diplomatic path to spare their countries the inevitable suffering that any war brings.

The 'motherhood' rationale for resistance was articulated during the mid-nineteenth century in the wake of the American Civil War when the 'Mothers' Proclamation', pledging to raise sons who would not take the lives of other mothers' sons was promulgated, and Mothers' Day declared as an anti-war holiday. It continued into the twentieth century and found its manifestations in such movements as the US Women Strike for Peace, a movement initiated to protect children from the health consequences of nuclear testing that brought about the 1963 Test Ban Treaty and the Soldiers' Mothers' Movement in Russia, through which women resisted their sons' serving in the armed conflict in Afghanistan in the 1990s.[17] More recently, in 2006 the organizers of Code Pink, a women's group organized in opposition to the Iraq War, circulated the Proclamation in observance of the third anniversary of the American invasion of Iraq, reminding the public that Mothers' Day had political significance beyond the commercialism and sentimentality that it has come to manifest.[18]

While it was evident that the motherhood concept was an organizing principle for such actions, feminist peace scholars and educators generally refuted it as being inconsistent with the theory of gender as a socially or culturally constructed category of human identity as indicated in the definition used in the previously cited report from the Office of the Swedish Government. While not uncontested, this argument gained ascendancy in the growing field of peace knowledge that focused on women's roles in and perspectives on war and peace. We, the authors, do not deny the differences in behaviours and inclinations that research suggests may be biologically based. So, too, we find interesting and potentially useful toward our own purposes of challenging the patriarchal paradigm of enforced heterosexuality, male dominance and militarized security, the theoretical propositions published by Myra J. Hird of Queens University in Canada:

> In contemporary society, the conceptual division between 'sex' as the biological differences, and 'gender' as the social, cultural, economic and political differences is largely taken for granted . . . current concern with the fragmentation of identities is crucially linked to questions concerning the continued viability of [this differentiation]. . . Nature . . . offers shades of difference and similarity much more often than clear opposites.[19]

As peace educators, we find this discourse on diversity in sex and gender promising of new possibilities into the many forms of diversity which we believe must be understood and defended against the onslaughts of fundamentalist reductionisms in the realms of gender, culture and religious and political ideology. In fact, we expect that wider and deeper enquiries into the political valences of gender will offer possibilities to educate for a humanly diverse as well as a more just and less violent global order.

With regard to the issues raised by the relevance of motherhood to gender and peace, we tend to believe it is the experience rather than the biological fact of motherhood, the learned caring and nurturing more than the biology of reproduction that influences mothers' pleas and actions for peace.[20] The biological factors under discussion indicate that the evident differences between men and women in regard to war and peace are far more complex than either of the two explanations of biology or social construction of gender or men's and women's actual roles in conducting war can account for.[21] This complexity, as we will see below in the account of the emergence of masculinities studies, is what gives this area of peace knowledge its special cogency for peace education. The multiple concepts and constructions of masculinities in various cultures, and during different historic periods, not only continue to challenge biological determinism and essentialism, they illustrate that human behaviour and characteristics are susceptible to the influence of context and circumstance and, we believe, can be affected by intentional education as much as by traditional socialization.

Peace education is concerned with developing pedagogies that enable learners to think in terms of complexities beyond the standard curricula on controversial issues, which usually teach students to consider little more than the two major opposing positions involved in the public discourse on the issues in question. It also seeks to enable learners to confront and explore some highly charged social issues that have personal valence for most people in as deeply reflective and socially responsible a manner as possible. Gender, and the contending theories about its formation and significance, is such an issue.

It is well known that peace education has been influenced by Freirean pedagogy.[22] The Brazilian educator, Paulo Freire, advocated practice of a dialogic pedagogy of reflection and action that was one of the foundations of critical pedagogy practised by many peace educators. But it is not so widely known that feminist pedagogy that addresses the significance of the personal dimensions to classroom discussion and learning has also had a profound effect on the work of many peace educators. In this regard, the work of Belenky et al. described in *Womens' Ways of Knowing* and the work of Carol Gilligan on gender differences in moral decision making are very relevant to peace education practice.[23] Gender differences in ways of learning and knowing, which we believe to be, largely but not entirely, the consequence of gender relations and the differences in the socialization experiences of boys and girls, provide some of the multiple ways of thinking that are essentially human. They offer the same possibility as cultural differences for broadening the learning and knowing repertoire necessary to understanding and analysing the complexities of the challenges of overcoming violence and achieving peace. Gender differences are a primary basis for understanding both multiple ways of knowing and varying perspectives on peace problems.

For feminist peace scholars these complexities were further evidence of the need to include in the growing 'canon' of peace studies the issues and perspectives they had argued to be integral to addressing the central purposes of the field, developing the knowledge necessary to reduce violence and advance justice. They argued that the failure to include these considerations militated against achieving the purposes for which peace knowledge was being produced and advanced through research and education. It took over a decade of professional discussions and arguments to gain general recognition of the cogency of the feminist arguments. Some specifics of these developments will be noted below as we discuss some of the political dimensions of gender and peace.

Connecting women, war and political participation

The national and military valorization of motherhood was poignantly evident during the two world wars of the twentieth century. The value that patriarchal, nationalist popular culture placed on motherhood and its vital contribution to the maintenance of fighting forces served as a means to deflect the potential influence of the more political anti-war arguments women were advancing and to impede the drive for women's suffrage, seen as a way for women to have more political influence over war, peace and other public matters. Lack of the vote, however, did not prevent American and European women's active political involvement, not only in forms of passive resistance, but in instances of political intervention such as the aforementioned international women's campaigns to avert the First World War that produced the Women's International League for Peace and Freedom (WILPF). Launched in this Euro-American peace initiative, WILPF now has national chapters throughout the world, with significant leadership from developing countries.[24]

WILPF, in a framework of values of justice and peace, made a significant contribution to the development of the integrated, holistic approach that the international peace education movement began to advocate in the 1980s. From its earliest days WILPF made clear connections between what later became recognized as the integral relationship between peace and human rights and contributed to the growing belief that more democratic governments would be less likely to engage in warfare.[25] This argument, advanced by others, has also been put forth by feminists who argue that the extreme underrepresentation of women in most spheres of government documented in UN studies precludes claims of the majority of states to be democracies.[26] Interpretations of the rationale for the Second World War, which saw the Western democracies allied in the war, tended to strengthen rather than undermine the argument since the popular interpretation was that these nations had taken up arms to defend democracy against dictatorship. This argument, along with the 'gender bending' contributions women made to the successful conduct of the war, was taken up by some in the women's movement in the post-Second World War period in a new phase of feminism. What was to become the international women's movement along with anti-colonialism and anti-racism movements, arose to demand the fulfilment of the promises of the avowed purposes of the war, to defend democracy and, in the aftermath, to assure human rights as one means to prevent further wars.[27] The issues of anti-colonialism, and to some extent issues of racial justice, found their way onto the research agendas and into the syllabi of peace scholars, but such was not the case with feminist or women's issues. Well into the 1970s questions that we now refer to as gender issues were considered by all but a very few peace researchers – those few were mainly feminists – to have little or no relevance to peace. In the first three editions published in 1972, 1978 and 1981 of the compendium of peace studies syllabi, Peace and World Order Studies, no courses on women's or gender issues or approaches were included. The next issue, published in 1983 – the only one edited by a woman – contained five syllabi on the topic in the section with the least entries of any of the topics included. In the edition of 1989, the topic is one of four sections containing only three syllabi – the other three being: ecological balance, alternative futures, education and teacher training, all topics which the gender perspective on peace education considers integral to the holistic approach it favours.

Through these two decades – the 1970s and 1980s – feminists and activists with WILPF in the lead insisted on a significant, undeniable interrelationship among the various justice issues of the post-war era that ultimately became the domain of positive peace. One of the unifying concepts was exclusion from and marginalization in politics of disempowered groups. Most of the groups becoming engaged in struggles to achieve a voice in policy-making, participation in their own governance, their places on research agendas and in university and school curricula that previously had been for the most part excluded from all these policy realms. Some saw this exclusion as the intentional dominance of the powerful over the powerless to maintain their privileges, rationalized by their greater capacity for the exercise of power. But others began to take a more system-based view, suggesting that the international power-based system itself was the major impediment to justice and peace, bringing the question of alternatives and system change into classroom enquiries and to the design of research projects.[28] The questions that formed this enquiry lead to theorizing the links among these forms of exclusions, the economic and political oppressions they rationalized and the institution of war, and, ultimately, to a more systematic analysis of patriarchy and its hold on so many social and institutional systems from school curricula, to church hierarchy, to the corporate world, governmental structures and the security establishment.

Advances in international standards: women's equality and peace

WILPF, along with various other women's organizations, took a leading role in the activities surrounding the United Nations' International Decades for Women from 1975–85, 1985–95. Under the general themes of equality, development and peace, concerted efforts were made by the UN and associated NGOs to advance women's legal equality, political participation and involvement at all levels of economic development from planning through assessment. It was in the arena of development that the negative consequences of gender inequality and gender-biased cultural practices became so evident. Issues of advancing the roles and participation of women in the UN system and setting standards to increase their participation in the politics and economies of the member states achieved wider public attention. They were also given more consideration in the field of peace knowledge by those who believed that the UN diagnosis of the relationship between gender and development and the assessments of the consequences of women's marginalization in the development process vividly illustrated the concept of structural violence.

Severe critiques of the almost total lack of attention to the actual effects of prevailing development policy on women – similar to criticisms still raised today about globalization and the economic burdens it imposes on the poor, especially women – were most acutely evident in such basic practices as the UN accounting system that failed to include the unpaid work of women that formed the very foundations of a society's capacity for economic production.[29] Especially forceful criticisms came from scholars of women's productive activities. A pioneering work in this field was Ester Boserup's 1970 study on women in development.[30] The research on women's economic impoverishment and exclusion from economic policy-making was to become a significant factor in both feminist and human rights arguments on the definitions of human security and what comprises it that arose in the 1990s.

For our purposes of illuminating the peace knowledge consequences of these exclusions, the most significant critiques came from feminist political scientists and international relations scholars. We find the most relevant to our perspective to be the works of Cynthia Cockburn of the UK and Anne Tickner and Cynthia Enloe of the US, who offer strong argumentation for much of what peace research and most of the peace movement consider wrong-headed and destructive policies and practices in the international system. They suggest that the failure to give adequate consideration to alternatives to the politics of force can be attributed to a significant degree to the limitation on and in many cases exclusion of women and women's perspectives from the security policy discourse.[31] These assertions informed the efforts of UN-associated NGOs to convene the October 2000 open session of the Security Council that issued Security Council Resolution 1325 (SC 1325), calling for the equal representation of women in peace and security negotiations and policy-making.

Gender exclusion refers not only to lack of women's participation, but also and especially ignoring the human consequences of gender-blind policies as they are experienced by both men and women. Such exclusion has also negatively impacted men, especially those at lower levels of political power, a problem not yet systematically addressed. Recognition of the impact of gender exclusion set into motion innovations in UN policy and norm setting that reciprocally affected and were affected by women's studies and a bit later by feminist scholarship such as that noted above.

The most significant of UN normative gender standards were the Convention on the Elimination of All Forms of Discrimination against Women (CEDAW 1980), the Declaration on the Elimination of All Forms of Violence against Women (1993), the Beijing Platform for Action (1995) and Security Council Resolution 1325 (2000).[32] These documents constitute a line of awareness and assertion of public responsibility for the achievement of women's equality in political, economic, social and cultural arenas, complementing and extending the preceding major emphasis on legal equality – although this still remains a significant and controversial issue in various societies. With the latter two documents, protection of women from gender-based violence, including and especially military violence, was designated as a fundamental human right. The inclusion of women in peace and conflict negotiations and security policy-making was declared by the UN to be essential to democracy and the achievement of this right. SC 1325 has become an important basis of action to implement all these gender-relevant international norms, serving as a political tool for international peace groups as well as women's NGOs. It is also a powerful example of collaboration between NGOs and the UN, and between women and men. The developments making the resolution possible were set in motion in 1999 by Anwarul K. Chowdhury, who was then the UN Ambassador from Bangladesh and president of the UN General Assembly. His words quoted below attest to his commitment to its purposes:

> The potential of Resolution 1325, its implications and impact in real terms are enormous. That women make a difference when in decision- and policy-making positions is no longer in dispute. When women participate in peace negotiations and in the crafting of a peace agreement, they keep the future of their societies in mind. They have the broader and longer-term interest of society in mind. Whereas, historically in post-conflict situations, men are interested in ensuring that the peace process will give them the

authority and power that they are seeking. A lasting peace cannot be achieved without the participation of women and the inclusion of gender perspectives and participation in peace processes.[33]

Thus, through this human rights route over the terrain of positive peace, the issue of gender as it relates to negative peace, the actual gendered experiences and consequences of war and peace within the sphere of traditional concepts of security became an important focus of the international gender discourse. With a particular focus on the multiple forms of sexist violence suffered by women in most societies and the effects of armed conflict on women, came recognition that these multiple forms of violence both in times of apparent peace as well as in times of war were interconnected in a global culture of violence. These trends illuminated and brought wider attention to the gender inequality–war interconnections. Understanding the interconnections in turn led more feminist scholars, researchers and peace activists, among them those in the Peace Education Commission of the International Peace Research Association, to adopt as a working premise the assertion that gender violence is one component of an essentially violent patriarchal international system. These interconnections were integral to a statement from the 1983 consultative meeting of what was to become IPRA's Women and Peace Commission. The statement identified the interconnections as 'a continuum of violence which links the violence against women to the violence of war.' The consultation also asserted that there were, 'connections between patriarchy, militaristic structures and values and direct violence'.[34] The assertion was that patriarchy has been maintained through the monopoly on power held by the men at the top of the hierarchical order, rationalized by a claim of male superiority. The power is manifest in the hierarchy's control of force. These assertions were later to become the subject of further analysis by masculinities scholars in exploration of the connections between masculine identities and aggressivity. Some of their conclusions will be elaborated on. Similar assertions were also echoed in a statement from a preparatory meeting for the Beijing Fourth World Conference on Women organized by the United Nations Division for the Advancement of Women in December 1994.[35]

During the 1980s, when there was a quantum leap in literature on women, peace and security, there was also a wider acknowledgement that violence, the institutions, habits of mind and behaviours that perpetuate it comprise what had been defined as the 'war system'.[36] We now argue that war is an essentially patriarchal institution. But patriarchy itself was not the subject of wide study for some years to come. Only now is it emerging as a central focus among scholars in masculinities studies, feminist peace and human rights activists whose analytic attention has turned to a more concentrated and systematic consideration of patriarchy as it manifests in contemporary institutions, policies and phenomena.[37]

We use the phrase 'apparent peace' above to describe the context for which violence against women occurs outside actual war and to call attention to the ongoing conditions of structural violence endured by vulnerable groups under the present global economic system, also, and especially, to take note of the gendered nature of the social and cultural violence that has been described as 'the war against women'.[38] This war rages in most times and places whether or not societies are engaged in armed conflict. We would argue that there has been an invisible theatre of combat in this gender war, 'the war against men'. Patriarchy is an 'equal opportunity' destroyer of both women and men. As we recommend below, an inclusive gender perspective that takes into account patriarchy's disadvantages to both men and women offers a unique opportunity to engage in transformational learning toward a peaceful, just and gender equal global order. We believe that a transformation process would require the extension of human rights standards intended to achieve gender justice to include all men and women of all sexualities, gender orientations and identities.[39]

Violence against women: gendered link between human rights and peace

CEDAW, the Convention on the Elimination of All Forms of Discrimination Against Women, the 1980 'women's human rights convention', was a culmination of the campaign for equality women's groups have been waging since the founding of the United Nations. It comprises a review of most of the forms of discrimination and oppression of women as they had been perceived and studied to that point. Its emphasis on the economic, social and cultural factors underlying the lack of legal and political equality echoed the concerns of the larger human rights movement that this sphere of rights had too long taken a back seat to civil and political rights. The separation between the two spheres of human rights impeded the holistic view of the field that a growing number of human rights advocates argued to be essential to the institutionalization and realization of universal human rights. It became the preferred framework for the UN's human rights efforts when it was noted as constitutive to the field in the final document of the 1993 International Conference on Human Rights held in Vienna. As peace educators, we advocate this holistic perspective as a comprehensive framework for the study of positive peace, arguing that the realization of human rights is the most practical means to the achievement of positive peace. We also consider that a holistic human rights perspective is integral to a truly inclusive gender perspective that in the mode of holism includes the whole spectrum of sexualities, heterosexual, transsexual, bisexual and homosexual, all gender identities. CEDAW is not adequate to the fulfilment of human rights as they would pertain to all these groups; nor does it address the problem of gender violence of any type, not even that perpetrated against women that became a focus of a women's human rights campaign in the next decade.

The origins of the Declaration on the Elimination of Violence against Women, issued by the Vienna International Conference on Human Rights in 1993, initially lacked systematic focus on the institution of war, but it achieved a major breakthrough in demonstrating that the phenomenon of gender violence was global, pervasive and constituted a long-ignored gross violation of human rights. It eliminated the distinction between women's rights and human rights that had ghettoized gendered aspects of both the discourse on human rights and the struggle for their universal realization. The Beijing Platform for Action, the product of the 1995 Fourth World Conference on Women, viewed as a human rights document made the connections that irrevocably integrated the issue of war into the analysis of and action on issues of gender equality. It paved the way for the campaign organized and conducted by women's NGOs for an open session of the Security Council on 'Women, Peace and Security', which in Resolution 1325 called for the representation of women in all matters concerned with peace and security official UN policy.[40]

The declaration and the resolution are clear illustrations of the ways in which women's movements have bridged the gap between civil society and the interstate system, and achieved a Freirean integration of research, education and action. In the early 1990s, the statistics on violence against women became the subject of even the popular press, producing some governmental response among Western states. Grassroots women's organizations throughout the world gathered multiple thousands of signatures calling for the international legal acknowledgement that gender violence was in serious contradiction of the international human rights norms.[41] The signed petitions were delivered to the UN Secretary General and facilitated the agreement to the declaration by the Vienna Conference on Human Rights, further strengthening the claim that women's rights are human rights, articulated in the 1995 Beijing Declaration that introduces the Platform for Action (BPFA). In recent years that has been the discussion of the development of a legally binding international convention on gender violence, so that its prohibition would be established within the body of international human rights treaty law. The Global Framework of the Beijing Platform is organized around 12 areas of critical concern, three of which provided the precedents that made possible SC 1325. The areas of concern referring to violence against women, women and armed conflict, and women in power and decision making make up the main substance and imperatives put forth in that Security Council resolution that in terms of gender and peace is the most signifi-cant international document issued to date. The Platform offers an illuminating definition of violence against women, bringing specificity to the more abstract definition of the Declara-tion on Violence against Women. For peace educators it is a useful tool for demonstrating how conceptual definitions of problems such as gender injustice can and should be derived from and help to explain the lived realities of those who suffer the problems.

With the two short and simple statements quoted below, the Beijing Platform for Action demonstrates international acceptance of an inclusive concept of gender as a social construct, indicating it is a requisite factor of consideration in all areas of critical concern:

> the differences between women's and men's achievements are still not recognized as the consequences of socially constructed gender roles rather than immutable biological differences.[42]

An even more significant statement supporting our assertion of the inseparable integral inter-dependence between gender equality and peace first argued as between women's equality and peace by one of the authors is articulated in the Platform quote below:[43]

> The maintenance of peace and security at the global, regional and local levels, together with the prevention of policies of aggression and ethnic cleansing and the resolution of armed conflict, is crucial for the protection of the human rights of women and girl-chil-dren, as well as for the elimination of all forms of violence against them and their use as weapons of war.[44]

The assertion reflected in this quote, as it is in SC 1325, is that viable peace in the absence of democratic politics, providing equal participation to all citizens, is not possible. The une-qual representation of women in policy-making is a serious obstacle to peace as indicated in this quotation. Without significant representation of women in the political process, abuses listed are not likely to be adequately addressed. The emergence of these concepts that linked women's situation to peace and violence against women to the larger systems of structural and armed violence and the developments that introduced them into the actions of inter-national civil society and the policies of the UN system were – to an extent that may not exist around any other global issue – informed by the involvement of feminist scholars and peace researchers. A symbiotic partnership among the UN agencies such as the Division for the Advancement of Women, UNIFEM (the women's development agency), UNESCO, women's organizations and the academy, produced problem-relevant policies, sharpened research questions, enriched courses with contemporary international developments, and gave this arena of peace research significant valence in international politics. As noted above, these years, the 1980s in particular, saw a plentiful harvest of literature on women, war and peace and women's human rights that brought a number of scholars together as participants in international civil society, further internationalizing the field, strengthening its global perspective and enriching courses in women's studies and peace studies with research and theorizing around the long-neglected sphere of gender and peace. It also offered particularly fruitful substance for pedagogical developments in peace education, especially among those practitioners who perceived human rights as essential and integral to the field.[45]

From our perspective, this literature's relationship to developments in international civil society and their combined relevance to peace education and the deconstruction of patriarchy, especially, as noted, the feminist critiques of prevailing international relations theory and peace research perspectives, are the most significant. When viewed in terms of the consequences of the lack of women's perspectives and consideration of women's experiences in the analyses and prevailing theories of international relations and interstate conflict since the end of the Second World War, these critiques significantly compromised the conclusions and paradigms in which international security policy was made, analysed and assessed.[46] While there are now various critiques of the realist school of international politics, feminist scholar Jane Tickner offered a groundbreaking perspective that remains relevant to our concerns:

> In realism's subject matter, as well as in its quest for a scientific methodology, we can detect an orientation that corresponds to some of the masculine-linked characteristics . . . such as the emphasis on power and autonomy and claims to objectivity and rationality. But among realism's critics, virtually no attention has been given to gender as a category of analysis. Scholars concerned with structural violence have paid little attention to how women are affected by global politics or the workings of the world economy, nor to the fact that hierarchical gender relations are interrelated with other forms of domination they do address.[47]

Feminist criticisms such as Tickner's were among the most challenging levelled at the realist school of international politics. Their work was prescient, anticipating criticisms that now are voiced even in mainstream discourse. Similar interpretations of the international significance of hierarchical gender relations later emerged in masculinities studies. Together they have made a significant place for gender in the global peace movement. The Hague Agenda for Peace and Justice in the 21st Century, issued by the end-of-century civil society peace movement conference held in the Netherlands in 1999, put an inclusive gender perspective in a prominent place in a statement that echoes many similar criticisms of the realist – we would say patriarchal – paradigm of international relations:

> The costs of the machismo that still pervades most societies are high for men whose choices are limited by this standard, and for women who experience continual violence both in war and peace. The Hague Appeal for Peace supports the redefinition of distorted gender roles that perpetuate violence.[48]

Toward an inclusive gender perspective: the emergence of masculinities studies

From the earliest days of women's striving for equality there have been men who accepted the arguments, sympathized with the goals, and some few joined in the efforts. Clearly, without cooperation from a significant number of men in the respective systems, women's national political rights would never have been legally established nor would any of the international gender-equality norms been introduced into the body of international human rights standards. While some men ridiculed, reviled and resisted, some also publicly and vigorously assisted. While some men sought to understand and respond to men's violence against women, others felt threatened by changes bringing a wider range of life choices to women. These challenges produced several distinct responses, some of them referred to as men's movements. In the US, phenomena such as 'Iron John' encouraged men to reclaim their traditional 'male values' of courage, assertion and leadership. Other American initiatives such as the 'Promise Keepers' and the 'Million Man March' called for re-assuming the responsibilities of fatherhood and family. These developments were largely in response and reaction to what were seen as the social and cultural dislocations brought about by women's movements in general and feminism in particular. They focused on men's self image and to some degree on reclaiming male pride of place in traditional society. Such projects we would describe as masculinist.[49] Masculinism is the reassertion of the masculine characteristics and values of the patriarchal gender order. Australian scholar R.W. Connell writes of the way in which that order is now global and profoundly affected by globalization in a way that reflects present power relations in the international system:

> Clearly, the world gender order is not simply an extension of traditional European-American gender order. That gender order was changed by colonialism, and elements from other cultures now circulate globally. Yet in no sense do they mix on equal terms, to produce a United Colors of Benetton gender order. The culture and institutions of the North Atlantic countries are hegemonic within the emergent world system. This is crucial for understanding the kinds of masculinities produced within it.[50]

As so much of the women's movement focused on women's distinct and separate experience, some men's approach to gender issues also emphasized the injustices integral to gender roles focusing on the particular experiences of men. As noted, one strand of the men's movements was related to perceptions that loss of exclusive right to certain social functions and positions was imposing inequality on men. But only masculinities studies worked within a relational or systemic framework that provides an inclusive gender perspective. As Connell states, 'Masculinities do not first exist and then come into contact with femininities; they are produced together in a process that constitutes a gender order.'[51]

Another strand of men's response to the gender problematic, the White Ribbon Campaign, a Canadian organization responding to the growing body of data and policy concern with violence against women, took an approach of acknowledging individual responsibility for and societal acceptance of violence against women in North America.[52] Some masculinities scholarship, as did some feminist theory, contextualized gender violence with a framework of violence in a male-dominated hierarchy. Michael Kaufman describes interrelationships among forms of men's violence:

> Men's violence against women does not occur in isolation but is linked to men's violence against other men and to the internalization of violence that is a man's violence against himself . . . male dominated societies are not only based on a hierarchy of men over women but some men over other men. Violence or the threat of violence among men is a mechanism used from childhood to establish that pecking order.[53]

Other male activists and scholars looked to the socialization of men, in the framework of gender as a social construction, undertaking research that became the foundation of masculinities studies. The social construction theory provided a foundation for masculinities studies to explore the cultural, social and biological influences in the formation of masculine identities. They enquired into influences from historical myths, cultural messages, family, biological assertions, ritual, laws, customs, media and sports on male assertiveness and claims to power. Taken together, these messages formed expectations of how a man should behave. Peace scholars were particularly concerned with the dominant masculine identities that reinforced social hierarchies and the exertion of power by men at the upper levels of hierarchies over women and other men. Gender identities such as the warrior, breadwinner or adventurer, and characteristics such as valour and toughness, served to inspire violent approaches to dealing with conflict and legitimated militarized approaches to peace and security.[54] During the world wars, joining the army was a rite of passage to full American manhood – a phenomenon not unique to the US, as has been documented by Turkish and Israeli scholars.[55] The manhood myth of the warrior was confronted during the Vietnam War as the anti-war movement decried sending a generation of young men to die in an unjust war. This issue, along with the mandatory military conscription, opened a small window for challenging the valorization of war in forming men's identities. It also manifested another problem as US military recruitment practices began targeting poor, urban and rural youth, particularly African Americans, demonstrating hierarchies among men based on race and socio-economic status.

Over the 1990s and the first decade of this century, scholars began to consider the concept of 'multiple masculinities' in which gender could be seen as constructed differently in different contexts, cultures, historic periods, and under unique circumstances. Multiple masculinities were defined establishing alternatives to the concept of the masculine ideal as the warrior. Especially in times of war, masculinity norms are strongly influenced by patriotism and military service, nurturing strong hero and protector identities, and denigrating male war resistors as less masculine, often meaning humanly inferior. Even in less conflict-plagued times, hierarchies exist among masculinities, and in most contexts a hegemonic or most desired form of masculinity emerges.[56] Within the hierarchies privileged exemptions from the ideal are possible. During the Vietnam War, for example, white middle-class American men could forestall, even avoid, going to war by going to college. Upon graduation, the privileged were more likely to gain important positions in society. The poor who served in the military often returned to a jobless civilian life. Hierarchies among masculinities involving race and class as manifest in military service, are further evidence that gender is as rooted in social constructs as it is in biology. The Vietnam War also made more evident the relationship between gender and the institution of war and demonstrated the possibility that both gender inequality and war are amenable to change through socialization and education.

Most masculinities studies were undertaken in the light of the social construction theory of gender. The gendered nature of various institutions and other social arrangements was illuminated, exposing the power and subordination arrangement of patriarchy as one that exists and is sustained largely through the unequal status of men and women. Gender inequality, as asserted earlier by feminist scholarship, an assertion now shared by masculinities studies, pervades virtually all formal and informal institutions, playing a significant role in sustaining the gendered world order and the institution of war. Therefore, any approach to the transformation of the war system will require taking into account the gendered nature of the entire system, inclusive of all the component institutions, social, economic and political. In sum, it calls for a broad and critical social education. We advocate for the inclusion and mainstreaming of gender in all social education, as has been advocated for UN policy and programmes. Gender mainstreaming is:

. . . assessing the implications for women and men of any planned action, including legislation, policies and programmes, in any area and at all levels . . . making women's as well as men's concerns and experiences integral [to education as well as policy-making] . . . so that woman and men benefit equally. The ultimate goal is gender equality [and positive peace].[57]

Especially in the realms of peace studies and peace education, a focus on developing new thinking about gender should become integral to all study and enquiry, cultivating learning that will enable men and women to understand how their gender identities are informed by and sustain the larger system of violence in which war and all forms of gender violence are embedded. A major task is raising awareness regarding the gender and peace problematic and how all are implicated in it. Women need not perceive themselves as subjects of discrimination or oppression to understand their subordination in the patriarchal hierarchy. Most men do not identify themselves, nor do they perceive their actions, as sustaining gender disparities. Education should elicit understanding of the complex realities of gender inequality. Men do not need to directly contribute to or behave in ways that sustain patriarchal society to the beneficiaries of male privilege. Building awareness of the patriarchal structures that account for gender disparities and male privilege are core learning goals of an inclusive gender perspective in peace education.

We think it significant that it was in the field of education that some of the earliest and most significant work on gender disparities was conducted. It is, therefore, not surprising that some of the leading scholars in masculinities studies are from the discipline of education. Indeed, as noted earlier, the first formal discussion of these issues within the International Peace Research Association were initiated and introduced to peace researchers by IPRA's Peace Education Commission. One of the first works in the field was by the distinguished Norwegian educator Birgit Brock-Utne, a member of that commission, and had concluded that the socialization of boys in ways that promoted cooperation and care for others as valorized in girl's socialization had significant potential as a means to educate for peace.[58] Male socialization became a fruitful area of enquiry pursued as well by American educators and introduced into international research and policy discussion by UNESCO.[59]

Reflection on the insights and knowledge produced by masculinities studies and their potential integration into an inclusive gender perspective in peace studies and peace education is one of the main tasks that should be high on the agenda of peace knowledge professionals. We need to take into account all of the complexities constitutive to gender and peace. Peace education could utilize the framework of patriarchy to illuminate various forms of hierarchy and to reveal the relational view of gender in which masculinities and femininities – as described above in the quotation from Michael Kimmel – are defined in terms relative to each other in a social construct built into institutions, cultures, power relations and social arrangements. In this context gender construction can be seen as varied, active and dynamic, an example of possibilities for truly significant change in the human condition. Whereas gender roles were formerly defined as dichotomous and static, they may now be conceived as mutable and subject to intentional, normative change. As social constructs, gender roles and relations are revealed to be the product of masculine and feminine identities being formed in parallel social processes. Neither these qualities and identities nor attitudes toward violence and war are formed in isolation from their social and cultural contexts. To understand the contexts toward changing them, it is essential to understand gender and the gender order conditioned by patriarchy.

Moving toward an inclusive gender perspective requires institutionalizing democratic practices and relations that promote tolerance of a range of sexual and gender identities, understanding the significance of gender to the social order and recognition of the potential peace contributions of what have been previously defined as masculine and feminine qualities. Peace education can play an important role in fostering this perspective through developing critical enquiry that examines various gender identities for both the positive gender attributes that can contribute toward nurturing a culture of peace, and the negative attributes that sustain and promote a culture of violence. Through such a process, conducted in open discourse, respectful of difference, learners may gain confidence in their own critical abilities and a sense of personal responsibility for the achievement of a just social order that could enable them to challenge the gender orders that have so long stifled the aspirations of men and women. As growing awareness of and action on the subordination of women produced historic strides toward gender equality, study of the consequences men suffer in a system of inequality can bring about new strides toward the authentic and inclusive human equality we are denied by patriarchy.

Challenging the patriarchal paradigm: gender equality and human security

Peace educators and peace researchers favouring holistic and integrated approaches to the tasks of building and transmitting peace knowledge have for some time focused attention on paradigms as heuristic devices to clarify characteristics and components of systems of thought, the cultures that produced them and the institutions that sustain them. Until the advent of the concept of a culture of peace, promulgated by UNESCO, the objective had been to develop knowledge to facilitate change in peace and security policies and institutions that would reduce violence and increase justice. Among some of the feminist scholars and activists who have recognized gender equality as a requisite for peace, the premise of the social construction and cultural derivation of gender is now leading to a more focused enquiry into patriarchy itself and how, as we have noted, it is manifested in various contemporary institutions, in cultural practices, both traditional and contemporary, and in social behaviours and relationships. This enquiry – like that which led to the normative and policy changes regarding gender violence and women's political participation – has been taken up mainly by feminist human rights activists. They argue that the achievement of full and authentic gender equality calls for an enquiry into assumed, enforced and encoded inequalities of the patriarchal paradigm within which neither men nor women are fully free human beings. The patriarchal system is not only a source of gender violence and inequality but of many egregious human rights violations, oppressive to both men and women. We would add to that argument that it also constitutes the most fundamental impediment to peace at all levels of the social order. The failure to name it as such, to fully analyse it as a primary obstacle to the kind of just global order that most would agree to be peace, is what keeps us caught in the war system and mired in the global culture of violence which it nurtures and by which it is nurtured.[60]

A major action research project to remedy this failure is being undertaken by the People's Movement for Human Rights Education (PDHRE), an NGO that advocates for human rights learning as the means to capacitate populations to achieve social justice, economic equity and political agency. In a document circulated to NGOs and UN agencies, PDHRE states a rationale for the project to which we would adhere and which we would augment:

> Throughout recorded history in most human societies some form of patriarchy has prevailed, reinforced by cultural values derived from systems of male dominance. It has

been so commonly and continually practiced as to appear natural rather than a humanly constructed social order that is both changing and changeable. In its present forms patriarchy has become more an ideology and belief system than the explicit social and political systems of earlier times. Even in countries where legal equality of women and men has been established, the deep psychological and cultural roots of patriarchy survive as a belief system in the minds of many women and men. [It] asserts the superiority of all males to all females and arranges this fundamental inequality in a hierarchal order in which middle aged men now hold primary power over all others, controlling economies, militaries, educational and religious institutions. Men in general are more powerful and advantaged than women. Western men have more power in the global order than men from other world regions. Women of higher economic class have power over both men and women of lower income and poverty status. At the very bottom of this hierarchy are the vulnerable and oppressed of the world, most the aged, all children, and women; with most vulnerable being aged, poor women. [Global] threats are made the more complex and difficult to address because of the limits imposed on human capacities and creativity by the gendered power divisions that comprise [patriarchy.] [It] is the antithesis of the ideology of human rights . . . human rights is the core of an alternative belief system that can transcend the limits [patriarchy] imposes on the realization of human possibilities and the enjoyment of human dignity.[61]

This statement comprises the normative core of an alternative to the patriarchal paradigm. Human rights, as we have seen, are the inspiration and the practical tool for confronting and overcoming injustice. They have provided the most significant progress to date in gender equality. But, in and of themselves human rights, even under stronger possibilities for enforcement, cannot transcend the violence problematic of patriarchy. Patriarchy maintains itself not only through the patriarchal mindset that has prevailed through centuries, but also and more evidently through the power of armed force, most especially that which is conducted by the hands of the state, exercised through police and military, mirrored in the use of force by nonstate actors. Clearly the state itself is a patriarchal institution, and those who aspire to its powers also manifest patriarchal characteristics such as control, force used in self-interest and disregard for the humanity of others. So, an alternative paradigm must elaborate an alternative to military security, pursue the reduction of violence through the reduction of armed forces and weaponry and seek to assure the human dignity of all.

If human rights can be the instruments of progress as it has, even within the patriarchal paradigm, under an effort to simultaneously reduce the primary tools and means of violations while advancing the realization of human rights, the international norms and standards are far more likely to provide actual human security. As peace educators, we endeavour to introduce consideration of these possibilities and to pose elements of the kind of enquiry PDHRE now invites civil society groups throughout the world to engage in as a form of human rights learning. Human rights learning and study of the conditions and possibilities for human security are central to peace education.

We believe that gender can serve as the conceptual core of a comprehensive study of these issues, exploring the problems, the possibilities, the institutions, the values, the concepts and the human experiences that comprise the complexities of the peace problematic. We hope that the field of gender and peace will become central to all realms of peace knowledge, and that all who seek ways to peace through these realms will join in a global enquiry into possible alternatives to the patriarchal paradigm. This paradigm conflates hierarchy with order and command of armed force with virtue as it coerces others into its own image. An alternative human equality paradigm rests on authentic democracy, nonviolent approaches to conflict and assurances of the human dignity of all.

Notes

1 Goldstein, J. (2001) *War and Gender*, Cambridge: Cambridge University Press.
2 Kaufman, M. (1999) *The Seven P's of Men's Violence*, at: http://www.whiteribbon.ca.
3 As it is referred to in a series of compendia of peace studies course outlines, see: Thomas, D. and Klare, M. (eds) (1989) *Peace and World Order Studies: a Curriculum Guide*, 5th edn, New York: World Policy Institute. This is the final of five editions issued by several publishers.
4 For distinctions among the realms of peace knowledge, see: Reardon, B. (1998) 'The urgency of peace education: the good news and the bad news', *Japan Peace Studies Bulletin*, 17, at: http://www-soc.nii.ac.jp/psaj/05Print/e_newsletter/1998/reardon.html.
5 The master comprehensive work in women's history by a peace researcher is: Boulding, E. (1976) *The Underside of History*, Boulder, CO: Westview Press.
6 This work, led by the Center for Women's Global Leadership at Rutgers University, was disseminated through the annual trainings on the human rights of women they conducted for women activists from the global south and women's NGOs associated with the United Nations.
7 Such arguments inform: Easlea, B. (1983) *Fathering the Unthinkable: Masculinity, Scientists and the Arms Race*, London: Pluto Press, and Cohn, C. (1987) 'Sex and death in the rational world of the defense intellectuals', *Signs*, Winter: 687–718; and Fox Keller, E. (1983) *A Feeling for the Organism*, New York: W.H. Freeman and Co.
8 Course syllabi demonstrating this inclusive, integrative approach developed by the authors are available at: www.tc.edu/PeaceEd/portal.
9 Gerd Johansen-Latham, translated by Stephen Croall (2005) *Patriarchal Violence – An Attack on Human Security*, Stockholm: Government Offices of Sweden.
10 The four peace activists were kidnapped on 26 November 2005.
11 See especially: McAllister, P. (1991) *The River of Courage: Generations of Women's Resistance and Action*, Philadelphia, PA: New Society Press.
12 Harvey Mansfield, the author of the recently published *Manliness* in a radio interview with New York Public Radio's Leonard Lopate on 21 March 2006, opined that it is women's task to civilize men. Mansfield, H. (2006) *Manliness*, New Haven, CT: Yale University Press.
13 Dworkin, A. (1974) *Woman Hating*, New York: E. P. Dutton & Co., Inc.
14 Members of both of these movements informed one of the authors that their frameworks were consistent with the arguments and analysis put forth in: Reardon, B. (1995) *Sexism and the War System*, New York: Syracuse University Press.
15 New Profile (2006) at: http://www.newprofile.org/default.asp?language=en. For more on Okinawan Women Against Military Violence, see: Akibayashi, K. (2001) 'Okinawa Women Act Against Military,' unpublished doctoral dissertation, Teachers College, Columbia University.
16 Sylvester, C. (1989) 'Patriarchy, peace and women warriors', in L. Rennie Forcey, (ed.) *Peace: Meanings, Politics, Strategies*, New York: Praeger P.
17 See: Swerdlow, A. (1993) *Women Strike for Peace: Traditional Motherhood and Radical Politics in the 1960s*, Chicago: University of Chicago Press; and Zdravomyslova, E. (1999) 'Peaceful initiatives: the Soldiers' Mothers Movement in Russia', in Breines I. et al. *Toward a Women's Agenda for a Culture of Peace*, Paris: UNESCO.
18 Code Pink, at: http://www.codepink4peace.org.
19 Hird, M.J. (2005) *Sex, Gender and Science*, New York: Palgrave Macmillan, 24–5.
20 See: Ruddick, S. (1995) *Maternal Thinking: Towards a Politics of Peace*, Boston, MA: Beacon Press; Noddings, N. (1993) *The Challenge to Care in Schools: An Alternative Approach to Education*, New York: Teachers College Press; Noddings, N. (1984) *Caring, a Feminine Approach to Ethics and Moral Education*, Berkeley: University of California Press; and Hamburg, B. and Hamburg, D. (2004) *Learning to Live Together*, New York: Oxford University Press.
21 A relevant discussion of testosterone and aggression is found in Goldstein, op. cit., 148–53.
22 Freire, P. (1970) *Pedagogy of the Oppressed*, New York: Herder and Herder.
23 Belenky, M.F., McVicker Clinchy, B., Rule Golberger, N. and Mattuck Tarule, J. (1986) *Women's Ways of Knowing: The Development of Self, Voice, and Mind*, New York: Basic Books. See also: Gilligan, C.

(1993) *In a Different Voice: Psychological Theory and Women's Development*, Boston, MA: Harvard University Press.

24 Foster, C. (1989) *Women for all Seasons: The Story of the Women's International League for Peace and Freedom*, Athens: University of Georgia.

25 The integral and essential relationships among peace, human rights and gender equality are foundational to the UN Charter and the Universal Declaration of Human Rights.

26 See: Gierycz, D. (1999) 'Women in decision-making: can we change the status quo?', in I. Breines et al. *Toward a Women's Agenda for a Culture of Peace*. The argument that democracies don't wage war on each other has been advanced by Rudolf Rummel, author of Rummel, R.W. (1994) *Death by Government*, New Brunswick, NJ: Transaction Publishers.

27 How the society reneged on this promise and the meaning of the war work experience to the modern women's movement is dealt with in Honey, M. (1984) *Creating Rosie the Riveter: Class, Gender and Propaganda During World War II*, Massachusetts: University of Massachusetts Press.

28 Notable among these was the World Order Models Project. Most active during the 1970s and 1980s, it brought together an international team of scholars to research and propose alternatives to the existing order.

29 See: Waring, M. (1988) *Counting for Nothing*, Wellington, New Zealand: Bridget Williams Books Limited.

30 Boserup, E. (1970) *Woman's Roles in Economic Development*, New York: St Martins Press.

31 The work of Cynthia Enloe, J. Anne Tickner and Cynthia Cockburn have been especially helpful. Their arguments are among the influences leading to our advocacy of the inclusion of gender perspectives in the study of and enquiry into all issues of peace, security and other related topics of the peace problematic. See especially, Enloe, C. (1989) *Bananas, Beaches, and Bases: Making Feminist Sense of International Relations*, Berkeley: University of California Press; Enloe, C. (2000) *Maneuvers: The International Politics of Militarizing Women's Lives*, Berkeley: University of California Press; Cockburn, C. (1998) *The Space Between Us: Negotiating Gender and National Identities in Conflict*, London: Zed Books; and Tickner, J.A. (1992) *Gender in International Relations*, New York: Columbia University Press.

32 We do not list the documents issued by the UN women's conferences of 1980 and 1985 for we do not find that they made substantive contributions to either the knowledge or normative base of an inclusive, holistic approach to gender and peace. The 1985 Forward Looking Strategies, however, did note that violence against women was an obstacle to peace (paragraph 258).

33 Anwarul K. Chowdhury, United Nations Under-Secretary General, Presentation at the 816th Wilton Park Conference, Sussex, England, 30 May 2005.

34 International Peace Research Association (1983) *Conclusions of the Consultation on Women, Militarism and Disarmament*, Hungary: Gyor, 3.

35 United Nations Division for the Advancement of Women, 'Report of the Expert Group Meeting on Gender and the Agenda for Peace', United Nations Headquarters, New York, 5–9 December 1994.

36 Reardon, *Sexism and the War System*, op. cit.

37 The first and definitive work on patriarchy was by historian Gerder Lerner. Lerner, G. (1986) *The Creation of Patriarchy*, New York and Oxford: Oxford University Press. It is Lerner who made the clearest distinction between sex as biologically determined and gender as a cultural construct.

38 French, M. (1992) *The War against Women*, New York: Summit Books.

39 We recognize that this chapter does not deal with human rights violations and violence against persons of other than heterosexual identities, but we believe it is a significant manifestation of gender violence, also largely attributable to patriarchy.

40 An open session of the Security Council is one in which non-member states and UN staff may address the Council. These sessions are often preceded by preparatory non-formal sessions in which Council members who wish to do so hear from NGOs qualified in the subject of the open session. The People's Movement for Human Rights Education (PDHRE) developed a workbook using the comprehensive framework of the BPFA that demonstrates the holistic nature of human rights as a tool for action in the achievement of full equality [PDHRE (2003) *Passport to Dignity*, New York: PDHRE]; this issued Resolution 1325 on Women, Peace and Security. See: United Nations (2000) *Security Council Resolution 1325*, at: http://www.peacewomen.org/un/sc/1325.html.

41 See: Heise, L. (1994) *Violence Against Women: The Hidden Health Burden*, Washington, DC: World Bank.

42 Beijing Platform for Action, Global Framework, para 27.

43 Reardon, *Sexism and the War System*, op. cit.

44 Beijing Platform for Action, Global Framework, op. cit., para 12.

45 See: Reardon, B. (2005) 'Peace and human rights education in an age of global terror', in *International House of Japan Bulletin*, 25, 2.

46 See especially the work of Spike Peterson and J. Anne Tickner. Peterson, V.S. and Runyan, A. (1999) *Global Gender Issues*, Boulder, CO: Westview Press; and Tickner, J.A. (1992) *Gender in International Relations*, New York: Columbia University Press.

47 Tickner, op. cit., 14.

48 Hague Agenda for Peace and Justice for the 21st Century: Root Causes of War/Culture of Peace Agenda, at: http://www.haguepeace.org/index.php?action=resources.

49 We take this term from the language of the Japanese scholar, Kinheide Mushakoji, who used it in summarizing the gender perspective assertions regarding male dominance made in an international scholars' statement to the Independent Commission on Human Security in 2003. It is also used by many masculinities scholars.

50 Connell, R.W. (1998) 'Masculinities and globalisation', in *Men and Masculinities*, I, 1: 3–23.

51 Connell, op. cit., 7.

52 The White Ribbon Campaign was launched in Canada to build awareness and responsibility among young men.

53 Kaufman, op. cit., 1.

54 An excellent study on how men form their gender identities and how those identities influence their behaviour was conducted by peace educator, Ian Harris. Harris, I. (1995) *Messages Men Hear*, London: Taylor and Francis.

55 Altinay, A.G. (2004) *The Myth of the Military-nation: Militarism, Gender, and Education in Turkey*, New York: Imprint & Houndmills; and Gor, H. (2003) 'Education for war in Israel: preparing children to accept war as a natural factor of life', in K. Saltzman and D. Gabbard (eds) *Education as Enforcement: The Militarization and Corporatization of Schools*, New York: RoutledgeFalmer.

56 R.W. Connell has been influential in the development of masculinities and gender studies, particularly through contributions to theories of multiple masculinities. See: Connell, R.W. (2000) *The Men and the Boys*, Berkeley: University of California Press.

57 United Nations, Economic and Social Council (1997) *Draft Agreed Conclusions on Mainstreaming the Gender Perspective into All Policies and Programmes in the United Nations*, Paris: UNESCO.

58 Brock-Utne, B. (1989) *Feminist Perspectives on Peace and Peace Education*, 1st edn, New York: Pergamon Press; and Brock-Utne, B. (1985) *Educating for Peace: A Feminist Perspective*, New York: Pergamon Press.

59 See: Miedzian, M. (1991) *Boys will be Boys: Breaking the Link Between Masculinity and Violence*, New York: Lantern Books; Breines, I., Connell, R. and Eide, I. (2000) *Male Roles, Masculinities and Violence: A Culture of Peace Perspective*, Paris: UNESCO; and Reardon, B. (2001) *Education for a Culture of Peace in a Gender Perspective*, Paris: UNESCO.

60 A fundamental aspect of the core argument in Reardon's *Sexism and the War System* regards the relationship of reciprocal causality that exists between women's oppression and war.

61 People's Movement for Human Rights Learning (2006) *Transforming the Patriarchal Order to a Human Rights System: A Position Paper*, New York: PDHRE.

39 Competing discourses of aggression and peacefulness

Majken Jul Sørensen

The existence of peaceful societies challenges persistent myths of innate human aggression that have so long prevailed in Western society. Here, case studies of the Inuit and Semai Senoi will be used to illustrate how perceptions of aggression and peacefulness are social constructions, and how Western societies can learn other approaches to violence, conflict, and aggression from these indigenous, peaceful communities.

Anger is an inner feeling that all human beings experience from time to time, but how we learn to deal with this emotion varies across time and culture. Anger should be separated from aggression, which is a learned way of behaving that can, but does not have to, result in violence. In many parts of the world, it is a persistent myth that aggression and violence are an inevitable part of human life and "human nature." For a long time it was, and in some places it still is, "common knowledge" that human beings have an innate aggressive drive; in its most extreme forms, this is known as "biological determinism." In their introduction to the book *Societies at Peace,* Signe Howell and Roy Willis write a comment that is useful to keep in mind: "It is undeniably the case that in Western society, aggression is regarded as part of human nature. But perhaps this tells us more about Western society than about human nature."

The easiest way to challenge the allegation that humans are aggressive is to pay attention to some of the peaceful societies or cultures of peace that have relatively low levels of aggression, violence, and conflict, and how they choose to handle their anger when it arises. Although these people are few in number, their very existence counters all claims about innate aggressive drives. Howell and Willis show how an *a priori* assumption about innate human aggressiveness has led generations of researchers to look for aggression, and categorize peaceful people by their lack of aggression instead of enter into these peoples' own universe to see what is important to them. They and other anthropologists have taken another point of departure – the innate human sociality, an *a priori* assumption that human beings will always be part of their community, with relations in the community fostering different values. Human beings are born with capacities and potentialities for both aggression and peacefulness, but it is socialization within a particular set of values that determine in which direction we will go – peacefulness or aggressiveness.

If we want to develop more peacefulness in the "Western world," it can be useful to see what we can learn from societies already practicing a more peaceful lifestyle. I will give examples of different ways the Semai Senoi, an indigenous people from Malaysia, and the Inuit, the original inhabitants of Greenland, northern Canada, and Siberia, traditionally handled conflicts. Not because we should copy their way of life and conflict resolution mechanisms, but because we have something to learn from their attitudes to aggression, violence, and conflict, which can complement theories of modern Western conflict resolution.

Some short overview of peaceful societies exists. In *Peaceful Societies*, David Fabbro has defined peaceful societies this way: First, the society has no wars fought over its territory. Second, the society is not involved in any external wars. Third, there are no civil wars or internal collective violence. Fourth, there is no standing military-police organization. Fifth, there is little or no inter-personal physical violence.

To understand Semai approaches to aggression, violence, and conflict, we must try to enter their perception of the world. This is just a very brief introduction based on the writings of Clayton A. Robarchek, the researcher who has written most extensively about the Semai and who has lived together with them for several years. He has remarked that one of the most striking things about Semai society for an outsider is the very low level of emotion that is expressed in everyday life – the only exception being fear. All threats, for example, from spirits and wild animals, are kept away by magic and rituals, and children learn from birth to fear almost everything – especially thunderstorms and strangers. Storms happen frequently in tropical Malaysia, and cause panic among the Semai every time. Children learn to associate all emotional arousal with fear – so when they experience any arousal, be it joy, anger, or grief, their first reaction is fear of this emotion.

Because the world is perceived as dangerous and human beings as almost helpless, the only thing that makes it possible to survive is for the community to stick together and for people to help each other. Food sharing plays an important practical and symbolic role within the community, and mutual aid, generosity and harmony is valued above anything else. Helpfulness is also reinforced because the Semai believe that unfulfilled wishes – for food, sex, or anything else – make people vulnerable to attack by animals or spirits that can cause illness or death. They are scared of wishing or longing for anything, because a person is responsible for keeping his or her desires under control. But people also go to great lengths in sharing what they have and keeping promises to avoid putting others (and thereby the community and themselves) in danger.

The way children are socialized to fear all emotions also leads to fear of anger and conflict. The Semai do not separate between the concepts of anger, violence, and conflict as Western conflict resolution literature does – all of them are seen as intertwined and perceived as dangerous. It is believed that anger can cause the death of another person. The Semai do what they can to avoid all forms of conflict, because it is more important to keep the community together (the only protection in a dangerous world) than personal interest and annoyances. When Robarchek asked people to complete sentences about what they feared most, the answer more frequent than spirits, tigers, and death combined was "becoming embroiled in a dispute." Conflict does occur, however, over big and small things like unfaithfulness, gossip, theft of fruit, or a kinsman's goat destroying the crops. Because there is nobody to enforce punishment in this egalitarian society, disputes between individuals threaten the unity of the community.

The Semai have developed a special formalized way of dealing with conflicts, which is called *becharaa*. If disputes develop, they are considered to be the responsibility of the whole community, and everybody has a duty to report a conflict they see develop to the headsman, who can then arrange a *becharaa*. This begins as an informal gathering for the whole community. Both the beginning and ending of the *becharaa* consists of long monologues by the headsman, where the harmony, mutual aid, and necessity of maintaining the group's unity is stressed again and again, and anecdotes about situations where people helped each other are told to reinforce the feeling that usually people help each other, and conflicts are the deviation. The parties to the conflict and members of their extended families do most of the talking, but there is no direct confrontation or display of anger. All possible explanations for the acts that caused the conflict are explored, as well as contradictory explanations, and it can look as if the parties talk past each other and do not address what the other just said. The *becharaa* goes on until nobody wishes to say anything else, and that can be several days.

Before the closing monologue, the headsman voices the group's consensus about the conflict, and lectures one or both parties about their guilt and what they should have done differently. Sometimes he imposes a small fine, which is often returned to the guilty party again. When the *becharaa* has ended, the matter can never be raised again. According to Robarchek, the *becharaa* serves the purpose of talking the conflict to death. Because the Semai fear all emotional arousal, they talk about what scared them over and over again. That is why the *becharaa* has some "irrational" elements (to Western eyes) – that contradicting explanations are given, that people repeat the same stories over and over again, that there is no time limit. But for the Semai, the *becharaa* is not finished as long as the conflict can still bring out any emotions in anybody.

Jean L. Briggs has written about the handling of emotions, including anger, in the Inuit camps in northern Canada where she lived for several years. There are many similarities between the Inuit and Semai in their demand for self-restraint and emotional control, and they share common values about the danger of aggression and the importance of the community. Other parts of their societies are very different, like their socialization process and their living conditions.

Bruce Bonta has tried to systematize peaceful societies' ways of dealing with conflict, and his category "self-restraint" is useful to describe how both the Semai and the Inuit use self-restraint and emotional control to avoid conflicts and prevent escalation in their societies. Harmony and the community are in both places considered more important than the individual. Semai keep their expectations low to avoid disappointments (and thereby danger), and the Inuit prevent rejections (and thereby potential conflict) by never asking for something they are not sure of getting. For the Inuit, another strategy is to hint at expectations instead of asking directly, and problematic issues about receiving and giving can also be hidden by a joking facade – in awkward situations people will say "I was just joking," and in this way, use ambiguity to prevent conflict.

"Separation" is an approach used by nearly half of the 24 communities that Bonta compares, and although Bonta does not point out the Inuit in this connection, Briggs mentions separation as something that happens in Inuit society to avoid confrontations. Withdrawal from conflict is very much favored by the Inuit, for either the angry person will leave for several hours or days, or everybody else will leave him – ostracism is the ultimate sanction. Gossip and ostracism are used against people who do not conform to a society where the ideal is to be generous, protective, happy, helpful, smiling, and even-tempered. One of Briggs' books about emotions in Inuit society is called *Never in Anger*. This does not mean that Inuit do not feel anger, but that they are socialized to control it to a degree we in the Western world call extreme. Any sign of anger is strongly disapproved of, and other feelings viewed as negative are greed, jealousy, stinginess, and bad temper. Because independence is also highly valued, a family that does not get along with the others can always leave and live somewhere else, either permanently or during the summer and autumn.

According to Briggs, withdrawal serves four different purposes in a conflict. It avoids them in the first place, like the self-restraint mentioned earlier; it expresses fear or disapproval of an angry person; it is a way of solving the conflict; and finally it can be a sanction. I disagree with Briggs that it "solves" the conflict; I would prefer to say that it takes away the immediate tension and prevents escalation. To apply the word "solution" usually requires an active engagement with the conflict.

But what use are the experiences of the Inuit and Semai for the Western world? It is not practically possible or (for most people) desirable to live in a world like theirs without modern comforts, and few people would accept the fear, superstition, or emotional control that are very deep in these societies. Other societies with low levels of physical violence have very sharp gender roles or practice other types of structural violence. It is important not to romanticize their lifestyle, and trying to copy them directly is meaningless and likely to bring other problems into the modern world. These peoples are still significant to us today, however, even if they are few in number. As we have seen, their very existence rejects the innate aggression myth, but they also challenge ideas about looking at conflict as something "healthy."

Bonta makes some interesting observations about the role of peacefulness in peaceful peoples' societies. They do not, for instance, see conflict as inevitable or constructive the way it is commonly perceived in Western conflict resolution, which often writes about the inevitability of conflict, and sees violence as the major problem in modern conflicts. An example of this is Kaj Björkqvist in *The Inevitability of Conflict, But Not of Violence*. The title itself reveals this position. Similar views can be found in almost all modern conflict resolution literature, and some even describe conflict as something positive that encourage creativity and problem-solving skills. It is important to be aware that the two indigenous peoples described here do not make this distinction to the same degree. On the contrary, they consider it to be only negative, something they go to a great length to avoid, and try to resolve as quickly as possible if it occurs. They are aware that conflict happens in their societies, but they will never consider it to be something useful to learn from. Even more important, they do not see peacefulness as an ideal they are striving for – they are peaceful. Bonta writes: ". . . their peaceful conflict resolution practices are fostered by their beliefs in peacefulness, which are in turn bolstered by the successful practices." For the Semai, violence is simply not an option in their construction of reality, and there is nobody to learn violent behavior from.

A distinction between two things should be made here. First, the peaceful societies do not separate between violence and conflict, and second, they see themselves as actually practicing peacefulness here and now. It is not just something they striving toward. In contrast to Bonta, I do not think it is their lack of distinction between conflict and violence that makes the peaceful societies so special, but instead their belief in their own peacefulness. It is not the lack of distinction we in the Western world need to learn from, but the belief in peacefulness that becomes a self-fulfilling prophecy, just like a belief in aggression becomes a self-fulfilling prophecy in the Western world. It makes sense to separate between the two different phenomena conflict and violence, but to also learn from the Inuit and Semai the importance of changing our worldview of who we are. If we stop seeing ourselves as being violent, it will be easier to stop behaving violently and in that way, we reinforce the worldview of ourselves as peaceful, which is what the Semai and Inuit do.

Robarchek has also done research among one of the most violent people, the Waorani in Ecuador, and compares the Waorani and the Semai worldviews in the article "Reciprocities and Realities: World Views, Peacefulness, and Violence among Semai and Waorani." These two groups live in almost the same physical surroundings, yet their view of this world is completely different. Whereas the Semai view the world as a fearful place, where people only have a chance to survive if they cooperate in close communities, the Waorani do not share this perception. They value individualism and self-reliance highly and feel completely capable of surviving in their environment. Seen with Western eyes, however, the Waorani's world is much more dangerous than the Semai's. First of all, they have an extremely high homicide rate, and in addition, their feeling of capability means that they support each other very little, as in instances of illness or childbirth that, to other people, appear to be dangerous and vulnerable situations. It would be interesting to know to what degree this feeling of capability and emphasis on individualism (that are also present in Western society) go together with high rates of violence, but so far this has not been explored across a large number of societies.

What I have presented here can be understood as what in social constructionism and discourse analysis is called "competing discourses" about how we should understand aggression and violence. In most places, the hegemonic discourse is to view aggression and violence as unavoidable parts of human nature that should be kept under control. This worldview places certain limits on how it is even possible to imagine a world with less violence, and how to work toward that goal. A competing discourse, represented by Semai and Inuit constructions of themselves as peaceful, opens up completely different ways to deal with anger, aggression, conflict, and violence. When it is not considered a possibility to use violence in a conflict because you believe yourself to belong to a peaceful people, then you also see a very different reality with less violence. When we understand our attitudes to aggression and violence as social constructions, images of the world that we have created, it also follows that these ideas can be deconstructed and it opens the possibility for change and learning new ways of behaving toward each other. It is, of course, utopian to imagine that this would happen overnight, but a first step is to acknowledge that there is nothing inevitable about the world as it is now.

In Fabbro's definition of peacefulness presented earlier, the absence of structural and cultural violence was not a criterion for being considered peaceful, and I have only been concerned with attitudes to direct, physical violence. An analysis of the discourses of structural and cultural violence both within Western society and peaceful societies would be a necessary next move to deconstruct perceptions of all kinds of violence, but one step at a time. Compared to today's world, it would be a big improvement if we could just reject direct violence and aggression as part of our "nature" and make peacefulness become a self-fulfilling prophecy.

Recommended readings

Björkqvist, Kaj. 1997. "The Inevitability of Conflict, but Not of Violence: Theoretical Considerations on Conflict and Aggression." in Douglas P. Fry & Kaj Björkqvist (eds.), *Cultural Variation in Conflict Resolution: Alternatives to Violence*. Mahwah, NJ: Lawrence Erlbaum Associates.

Bonta, Bruce D. 1996. "Conflict Resolution among Peaceful Societies: The Culture of Peacefulness." *Journal of Peace Research*, 33(4): 403–420.

Boulding, Elise. 2000. "Cultures of Peace: The Hidden Side of History." *Syracuse Studies on Peace and Conflict Resolution*. Syracuse, NY: Syracuse University Press.

Briggs, Jean L. 1979. "The Creation of Value in Canadian Inuit Society." *International Social Science Journal*, 31(3): 393–403.

Briggs, Jean L. 1970. *Never in Anger: Portrait of an Eskimo Family*. Cambridge, MA: Harvard University Press.

Briggs, Jean L. 1994. "'Why Don't You Kill Your Baby Brother?' the Dynamics of Peace in Canadian Inuit Camps." in Thomas Gregor (ed.), *The Anthropology of Peace and Nonviolence*. Boulder, CO: Lynne Rienner Publishers.

Fabbro, David. 1978. "Peaceful Societies: An Introduction." *Journal of Peace Research*, 15(1): 67–83.

Howell, Signe and Roy G. Willis. 1989. "Introduction." in Roy G. Willis (ed.), *Societies at Peace: Anthropological Perspectives*. London and New York: Routledge.

Robarchek, Clayton A. 1997. "A Community of Interests: Semai Senoi Conflict Resolution." in Kaj Björkqvist (ed.), *Cultural Variation in Conflict Resolution: Alternatives to Violence*. Mahwah, NJ: Lawrence Erlbaum Associates.

Robarchek, Clayton A. 1979. "Conflict, Emotion, and Abreaction: Resolution of Conflict Among the Semai Senoi." *Ethos,* 7(2): 104–123.

Robarchek, Clayton A. 1977. "Frustration, Aggression, and the Nonviolent Semai." *American Ethnologist,* 4(4): 762–779.

Robarchek, Clayton A. 1986. "Helplessness, Fearfulness, and Peacefulness: The Emotional and Motivational Contexts of Semai Social Relations." *Anthropological Quarterly*, 59(4): 177–183.

Robarchek, Clayton A. and Carole J. Robarchek. 1998. "Reciprocities and Realities: World Views, Peacefulness, and Violence among Semai and Waorani." *Aggressive Behavior*, 24: 123–133.

40 Gender, conflict, and social capital

Bonding and bridging in war in the former Yugoslavia

Maja Korac

The 1990s are marked by unprecedented mobilisation for armed conflict at the local or state level. With 44 countries, or 25 per cent of the world's states at war during this period, the world experienced more violent conflict than ever before. Conflicts of the 1990s are often called *new wars* (Kaldor 1999; Duffield 2001) as they are importantly shaped by the processes of globalisation, structural changes in the world economy and politics, that is, by the emergence of the "new world order." This type of war is characterised not only by the new, unconventional forms of warfare, but also by the changed form and nature of mobilisation for both forging war and promoting peace. The nature and forms of mobilisation in this type of conflict range from local or national to transnational or international.

Duffield (2001) defines new wars as *network wars* referring to the links and connections formed within states as well as at local-global levels, which are central to mobilising people/fighters as well as securing arms and other resources for this type of war. The centrality of networks to this type of war, however, goes beyond mobilising and resource factors. They are critical for how this type of conflict spreads and takes root in society causing widespread victimisation of populations for prolonged periods. Conflicts of the 1990s have been internal and overwhelmingly marked by the divisive politics that have transformed ethnicity into an effective weapon of war. Reshaping social networks and links at the communal level is central to constructing these wars as "ethnic" or "religious." Duffield (1997) and Kaldor (1999) point out that one of the highest and the gravest costs of new wars is the destruction of social networks and local communities caused by the divisive identity politics of this type of war. By spreading fear and hatred among populations at a communal level, political elites and local warlords mobilise them for support of, and engagement in, violent conflict, and effectively use ethnicity as a tool of war. Goodhand and Hulme (1999: 17–18) point out that "[i]n contemporary conflicts, 'the community' represents the nexus of conflict action." It is at the communal level, they emphasise, where most of the physical violence and suffering occurs (ibid.).

The destruction of social networks at the communal level is about undermining trust and webs of support embedded in (local) social connections tied through local institutions as well as other, informal ties such as family, friendship links, and other forms of sociability and communal links. As these types of bonding and bridging social links are important sources of individual and group identities, as well as social stability and cohesion, their destruction is critical for implementing and spreading divisive politics of new wars and for mobilising support for them. Through various social and political mechanisms, the trust which these connections engender is gradually replaced by fear of a neighbour, friend, fellow co-worker or colleague, and often a relative or a family member, all of whom become labelled as the "Other" within the divisive, exclusionary discourse of new war. This type of discourse prescribes and imposes legitimacy of one type of bond, most often ethnic understood as primordial, and requires destruction, to the point of annihilation, of any bridging connections between diverse individuals and groups at the communal, local level, and beyond.

If undermining trust and webs of social support is central to the development and spreading of new wars, regaining, recreating, and developing new basis of trust is critical for building "viable constituencies for peace" (Goodhand and Hulme 1999: 18), hence, for conflict resolution and any lasting, sustainable peace. Such "islands of civility" (Kaldor 1999) consisting of individuals and groups promoting inter-group, cross-ethnic bridging connections and civic, rather than ethnic politics, exist or have the potential to emerge in the context of new war. It is critical, therefore, to acknowledge and support their existence or to identify social and political forces and spaces within which they have the potential to emerge, as well as to develop strategies to promote them. The character of connections underpinning this type of mobilisation in a new war are importantly about recreating old or developing new basis of trust between groups constructed by political elites and warlords as ethnic and opposing. In this sense, these inter-group links are primarily *bridging* in nature aimed at establishing bonds across difference and (ethnic) boundaries, rather than embedded in them. Much of these processes concern identity as well as politics, and are about the *politics of identity* rather than identity politics. This latter distinction is important as it points to the *bottom-up* processes through which local people challenge, subvert, and contest structures of power that constrain their social lives (Hill and Wilson 2003: 2). This process is in opposition to the top-down processes of identity politics whereby various political, social, and economic entities and elites attempt to mould collective identities into fixed and "naturalized" frames (ibid.).

The emphasis on social networks and trust as the entry point into the analysis of the new type of war, links social capital to the mechanisms and processes underpinning the ways in which they unfold, develop, and are made to last for prolonged periods of time or are undermined from within. The recognition of this link provides a useful conceptual framework for exploring how social networks and trust are reshaped in this type of conflict. It facilitates understanding of their role in spreading new war as well as in forging peace. Social capital is thus understood here as social-relational concept, encompassing norms of reciprocity and trust (Coleman 1990). To reveal and understand how social capital translates into social and political engagement for war or peace it is important to identify conditions shaping norms of reciprocity and facilitating the development of different forms of trust in specific contexts.

I will develop further some of these points conceptually as well as empirically in reference to my research on the violent disintegration of Yugoslavia in the 1990s. By looking (back) at the processes that led to the formation of ethnicised states in the region, I explore the role of social capital, its bonding and bridging qualities, in setting the stage for spreading ethnic hatred and fuelling violence in this conflict, as well as in opening up spaces for reconciliation and conflict resolution. In doing this, I am particularly interested in examining the gender dimensions of these processes.

From cross-ethnic bridges to ethnic bonds: gender and the process of naturalising trust and reciprocity

Ethnicity, understood as a set of fixed and *naturalised* (ethnic) ties and bonds defined by "common blood and origin" had been at the centre of attention during the violent disintegration of Yugoslavia. Conflict was most often described as *ethnic* war attributed to "the centuries of animosity" among the peoples of the Balkans and inequality marked by ethnicity. A more careful and informed analysis of the situation in the country demonstrates, however, that in ethnic terms Yugoslavia was, as Woodward (1995: 32) noted, a land of minorities, in which most local communities and large parts of the country were ethnically mixed, and no group had more than a regional majority. These ethnically mixed local communities were sites not just of peaceful multicultural co-existence, as known in the West, but of genuine cohesion exemplified in the high percentage of ethnically mixed marriages and people of ethnically mixed backgrounds (Kaldor 1999; Korac 2004; Morokvasic-Müller 2004).[1] Moreover, the primary social divisions and inequalities of the pre-war Yugoslavia "were not defined by ethnicity but by job status and growing unemployment" (Woodward 1995: 44). Thus, the social fabric of life at the communal level was importantly cross-ethnic, as were the socio-economic divisions and inequalities. How had these bridging social relations that allowed for the formation of specific forms of reciprocity and cross-ethnic trust been reshaped into bitter ethnic divisions and seemingly impermeable boundaries? What type of trust and reciprocity is shaped by this kind of boundary formation? How are these processes gendered?

In answering these questions it is necessary to examine, albeit briefly, the intersection of socio-economic and political factors and conditions of the 1980s, and explore how these led to the development of divisive identity politics and to the centrality of ethnic rather than civic politics in the region. A socio-economic crisis in Yugoslavia emerged in the 1980s and was linked to the reprogramming of the country's foreign debt. The latter was dictated by the IMF and the World Bank which, following the world oil crisis of the mid 1970s, put pressure on the then Yugoslav government to introduce austerity measures and restructure the economy. The effects of these measures and the crisis that followed were visible and demoralising as millions of people were experiencing a substantial decrease in their standard of living and an equally high percentage had lost their jobs. Structural limitations of the Yugoslav economy, which had relatively limited elements of market economy, as well as the country's inadequate political decision-making structures, in conjunction with the structural changes in the world economy and politics, led the society to a deep crisis. The resulting economic, social, and political restructuring caused a gradual dismantling of state socialism.

These processes triggered the onset of a personal and collective identity crisis for the population in the region. They also heightened people's sense of economic and social insecurity, because they were no longer protected by the shield of the socialist state. Ethnicity and ethnic (be)longing articulated and tied through nationalist claims for ethnic purity of their territories had a powerful appeal, as it promised millions of people a sense of belonging and security at the time of radical change. The post-socialist nationalists skilfully manipulated this sense of disorientation among the population. By seeking political power over sub-federal territories,[2] they aggressively sought to create a base for an ethnic identity that would support their projects of ethnically exclusive states. Given the cross-ethnic character of social relations and ties in the country as well as the actual ethnic mix of population territorially and geographically, the nationalists' aim for "ethnically pure" states required a radical shift in discourse. History and language were to be purged of any notion of peaceful co-existence, as cultural "cleansing" was a precursor to war. In the process, cross-ethnic links, cooperation, and historic ties were replaced by the essential notion of ethnic difference. Ethnic groups, the post-socialist nationalists claimed, were tied with a "common blood" and "common destiny" which form the *natural* basis for cooperation, reciprocity, and trust. Any other types of bonds were perceived as a *threat* to the historic, cultural, and territorial claims of the ethnic collective. Within the political nationalistic discourse and, consequently, the public realm, cross-ethnic links were treated as suspicious or more often as a dangerous aberration away from the natural and *normal* ethnic ties and bonds based on shared tradition, religion, and culture.

Despite the political claims made by politicians, multi-ethnic Yugoslavia was still a reality in the lives of its individual citizens in 1990–1. A survey of 650 refugees in Serbia, originating from 52 ethnically heterogeneous communities in Croatia, showed that the disintegration of their communities was not the result of ethnic tensions in their day-to-day lives in the experience of those surveyed (Milivojevic 1992). Rather, it resulted from political pressure orchestrated by the political elites and their nationalistic parties causing fear among the local citizens. This type of pressure gradually led to ethnic tensions, conflict, and their flight to Serbia (ibid.).

In this survey two-thirds of the respondents came from minority groups in their communities. Some 86 per cent of them had ethnic origins that differed from those of their neighbours, while 96 per cent had established friendships and 66 per cent had family relations with members of other ethnic groups. Fully 60 per cent denied the existence of ethnic divisions or intolerance in their communities and 77 per cent had not had personal conflicts with members of other ethnic groups. While 5.5 per cent judged the atmosphere to be one of ethnic division and intolerance, only 1.2 per cent were able to give evidence of personal conflicts with members of other ethnic groups, and a mere 0.8 per cent were able to give evidence of collective forms of such conflict (Milivojevic 1992). These data describe the situation in ethnically mixed communities in Croatia before the first multi-party election campaigns in the region, in the winter of 1990. According to the same survey, from that time on, the situation started to change, and relations with neighbours, friends, and even relations among family members deteriorated.

My own research revealed a similar pattern.[3] For example, Goca, a Bosnian Serb woman from eastern Bosnia-Herzegovina, a teacher, portrayed the situation in her town a few years before her flight:

> In our street, the neighbours were mostly Muslims [. . .] Those seven, eight Muslim homes around us, we didn't celebrate any holiday [religious] alone, our neighbours, all of them would come, wish us a happy holiday, but also, not a *Bairam* [Muslim religious holiday] passed without us wishing them a happy holiday [. . .] Believe me that we, from [her hometown], neither Muslims nor Serbs, didn't want war [. . .] We couldn't conceive there'd be a war, that I'd run away from my Muslim neighbour. And I also know that my closest Muslim neighbours didn't think so [. . .] Actually, two years before the war [the war in Bosnia-Herzegovina started in April 1992], something changed in the people, you'd talk with your friends, but there were some things you'd not talk about [. . .] You could feel it in the school [where she worked as a teacher], that parents were choosing a Muslim, a Serb teacher. That grieved me very much [. . .] In the circle of people with whom me and my husband were friends [. . .] the people started wondering the last two years what was happening, when those national parties won in our Bosnia [in 1990].
>
> (personal communication, summer 1995)

Similarly, Branka, a Croatian Serb woman from eastern Croatia, explained the situation in her hometown before flight:

> You couldn't feel it [ethnic intolerance] at all, nor did anyone ask you what you were [in terms of one's ethnic origin]. I don't know [. . .] I didn't feel that we [Serbs in her hometown mostly populated by Croats] were being treated differently, we're this and you're that. Not until Tudjman's [the then President of Croatia] Croatian Democratic Union [HDZ party] started, those elections, then they went completely crazy. Maybe you wouldn't have paid so much attention to it, but there is this fear, the fear your parents passed on to you 'cause they have gone through some things [during the IIWW].[4]

Like, here it is [nationalism] rearing its head again. Then the media, since we could only watch Channel 1 of the Belgrade and Zagreb state TV.

(personal communication, summer 1995)

Politicians engineered war propaganda, targeting the voters who, in 1990, at the time of the first multi-party elections in the country, were still ambivalent and did not make a clear choice for nationalists and independence (Woodward 1995: 118). The process was not smooth, as it took time and a lot of war propaganda to recreate "national enemies" and to develop paranoia within ethnic collectives. As in other conflicts constructed as ethnic strife, for example in Rwanda, the role of the media was central to spreading fear and hatred among populations at the communal level.[5] As Parin (1994: 41) pointed out, television and radio were tightly controlled and were "serving the populace a diet of lies, invention, and propaganda, sometimes horrifying, sometimes sentimental." The "television war" and the media war started long before the outbreak of the armed conflict.[6] In his analysis, Parin (ibid.) refers to a statement of Marco Altherr, the then Head of the International Red Cross delegation in the former Yugoslavia, in which he asserts that television was in large measure responsible for atrocities on both sides of the conflict in Croatia, "by having aroused instincts of revenge and unleashed reciprocal acts of retribution."

In their rhetoric, the post-socialist nationalists claimed that the "unnatural" socialist regime had replaced religion, tradition, shared blood, and kin for the emancipation of the working class, women, and proletarian internationalism. The nationalistic discourse, for its part, offered a set of values constructed as traditional, which could easily be perceived as *natural*. According to these "new" values women were expected to take on the responsibilities for the (re)production of the group, as well as custody of cultural values and identity. Policies were introduced encouraging the population growth of the "right kind" in the name of "national security" (Korac 1996). Many authors have emphasised that women are central to producing and maintaining cultural and group identity (e.g. Yuval-Davis and Anthias 1989; Yuval-Davis 1997; Walby 1992). During the growing process of militarisation associated with the escalation of armed conflict, women often become specifically targeted because of these roles. This is because identity politics of new wars constructed as ethnic strife assign women with "honourable" roles as "Mothers of the Nation" and "Symbols of the Nation."[7] They became increasingly seen as precious property to be controlled and "protected."

In this type of conflict, women are seen as precious property of both the "enemy" and the nationalists. Their bodies become territories to be seized and conquered. Testimonies of the raped women in the war in Bosnia-Herzegovina show that conquering women's bodies did not primarily mean sexual violence against them, but a pattern of revenge and aggression resulting in the physical victimisation of women (Stiglmayer 1994: 118). Physical and sexual violence against women in war (and in peace) serves as a "method" of "disciplining" women who fail to behave "properly." Women are "disciplined" by men of the opposed ethnic group because they are loyal to their husbands and community.[8]

Rape in war constructed as ethnic strife is also a powerful symbolic weapon against the "enemy." The woman, as a symbol of the nation, as pointed out earlier, depicts the "Motherland" as a spatial metaphor, an embodied femaleness. Rape of the woman's body/nation, by planting alien seed, disrupts the maintenance of the collective. This logic leads to interpretations of rape as *ethnic harm*, rather than a violent assault on women's rights to reproductive self-determination, through the violation of women's bodies and control of their lives. Rape is also an effective weapon of territorial "cleansing," since men in patriarchal cultures will not return to the communities where they have been "humiliated" by the rape of "their" women

(Korac 1999). The very logic of rape as a weapon in the brutal strategy of "ethnic-cleansing," as Meznaric (1994: 79) explains, rests upon "the use of gender as a means to control communication and to sharpen the boundaries between two opposed ethnicities."

The rape of women "belonging to the enemy" carries an important symbolic message from men to men. As Seifert (1994: 58) points out, it communicates to men of the opposing group that they are unable to defend their women. Therefore, she argues, sexual aggression towards women in war results, at a symbolic level, in wounded masculinity, marking men as "incompetent" in their role as protectors of their women (Seifert 1994: 58). Rape and sexual violence in war also functions as an important mobilising element for furthering militarisation of ethnic collectives. In war masculinity is predominantly equated with militarised aggression. Consequently, men are under constant pressure to prove their manhood by joining the military and by committing various acts of violence, importantly including sexual violence. Militarised violence, therefore, becomes the process within which men can ultimately prove their "wounded" masculinity.

Reshaping social relations marked by cross-ethnic ties and the creation of ethnic tensions, hatred and (militarised) violence was, therefore, a profoundly gendered process. Due to the patriarchal backlash of the transition period briefly outlined here, the notions of femininity and masculinity had been gradually reshaped and closely linked to the notions of ethnic purity, identity, and authenticity. This change and the resulting shift in the dynamics of gender relations of power were central to instigating (militarised) war violence. Women and men had gradually become mobilised and engaged with war through their reshaped gender roles. Their fe/male bodies, feminine and masculine, had been critical both symbolically and physically for naturalising ethnic bonds and the creation of new ethnicised forms of statehood.

In this sense, both women and men as specifically located and positioned gendered actors played active, albeit different, roles in this war. They also responded to the conflict in different ways. While some became actively involved in waging or supporting war, others sought alliances across conflict imposed divisions and demarcation lines organising themselves against war. I will examine both the conceptual and context specific reasons why (some) women opted for alternative political mobilisation during the violent disintegration of Yugoslavia, and became involved in anti-war initiatives *as women*. Their activism, I argue, had an important potential in conflict resolution although it was never fully acknowledged and adequately supported.

Recreating cross-ethnic trust: bottom-up identity work of anti-war women's groups

During the 1990s, there were a number of women's groups in Serbia (e.g. Women in Black Belgrade,[9] and Autonomous Women's Centre Belgrade), Croatia (e.g. Centre for Women War Victims Zagreb), and in Bosnia (e.g. Medica Zenica, and Women for Women, Sarajevo), which can be regarded as some of the very few "islands of civility" (Kaldor 1999). The work of these groups was aimed at re-establishing cross-ethnic ties and forms of trust, as these women recognised quite early on the centrality of maintaining old and developing new connections across ethnic lines and boundaries of the new ethnicised states.

The awareness of the centrality of inter-group connections across the ethnic divide for conflict resolution and post-conflict reconstruction prompted these anti-war women's groups to embark upon work with refugee women and women survivors of sexual violence in war. As these women have been the most violently affected by the exclusionary ethnic politics and nationalism in the region they were in the greatest need of support to overcome their experiences of victimisation as an ethnic "other." They were also those who, as it was then hoped, would eventually return to their homes and thus actively engage in re-building their multi-ethnic communities. The work with women who were subjected to sexual violence was particularly important because of the social and political implications of sexualised forms of violence in this type of conflict, as outlined earlier. Anti-war women's groups argued that women who were subjected to sexual violence in the conflict were further victimised by the aggressive politics of their governments and their media machines.[10]

In response to the processes of "othering" members of different ethnic groups, anti-war women's groups put emphasis on establishing multi-ethnic self-help groups for exiled women. This was regarded as critical for their overall wellbeing as it was considered that coming to terms with individual traumatic experiences is importantly linked to the process of group reconciliation. By implementing this approach they combined provision of humanitarian assistance with psycho-social and political work with victimised women. Women activists not only aimed to provide support by collecting and delivering aid, such as food or clothing, or by helping these women to find work and by offering them legal advice. Rather, the work of anti-war women's groups put strong emphasis on the importance of re-establishing destroyed connections across the ethnic divide, which they considered a critically important source of individual and group identity formation. This work demonstrated that women of different ethnic backgrounds, with diverse experiences of victimisation, could establish and maintain relationships of mutual respect. This was considered a starting point in (re)developing relationships of trust, which is a critical first step in overcoming divisions and fragmentation caused by exclusionary and nationalist politics of war (Boric 1994; Cockburn 1998; Korac 1998c).

In helping victimised women to come to terms with their traumatic experiences, some women's groups introduced discussion groups and writing workshops. This was regarded as yet another way of initiating a gradual and often painful process of (re)establishing respect and trust in the "other" side of the ethnic divide. In these workshops refugee and non-refugee women talked about family, friendship, and other social ties in their communities. After years of the divisive identity-politics of war and experiences of victimisation because of their ethnicity, these discussions provided a supportive context permitting women to remember the inter-ethnic links they had before the war, as well as those forged during the conflict, their flight and its aftermath. In doing so they actively explored the issues of loss, anger, hatred, and guilt. An activist of the Women in Black Belgrade explained, "the women have every right to their bitterness towards people from other ethnic origin," and that is why the exploration of their feelings was so important (personal communication, summer 1995). However, the discussion groups and written accounts were typically characterised by emerging stories and memories of life as it was before the war, and would gradually lead to the recognition of good and trusted neighbours, friends, and relatives whom the war turned into enemies, some real and some imagined. This practice was invaluable because it enabled the women to create a social space in which they were *allowed* to remember good and trusted people at the other side of the ethnic divide. Within the context of identity politics of war that promoted hatred and fear of an "other," defined as a member of the opposed ethnic group, this was regarded as a highly subversive activity. More importantly, because these women had traumatic experiences during the conflict because of their ethnicity, this process was a highly valuable step towards the reconciliation and healing. This process proved to be critical for many of the victimised women in dealing with their feelings of hatred and bitterness. It led to questioning issues of identity and belonging, as they were shaped by the divisive politics of conflict as well as their war experiences.

Through this type of "identity work" both refugee and non-refugee women started developing positive and constructive approaches to crises, and created spaces for mutual understanding and ongoing productive exchange. One of the women active in Autonomous Women's Centre Belgrade explained how each and every one of the women involved in this process aimed at building trust in the "other" side through their willingness to hear what the other side had to say, and through their trust that the other side is equally willing to hear them (personal communication, summer 1995). This type of communication and exchange created spaces in which women were positioned in a compatible way, and where the nationalist discourse of "right" and "wrong" ethnic belonging did not exist. Women's experience of exile and their involvement in work organised by anti-war women's groups in the region exposed the hollowness of essentialist beliefs in the "common destiny" of ethnic collectives and related narratives.

This process of women organising against war and the effort of keeping lines of communication open was not problem-free. It caused at times internal tensions and divisions.[11] The spread of war, distraction, and various forms of victimisation of different ethnic groups in the region were new experiences for these women. During the early years of the conflict, they found them almost impossible to share. Their first meetings with women from "the other side" marked the beginning of a painful, yet an overall successful process of reconciliation of differences embedded in "relational positionality" of these women (Stasiulis 1998). Relational positionality is a concept which refers to: "the multiple relations of power which intersect in complex ways with position of individuals and collectives in shifting and often contradictory locations within geopolitical spaces, historical narratives and movement politics" (Stasiulis 1998: 16–17). Although the tensions and divisions resulting from women's differentiated positioning and experiences of war and violence have become more widely/internationally known, their courageous and persistent initiatives to keep communications across the ethnic divide open were left largely unacknowledged. However, connections across the ethnic divide did not only survive, but also grew with the escalation of war violence and the growing numbers of refugees in the region.

The email link *Za mir* [for peace], which was almost the only means of communication within the war-torn region during the years of armed conflict, was one of the important ways of exchange among these women. It enabled women activists to share experiences and newly acquired knowledge concerning their work with refugee women and survivors of sexual violence in war. It also facilitated the establishment of new contacts and friendships, as well as the nurturing of established ones. Moreover, Women in Black Belgrade were involved in establishing a wider network of anti-war women's groups, consisting of women from the region as well as internationally. This has resulted in an annual meeting of women's solidarity against war, nationalism, and violence. Between 1992 and the early 2000, this international meeting was held every summer in Serbia, each meeting followed by a published report entitled *Women for Peace*. During the years of the armed conflict (1991–5), participation at these meetings was highly risky for many women coming from territories directly affected by armed conflict. It involved not only a laborious process of obtaining travel documents, but also long, exhausting, and often dangerous journeys. Moreover, these women were regarded as "disloyal" and subversive to the political interests of their "countrymen" and the state, because of their participation at these meetings. Thus, they were often in danger of being socially and politically stigmatised in their places of origin and of losing their jobs (personal communication with participants of the 6th Annual Meeting of Women's Solidarity Against War, Nationalism and Violence, held in Novi Sad, Serbia, August 1997).

Women-as-women cross-ethnic organising and reconciliatory potential: concluding remarks

It is not surprising that (some) women in the region had been actively involved in the grass-roots work of keeping lines of communication open since the very beginning of tensions and turmoil leading to war. Cockburn (1998: 44), in her analysis of women's "bridge-building" projects in Northern Ireland, Israel/ Palestine and Bosnia-Herzegovina, points out that feminism understood as anti-essentialist and democratic, that is – inclusive of women differently situated in ethnic, class and other structures, tend to "immunize" women against regressive constructions of ethnic and national identity characterising conflict constructed as ethnic, religious, or communal strife. "If you pick a non-primordial gender card," she claims, "you are less likely to reach for a primordial national card" (ibid.). Cockburn further argues that such a gender critique reveals the seductive notions of the words "community," "country," and "people" invoked in nationalist discourse, which hide within it gender and class inequalities. She goes on to explain how anti-essentialist and democratic feminism helps (some) women to reveal the contradicting nature of the seemingly innocent notion of "home" that conceals confinement, divisions, oppression, and violence, and points out that such women are "the more likely to be sceptical of 'homeland'. If you see home as a 'golden cage' you may suspect that homeland too has its contradictions" (Cockburn 1998: 45). For these reasons, she concludes, a feminist analysis "makes women question the pursuit of political movements by violent means" (Cockburn 1998: 45). This and other similar feminist analyses emphasise that women are not "natural peacemakers" and that they can indeed be deeply involved in nationalist projects and politics. These analyses point out, however, that because women have not been exposed to masculine socialisation, they may be better positioned than men to question the values of a male-dominated society and to formulate a transformative, non-violent vision of conflict resolution (Carter 1996; Women in Black Belgrade 1994, 1997). Studies of conflicts in Colombia and Guatemala also support this argument and demonstrate that women's organising tends to produce greater peace-facilitating social capital than men's groups (Moser and McIlwaine 2001).

Women's organising against divisive politics and war violence in Serbia and other parts of socialist Yugoslavia had started quite early on, before the armed violence began. Feminism has a long history in the region, and feminists were the first to initiate an organised women's resistance to nationalism, violence, and war.[12] The emergence of nationalism and nationalist discourse left women increasingly "displaced" from participation in the labour force; it "planted" them back into the family and household. These developments were coupled with a decrease in woman's political participation.[13] As women were losing out in economic, social, and public life, and when their reproductive rights and freedoms came under attack by nationalists who saw women as biological reproducers of their nations, previously loosely linked women who called themselves feminists began to organise. Although these groups were small and coming from the political margin, they were among the first to publicly voice their opposition to nationalist politics, their tactics of spreading fear and hatred and to the process of militarisation in the region.

One of the groups these women formed in Belgrade was "Women in Black Against War," as mentioned earlier. These women were publicly protesting against the Serbian regime, nationalist politics, and war, and were pressing for creative diplomacy and arguing for a voice for democratic women's groups and other nongovernmental organisations in negotiating a cessation of hostilities in the country. The first vigil of Women in Black (WiB) Belgrade was held on 9 October 1991, and it remained the only permanent anti-war public protest to this day. This was not the only anti-war and peace initiative started by women, in fact, women launched almost all the early peace initiatives in Belgrade and Serbia (Mladjenovic 2003). Mladjenovic (ibid: 41) argues that the reasons for women making up the majority in the early peace initiatives were threefold. Their gender position made it safer for them to act against the regime, as men were under threat of forced mobilisation. Also, their experience of doing unpaid work in the household made them more open to engagement in unpaid, volunteer work in the peace movement. Finally, their knowledge of "making do with less" facilitated their engagement in horizontal, non-competitive activities. Further, and in reference to research on gender, social capital and political participation, in any society women are more likely to be active in the more informal reaches of politics, such as peace movements, rather than in a more formal political arena (Lowndes 2006).

Through this kind of communication and activism these women became engaged in *bridging* initiatives and practices aimed at establishing bonds across difference and (ethnic) boundaries. The practice does not imply, however, abandonment of one's own "roots" or sense of identity and belonging. In this sense, bridging and bonding are not "either-or" categories (Putnam 2000: 23). Rather they involve the simultaneous processes of "rooting" in one's own membership and identity, and "shifting" in order to put oneself in the situation of other participants in the process or communication. This type of practice often pursued by women's groups has been termed *transversal* politics by Italian feminists.[14] This type of resistance to war that emerged initially among rather small and marginal groups of middle-class women who considered themselves feminists had been gradually, yet crucially, shaped and empowered by the experiences of refugee women who have been victimised by war in various ways. Their joint and successful efforts in organising multi-ethnic self-help groups remained a unique attempt in developing elements of a culture of reconciliation in the region. Although important, these groups and their work remained marginal within the "mainstream," male-dominated alternative political initiatives in the region as well as internationally.

This piece has aimed to contribute to gendered analyses of conflict and social capital by examining how the process of mobilisation of social capital for war or peace is gendered and context-specific. My analysis has also supported substantial empirical evidence that women-as-women organising in specific contexts promotes civic bridging links and supports a type of alternative politics that is embedded in cross-ethnic and cross-boundary trust and reciprocity. This type of links and communication are central to the reconciliation processes, conflict resolution, and post-conflict reconstruction. Further research and analysis is required to uncover other links and factors affecting these (gendered) processes in order to identify and support the ones which represent a resource for democracy and peace.

Notes

1 At the time of the 1981 census, the number of people in ethnically mixed marriages and from ethnically mixed backgrounds was greater than the number of ethnic Albanians living in Kosova, Montenegrins, Macedonians, Bosniaks, and Slovenes (Petrovic 1985).

2 Denitch (1972) explains how the Yugoslav system of decentralisation was based on the identification of leadership, not with ethnic, but with geopolitical (republic) interests. Given that none of the republics was ethnically homogeneous, the local leadership was formed within the republics. Such formed leadership, in time, became the leadership on the federal level, but its power base remained in the republics. Denitch rightly argued, back in the 1970s, that this system had "a build-in tendency to develop localism and to encourage nationalistic demagoguery" (1972: 34).

3 Empirical data used in this chapter were collected between 1994 and 1997 as part of my PhD research project entitled *The Power of Gender in the Transition from State Socialism to Ethnic Nationalism, Militarization, and War: The Case of Post Yugoslav States*, York University, Toronto (Korac 1998a).

4 During the Second World War and the socialist revolution in Yugoslavia (1941–5) massacres of civilians took place throughout the region. Some of the worst were committed by the *Ustashe*, pro-Nazi Croats, against the Serbian population in Croatia and Bosnia-Herzegovina. The Ustashe also murdered left-wing Croats and the Jews and Gypsies who came under the jurisdiction of the independent Nazi-state of Croatia. One of the most notorious death camps in this state was run by the fascist Ustashe at Jasenovac, where hundreds of thousands of Serbs were slaughtered between 1941 and 1945 (Denitch 1994: 30). As Parin (1994: 39) pointed out, the independent Croatia of the 1990s was compared by many Serbs living there to the fascist, puppet Croatian state created during the Second World War. He also emphasised that the then Croatian government did not do anything to distance itself clearly from the crimes of fascism (ibid.).

5 For more information on the role of the media in the conflict in Rwanda see Malvern (2002) and Des Forges (2002).

6 For more information on the role of the media in the Yugoslav conflict, see Žarkov (2007).

7 Gender dimensions of identity politics of new wars in general, and in Yugoslavia in particular, are more complex and go beyond the notion of women as "Mothers of the Nation." For an in-depth analysis of how identity politics of conflict in Yugoslavia had shaped notions of femininity and masculinity, and the roles of women and men see Žarkov (2007).

8 This has been well-documented in testimonies of raped women in Bosnia-Herzegovina (Stiglmayer 1994: 136).

9 "Women in Black against War" started in Israel/Palestine in the late 1980s, and quickly spread to Italy, and on to Belgrade, London, Toronto, and other centres. By the late 1990s, it had become a worldwide network of anti-war and anti-nationalist women.

10 For more on these types of victimisation see Korac (1998b).

11 For more on the issue of internal tensions and divisions see Benderly (1997) and Korac (1998a: 35–46).

12 For more on the history of feminism before the conflict see Benderly (1997), Korac (1998a), and Papic (1995).

13 For more on how women were losing out in economic, social and public life see Milic (1996) and Korac (1998b).

14 Nira Yuval-Davis (1997) developed conceptually this well-known strategy of feminists worldwide and emphasised the centrality of the processes of "rooting" and "shifting" for this type of communication and exchange.

References

Benderly, J. (1997) "Rape, feminism, and nationalism in the war in Yugoslav successor states," in L. A. West (ed.), *West feminist nationalism*, London: Routledge.

Boric, R. (ed.) (1994) *Edited volume: centre for women war victims*, Zagreb: Women's Information and Documentation Centre.

Carter, A. (1996) "Should women be soldiers or pacifists," *Peace Review*, 8(3): 31–6.

Cockburn, C. (1998) *The space between us: negotiating gender and national identities in conflict*, London: Zed Books.

Coleman, J. S. (1990) *Foundations of Social Theory*, Cambridge: Belknap Press of Harvard University Press.

Denitch, B. (1972) "Social structure: strengths and stresses," in G. M. Raymond (ed.), *Proceedings of the Sixth Pratt Planning Conference* held on 7 March 1972 in New York City, pp. 34–6.

—— (1994) *Ethnic Nationalism: The Tragic Death of Yugoslavia*, Minneapolis and London: University of Minnesota Press.

Des Forges, A. (2002) "Silencing the voices of hate in Rwanda," in M. E. Price and M. Thomson (eds), *Forging peace: intervention, human rights and the management of media space*, Edinburgh: Edinburgh University Press.

Duffield, M. (1997) "Ethnic war and international humanitarian intervention: A broad perspective," in D. Turton (ed.), *War and ethnicity: global connections and local violence*, New York: University of Rochester Press.

—— (2001) *Global governance and the new wars*, London: Zed Books.

Goodhand, J. and Hulme, D. (1999) "From wars to complex political emergencies: Understanding conflict and peace-building in the new world disorder," *Third World Quarterly*, 20(1): 15–26.

Hill, J. D. and Wilson, T. M. (2003) "Identity politics and the politics of identities," *Identities: Global Studies in Culture and Power*, 10: 1–8.

Kaldor, M. (1999) *New and old wars: organised violence in a global era*, Cambridge: Polity Press.

Korac, M. (1996) "Understanding ethnic national identity in times of war and social change," in R. B. Pynsent (ed.), *The literature of nationalism of nationalism: essays on east European identity*, London: Macmillan.

—— (1998a) *The power of gender in the transition from state socialism to ethnic nationalism, militarization, and war: the case of post Yugoslav states*, unpublished thesis, York University, Canada.

—— (1998b) "Ethnic nationalism, wars and the patterns of social, political and sexual violence against women: the case of post-Yugoslav countries," *Identities*, 5(2): 153–81.

—— (1998c) *Linking arms: women and war in post-Yugoslav states*, Women and Nonviolence Series, No. 6. Uppsala: Life&Peace Institute.

—— (1999) "Refugee women in Serbia: their experiences with war, nationalism and state building," in N. Yuval-Davies and P. Wierbner (eds), *Women, citizenship and difference*, London: Zed Books.

—— (2004) "War, Flight and Exile: Gendered Violence among Refugee Women from Post-Yugoslav States," in W. Giles and J. Hyndman (eds) *Sites of Violence: ender and Conflict Zones*. Berkeley: University of California Press.

Lowndes, V. (2006) "It's not what you've got, but what you do with it: women, social capital, and political participation," in E. Gidengil and B. O'Neill (eds), *Gender and social capital*, New York and Oxon: Routledge.

Malvern, L. (2002) "Missing the story: the media and the Rwanda genocide," in C. McInnes and N. J. Wheeler (eds), *Dimensions of military intervention*, London: Frank Cass.

Meznaric, S. (1994) "Gender as an ethno-marker: rape, war, and identity politics in the former Yugoslavia," in V. M. Moghadam (ed.), *Identity politics and women: cultural reassertions and feminisms in international relations*, Boulder: Westview.

Milic, A. (1996) "Nationalism and sexism: Eastern Europe in transition," in R. Cap Ian and J. Feffer (eds), *Europe's new nationalism: states and minorities in conflict*, Oxford: Oxford University Press.

Milivojevic, Z. (1992) "Research on displaced persons from Croatia, 1991," paper presented at the Conference on Mass Migration in Europe, Vienna, March.

Mladjenovic, L. (2003) "Women in Black against war (Belgrade)," in W. Giles, M. De Alwis, E. Klein, N. Silva, M. Korac, D. Knezevic and Z. Papic (eds), *Feminists under fire: exchanges across war zones*, Toronto: Between the Lines.

Morokvasic-Müller, M. (2004) "From pillars of Yugoslavism to targets of violence: interethnic marriages in the former Yugoslavia and thereafter," in W. Giles and J. Hyndman (eds), *Sites of violence: gender and conflict zones*, Berkeley: University of California Press.

Moser, C. O. N. and Clark, F. C. (eds) (2001) *Victims, perpetrators or actors? Gender, armed conflict, and political violence*, London: Zed Books.

Moser, C. and McIlwaine, C. (2001) *Violence in a post-conflict context: urban poor perceptions from Guatemala*, Washington, DC: World Bank.

Papic, Z. (1995) "Women's movement in former Yugoslavia: 1970s and 1980s," in M. Blagojevic, D. Duhacek and J. Lukic (eds), *What can we do for ourselves*, Belgrade: Centre for Women's Studies, Research and Communication.

Parin. P. (1994) "Open wounds: ethnopsychoanalytic reflections of the wars in the former Yugoslavia," in A. Stiglmayer (ed.), *Mass rape: the war against women in Bosnia-Herzegovina*, Lincoln and London: University of Nebraska Press.

Petrovic, R. (1985) *Etnicki mesoviti brakovi u Jugoslaviji [Ethnically mixed marriages in Yugoslavia]*. Beograd: Institut za socioloska istrazivanja Filozoskog fakultetau Beogradu.

Putnam, R. D. (2000) *Bowling alone: the collapse and revival of American community*, New York: Simon & Schuster.

Seifert, R. (1994) "War and rape: a preliminary analysis," in A. Stiglmayer (ed.), *Mass rape: the war against women in Bosnia-Herzegovina*, Lincoln and London: University of Nebraska Press.

Stasiulis, D. (1998) "Relational positionalities of nationalism, racism and feminism," paper presented at the 10th Annual Interdisciplinary Feminist Colloquium, York University, Toronto, March.

Stiglmayer, A. (ed.) (1994) *Mass rape: the war against women in Bosnia-Herzegovina*, Lincoln and London: University of Nebraska Press.

Walby, S. (1992) "Woman and nation," *International Journal of Comparative Sociology*, 32(1–2): 81–100.

Women in Black Belgrade (1994) *Women for peace*, Belgrade: Women in Black.

—— (1997) *Women for peace*, Belgrade: Women in Black.

Woodward, S. (1995) *Balkan tragedy: chaos and dissolution after Cold War*, Washington, DC: The Brookings Institute.

Yuval-Davis, N. (1997) *Gender and nation*, London: SAGE.

Yuval-Davis, N. and Anthias, F. (eds) (1989) *Women-nation-state*, London: Macmillan.

Žarkov, D. (2007) *The body of war: media, ethnicity, and gender in the break-up of Yugoslavia*, Durham and London: Duke University Press.

41 Peaceful societies and everyday behavior

Elise Boulding

Let us begin by remembering that there is no such thing as a conflict-free society. Conflict is ubiquitous. That ubiquity stems from the basic fact of human individuality and difference in the context of limited physical and social resources. Conflict itself should not be confused with violence, which is taken here to mean the intentional harming of others for one's own ends. The differences in wants, needs, perceptions, and aspirations among individuals and among groups, stemming from individual uniqueness, require a constant process of conflict management in daily life at every level from the intrapersonal (each of us has many selves), to the family and the local community, and on to the international community. What keeps this unceasing process of conflict from degenerating into the war of each against all is the equally ubiquitous need of humans for one another, for the social bonding and nurturance without which no society could function. From this perspective, there is no society without significant elements of peaceableness.

Hans Hass has undertaken a remarkable documentation of the universality of human responsiveness to other humans.[1] Traveling around the world with his camera, he has photographed a series of expressive human gestures – smiling, greeting with glad surprise (eyebrows raised), comforting another in grief by having the griever's head resting on the comforter's shoulder, reaching out to protect a child in danger – in settings as far apart as Kenya, Samoa, and France. In cultures that practice disciplined control over such expressive gestures, one finds their fullest expression in children who have not yet learned the discipline.

Hass points out that children learn early how much a smile can do. Why do we humans smile so much? "Because we are not, basically, unfriendly creatures. Thus our smile is a means of eliciting contact readiness with others and of conveying our accessibility to contact."[2] A smile serves as a social bridge builder.

This universal need for bonding can be thought of as the key to the survival of the human species. It is what draws humans toward negotiating with one another in the face of conflicting interests, needs, and perceptions, whether in settings of family, neighborhood, workplace, or public institutions. The very existence of war and social violence, however, tells us that

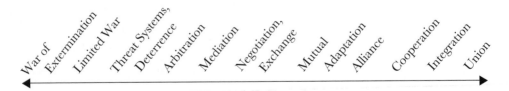

Figure 1 The conflict continuum

negotiation is not the only response to conflict. In fact, we may think of responses to conflict as falling on a conflict-management continuum from destruction of the adversary through a range of mediating-negotiating behaviors to complete union with the other.

Peaceful behavior in everyday life: cultural concepts

Some societies tend toward the aggressive end of the conflict management continuum in · their behaviors, others toward the integrative, with many societies falling somewhere in the middle. The historical reasons why different groups pattern their responses to conflict differently lie beyond my scope here, but former warrior societies have been known to change and adopt more peaceable ways. We have also noted that warrior societies of the past have all had images of living in peace. The wars of ancient China did not prevent Chang Huen-Chu from writing: "Heaven is the father and Earth is the mother . . . wherefore all included between Heaven and Earth are one body with us and in regard to our dispositions, Heaven and Earth should be our teachers. The People our brothers and we are united with all things."[3] This theme of being kin with all peoples and with earth itself is rooted in a basic experience of the social bonds of kinship and intergroup alliances and the need for mutual aid systems in order to survive, whether in inner cities or on over-stressed farmlands. The peaceful elements of religious teachings strengthen that social bonding. The women's culture also strengthens that bonding, sharing with the religious culture a primary-level responsibility for the well-being of a people. Women's cultures everywhere are an important source of the work of nurturance of a society; a reservoir of experience and knowledge in the bearing and rearing of children; in the healing of the sick; in the growing, processing, and actual serving of food; and in the providing of clothing and shelter. Traditionally, women have had the more difficult role in marriage partnerships through the widespread practice of the woman's moving to the male partners community and being expected to serve as communication channel and conflict resolver when differences between the communities arise. It is very often, therefore, women who have had the most experience in doing the background work for negotiation and mediation.

The role of infants and young children in the gentling of the human species is often understated. Adults everywhere tend to respond to infants with smiles and modulated voices. Watching small children discover with delight the most ordinary and humdrum items of daily existence literally refreshes adults, as does seeing children at play, creating a wondrous imaginary world that has no purpose but itself.

Through most of human history people have lived in rural settings and in small-scale societies. Just as each familial household develops its own problem-solving behavior, so each social group has developed its own strategies of conflict resolution over time, uniquely rooted in local culture and passed on from generation to generation. Similarly, each society has its own fund: of adaptability, built on the knowledge of local environment and life-world and the historical memory of times of crisis and change. Such knowledge and experience are represented in familial households as they are organized into communities. The knowledge is woven into religious teachings, into the music, poetry, and dancing of ceremonies, celebrations, and play. It is present in women's culture, in the word of work, in traditional decision-making assemblies, in environmental lore, and in the memory of the past. These are the hidden peacebuilding strengths of every society.

As societies become more complex and elites become differentiated from "common people," center-periphery problems based on mutual ignorance develop. Elites not only cease to share locally based knowledge but cease literally to share a common language with locals.

Traditional conflict resolution methods then break down, and new ones are slow to develop during prolonged periods of transition. Since in this last decade of the twentieth century there are only 188 states in the world and "10,000 societies"[4] – ethnic, religious, and cultural groups with significant historical identity – this breakdown of communication and lack of common conflict management practices between ethnic groups and the larger states of which they are a part is one of the major problems contributing to current levels of intrastate as well as interstate violence. Rediscovery of the hidden strengths of local cultures is one important aspect of peace building for this painful transitional period in contemporary history.

Given the diversify of negotiation and conflict-resolving behaviors that go on every day in every household and every community in the 188 states of the present international order, how can everyday peace behaviour be illustrated? This will be handled here in two ways. First, the character and dynamics of everyday peace behavior will be highlighted by choosing societies that set a high value on peaceableness and examining how they go about their conflict management/avoidance interactions as adults and how they train their children to such behavior.[5] Next, we will take a look at peace behaviors to be found in societies in general, common elements underlying wide differences in cultural patterns. The advantage of beginning with societies that are known to be peaceful is that this approach offers behavioral specificity. It highlights the strategies and skill-based nature of peaceful behavior and its dependence on an explicit set of values about nonaggression. Only after that will we go on to see how families in every society, in fact, give some degree of skill training to children to achieve the accepted norms of conflict resolution behavior, whatever they may be. This is the basic process of socialization at work.

In this pursuit of local strengths in peaceableness, we will examine peace behaviors in two types of societies that are alive and functioning at the present time: (1) small preindustrial societal groups that maintain a distinctive identity and yet also have some degree of contact with the larger world and its urban centers and (2) interfaith Irish and North American Anabaptist "peace church" communities that function actively within industrial core societies but have distinctive lifeways that mark them as separate subcultures within those societies.

The behavioral dynamics of peaceableness in selected contemporary societies

The societies selected here set a high value on nonaggression and noncompetitiveness and therefore handle conflict by a variety of nonviolent means. The four tribal societies to be examined are the Inuit of the Canadian part of the circumpolar North, the Mbuti of the northeastern rainforests of Central-African Zaire, the Zuni of the desert Southwest of the United States, and the mountain-dwelling Arapesh of New Guinea. Each has a distinct and sensitive relationship with its bioregion. Each has distinctive ways of child rearing that produce distinctive adult behavior, but they vary in the degree to which these skills are conflict-suppressing or conflict-resolving, and in the degree to which the skills are based on a strongly dichotomous ingroup-outgroup way of thinking in relation to neighboring peoples. Where there is a strong dichotomous sense, people are free to be aggressive with outsiders and are expected to be peaceful only in their own community. Where attitudes are more inclusive of other peoples, peaceful behavior is extended to outsiders.

The Inuit

The Inuit live in the circumpolar North, spread out from eastern Siberia through Greenland and Canada to Alaska. They survive a harsh and unforgiving winter cold through cooperation and social warmth, a warmth that extends to the baby animals that children bring home from the icy outdoors to cuddle. Violence and aggression are under strong social prohibition. The social values are centered on (1) *isuma*, which involves rationality, impulse control, thinking problems through calmly and being able to predict consequences of behavior, and (2) *nallik*, which is love, nurturance, protectiveness, concern for others' welfare and total suppression of hostility.

The distinctive childrearing that produces these rational, compassionate, controlled adults revolves around what Briggs calls *benevolent aggression*.[6] This involves an unusual combination of warm affection for infants and a complex kind of teasing that creates fear in children and then teaches them to laugh at their fears. The title of one of Briggs's studies, "Why Don't You Kill Your Baby Brother?" suggests the extremes to which teasing goes, seen from a Western perspective. That it works – in the sense that it produces people with both *isuma* and *nallik*, and a remarkably peaceful society – I would ascribe to the fact that young children are far more socially perceptive, far more sophisticated in their assessment of social situations, than adults usually give them credit for and that they very early figure out what is going on and learn to respond creatively.[7] Although it is a tricky kind of socialization that one can imagine going wrong with some individuals, it does make children self-reliant problem solvers with a well-developed sense of humor, who are affectionate and acutely aware of the disciplined anger-control processes going on inside themselves and others. Girls and boys get the same type of socialization, and Inuit men and women are equally resourceful. There is also a parallel process of much fondling of infants and baby arctic animals, much food sharing and communal eating, much laughter and playfulness. This unusual combination of affection and teasing seems to lead to a high level of conflict awareness and an equally high level of skill in problem solving. The skill of handling conflict playfully, as in song duels (or drum matches) between offended parties, and other similar rituals, produces enjoyable public events rather than battles.

There is no basic we-they, in-out dichotomy, so the conflict management skills are in theory extendable to conflict with non-Inuits. Conflicts with less aware parties such as the Canadian government suggest limits to this. In recent years the Inuit have suffered much from forced government resettlement projects and now have their share of problems with unemployment and accompanying dysfunctional behavior. However, it is also noteworthy that an Inuit, Mary Simon, was chosen as Canada's first circumpolar ambassador. With her colleagues in the Council of Arctic Peoples she has shown the hidden strengths and resourcefulness of traditional Inuit culture by applying them to the protection of the fragile arctic environment and the creation of new spaces for reconstructed life ways to enable limits to maintain a viable society.[8]

The Mbuti

The Mbuti are hunter/gatherer, rainforest-dwelling Pygmies in northeastern Zaire (now the Congo) who have long had periodic contact with Bantu villagers; they have been movingly described by Tumbull.[9] The basis for their peacefulness is their relationship to the rainforest – their mother, father, teacher, and metaphoric womb. The family hut is also symbolically a womb. Children grow up listening to the trees, learning to climb them early so they can sit high above the ground, listening to wind and waving branches. Mbuti is a listening culture but also a singing and dancing culture, as adults and children sing to and dance with the trees. *Ekimi*, quietness, is highly valued, as opposed to *akami*, disturbance. This preference for quietness, harmony, is reinforced at every stage of life, yet does not preclude children's rough-and-tumble play and a lot of petty squabbling among adults, which tends to be controlled by ridicule. Although children are slapped to control forbidden activities and nuisance behavior, they are also taught interdependence and cooperation. Adults seem to enjoy horseplay and noisy dispute. Semi humorous "sex wars" in which men and women line up for a tug-of-war between the sexes serve as tension dissipaters – the tugs-of-war break up with much laughter. They are also an indication of the companionable equality between women and men. Most groups have a "clown," one person whose antics also help keep conflicts from getting out of hand. For all the squabbling, disagreements rarely get serious.

The contrast between the forest as womb and the love of the silences of the forest, on the one hand, and, on the other hand, the frequency of arguing and the use of joking and ridicule to keep it under control, is an interesting one. The Mbuti themselves value "letting it all hang out" (in modern parlance), not letting conflicts fester. There seems to be a nature-based social equilibrium here, based on a combination of listening, singing, dancing, and squabbling that is not easy for Westerners to understand.

The Mbuti, like the Inuit, have faced a modernizing national government that is destroying their environment and requiring adaptation to the limit of their capability. Worse, their forest home is being overrun by soldiers and guerrillas. Nevertheless, the Mbuti "we" is an inclusive *we*. This suggests potential for some degree of long-term survivability as they link with other rainforest peoples in the new transnational indigenous peoples networks, but the destruction of their lifeways as a by-product of widespread civil wars in the Great Lakes region of Africa is a very serious threat.[10]

The Zuni

The Zuni live in the arid mountain canyon country of western New Mexico in the United States, many of them on a Zuni Indian reservation. A matrilineal society noted for its peaceful life ways, its arts and crafts, and its antipathy to overt violence, the Zuni are well known through the writings of Ruth Benedict.[11] As with the Mbuti, the love of harmony is based on a sense of oneness with nature and a sense of place, yet that love of harmony dots not preclude habits of gossip and quarreling.

The war gods that once ensured tribal survival in a period of warfare are now thought to be channeling their sacred energy into the peaceful well-being of the Zuni. Earlier ingroup-outgroup attitudes that kept the warfare going are no longer salient. The culture devalues authority, leadership, and individual success. No one wants to stand out. There are rituals for sharing, for healing, for conflict resolution, which help children to learn appropriate group behavior. Problem-solving skills are highly developed but without any counterpoint of individualism. There is continued skill transmission of the remarkable environmental knowledge that enabled a rich Zuni culture to develop in a very arid environment, including traditional agriculture and irrigation practices that are only now coming to be understood by Westerners as representing a very sophisticated technology.

Children, after a very permissive nurturant infancy, are disciplined by masked demons who make an appearance to scold them for fighting. Sudden withdrawals of goodies by adults prepare children for social obedience and nonaggressive behavior. Zuni youth therefore do not respond well to the incitements to individual achievement and competition in use by Anglo teachers in Zuni schools, although group performance levels are high. The economic, social, and political influence the Zuni have been exposed to in the past half century have heavily stressed the Zuni value system and have increased local conflict levels. However, the traditional Zuni skills of cooperation are reasserting themselves in very interesting tribal developments, including the launching of a comprehensive Sustainable Development Plan built on a combination of traditional knowledge of the desert environment and new scientific knowledge, which it is hoped will initiate a renaissance of the Zuni way of life.[12]

The Arapesh

The mountain-dwelling Arapesh are one of the many tribes living in the highly diverse archipelago of New Guinea, an area divided by successive colonial occupations and now consisting of independent Papua New Guinea and an Indonesian-claimed province, West Irian. Much has changed since Margaret Mead's study of them in 1930,[13] so it should be noted that it is the 1930s Arapesh being described here. These people had in common with the North American Zuni a distaste for standing out, a preference for conformity, and a rejection of violence in the community. This rejection, however, was accompanied by actual hostility towards outsiders, and little emphasis on dealing with conflicts in a problem-solving way.

Arapesh children grow up experiencing cooperation as the key mode of life. All tasks are group tasks. Any one household will plant many yam gardens, each with a different group of households. (We now know that this represents a very sophisticated adaptation to a region with great diversity in soil quality and many microclimates at different altitudes in a bewildering variety of microecosystems. Spreading the risk of poor crop yields over many garden plots planted in different locations at different times during the year ensures that there will be some food at all times.)

For the children, every person in the village is thought of as a relative. Everyone is to be trusted, shared with, loved – children are lent about in a world filled with parents. Children are taught to express anger without hurting anyone and are never allowed to hit a person. This means that conflict is not addressed. The only need for leadership is for ceremonial feasts. The person chosen to be a feast giver (someone already recognized as having regrettable but useful aggressive tendencies) gets special training for his role by the community and has a feast-exchanger partner in a neighboring clan. This is the one accepted competitive relationship, and competition between feast givers from different clans can be fierce and aggressive. The feast giver does not, however, enjoy his role (at least is not supposed to) and is allowed to retire into gentleness when his oldest son reaches puberty. Although feast givers are generally men, there is a minimum of sex-role differentiation or dominance patterns. There are, however, certain culturally allocated specializations. Color painting, for example, is done only by men.

The major negative factor in the society is fear of sorcery, which is thought to come from outside enemies who have somehow gotten hold of an individual's personal "dirt." Even nature-caused crop failures are thought of as sorcery-induced. There are no gradations in social relations – only friends (insiders) and enemies (outsiders). The Arapesh, thus left without any patterns for incorporating the other, the different, the stranger, into their lives, are very vulnerable in the turbulent struggles between tribes, against present and former colonial authorities, and against powerful mining companies destroying mountain environments through open-pit copper and gold mining.

In the four peace-valuing societies we have looked at so far, we have seen a pattern of bottom-line nurturance and sharing behavior experienced from childhood. Sex-role differentiation has been minimal. However, there has been considerable variation in the ways conflict is managed, from avoidance and suppression, as among the Zuni and Arapesh, to acknowledgment of and socialization for managing conflict, was with the Inuit and Mbuti. But all the societies, at the times their behavior was recorded, were living in relative isolation from the urban and industrial centers of their respective countries. Now we turn to two cultures located within politically modernized states; the rural Irish of Northern Ireland and the Anabaptist cultures of the historic peace churches in the United States, both rural and urban.

The rural Northern Irish

Some of the rural communities of Ulster exemplify the possibility of nonviolence emerging from violence. The extremes of physical aggression experienced in urban areas are rejected by both contending parties – Catholic and Protestant – in some rural areas. In the communities described in Bonta's collection of studies, the Protestants have abandoned their former "superior" socioeconomic statues for a more egalitarian stance *vis-à-vis* the Catholics, and communities of both faiths work very hard at developing many joint activities.[14] They deliberately form nonsectarian groups, so as to prevent the religious polarization prevalent elsewhere in Ulster. They have very selfconsciously chosen bridge building across cultural and religious differences. Joint activities for children and youth as well as adults are carefully planned. Hostile behavior is quickly dealt with in the interests of community harmony. Social, economic, and cultural functions that involve cooperation of Catholic and Protestant farmers and business people are given high priority, and people strongly value good-neighborly relations. When violence does occur, it is blamed on outsiders. While locally inclusive in their peacebuilding, they are threatened and vulnerable in the face of the larger-scale violence taking place in the region. The success of current negotiations in the 1990s between the two parts of Ireland and Britain may depend on the extent to which other areas are willing to accept peaceful interfaith communities as role models for relations on a larger scale.

The Anabaptist/historic peace church communities

Anabaptism has its roots in fifteenth- and sixteenth-century movements – partly originating in the Swiss Alps – to defy all outward authority (including infant baptism, which forcibly incorporated each newborn into the local religious power structure). These movements produced a type of early-Christian pacifism as they spread through Europe. In the seventeenth century (and later), many of these Anabaptists migrated to the Americas in search of religious freedom and freedom from military service. The three main communities presently active in the Americas, known as the historic peace churches, are the Brethren, the Mennonites, and the Quakers. Other smaller communities include the Amish, the Doukhobors, the Moravians, and the Hutterites. We will focus here on the three major Anabaptist communities. Traditionally abstaining from political action because of their rejection of military service[15] they have nevertheless become increasingly involved in various types of pubic activity to remove social and economic injustice and to bring and end to war as an instrument of state policy. In the Second World War, the three faith communities in the United States cooperated to administer Civilian Public Service Camps for their own young men and other conscientious objectors as an alternative to military service.

All three communities hold to the testimonies of simplicity, gender and racial equality, and personal and social nonviolence, yet find themselves an increasingly urban and middle-class that stands in contrast to the communities' more rural origins. Their challenge is not only to develop strategies for living their witness; increasingly, in the twentieth century, they have sought to find ways to work for their vision of a "peaceable kingdom" on earth and to rear their children to carry on efforts for social transformation of an increasingly violent larger society.[16]

The three faiths differ in degrees of hierarchical authority, with the Quakers as the most egalitarian, having no "hireling shepherds" (as ministers are traditionally referred to among Quakers).[17] All three faiths stress democratic participation of all members, including women, and decision making at the local level. Quakers, however, in the absence of authority figures, developed a special consensus approach to decision making based on the "sense of meeting," as members sought divine guidance on what was to be done in the face of conflicting views of participating individuals. The refusal to use voting procedures and majority rule meant that decisions could not be taken until either all members reached agreement or dissenters were willing to "stand aside."[18] What is particularly interesting about the consensus method is that it respects the presence of conflict and allows for the full airing of differences. It also depends on a disciplined spiritual maturity of members of the community, a common acceptance of collective inward illumination of the group, and great skill in intellectual discernment and interpersonal and intergroup communication. This is a tall order for any group, and therefore great importance is given to the religious education of the children of a Meeting. They must be prepared not only to carry on the consensus process within their Meeting but also to carry Friends' testimonies into the larger society in an active pursuit of social and economic justice and peace. Although consensus is specifically Quaker, the educational practices described here are also common among Mennonites and Brethrens.

Anabaptist testimonies begin in the home. While individual families certainly fall short of the ideal, spouse relations (based on a full and equal partnership) and parenting are taken seriously by both parents. An important part of parenting is the cultivation of the divine seed in each child, so times of silent worship in the home, as well as discussion and reading, help prepare children for their responsibilities. Explicit training in nonviolent responses to conflict and alternative ways of dealing with conflict are emphasized. Conflict suppression is not encouraged. Rather, children are urged to "work things out." All this is in the context of an affectionate family life and a nurturant local Meeting. "The chief enjoyment of Friends is connubial bliss," wrote an eighteenth-century observer of Quakers, and although divorce takes its toll in every religious community today, Anabaptist families on the whole have an enjoyable family life. On the other hand, Anabaptist adults – and children too – also carry a certain load of guilt. Given their acceptance of responsibility for peace and justice in the world but the reality of the huge gap between what any individual or family or Meeting can do and what is needed, guilt is inevitable. A healthy family and a healthy Meeting keep a sense of humor about this. Laughter is an important safety valve. So are imagination and skill in organizing useful local service projects that can absorb individual energies creatively.

An important institution in the local communities of all three faith groups is the Sunday School (by Quakers called the First Day School), where adults of the congregation do their best to supplement the work of the member families by preparing children and young people spiritually, intellectually, and in terms of social skills, specifically for peacemaking. Community history and the stories of Quaker, Mennonite, and Brethren heroes and heroines are an important part of this education.

While the forms of worship of the three faith communities are different, all three have a strong emphasis on family life, individual spiritual development and training for social service and peacebuilding. All three have developed remarkable service bodies that do peacebuilding around the world, and Brethren and Mennonites are particularly strong in nonviolence training for their youth in preparation for giving a year or more of service in their own country or abroad. The Children's Creative Response to Conflict Program, now used in elementary and middle schools in a number of countries, was first developed by Quakers to help children deal with conflict.[19] A similar program, Alternatives to Violence, was developed to prepare prisoners for life after prison. Each faith supports outstanding schools and colleges that educate young people who seek an active and participatory learning experience.

Because all three Anabaptist communities are committed to the work of social transformation towards peace and justice for all people, "enemy" concepts are not used nor is the language of fighting. There can be no enemies, only strangers with whom a relationship needs to be developed. Peacemaking is seen as building bridges across differences, finding solutions to the problems of all disputants in ways that injure none, and refraining disputes so common interests can be discovered.

The world sometimes overwhelms the sense of faith-based identity, and callings can weaken. Also, individuals can feel hopelessly compromised by the world they are trying to change. To deal with these problems, the three historic peace churches formed the coalition "New Call to Peacemaking" several decades ago in order to strengthen each other's resolve to carry on peacemaking activities. Currently they jointly support the training and deployment of unarmed peace teams in situations of serious violence in Africa, Central and Latin America, and the Middle East.

Peace behaviors that can be found in any society

Microsocieties such as we have been examining, which take peace and nonviolence as primary organizing values of their lifeways, are rare in the closing years of the twentieth century. Most of humanity lives in societies marked by increasingly high densities of weaponry, from handguns to bombs to the terrors of chemical and biological weapons. But underneath the layers of violence each society, without exception, has its peace behaviors, precious resources that can be available to help bring about new and gentler forms of governance locally and on a larger scale in the next century.

Where do we find these behaviors, these peace culture resources? In the recurring cycles, rhythms, and rituals of human celebration, with its feasting, singing, dancing, and sharing of gifts. In the reproductive cycles of human partnering, of birthing, of family maintenance as the years go by, and the completion of dying – in the cycles that bind people together across kin groups. In the succession of woundings and healings of human bodies as they move through life's dangers in those cycles. In the labor to produce sustenance from the earth. In the daily round of trade, the barter and exchange of goods and services. And, perhaps most wonderful of all, in human play – the playing of games, the play of artistic creation, the play of the mind in the pursuit of knowledge. Let us explore each in turn.

Partnering and reproduction

The familial household is the most adaptive of human institutions, expanding and contracting through history according to changing social conditions from individual units consisting of a single person or a couple to the 200-person multifamily commune, the *frérêche* or *zadruga* common in parts of medieval Europe, or the monastic households of monks or nuns. Different social patterns develop in different times and places. While the human capacity to love is not necessarily the basis for partnering, that capacity to love mellows many a marital companionship over time, whatever the nature of the original marriage arrangements. The newborn infant depends on that capacity to love for survival; for the little ones that do survive, love can multiply as mothers and infants interact. Love can multiply as fathers and infants interact too, and it is noteworthy that in all the peaceful cultures described earlier in this chapter, fathers played an active role in parenting the young. Infants and children have a gentling effect on adults everywhere, as the Hass photographs show, but this gentling effect can be enhanced or reduced by childrearing customs. There are societies where fathers ignore children until they reach the age of six or so, and then suddenly reach in to remove little boys from their all-women's world and put them in an all-men's world, to be raised to be fierce and manly. The attention that fathers give to their sons under these conditions hardly has a gentling effect on either generation.

How some societies become harsh and punitive, or withdrawn and fearful, rather than peaceful and trusting is beyond my scope here. However, one significant step toward a gentling society is the creation of social arrangements that provide for both parents to spend more time with infants and small children. Another is giving skill training in handling interpersonal conflicts, again as we have seen in the societies already examined. Such training has a multiplier effect on peaceableness in a society, since the interpersonal skills learned in families are then used in the community as well. The limits to the skills of diplomacy and negotiation exercised at the intergroup and international levels are set by each society in the family arena where they are first learned.[20]

Production and sustenance

In societies where nature is both parent and teacher, where a close attunement to the environment patterns the ways of obtaining food and other resources, the skills of listening to nature and the skills of listening to fellow humans are closely related. Because nature is unpredictable, human interdependence and resource sharing means survival in times of drought, flood, or earthquake. Finding ways to make that interdependence a visible reality in complex societies where rich and poor do not interact, and finding ways to listen to the natural environment on city streets, is a challenge for the inhabitants of industrialized states – and a challenge that peace activists accept. They are constantly seeking ways to dramatize the reality of human interdependence for the basic necessities of life.[21]

Celebration and ritual

Celebrations are the play life of a society, occasions for embodying the experienced beauty of both inner and outer lifeworlds in song, dance, poetry, and the creation of symbolic imagery. They are also occasions for reaffirmation of identity and social values.[22] At their best, feasting and gift giving emphasize sharing and reciprocity, a sense of the community as one family. When sharing and gift giving have a character of spontaneity and exuberance, and singing and dancing are freely and widely participated in, then celebration is a powerful reinforcement of peaceful and caring community relations. It becomes a time of letting go of grudges, of reconciliation among persons whose relations may have become strained. To the extent that there is a clearly defined articulated basis for the celebration, patterned in ritual, it also becomes a reconnection with creation itself, a reminder of the oneness of the cosmos and all living things. It becomes a time for the making of vows to undertake difficult tasks to serve the community. Celebrations mark the rites of passage from birthing to childhood to puberty to adulthood. They mark wounding and healing, and they mark dying. They also mark the great historical moments of the remembered past, and the great traumas.

The quality of the peace culture in any given society can be found in its art forms. The visual, the kinetic, and the audial arts are interpenetrating expressions of the joys, sorrows, and spiritual intuitions of humans us they participate in the lifeworlds of the planet and beyond. Art forms that enhance the capacity of the human senses for experiencing and relating to those lifeworlds are part of the very core of a society's peace culture. Art forms that constrict the capacity to relate to those lifeworlds reflect, on the other hand, a culture of violence.

In short, when celebrations lose their playfulness, when art forms constrict the capacity for relationship, when gift giving becomes carefully calibrated exchange, when performing becomes competitive, then they lose their character of replenishing the human spirit and are a poor source for general peaceableness.

The role of religious belief and practices in building the habits of peace in daily life has already been discussed. When those religious rituals that emphasize a loving, forgiving God and loving and forgiving relations among humans are given primacy, when women and men are seen as partners with equal voices in a community of faith that seeks social and economic justice for all people, and children learn nonviolence, then religious practices and rituals will contribute to peace. Yet most contemporary societies have a diversity of religious communities, including some that emphasize holy war and strong exercise of patriarchal authority. It can certainly not be said that all religious groups will be oriented towards peacemaking.

Trade and exchange

The words "nurturance" and "caring" have been used a great deal. It must be recognized, however, that nurturance and caring do not have to characterize all social interactions in order for them to be regarded as contributing to social peace. The establishment of trade relations with neighboring and more distant social groups contributes to the mutual well-being of participants when each has something the other wants – even in the absence of other elaborating behaviors (as in the famous anthropological examples of silent trade). What is necessary is that each party see the exchange as fair and reasonable, as mutually beneficial. In fact, much gift giving is actually exchange in this sense, as Mauss makes clear.[23] Sahlins points out that the practice of trade became a creative alternative to simply raiding one's neighbors – a habit that, unfortunately, can easily lead to more or less continual warfare.[24] By the same token, trade has a quality of fragility about it – if either party is dissatisfied, there is always the possibility of reverting to war. Ceremonial gift giving lies at a point somewhere between the trade that is a substitute for war and more spontaneous sharing.

The line between ceremonial gift giving, which is a periodic redistribution of wealth that keeps a certain balance over time of giving and receiving, and gifts given more spontaneously and without mental calculation about future benefits is impossible to draw, and the effort probably makes no sense. A response of spontaneous gratitude on the part of the recipient of a gift may also have incalculable value and be considered in itself a return "gift." The fact that we speak of "exchanging gifts" at certain holiday seasons suggests that, for the most part, some degree of exchange is assumed in gift giving, in fact it is worth noting that marketplaces often have an air of festivity about them even when all transactions are apparently commercial. What actually happens in many situations involving human exchanges, whether of service or goods, is that a reciprocity multiplier effect is at work.[25] Each person throws in a little extra for "good measure," whether the extra quarter-ounce of meat on the butcher's scale or a warm smile to the clerk at the checkout counter. It is the reciprocity multiplier effect that ensures that trade will further continuing goodwill among the parties involved and helps them deal resourcefully with conflicts when they do arise.

Play of the imagination

Celebrations have been referred to as society at play. But play by its very nature performs a serious creative function for each community, as Huizinga has pointed out.[26] Taking place outside the realm of everyday life, play nevertheless creates boundaries, rules, and roles ("let's play house – you be the daddy and I'll be the mommy"), and structures spaces within which children can create their own realities in fantasy. Mary Reilly emphasizes the importance of play in learning nonviolence and self-control.[27] Watching infant monkeys at play, she comments on "the conversion of aggression into social complexity" as the monkeys learn control over their movements in the course of rough-and-tumble activity. When children's rough-and-tumble play dissolves into tears because a child is hurt, the same learning can take place.

The fact that play space is also space in which children can practice grownup activities does not take away from the fact that play is done *for its own sake,* "for fun." This makes "playing" important for adults, who tend to be excessively tense and serious about many of their activities. Competitive sports and spectator games may work against the spontaneity of play, for both players and watchers, but the rudiments of play survive as the popularity of spectator sports suggests. Yet there are other, less obvious forms of play. Some are highly developed: the mind at play in science; "the muse" at play creating poetry, music, painting, sculpture; the body at play in song, dance, and drama. Play goes on at the grassroots level in the folk culture of each society, and it goes on among the elites as well, hut the play of each tends to take separate forms in terms of style, language, and content. It is rime to rediscover all the different forms of play, including artistic and scientific play, and find ways to release them into a shared celebration of play in public spaces. We cannot ignore that some art, and some sports, have become so violent that they have lost their character of play. The recovery of play as fun, a basic heritage of every society, is the best answer to that violence.

One way to think about play is that it allows the imagination to fantasize alternatives to everyday reality. These alternatives maybe thought of as images of possible futures. A society that encourages the play of the mind encourages the exploration of other and better ways of ordering life ways. We have already mentioned Polak, the Dutch historian who discovered through his macrohistorical studies that societies tended to be empowered by positive images of the future. The visions themselves could act as magnets, drawing forth behaviors that could bring the envisioned future into being.[28] Polak wrote *The Image of the Future* in 1950 for a war-paralyzed Europe, as a call to begin imaging how things could be, to create visions that could inspire actions. A half century later we have once more reached a state of social despair, in countries of both the North and the South. What are the possibilities for the twenty-first century? The task of shifting the cultural balance away from violence and toward nonviolence is a challenge for all – whatever one's walk of life, one's age, one's gender, wherever one lives on the planet we call home. The range of human activity that can be retuned to contribute to peace building is vast. The only limitation on that retuning is the willingness to liberate our own imaginations.

Notes

1 Hans Hass. *The Human Animal: The Mystery of Man's Behavior* (New York: G. P. Pulnam's Sons, 1970).
2 Hans Hass, *Human Animal,* 123.
3 This passage is found in Leonard Tomkinson, *Studies in the Theory and Practice of Peace and War in Chinese History and Literature* (Shanghai: Friends Center, Christian Literature Society, 1940).
4 The "10,000 societies" is a term sometimes used by anthropologists to refer to the large number of

separate ethnic groups spread across the globe. Estimates of the actual number of societies range from 5,000 to 7,000, varying according to the criteria used for counting.

5 In making choices on which peoples to select and what social practices are most significant in generating societal peaceableness, I have drawn heavily on the selection of anthropological studies of peaceful societies prepared by Bruce D. Bonta and published as *Peaceful Peoples: An Annotated Bibliography* (Metuchen, N.J.: Scarecrow, 1993). I wish to express my appreciation here for his outstanding work.

6 Jean Briggs, *Never in Anger: Portrait of an Eskimo Family* (Cambridge, Mass.: Harvard Univ. Press, 1971). See also Briggs's "The Origins of Nonviolence: Inuit Management of Aggression," in *Learning Non-Aggression: The Experience of the Non-Literate Societies*, ed. Ashley Monlagu (New York: Oxford Univ. Press, 1978), 54–93.

7 Susan Isaacs, *Intellectual Growth in Young Children* (London: Routledge & Kegan Paul, 1930). Note also Elise Boulding, "The Nurturance of Adults by Children in Family Settings," in *Research in the Interweave of Social Roles*, ed. Helen Lopata (Greenwich, Conn.: JAI Press, 1980), 167–89.

8 Clyde H. Farmsworth, "Envoy Defends World of Eskimo" *New York Times*, Feb. 22, 1995.

9 Colin Turnbull, *The Forest People* (New York: Simon & Schuster, 1961).

10 In 1991 the first representative of the Central African Forest Peoples made his way to Geneva to create linkage with the UN Working Group for Indigenous Populations. Since then, the newsletter of the International Work Group for Indigenous Affairs (IWGIA) is reporting increased activities among the African rainforest peoples. A linkage with other rainforest peoples took place during the 1993 International Year of the World's Indigenous Peoples. See the IWGIA Newsletters (Copenhagen), nos. 2 and 3 (1993).

11 See especially: Ruth Benedict, Patterns of Culture (Boston: Houghton Mifflin, 1959). See also Irving Goldman, "The Zuni Indians of New Mexico," in *Cooperation and Competition among Primitive Peoples*, ed. Margaret Mead. (New York: McGraw-Hill, 1937), 313–53; John Whiting et al., "The Learning Values," in *People of Rimrock: A Study of Values in Five Cultures*, ed. Evon Vogt and Ethel Albert, (Cambridge, Mass: Harvard Univ. Press, 1967). 83–125.

12 For an account of new Zuni developments, see Derek Denniston's "High Priorities: Conserving Mountain Ecosystems and Cultures," *World Watch Paper* 123 (Feb. 1995): 50–51.

13 Margaret Mead, *Sex and Temperament in Three Primitive Societies* (New York: Mentor, 1950).

14 Bonta, *Peaceful Peoples*.

15 Although Pennylvania was a colony founded by Quakers, and Quakers originally constituted a majority in the colony's legislative assembly, the issue of voting appropriations to fulfill military obligations to the king during the French and Indian Wars led most Quakers to resign from the legislature in the later years of the colony.

16 Among studies on the Anabaptist communities, see James Juhnke, *Vision, Doctrine, War: Mennonite Identity and Organization in America*, 3 vols. (Scottdale, Pa.: Herald, 1986); Duane Friesen, *Christian Peacemaking and International Conflict* (Scottdale, Pa.: Herald, 1986); and Elbert Russel. *The History of Quakerism* (New York: Macmillan, 1992).

17 During the nineteenth-century evangelical revival in the United States, a certain number of Quaker meetings shifted to the more usual pattern of having ministers, to cope with the rapidly growing numbers of adherents.

18 The consensus process does not lead to speedy decisions. It took one hundred years from the first proposal was made to abolish slaveholding among Friends to the time when Friends were able to unite in accepting this as a Quaker witness.

19 The Children's Creative Response to Conflict Program is now housed with the Fellowship of Reconciliation, Box 271, Nyack, NY 10960.

19 Elise Boulding, "The Family as a Small Society," and "The Family as a Way into the Future," in *One Small Plot of Heaven: Reflections of a Quaker Sociologist on Family Life* (Wallingford, Pa.: Pendle Hill, 1989).

20 A number of organizations work to spread this sense of ecological interdependence, and they all publish newsletters. U.S. mailing addresses for a few: International Society for Ecology and Culture, P.O. Box 9475, Berkeley, CA 94709; RAIN, The Planet Drum foundation, P.O. Box 31251, San Francisco, CA 94131; Ocean Arks International, One Locus St., Falmouth, MA 02540; World Neighbors, 4127 NW 122 St., Oklahorna City, OK 73210–8869.

21 For examples, see McKim Marriott, "The Feast of Love," in *Krishna Myths, Rites and Attitudes*, ed. Milton Singer (Chicago: Univ. of Chicago Press, 1968). See also Richard Lannoy, *The Speaking Tree: A Study of Indian Culture and Society* (London: Oxford Univ. Press, 1971).

22 Marcel Mauss, *The Gift: Forms and Functions of Exchange in Archaic Societies* (New York: Norton, 1971).

23 Marshall Sahlins, *Stone Age Economics* (New York: Aldine-Atherton, 1972).

24 Alvin Gouldner, "The Norm of Reciprocity," *American Sociological Review* 25 (1960): 161–78.

25 Johan Huizinga, *Homo Ludens: A Study of the Play Element in Culture* (Boston: Beacon, 1955).

26 Mary Reilly, ed., *Play as Exploratory Learning* (Beverly Hills, Calif.: Sage, 1974).

28 Fred Polak, *The Image of the Future*, trans. Elise Boulding (San Francisco: Jossey-Bass/Elsevier, 1972). This is a one-volume abridgement of the full two-volume translation of the original Dutch (Dobbs Ferry, N.Y.: Oceana Press, 1961).

PART 6: BUILDING INSTITUTIONS AND CULTURES OF PEACE

Suggestions for further reading

An Agenda for Peace – Preventive diplomacy, peacemaking and peace-keeping: http://www.un.org/Docs/SG/agpeace.html

Boulding, Elise. *Cultures of Peace: The Hidden Side of History.* Syracuse, NY: Syracuse University Press, 2000.

Dayton, Bruce W. and Louis Kriesberg (2009). *Conflict Transformation and Peacebuilding: Moving from Violence to Sustainable Peace, Security and Conflict Management.* London, New York: Routledge.

Lederach, John Paul (1997). *Building Peace: Sustainable Reconciliation in Divided Societies.* Washington, D.C.: United States Institute of Peace Press.

Lederach, John Paul (2005). *The Moral Imagination: The Art and Soul of Building Peace.* Oxford, New York: Oxford University Press.

Lederach, John Paul (2002). *A Handbook of International Peacebuilding: Into the Eye of the Storm.* First edition. San Francisco: Jossey-Bass.

Ross, Marc Howard (2009). *Culture and Belonging in Divided Societies: Contestation and Symbolic Landscapes.* Philadelphia: University of Pennsylvania Press.

Zelizer, Craig and Robert A. Rubinstein (2009). *Building Peace: Practical Reflections from the Field.* Sterling, VA: Kumarian Press.

Websites

Journal of International Peacekeeping: http://www.internationalpeacekeeping.org/

Journal of Peace Education: http://www.tandf.co.uk/journals/titles/17400201.asp

The Journal of Peacebuilding & Development: http://www.journalpeacedev.org/

SCR Resolution 1325: http://www.unifem.org/gender_issues/women_war_peace/unscr_1325.php

The UN Peacebuilding Commission (PBC): http://www.un.org/peace/peacebuilding/

Questions for reflection and discussion

1   What are the main challenges for external actors who wish to build new states and state-structures?

2   What are the main arguments in favour of and against designating a specific role for women in conflicts?

3   Can peaceful societies function as a good model for all societies? Or are they too dependent on a specific context?

4   What kind of impact might the inclusion of peaceful ways of handling conflicts in school curricula have on large-scale social conflicts?

5   Discuss different peacebuilding efforts and the effects they might have after wars have ended.

Index